Unilever Overseas

Unilever Overseas

The Anatomy of a Multinational
1895-1965

D. K. FIELDHOUSE

CROOM HELM LONDON
THE HOOVER INSTITUTION PRESS
Stanford, California, USA

© 1978 D. K. Fieldhouse
Croom Helm Ltd, 2–10 St John's Road, London SW11

British Library Cataloguing in Publication Data

Fieldhouse, David Kenneth
    Unilever overseas. – (Hoover Institution on
    War, Revolution and Peace. Publications.)
    1. Unilever Limited
    2. Underdeveloped areas – Economic conditions
    I. Title   II. Series
    338.8'8   HC59.7

    ISBN 0–85664–805–1

Hoover Institution Publication 205
Hoover Institution Press
Stanford, California 94305
ISBN 0–8179–7051–7

Printed and bound in Great Britain

Printed in Great Britain by offset lithography by
Billing & Sons Ltd, Guildford, London and Worcester

Contents

TABLES

FIGURES

MAP

TO EDGAR GRAHAM

Notes on Terms used in the
Text and Tables

Unilever uses a number of words and phrases as terms of art whose meaning is not necessarily self-evident. The most important of these are explained in Chapter 2, pp. 57–59. Some others are listed below:

à façon: a system by which Unilever arranges for some other firm to manufacture Unilever branded goods on their behalf, usually on a cost-plus basis.

'Concern': a generic term deriving from Lever Brothers and later adopted by Unilever to indicate the business as a whole. Thus 'the concern', 'concern soap'.

'Detergents' include soap, soap powders and scourers such as Vim as well as non-soapy synthetic detergents (NSDs) such as Omo. NSDs were only introduced after 1945 and thereafter the term 'detergents' is normally used to cover these as well as true soaps.

'Edibles' (edible fats and oils) include all products based on vegetable oils, such as margarine, baking fat, vegetable products/vanaspati/ghee substitute and dairy products.

'Foods' include frozen foods, dehydrated and canned foods (soups, vegetables, fish, fruit), mayonnaise, jam, fruit drinks, desserts, puddings, tea, ice-cream, sausages, meat, etc.

'Toilet preparations' include toothpaste, tooth-powder, toilet powders, face creams and lotions, hair shampoos, scents and shaving sticks. Sales volume of these is often expressed in 'gross' = 144 units.

'Ton', 'Metric Ton'. In the records it is not always clear whether a 'ton' is metric (2204.6 lbs) or avoirdupois, and if the latter whether

1

a long ton (2240 lbs) or a short ton (2000 lbs). The convention adopted in this book is to assume that, unless they are stated to be metric tons, all tons are long tons. In some instances this may be wrong but for the purpose of indicating sales volume the difference is of no importance.

'Gross Capital Employed' (GCE): average fixed assets (valued at remainder life replacement value) and working capital (stocks, debtors less creditors) employed in the business.

'Nett Sales Value' (NSV): turnover in money terms excluding sales taxes, deducting rebates, deducting cash discounts.

Abbreviations Used in Tables

n/a = not available or not relevant
— = there is known to be none
(—)= undefined loss

Preface

The official history of Unilever as a business enterprise has already been written by Charles Wilson in *The History of Unilever* (2 volumes, London, 1954) and *Unilever 1945–1965* (London, 1968) and, although there is some overlap, this book does not attempt to cover the same ground. But Wilson was prevented by shortage of space from writing a detailed account of the growth of Unilever as a multinational company, expanding through a multiplicity of overseas subsidiary companies. My study is therefore complementary to his. Taking a limited number of overseas subsidiaries (eleven manufacturing companies and two vegetable oil plantations), my object is to test some of the generalised statements made about the character of direct foreign investment in less developed countries (LDCs). My position differs from that of Wilson in two other respects. First, my starting point and main interest lie in the colonial or ex-colonial territories in which these Unilever subsidiaries operated, not in Unilever as a business organisation. Second, this book was not commissioned, is not official and the opinions expressed do not necessarily express Unilever's views on any issue.

The most important feature of the book is the large amount of original material from the Unilever archives it contains; and since the basis on which an independent researcher is permitted to use and publish confidential material of this type is vital to his credibility, it is necessary to state precisely the conditions on which I was allowed to do this. The book grew almost accidentally out of conversations I had with Edgar Graham, a Director of Unilever while he was a Visiting Fellow of Nuffield College, Oxford, and now Chairman of the Overseas Committee, about the role of multinationals in less developed countries and the problems of obtaining access to the papers of companies such as Unilever that operated there. He agreed to ask for me to be given permission to use the Unilever archives to look into certain specific questions relating to West Africa; and in course of time and further discussion this limited idea developed into a larger project to study a cross-section of Unilever manufacturing and plantation subsidiaries. It was on this basis that the Special Committee of Unilever gave me unrestricted access to all Unilever records up to 1965, then only seven years past. The one condition imposed was that the Special Committee had the right to read my eventual manuscript in draft before publication and to insist on the removal of any passages 'consisting of, or based on, material taken from Unilever's private archives (as distinct from other material freely available to the public)'. Beyond that Unilever imposed no restrictions and took no responsibility for what was contained in my book or for its publication; but because I experienced difficulty in obtaining a research grant, the company agreed to provide a room in Unilever House and to make funds available to pay a research assistant of my choosing. Subsequently the company met the cost of my visiting its Rotterdam headquarters and four companies overseas. I am immensely grateful for this help and for the tolerance the company showed to an outsider who asked them to probe their records to satisfy his curiosity; but I must state categorically that none of this has influenced my attitude to the history of these Unilever companies. I am glad also to be able to say that I have not been asked to omit or change anything I wished to publish except on the ground that it might be embarrassing to individuals or to third parties, not to Unilever as such. Conversely Unilever takes no responsibility for any of the opinions stated, nor does it guarantee the accuracy of the facts or statistical data I have taken from their records.

On the other hand I have received much help from many Unilever people, essential because an historian with no business experience finds it very difficult to understand the activities, even the terminology, of a business firm. My main gratitude must be to Edgar Graham who has fought my battles, read every word of the book at least twice in draft and made many valuable **comments**. For these reasons the book is dedicated to him. I am also grateful to Sir Ernest Woodroofe who was Chairman of Unilever Ltd when I was given permission to do this work and who read some parts of it; and to Sir David Orr and Mr Frans Van den Hoven, the present Chairmen respectively of Unilever Ltd and Unilever NV. The number of other present or retired members of Unilever who have given me information or advice is too long to list, but I am particularly grateful to Mr Andrew Knox, one time Chairman of the Overseas Committee, who made valuable comments on several chapters; Miss Hilary Kinghorn of the Overseas Committee, who acted throughout as general administrator of my project; Mr Brian Borthwick, also of the Overseas Committee, who gave much advice on technical and accounting questions; Dr Arie Braakman, who organised my visit to Unilever NV in Rotterdam in 1975; and Miss Maureen Staniforth, Librarian of the Information Department in Unilever House, London, who helped me in many ways. I must also thank the Chairmen and Boards of the four Unilever overseas companies—Hindustan Lever, India, Lever Brothers (Pakistan) Ltd, Unilever-Is, Turkey and Unilever Indonesia—which I was able to visit in order to discuss aspects of the draft chapters I or my wife had written on their companies. In each place we had long and vigorous discussions with past and present members of the local management and others connected with these subsidiaries, most of them indigenous. Nothing did more to clarify my mind on the role of a multinational in less developed countries and the only significant interpretative changes I made in the draft chapters resulted from these discussions and related mainly to relations between a subsidiary and its host society. It was unfortunately impracticable for me to visit any of the other Unilever companies included in this book, but the relevant chapters were sent in first draft for comment by the existing management and, where possible, by others who worked in these companies before 1965. They were able to suggest valuable points of detail or interpretation, but I never accepted comment of this kind when it appeared to conflict with the written evidence.

Rather than write a separate note a short comment on the sources used can be included here. The book is almost exclusively based on confidential material in the possession of Unilever. The company does not possess an archive in the sense that the records of its past activities are catalogued, arranged and available for research purposes. For this reason, and also because the Unilever records are not generally available to students, I have followed Wilson in not giving references to the Unilever sources used in writing the text and compiling the tables. The materials I used, however, fall into four categories and it is usually obvious from the text which of these is the source for a particular statement or fact.

1. The Leverhulme Correspondence. This consists of the business correspondence of William Lever, the first Viscount Leverhulme. Wilson (*History*, I, p.x) mentions finding some 30,000 files of correspondence and papers and these were listed. By the time I came to work on them some twenty years later a considerable proportion of the files then listed were missing and could not be traced; but fortunately enough were still available to provide evidence on most, though not all, the important developments in which I was interested during Leverhulme's lifetime.

2. The minutes of a succession of committees of the Board of Lever Brothers and later of Unilever, which start with the Policy and Tactics Committee in 1912 and continue from 1925 with the Directors' Conference. On the Dutch side of what became Unilever there are minutes of various committees of Van den Berghs and of Jurgens and from 1927 of Margarine Union and Margarine Unie into which they merged.

3. Minutes of the Special Committee's meetings with various executive groups. These begin from 1930, when the Special Committee was revived, and continue to the present. They are carefully indexed and provide the most authoritative and confidential evidence of the decision-making process at the highest level. For the present study the relevant series of minutes were those of meetings between the Special Committee and the Overseas Committee and from 1955 also the Plantations Executive, later Plantations Group.

4. Records of the Overseas Committee, Unilever Export Ltd and Plantations Group. The first of these goes back to the 1920s, before the Overseas Committee as such was set up. The very extensive surviving material consists mainly of dossiers prepared for individual directors and others from Lever Brothers to take on visits to the overseas companies and of the reports they wrote on their visits. Until about 1939 both dossiers and reports were usually voluminous: a single report might contain 200 pages of typescript and provide detailed statistics on all parts of a business. During the Second World War few visits were made or reports written; and after 1945 improved communication had the result that visits became much more frequent, information could be sent very quickly by air mail, telephone or telex, and the length and substance of directors' reports were greatly reduced. Unfortunately this resulted in far less information surviving for the historian. The earlier reports are a mine of information; but since Unilever destroys routine correspondence after five years, almost none of the Overseas Committee's post-1945

correspondence, which presumably contained much the same information as in earlier reports, is now available. Hence the paradox that there are more gaps in the surviving information for the period 1940 to 1955 than for the two decades before 1940. Fortunately Plantations Group has so far kept all its correspondence with the plantation companies from its formation in 1955. As for Unilever Export Ltd and its preceding organisations in Lever Brothers and the Dutch companies, the records are very patchy before the 1950s. The only statistics that could be discovered on Lever exports before 1929 and on Unilever soap exports thereafter were in six ledgers found in a broom cupboard in Port Sunlight. These were copied and have been used where relevant, but there are very large gaps. On the Dutch side valuable material on exports to many countries was found for the years 1923 to 1929, but thereafter the only surviving data before the 1950s appears to be for 1937-8.

In addition to the material available in the London and Rotterdam headquarters of Unilever there are, of course, records in the head offices of the overseas companies, and where the evidence available in Europe was inadequate these companies were asked to fill gaps. They were able to provide valuable information on many points but in most cases they too had not kept earlier records. Thus a general comment on the sources available for writing this book might be that, while they are voluminous on some companies and for some periods, they are patchy and there are frustrating gaps, indicated in the tables by n/a to mean either not available or not relevant. I had access to whatever could be found and much effort was spent on searching; but there are aspects of the history of Unilever overseas which are likely to remain unknown.

Unilever did not, however, operate in a vacuum; and since I approached this study from the standpoint of the individual overseas companies, it would have been desirable to embed each of them in a detailed study of the country in which it operated. Thus Hindustan Lever should form part of a study of the industrial development of India from the second decade of this century. But there are studies here of thirteen companies in twelve countries. To study the background of each of these countries in detail, using primary sources, would have made this the research work of a lifetime and must have resulted in perhaps a dozen monographs. I therefore had no difficulty in resisting this temptation. It was more disappointing that in the end I found that space made it impossible even to provide a sketch of the social, economic and political background for most of these countries. I have therefore had to assume some knowledge of the historical environment in which each of these companies operated.

Even though the original materials available in Unilever House were less complete than I had expected, it would have taken a very long time for me, working in Oxford and visiting Unilever House as often as I could, to have read through all the available records on these thirteen companies. I am therefore very grateful to Miss Elaine Moore who acted as my part-time research assistant for the first three years and did much of the spade work in discovering, carding and transcribing relevant material. Miss Moore had hoped to write a study of three Unilever companies in Latin America which would have formed part of Chapter 7 together with Turkey; but in the end other commitments prevented her from completing this study in time for publication as part of this book. This is unfortunate on two counts: the activities of multinationals play a central role in the current literature on 'under-development' in Latin America; and these countries, along with Turkey, would have been the only hosts to Unilever companies included in this book which were not European colonial dependencies at some period during the twentieth century. Miss Moore nevertheless hopes that she may eventually be able to complete and publish this study separately and some statistics for Latin America are included in Tables 10.1 and 10.2 in the last chapter. After she ceased to work on the project in 1975 my wife, Sheila Fieldhouse, took over the research work in Unilever House and she has also written Chapter 7 on Unilever-Is in Turkey. I am grateful to her for her help and for tolerating my preoccupation with Unilever. I am also grateful to Nuffield College for its support and to my two successive secretaries there, Mrs Eileen Jenkins and Mrs Sheila Hazelden, who between them typed the book. Mr Maurice Scott kindly read Chapter 10 and helped to sharpen the argument, but he has no responsibility for the end result. Finally I must thank the Hoover Institution, Stanford University, which gave me a Visiting Fellowship there in 1976/7 to enable me to complete the first draft of the book; and in particular Professor Peter Duignan and Dr Lewis Gann, Senior Fellows of the Institution, who gave me valuable advice on the African sections. The number of others who have helped by reading drafts or giving advice is too long to list; and I must conclude that the obligations incurred in writing a book of this kind must outweigh its value.

D. K. Fieldhouse
Nuffield College, Oxford

February 1978

1

Introduction

The aim of this book is to study in as much detail as space and the available evidence make possible the activities of Unilever in a number of countries in the less developed world. The frame of reference is the role of an 'international' or 'multinational' company or corporation because this has become a central issue in the controversy over the relations between 'rich' and 'poor' countries.[1] The subject can be approached from many angles but to the historian three questions are of particular importance. First, why a capitalist firm should choose to invest capital in productive enterprises overseas rather than export products from its home base. Second, the character of the subsidiary companies as business enterprises and how profitable they proved to be from the standpoint of the home investing company. Finally, what effects the investment had on the host country. This book asks and as far as possible answers these three questions in relation to a selection of Unilever subsidiaries in Africa, Asia and the South Pacific.

The three problems are deceptively alike but in fact differ widely in complexity and therefore the way in which they must be handled. Consider first the question of motives. These might be of many sorts, depending on the character of the parent enterprise and its needs; and this makes it important to decide at the start which category best fitted Unilever. Looking at international companies in the broad, and ignoring portfolio investments, it is possible to define four main motives for making a productive investment overseas, each of which is likely to result in a different style of subsidiary. Using Professor Reuber's terms,[2] the first three are 'export-oriented', the fourth 'market-development' investments. First, there are companies whose main purpose is the extraction, processing and eventual sale overseas of commodities that are found only in particular countries, typically petroleum, metal ores or mineral fertilisers. Although some of these, notably the big American oil companies, began by extracting and refining petroleum at home and exporting their products, most such companies invest in leases of oil wells, in gold or copper mines, phosphate and bauxite deposits because they need these things to operate at all or at the least to enlarge the scope of their activities. They have, moreover, to be international corporations because they exist to extract and transfer natural endowments from where they are found to where they are consumed: by their very nature they are therefore 'export-oriented'. This is not, of course, to imply that such enterprises are always necessary for the exploitation of these resources. Initially, when a new supply is discovered or a demand first arises, big international companies are often the only source of immediate and sufficient capital and know-how to make rapid development possible: the recent example of North Sea oil indicates that this dependence is not restricted to less developed countries (LDCs). But over time the role of the international company can be, and often has been, taken over by local governments or indigenous companies; and this leaves the foreign firm with a different and more restricted role— that of buying the product and distributing it in other countries. Thus petroleum companies have in general had to change from extraction to refining and distribution; and, in so far as they may then, in a particular country, be restricted to importing and refining petroleum bought overseas for local consumption, they change their role from being export-oriented to market-development.

A second type of export-oriented multinational grows (or possibly buys) agricultural commodities in one place for resale or use else-where. Typically such firms might establish and run plantations producing vegetable oils, rubber, tea, cocoa or tropical fruits. These enterprises have to be overseas because climatic and other conditions essential for these products do not exist in the temperate countries of Europe and North America which are the main consumers. Foreign direct investment was necessary in the first instance because most of the countries in which it was possible to grow such things possessed neither the capital nor the know-how to do so: often the plant or tree was brought in from somewhere else. Beyond this the motive for investment varied. On the one hand a foreign company might merely produce in order to sell elsewhere; alternatively it might produce materials needed for its own production of other things; and in that case the function of the overseas investment would be vertical integration whose function was to ensure a sufficient supply of essential raw materials or intermediates at a price unaffected by market fluctuations. By this means a manufacturing concern might hope to increase its ability to compete with rivals who depended on the commodity market for their inputs; though such a strategy might prove counter-productive if the market fell to the point at which commodities could be bought more cheaply than they could be produced on plantations owned by the multinational manufacturing company.

The third type of multinational is primarily a manufacturing enterprise with its main factories in the home country and the developed countries of Europe and North America, where it also sells most of its products. Its motives for setting up subsidiary manufacturing or assembly plants overseas are to take advantage of more favourable production factors there (raw materials, labour supply, special tariff concessions, etc.) in order to produce part or all of the product for the home or overseas markets. These subsidiaries are therefore export-oriented. Thus an American electronics company may decide to build and run a factory in South Korea, Hong Kong or Taiwan because it is cheaper to send and assemble American-made components there and then transport the finished or partly finished product for sale in the United States than to carry out the whole operation at home. Alternatively it may be advantageous to carry out the whole manufacturing operation in one of these places, using only foreign capital and know-how. For this type of multinational the non-communist world forms a single industrial system in which capital is employed and products sold wherever production costs are lowest and the market most favourable. Decisions to invest overseas thus form an integral part of a global production strategy and individual subsidiary companies have little or no autonomous function.

Finally there is a different kind of industrial concern which sets up production facilities overseas but does so to manufacture goods for the market of the country in which the subsidiary is located rather than for export overseas. These are 'market-development' enterprises. The contrast with the previous three types stems from the nature of the benefits looked for by the investing company. In this case the host country may possess no peculiar advantages as a site for manufacturing: no particularly cheap raw materials, a labour force no cheaper (taking wage rates in relation to efficiency) than in the multinational's home country, and no special tax or other benefits. It might, therefore, have been expected that the foreign industrial enterprise would prefer to manufacture its products at home and export them to such a market, and the reasons for not doing this but investing in local production have to be explained. The classic reason would be a discriminating import tariff which penalised imported manufactures as against imported raw materials, probably with the aim of stimulating industrialisation or helping existing local producers. Alternatively, even under more or less free trade conditions, high freights on imports to countries which possessed the raw materials needed to make a particular product might tilt the balance in favour of local production. There are many other possible factors: the common denominator is that in every case a multinational invests in local production for the local market alone (and possibly for its immediate neighbours). Such investment is typically a defensive strategy, often adopted by firms which have established international export markets for branded products and then find that they have to jump protective walls to compete with local competitors.

But not all market-development enterprises have defensive aims. Where a large industrial concern in Europe or America wants to widen its market overseas and finds that there are already well established producers in a potentially attractive overseas market, it may decide that the only way in which it can enter that market at all is to build a factory there or (more commonly in developed countries) to buy out an existing manufacturer, taking over his goodwill as well as his productive facilities. Investment of this kind is normally more expensive because of the cost of the goodwill. It is probably also less constructive from the standpoint of the host country because there may be no nett addition to its productive capacity; though in principle a take-over should release local capital for alternative productive use in the host country. In addition local manufacture by a multinational may result from an invitation by a host government which wants to expand the local industrial base. From the standpoint of the investing foreign company such a subsidiary may represent either an expansion of its total market or a defence of its established goodwill; but in either case it is likely to be market-development not export-oriented in character.

If we consider how Unilever fits into this spectrum it is obvious, given the nature of its products and activities in Europe and America, that the first possibility can be excluded at once: Unilever was never concerned with the extraction or distribution of minerals, etc. Nor was the 'concern' (a generic term often used as shorthand in Unilever for the business as a whole and used in the same way in this book) likely to be attracted by the third option—distribution of manufacturing processes between plants in different countries for consumption elsewhere; but this requires explanation. The main reason is to be found in the nature of the company's basic products: soap, non-soapy detergents (NSDs), dental and toilet preparations, margarine, cooking fats and oils, frozen and canned foods and marginal products such as cattle feed and paperboard. What all these had in common was that production was virtually a single continuous process in which the raw materials (vegetable oil, animal fats, chemicals, etc.) were, so to say, boiled up together in a vat and came out as a finished product. In such an industry there was no scope for moving components round the world in search of clever hands who would put them together for low rewards. Moreover, freight on these raw materials to the Lever soap works in Britain or the Van den Bergh or Jurgens margarine factories in Holland was so small in relation to the value of the product that there was no advantage in manufacturing these products in the tropical countries from which they came in order to distribute the product throughout the world. In short, the nature of the Unilever business ensured that the company's first preference would usually be to manufacture all its products in its home factories, whether for consumption in the home market or for export. It had no incentive to establish export-oriented subsidiaries round the world.

There thus remain only two actual grounds for setting up Unilever subsidiaries: production or purchase of agricultural commodities for use or sale elsewhere and manufacture for local consumption. The first was the less important. Lever Brothers owned and operated plantations (in varying forms) in the Solomon Islands from 1903, in the Belgian Congo (Zaire) from 1911, in West Africa from the 1920s and in South-east Asia from after the Second World War. It also traded in vegetable oils and other tropical commodities, mainly from Africa, which were bought by a number of trading companies owned by Lever Brothers and either used by the concern's own factories or sold on the market. It will, therefore, be necessary to discover why a manufacturing enterprise of this kind should have diversified in this way, and in particular whether such investment was intended to result in vertical integration from, say, Lever's coconut palms to Lever's Lux Toilet Soap.

Whatever their functions, plantations were a very small part of Unilever's overseas investment compared with their soap and margarine factories. Lever Brothers began to build or buy soap factories overseas as early as the mid-1890s and after the merger with the Dutch margarine companies in 1929 margarine production was begun in several countries in which a market existed or could be created. Virtually without exception these factories existed to serve local consumers. They were classic examples of market-development enterprises and formed the heart of Unilever as a multinational. A large part of this book is therefore devoted to examining the grounds on which these subsidiaries were set up in a cross-section of either 'new' or 'developing' countries in different continents, how they performed and what significance they had for the countries in which they operated. Of the eleven manufacturing companies examined, only two—in Kenya and Ghana—can in any sense be described as government-initiated, and then only with reservations. Nevertheless these make it possible to consider the significance of this special dimension to the general category of manufacturing subsidiaries whose function was to produce for the local market.

The second basic question to be asked about multinationals is how they run their subsidiaries and how profitable they find them. The literature on multinationals provides a large number of specific questions under these heads and, in so far as the available evidence makes it possible, an attempt will be made to answer some of these as they relate to Unilever enterprises in the concluding chapter. At this point it is proposed merely to signpost some of the more important features to be looked for in the case studies of individual overseas companies.

First in order of importance is the relationship between the subsidiary and its metropolitan master. Much of the published literature appears to assume that a wholly-owned industrial sub-sidiary (or affiliate, as it is often called) is merely a productive machine, run from the centre, making only those products and brands the metropolitan company makes and which it is allowed to duplicate, mindless and characterless. This may, indeed, sometimes be the case. But it is not necessarily or invariably so and variations in the centre–subsidiary relationship are one of the most important features differentiating one multinational from another. The issue is important because the degree of autonomy and business personality a subsidiary is allowed to develop may make a critical difference to its ability to integrate with the economy and society of the host country. Thus, a locally registered company which is substantially free to determine what products the local market will accept, to diversify along lines favoured by the host government, to use local inputs and so on, is a significantly different thing from a company which is not locally registered, makes, say, one aerated soft drink (using imported ingredients) to international specifications, and is not allowed to widen its product range.

Closely connected with autonomy is what is commonly called 'socialisation' or 'localisation' of a subsidiary. Although this could be taken to include autonomous development along lines determined by the needs and conditions of the host society, it is normally taken to imply local participation in the equity of the local company and the employment of nationals of the host country up to the highest levels rather than continuing use of expatriate management. How important these developments may be is central to the main debate over the character of multinational companies. Those who believe such enterprises are exploitative under all conditions argue that it makes little difference whether some of the capital is locally owned so long as control is retained by foreign capital and that an indigenous manager is no less an agent of foreign interests than an expatriate. There is, however, an alternative view that the best way in which a developing country can obtain the benefits of foreign capital without commitment to perpetual acceptance of an alien segment in its economy is to insist that foreign ownership of the capital is progressively eliminated by sale of shares to the local government or its citizens and that the local management comes gradually to consist of nationals as a sufficient number of qualified managers is created. In examining the history of these Unilever companies the points to be looked for are, therefore, if, when and to what extent shares in the subsidiary became available in the local stock market; when and at what pace nationalisation of the management took place; and finally, what effects either or both of these had on the character of the company.

A third way in which multinationals and their subsidiaries can be differentiated is by their financial arrangements. The early Marxist theory of imperialism as evolved by men such as Rudolf Hilferding and V. I. Lenin[3] was based on the assumption that imperialism was the product of surplus capital (in modern terms, excess liquidity) in the developed countries seeking profitable openings overseas; and their arguments were supported by statistics showing a massive outflow of investments in the later nineteenth century. Later Marxist theorists, however, have observed that much of this early capital outflow went into communications or loans to governments rather than into productive enterprises still owned by foreign capitalists. They have, therefore, constructed an alternative hypothesis that modern capitalists do not invest large sums overseas. They set up foreign enterprises because they see an opportunity to make profits without risking their existing capital, putting in technology and managerial skills but borrowing capital from local banks or governments anxious to stimulate industrialisation. They can then repay the relatively small initial debt from profits and depreciation. Subsequent profits are sent abroad and thus constitute a nett drain on the resources of the host country which has, so to speak, been conned into providing the capital on which it is now required to pay interest. Whatever the utility of this particular argument, the underlying issue is important and must be investigated in detail: how did Unilever build up the capital of its overseas subsidiaries and had investment decisions any connection with the company's liquidity at a particular time?

The third and most controversial issue connected with the role of the multinational in less developed countries is closely related to its finances—the benefits received respectively by alien capital and the host society. So far as the multinational is concerned the question is essentially relative: were the profits made in relation to capital employed greater in one subsidiary than in another and in subsidiaries than in the home company? The statistics published in this book show that there were very wide variations in profitability between one company and another and within any one company over time. The reasons for these variations must be looked for and their significance considered. But a far more difficult issue is what a host country gains or loses from the presence of a foreign subsidiary. Since this is one of the most controversial and highly technical points in debate between economists specialising in the theory of growth and among proponents of under-development (or dependency) theory, it would be presumptuous for an historian using evidence drawn from a single Anglo-Dutch company to think that he can produce any generally satisfactory answer. Equally, however, it would be cowardly to make no attempt to assess the contribution made by Unilever's industrial and plantation enterprises to the economic growth of the countries in which these were situated. Some generalised comments will be made in the individual chapters; and in the concluding chapter a more methodical attempt will be made to test the utility of these subsidiaries using the criteria defined by Professor Reuber in his *Private Foreign Investment in Development* and in comparison with the aggregated evidence he obtained from a large number of foreign companies operating in the less developed world.

These are some of the main conceptual issues that stem from contemporary analysis of the role of multinationals. But this book is not entirely or even primarily concerned with contemporary issues: it is an attempt to trace the development of Unilever as a multinational company from the first steps taken by Lever in the early 1890s (1895 is taken as a convenient starting date because in that year Lever bought a factory site at Balmain, Sydney, on which the first of the overseas companies studied in this book was later built) to 1965, a date chosen merely to provide a reasonable *cordon sanitaire* between the end of the book and the date of its publication. To the historian this time factor adds a critical dimension to the study of a multinational. In 1895 the partition of Africa, where many of the Unilever subsidiaries were eventually to be placed, was still incomplete: according to Lenin, even the time at which, in his estimate, capitalism definitely reached its 'highest' stage of 'imperialism' was still five years in the future. Mira Wilkins in her excellent study of *The Emergence of Multinational Enterprises* suggests that, although a number of American firms had already established manufacturing subsidiaries overseas, notably Singer Sewing Machine, who may well be entitled to be called the first multinational by virtue of starting to assemble machines in Britain in 1867, the first main period of American overseas direct development began only about 1893. If Lever Brothers was not the first multinational it was certainly one of the first generation of capitalist concerns to manufacture in a number of countries.

The history of Unilever as a multinational enterprise from the 1890s to 1965 thus spans most of the time period in which such companies have existed and it is obvious that the conditions in which they operated changed fundamentally during that time. Many of what are now independent states in Africa and Asia went through two transformations in that period: from a number of independent indigenous units they were integrated, often arbitrarily, into colonial territories, and then, at different times after 1945, became sovereign states of a more or less Western type. While they were undergoing these political changes, their economic systems were first brought into close or closer contact with the international market and then partially restructured to meet its demands. By the 1960s their newly independent governments were trying to undertake a still more radical reconstruction in order to break free from what many of them regarded as undesirable dependence on foreign capital and overseas markets and to achieve what the development economists called 'sustained economic growth'. Time and change were inevitably factors influencing the attitude of European and American capitalism to these African, Asian and Pacific countries. Territories which might offer no attractions to a possible foreign investor in, say, 1910, might have become very attractive under the totally different conditions of the 1960s. Conversely, the grounds on which a decision was taken to invest in a palm oil plantation before 1914 might no longer seem relevant by the 1930s. In short, the history of a multinational, which alone can explain why it became what it is in the present, must be written in dynamic terms against a changing environment; and it is a main aim of this book to emphasise how greatly the character of Unilever and its activities overseas changed over time.

Change was continuous; but for most of the countries studied here there was one change that was more important than any other in this period—the transition from colonialism to independence. It is no accident that 12 out of the 13 subsidiary companies examined in this book were in countries which were British, Dutch or Belgian colonies for part at least of the twentieth century. Since the aim of the book is to study the role of a multinational in less developed countries, the majority of subsidiaries in Europe and North America were automatically excluded. Since it was desirable to choose countries in which there had been a subsidiary for as long a time as possible (to emphasise the process of time and change), as many as possible were selected which had Unilever subsidiaries before 1939; and of the countries in which there were manufacturing subsidiaries then, only Siam, China, Argentina and Brazil were not then colonies. The first two were excluded because of problems relating to sources and access, the last two for reasons explained in the Preface. Thus all but one of the subsidiaries included were for much of the time European dependencies: Turkey is the only exception, and this has been included partly because it demonstrates important aspects of establishing and operating a subsidiary in a country which had never been a dependency. Colonialism and decolonisation are, therefore, major themes in this book; and one main aim is to investigate whether colonialism was attractive to a foreign firm contemplating overseas investment and, conversely, whether decolonisation deterred new investment and adversely affected the operations of existing enterprises.

Colonialism is a very general concept, and within the list of colonial dependencies examined here there are three distinct categories. The first consists of Australia and South Africa. At the time when Lever first built or acquired factories in these countries they were self-governing British Dominions, founder members of what was later called the British Commonwealth. Although these, along with Canada, New Zealand and Newfoundland, were not permitted to act as fully sovereign states until 1931, they had almost complete autonomy in domestic affairs, and in particular control over tariff policy, at the time when the first Lever companies were set up there. They were also, of course, relatively affluent societies judged by per capita incomes, and to this extent were not 'under-developed' countries in the modern sense. The grounds for including them in this study are set out in Chapter 3: in brief, they were among the first generation of non-industrialised overseas countries in which Levers set up manufacturing subsidiaries. They therefore provide a model of the attractions that drew foreign industrialists to invest in local manufacturing in this first period during which the multi-nationals were expanding overseas and of the techniques then used to set up an overseas business. Their later history, although in many ways similar to that of Unilever subsidiaries in Europe and North America, demonstrates the lines on which such a subsidiary was likely to develop, and this provides a frame of reference for the development of other Unilever subsidiaries in less affluent overseas countries.

The second group of countries and companies studied consists of India (including Pakistan after 1947), Indonesia and Ceylon. They are important because it was in these places, together with Latin America, China and Siam, that the second generation of Unilever manufacturing subsidiaries was established, mostly between 1920 and 1940, and because direct investment in such countries was almost unprecedented.[4] Hitherto European and American capitalism had concentrated almost entirely on the much more affluent countries of Europe, North America and the British settlement colonies because all offered sizeable markets, conventional facilities for the transport and sale of products and, perhaps most important, substantial import tariffs to protect infant industries against foreign competition. By contrast India, Indonesia and Ceylon were all colonial dependencies. Their per capita incomes were very low by European standards, consumption patterns and systems of product distribution were very different, and until these two decades none had been allowed a protective tariff. For a manufacturing company such as Unilever to set up manufacturing subsidiaries in such places marked a significant extension of the range of activities of a multinational whose subsidiaries normally manufactured for local markets. It is therefore very important to discover why, during the two decades after 1920, Unilever should have decided to invest in factories in these three countries. But these companies are also important because their history covers a relatively long time-span— in the case of India over 40 years. This provides evidence on how the concern dealt with the special problems of operating in an environment very different from that in Europe and above all on the consequences of decolonisation. India, Pakistan and Ceylon were sovereign states for nearly two decades of the period covered by this book and there is no better evidence on how independence affected the relations between the government of a sovereign developing country and the subsidiary of a multinational.

The third group consists of four manufacturing companies in Africa—in Nigeria, Zaire, Ghana and Kenya—and one in Turkey. Strictly speaking these do not all belong to the same time period: the Nigerian and Congo companies were founded in the early 1920s, and this in itself is surprising and requires explanation. But in fact, as will be seen in Chapter 6, these two were special cases: they were not part of a wider project for manufacturing in tropical Africa, and their development into substantial and genuinely import-substituting subsidiaries only took place after 1945. At this stage they were joined by the other African companies included in this group; and in this sense all four companies represent aspects of the most recent phase of the expansion of multinational companies in the least developed countries. Their history throws light on why, at this comparatively late stage, so much foreign investment came to be made in industry in Black Africa and on the significance of political independence.

All the companies mentioned so far were manufacturing subsidiaries producing for the market of the host country. Yet Unilever
also had overseas subsidiaries which were export-oriented: plantation
companies and one very large trading company, United Africa
Company (UAC), which, until the 1960s, was primarily concerned
with the purchase and export of tropical commodities and the
import and distribution of a wide range of 'trade goods'. The
reasons for not including UAC are that it was too large and
specialised a venture with too few structural links with the rest of
Unilever to be dealt with in the same book as all these other
companies. But the plantations pose a significant and also manage-
able problem: why did this manufacturing enterprise undertake
the production of vegetable oils and, although much later, other
tropical commodities? There are two obvious alternative explanations: vertical integration or horizontal diversification; and in
Chapters 8 and 9 evidence on the Unilever plantations in the
Solomon Islands and Zaire are used to provide answers. But the
history of the plantations has a wider historical interest. They were
a far more important element in the general history of these two
societies than a manufacturing subsidiary could be, and their
development is therefore recounted in rather more detail. At the
end of Chapter 9 the record of these plantations is compared
briefly with that of other Unilever commodity producing ventures
and some general conclusions are put forward about the profitability of commodity production as a form of direct foreign investment in the second half of the twentieth century.

One main aspect of this book is to emphasise the importance of
time and change in the study of multinational companies. A second
is to demonstrate that the history of a multinational is not merely
that of the parent company. It is necessary to emphasise this point
because almost all the literature deals with multinationals as unitary
enterprises, often taking many multinationals as a statistical
aggregate. For the economist aggregates and averages may be
sufficient; but for the historian who wants to know how things
became what they are they do not explain anything. It has been said
above that the degree of autonomy possessed by the subsidiary of a
multinational is a critical factor in assessing its character, and
particularly its relations with the host country. But historically the
importance of studying each subsidiary separately is more
compelling: no two subsidiaries, at least those of Unilever, were
the same in origin, character or performance. Some were successful

and profitable, others remained stunted and of little value to the parent company. Some manufactured a narrow product range, others diversified broadly, even beyond the limits of the technology possessed by the parent company. Yet in the published reports of this as all other multinationals and in the statistical tables of most studies individual success or failure is commonly buried in anonymous totals.

This is to ignore or to conceal the realities. The fact that each subsidiary is a separate business enterprise becomes obvious the moment one examines the records in Unilever House. Apart from the minutes of central committees and boards who survey the whole business from the highest level, the records are arranged by separate overseas companies, just as the records of the British Colonial Office, with which many interesting analogies can be drawn, were arranged by individual colonies. The reasons are the same. The subsidiary, like the colony, was a distinct legal personality. Most Unilever subsidiaries were registered in the country in which they operated. They had their own chairmen, boards, managing directors and management; and although there was considerable mobility between companies, individuals might spend a decade or more working in a particular country. From the start William Lever emphasised that each local management must take its own decisions in the light of local circumstances. He did not invariably respect his own principle and central control was always an important fact—how important remains to be judged in the light of the evidence. But time was on the side of individuality. As particular countries strengthened their control over their economics and as the localisation of management and, in some cases, also the capital of subsidiaries increased, so the particularism of each overseas company became more marked. It would, therefore, have been a practical impossibility to have studied or written this history as a single narrative. A multinational is the sum of its parts and the relationship between centre and subsidiaries is one of the most important aspects of the study.

This is why this book consists of separate chapters or sections of chapters on each of the chosen Unilever subsidiaries. No two are identical; but in the nature of things they had common characteristics. They made many of the same products in much the same way; their accounting systems were as alike as the central accounts departments could persuade local accountants to make them; the interchange of managers and the training of junior staff overseas tended to produce recognisable 'Unilever' men. Hence, while emphasising the essential individuality of each company, it is also important to look for similarities and common influences. In the concluding chapter an attempt will be made to strike a balance between the common and contrasting features of these thirteen Unilever overseas subsidiaries.

The book, then, is an attempt to treat an Anglo-Dutch multi-national company as part of the history of western activity in the less developed world during the seventy years before 1965. The questions posed and the way the material is treated are both characteristic of the approach of an historian rather than of an economist or sociologist; and in the nature of historical research, the evidence is more important than the conclusions drawn from it. If the book does no more, it should provide a body of new information which will be of use to others working on the character of multinational companies or on the history of the individual countries in which Unilever operated.

2

Metropolitan Unilever:
the Central Organisation

The character of any institution lies in its functions and the accumulated conventions which determine how these are carried out, not in its formal structure. Charles Wilson has authoritatively described the administrative system of Lever Brothers to 1929 and that of Unilever after Lever Brothers merged with Margarine Union and Margarine Unie, and certain aspects have been dealt with in greater detail and with considerable panache by Andrew Knox in his autobiography, *Coming Clean*.[1] These, together with the life of his father by the second Viscount Leverhulme[2] and the original material in the archives of Unilever House, provide the material for the sketch given in this chapter. There is little here that is entirely new and this summary has two limited functions: to introduce institutions and administrative practices which will be referred to in later chapters; and, most important in a book which concentrates mainly on Lever/Unilever overseas subsidiaries, to describe the central structure of authority and control which linked the periphery with the centres of power in this multinational company. No account is given of the Dutch companies before 1929 because they possessed no overseas subsidiaries and because the central agencies for controlling overseas enterprises that Unilever used after the merger were simply taken over from Lever Brothers.

The administrative history of Lever/Unilever to 1965 falls into three distinct periods and this account will follow the same pattern. The first covers the lifetime of William Lever (created a Baronet in 1911, a Baron in 1917 and a Viscount in 1922, but hereafter referred to as 'Lever' irrespective of date and his status) from his founding of Lever Brothers Ltd in 1890 to his death in 1925. During these

24

thirty-five years Lever Brothers can be described in terms of a conventional late-nineteenth-century company which expanded its industrial and commercial activities and founded or acquired a number of subsidiary 'associated companies' (to use Lever's own invariable term) without changing its original administrative structure. The second period began in 1925 and lasted until 1945. In the early years a collective management replaced a single entrepreneur and consultative and decision-making bodies grew in number and importance. But far greater changes resulted from the formation of Unilever in 1929/30 since it was then necessary to establish institutions capable of co-ordinating two completely different organisations with branches both in Europe and overseas. The main innovations were complete by 1931 and with few changes lasted until 1945. This administrative revolution was accompanied by parallel changes in industrial organisation. During the 1930s a major rationalisation was carried through in Britain, Europe and many overseas countries whose general aim was to close down small factories and wind up obsolescent companies, consolidating production into a minimal number of units and transferring trademarks, patents and goodwill into a single central pool. It was at this stage, therefore, that Unilever began to look like a single federal enterprise rather than a loose confederation which could have been dismantled without much difficulty. The third and still continuing phase began after the Second World War. Institutionally its dominant feature was the proliferation of new administrative agencies whose function was to attempt to impose rationality—co-ordination was the vogue word—on a business which was growing so fast in size, capital employed, range of products and number of individual units that it was liable in due course to become uncontrollable. For the overseas companies with which this book is concerned the main question in this period was whether their traditional autonomy would survive the pressure towards greater uniformity and centralisation resulting from increasingly sophisticated technology and immensely improved communications.

1890–1925[3]

Until Lever's death in 1925 control of Lever Brothers was so completely in his hands that the institutions through which he chose to run his business may seem unimportant. Yet this is not so. Lever devolved a considerable amount of responsibility to individuals and organisations both in Britain and overseas on the general principle that a man should be left to get on with his job until and unless he did it unsatisfactorily and many of the practices and institutions he established survived his death and later became intrinsic to the running of Unilever in Europe and overseas. It is, therefore, necessary to describe the more important features of the Lever business before 1925, and in particular those which related most closely to the overseas companies described in this book.

Lever set up his first business, a wholesale grocery called Lever & Co., in 1877 and it was this company that in 1884 registered the trademark 'Sunlight Soap' on which much of his future success was built. It is not clear when Lever Brothers was set up, though the lease of a factory at Warrington, where Lever made his soap from 1885 to 1889, was in that name; and Lever Brothers Ltd was not registered as a private limited company until May 1890. In 1894 it was converted into a public limited company with an authorised capital of £1,500,000, half ordinary shares, the rest 5 per cent preference shares. It is important that from the start all the ordinary shares were owned by Lever and three or four others, and that he bought out all these by 1902, offering them preference shares on favourable terms. His aim was not to hold legal control of the company, since preference shareholders had precisely the same voting power as ordinary shareholders, but to possess the moral claim to determine policy on the ground that, provided his preference shareholders always received their dividends, the marginal risk lay with him alone. Wilson's statistics of capital employed in Lever Brothers from 1894 to 1929[4] show that as late as 1905 ordinary shares at £1,850,000 plus capital reserves at £315,757 outweighed preference shares at £2 million. But from 1906, as he sold an increasing number of preference shares to finance expansion at home and overseas, the balance of share ownership changed. In 1910 Lever converted £850,000 of ordinary shares into a new category of 15 per cent cumulative preferred ordinary shares which, as will be seen later, he used as a means of acquiring control of companies in Australia, South Africa and elsewhere by exchange of scrip without having to issue more preference shares in Britain. By 1921 his ordinary shares were £2,280,000 plus £809,815 reserves out of total capital of £51,792,177, which now included loan capital (debentures) of £4 million; Lever's personal holding was down to 2 per cent.

It is not suggested that Lever's control in any sense declined in proportion to his stake in the equity of Lever Brothers. His personal ability and force, which remained almost unchanged to the end, coupled with the fact that he was the creator of the business and remained the only ordinary shareholder, ensured that until at least 1921 he was able to determine policy in almost all matters without serious question. It is also obvious that as the business grew it was bound to need a larger and more sophisticated administrative and decision-making system. Nevertheless the time-table of the evolution of advisory and decision-making bodies within Lever Brothers roughly paralleled the changing balance of share ownership; in the process Lever Brothers gradually changed from being a public company run like a private venture into something close to a conventional modern company with a collective professional management.

In this process there seem to have been two milestones, in 1912 and 1921. Until 1912 Lever Brothers was run very simply. There was a Board of Directors, four in 1894, eight from 1897. Initially these included Lever's father and brother and P. J. Winser, the Port Sunlight Works Manager. In 1917, however, when the other Levers left the Board, a critical change took place. Thereafter virtually all directors were full-time managers, either in Lever Brothers itself or in other companies which it absorbed; that is, there were no honorific or part-time directors, and none voted onto the Board by the preference shareholders, as was common in America. It was not until the merger with the Dutch margarine companies in 1929 that Unilever had a part-time director and not until 1937 that the category of 'advisory directors' was created. This convention (it was no more, since the shareholders could destroy it by electing non-official directors at any annual general meeting) is very important for understanding the character of Unilever. It began because Lever did not want the advice of outsiders or need their reputation to enhance his company's status: he wanted employees. It continued because the management fully satisfied the shareholders. But by Lever's death it was a basic assumption that the Board should be a body of full-time experts whose opinions were valuable because they were directly responsible for some part of the business. The fact that almost all directors rose to that position by working for a lifetime in the concern meant also that they developed a very strong *esprit de corps* and a set of common assumptions; and the continuing convention that directors and chairmen should, with very few exceptions, be drawn from the higher management (D'Arcy Cooper was the only chairman of whom this was not true, and he came into the business after 1920 under conditions of crisis) also meant that every new management recruit carried a baton in his knapsack.

It is, therefore, not surprising that, with a Board consisting of employees who held their posts at Lever's pleasure and could be (and sometimes were) dismissed, there was little collective control of policy in the early days, certainly until 1912. Lever's son described the system as it was before 1914 as follows:

> Board meetings, except for the transaction of purely formal and legal business, were hardly ever held. Each director had a particular section under his care, and was in almost daily consultation with the Chairman, who alone guided the policy of the entire business. It has been said that Lever could not work with other men except as their chief.[5]

But even before 1914 changes were on the way. As the size of the firm increased, and because Lever was frequently abroad, he found it necessary to set up a number of committees whose function was either to share responsibility in advising the Board on major matters or to co-ordinate the commercial activities of different parts of the business. The most important was the Policy and Tactics Committee (PTC) of the Board, whose surviving minutes began in 1912. It was renamed the Policy Council (PC) in 1918 and lasted until 1921. These committees were virtually coterminous with the Board: each had nine members in 1912, rising to over twenty in 1921. The difference was that the Committee was an informal body which might include men who were not legally directors and could advise without taking formal decisions. From about the same time (though it has not been possible to establish the precise date when it began) Lever set up a Finance Committee whose functions and powers he defined clearly in a letter written in February 1915 to his son, Hulme Lever, who had been appointed its chairman.

> I am now signing certain notes in connection with the Foreign and Colonial Associated Companies, which notes are calling for capital expenditure and which require to be signed by a Director. I am merely doing this at present in the absence of Mr Tillotson, and I want to explain that my signature of course is merely following the routine of our firm, which is that all requisitions for capital expenditure must be signed by a Director. In view of

the fact that I am signing these notes some confusion might arise if I did not explain the position, which is that all requisitions for capital expenditure must come before the Finance Committee, of which you are Chairman, but these requisitions can only come before the Finance Committee after being signed by a Director. The Finance Committee will consider these requests and the responsibility resting on the Finance Committee is not only to consider the application but to consider how the money can be provided to meet such capital expenditure. The Finance Committee are quite in order in turning down any request for any reason whatever, and certainly, however important and urgent a requisition may be, it becomes the duty of the Finance Committee to turn it down in the event of their feeling that the financial resources of the firm during the period when this capital expenditure would require to be made do not justify such expense being incurred.

The course to take with items that are rejected is that they go back to the Director who made the requisition. The Director who made the requisition can then ask for them to go before the whole Board of Directors at the next Directors' Meeting, when in the opinion of the Director who made the requisition, the capital expenditure was such that he would not himself incur the responsibility of acquiescing in the abandonment of the proposal he had made. Thus the taking of the matter before the whole Board of Directors, will free the members of the Finance Committee from responsibility in the action they have taken and will also free the Director making the requisition from responsibility and the final responsibility will then rest, as it ought to do, on the Board of Directors as a whole and not on the Finance Committee or the individual Director. Both the individual Director and the Committee must retain full liberty of action in these matters—the one to propose, regardless of whether the money can be found or not, which cannot be really his immediate concern, and the Finance Committee to reject if in their opinion there will be difficulty in providing the money, or for any other reason.

Judging from their minutes, these committees played an important role in the decision-making process from 1912 to 1921. Lever was often not present—in fact he may well have made a point of leaving his directors to thrash out questions without, as it were, looking over their shoulders to see what he thought; and this also left him uncommitted to any recommendation they might make. On specific issues, particularly when a project was likely to absorb a lot of capital and would involve further sale of preference shares, both committees were ready to express strong views: for example, further investment in the Congo plantations between 1915 and 1918 at a time when Lever Brothers was short of capital and Huileries du Congo Belge (HCB) was making continuous losses. Lever was probably influenced by the views expressed: he certainly read the minutes carefully and commented extensively in margins and across the page. But in the last resort he almost certainly took all final decisions, often deliberately leaving a committee in ignorance of what he was doing, as with the purchase of shares in a rival South African company in 1915.[6] It was not until 1920, when his judgement could reasonably be faulted on the purchase of the Niger Co., that anything like a collective decision-making process was established.

A number of other committees were set up in the decade after 1912 whose function was to co-ordinate action rather than to consider policy. These consisted of the heads of the various departments of Lever Brothers or its associated companies in Britain which had common problems. In addition there were by then Group Boards, formed to supervise the activities of 'associated companies' in which Lever had bought a stake but which remained autonomous. Within Lever Brothers the real work was done by the departments at Port Sunlight—the Buying Department, Export Department, Foreign Associated Companies Department and so on—which were the nucleus of the larger organisations such as the Overseas Committee and United Exporters which will be described below.

For the overseas companies with which this book is primarily concerned, the Lever administrative system in Britain had limited interest: their local managements were expected to get on with their own work and were left to do it, provided they complied with all the rules and sent back weekly, monthly, quarterly and annual estimates and reports. These companies were supervised by a group of Lever Brothers directors or very senior executives in Port Sunlight (or London after the central administration moved there in 1921). Until 1915 J. L. Tillotson, one of the earliest of Lever's directors, had the title of Director of Imperial and Foreign Departments. After his death in that year responsibility was transferred to a group of three. By 1919 they were called collectively the Foreign Associated

Companies Control Board. Each had the title Director Overseas Companies (DOC) and they divided Lever Brothers' overseas interests between them. Thus in 1924 C. E. Tatlow was in charge of DOC department A, which was responsible for South Africa, France, Belgium, Nigeria and the Belgian Congo; A. C. Knight (who was not a director and was forced to resign after a disagreement with Lever that year) had DOC B, looking after China, Japan and India; and H. G. Hart looked after DOC C (though according to Knox he insisted on calling it H in case he was thought junior to those in charge of DOC A and B), which covered America, Scandinavia and Holland. These men were responsible for all Lever Brothers activities overseas, including exports. Only the two commodity enterprises in the Belgian Congo and the Solomons, the first with direct links to Lever, the second under the Australian company, together with the West African trading companies eventually incorporated with the Niger company, escaped the DOCs.

This system of appointing senior Lever men to take specific responsibility for particular overseas interests was the nucleus of the later system by which Lever/Unilever kept in touch with its overseas subsidiaries through the Overseas Committee (OSC) and individual directors. Yet so long as he lived Lever himself remained the dominant influence in this field also. He corresponded direct with the local managing directors or chairmen, reviewed their perform-ance, approved or disallowed their estimates and visited them from time to time to take the big decisions. Until 1925 these associated companies in fact remained so many individual enterprises linked through him rather than united as part of a single Lever commercial organisation in a particular country. It was therefore only after his death that the DOC system could evolve into a fully responsible mechanism for the central control of the overseas subsidiaries and at the same time restructure all Lever interests within a particular country.

Until about 1919 Lever Brothers can thus be seen as a very large soap manufacturing enterprise which had enlarged its share of the soap market in Britain, Europe, North America, Australia and South Africa by building factories and acquiring or merging with local competitors and had also begun to diversify into other but still organically related fields such as the West African palm oil trade, plantations, margarine manufacture, oil milling, etc., but one which nevertheless remained essentially unitary in conception. From

1919 all this changed rapidly. The story of Lever's acquisitions in the next three years, which included buying control of the only two remaining large soap companies in Britain, Gossages and Crosfields, the Niger Company, Sanitas Disinfectant Co., Trufood Ltd, a fleet of Scottish fishing trawlers and a chain of fish shops, a soap company in India, an oil refining business in the Philippines and founding two soap companies in Nigeria and the Congo, has been told by Wilson. [7] These purchases had irreversible consequences. Lever Brothers took the critical step over the threshold from being essentially a unitary enterprise into being a horizontally diversified conglomerate of great complexity. As a direct consequence the still primitive structure of administration and control at the centre proved inadequate and new systems of consultation and administration began to evolve from 1921. Thereafter the process was continuous but it is convenient to break this account in 1925 because Lever's death marked the most important turning point since the founding of the business.

It is difficult to be certain who was responsible for the administrative innovations that began in January 1921, but it is probable that they were initiated by Francis D'Arcy Cooper who, as a member of Cooper Brothers and Co., the accountants who had worked for Levers for a long time, was asked in 1920 to tackle the major financial problems resulting from the purchase of the Niger Co. The first step was to set up a new collective leadership and to locate this in London rather than Port Sunlight. This was the Special Committee which first met in January 1921. It had four members—Lever, his son Hulme Lever, Harold Greenhalgh and John McDowell, two of the most experienced and trusted directors. These had power 'to co-opt any professional gentleman not being a director of the Company to assist and advise them'—presumably Cooper. The Special Committee did not necessarily replace the existing Policy Council, but in fact this ceased to meet after July 1921 and nothing like it was revived until 1925, when the Managing Directors' Conference was set up to perform a similar role.

The Special Committee was to become the most important feature of Unilever's administrative history; but its immediate function was more limited—to ensure that Lever acted only on proper advice and after mature consideration; and he seems to have accepted the new situation generously and fully. During the next four years he wrote a large number of letters to his 'colleagues' on the Committee from wherever he happened to be—Scotland, Port

Sunlight, Africa; and while he never hesitated to put his own viewpoint, the underlying assumption was always that the Committee now had full executive authority even in his absence and, even more important, that all decisions must be collective. His attitude is well summarised in three letters to the other members (who were joined by D'Arcy Cooper when he became a director in 1923), the first two written in 1923, the third in 1924. The first was to Greenhalgh, dated 26 April 1923:

> I can assure you that yourself and other members of the Special Committee are of the greatest help to me and I am anxious to avail myself to a still further extent of this help. It is not that I am feeling in any way unequal to the work at present but that I am conscious that very often after seventy changes come very suddenly and I am anxious to consider the business first, foremost and all the time. It is always a great pleasure to me to fulfil all the duties I perform but I have no right to indulge in my preferences. It was for this reason that I bought the Island of Lewis thinking that I could then be at a distance and yet sufficiently near to be reached immediately by cable and in a couple of days by post.

The next day he wrote again emphasising that all letters relating to the business should be read and commented on by the other members of the Special Committee and should then be sent to him. The third, written a year later on 14 June 1924, sets out his views, after three years' experience of the new system, in more detail.

> My dear Colleagues,
>
> I am very anxious to more clearly define my position in relation to the Special Committee. I am certain that it is your wish also that I should do so.
>
> On many occasions I am asked as to my views on matters. If, after I have expressed these views, no comment is made upon them I take it for granted that we are united on the subject, but it often happens I am certain that on further consideration other points of view occur to some one or all of my colleagues which would modify their previous assent. This is greatly to the advantage of the business that it should be so, but what I want is that when on afterthought a modification of the original idea is

thought advisable, I should be informed of that forthwith, because I might have other views to put before my colleagues that I did not bring forward at the time because we were all agreed but which I ought to have an opportunity of bringing forward if further thought on the matter gave to any of my colleagues or all of my colleagues a changed opinion. In short, what I want is to have the benefit of as wide a diversity of opinion as possible given without hesitation, and equally I want that if no diverse opinion is expressed at the moment in consultation to feel that we are united upon the policy that was not dissented upon but it would not be in the interests of the business that afterthoughts should be excluded; therefore afterthoughts must be an important part of our policy and should be admitted if not too late, that is if action has not already been taken upon the lines agreed upon. These afterthoughts to be communicated to myself; they will always be welcome and always receive the fullest consideration, but if no afterthoughts reach me I want to feel that we are united and that the matter will go through, whatever it may be, upon the lines we have discussed and apparently agreed upon.

This marked a major step in the evolution of Lever Brothers from personal to collective leadership. 1921 to 1925 saw other important changes. Psychologically the most significant was possibly the transfer of Lever Brothers headquarters from Port Sunlight to De Keyser's Hotel, Blackfriars, early in 1921, on the site of the present head office of Unilever, built in the early 1930s. Lever had had a London office for a long time, but the transfer of the main administration symbolised the transformation of a Lancashire soap business into an international enterprise. Of greater practical importance, however, were the first steps taken during and after 1923 towards rationalisation of the multifarious industrial and other enterprises founded or acquired by Lever. To this point almost all had retained their legal identity and autonomy, each with its own board, management, factories, sales force and so on. In many respects all these survived until the 1930s for Lever had developed a strong dislike in his later years of what he called 'scrambling eggs' and this bolstered the natural aversion of the management of associated companies to losing their independent existence. But from 1923 the cost and inefficiency of this situation became increasingly obvious and in the next two years two innovations of considerable later importance were made.

The first, in 1923, was to remodel the existing Group Boards. In the past individual manufacturing companies had been grouped territorially, irrespective of what they made; they were now grouped by product, and this led to the system of Product Executives developed in the 1930s. The second, in 1923 and 1924, was a major attempt to break down the separatism each associated company in Britain showed over its export trade. This was most acute and ridiculous in the soap business. Since 1919, when Lever had gained control over William Gossage and Sons of Widnes and Joseph Crosfield and Sons of Warrington, his greatest surviving rivals, these and Lever Brothers had retained their own sales systems at home and abroad. At home the central Lever Brothers committees could without too much difficulty impose some uniformity on prices, discounts, credit terms and so on; but in overseas markets each company continued to operate quite independently and to compete fiercely. Even Lever, who was keen to stimulate competition 'within the family', saw the need for co-ordination. In 1919 he began to work on the problem of overlapping sales of Lever and associated company products in a given country; there must be a clear demarcation between that company's exports from the UK, goods from another subsidiary and the local manufacturing company as regards use of trademarks and brand names. In 1923 he turned to cut-throat competition between the Lever Bros, Gossage and Crosfield export departments in overseas markets. Their 'continual jealousy' prevented an agreed policy to promote total sales and maximise profits and laid the way open to foreign competition. His proposed solution was to create a single head of the 'export' business for all the Lever soap companies in Britain. But the outcome was less radical and quite unsatisfactory. In place of a single autocratic controller, who would not have been acceptable to the various boards at this stage, an Export Control Board (renamed the Export Committee in July 1925 and still later known as the Export Executive) was set up in 1924, consisting of the heads of the export departments of each company, with C. H. Hamilton (Chairman of Gossages) as chairman. It met periodically in London and attempted to sort out conflicts and duplication of effort; but the evidence suggests that it achieved very little. In 1928 Andrew Knox described current practice as follows:

There is no disguising the fact that in export markets . . . our three chief companies spend most of their time competing against each other rather than finding new business for the Family as a whole: while we have one united interest, we have no common policy.[8]

Possibly as a result of Knox's letter a much more radical approach was then adopted. The Export Control Board's successor, the Export Committee, was replaced by a new unitary executive department called United Exporters Limited (UEL) whose directors were drawn from the highest levels of the Lever system to place them above the petty wrangling of their respective export departments: the chairman was D'Arcy Cooper, by then Chairman of Lever Brothers, and his colleagues were the chairmen of Gossages and Crosfields and two directors of Lever Brothers. Thereafter all overseas sales were handled from London and the individual soap factories (until Gossages was closed down in the early 1930s) became merely manufacturing units within an increasingly consolidated single business. In this way the evolution of Export symbolised the evolution of the old decentralised Lever Brothers into the new Lever/Unilever organisation built up in the years 1925 to 1940.

1925–45

The dominant trends in Lever Brothers after 1925 were the rapid evolution of a conventional modern collective system of corporate management followed by rationalisation of the means of production and distribution. The first process was far advanced by the time of the merger with the Dutch margarine companies in 1929, when the Lever administration system had again to be modified, though not fundamentally changed; the second took place almost entirely after 1930.

Because Lever's personal power had, so to speak, been partly put into commission in 1921 and because his son, the second Viscount Leverhulme (hereafter Leverhulme), though always an active member of the company, preferred not to become chairman, taking the title of 'Governor', control of Lever Brothers passed to the Special Committee as a collective leadership rather than to a single chairman when Lever died in 1925. A further sign that decision-making was to be more widely dispersed was the resuscitation of the old PTC or PC, though now called the Managing Directors' Conference (hereafter MDC, though it was later called the Directors' Conference). It started to meet in May 1925 as a committee of the whole Board after the Board's weekly meetings, and it kept full minutes. On the whole its function seems to have been to disseminate information and ensure that directors could see the business as a whole rather than to act as a genuine decision-making body; but it could and did debate issues and might be asked for collective advice if the Special Committee wanted a general opinion.

Below these two, which dealt with any and all Lever business, other more specialised committees were now established or continued in modified form. All were intended to strengthen the control of the centre over the particularism of individual companies and organisations. Thus the Sales Executive Committee, to reduce competition in the domestic market, and the Capital Expenditure Committee were both set up in May 1925. They were followed in October 1926 by the Overseas Committee, and this requires more detailed description because it plays so large a role in this book. In one sense it was not new because it merely took over the work of the existing DOC departments and with them the three directors in charge, Greenhalgh, Tatlow and Hart, together with Charles Cole, previously assistant to DOC/B, as Secretary. But three things gave the new committee a different significance. First, it was to act collectively, meeting daily and dealing with all questions of principle which came up for consideration by the three overseas departments. Second, the committee was to set up subordinate departments, each dealing with one subject for all overseas companies under the committee's control—thus cutting across territorial boundaries for the first time. Finally, the Export Committee was to come under Overseas Committee to ensure that the exporting and manufacturing of soap overseas should be seen as complementary and not competing activities. A single body could now judge at what moment, if ever, it became more advantageous for Lever as a whole to make something locally rather than import it from Britain. In this way the essential unity of decision-making, which had once been held by Lever in person, was re-embodied in a committee whose members were indifferently concerned with exporting and import-substitution.

Three years after the Overseas Committee was born Lever Bros was forced by the merger with the twin Dutch companies, Margarine Union Ltd and Margarine Unie NV, to undertake a far more difficult administrative reconstruction which established patterns that lasted until the 1960s and beyond. It would be impossible here to explain in detail why these two very dissimilar combines—one essentially a soap business, the other predominantly concerned with edible oils and fats—came together to form a still larger combine. The story has been told in detail by Wilson[9] and it is necessary here only to describe its consequences for the new 'Unilever' as an international enterprise.

The fusion of Lever Brothers and Margarine Union/Unie was basically the outcome of growing competition between two large enterprises which used the same raw materials and were beginning to encroach on each other's markets. Levers had been persuaded, without much difficulty, by the British government to start making margarine in 1914. Their Planters Margarine had done reasonably well during the First World War and, although it was generally a loss-maker during the 1920s, it represented a modest challenge to the Dutch margarine companies in the British market. On the other side the four Dutch margarine and edible oil companies—Jurgens, Van den Berghs, Hartogs and Calvé Delft—which had merged in 1927–8, had their own soap interests; and when they were joined in 1928 by the two eastern European firms, Centra and Schichts, their combined soap sales constituted a threat to Levers' European soap companies. But when Margarine Unie began negotiations with Levers in 1928 they at first intended only to eliminate overlapping by arranging for the sale of Levers' margarine interests to Margarine Union: the reciprocal sale of all Margarine Unie's soap interests came up on Levers' initiative in the course of negotiation. This, however, proved an unsatisfactory solution for there were many industrial and other indivisibilities on each side and the idea of a total merger grew out of frustrating attempts to solve the problem of who should sell what. On 8 August 1929 a short document known as the Heads of Agreement laid down the basic principles on which the new combination was to be based. The two groups would form a federation consisting of two new companies, one English, the other Dutch. Margarine Union, the existing British-registered company established earlier by Jurgens and Van den Berghs, changed its name to Unilever Ltd and acquired the whole of Lever Brothers ordinary shares in exchange for Margarine Union shares. Lever Brothers thus became a wholly owned subsidiary of Unilever Ltd, but retained its legal identity and preference capital. Margarine Unie changed its name to Unilever NV. One vital principle on which the Dutch combines had been based—equalisation of dividends between Margarine Union and Unie—was retained and this meant that a transfer of shares from London to the Rotterdam headquarters of Unilever NV or back again might become necessary. But the important thing was that, by an ingenious legal device, itself made necessary by the tax and company laws of Britain and the Netherlands, it had proved possible to form a merger between two already very complex organisations without subordinating one to the other.

The merger eliminated competition but it did not solve the problem of how the federated businesses were to be run. A solution was found by adopting one unusual administrative device from each side. From the Dutch combine, Unilever adopted the practice of having two boards of directors, one for Limited, the other for NV, consisting of the same men but with different chairmen. From Lever Brothers Unilever took over the Special Committee as a unique instrument for imposing collective control at the top. This did not in fact operate immediately: from 27 October 1929 to the end of August 1930 the still coalescing business in England was supervised by an 'Executive Committee'; and even when the new Special Committee came into existence in September 1930 it was twice the size of the old—four men from each side of the business. There was therefore the risk that the expanded committee would institutionalise the diversity of Unilever as an amalgamation of recently fused and imperfectly homogenised European and British family enterprises, the former still led by members of the Jurgens, Van den Berghs, Hartog and Schicht clans.

This danger was averted by the emergence from the start of Francis D'Arcy Cooper as the dominant personality of the new Unilever and his success in making London the acknowledged centre of the whole concern. Since Cooper held undisputed control over the largest single unit in Unilever, was accepted as an outstanding businessman and, perhaps most important, was neutral as between Van den Berghs, Hartogs and the rest, he was well placed to assert his position as effective head of a federal enterprise. True unity of direction came later, when Cooper was able first to persuade the Dutch families to stop voting on the Board and the Special Committee as family groups and then to reduce the size of the Special Committee to four—still two Dutch and two British. It was nevertheless by no means certain that London would become the administrative and symbolic centre of this multinational commercial empire and for some time the combined boards of Limited and NV met every two months in various cities in Britain and on the continent. This was obviously too inconvenient to last. Board meetings were reduced in number and the Lever Brothers Directors' Conference was adopted as a committee of the whole, meeting in London because the headquarters of both Margarine Union and Levers were there. In the end Cooper was able to persuade the continental directors that it would be convenient if the Board followed the Conference to Blackfriars. Thus by 1931 the future pattern was visible: a modified Special Committee and an enlarged Directors' Conference running a world-wide business from London with an additional headquarters in Rotterdam. To symbolise the new situation a new Unilever House was built on the existing site at Blackfriars which provided an impressive Board room and offices for the Special Committee, the majority of directors and those administrative departments which served the combine as a whole. A rather smaller building was put up in Rotterdam which provided for those directors and administrative departments which were primarily involved in the continental side of the business.

Yet this alone does not explain why the fusion worked so well. To the British historian looking at the concern from the outside it seems that the main reason why there was so little friction over issues such as language and so little apparent resentment at the dominance of London was the extraordinarily non-parochial character of the Dutch part of the concern. Far more international in outlook than most in Britain, speaking English, French and German where most Englishmen spoke only English, the Dutch obviously made a very large contribution to the success of Unilever as a bilingual international enterprise.

Goodwill and an ingenious solution to the problems of top management could not by themselves solve the technical problems of how to run so large and overlapping a collection of businesses at a time of acute recession. Two things had to be done: to rationalise a multiplicity of individual industrial and commercial units within both halves of Unilever; and to evolve a pyramidical structure of command to provide effective control of broad policy at the top while allowing reasonable flexibility at the bottom. Wilson has described the process of rationalisation in Britain and Europe,[10] and since this only affected the overseas companies in so far as it provided a model for their own reorganisation, it is proposed to concentrate on administrative change.

Ignoring the multitude of short-lived committees set up in the early days, the essential features of the Unilever administration structure in the mid-1930s and down to 1945 were as follows. Below the Board and the Special Committee was the Directors' Conference which met weekly and acted as a centre for the dissemination of information and exchange of opinions. Its functions were extended because the Finance Committee was abolished in 1931 and all capital expenditure proposals had to go to the Conference. At the same level, in that they served all Unilever companies, were a number of service departments and specialised advisory committees, some in London, others in Rotterdam. Below these Unilever divided into four partly autonomous segments whose top management met round the table of the Conference. Essentially the division was geographical: Britain, the continent, overseas manufacturing and plantation companies (excluding those in West Africa) and the United Africa Company. All but the British section were run by collective executives: the Continental Committee, the Overseas Committee and the Board of UAC. The domestic British business continued, as before 1929, to be run by group executives divided according to product, such as the Home Soap Executive. Below each of these four committees, boards or executives stood the management of individual home, continental or overseas companies, factories, plantations or trading firms. The pyramid was complete and the system of control proved adequate until the business began to expand again and diversify after 1945.

For the present study the Overseas Committee is, of course, the most important part of the new structure; and it is significant that of all parts of the old Lever Brothers this seems to have changed least as a result of the merger of 1929. Indeed Andrew Knox, who was associated with OSC throughout this period, does not mention any effect the merger had on the Committee or its functions. One main reason for this was that in 1929 the Dutch companies had no active overseas manufacturing or plantation subsidiaries, another that the margarine export trade continued to be handled by the Continental Committee. Thus OSC was left to supervise the existing Lever manufacturing and other subsidiaries, together with exports of Lever products through UEL which remained under the supervision of OSC. The main difference was that the Committee as reconstituted in 1931 contained two senior representatives of the continental companies—Sidney Van den Bergh and Georg Schicht —to balance Greenhalgh as Chairman and Tatlow. Charles Cole remained Secretary and provided continuity. Apart from their personal abilities (and the mind of Sidney Van den Bergh in

particular is stamped across the records of most of Unilever's
overseas activities until his resignation in 1963), the accession of
representatives of NV had the immense advantage that these men
understood the edible oils and fats business better than most British
members at a time when the overseas companies were beginning to
diversify into these fields.

Between 1931 and 1943 only two significant changes were made
in the character of OSC, one substantive, the other terminological.
The substantive change came in November 1932 when it was
decided that the Committee should no longer act collectively when
it held its frequent meetings with the Special Committee to discuss
estimates, capital proposals and so on. The overseas companies
were once again, as before 1926, divided into lists, which cut across
geographical lines, and each of the four directors became primarily
responsible for one list of companies. He visited each country about
once every two years, writing a substantial report on their activities;
and he was expected to speak for them on the Committee, at the
Conference and in meetings with the Special Committee. This
specialisation led later to the concept of 'Contact Directors' which
is described below.

The terminological change came in July 1938. As a result of the
depression the continental companies allocated to Unilever NV in
1929 were earning much less than those allocated to Unilever
Limited. To maintain the principle of equal dividends without
straining the tax laws it was decided to reconstruct the legal company
structure and to transfer a number of companies whose shares were
on the books of Unilever Limited to those of Unilever NV. Unilever
Ltd and Unilever NV were formally dissolved and re-emerged as
'Lever Brothers and Unilever Ltd' and 'Lever Brothers and Unilever
NV'. The subsidiary companies whose shares were transferred to
Holland were chosen so that they included all those outside the
British Empire and Commonwealth: that is, the USA, the
Philippines, China, Siam, Indonesia and Latin America. This
divided the OSC's old empire and the Committee was in fact
technically dissolved. An Empire Overseas Committee, consisting
of the three British members of OSC—Tatlow, Barnish and Hansard,
plus W. P. Scott of UEL, retained responsibility for all British
territories while the old Continental Committee, renamed Unilever
NV (Continental and Overseas) Committee and with Sidney Van
den Bergh as one of its members, took control of all non-British
overseas companies. For an integrated Anglo-Dutch company this

was theoretically a step backwards; but in practice the change made little difference since both OSC and Continental and Overseas Committee (COC) were based in Unilever House and both reported to the Special Committee and Directors' Conference.

In any case this restructuring proved to be short-lived. Once war was declared a year later in 1939 the distinction between the two Overseas Committees appears to have been dropped: by November 1939 minutes of meetings of the Special Committee with directors concerned with overseas companies were said to be 'with the Overseas Committee', irrespective of what territory was involved. The occupation of Holland by the Germans in 1940 meant in any case that the whole Unilever system outside occupied Europe was run from London; and restrictions on communications between Britain and other continents left many overseas companies in partial isolation. It is not clear from the records which London director kept an eye on which overseas company from 1940 to 1943, but the Overseas Committee continued to function under its Secretary, Charles Cole. In January 1942 Lawrence Heyworth told the Special Committee that the overseas organisation needed improvement; but it was not until October 1943 that the Directors' Conference formally approved a new system. Its essential feature was that all continental and overseas companies were divided between four 'Co-ordinating Directors'—A. Hartog and J. L. Polak from the Dutch side, J. L. Heyworth and R. H. Muir from the British. The Overseas Committee, consisting of Polak and Muir, continued only until these directors had taken up their duties. A new marketing department took over the routine work of the old OSC, and the OSC Sales and Technical Staff provided the nucleus of a new Marketing Advisory Division and a Technical Division in Unilever House. In the same period most of the overseas companies were organised into four groups, each with its marketing, technical and accounting services, centred on Buenos Aires, Durban, Bombay and Sydney. Trinidad, Nigeria and the Congo were supervised from London by one of the Co-ordinating Directors. It is not surprising that there are few records relating to the overseas companies in Unilever House for this period: essentially they had to go their own way and make do as well as they could.

The war thus seemed to have destroyed the unity of the old OSC. The Co-ordinating Directors of 1943 proved not to be merely a wartime expedient for they were reorganised in January 1945, given the name 'Contact Directors' and the individual responsibility for companies allocated to them was defined by Special Committee as a long-term practice. The Secretariat that served the Contact Directors was still the OSC staff under Charles Cole, and this provided essential continuity and some co-ordination; but when the Special Committee met to consider overseas estimates, etc. it was with those 'Contact Directors' responsible for those companies as individuals. It is an important, though difficult, question what effect these changes had on the character of Unilever's relations with the overseas subsidiaries. Wilson writes of the evolution of the Contact Directors as if they represented a deliberate new approach worked out during the Second World War which 'envisaged the abolition of control such as the Continental and Overseas Committees had exercised over the affairs of foreign and overseas associated companies. . . . So far as possible, the local management were to be left to themselves, for it was of the essence of the plan that it recognised that in many respects the local man knew his problems and the answers to them better than anyone in London or Rotterdam.' This implies a substantive change of approach from a relatively centralised to a federative international enterprise, though Wilson qualified this by pointing out that 'many of these principles had their roots in the past'. Nevertheless his conclusion was that 'The new policy envisaged a partnership between centre and perimeter, rather than a dictatorship of above to below'.[11] Wilson may have had access to information on the intentions of men in the mid-1940s which is not now available: all three Heyworth brothers are dead and no private correspondence survives. But the primary material on which this book is based suggests that this is a misleading interpretation of the Contact Director system. First, the autonomy of overseas 'associated companies' had been one of Lever's first principles and the amount of central control had never been great. Second, the restructuring of the OSC in the 1940s on which Wilson based his argument was initially a wartime expedient to provide some substitute for super- vision from London when this could not be done in the normal way. Finally, the new terminology did little more than recognise the fact, admitted as early as 1932, that the OSC as a whole could not know enough about each overseas company to adjudicate collectively on questions of detail. The individual responsibility of directors for particular companies established then was precisely the responsi- bility held by Contact Directors after 1945.

In fact the real significance of the creation of Contact Directors for overseas companies was that it formed part of a wider post-war unification of Unilever by abolishing the distinction between 'British', 'European' and 'Overseas' enterprises. A detailed plan promulgated after considerable discussion in April 1949 envisaged that the whole Unilever system (as always excluding UAC) would be unified at the top by a system of Contact Directors, each taking responsibility for a different segment of the concern. The main distinction would be between the British and all other parts of the business. By that time all productive enterprises in Britain had already been 'scrambled' and reorganised along product lines: hence there was now a Contact Director for each of the Home Executives —soap, oil-milling, margarine and food. Since the continental and overseas units were still organised on a national and company basis, these had Contact Directors for areas: two for West Europe, based on Rotterdam, five others for the rest of the world. Lever Brothers (India) Ltd was therefore on a par with, say, Huilever in Brussels. R. H. Muir would speak for the first, F. J. Tempel or W. A. Faure of Rotterdam would speak for the second. How these Contact Directors fulfilled their linking functions was left to their discretion: as the Special Committee minute said, 'a uniform approach to this problem was not possible, as the management in some places were young and inexperienced . . .'. But for all companies the old rule laid down by Lever from the start was to be observed: 'the local management should be encouraged to take their own decisions, even at the risk of making mistakes'.

All this seemed to reflect a conscious attempt to return to the atomised Lever industrial empire of the pre-1930s with its emphasis on individual responsibility among directors and the autonomy of particular subsidiaries. Yet even in rationalising the system worked out since 1943, the Special Committee minutes of April 1949 placed heavy emphasis on collective responsibility and consultation. 'The principle of the joint responsibility of Contact Directors was fully understood, but it was obviously undesirable that all should attempt to take responsibility for each matter of detail.'

Again,

It would be the responsibility of each of these Directors to see that any matter of importance concerning his territories should be discussed with his colleagues. The success of the system depended upon free and frank discussion, so as to derive the maximum amount of benefit from their collective experience.

The scheme provided no institutional framework for such consultation or for the dissemination of paper; but this was the germ from which the later evolution of the Contact Directors into a revived Overseas Committee was to grow.

1945–65

In the mid-1940s Unilever, for all its size, was still a comparatively simple business. First, although Lever Brothers was a diversified business from the early 1920s, diversity was qualified in two respects: it was the result of the eclectic interests of Lever rather than of deliberate corporate policy; and the number of brands within the production categories, as is clear from Wilson's diagrams, was still comparatively limited.[12] Second, the number of overseas companies was still small: only about fourteen manufacturing subsidiaries altogether in 1938. In that year 60 per cent of Unilever's turnover of under £200 million and almost all the profits came from edible fats, soap and the activities of UAC and plantations. Toilet preparations provided only 1 per cent and foods 11 per cent of turnover.

By 1965 Unilever was a much bigger and immensely more complicated enterprise and this had major consequences for its overseas operations. Growth had occurred in three main directions. First, the number of products had expanded and the composition of each category had changed. Non-soapy detergents (NSDs)—that is, synthetic washing and scouring products—which had accounted for only 8 per cent of 'detergent' sales in 1950 by volume, were 56 per cent of detergent sales by 1965. 'Foods' now included a very wide range which had been expanded since 1938 by the development of dehydrated soups, frozen foods and ice-cream. Products such as chemicals, packaging materials, plastics, etc., categorised as 'miscellaneous', had declined between 1938 and 1965 from 17 per cent to 9 per cent of total sales by value, though their sales value had risen absolutely and the range of products was immensely greater. It is not within the scope of this study to account for this diversification in Unilever's business after 1945 and Wilson has analysed it in detail. But from the standpoint of Unilever as a whole these developments had one major consequence: they made it impossible indefinitely to preserve the relatively simple production and control system which has been described above. Innovation and diversification on this scale demanded far more planning and research than ever before and the adoption of relatively advanced and expensive new technologies implied allocation of resources on an international basis rather than within the framework of individual historic companies or national product groups. It would, for example, have been extremely wasteful to have multiplied research laboratories indefinitely, and this meant that the provision of research services to enterprises in different centres had to be co-ordinated. Thus the main new need and achievement of Unilever as an administrative structure after 1945 was greater co-ordination; and this meant in some degree subordinating all parts of the business which made the same thing or needed the same service to a central co-ordinating authority. Such co-ordination, it must be emphasised, was quite a different thing from the provision of common technical and advisory services, which had been available to factory, company and group managements from the early days and which survived into the new era. Co-ordination meant central control: only a comparatively few marginal activities of Unilever in Britain and Europe remained under the direct executive authority of the UK and continental groups rather than under supervision by the new co-ordination organisation by 1967. This was to make eggs into an omelette rather than merely to scramble them.

The effects of these developments—both diversification and the growth of co-ordination on overseas companies—were evident in many ways, but two stand out. First, the tendency of the parent companies towards growth in Europe through diversification and the adoption of new higher technology was repeated, at least in part, overseas. The pattern would not be identical, given wide differences in the size and sophistication of markets; but any overseas company which found itself coming up against barriers to further growth along established lines was now free to call upon an expanding range of technologies and brands already available in Europe. It will be seen that as a consequence the profiles of most overseas companies tended to change after 1945 as indistinct shadows of the business in Europe.

The obverse of this trend was that the overseas companies were likely to become more dependent on the know-how concentrated in the home companies. In the past an Australian or Indian company, once established, needed to call for visits by technical experts from Europe only when they ran into difficulties or were introducing a new product, and this was infrequent. But if, after 1945, Unilever Australia wanted to manufacture, say, dehydrated soups or NSDs, both requiring new technology, they could best do so with the help of experts and equipment from Europe; and since such a new departure usually involved considerable capital investment and at the same time was likely to affect the established export market of Unilever factories in Europe, London alone could decide whether local manufacture was justified by reference to Unilever's international interests. In short, the price of diversification by means of instant imported technology and capital was much the same for a Unilever subsidiary as it was for a less developed country—increasing dependence on the source of capital and skills.

During the two decades after 1945, and especially after about 1955, the tension between local autonomy and the control inseparable from the importation of new techniques and capital constitutes a major theme in the history of Unilever overseas. The results were neither uniform nor simple and the position was confused by the simultaneous transition of many of the colonial territories in which Unilever had subsidiaries to political independence. These developments tended to collide and cancel each other out. On the one hand new technology certainly led to much greater day-to-day involvement of the centre in the affairs of subsidiaries; and, as Knox wrote in the early 1970s, 'nowadays the management of a company such as Unilever Australia would be lucky to have a single week in the year (except perhaps at Christmas and New Year) without someone from head office about the place'.[13] Taken sufficiently far this would mean that local managements would become mere machine minders and ledger fillers, the antithesis of the basic Lever conception of 'associated companies'. But by a peculiar coincidence the newly independent sovereign states in which many Unilever subsidiaries operated were now bringing pressure on foreign-owned firms to integrate themselves more closely into the host economy. For example, they were asked to allow local participation in the equity, to increase the proportion of native managers, to use local raw materials, to sell at controlled or agreed prices and to make those things the government thought the country needed or could afford to consume. The case studies in this book give some indication of what results such pressures had and how far they offset the natural tendency of the subsidiaries of a multinational to follow the production patterns of its parent and be controlled by it. In the final chapter an attempt will be made to assess how far this new economic nationalism counterbalanced the equally new tendency towards central control within the Unilever system.

It remains briefly to outline the changing administrative structure of Unilever from the mid-1940s to 1965 with special emphasis on those aspects which most affected the overseas companies. At the top the Special Committee perhaps changed least. On the death of the second Viscount Leverhulme in 1949 the number of its members was reduced to three because the third Viscount chose to become an Advisory Director rather than Governor. Thereafter the conventional formula was that the Board would annually elect to the Committee the Chairmen of Unilever Limited and NV and the Vice-Chairman of Unilever Limited or NV. The role of the Committee after 1945 was, as always, to see the whole business in perspective and the accelerating expansion of this period made this increasingly difficult. Their solution was to hold regular meetings with the directors and other senior executives in charge of each operating segment of the concern as often as possible. The pattern changed as the structure evolved. As some indication, the Special Committee files for the years 1952–4 show that they had regular meetings with at least fifteen separate executive or administrative groups, whereas in 1937 they had similar meetings with only seven and it must be assumed that this total is incomplete. In addition to these regular (commonly monthly) meetings, the Committee undertook three major annual reviews which covered the whole business. These were the Annual Operating Plans of all companies, which covered estimates of prospective sales and costs which, when approved, became formalised as the traditional 'pro forma' or target of Lever's terminology; the Annual Capital Expenditure Budget; and the Annual Review of Remuneration and Selection of Top Management.[14] Such reviews were by no means a formality: the Committee frequently insisted on changes in the proposals before them. Apart from these routine meetings and surveys the Committee operated very flexibly and placed heavy emphasis on personal contact with senior management. Thus overseas chairmen with specially important projects would accompany a member of the Overseas Committee to the Special Committee and be able there to present their case. Although the Committee avoided formality, detailed and highly confidential minutes of meetings with executives were taken continuously from 1930, though no minutes of meetings of the Committee alone were kept until the 1970s. For the historian these minutes are the best evidence of the intentions of the official mind of Unilever.

The Board and the Directors' Conference remained substantially unchanged after 1945 but the rest of the administrative system altered considerably to match structural change in the business. Wilson has described this process and the evolving structure can best be understood from the diagrams he provides and, for the early 1970s, from Figures 1, 2, 3 and 4 below.[15] Down to 1965 the key units below the Board—the Management Groups—were still based on geography rather than product. In 1949 there were four main Management Groups: UK Co-ordination; Contact Directors, Rotterdam; Contact Directors, Overseas; and the Board of UAC. After 1949 the main change was the evolution of 'Co-ordination' whose objectives have already been outlined. The aim was initially to superimpose a system of advisory committees and supporting specialised administrative units on top of the existing production units which were territorially oriented. Starting in 1959 a number of these co-ordinating units were established to ensure uniformity of practice, quality, etc., in the main Unilever brands. By 1965 there were six of these: Food I (edible fats), Food II (other foods), Chemicals, Detergents (soap and NSDs), Toilet Preparations and Paper, Printing and Packaging. At this stage these were essentially advisory bodies: the lines of executive control ran from the main Board through the appropriate Management Group to the individual manufacturing company. The big change took place in 1966/7, after the period covered by this book. Supervision of the main 'international' brands was then transferred from individual operating companies to the appropriate 'Co-ordination' in London and Rotterdam: the UK Committee and Continental Group, Rotterdam, retained executive control only over Unilever companies in certain countries which did not manufacture standard international lines and over other companies in the UK and elsewhere which produced articles not so far covered by a co-ordination unit. The effect was that one or more directors was now directly in charge of the production of a particular product wherever it was manufactured. As Wilson put it, 'the aim was to place on the co-ordinator the responsibility for formulating policies that would stimulate expansion in his group of products anywhere in the world where opportunity offered'.[16]

Within this changing framework the developments that most affected the overseas companies described in this book, all of which were formally excluded from the co-ordination system, were the evolution of the Contact Director system of 1945–9 into a reborn Overseas Committee; the parallel restructuring of United Exporters

Figure 1   The Structure of Unilever, 1973

UNILEVER IDENTICAL BOARDS
SPECIAL COMMITTEE

SECRETARIAT

CONCERN DIVISIONS
CHART 6

AUDIT
COMPANIES' SECRETARIAL
CORPORATE DEVELOPMENT
FINANCE
ECONOMICS
MARKETING
ORGANISATION
ENGINEERING
PENSIONS
PERSONNEL
RESEARCH
PATENTS

REGIONAL DIRECTORS EUROPE
CHART 3

EUROPEAN LIAISON COMMITTEE

NATIONAL MANAGEMENTS IN

Austria, Belgium,
Denmark, Finland,
France, Germany,
Greece, Ireland,
Italy, Netherlands,
Portugal, Spain,
Sweden,
Switzerland,
United Kingdom

NATIONAL CONFERENCES

CO-ORDINATION
CHART 2

ANIMAL FEEDS
CHEMICALS
DETERGENTS
EDIBLE FATS AND DAIRY
FOOD AND DRINKS
MEAT PRODUCTS
PACKAGING, PRINTING
PLASTICS
TOILET PREPARATIONS

COMPANIES IN

Austria, Belgium,
Denmark, Finland,
France, Germany,
Greece, Italy,
Netherlands, Spain,
Sweden, Switzerland,
United Kingdom

OVERSEAS COMMITTEE
CHART 4

COMPANIES IN

Argentina, Australia,
Brazil,
Central America,
Chile, Colombia,
East Africa, Ghana,
India, Indonesia,
Japan, Malawi,
Malaysia, Mexico,
New Zealand, Nigeria,
Pakistan, Peru,
Philippines,
Singapore, South Africa
Sri Lanka,
Thailand, Trinidad,
Tunisia, Turkey,
United Kingdom (UELI),
Venezuela, Zaire

UNITED AFRICA GROUP
CHART 5

OPERATIONS IN

Arabian Gulf, Belgium,
Burundi, Canary Islands,
The Gambia, Germany,
Ghana, Hong Kong, Italy,
Japan, Kenya, Morocco,
Nigeria, Rwanda, Sierra
Leone, Solomon Islands,
Tanzania, Uganda, United
Kingdom, U.S.A.,
Zambia
Ex-French Territories:
Belgium, Cameroun,
Centralfrique, Congo,
Côte d'Ivoire, Dahomey,
France, Gabon, Haute
Volta, Mali, Mauritania,
Niger, Senegal, Tchad,
Togo, Zaire

PLANTATIONS GROUP

PLANTATIONS COMPANIES IN

Belgium,
Cameroun,
Malaysia,
Nigeria,
Solomon Islands,
Zaire

COMPANIES IN

Canada,
U.S.A.
Chart 4

SSC&B LINTAS INTERNATIONAL

AGENCIES IN

Argentina,
Australia,
Austria,
Belgium,
Brazil,
Denmark,
Finland,
France,
Germany,
Ghana,
Greece, India,
Indonesia,
Italy,
Malaysia
Netherlands,
New Zealand,
Nigeria,
Portugal,
Sierra Leone,
South Africa,
Spain, Sweden,
Switzerland,
Thailand,
United Kingdom

51

Figure 2 Product Co-ordination in Britain and Europe, 1973

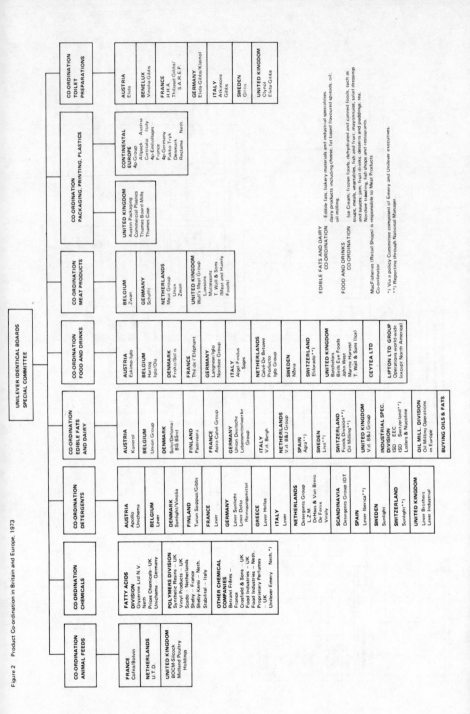

Figure 3   Companies under the Overseas Committee, 1973

UNILEVER IDENTICAL BOARDS
SPECIAL COMMITTEE

OVERSEAS COMMITTEE
LONDON

NORTH AMERICA

CANADA
Company	Coding
Lever Brothers	D, T
Lever Detergents	C
Hartchemical	F3
Hygrade Foods	D
Monarch Fine Foods	F1
Myriad Detergents	
New Foundland	D
Margarine	F1
Shopsy's Foods	F2, F3
Woodbridge Moulded Products	P
A&W Foods Services	
Thomas J. Lipton	F2, F3
Jackson	
Langs	
Puritan	

U.S.A.
Company	Coding
Lever Brothers	C, D, F1, F2, T
Thomas J. Lipton	F2
Good Humor	
Knox	
Lipton Pet Foods	
Morton House	
Penn Dutch	

ARGENTINA
Company	Coding
J. & E. Atkinson	D, T
Lever Y Asociados	D, T, F1

AUSTRALIA
Company	Coding
Beacon Research	
E.O.I.	F1
Interpack Australia	P
J. Kitchen & Sons	D
Lever & Kitchen	D
Rexona	D, T
Rosella Foods	F2
Streets Ice Cream	F2
Unilever Australia	T
Hillcastle	h
Lever Industrial	

BRAZIL
Company	Coding
Industrial Gessy Lever	D, T, F1
S.A. de Perfumerias	D, T
J. & E. Atkinson	

CENTRAL AMERICA
Company	Coding
Distribuidora S.A.	D, F1, F2, T
Industrias Unsola	

CHILE
Company	Coding
J. & E. Atkinson	T
Indus Lever	D, F1, T

COLOMBIA
Company	Coding
Productos Lever/Copra	D, F1, T

EAST AFRICA
Company	Coding
East Africa Industries	D, F1, F2, T
Uganda Associated Industries	D, F1

GHANA
Company	Coding
Lever Brothers (Ghana)	D, T, F1

INDIA
Company	Coding
Hindustan Lever	C, D, F1, T
Indrapori	D, F1, T

INDONESIA
Company	Coding
Unilever Indonesia	D, F1, F2, T

JAPAN
Company	Coding
Hohnen-Lever	D, F1

MALAWI
Company	Coding
Lever Brothers (Malawi)	D, F1, F2, T

MALAYSIA
Company	Coding
Lever Brothers (Malaysia)	D, F1, T
Wails Fitzpatrick's	F2

MEXICO
Company	Coding
Productos Lever	D

NEW ZEALAND
Company	Coding
Birds Eye Foods	F2
New Zealand	
Knights New Zealand	D, T
Levers New Zealand	D
Unilever New Zealand	

NIGERIA
Company	Coding
Lever Brothers (Nigeria)	D, F1, F2, T

PAKISTAN
Company	Coding
Lever Brothers (Pakistan)	D, F1, T

PERU
Company	Coding
Indusa	D

PHILIPPINES
Company	Coding
Philippine Refining	C, D, F1, F2, T

SINGAPORE
Company	Coding
Lever Brothers (Singapore)	F1, D
Wails Fitzpatrick's	F2

SRI LANKA
Company	Coding
Lever Brothers (Ceylon)	D, F1, T

SOUTH AFRICA
Company	Coding
Consumer Research Services	T
Elida Gibbs	C, D
Hudson & Knight	F1, F2, h
Lever Brothers	D
Lever's Stock Feeds	A
Meirose Foods	F1
Suicase & Chemical Industries	C
T Wall & Sons	F2
Van den Bergh & Jurgens	F1, F2
S.A. Warehousing Services	
Unilever South Africa	

THAILAND
Company	Coding
Lever Brothers (Thailand)	D, F1, F2, T

TRINIDAD
Company	Coding
Lever Brothers West Indies	D, F1

TUNISIA
Company	Coding
Unilea Tunisie	D, T

TURKEY
Company	Coding
Lever Brothers (Turkey)	D,
Unilever Is.	F1
G & A Baker	D, T

UNITED KINGDOM
Company	Coding
Unilever Export	C, D, F1, F2, T

VENEZUELA
Company	Coding
Lever	D, F2, T

ZAIRE
Company	Coding
Marsavco Zaire	D, F1, T
Zapak	P

A – Animal Feeds
C – Chemicals
D – Detergents
F1 – Edible Fats and Dairy
F2 – Food and Drinks
F3 – Meat Products
P – Paper, Printing & Packaging
T – Toilet Preparations

OTHER CODING
h – Non-Distributive Trade

53

Figure 4   The United Africa Group, 1973

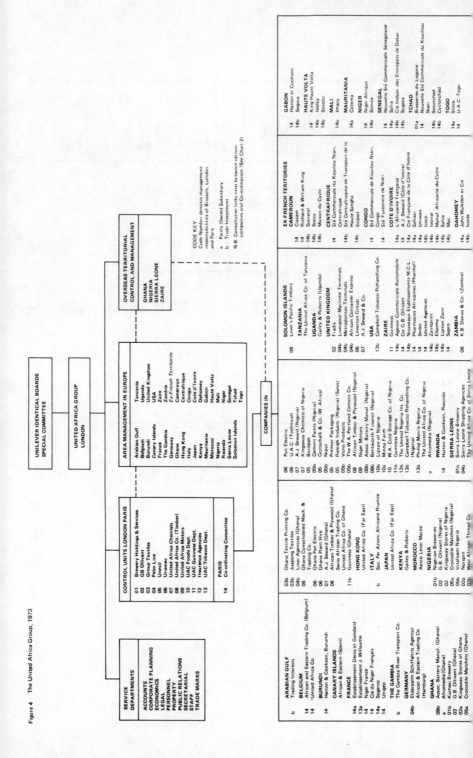

into Unilever Export in 1945–6; and the establishment of Plantations as a separate and similar, though much smaller, supervisory mechanism. The second of these has already been mentioned and it is described in some detail by Knox, who was Chairman of Unilever Export from 1952 to 1961.[17] For the overseas manufacturing companies the dominant fact of this period was the rebirth of the Overseas Committee. As so often in administrative history this seems to have been the result of evolution rather than deliberation. It has been seen that even in 1949 the Special Committee, while dividing the overseas possession between Contact Directors who were to take individual responsibility for particular companies, emphasised that they also had collective responsibility for all non-British companies except UAC. It was therefore not surprising that after 1949 the Contact Directors, according to Knox, 'slipped back into a committee form of working'[18] long before there was again an official OSC. In course of time, also, a practical distinction came to be made between 'the Overseas Contact Directors' and those for Continental countries. In 1954 the Overseas Committee was again formally constituted, though still as the sum of the activities of individual directors rather than as a collective unit and without a chairman. It was at the suggestion of his colleagues in 1957 that Knox became the first Chairman of the Committee since 1943 *de facto*, and the Special Committee formally established the post in January 1958. The Chairman's new status had the advantage in terms of an institutional pecking order that it put him on a par with other Unilever directors who were in charge of major administrative units such as UAC or an Executive Group in Britain and this gave more weight to the needs of the overseas associated companies. The Special Committee noted this at the time: 'This appointment would simplify the Overseas Committee's relationship with the Service Departments and Divisions, and would make possible a greater measure of co-ordination in the work of contact with the overseas companies.'

The reconstitution of the OSC and its chairman were not momentous events in the history of Unilever overseas for individual members of the Committee continued to take special responsibility for particular overseas companies; but collectively the Committee was able to ensure that the special needs and problems of those companies were given proper attention in a way individual directors using the general Unilever secretariat and specialised agencies might have found difficult. The aim of ensuring an overall view was furthered by deliberately allocating overseas companies to individual directors on an apparently random basis, so that one man might be responsible for a group of companies ranging from Latin America to South East Asia. This marked a change of policy though a return to the practice of the 1930s: since 1949 individual Contact Directors had as far as possible been allocated neighbouring countries. Knox, who constructed the new system, rationalised it on the grounds that if a geographical division was established, individual Contact Directors might 'lose interest in the rest of the world, or begin to think that they knew better how to tackle the problems of their countries than their colleagues and even than their Chairman!'[19]

To the student of modern British colonial administration the functions and techniques of the OSC seem very familiar, despite differences of scale and the fact that Colonial Office officials, unlike Contact Directors, very seldom visited their overseas charges in person. Like the Colonial Office, and still more the Dominions Office of the 1930s and 1940s, the OSC had five main functions: collectively, to take responsibility for all overseas companies within its executive Management Group; to handle the flow of correspondence between each overseas unit and all London and Rotterdam departments; to act as sponsor for the overseas companies' interests and proposals; to promulgate new ideas of possible interest to subsidiaries and conversely to process proposals for investment, new brands, etc. put up by overseas companies; and finally to deal with personnel matters, ranging from appointments to senior posts to the details of remuneration and home leave. Over time, and particularly after 1945, the means of keeping in touch changed as communications improved. The infrequent, formal and often extended visits made by a London director were replaced by frequent and usually brief trips made not only by a director but also, increasingly, by experts from the specialised service departments and, after 1965, from the 'Co-ordinations'. More important, whereas once the views of overseas managements were put to the centre only in letters and through reports of visiting directors, by the 1960s every overseas chairman visited London at least once a year, reporting on his business and presenting his proposals in person. Such contacts were of great importance in a business of this kind, particularly as the overseas managements became increasingly non-European. It was perhaps the most important achievement of the OSC and its supporting organisation in Unilever House that by the 1970s they appeared to have established a network of close personal and, as far as possible multilateral, relationships between themselves and their overseas dependencies.

Apart from the appointment and supervision of overseas staff the main preoccupation of OSC was, of course, to ensure that Unilever obtained the greatest possible advantage from its investment in these overseas companies. This meant constant review of every detail of an overseas company's activities, ranging from margins on toilet soap to the prospective return on a proposed investment of several million pounds in a new factory. To make such supervision possible it was essential to impose uniform procedures throughout the overseas companies, particularly concerning accounts, trading reports, methods of costing projects and calculating returns. Lever companies thus developed from a very early period, certainly before 1914, a common vocabulary which the new entrant, like the historian, had to learn before he could understand how the system worked. It is impossible here to describe all these various techniques and in any case these varied substantially over the time period covered by this study; but it is essential to explain the main accounting terms that are referred to in the text and tables, since these are terms of art and are specific to Unilever. Unilever used three forms of accounts for different purposes. These were as follows:

1. 'Statistical Accounts', forming part of the system of internal management reporting, whose purpose was to express financial information in the form that most clearly indicated the economic performance of any part of Unilever and was identical as between any two companies wherever they might be. Three of the conventions adopted, especially since the mid-1950s, need particular comment because they affect the statistical data used in this book. First, 'statistical tax' was calculated on the assumption that all the profit made in a particular year would be distributed as dividends and the 'nett profit (result) after tax' therefore represented the potential nett return to Unilever from the operations of a single company in one year. Second, 'Gross Capital Employed' (GCE) was calculated as the average for the year and the value of the fixed assets was put in on the basis of a proportion of the replacement cost rather than the historic cost. Finally, some 'Head Office Charges' were imputed to particular companies to spread the overheads of the Unilever Ltd and NV headquarters over the business as a whole, even though in many cases no actual financial contribution was made by a subsidiary.

It is not clear from the records when these internal accounting conventions were first used or how consistent they have been over time. There are statements of accounts on a 'white sheet basis' (which incorporate some of these measurement techniques) for several of the companies included in this book for most of the 1930s, but I was unable to find any such statements between 1940 and about 1956. This may have no significance and may result from the accident that these statements were not kept. But from 1956 to 1965 I was provided with statements of this kind, known as 'trading summaries', for all these companies and I have used this material because it provides the best indicator of economic performance. Where this is done for any period the term 'nett profit (result) after statistical tax' is used to distinguish these figures from the 'nett profit (result) per accounts' which is defined below. I have also restricted the term 'Gross Capital Employed' to the totals calculated on the basis described above, using 'Capital Employed' (CE) for all periods before 1956 when it is not clear how the total was reached.

2. 'Local Financial Accounts' are prepared by individual companies in accordance with their local tax laws and may differ significantly from the 'statistical accounts' described above. The 'trading profit', arrived at after deducting all commercial costs from the 'nett sales value' (NSV) for a year, is the same in both cases; but the 'nett profit (result) per accounts' ('accounting profit' in the tables printed in this book) is arrived at by deducting whatever sums were actually payable in respect of that accounting year as taxes, interest, etc. and after taking account of other financial items such as income from subsidiaries of local companies. Since the tax payable may be affected by losses carried forward or by decisions regarding what proportion of profits to distribute as dividends, both the tax payable and the nett profit will probably differ from sums included in the Statistical Accounts. In the Financial Accounts, also, the figure for Capital Employed will normally be calculated on a conventional accounting basis: that is the historic cost of fixed assets less depreciation plus the book cost of stocks nett of debtors and creditors; and these will be calculated for the last day of the accounting year, normally 31 December. Copies of these Financial Accounts are sent by each company to its Head Office, that is, either Unilever Ltd in London or Unilever NV in Rotterdam, according to which of these held the shares of that subsidiary.

In this book I have had to use these local Financial Accounts extensively. Before 1956 they are usually the only accounts available and even after 1956 it is necessary to use the 'nett profit (result) per accounts' figure to show how the profits actually available were allocated as between dividends, taxes, investment, etc. Strictly speaking when calculating the return to capital using these 'accounting profits' the figure for capital employed should be the accounting capital at the end of each year; but to save space in the tables I have normally used the Gross Capital Employed taken from the Statistical Accounts from 1956 to 1965.

3. 'Unilever Financial Accounts' are the same local Financial Accounts, adjusted, if necessary, to bring them into line with UK and Netherlands financial accounting laws for consolidation into the annual accounts of Unilever Ltd and Unilever NV. These figures have only been used in Table 10.2 in the concluding chapter.

In writing this book a serious technical problem was that before the mid-1950s it was necessary to use whatever financial and other data happened to be available in the archives of Unilever Ltd and NV in London and Rotterdam and of the overseas companies. It is obvious from the gaps in some tables that much information has not survived. In many cases where there were statements of 'profit' or 'capital employed' it was not clear how these were calculated, and the further back in time, the less likely it was that anyone could confidently explain contemporary accounting conventions. It must, therefore, be said that much of the data on profitability before the mid-1950s, and in particular calculation of the return to capital, is liable to error resulting from my misinterpreting the available data; and this is particularly relevant to statements covering long periods of time during which accounting conventions may have changed substantially. It must also be said that in many cases there were inconsistencies between two statements of the same thing, whether of the volume of sales, NSV or results. In such cases I had to judge which seemed the more realistic figure and I was encouraged by Andrew Knox's comment that in his experience there was 'a strange but, in my observation, absolute rule, namely that head office records of an operating company's activities will never agree with those of the company concerned. The difference may be marginal and irrelevant but will always exist.'[20]

One other feature of the accounts requires comment because the subject is widely emphasised and commonly incorrectly treated in the literature on multinational companies: financial transactions between different parts of a single business, and in particular interest payments, the price of goods transferred from one part to another, royalties and service fees. Unilever practice on all these was consistent and straightforward, based on the principle that no one part of the concern should obtain an advantage at the cost of another. Borrowing by a company from Unilever Limited or NV incurred interest at current bank rates. The price of raw materials and intermediates transferred within the concern was fixed at cost plus a commission or a profit, commonly 5 or 6 per cent. Royalties were more complicated. The concept of a royalty is, of course, that the user of a trademark or a technique pays a fee to its owner, and in the case of a multinational this involves a payment from a subsidiary to its parent. Unilever practice on this changed over time. Because in many cases a local factory and subsidiary company grew from an established import business whose goodwill consisted of the reputation of concern brands, this goodwill and these brand names were commonly incorporated as original assets in the capital of the new manufacturing company. In this case no royalty was ever paid. But over time, and as the number of new Unilever brands and patents and their technical sophistication increased, it was sometimes thought better to allow local manufacture on licence and so to charge royalties. These were paid at fixed rates and were never used to adjust tax liabilities as between one company and another. Under modern conditions such royalty payments normally require the formal agreement of the host government. Finally, service fees are comparatively recent in Unilever practice. From about 1960 it became standard practice to charge a proportion of the overheads of the 'home company' (i.e. London or Rotterdam) to each overseas company on the principle that these central administrative organisations and research facilities existed only to serve the multiplicity of subsidiaries. As has been seen, 'Home Overheads' had previously been imputed in the Statistical Accounts; but now, and largely because of the growing trend towards third party participation in the equity of overseas subsidiaries which meant that Unilever had for the first time to share local profits with local shareholders, it became significant to distinguish precisely for which part of the concern costs were incurred and to charge them accordingly. For these reasons the Special Committee formally minuted in October 1960 that 'as a general rule Overseas Companies should be asked to pay service fees to London for specialist services, particularly in view of the probable extension of local participation'. Putting this into practice always depended on the agreement of the local tax authorities and there were complications where there were already local shareholders who might stand to lose from the insertion of an additional pre-tax cost. Thus Hindustan Lever never transferred anything except post-tax dividends. But where government and shareholders agreed, service fees began to be charged at various times from 1961 on the basis of about 1 per cent of NSV.

The Overseas Committee in its various forms and under different names was, by definition, exclusively concerned with the Lever/Unilever overseas empire. But it never possessed an exclusive control over all the concern's overseas interests. OSC never took over the Niger Company/UAC and the position of the plantations varied over time. UAC is not studied in this book, for reasons similar to those which explain why it remained outside the orbit of OSC. It was a highly specialised African trading business whose traditions had been built up in West Africa in the nineteenth century and it had almost no organic link with Lever/Unilever as an industrial complex. Lever had bought the Niger Company as a going concern (though one on the verge of floundering). He had amalgamated it with the relatively small African trading companies he already owned and, apart from placing two Lever directors on the board to improve its efficiency, he largely left its management intact. When the Niger Company merged with African and Eastern in 1929 to form UAC its autonomy was, if anything, increased because initially Unilever owned only 50 per cent of the shares. Although this proportion rose to 80 per cent in 1931 and to 100 per cent in 1945, UAC remained a monolith too diverse even for Unilever fully to ingest. And so it remained to the 1960s. UAC had its Chairman and Board, of which the Special Committee were members, and had representative directors on the Board of Unilever. There were many points of contact between UAC and other Unilever enterprises, and a number of these links will be mentioned in later chapters, in particular with the West African Soap Co., Unilever-Is in Turkey and the Solomon Islands timber project of the 1960s. Yet to the end of the period UAC remained an empire within an empire or, as Knox described it in 1948, 'a constellation: shining particularly brightly at that time, a large group in itself, managed separately from Unilever up to Board level'.[21]

The position of the plantations in Africa and the East in the Unilever administrative system was complicated and variable. Until 1955 there was never any one committee or secretariat in London which dealt solely and specifically with the plantations in the way that individual directors or the OSC looked after manufacturing companies. The historical reasons for this were that until the 1920s there were only two Lever plantations—Lever's Pacific Plantations Ltd (LPPL) in the Solomons, and Huileries du Congo Belge (HCB) in the Belgian Congo. Two plantation companies did not warrant a special departmental organisation and in any case each of these had a special intermediate relationship which made detailed supervision from London unnecessary. LPPL was always run by and from Lever Brothers Ltd in Sydney and eventually became a subsidiary of the Australian business. HCB was a Belgian registered company and its headquarters had by Belgian law to be in Brussels. From the 1920s additional vegetable oil plantations were established, first in Nigeria and the Cameroons, then, after 1945, in Malaya and Sabah. Taken together with LPPL and HCB these might have constituted the basis for a unified plantation organisation; but because all these were started and originally run by UAC, as part of a single UAC subsidiary, Pamol Ltd, this was not thought necessary. In the mid-1950s, however, with the tendency for Unilever House to base administrative divisions on function, it was at last decided to bring together all the plantation companies under a single central executive, comparable to one of the home executives, and thus concentrate all the concern's know-how on plantations. The first head of the new Plantation Executive set up in 1955 was D. L. Martin, a UAC man with wide experience of plantations, helped by Colin Black, previously the Managing Director of the Lever soap factory at Apapa, Nigeria, and so an Overseas Committee man. Thereafter the Plantation Executive, promoted to 'Group' in 1957, though not technically a committee of the Unilever Board as OSC was, dealt directly with the Special Committee in monthly meetings and controlled all plantations independently.

What, then, was Unilever? Was it merely a holding company, a vast trust owning all (or a majority) of the shares in an extremely diverse collection of productive enterprises throughout the world on which it levied tribute and to which it contributed little? Or, at the other extreme, was it a highly integrated industrial machine which as far as possible grew its own raw materials, transformed them into branded products wherever in the world seemed most profitable, advertised them through its own subsidiary, Lintas, and sold them in whatever market offered the highest prices? The pattern that will emerge from the studies in this book lies somewhere between these extremes. Unilever was never planned: Topsy-like it just grew. But this does not mean that Unilever was ever merely a holding company: Unilever House did much more than count the dividends it received. At every stage, from the early days of William Lever in Britain and the various Dutch families in the Netherlands, the men at the top expected to play a dynamic role in running all parts of the business. The means changed over time as the concern grew, and this chapter has surveyed some of the mechanisms of control. What has not been examined, but is well described by Wilson, is the immensely important role played by the technical services, and particularly the research laboratories, in Britain and the Netherlands. In fact what gave a Unilever subsidiary its special character was the composite of these influences—the patterns of business practice, the technology, the style of management—which were developed in Britain and the Netherlands and built into every overseas subsidiary. These were the positive and continuing inputs which justified the charges made for 'Home Overheads' and 'Service': they were what made Unilever a multinational enterprise, not an international holding company.

Unilever, in fact, was a federal enterprise in which, as in all federal systems, power and responsibility were divided between the centre and the periphery. It is one of the aims of this book, and a main reason why it concentrates on individual overseas companies rather than on the concern as an aggregate, to discover where the balance lay; and a major conclusion will be that one reason why Unilever is so comparatively welcome and also successful as a foreign capitalist enterprise in the less developed world is that its tradition and character have enabled it to strike an exceptionally good balance between the two extremes of over-centralisation and inadequate support of its subsidiaries.

3

Unilever in Australia and South Africa

In a book primarily concerned with the activities of a multinational company in less developed countries, Australia and South Africa may seem out of place. Yet it was in these places, along with Canada, the USA and parts of Europe, that Lever Brothers first established overseas manufacturing subsidiaries and it was there that the model of a Lever and later Unilever subsidiary evolved. In their origins one can see the motives for adopting local manufacture as an alternative to exporting from Port Sunlight and the path they beat out came to be regarded as the norm. For this reason, also, they provide a contrast with other concern companies that were founded later in less developed countries and which found it impossible to follow the same evolutionary pattern. It is proposed to describe the development of these companies in Australia and South Africa separately and briefly. Each section will be divided into three chronological parts indicating the three 'ages' of a typical manufacturing subsidiary to 1965: from the start of 1914, to show how and why the company was established; from 1914 to 1945 to show how they operated in what will be described as their 'classical' period; and finally from 1945 to 1965, when the main themes are rationalisation, diversification and integration with the host society.

Australia

(a) Origins of the Business, 1888–1914

The first step towards the establishment of Unilever Australia Proprietary Limited, as the Australian business was called by 1965, was taken in December 1888 when an office of Lever Brothers was

64

opened in Sydney. It had a double function: to repack and distribute throughout the Australian colonies the imported products of Port Sunlight; and in return to buy and transmit copra from the Pacific Islands and Australian tallow as raw materials to Port Sunlight. This second function is the key to future developments. The availability of raw materials did not necessarily induce Lever to move from import to local manufacture in any country; but, judging by his general practice in Europe and North America during the 1890s, this, when coupled with a promising local market and substantial import tariffs, was likely to lead to a Lever factory. Unfortunately it is impossible to determine precisely when and on what grounds Lever decided to manufacture soap in Australia because evidence for the 1890s is very limited. The basic facts are as follows. Lever visited Australia in 1892 and noted in South Australia that, whereas the tariff on imported soaps in that colony was an almost prohibitive 4d a pound, this would have been only 1d a pound if the brand name had been stamped on the soap in the colony.[1] He visited Australia again in 1895 and reorganised the system of agents through which his imported products were distributed in Sydney, Melbourne and Adelaide. While in Sydney he bought a site, with a water frontage, at Balmain. He had done the same in Toronto in 1892 and it seems to have been his normal practice by this time to buy land in places where he might eventually wish to build a factory as a precautionary measure. At Balmain a copra crushing mill and oil tanks were immediately built but work on a soap manufacturing plant there did not begin until 1899, possibly stimulated by the then certainty that the Australian colonies would form a federation and that its tariff policy would follow the protectionism of Victoria and South Australia rather than the free trade of New South Wales. Work was completed and the factory started operating in October 1900, the same month as the Toronto factory. Soap works and copra mill were owned by a new company, Lever Brothers Ltd (Australia) (hereafter LB(A)) which was incorporated in New South Wales as an Australian enterprise on 31 December 1899. The nominal capital of £A600,000 was wholly owned by Lever Brothers; but with a local chairman, board of directors and Australian registration it was, at least in principle, what Lever maintained all his 'associated companies' should be— autonomous and indigenous, able to understand and respond to local conditions in a way the management at Port Sunlight could not.

In practice, however, LB(A) had very little independence, and this was typical of most Lever subsidiaries during Lever's lifetime. To start with, it could export manufactures only to New Zealand and the South Sea Islands. This rule, common to most Lever subsidiaries, was intended to ensure that local factories did not infringe markets served by Port Sunlight and create problems with brand names, etc. A more important and typical limitation was that the local Board ceased to exist in 1903. The reasons are obscure but may have been connected with Lever's visit to Balmain in October 1901 which resulted in two of the four local directors being recalled to Port Sunlight. In 1902 Lever appointed Joseph Meek Managing Director of LB(A). He had complete trust in him and Meek held the job for 21 years; but in 1904 the company's Letters of Association were altered so that meetings of shareholders and directors could be held either in Australia or in England. Since Lever Brothers were the only shareholders and Meek was the only director resident in Australia, it seemed logical for all company meetings to be held in England: and so from 1905 to 1922 they were. LB(A) thus became merely a factory and oil mill run by a resident managing director who received detailed orders from England and was inspected periodically by Lever or some other senior Port Sunlight executive. Given the small scale of the business this was a reasonable policy; on the other hand it reduced the ability of the Australian management to think and plan in local terms to meet the special needs of the Australian market and was inconsistent with Lever's strong belief in the importance of leaving responsibility with the local management.[2] In the long run such a degree of centralisation in an international business was not typical of Levers or Unilever and would not have been successful.

Once launched, and then in effect gelded, LB(A) had an unspectacular history until 1914. One by one all the main Lever products came to be made at Balmain. New South Wales was the main market but there were agents in other Australian states and in 1911 the first branch office was opened in Melbourne to handle sales in Victoria. But by 1912 Lever realised that his larger aims were not being achieved. Balmain had been designed to replace Port Sunlight as a base from which, using local raw materials, exploiting the new federal tariff and reducing transport costs, Levers could penetrate and take over the soap market in all the Australian states from the established indigenous manufacturers.

This did not happen. Levers made virtually no dent in the soap empires owned by J. Kitchen and Sons in Victoria and W. H. Burford and Co. in South Australia. The reasons are obvious but important, because they are common to most of the developed countries in which Levers tried to establish local manufacture. Kitchens and Burfords produced parallel products of closely comparable quality to those of Levers. Being local producers using largely local materials such as tallow they could economise on transport costs; and being long established they had a firm hold on the loyalty of wholesalers, retailers and consumers. Even the most intensive promotional effort could not have given Levers more than a token share of these virtually saturated markets. Yet expansion beyond New South Wales was essential. In 1913 LB(A) was selling a mere 4,000 tons of soap, less than had been planned in 1900 and far too narrow a base for a really profitable business. Something had to be done.

It is important that Lever's first reaction was that he should build his own factories in each of the other states to challenge local manufacturers on their own ground on the assumption, as he wrote to Meek in 1912, that, in a country where distances were so large, 'separate centres of soap manufacturing is the soundest policy'. He seems, however, to have been persuaded that the local manufacturers were too strongly entrenched to be destroyed in this way and that they would have to be bought out. When he next visited Australia, in March 1914, he therefore laid foundations for a merger with Kitchens and a take-over of Burfords; and since the character of these firms affected the future pattern of the business, it is necessary briefly to describe their origins.

In 1914 the Kitchen business was by far the largest soap and candle manufacturer in Australia. Founded as a small tallow and candle firm at Melbourne in 1856, it had grown by somewhat the same methods as Lever had used in Britain—promotion of branded quality products coupled with the acquisition of rival firms. In New South Wales there was now Kitchen and Sons Ltd, Sydney, originally the Sydney Soap Company, in which Kitchens had acquired a majority interest in 1888. In Queensland Kitchens owned the Ross Soap Co., bought in 1909, a 50 per cent share in the Brisbane Soap Co., and the Apollo Co., acquired with its parent, the Apollo Candle Company of Melbourne, in 1884. There were other Kitchen factories in South and West Australia and Kitchens also owned the

Neptune Oil Co. Ltd and the Commonwealth Copra Co. Ltd, established in 1908 to produce and mill copra in Papua. Kitchens were market leaders in Victoria, Queensland and Tasmania, ran second to Burfords in South Australia and were in strong competition with Levers in New South Wales. It would have been difficult for Levers, still a minnow in Australia, to swallow this industrial whale and it is important to discover how they were able to do so.

Kitchens' motives for selling are not clear. Wilson suggests that they had a bad year in 1913:[3] their unpublished house history on the other hand suggests that association with Levers was welcomed because it would enable Kitchens to use the new patented method of hydrogenating oil and would result in 'a considerable strengthening of the business as a whole'. Perhaps equally relevant was that the Kitchen family would be able to cash in on the fruits of its efforts over the previous half century by selling part or all of the business to Levers. The agreement worked out in 1914 involved in the first stage a revaluation of Kitchens' assets and an increase in the nominal capital of J. Kitchen and Sons Ltd, Melbourne, from £A250,000 to £A401,902, consisting of 100,488 shares of £4. The shares of Kitchen and Sons Ltd of Sydney remained unchanged. Lever decided to acquire control of both companies and in May 1914 he offered two alternative proposals to Kitchens. By the first, Levers would secure only a half interest in both businesses, by the second a three-quarter interest. Either way, Kitchen shareholders would be paid in Lever Brothers 15 per cent cumulative preferred ordinary shares. These would be valued at £2 5s 0d and Lever offered to buy part of these shares back from Kitchen shareholders by 1 December 1914 if they chose to accept the option, or later at agreed prices. The smaller deal therefore involved about £136,000 cash, the larger £236,000. The Kitchen family would continue to have both a financial stake in their business—a quarter of the shares at least—and virtually complete freedom in running it. The only link between the boards and managements of the two main Kitchen companies and LB(A) would be a Central Management Board of four which would contain two directors from Kitchens, plus Meek, and Bowen of Burfords. Thus the total effect would be that, while Kitchens continued to run their own business and to receive salaries and other perquisites, Levers would have taken over the risk on half or three-quarters of the capital.

This was an attractive proposal and it is not surprising that in

November 1914 the Kitchen family shareholders offered 'unanimously', though in fact after a major internal division, to accept the larger offer which gave Lever Brothers Ltd 83,839 shares in J. Kitchen and Sons Ltd, and £A37,621 of the shares in Kitchen and Sons Ltd, of Sydney. Lever was delighted with 'a most excellent transaction, not only on its own merits, but because of its consolidation of our Australian undertakings'. He admitted that he might have to find a lot of money 'sometime', as Kitchen holders of the Lever cumulative preferred ordinary shares chose to cash them; but he felt that it had been right to take an opportunity 'that would never have come again, and I am sure that we have taken the wisest course notwithstanding that it means committing ourselves to obligations spread over a number of years'. He had to find £45,000 in 1915 to redeem 20,000 of the Levers' shares and over the next eight years he spent a great deal more on redeeming further Lever shares and buying out remaining Kitchen shareholders. Significantly, it was Lever's clear intention in Australia, as in all other countries, that if possible all shares and subsidiaries should be owned by Levers or by 'those interested who are actively engaged in the business, or relations and friends of those actively engaged in the business'. It took some years to achieve total control of Kitchens but it had been done by 1923.

The evidence on how W. H. Burford and Sons Ltd was acquired is much less complete. The firm had been founded in 1839, in the earliest days of the South Australian settlement, and had grown with the colony. By the end of the century it dominated the South Australian and West Australian markets and, as has been seen, competed in the South-eastern states with Kitchens and Levers. From Lever's point of view acquisition of Burfords was critical if he was to exploit the opportunities provided by buying Kitchens. In December 1914 he therefore acquired the whole of the 90,000 £1 ordinary shares and 25,000 of the 5 per cent first preference shares, leaving a substantial number of preference shares still held by third parties. Like Kitchens, Burfords was left as an autonomous enterprise loosely connected with the other concern enterprises through the Central Management Committee.

Acquisition of Burfords virtually completed Lever's Australian empire as it was to remain until after 1940. Only a few minor organisational changes were made which can conveniently be summarised at this point, although they lie well beyond 1914. The main trend was towards simplification of the companies' legal structure without destroying the commercial independence of each enterprise. The critical year was 1924 when Lever visited Australia to establish his co-partnership scheme, a design for giving employees a direct interest in the prosperity of the business. He took the opportunity to restructure the concern's holdings in Australia, and in December 1924 a new company, Australian Producers Co-partnership Pty Ltd, was established with a nominal capital of £A10,000 (of which only two £A1 shares were ever issued), as a holding company to supervise all parts of the business and to organise the co-partnership scheme. Essentially the Central Management Board remained what it had always been—a confederation of heads of member companies—but with F. W. Kitchen as Chairman and Bowen and J. L. Heyworth (replacing Meek as Chairman of Lever Brothers Ltd (Australia)) as original members. The co-partnership scheme came to nothing for Lever died the next year; but the new holding company survived and in 1932 was re-named Associated Enterprises Pty Ltd (AEP), which in turn was re-named Lever Associated Enterprises Pty Ltd (LAEP) in 1944.

These changes had no necessary effect on the autonomy of the various companies; but in 1924 the infrastructure was also simplified. Most of the Kitchen companies lost their individuality and were absorbed—by internal share purchases—into a new holding company, J. Kitchen and Sons Pty Ltd, incorporated in Victoria, which became the main Australian holding company for all Lever Brothers interests. The position was thereafter as follows. Under the general wing of the new Australian Producers Co-partnership Pty Ltd, there were three main soap manufacturing companies: Lever Brothers Limited (Australia), J. Kitchen and Sons Pty Ltd, and W. H. Burford and Sons Ltd. The total capital at book value in 1927 was £A1,671,890 though if additional finance obtained from loans, creditors and use of reserves was taken into account the total capital employed would be substantially higher. In addition there were other enterprises linked only with these companies by the accident that they were wholly or partly owned by Levers: Levers Pacific Plantations Limited, which now incorporated Kitchens Commonwealth Copra Company, with book capital of £A572,500; Trufood of Australia Limited, in which Levers held £A36,427 out of a total capital of £A150,000; and shares nominally worth £A2,046 in the Commonwealth Oxygen and Accessories Limited, a subsidiary of British Oxygen whose shares Levers sold in 1934. Essentially, then, the Lever business in Australia remained what it had been in

1914: a soap, candles and edible oil enterprise built up by mergers with dominant rivals but with minimal changes in the structure of its component parts.

(b) The 'Classical' Period, 1914–45

The thirty years after 1914 can be regarded—and will be treated here—as the 'classical' period of the Australian business:

Table 3.1 : Australia: All Companies' Trading Summary, 1923–47, (£A,000)

Year	A Trading profit before tax	B Nett accounting profit after tax	C Nett profit after statistical tax	D Capital employed	Nett yield B/D %
1927	n/a	328,239	n/a	3,510,656	9.3
1928	n/a	274,288	n/a	n/a	n/a
1929	n/a	251,363	n/a	n/a	n/a
1930	n/a	232,611	n/a	2,307,022	10.1
1931	n/a	297,124	n/a	n/a	n/a
1932	227,026	194,088	167,999	3,109,252	6.2
1933	200,073	165,113	148,005	n/a	n/a
1934	380,742	304,802	274,884	n/a	n/a
1935	546,990	446,277	404,555	n/a	n/a
1936	562,975	515,796	444,383	3,021,000	17.1
1937	558,675	508,684	401,354	3,437,048	14.8
1938	474,772	440,471	379,819	3,484,993	12.6
1939	597,690	n/a	n/a	n/a	n/a
1940	n/a	n/a	n/a	3,652,486	n/a
1941	700,000	259,407	n/a	n/a	n/a
1942	n/a	n/a	n/a	n/a	n/a
1943	n/a	n/a	n/a	n/a	n/a
1944	516,000	n/a	188,300	3,475,000	n/a
1945	587,000	253,100	n/a	n/a	n/a
1946	271,000	n/a	n/a	n/a	n/a
1947	358,000	n/a	n/a	4,372,000	n/a

'classical', that is, in that it reflected and fulfilled Levers' specific objects and also in that soap remained the main prop of the business. In another sense, also, this was a classical period for the operations of a multinational company overseas. Except for the war years 1914–18 and 1939–45 and their immediate aftermaths, there was

Table 3.2 : Australia: All Companies' Sales Volume of Main Products, 1923–46

Year	Soap	Share of market	Toilet preparations	Edible fats and glycerine	Foods
	Tons	%	£A	Tons	Tons
1923	23,844	n/a	n/a	n/a	1,794
1924	24,947	n/a	n/a	n/a	1,737
1925	25,248	n/a	n/a	n/a	1,510
1926	25,808	64	n/a	n/a	1,774
1927	26,293	56	n/a	n/a	1,958
1928	29,074	57	n/a	n/a	n/a
1929	30,138	55	n/a	2,878	n/a
1930	30,016	56	n/a	2,892	2,104
1931	29,657	56	29,635	3,539	n/a
1932	28,163	57	63,122	3,079	n/a
1933	29,799	62	70,409	3,264	n/a
1934	30,298	64	51,776	4,272	n/a
1935	32,732	64	52,757	5,058	n/a
1936	34,770	63	53,672	5,442	n/a
1937	36,139	n/a	38,681	6,433	n/a
1938	39,229	n/a	33,574	8,122	n/a
1939	n/a	n/a	35,674	8,279	n/a
1940	n/a	n/a	66,300	10,254	n/a
1941	n/a	n/a	n/a	12,214	n/a
1942	n/a	n/a	n/a	9,543	n/a
1943	n/a	n/a	n/a	9,850	n/a
1944	n/a	n/a	n/a	10,143	n/a
1945	52,105	66	n/a	9,388	n/a
1946	49,430	77	204,088	6,586	n/a

virtually no political influence in Australia on what the concern did with its capital and earnings. This is, therefore, a very useful period to use for measuring the performance and assessing the characteristics of this subsidiary under virtually optimal operating conditions in an 'open' economy.

The most striking feature was stability and lack of major structural change. Taking capital employed as one yardstick, there was remarkably little increase in this period. The nominal capital of the Kitchens, Levers and Burfords businesses in 1914 was £A1,251,950. In 1927 it was £A1,850,000 and in 1947 £A3,546,000. It is more difficult to assess the growth of capital employed since no figures are available for the early years, but, as can be seen from Table 3.1, there was no increase between 1927—£A3,510,656—and 1944—£A3,475,000, though this was raised to £A4,372,000 by 1947. Turnover increased more substantially. Table 3.2 shows that sales of detergents by volume more than doubled between 1925 and 1945, and that, at their wartime peak, sales of edible oils were some three times their volume in 1930. The fact that these products were still much more important than any others in the mid-1940s is also significant. In 1945 out of total profits of £A253,100, £A231,100 came from detergents, £A6,000 from edible fats (though this was abnormally low), £A1,250 from toilet preparations, £A375 from oil and cake, and £A14,375 from 'sundries and other trade'. Clearly this was still an industry based on soap, with edible oils a very poor second and other products of virtually no significance.

Structurally also change was slow, though it had begun by 1946. By then all the companies were at one or two removes subsidiaries of J. Kitchen and Sons Pty Ltd, which in turn was a wholly owned subsidiary of Unilever Ltd, apart from £A13,000 of third party shares in Burfords still not acquired by Unilever. But this had little functional significance. The essential fact was that until 1941 each original company continued to manufacture its own brands in its own factories and, with the exception of Burfords, to sell through separate marketing companies. At the highest level there was first the Central Management Board, then the board of AEP. This met periodically, but of the four directors two were usually in Sydney and two in Melbourne, so there was no continuous consultation between the heads of the business. Nor was there any centralised technical control, research or raw material buying, though from 1931 Lintas handled advertising for all these companies, and there was a limited overlap in the selling forces and some interchange of brands. But there was still internal competition and very little attempt had been made by 1939 to rationalise Unilever's Australian business. In 1934 marketing of all edible fats and oils was consolidated in a single enterprise called Edible Oil Industries Pty Ltd (EOI), but production was left with the three original companies. The Burford factories had been condemned by successive London visitors for a decade before they were handed over to be run by Kitchens in 1937: even then they survived because it seemed impossible to find buyers who would pay a satisfactory price. Such conservatism requires explanation. Until 1925 the major obstacle was Lever's dislike of 'scrambling eggs'. After his death the way was open but incentives were lacking. Even during the slump, sales volume dipped only by about 2,000 tons of soap a year; and, although profit margins suffered more, they recovered by 1934 and rose to new heights in the following years. With over 60 per cent of the Australian soap market and a yield of over 10 per cent on the now heavily depreciated capital, Unilever was content to leave well alone. And in addition to these commercial considerations, Fred Kitchen was Chairman of the whole business until his death in 1940 and radical reconstruction, involving destruction of the individuality of his family firm, had to wait until he was no longer running it.

One sign of this conservatism was that before 1940 the Australian management showed no desire to diversify their business in order to deploy their capital and skills outside the limited local market for soap and candles. Yet it was evident well before 1940 that a company such as Unilever which owned so wide a range of technologies and brands covering so large a number of different products in other parts of the world was unlikely to allow a subsidiary in as affluent a country as Australia to stick to the soapmaker's pans indefinitely; and because the roots of later diversification, here as elsewhere, lay in this treasure trove of international brands it is important briefly to trace the first steps taken by the Australian companies before the Second World War towards a wider product base.

For any Lever/Unilever subsidiary based on soap the logical first step towards diversification was margarine and cooking fats. Australia, however, presented difficulties which were common in many other developed countries with established dairying industries: all margarine was suspect and table margarine (the most profitable form) was regarded as virtually immoral because it threatened the livelihood of the farmer. Before 1939 and wartime restrictions the only legal controls on margarine manufacture and sale in Australia were regulations imposed by individual states on quality, presentation, etc.; but the Unilever companies were afraid that if they sold their own brands of table margarine their much more important soap trade would suffer, especially in the dairying districts. The concern therefore concentrated on bulk hardened fat and unbranded cooking margarine. Initially these were sold mainly to the cake and biscuit trade, but increasingly during the 1930s hardened fat was sold to small local manufacturers (or, more accurately, blenders) of table margarine who were given technical advice on how to add water, flavour, etc. to the bulk fat and who sold under their own brand names. For the same reason when, under slump conditions during the early 1930s, Unilever came to consider a merger with their main local competitor in the field of hardened fats, the Marrickville Margarine Company, the proposal was rejected. Instead the two firms made a quota agreement. Unilever got most of the bulk fat market—94 per cent—while Marrickville took most of the table margarine market. The original agreement was later modified to accommodate other producers, but it had important consequences. During the 1930s it enabled Unilever to increase the volume of its edible oils and fats sales from 2,892 tons in 1930 to a pre-1946 peak of 12,214 tons in 1941, while maintaining reasonable profit margins. The longer-term consequences were less satisfactory. As will be seen later, when first the federal government and, after the Second World War, the state governments came to impose formal quotas on table margarine manufacture, this was done on the basis of sales during the 1930s; and since the concern had then sold very little table margarine it received a very small quota. In the 1950s, when margarine came to be accepted as a respectable product, the ironical situation arose that the world's largest single manufacturer of table margarine found itself trying to buy out the small blending companies which it had helped to establish in the 1930s in order to obtain their quotas of one or two hundred tons a year.

Partially blocked in this field, Unilever had to look to other products if it was to diversify. As a conscious policy horizontal diversification was not, in fact, characteristic of this or any other concern subsidiary in the 1930s. Yet AEP was in a limited sense already diversified before 1945; and because the way in which this diversification, so to speak, crept up on the local management because it was part of a much larger international organisation, it is necessary to describe briefly how this happened.

In Australia the initial movement into toilet preparations and foods—which were to be the main new fields of development there as in many other Unilever subsidiaries—derived from the fact that parent companies owned by Levers in Europe happened to have their own branches or established markets in Australia. Long before AEP saw any advantage in switching its main drive from soap and edible oils into these fields, the local management found itself obliged willy-nilly to take some interest in these collateral relations. In the early 1930s Lever interests in Australia were a widely assorted bunch. Two can be dismissed briefly. Levers Pacific Plantations Pty Ltd (LPPL) was technically a subsidiary first of Lever Brothers (Australia), then of Kitchens; but it was effectively a quite distinct enterprise which was associated with AEP mainly to provide it with managerial supervision and a secure market: it will be considered in Chapter 8. We can also ignore Commonwealth Oxygen Accessories Ltd, a subsidiary of British Oxygen, in which for a short time Levers had a holding but in which they took no direct interest. This leaves seven enterprises which Unilever controlled or partially controlled in Britain or America and which had subsidiaries in Australia.

First in chronological order was Trufood of Australia Ltd, with a factory that manufactured powdered milk at Glenormiston. Lever acquired a minority interest in this when he bought Trufoods in Britain; but no structural connection was established with AEP and dried milk never became part of the post-1941 strategy of diversification into foods. By that time, however, AEP found itself involved in toilet preparations, again because Levers had taken over or controlled companies in Europe or North America which had their own subsidiaries in Australia. Rexona Proprietary Ltd was acquired in 1929. It was a small enterprise making and marketing toilet soaps and medicated ointments. Lever men were for some time baffled as to what to do with these assets but eventually made some Rexona products at other concern factories and used Rexona as a selling organisation for toilet preparations. J. and E. Atkinson Pty Ltd, the Australian subsidiary of Atkinsons which had come into the Lever system with Crosfields, was established in Sydney in 1931 'to take advantage of a sudden prohibition of imports' during the slump. It had no structural connection with the rest of the Unilever business in Australia but was made a subsidiary of Kitchens. Then there were toothpastes. D. and W. Gibbs was taken over by Lever as part of Prices Candles in 1919 and thereafter Gibbs Dentifrice and Gibbs Dental Cream were made by Levers at Balmain. Pepsodent joined the family in 1944 when Unilever acquired the parent company in America. Gibbs had never been able to compete in Australia with Colgate, but Pepsodent was a popular brand which might well enable AEP to diversify success-fully in this direction.

These Unilever subsidiaries provided the Australian business with the brands and goodwill necessary to launch out into toilet prepara-tions if it decided to do so; and after 1945 AEP did, in fact, do this. But by that date convenience foods had become a major pre-occupation with Unilever in Europe and America and the last two enterprises launched or projected by 1945 to make use of existing concern know-how in Australia were concerned with tea and frozen vegetables. Van den Berghs had bought a minority interest in Liptons, the tea and grocery business, in 1927 and this passed to Unilever. In the early 1930s the British management of Liptons, which Unilever did not control, decided to enter the Australian market. Harold Greenhalgh advised against this on the ground that the established Australian tea firms, Bushells and Robur, were too well entrenched, and experience proved him right: Liptons made regular losses in Australia and obtained only a minute share of the market. In 1946, when Unilever bought a controlling interest in Lipton's American business, they also bought out the Australian business and formed a new Lipton company there, in which Unilever held 75 per cent of the equity, in the hope that tea would provide Unilever with opportunities for growth. Its future was closely related in Unilever thought to that of convenience foods which, by 1945, were an important element of post-war planning. In 1943 Unilever had bought Batchelors, the British canned vegetable company, and also a majority of the shares in the UK subsidiary of the American frozen food company, Birds Eye. As early as 1944, before Birds Eye was actually in production in Britain, the Special Committee had decided that Australia appeared to offer 'a good prospect' for frozen foods and immediately linked Birds Eye with Liptons: 'a substantial development of Liptons tea is practicable throughout Australia; this would support a selling organization which would carry other food lines, and at the same time, make a very satisfactory profit for the Lipton Company on tea'.

These hopes proved to be dupes: yet the projections Unilever made for Liptons and Birds Eye in Australia in 1944 mark the end of the 'classical period' of the Australian business and the start of its post-war evolution. The essential point is that for the first time Unilever was planning to broaden the product range of its main Australian subsidiary not because there happened to be an existing business brought into the Unilever system as a by-product of transactions elsewhere but because it was now becoming Unilever policy to look for opportunities to expand and diversify in all countries that offered market opportunities. Whatever the outcome of these particular projects (and it will be seen that some were disastrous), 1944 marks the beginning of the end of the old and comparatively static Lever/Kitchen/Burford enterprise.

(c) *Rationalisation, Diversification and Integration, 1945–65*

Although from this standpoint it is logical to start the last phase of Unilever's development in Australia, its 'modern' phase, from 1945/6, on other grounds 1939 or 1941 might be taken as the terminal date for the 'classical period'. The coming of the Second World War, particularly the Pacific war, radically altered the economic environment in which Unilever had to operate, and it was not until the mid-1950s that Australia became once again a fully 'open' economy. The war, in fact, gave Australia many of the characteristics of a 'managed' economy of the type normal in most of the less developed countries (LDCs) studied in this book. Corporate taxation rose from about 20 per cent of trading profit in 1938 to over 60 per cent in 1944 and then stabilised at around 40 per cent by 1956. These rates were not high by the standards of many LDCs after 1945, but they made it difficult ever again to provide as high a nett return as in the halcyon days of the mid-1930s. Equally important were the physical controls introduced during the Second World War, many of which lingered on to the end of the Labour era in 1949 and then gradually disappeared. Among the more important of the powers taken by the federal government were control of wholesale and retail prices, allocation of raw materials, restriction of internal transport, bulk buying of some imported foods including tea and allocation of quotas to makers of table margarine on the basis of pre-war performance. The dismantling of these controls took a surprisingly long time after the war and as late as January 1953 it was estimated that price controls alone were likely to cost the Unilever business between £A320,000 and £A450,000 in that year. Price controls persisted after 1955 in Queensland and South Australia, both of which had Labour governments; some federal controls, such as import licensing, continued until 1960; and the quota system for table margarine persisted in all states in 1965. But in most respects Australia was once again an 'open' economy by the late 1950s.

This had a very important impact on the character of the Unilever business and how it was seen from London. Australia was once again a place where Unilever could undertake development in a familiar climate. Security for their capital, freedom to move capital and profits at will, the end of controls on imports and prices were the foundation of business confidence and were accepted as compensation for the comparatively low profits the Australian business provided in most years after 1945. These things make it possible to treat the Australian companies after 1945 as a model of the 'natural' evolutionary tendencies of a typical Unilever subsidiary in this third period and therefore as a foil for concern companies in different environments. Three main themes dominate the records: the rapid growth of turnover and the range of products; the problem of relations with the host society; and profitability. The last of these will be examined later in this chapter in conjunction with South Africa: the other themes will be considered in that order.

The most important features of the growth of the business between 1946 and 1965 were, first, centralisation and rationalisation; second, diversification of the product range. The first deliberate step away from the 'no scrambled eggs' policy imposed by Lever was undertaken in the early 1940s after the death of Fred Kitchen. The central executive of AEP, renamed Lever Associated Enterprises Pty Ltd (LAEP) in 1944, took over the duties of the chairman and directors of each of the subordinate companies, together with the technical direction which determined the character and composition of the products made by each company. This was the first step towards full amalgamation of all the Australian enterprises, but it was a very small step. It did not centralise or rationalise manufacture and it left the marketing organisations intact. In 1947 there were still ten Unilever factories, four major and six minor, and six selling organisations with still another one in process of formation for foods. The following year London at last decided to act on proposals for rationalisation that went back to the early 1930s: the six small factories were to be closed at once and the Burford factory at Adelaide and the Kitchen factory at Brisbane were to follow these in due course. It was not until 1962, when declining profit margins made economies vital, that the possibility of further rationalising production was conceived. G. W. E. Barraclough, Chairman of Unilever (Australia) Proprietary Ltd (UAP), which had become the holding company for all Unilever interests in Australia in 1956, then floated the idea that all the various production functions should be integrated on a product basis, as had long ago been done in Britain. Balmain would become the only manufacturing centre for detergents, toilet preparations and edible fats (each with its separate factory), while the Kitchen factory at Melbourne would become the sole centre for foods, excluding ice-cream. After further preparation these concepts were accepted by the Special Committee in December 1964 and January 1965. The capital cost was estimated to be £A560,000 and the gross annual savings £A312,000. With other savings resulting from further integration and elimination of duplication of functions this was described by Andrew Knox and A. J. Caron, when they visited Australia in 1965, as 'a real break through in the matter of overhead expenses'.

The second major development after the Second World War was horizontal diversification: the aim of this account is to demonstrate why this occurred and what success it achieved. Although the details are specific to Australia, it will be seen later that the underlying factors were common to most overseas subsidiaries in this period; and the Australian experience will therefore serve as a model.

It has been seen that the first deliberate decision to undertake diversification in Australia as a matter of policy occurred in 1944. This decision was taken in London and as far as can be judged had little to do with the specific needs of the Australian business: it was policy to promote frozen foods in all countries that offered a viable market. But there were also reasons specific to the Australian business, which were essentially that the scope for increases in the sale of detergents and edible oils, the pillars on which the enterprise had been built, was becoming limited. In 1949 F. D. Morrell, who, as a one-time chairman of the Australian companies but now based on London, was in a good position to know, summarised the motives that resulted in diversification as follows:

Our future in the soap trade is limited by the fact that we already have a very large share of the business. The availability of raw materials and the politics of the Dairy Industry set a similar limit to edible fats and margarine. It was therefore decided after the war to attempt to develop a foods business, as the most likely means of expanding the Concern's interests in a young and growing market where the consumers are comparatively wealthy and have a high standard of living.

Clearly the interests of the centre of Unilever, anxious to make maximum use of new products and technology throughout the world, coincided with the needs of the Australian subsidiaries, which had long ago probed the limits of conventional product markets, found traditional overseas markets for Kitchen products (notably in Indonesia) being closed and by about 1951 had reached something like a plateau in the volume of soap sales. But this is not to say that diversification provided easy solutions; and to demonstrate some of the problems involved it is proposed briefly to survey Unilever Australia's experience with detergents, edible fats, toilet preparations, foods and ice-cream between 1945 and 1965.

In the mid-1940s Unilever made three assumptions about the prospects for detergents in Australia: that the concern would retain a predominant share in the local market, the only serious challenge coming in toilet soaps; that growth in the soap market would be sluggish; but that once wartime controls were removed detergents would once again become very profitable and be the backbone of the group's earnings. Up to a point the first of these projections proved correct: Unilever remained king of soap. But between 1959 and 1965 the situation deteriorated rapidly as the concern's market share of detergents of all types fell from 72 per cent to 59 per cent and seemed in danger of further decline. The trouble did not lie so much in toilet soaps, over which Unilever and Colgate fought a drawn battle, but in the increasing importance of non-soapy detergents (NSDs) which, being new, offered Colgate the chance to challenge Unilever's dominance of the soap powder market (Rinso, Persil). In the early 1950s Unilever hesitated to invest in NSD production in Australia. Colgate got in first with Fab and this still had a slight edge over Unilever's Surf in the mid-1960s. Significantly in 1963 Unilever held only 33 per cent of the new liquid detergent market, again due to competition from Colgate and others. In short, Unilever could not sustain the predominant position it had built up by buying out all major rivals half a century earlier. Meantime fears that the Australian soap market would expand slowly had proved correct; and this helped to falsify

Table 3.3 Australia: All Companies' Trading Summary, 1946–65 (£A)

Year	A NSV	B Gross profit	C Trading profit before tax	D Nett accounting profit after tax	E Nett profit after statistical tax	F GCE (average for year)	Yield after stat. tax E/F%
1946	n/a	n/a	271,000	n/a	n/a	n/a	n/a
1947	n/a	n/a	358,000	n/a	n/a	4,372,000	n/a
1948	n/a	n/a	548,000	n/a	n/a	n/a	n/a
1949	n/a	n/a	188,000	n/a	n/a	n/a	n/a
1950	n/a	n/a	n/a	318,000	n/a	n/a	n/a

Year						
1951	11,485,000	n/a	771,000	208,600	n/a	n/a	n/a
1952	13,303,000	3,136,341	524,000	230,200	n/a	n/a	n/a
1953	14,769,000	4,625,922	1,293,000	702,500	737,000	11,589,000	6.4
1954	16,896,000	4,705,444	1,367,000	1,130,000	1,285,000	11,254,000	11.4
1955	18,006,000	5,060,000	1,461,000	1,010,000	1,191,000	13,020,000	9.1
1956	19,416,000	5,374,306	1,449,000	988,000	869,000	14,232,000	6.1
1957	20,325,000	6,187,441	1,998,000	1,416,000	1,249,000	13,977,000	8.9
1958	20,971,000	6,468,000	1,750,000	1,204,000	1,094,000	14,961,000	7.3
1959	23,288,000	7,993,000	2,217,000	1,432,000	1,386,000	15,828,000	8.8
1960	26,149,000	9,980,000	2,342,000	2,292,000	1,405,000	16,898,000	8.3
1961	26,888,000	9,993,000	1,409,000	860,000	845,000	18,800,000	4.5
1962	29,800,000	11,908,000	2,730,000	1,508,000	1,712,000	21,200,000	8.1
1963	33,300,000	13,122,000	2,577,000	1,413,000	1,596,000	24,300,000	6.6
1964	36,100,000	13,002,000	2,113,000	1,072,000	1,340,000	28,000,000	4.8
1965	39,295,000	13,818,000	2,084,000	941,000	1,285,000	29,216,000	4.4

Table 3.4   Australia: NSV and Volume of Main Products, 1946–65

Year	Detergents Tons	Detergents £A,000	Edible fats Tons	Edible fats £A,000	Toilet preparations £A,000	Foods £A,000	Foods[b] Ice-cream £A,000	Total[a] NSV £A,000	Trading profit before tax as a % of NSV
1946	49,380	n/a	6,493	n/a	204	n/a	n/a	n/a	n/a
1947	46,466	n/a	5,473	n/a	222	n/a	n/a	n/a	n/a
1948	56,324	n/a	10,207	n/a	279	n/a	n/a	n/a	n/a
1949	58,966	n/a	13,376	n/a	279	n/a	n/a	n/a	n/a
1950	66,733	n/a	11,243	n/a	353	n/a	n/a	n/a	n/a
1951	73,702	n/a	13,175	n/a	406	n/a	n/a	11,485	6.7
1952	68,255	8,996	12,278	2,311	457	1,683	n/a	13,303	3.9
1953	69,913	9,614	11,943	2,330	477	1,866	n/a	14,769	8.7
1954	77,337	10,640	12,422	2,442	483	2,266	n/a	16,896	8.1

Year								
1955	79,068	11,276	11,926	2,373	493	2,370	n/a	18,006	7.0
1956	78,557	11,473	13,369	2,761	564	3,076	n/a	19,406	7.5
1957	81,940	12,591	13,071	2,096	708	2,828	n/a	20,325	9.0
1958	82,351	13,809	13,403	2,734	797	1,874	n/a	20,893	7.0
1959	83,420	14,974	14,649	3,172	849	2,194	435	23,387	9.0
1960	83,724	15,501	16,588	3,680	1,153	2,070	1,972	26,653	8.0
1961	74,793	14,155	15,887	3,570	1,455	2,310	3,490	26,888	5.0
1962	73,940	14,799	16,160	3,591	1,523	2,800	4,719	29,787	9.0
1963	77,035	15,854	17,518	3,848	1,682	4,250	5,280	33,328	8.0
1964	70,131	15,154	18,324	4,054	1,675	6,785	5,898	36,097	6.0
1965	69,950	16,734	18,354	4,322	1,623	7,206	6,632	39,295	5.3

[a] The total includes other parts of the business. The figures in this column were taken from a different source from those in the other columns, which explains why the total is inconsistent with the sum of individual columns.

[b] 'Foods' includes Liptons tea to 1957, after which tea was sold by a separate Lipton organization. This accounts for the drop in NSV of Foods 1957–8.

expectations of high profits. Whereas in 1946 detergents provided some 84 per cent of nett profits, by 1964 they provided only 49 per cent. Between 1954 and 1964 the nett return to capital employed in detergents declined from 12.8 per cent to 6.8 per cent. These trends both explain and justify Unilever's determination to diversify.

Table 3.5   Australia: Comparative Profitability of Main Products, 1954—65 (Nett profit after statistical tax as a % of gross capital employed for each product)

Year	Edible fats	Ice-cream	Foods	Deter-gents	Toilet prepara-tions	Chemicals	Printing paper, etc.
1954	0.4	n/a	(—)	12.8	7.1	0.8	3.5
1955	(—)	n/a	n/a	8.2	6.7	n/a	n/a
1956	1.0	n/a	n/a	7.2	0.9	3.5	(—)
1957	2.1	(—)	(—)	11.8	12.3	4.5	1.7
1958	(—)	(—)	(—)	10.1	10.0	3.5	3.4
1959	(—)	(—)	(—)	11.8	9.2	7.2	5.0
1960	3.5	0.9	9.7	9.2	13.1	3.8	10.9
1961	1.4	8.5	6.8	5.4	4.6	(—)	5.4
1962	7.1	7.7	(—)	11.7	(—)	2.0	4.8
1963	8.0	8.5	(—)	9.5	(—)	1.0	4.4
1964	7.3	7.6	(—)	6.8	8.6	6.5	(—)
1965	3.8	7.0	(—)	6.9	13.8	5.3	4.2

[a](—) = Loss.

[b]*n/a* means not available or not relevant.

The other original, though much less important, pillar of the Australian business had been edible fats. Because of governmental restrictions on table margarine Unilever concentrated mainly on cooking fats: as Morrell summed it up in a report of 1949, 'we sell to bakers, pastrycooks and manufacturers'. This was a reasonably profitable business before the Second World War and again after price controls were removed; but by the later 1950s the market was virtually static and profitability went down as the blended margarine industry, which consumed Unilever hardened fats, declined. The only solution lay in expanding the table margarine market, for a branded product offered potentially much higher profits than the bulk sale of edible fats; and in a genuinely open market it is probable that long before 1946 Unilever would have become market leaders with Stork or some similar quality margarine. The prospects therefore depended entirely on liberalisation of the table margarine quota system. From 1952 Unilever men began to express some optimism on the prospects because, as butter prices rose, the potential demand increased; and from 1955, when the individual states took over control of quotas from the federal government, quotas did in fact increase slightly. But they were still too small to justify large-scale production of table margarine and Unilever therefore attempted to buy quotas from existing producers. This was an expensive process and by 1965 Unilever's production was still ludicrously small. Unless conditions improved considerably edible fats, like soap, offered Unilever no escape from the problems of a limited market.

Toilet preparations also proved disappointing. From 1944 Unilever opinion was generally enthusiastic about the prospects: the aim was to increase the concern's market share from 3 per cent or so to between 15 per cent and 20 per cent 'by developing Atkinsons in the Yardley class and Rexona in the "shilling" class'. New lines would be started, consumer reaction efficiently tested, production concentrated at Balmain. Something was achieved but toilet preparations failed to become a pillar of Unilever Australia. Atkinsons never fulfilled expectations and in 1948 J. H. Hansard of the Overseas Committee favoured winding it up. It survived but never did well. The big battle took place over toothpaste. In 1949 Gibbs SR had 15 per cent of the market and Pepsodent 12 per cent, both behind Ipana, Colgate and Kolynos. By 1963 the total Unilever share of the market was down to 12 per cent, and its American rivals were rampant. Unilever's failure in toilet preparations, however, was relative rather than absolute. As Tables 3.4 and 3.5 show, turnover doubled between 1959 and 1964, helped by some successful hair preparations and other minor products; and although performance was erratic due to recurrent bouts of heavy promotional expenditure, profits were satisfactory in several years. The real failure was that toilet preparations could not provide a satisfactory field for expansion: in 1964 turnover was only about one-tenth that of detergents and a quarter of foods, even excluding ice-cream. It is difficult to be sure of the causes of this relative failure: the Unilever records abound with different explanations and formulae for success, but none seemed to solve the problem. Perhaps the main explanation is that in this field Unilever had no particular advantage over its main rivals, the big American firms: it had not been first in the field; its products were no better than (if indeed as good as) those of its rivals; and there was no possibility of buying out competition. It did reasonably well but could not repeat the triumphs of an earlier age in other products.

Given these various difficulties in detergents, margarine and toilet preparations, foods other than edible fats remained the best hope for expansion in Australia after 1945. Here Unilever might be able to get in first, at least on a large or national scale: the difficulty was to find those things which it was practicable to produce and profitable to sell in Australia, and these might be very different from what was made and sold in Europe and North America. In terms of this search the twenty years after 1945 fall into two unequal halves, dividing in 1957–9. In the earlier period Unilever attempted to develop Lipton's tea, cornflour, frosted vegetables, dehydrated packet soups and dessert mixes. By 1957 Unilever Australia had lost faith in tea, which was handed back to the parent board of Liptons to run; and by 1959 it had been decided to sell the Birds Eye frosted pea enterprise also. The second period thus saw a renewed search; and by 1965 the main emphasis had been placed not on novelties or products built up in Australia by Unilever, but on ice-cream and canned fruit, both of which had been made and sold there for a long time and which Unilever bought into at massive cost. It is thus necessary to explain the failure of tea and frosted vegetables and the decision to go for safe established lines.

The reasons for the failure in tea lay outside Unilever's control. So long as the government acted as sole importer and fixed profit margins to distributors, it was virtually impossible for Unilever to spend sufficient money on promotion to establish its brands without making a loss. Even when state importing ended in 1950 the price controls operated by all states ensured that tea would be a loser; and although Unilever persevered with tea as one of the products sold by its marketing company, World Brands, until 1957, two years after the end of price controls in New South Wales and Victoria, losses continued. At that point World Brands gave up tea and Liptons took over.

Unilever had been unlucky in that their drive to enter the tea business coincided with government controls which made it almost impossible for new firms to enter a crowded retail market. Other products marketed by World Brands in this period were not handicapped in the same way and had the chance to scoop the market by pioneering. The first two products introduced were both derived from Unilever products developed elsewhere: a cornflour dessert mixture called Mellah, from North America, and dehydrated soup developed by Liptons in the USA. Mellah and other minor food products achieved a reasonable turnover in the 1950s but also made consistent losses. Dehydrated soup was a winner from the start. Turnover rose from £A408,139 in 1952 to £A886,206 in 1957 and pre-tax profits from £A63,044 to £A90,473. But the real disappointment was frozen foods. Unilever tried very hard to make a success of these and London confidently expected year by year after 1945 that production was about to begin. But preparations took time. A growing area had to be found which would provide a sufficient volume of peas. Then Unilever had either to build a freezing factory or go into partnership with some existing firm, such as a cannery. Finally it was necessary to establish retail outlets and provide retailers with refrigerated cabinets. By 1948 production was starting at Batlow, 270 miles south-west of Sydney, on the basis of a co-packing agreement with the Batlow Packing House Co-operative Limited, a cannery established in 1923. Contracts were made with local farmers to grow peas and other vegetables and the company was thinking of leasing land on which to grow crops on a contract basis. In 1949 Morrell was optimistic about the prospects, but the promise was never fulfilled. First the supply of vegetables proved inadequate, and Birds Eye had to move to Bathurst, in New South Wales, in 1953. Two years later a co-packing agreement was made with a local canning firm, Edgell, which had farms in Bathurst and in Devonport, Tasmania. Optimism was generated by the first small profit, made in 1956; but by 1959 this had dissipated after further losses and inability to sell the whole output. At this point Unilever had three options: to soldier on, in the hope that both supply and demand problems could be solved; to wind up altogether; or to sell out to Edgells on easy terms. The Special Committee adopted the last alternative. Edgells bought not only the Birds Eye machinery but also the right to use the brand name in Australia. The deal was concluded in March 1959.

It is easy to be wise after the event, but hindsight suggests that the decision to sell was a mistake. Accumulated losses were large but quite soon after 1959 the market for frozen foods expanded rapidly and it seems probable that Birds Eye might have made reasonable profits in the 1960s and 1970s. This was recognised, for when Edgells came up for sale in the early 1960s, Unilever made an offer, only to be outbid by a local rival. The purchase of Rosella, which is described below, would have been unnecessary if Unilever had held out or had later repurchased its Birds Eye enterprise. If the story has a moral, it may be that a multinational company, which is accustomed to building up the production and sales of a new enterprise quickly, is likely to become impatient when production is held back by the need to foster the agricultural sources of its inputs and when sales promotion meets conservative consumer resistance. Yet patience may not be enough: it will be seen that Unilever were patient with foods in India but received no reward.

1957–9 was, in any case, the time when Unilever had to face the fact that its original plan to expand and diversify in Australia by promoting new concern products developed in other countries appeared to have failed and would have to be replaced. It was at this point that the decision was apparently taken (though whether it was seen in this light is not clear from the records) to drop the policy of expansion at low cost through innovation and to go back to the original Lever technique of buying established local enterprises making products in which the concern was expert elsewhere, even though this involved considerable capital investment. For this reason the acquisition of three established Australian ice-cream enterprises—McNivens, Streets and Sennitts—between 1958 and 1961, followed by Rosella canned foods in 1963, marks an important stage in the history of Unilever Australia.

It may seem surprising, in view of the success and size of the Walls ice-cream business in Britain, that Unilever should not have considered entering the ice-cream market in Australia before 1958. The reasons can only be inferred, but the most likely is that Unilever subsidiaries normally manufactured only those concern products whose brand names and reputation had already been established overseas by means of initial imports from Britain or America. In Australia this had been true of soaps, toilet preparations, convenience foods and table margarine. Alternatively, they could continue to produce goods whose local markets had already been established by the local firms Unilever acquired, for example, the whole range of Kitchen and Burford soaps. But neither ice-cream nor canned foods fell into these categories. To export Walls ice-cream (or for that matter Batchelor canned vegetables) to Australia would at any time have been to send coals to Newcastle because there was locally made ice-cream and both fresh and canned fruit and vegetables. Only a few luxury food lines were ever exported there. Hence, neither Walls nor Batchelor brand names meant anything to Australian consumers and there was no point in manu-facturing either commodity in Australia until somehow these Unilever brand names and their reputation for quality had become established there. This might have been done by small-scale manufacture in the existing factories, but it would have been a very slow business, probably attended by consistent losses for a long time.

This may explain why ice-cream and canned foods did not feature in pre-1958 development plans; but it does not account for the purchase of firms producing these foods in the five years after 1958. The grounds for doing this are fundamental to the study of overseas subsidiaries of all multinational companies because it is one thing to invest in local manufacture of a product which is central to the parent business and which might be imported had import tariffs not been prohibitive, but quite another to diversify horizontally at high capital cost to produce goods which would not under any circum-stances have been imported. The records suggest that the main motive was to sustain the dynamism of the Australian business and also, as a secondary factor, to maintain the morale of the local management. By 1958 frozen foods and tea were clearly failures and expansion in table margarines were blocked by quotas. It was at this moment that the Australian management suggested buying their way into the ice-cream market as an alternative. London was cautious. It accepted the general principle that it was desirable to get into the ice-cream market in Australia in order to increase turnover, and also that it was more efficient to buy into existing firms than to start from scratch; but at the very least they wanted to be sure that the profits of any businesses bought would be reason-able. Negotiations for buying McNiven Brothers Limited, which happened to be on offer at that time, lasted from July 1958 to May 1959 and ended with Unilever buying the business for £A532,000, well above the £A400,000 originally put as a maximum by London; and at that price it was probably not a profitable investment on its own. Its value was simply that it provided a first foothold, some 10 per cent of the New South Wales market; and it would only be profitable if further capacity could be obtained. Early in 1960 Streets ice-cream, with 60 per cent of the New South Wales market, came up for sale. This involved a much larger investment, somewhere around £A4 million. Barraclough was authorised to bid up to £A4.5 million and in the end was able to outbid Krafts who were also in the market. A year later nearly another £A1 million was spent on buying Sennitts ice-cream in Victoria; and as an ancillary to this Unilever bought Gardiners Refrigeration Co. Propriety Limited, which supplied refrigerating plant to retailers at nominal rentals as an incentive to selling a particular brand. Thus within three years Unilever had come to control some two-thirds of the ice-cream market in New South Wales and a substantial part of the Victorian market. It was in fact these market shares, dependent on established brand names, that had been bought at such large cost, for it was soon decided to close down several of the existing factories and to concentrate production, at least for New South Wales, at the main Street factory at Turella. But at least Unilever had now achieved in the field of ice-cream roughly the same predominant position that they had much earlier acquired in detergents by buying out Kitchens and Burfords. It remained to be seen whether the results would be equally profitable.

To round off the story of diversification into foodstuffs, in 1963 Unilever bought Rosella, the large canned food and jam enterprise in Victoria, for £A4.5 million. Again the price represented a share of an established market rather than the intrinsic value of the assets acquired for, as R. H. Siddons said at the time, Rosella was an old-fashioned firm whose equipment and production methods would require considerable modification. The case for buying Rosella rested on two propositions: first, a 'wet foods' business was a desirable complement to the existing 'dry foods' represented by dehydrated soups; second, the success of Heinz and Campbells in Australia suggested that this was a market in which Unilever could compete successfully. Here again was an investment obviously designed to lay foundations for further diversification rather than to provide a high return on capital invested in the short run.

Thus by 1965 the balance of the Australian business had tilted decisively away from the original pattern. Some 25 per cent of concern capital was now in ice-cream and a substantial amount in other foodstuffs. Although the concept of diversification had been deliberately adopted in 1944, the eventual pattern, particularly the heavy dependence on ice-cream and canned foods, most certainly had not. This had been a reaction to the trend of events and particularly the failure of frozen foods. In changing their approach Unilever also had to accept a new investment strategy—heavy expenditure in buying out rivals rather than growth through the use of existing productive resources and Unilever brands. Obviously the new strategy involved considerable risks and it is important that Unilever was encouraged to take such risks by the fact that in Australia, at least, capital transfers were then still uncontrolled, so that, if experience showed that the new policy was misguided, it was at least theoretically possible to repatriate the new investment. But this was very much a last resort. The immediate aim was to check the downward trend of profits through horizontal diversification, and the interest of this development lies in whether or not it had this effect. Unfortunately the success or failure of the experiment lies beyond the limits of the present study.

A second major theme that comes into almost all the case studies in this book relates to the process of domesticating Unilever subsidiaries into their host societies; and in this integrative process two issues commonly arose: the extent to which management and senior technical posts were monopolised by expatriates, and whether the government or nationals of the host country owned or could own any part of the equity of the local company. These proved to be important issues in all less developed countries after the 1940s, but they were never significant in Australia or South Africa before 1965; and because this is one of the factors distinguishing Unilever subsidiaries in more developed from those in less developed countries, it is important to discover why this was so.

There were two good reasons why localisation of management was never an issue in Australia or in similar countries. First, large sections of the Unilever business were originally owned and run by Australians and these had never been replaced by Englishmen. Second, and of more general interest, there was never any reason why even the Lever component of the Australian business should not be staffed very largely by Australians. This was largely a matter of language, education and culture: an Australian of comparable experience was entirely interchangeable with someone born in Britain and there was no shortage of men with relevant qualifications. Conversely Australians did not resent the presence of British nationals in the Unilever business as an affront to the nation's

dignity. This made it possible for the Australian business to demonstrate two important and complementary features found in many
subsidiaries in countries where nationalistic impulses do not exclude
them: that the local management will be predominantly indigenous,
but that there may be expatriates from the parent concern or other
subsidiaries at any level. All native-born Australian managers were
given training and had periods of service in Europe or in other
Unilever companies and conversely there was always a minority of
men from other Unilever enterprises working in Australia. This was
policy, not accident, and the objective bears on the special character
of a multinational company. The vital need, if a subsidiary is not to
be merely a local enterprise carrying the name and trademarks of
a larger international corporation, is for it to remain in the main-
stream of development and to benefit from the parent company's
stock of skills; and this became progressively more important over
time as the subsidiaries needed to draw on the latest techniques in
the fields of frozen foods, convenience foods, etc. Because Australia,
once it had emerged from its wartime period of state control, became
an 'open' economy and society again, the Unilever companies there
were able to benefit from mobility among its staff.

The other issue was ownership of the share capital of the
Australian business. The immediate question is why Unilever was
anxious to hold 100 per cent of the share capital of its Australian
companies, how important an issue this became before 1965 and
why Unilever eventually retained 100 per cent control.

It was not, in fact, until 1957 that Unilever were able to buy out
the last Burford shareholders in Unilever Australia; and since these
had never been in a position to affect company policy, it is significant
that Unilever should have thought it worthwhile to pursue the
objective of total ownership of Burfords as well as of all other
companies they acquired in Australia over a period of more than
40 years. The reasons, which were equally applicable to all overseas
countries, can be summed up in the proposition that unfettered
decision-making required total control. Examples relating to
Australia can be given. It might have been embarrassing to face
opposition from shareholders in the various original companies to
rationalisation of the business after 1941, especially since this
involved destruction of family enterprises. More important, shareholders had a legitimate expectation of dividends and bonus share
issues, whereas it was basic Unilever policy in all countries to make

capital investment a first call on profits and capital reserves since distribution of profits as dividends or bonus shares normally attracted a higher rate of taxation. Finally, total control exempted the management from criticism at annual general meetings. All these were good reasons why Unilever preferred to hold 100 per cent of the shares in its overseas companies, even though only 51 per cent was needed to provide management control and in practice a much smaller proportion might serve.

There were, on the other hand, circumstances in which it might become desirable or necessary to sacrifice total ownership once it had been achieved. Before 1939 it is unlikely that this was even considered; but after 1945, and especially in countries with 'managed' economies and strong nationalist feelings, two grounds for partial disinvestment might arise: first, the need to raise money locally in order to avoid transferring hard currency which might not be allowed out again; second, strong pressure from host governments or local public opinion on whatever economic or emotional grounds. The first of these was never relevant in Australia before 1965; nor had any shares actually been sold there. But there was some feeling in the early 1960s that Unilever ought to offer part of its equity to the public; and it is therefore necessary to consider where this feeling lay and why it could be resisted.

The first recorded mention in the Unilever archives of the possibility of obtaining even a stock market quotation for shares in the Australian business is in December 1960, when R. H. Siddons raised the issue after a visit there. There was clearly an undercurrent of hostility among certain sections of Australian society which disapproved in general terms of foreign subsidiaries being wholly foreign-owned, and this was not restricted to left-wing intellectuals. For example, it was Mr McEwen, then Leader of the Country Party, who first used the expression 'selling a share of the farm', which passed into local idiom, when Unilever bought Rosella in 1963. The earlier acquisition of Streets ice-cream business was greeted by one newspaper with the headline 'Another good Australian company disappears into the Unilever maw'. There was more consistent, though less vocal, pressure from stockbrokers, presumably because they wanted another 'blue chip' stock in a rather thin capital market. A decade earlier these indications of Australian opinion would probably have been ignored by Unilever House; and it may be a reflection of developments in India and other less developed countries during the 1950s, some of which are described below, that by the 1960s Lord Cole, Chairman of Limited, should have been prepared to taken them seriously. In 1961 he told the Directors' Conference after a visit to Australia that 'perhaps we should think in terms of giving the Australian public some participation in the not too distant future'. He was not keen to do this and in 1961 commented that experience elsewhere suggested that to have part of the shares on the market might be 'immensely troublesome'. He thought it best to resist pressure for as long as possible but accepted that 'sentiment could be a compelling reason' for selling shares. A year later there was nothing to indicate how seriously Unilever should take expressions of public concern, but the company was asked to send written evidence to a government enquiry into the subject of foreign-owned subsidiaries. By 1965 the whole question had been complicated by the adverse balance of payments position of Australia which meant that the local government was likely to be critical if Unilever sold shares there and repatriated the proceeds. For this among other reasons no shares were sold in Unilever's Australian business by the end of 1965 nor, indeed, by 1977. Unilever Australia remained a wholly-owned Unilever subsidiary.

The significance of this for the present study lies in the circumstances that made it possible to avoid local participation. This was possible mainly because neither the Australian government nor public appear to have felt sufficiently strongly on the question to insist that this or any other foreign company must sell part of its equity; and this in turn reflected Australia's commitment to make conditions attractive for foreign investors. For their part, freedom not to sell shares coupled with freedom to remit profits, etc. were two grounds on which Unilever regarded Australia as an excellent investment area; and this explains why Unilever was prepared to provide the very large capital investment needed to purchase the various Australian companies bought in the early 1960s, even though the return to capital invested in Australia was significantly below that obtained in a number of other countries which were required to raise most of their own development capital. Australia, in short, generated business confidence and this placed it in a different category as seen by a multinational company from most of the other countries studied in this book.

South Africa

The two main grounds for including a short study of the South

African business are, first, to check that the Australian model is indeed characteristic of Unilever manufacturing subsidiaries founded in more developed countries before 1920; second, that South Africa might have been expected to constitute a special case, as a racially segregated society in which a white minority relied heavily on black labour but excluded blacks from political power and from the higher posts in government, industry and the professions. On the assumption that a proletariat of this kind should increase the profitability of capital investment, it is important to investigate whether the performance of Lever Brothers (South Africa) Ltd reflects this South African 'special institution'. As with Australia, it is not intended to tell a continuous story but to concentrate on three questions that were central at different times: the reasons for the first establishment of a Lever manufacturing company in South Africa and how it was built up before 1915; the characteristics of the business in its 'classical' period between 1918 and about 1945; and finally the nature and profitability of the company in the two decades after 1945.

(a) The Establishment of Lever Brothers in South Africa to 1915

The case of South Africa supports the generalisation that William Lever built up overseas manufacturing companies at the same time and by roughly the same means as he expanded his industrial base in Britain. It also shows that the motive was to expand the market for Lever brands in the face of local competition more effectively than he could have hoped to do by importing from Port Sunlight. Early events in South Africa paralleled those in Australia. First a market was created by importing Lever brands from Port Sunlight. Sunlight Soap was exported to South Africa through local agents as early as 1890 and in 1891 an advertising agent was sent on a visit to promote sales. Sunlight had two initial advantages: it was the first wrapped and branded soap to appear in South Africa; and local competitors had to pay £1 a ton import duty on the palm and coconut oil and rosin which, together with local tallow, were their main raw materials. Since the Cape and Natal then had low revenue-producing tariffs on manufactured goods, this meant that the small local soap producers had little or no advantage over importers. Only the Transvaal, which helped local producers with tariffs and monopolies on certain goods and where freight from the coast added considerably to the landed cost of imports, presented any serious problems for the overseas exporter. Thus, when Lever first

Table 3.6(a)   South Africa: Imports of Soap
from UK, 1910—21 (tons)

Year	Total	Gossages	Gossages' Share Per cent
1910	6,181	1,738	28
1911	5,102	1,570	31
1912	3,115	1,473	47
1913	2,339	1,086	46
1914	1,317	565	43
1915	1,394	222	16
1916	559	14	3
1917	475	3	1
1918	213	—	—
1919	130	—	—
1920	197	—	—
1921	102	1	1

Table 3.6(b)   South Africa: Sales of Soap and Edible Fats
and Oils, 1904—45 by all associated companies (tons)

Year	Sunlight	Soap Total	Edible oils and fats
1905	3,967	4,115	n/a
1906	3,513	n/a	n/a
1907	2,824	n/a	n/a
1908	2,694	n/a	n/a
1909	2,300	2,553	n/a
1910	2,554	n/a	n/a
1911	2,249	n/a	n/a
1912	2,898	3,472	n/a
1913	2,750	n/a	n/a

1914	2,707	n/a	n/a
1915	2,768	n/a	n/a
1916	2,694	n/a	n/a
1917	3,231	n/a	n/a
1918	3,202	n/a	n/a
1919	2,621	n/a	n/a
1920	1,835	n/a	n/a
1921	2,658	n/a	22
1922	2,937	n/a	93
1923	3,051	n/a	129
1924	2,786	n/a	149
1925	2,752	n/a	274
1926	2,717	14,126	333
1927	2,508	14,297	589
1928	2,801	16,197	776
1929	2,821	18,252	859
1930	2,809	18,142	865
1931	2,639	17,891	1,095
1932	2,127	19,583	933
1933	1,783	17,085	1,374
1934	2,144	18,572	1,966
1935	2,395	21,649	2,642
1936	2,436	24,969	3,793
1937	2,839	29,534	4,429
1938	3,055	32,904	5,348
1939	3,238	36,412	6,419
1940	3,357	34,606	6,619
1941	4,581	45,246	7,683
1942	6,408	48,857	7,906
1943	8,159	48,570	n/a
1944	8,589	49,698	n/a
1945	8,928	44,921	n/a

Note: To 1912 total soap sales are Lever imported or locally made soap. Thereafter the total includes the products of associated companies in South Africa.

visited South Africa in 1895 on his way to Australia, travelling energetically from Cape Town to Kimberley, Johannesburg and on to Durban, he grasped that this was, for the time at least, an export market rather than a place in which to build a factory. It promised, nevertheless, to be a very good export market since, although the total European population was under a million, European wages, particularly on the Rand, were exceptionally high; and he immediately took steps to create an efficient Lever organisation based on Cape Town. A permanent advertising agent was sent out in 1896 and in 1903–5, after the Boer War had greatly increased demand for Lever products, the previous system of importing through local agents was replaced by a Lever agency in Cape Town, with its own travelling salesmen. A local company was registered in Cape Colony in 1904 to safeguard Lever trademarks; and 1904/5, when 4,000 tons of imported soap were sold, proved to be the best year before 1917. Although, following his normal precautionary practice, a factory site at Salt River, near Cape Town, was bought in 1904/5, the success of the import drive suggested that this, like the site Lever had bought at Toronto in 1892, might not be used for an indefinite period, if at all.

But the conditions which had made South Africa so satisfactory as an import market proved transitory and by 1910 two major changes had occurred which forced Lever into local manufacture. The first was the growth of serious competition from local manufacturers in response to an expanding European population and an increasing number of African wage-earners in the mines. In the Transvaal the most important of these were the Transvaal Soap Co. (TSC) at Auckland Park and the New Transvaal Chemical Co. (NTCC), both of which dated from 1896, the period when President Kruger had been attempting to stimulate local industry by giving monopolies and tariff advantages. The TSC had been given a ten-year soap monopoly but was never very successful and after the Boer War was taken over by a firm of butchers who used their own tallow and fats to make cheap filled soaps with some success. The NTCC was a more serious rival. Its Chairman was Baron D'Erlanger and the company had been formed in England in 1896 to take over the existing Transvaal Chemical Co. which had a factory making chemicals, chemical compounds and soap at Delmore, near Germiston. After the war the business was built up by two brothers, Dr Jacques Schlesinger and Caesar Schlesinger, and from 1908 began to expand rapidly. A soap works was built at Jacobs on the outskirts of Durban, named the Natal Oil and Fats Industry Ltd (NOFI), soap making was started again at Delmore after a lapse, candle manufacture was begun in response to demand from the mines and the company entered the gold industry by investing in the Macharie Gold Mining Co. Ltd and erecting a gold recovery plant with sulphuric acid as a by-product. This was obviously no small backyard competitor and with its capital of £300,000 and substantial British backing it might well dominate the Transvaal soap market. By 1908, moreover, there were expanding soap works in Natal, notably the Durban Oil and Soap Co. Ltd (DOSCO) and the Natal Soap Works Ltd (NSW), which was founded and run by E. Anderson and E. L. Acutt.

These industrial developments alone might have been enough to force Lever to build or buy a factory in South Africa, but immediate action was forced on him by political changes which were about to tilt the scales decisively against importers. By 1909 agreement had been reached on terms for uniting the four South African colonies into the Union of South Africa which was brought into existence by British legislation in 1910. It was obvious that the Union would adopt the protectionist tariff of the Transvaal rather than the Cape's revenue-producing tariff; and with internal free trade and a railway freight union in prospect, the economic geography of South Africa was changing rapidly. The Transvaal would undoubtedly become the economic centre of the new state; and Durban, much closer to the centres of wealth than Cape Town, was likely to increase its importance both as a port and industrial centre. Precisely when Lever recognised the significance of these developments is not clear, though the account later compiled by the South African company states that 'by 1907 he had realised the time to undertake local production was near'. Certainly it was not later than 1909, for in that year H. Greenhalgh was sent to survey all possible sites for a factory and chose one at Congella, Durban, on the ground that the combination of a deep water port to handle imported raw materials, the railway to the Transvaal and cheap local coal made Durban the best single industrial centre to serve the whole of the future Union. Time was needed to build this factory, and since it was important not to allow competitors too great a lead, Greenhalgh completed arrangements to buy control of DOSCO, which was to make Lever brand soaps until the projected large Lever factory was built. At about this time, also, Levers bought £30,000 shares in the New Transvaal Chemical Co. 'in view', as Lever put it in 1911, 'of possible working arrangements with this Company in South Africa', which may have meant an *à façon* arrangement for manufacturing Lever products in NTCC factories.

By 1910, therefore, Lever was firmly committed to local manufacture of the main Lever lines in South Africa, and in January he summarised the factors which had forced him to be so, and incidentally to sell more Lever Brothers preference shares to meet the costs, in a letter to his broker, R. Nivison:

> With reference to South Africa, local Soap Works are springing up there at a great rate and competition is becoming very keen. South African colonists are at present mad upon local industries and are not only giving Protection by Duties but they are giving advantages in Railway rates and very serious advantages, viz., in many cases 25% rebate on goods manufactured in South Africa. All these together will mean an issue of £500,000 A preference shares.

His strategy appears to have been much the same as in Australia a decade earlier—to build a large soap factory at a single strategic point and from there to penetrate all other internal markets. In 1911, when a new company, Lever Brothers (South Africa) Ltd (LB(SA)), was registered in England with an authorised capital of £500,000 to replace the earlier company registered in Cape Colony, he still seemed confident in this strategy for in that year he sold his holding in NTCC on the ground that he no longer needed a working arrangement with them and did not believe in portfolio investments anywhere. Clearly he did not regard NTCC as a serious rival in the Transvaal for he commented that ending the arrangement would have no serious effect on them because their main interests were chemicals, candles and gold recovery rather than soap manufacture. But by 1912, when he again visited South Africa, Lever recognised that his single factory strategy would not work there any more than in Canada and the USA or, as he was just beginning to realise, in Australia. Distance, and therefore freight costs, to the Transvaal and the Cape were too high and local competitors were in a strong position to build up local brand loyalties. To achieve market leadership in South Africa he would therefore have to run his own factories in each of the three main centres; and, because his rivals had a head start, he would have to buy at least some of them to eliminate competition. In 1912, therefore, during this visit to South Africa,

Lady Lever cut the first sod for a small factory on the existing site at Salt River, Cape Town. This cost only £46,000 to build and went into production in June 1913. He also completed negotiations to buy the Transvaal Soap Co. for £25,000. His plan was to increase the capacity of this small factory, add a glycerine recovery plant, and use it to establish a market in the Transvaal. Levers would thus have three factories in South Africa, and could supply each main population centre without the handicap of freight costs from the coast; and it was on grounds of distance that Lever justified his actions to his British shareholders in 1912:

> It may look a little unnecessary to have three works in South Africa . . . but when I tell you that it takes the management four days to come from Durban to Cape Town and a day and a night in the train from Johannesburg to Durban, and when you consider that local management is generally required to be right on the spot, it is the only way really in which you can conduct the business.

So large an investment might have been expected to meet the needs of the South African business for the indefinite future; but unfortunately for Levers it quickly became clear that other firms were by then so well established that LB(SA) would not make easy profits. The results of the four factories built or acquired by Lever in the years 1911–14 were as follows (losses in brackets):

| | £s | | | |
Year ending in:	1911	1912	1913	1914
LB, Durban	(9763)[a]	3471	29197	4717
DOSCO	—	—	(189)	(969)
TSC	—	(144)[b]	(402)	(138)
LB, Cape Town	—	—	(1694)	(881)

[a] for nine months
[b] for three months

Although there were offsetting profits on lines still imported from Britain, these were very depressing returns on an investment of £500,000, and Lever had to analyse the causes. He pinpointed two: continuing strong imports from Britain and intensifying local competition. The pattern of imported soaps can be seen in Table 3.6(a). Clearly the new South African tariff, coupled with Levers' switch from imports to local manufacture, was rapidly reducing total soap imports; but it was significant that Gossages, which had a larger soap export trade than any other British company, were reducing their sales in South Africa very slowly. In 1913, however, in alliance with Crosfields, they hedged against the future effects of tariffs by acquiring a controlling interest in the Natal Soap Works, which continued to make its existing brands as well as Gossage, Crosfield and Erasmic brands. The result was a rapid reduction in soap imports, but also intensified local competition; and by 1913 this was the main problem facing Levers in South Africa.

Had the Natal Soap Works been his only significant rival, Lever might not have been seriously worried at this stage; but in addition NTCC, far from having no interest in soap manufacture as Lever had thought, now became a serious and aggressive competitor in Natal as well as in the Transvaal. In 1912 they bought the DOSCO factory site from Levers, who no longer needed it once their main Durban factory was completed. In 1913 they set up a whaling enterprise, the Premier Whaling Co., at Bluff, near Durban, to provide them with cheap oil for hardening. With its strong financial base in Britain and an able local management, NTCC was clearly prepared to fight Levers for the South African soap market, using low prices and very long credit to wholesalers as its main weapons. South Africa could not indefinitely support two firms of this size and type—or three including the NSW—unless they amalgamated or formed a ring.

This, of course, was much the same position as Levers reached in Australia at almost exactly the same time; and in both countries they eventually adopted the same solution of buying out their main local rivals. In South Africa the problem of NSW was easily solved by Levers buying 4,000 shares in 1914. This did not provide control, but it symbolised the nascent alignment of Levers with Gossages and Crosfields in Britain and resulted in agreed conditions and prices in South Africa until Levers took over the two parent firms in 1919. That left NTCC; and since this was not the subsidiary of a British business but an enterprise which had to stand or fall by its South African achievement, no easy accommodation was likely. Since, however, competition on agreed terms would benefit Levers with their established brand names, it was unlikely that NTCC would accept a price agreement. The choice was therefore between cut-throat competition to the death and buying the NTCC; and since Lever normally preferred to buy rather than to run the risk of an expensive fight, the central issue in 1912–15 was whether NTCC could be bought at a price Lever could afford to pay.

At the start this was by no means certain. 1912–13 were particularly difficult years for Lever Brothers, when issued capital was increasing fast and returns, particularly from overseas companies, were dropping. Lever therefore could not be certain that he could raise enough new capital to buy a majority holding in NTCC without affecting the credit of Lever Brothers and possibly splitting a Levers Board already divided over fundamental issues of policy. In the event Lever was lucky because in 1912–13 NTCC also were in serious financial trouble. They had increased their capital to pay for expansion, but had then been hit by a short-lived recession in South Africa and by a reduction in sales resulting from the strikes and riots on the Rand mines in 1913–14. In September 1913 Lever learned from a South African contact that 'they [NTCC] are in deep water. Dr [Jacques] Schlesinger is home either to sell to you or to raise more capital.' That appeared to put Lever in a very strong bargaining position; yet, assuming (as seems likely) that the first contacts with the Schlesingers were made in September 1913, it took him fifteen months to land his prey. There were several reasons for the delay: Lever's inability to pay in cash rather than by exchange of Lever Brothers stock; the high price demanded by the NTCC shareholders; and the complication of an additional demand made privately by the Schlesinger brothers for substantial compensation to themselves for an alleged secret process for treating low grade oils and for loss of future prospects in the business they had built up. Lever did not under-estimate the value of NTCC: he told the Policy and Tactics Committee in July 1914 that '[it] stood at the Gate of South Africa and was keeping profits down . . . [It] could make it unprofitable for us in South Africa as they had never listened to reason until now.' He had therefore offered 150,000 of his 15 per cent preferred ordinary shares for the 150,000 ordinary shares in the NTCC; 75,000 more of these shares for the 150,000 6 per cent NTCC preferred stock and 20,000 more for the Schlesingers' alleged secret process and interests. The main obstacle to agreement seems to have been the last of these. The Schlesingers demanded £100,000 in cash and Lever admitted that he was 'nervous when there were so many conditions attached and he did not like these wheels within wheels'. He continued to meet Caesar Schlesinger regularly over the next five months and the minutes of the PTC, to which he reported progress regularly—four times in the first three weeks of September 1914 alone—reflect an unusual uncertainty as to whether he was doing the right thing and what price he was wise to pay. The details of these negotiations need not be told here. The essential point is that by 24 September 1914 it had been decided in PTC to separate the price to be paid privately to the Schlesingers from that to be offered for the shares. The second depended mainly on whether the profits of NTCC would cover the cost of the interest Lever Brothers would have to pay on the new shares created and given in exchange for NTCC shares. On 24 September PTC agreed to a substantial offer of 300,000 Lever Brothers 6 per cent preference shares for the total NTCC capital, provided that Levers' accountants, Cooper Brothers, could investigate the NTCC accounts and reported favourably.

The report was available by December 1914; but when the PTC met to discuss the position, Lever was away and had refused to allow the Committee to see Coopers' report. The Committee was therefore in the dark, and after a long debate it decided, despite obviously strong doubts, to authorise Lever to make whatever arrangements he thought best. This paid off. On 6 January 1915 he made an agreement with NTCC by which the existing ordinary shares were converted into Lever Brothers 8 per cent convertible preference shares and the existing NTCC preference shares were left with their owners. 150,000 new NTCC ordinary shares were created which Lever acquired in exchange for 150,000 of his 15 per cent cumulative preferred ordinary shares. This gave him full control and the holders of NTCC preference stock were not bought out until the 1930s. There remained the private interests of the Schlesinger brothers; and three months later Lever induced them to accept 20,000 more of his 15 per cent cumulative preferred shares in compensation for their secret process (of which no more was ever heard) and business prospects. It was a key element in this agreement that the brothers would continue to run NTCC and its subsidiaries and that these would remain distinct from other Lever soap companies, just as he left the Kitchen family to run its business in Australia. Thus all that Lever had actually achieved was to prevent NTCC and its subsidiaries from carrying on cut-throat competition with him. Indeed this had been his only aim from the start: he had told the PTC in September 1914 that 'the benefit [of taking control of NTCC] would be practically nil providing they sold their Soap at a proper price'. His comment after the negotiations in March 1915 was that 'there can be no competition now between Lever Brothers and the Transvaal Chemical Co. [*sic*] as we own all the ordinary shares of the latter'; and although it took time and considerable pressure to induce the unchanged management of NTCC to fall into line, by 1916 they accepted the rule that the price of NTCC soap should not be more than 2s a case below that of Lever soap of comparable quality and that they must not give credit for more than 30 days.

1915/16 thus marked the end of the first stage of Levers' activities in South Africa. Within five years they had moved from being mere importers of soap to owning or controlling the great majority of the nascent local soap manufacturing industry. The only significant surviving competition came from the Natal Soap Works and a smaller factory owned by F. Ginsberg and Co. Ltd at Kingwilliamstown, which was then too small to worry about. As has been seen, NSW was by then Gossage and Crosfield property. Lever made a move to buy it in 1915 but failed. This might have been significant if NSW had attempted price-cutting, but in 1915/16 Lever organised a South African Soap Makers' Association to regulate minimum prices and selling terms. This ensured that, since imports had virtually stopped, the South African market could be made profitable for all concerned, and from then onwards the Lever and associated companies began to make reasonable profits.

These early developments are important in two respects. First, they gave Lever Brothers a hold on the South African soap industry which they never lost. Control never amounted to monopoly because, as immediately after 1919, new manufacturers were constantly springing up. But by establishing his brands and local factories so near the start of South Africa's economic and demographic development, Lever laid the foundations for enduring primacy. Of more general interest were the methods used to establish this position which, because they were almost identical with those adopted in Australia, confirm that this was the standard Lever approach in countries of this type during the first period of his overseas expansion: first an intensive import drive to establish Lever brands; then, when local competition and tariffs made local manufacture essential, building a single factory intended, like Port Sunlight, to supply the whole local market. When this strategy was

Table 3.7   South Africa: Lever Brothers (South Africa) (Pty) Ltd. Profits and (Losses) 1911—30 (£'000)

Year	A Nett accounting profit after tax[a]	B Capital employed	A/B %
1911	(9.7)	n/a	n/a
1912	3.5	250	1.4
1913	26.9	n/a	n/a
1914	4.8	n/a	n/a
1915	70	[1,000] [b]	7.0
1916	76	n/a	7.6
1917	57	n/a	5.7
1918	57	n/a	5.7
1919	44	n/a	4.4
1920	(3.3)	n/a	(3.3)
1921	79	n/a	7.9
1922	185	n/a	18.5
1923	168	n/a	16.8
1924	153	[1,300] [b]	11.7
1925	154	n/a	11.8
1926	163	n/a	12.5
1927	166	1,300	12.7
1928	131	[1,300] [b]	10.0
1929	122	1,160	10.5
1930	105	n/a	10.5

[a]There is some disparity between these figures and other contemporary statistics, probably due to incorporation of unstated profit or loss items in one or other account. They do not include Natal Soap Works 1919—26.

[b]The only firm data on capital employed is for the three years 1912, 1927 and 1929. In order to establish the order of magnitude of accounting profits, an approximation of the likely capital employed, based on various evidence, has been made. It has been assumed that from 1915 to 1923 CE was approximately £1,000,000 and from 1924 to 1928 approximately £1,300,000. For 1930, following the known reduction of CE in 1929, a figure of £1,000,000 has been adopted. These assumed figures are in square brackets.

found ineffective against entrenched regional competitors, Lever attempted to buy control of his main rivals by exchanging shares. But his aim was strictly limited to eliminating dangerous local competition. Acquisition of a controlling interest in these companies, including the Natal Soap Co. acquired in 1919 along with Gossages and Crosfields, did not result in integration and rationalisation of production. 'No scrambled eggs' had by this time become a central tenet of Lever's business philosophy, and, as in Australia, these 'associated companies' retained their legal and physical identity. Concentration of this complex industrial empire had to wait until the second stage of the story after Lever's death in 1925.

(b) Rationalisation and Consolidation, 1915–45

The 30 years after 1915 were a 'classical' period for Lever Brothers (South Africa) Ltd in the same sense as they were for the Australian business. The South African companies remained almost entirely what they had been intended to be—manufacturers of soap for local consumption without any significant diversification—and the main achievements of these years were to consolidate the many separate and independently operated companies into a single organisation, even though some companies retained a notional legal identity as dormant trademark companies, and to reduce a multiplicity of factories from seven to four, with plans for further reduction. In both respects the South African pattern of evolution very closely resembled that in Australia, Canada and indeed virtually all countries in the developed world. It is, therefore, necessary only to describe these developments in South Africa briefly, and mainly in order to demonstrate that the Australian pattern already described was in fact the norm.

Rationalisation of the hydra-headed business built by Lever did not, and in fact could not, begin until after his death. To the last he remained a firm believer in the commercial value of 'competition within the family' and in the over-riding value of the local goodwill generated by a factory and its trademarks. The first recorded proposal for a reduction in the number of South African factories came in 1921 from Caesar Schlesinger, by then overlord of the whole of Lever's South African business. Schlesinger argued that, in view of the sudden increase in local competition (which he ascribed to the influx of Russian Jews following the revolution) Levers and NTCC would have to cut costs and that one way of doing this was to reduce the number of factories from seven to three. In reply Lever sent him a characteristic lecture on the value of multiple local enterprises, and his letter is worth quoting extensively because it encapsulates this aspect of his business philosophy.

I have not found that one big centre for manufacturing soap has any economy to offer only [*sic*] when it is run to the full of its capacity. Smaller units run also at the full extent of their capacity are on the lowest basis of economic production. It is entirely a question of any works being run to its full capacity or only half its capacity. You will find that salaries of Managers for a large unit are almost automatically in proportion to the size of the unit. Giving English figures of salaries, one can get a general works manager for a small works for £300 a year. According to the size of the bigger unit, the salary of the manager would run anything up to ten times that amount, but the output of the bigger unit would not be ten times that of the smaller unit.

Equally there is a question of railway carriage to consider. I do not know how the figures work out in South Africa, but in the United Kingdom, Railway carriage before the War was always about double the cost of wages for the manufacture of soap—hence we have a great advantage in having a great number of Works scattered throughout the country. . . .I believe that the small individual companies represented by the four works you propose to close down would greatly assist you in meeting competition. It is never so effective for a big company to bring out a competing brand as for a small company to do so.

Whether or not Lever was right, the consequences for his South African business are clear. Between 1915 and 1925 the number of his associated companies and factories grew rather than diminished and their autonomy remained almost complete. The two new members of the 'family' were the Natal Soap Works, with a factory at Pretoria as well as at Durban, which came into Lever's hands through his acquisition of control of Gossages and Crosfields in 1919; and the New Prospect Soap and Chemical Manufacturing Co. Ltd at Denver, near Johannesburg, founded in 1918, which Lever bought out in 1924 because it seemed to threaten serious competition there. In 1926 this was renamed the Herald Soap and Industries Ltd. This purchase brought the total of Lever factories to eight, four in

the Transvaal, three in Durban and one in Cape Town; and whatever the case for acquiring the additional companies, each new acquisition increased the difficulty of driving so large a team, particularly when the only man with real authority in the Lever empire had to spend most of his time in Britain.

This problem was not, of course, special to South Africa; and in 1920 he applied there the same solution (or palliative) as he was to adopt in Australia three years later: he set up a Central Administrative Board. Its chairman was Caesar Schlesinger, who was given exceptionally generous financial conditions, including a share of profits, and there were four other members, two from NTCC and two from the Lever side. The Board met quarterly, rotating between the three main cities. But, as it had no defined powers or functions and no continuous existence or secretariat, it was quite unable to consolidate the Lever business; and on the first occasion, in 1921, that it decided to act independently, by reducing the price of most soaps and also candles to meet substantial price cutting by rivals, Lever was furious that he had not been consulted. One result was that Schlesinger lost Lever's confidence and was given notice in 1924. He was replaced by Goodall, a Lever man, in 1925; but the Board never seems to have achieved any real administrative mastery over its constituent companies. As its administrative costs were considerable it was an obvious target for the axe after Lever's death. The London Board condemned it in 1928 and it was abolished when Goodall retired in 1930.

The Board was virtually the only step Lever took to consolidate the South African business; but he was not necessarily adamant on the question of closing unprofitable factories. In 1921, in response to Lever's challenge to state which factories should be closed, Schlesinger had suggested closing both of those in the Transvaal which were not part of NTCC—the Transvaal Soap Co. and the Pretoria works of NSW. Lever reacted by considering the closure of NTCC's Delmore factory instead. In 1922 he closed down its gold recovery plant and is thought to have decided to close the rest of the works in due time. It survived him but was the first victim of the new centralising policy adopted immediately after his death.

What happened in South Africa after 1925 was, of course, part of a general re-examination and restructuring of the whole Lever system undertaken by the new chairman of Lever Brothers, D'Arcy Cooper, who had to consolidate after the financial disasters of the previous five years and did not believe in artificially prolonging the life of moribund associated companies. He visited South Africa in 1926 and action followed. The NTCC, which had made a substantial loss in 1925, was the first victim. In March 1926 the London Board decided to close its Delmore factory, on the ground that the Rand did not need four Lever soap factories and that to close the Denver factory would involve a capital loss. It also decided in principle to liquidate the NTCC; but further investigation seems to have made this unattractive, possibly for reasons connected with death duties payable on NTCC's holding of Lever's preferred ordinary shares. NTCC therefore survived until 1937 as a holding company, but its goodwill and trademarks were transferred at once to its own subsidiary in Durban, SAOFI, which was renamed the Surprise Soap Co. after its most popular brand of soap. This first slimming exercise was followed in 1937 by selling the Pretoria factory of NSW, leaving two factories in the Transvaal, three in Durban and one in Cape Town.

This, however, was the only real concentration of the South African business before 1930 and until then its confederate character remained intact. 1930 proved a major turning point. Opportunity for change was provided by the retirement due to age of Goodall as Chairman of the Administrative Board; but the incentive came from the rapid decline in profits since 1927 and the incipient international recession. The main architect of restructuring was Harold Greenhalgh, who, although one of Lever's most trusted servants, now accepted the need to adopt policies Lever would certainly have disliked. In 1929 he had decided to close the NSW factory at Durban; and, after a visit to South Africa in January/February 1930, laid down the broad lines on which the business should be—and in the event largely was—reorganised during the following decade. Levers should buy no more factories, close the NSW factory at Durban, transferring part of its production to Levers' Congella factory and the rest to Cape Town, and wind up the Administrative Board, leaving the Lever management at Durban with general oversight over the other companies and factories. The next stage would involve rationalisation of production to end duplication—all toilet soaps, for example, being made at Congella—leading ultimately to a total of three factories, one in each city. As to product strategy, looking at the remarkably static sales of Sunlight since 1907, Greenhalgh proposed greater emphasis on production of the cheaper 'filled' soaps (that is, with a lower fatty acid content) whose sales should increase with the rising number and incomes of Africans drawn into the European economy. This was also the most competitive sector of the soap market; but the large Lever works should be able to manufacture cheap soaps at a lower marginal cost than their many small competitors for whom these soaps were bread and butter. Provided no actual losses were made, a policy of selling cheap soaps at very low profit margins would check competition and the real profits could be made on quality soaps sold at a premium.

This programme was immediately adopted by the London Board and the main theme of the 1930s was its partial implementation. The first step was to reorganise the company structure. In 1930 the Administrative Board was abolished, Lever Brothers (SA) Ltd—the British registered company—became a holding company, and a new South African registered company, Lever Brothers (SA) (Pty) Ltd was set up. This became the controlling company for almost all Lever activities in South Africa and by 1938, after a progressive policy of rationalisation which need not be detailed, became the only manufacturing company, the rest being bought out by Lever Brothers and either suppressed or used as dormant trademark companies. By this time, also, productive capacity had been substantially rationalised. The two factories in Durban belonging respectively to SAOFI and NSW were closed, leaving the Congella factory, the Cape Town factory and two around Johannesburg—the Transvaal Soap and the Herald Soap companies. This left the question of whether to maintain one or more factories in the Transvaal, and if one, which of these or possibly a new factory altogether. In the mid-1930s the omens were that a new factory would be built on a site bought at Elandsfontein on the grounds that neither the Denver site of Herald Soap nor the Auckland Park site of Transvaal Soap was big enough to meet the entire needs of the Transvaal; but in 1938 Greenhalgh and D'Arcy Cooper decided that this would cost too much and instead capacity at Auckland Park was increased to meet the growing demand for cheap filled soaps.

Thus at the outbreak of the Second World War concentration and rationalisation had gone a long way. LB(SA) was now a single manufacturing company with a single sales force. The whole business was run from Durban, and, although the three other factories survived, it seemed likely that the Congella factory would become the main, and possibly the only, Lever factory in South Africa. In 1938 Congella made 13,742 tons out of total Lever production of

32,904 tons in South Africa, Cape Town 3,463 tons and each Johannesburg factory around 7,000 tons. But these totals understate the primacy of Congella. Not only did this factory make the whole range of Lever products then made in South Africa for the Natal, eastern Cape and part of the Orange Free State markets, it also supplied all the toilet soap, toilet specialities and edible fats and oils for the South African market. Conversely, while Cape Town made Sunlight, other laundry soaps and Lifebuoy for the western Cape market, the Johannesburg factories made cheap filled soaps exclusively. In the event the Second World War checked and reversed this trend towards concentration of production in Durban. Increasing demand for cheap soaps coupled with growing use of local rather than imported raw materials tended to shift the centre of gravity to the Transvaal. By 1942, after considerable capital expenditure, Auckland Park was producing 16,793 tons of soap to Durban's 18,101 tons and, more significant, was now making quality hard soaps for the first time. As E. Quin remarked after a visit in 1943, it was now inconceivable that the Durban factory should monopolise the manufacture of Sunlight and Lifebuoy for the Transvaal, and equally that Durban would ever become the sole manufacturing centre for South Africa. But it remained open whether the Transvaal would need two factories and if not whether Auckland Park alone could meet the needs of an expanding market.

By the early 1940s the Lever business in South Africa had clearly changed fundamentally; yet in one respect at least it retained its original character: it was still basically a maker of soap, with cooking oils and fats, but not margarine, as a second and comparatively unimportant second string. The main reason for this narrow product range and the lack of diversification was the restricted local market. With a total white population of only 1,722,660 in 1926 plus 7,394,094 Africans and 'coloureds' (1921 census), rising to 2,372,690 and 9,045,659 respectively in 1946 and with non-European wages very low (non-European factory wages averaged only £54 8s a year in 1938/9), South Africa was a much less attractive place in which to manufacture luxury goods than, say, Australia or Canada and not very different from New Zealand, where the product range was equally narrow. As a result virtually none of the specialised Unilever products which began to be made in Australia in the 1920s and 1930s were made in South Africa; and down to the early 1940s United Exporters in Britain continued to send such Unilever products as Gibbs toothpaste, Icilma toilet preparations, Atkinson perfumes and even Knights and Pears toilet soaps. The volume of these imports remained small and there seemed no strong probability that they would lay foundations for local manufacture.

This was not through oversight. In 1937 E. Fletcher of UEL considered further import substitution but concluded that the tariff on toilet preparations was too low and that consumer preference for imported goods remained too strong. A year later Greenhalgh projected local production of imported lines, but not for the time being. In fact it was the war which, by disrupting imports and increasing consumer demand, produced action. By 1943 there was a plant at the Durban factory making the standard range of Unilever toilet and dental preparations; and in that year the London Board was told that, after discussion with the South African Industrial Development Commission, it was proposed to investigate a number of possible new products, including margarine, frosted fruit and compound cattle cake. This marked a possible watershed; but margarine remained the key to successful diversification. Nothing had done more so far to prevent Levers from widening their product base than what amounted to a legal ban on the manufacture of margarine in response to the political power of the dairying interests. But from 1943 onwards margarine became a top priority in Unilever's forward planning and the impetus to diversification was increasingly strong.

To this point the Lever/Unilever business in South Africa conformed so closely to the conventional evolutionary pattern of similar enterprises in Europe, Australia and America that it might seem to lack special interest. What made it exceptional before and after 1945 was its remarkably satisfactory and consistent profitability, Lack of reliable data on capital employed and the complicated nature of the system of associated companies make calculation of the return to capital here, as in most overseas countries, largely conjectural before 1930; but from Tables 3.7, 3.8 and 3.9 at least two things are certain: losses were made in South Africa in only two years out of the 55 covered by this study; and from 1931–45 the average return (accounting profits) on capital employed was 13.4 per cent. If a reasonable guess is made at the capital employed from 1921–6 and from 1928–30, the average rate of return for the decade 1921–30 would be about 12 per cent. These are both impressive figures and pose two questions: first, whether South Africa was exceptionally profitable in comparison with other overseas companies studied here; second, whether its consistently high

Table 3.8 South Africa: Profits and Losses 1931–45 (£SA'000)

Year	Nett sales value	Nett accounting profit as % of nett sales value	Trading profit before tax	Nett accounting profit after tax	Nett profit after statistical tax	CE (1 January of year)	D/F %	Dividends
	A	B	C	D	E	F		
1931	n/a	n/a	142	105	n/a	938	11.2	n/a
1932	n/a	n/a	n/a	19	4	943	2.0	n/a
1933	n/a	n/a	n/a	60	44	[900]	6.7	n/a
1934	n/a	n/a	n/a	89	70	883	10.1	n/a
1935	903	n/a	n/a	146	119	933	15.6	77
1936	1,026	n/a	n/a	171	140	966	17.7	48
1937	1,295	n/a	244	247	210	1,046	23.6	225
1938	1,362	14.2	220	203	186	1,053	19.3	152
1939	1,488	19.1	317	284	246	1,091	26.0	177
1940	1,651	10.6	287	175	n/a	1,140	15.4	n/a
1941	2,138	10.1	462	216	n/a	1,189	18.2	n/a
1942	2,775	5.8	442	161	n/a	1,797	9.0	n/a
1943	3,651	6.6	604	241	n/a	1,657	14.5	n/a
1944	4,102	4.9	572	201	n/a	2,380	8.5	n/a
1945	4,081	4.9	436	200	n/a	2,269	8.8	n/a

profit levels can be attributed to low production costs, possibly associated with 'cheap' black labour. Comparative data on both questions is set out in Tables 3.9 and 3.10.

Table 3.9   South Africa: Nett Profit[a] in Relation to Capital Employed in Five Unilever Companies before 1945

South Africa — Lever Brothers (South Africa) (Pty) Ltd	
1921—30	12% (estimated)
1931—45	13.4%
Nigeria — (WASCO)	
1926—31	39.6%
1932—40	4.6%
Congo — (SAVCO) (before tax)	
1925—31	17.6%
1932—45	10.7%
Australia — Lever Brothers (Australia), Sydney	
1927—38	10.4%
India	
1935—8	Soap 13.8%
1935—8	Vanaspati 39%

[a]Nett profit after statistical tax.

On the first issue certainty is impossible because the data is defective. It seems reasonably certain that, of the four overseas companies which operated for a sufficient time before 1945 to provide useful evidence, South Africa provided the most consistently high post-tax return to capital employed, but that other companies gave considerably higher returns for limited periods. For example,

Table 3.10 Costs, Tax Rates, and Profits, Lever Brothers (Australia), Sydney, and Lever Brothers (South Africa) (Pty) Ltd 1936 and 1937 (£'000)

Year	A Capital employed	B Nett sales value	C Fixed expenses	D Advertising as % of nett sales value	E Fixed expenses as % of nett sales value	F[a] Tax as % of trading profit	G Nett profit after statistical tax as % of capital employed	H Nett result as % of NSV
(1)	*Lever Brothers Sydney*							
1936	1,119	751	92	18.0	12.2	20.4	21.2	31.7
1937	1,119	886	129	19.0	14.6	20.4	15.3	19.4
(2)	*Lever Brothers (South Africa) Pty) Ltd*							
1936	966	1,026	182	6.2	17.8	10.0	14.5	13.6
1937	1.046	1,295	214	5.0	16.5	10.0	20.0	16.2

Note: a. The figures in columns F and G are based on statistical tax liability, not taxes actually paid that year.

Savonneries du Congo Belge (SAVCO) did better than LB(SA) in the later 1920s but much worse between 1932–45. West African Soap Industries (WASCO) did spectacularly better in the 1920s but very much worse in the 1930s. The Indian figures cover only the first four years of local manufacture, but are higher than anything in the South African record. But for the present purpose the Australian figures, which cover the longest period, are the most significant. While the return was generally lower than for South Africa, it was not far below; and because in many respects the two enterprises were similar it is proposed to concentrate on the reasons for this margin of around 3 per cent in their profit figures.

Two good reasons why both had good post-tax profit figures in relation to capital employed were market dominance in soaps and very restricted new investment after the first foundation of the overseas company, coupled with maximum depreciation of the book value of the fixed capital, which naturally increased the return to investment. [4] But in considering why South Africa should have done better than Australia, there remains the possibility that this might be due to the fact, unique among these companies, that, while the Lever factories, in common with all others there, were largely staffed by Africans on relatively low wages, they were selling to predominantly white consumers whose average incomes were at least as high as those found in Europe or Australia. Since Marxists would argue that this combination of factors, by intensifying the exploitation of the labour force, would raise the profits of capital in South Africa above the norm, it is worth looking at the evidence on the Lever/Unilever business there more closely. Comparison with the Lever business in Sydney, Australia should clarify the position.

It is, of course, inherently improbable that use of 'cheap' labour in an African country would provide above average profit margins for a local business producing for the local market. The question will be considered more fully in relation to the East African business in a later chapter; but the main *a priori* arguments against this happening are as follows. First, soap making is a highly capital intensive business and wage costs constitute a relatively very small proportion of total production and distribution costs. Second, the number of workers employed in relation to the volume of output is directly related to wages and the efficiency of the work force. High wages invariably lead to a reduction of the numbers employed through mechanisation, provided the workers are competent to operate more sophisticated equipment. Low wages are normally associated with low technical and other skills and are therefore balanced by the need to employ more men than would be required if their skills were higher, and also by a relatively large and expensive supervisory staff. There are two situations, however, in which low wages might significantly affect profits in a business of this type. On the one hand, if low skills were associated with high wages, possibly because these were imposed by government, it would be impractical to install complicated equipment, labour costs would rise and profits would fall. Conversely, if factory workers possessed advanced industrial skills and experience which justified mechanisation and made possible a reduction of the labour force, but wages were arbitrarily depressed by legislation or binding social convention, then profits would be artificially increased. Because there were laws and conventions providing for job reservation and thus limiting wages paid to Africans, it is at least possible that the second situation may have existed in South Africa, provided, of course, that the labour force was sufficiently sophisticated to justify investment in advanced equipment. It is therefore proposed to analyse and compare the main constituents of Lever profits in the South African and Australian businesses in the mid-1930s (for which sufficient data is available) to test this possibility.

The facts are summarised in Table 3.10. Unfortunately no information has survived on the number of employees in either country in the mid-1930s, so it is impossible to compare productivity. But this is not, in fact, important. The key figure is total fixed expenditure (that is, excluding the cost of raw materials and advertising) because this includes the cost of all types of labour and allows for the degree of mechanisation as well as differential wage rates. It is clear from column E, which relates fixed expenses to nett sales value, that in these years (and in fact in most years for which data is available) fixed expenses were significantly higher in South Africa than in Australia, despite the fact that Australian wage rates were among the highest in the world. Clearly 'cheap' black labour did not provide low fixed production costs.

This, however, leaves unanswered the question of why South African profits after tax were on average above those made in Australia in the decades before 1945. It was not due to market shares being different, since the Lever companies in the two countries had roughly the same proportion of the soap market; nor to raw material costs, since both relied heavily on local tallow. In both countries the cost of transport from factory to market also tended to be high. But Australian companies suffered from three special disadvantages. In New South Wales at least competition from overseas and local rivals was sufficiently severe to demand large expenditure on advertising: 18 per cent of NSV in 1936, 19 per cent in 1937; whereas the South African companies could get away with 6.2 per cent and 5.0 per cent in these two years. Another factor was company taxation, which was twice as high in Australia as in South Africa at this time. Finally South Africa had been able to keep its capital employed very much lower than Lever Bros in Sydney in relation to the value of production. Thus, while lower factory overheads in Sydney offset higher taxation and gave this factory a good return on NSV, its relatively large book capital meant that it lost its advantage over South Africa in terms of the nett return to capital employed.

These differences were not, in fact, very great: the total Australian result summarised in Table 3.1 was worse than that for Sydney because other parts of the Australian business, notably Burfords in Adelaide, were less efficient. The conclusion must therefore be that the very satisfactory return Unilever received from their South African business represented the sum of a number of favourable factors which were seldom all present for so long a period elsewhere (it is significant that the slump affected the South African business much less than Lever enterprises in most other countries) but that it had no definable relationship to the employment of black African workers. Lever men at least had no illusions on this subject. Far from seeing low African wages and continued inequality as an asset to their business, they repeatedly stated their view that African advancement was an essential condition of any substantial increase in the company's sales and profits. A comment by Quin on his visit in 1943 may be taken as an expression of this consensus, then and later:

A very hopeful augury for the future lies in the fact that it is increasingly being appreciated by politicians, industrialists and the more enlightened sections of the general public that in the development of the backward non-European population lies South African's chief hope of progress and prosperity in the future. If the economic status of these people (who form almost

80% of the total population) were to be raised the internal market in South Africa would be expanded to many times its present size . . .

During the war-years [*sic*] considerable progress has in fact already been made in advancing non-European wage rates, the Wage Board having consistently increased rates in successive Determinations . . .

It is appreciated—though not perhaps as generally as it should be—that the mere raising of non-European wages will not in itself accomplish much, and may even have the opposite effect to that intended unless the efficiency of these workers is improved, and the Colour Bar restrictions relaxed so that non-Europeans can be employed on work that justifies higher wages. Essential pre-requisites to any general improvement in efficiency on [the part of] the non-European worker are improved housing, feeding, education and social services generally, and this is realised.

Quin was over-optimistic: the political watershed of 1948, when the Nationalists came to power, was to be followed by the reversal of many of the beneficial trends he depicted. But his approach underlines the central point that a multinational company whose profit comes from selling in the market where its manufacturing subsidiary is situated cannot regard low industrial wages as an asset, even though it may be compelled, by law or organised white labour, to pay wages in line with those in the host society. What little it might gain in its wage bill it more than loses from the general reduction of the capacity of the bulk of wage earners to buy its products.

(c) Diversification, Localisation and the Colour Bar, 1945–65

During the 1950s and early 1960s the two adjectives most commonly used by senior Unilever executives to describe the South African business were 'sound' and 'conservative'; and in conjunction these sum up the later history of the business pretty well. Knowledge of contemporaneous patterns of development in Australia makes it possible to add a third: 'evolving along conventional Unilever lines'. In fact, almost all the developments of these two decades were projected or readily predictable by 1944: further rationalisation of production to reduce the factories at Johannesburg to one and possibly also to close that at Cape Town; preservation of an established position as market leader; expansion of the edible fats and oils side if margarine manufacture was allowed; modest diversification into other established Unilever products as the market expanded, possibly by buying out existing enterprises; and, assuming all went well, maintenance of nett profits at around 10 per cent of gross capital employed. It was also predictable that Unilever would continue to regret the low incomes of blacks and 'coloureds' and their own inability in the face of government and white union pressure to promote Africans and 'coloureds' to higher levels in the work force, but that they would, in fact, do as the Romans did as the price of survival. Since all these retrospective predictions are correct, it is necessary here only to substantiate them briefly, considering in turn rationalisation of the business, diversification, race relations and profitability after 1945 in comparison with that of Unilever in Australia.

By 1945 LB(SA) had already been both rationalised and consolidated in the sense that the original collection of legally and functionally separate businesses had been homogenised into a single enterprise under unitary management. Indeed, the sales force had by then passed beyond this first stage in which a single organisation had replaced the many sales organisations inherited from the original associate companies: in 1944 it had been redivided along product lines. After 1945, therefore, rationalisation turned on three different issues. The first, reduction in the number of dormant trademark companies, needs no description: it followed the general trend within Unilever as a whole and had no significance for the conduct or profitability of the business. The other two questions were, first, whether to reduce the surviving four factories to three or less; and, when additional new businesses were acquired, in which Unilever had a majority interest, how closely these should be integrated into the existing business.

The old issue of how many factories to keep in Johannesburg and, if only one, which of the existing works or a new one on the Elandsfontein site, was further complicated by 1945 by the fact that an increasing proportion of total sales was now in the Transvaal and that much of the raw material came from the Belgian Congo rather than from overseas via Durban. Early post-war proposals for transferring the administrative headquarters of the whole business to Johannesburg came to nothing, but planning for the Transvaal took for granted that production facilities there would have to be increased very considerably. The Elandsfontein site was rejected on the grounds that it was now seen to be unsuitable for large-scale production (though it was not sold until 1964) and an alternative site bought at Boksburg. Major changes were postponed until 1954 because of the difficulty of getting finance and equipment for a new factory; but in 1951 the Denver factory and site were closed and a new plant, initially to manufacture margarine and oils and subsequently NSDs, was started at Boksburg. This came into production in 1956 but Auckland Park continued to produce soap until it was decided to sell it in 1968. By this time also pressure to close the Cape Town factory was building up on the grounds that, as G. D. A. Klijnstra said in 1963, it 'was becoming marginal if not uneconomic'. This view was repeated by Edgar Graham the following year: and, although Cape Town had not been closed down by the time this study ends, it was by then certain that the Unilever soap and edibles business in South Africa would be concentrated in two factories, at Durban and Boksburg.

A far more significant development, which very closely paralleled that in Australia, was diversification. Conceptually the starting point was a 'General Development Plan' which was prepared by the Overseas Committee and approved by the Special Committee in June 1944 as part of the major forward planning exercise undertaken that year and whose effects are evident in most parts of this book. The underlying assumption was a 'uniform increase in population over the three main centres' and a progressive increase in demand for soap and edible products 'due to steadily improving conditions of the natives'. On this basis it was planned to spend about £3 million (at current prices) over the next ten years, £800,000 at once, on expansion and diversification. For soap the aim was to achieve 75 per cent of the market and to increase the porportion of quality soap sold. Sales of edible fats and oils were expected to rise to about 8,000 tons; but the main hope was that the South African government might for the first time allow manufacture and sale of margarine. The existing range of locally manufactured toilet preparations would be maintained and possibly expanded. But totally new products were not thought promising. The governmental Industrial Development Commission was keen that LB(SA) should expand from their limited production of meal (a by-product of milling) into composite cattle feeds as part of a government sponsored enterprise called NASFEEDS, but Unilever was not at all sure that this would be profitable at the prices the government seemed likely to set for the product. As for human foods, the Special Committee made no projection on the ground that South Africa was not yet a satisfactory market for ice-cream or the frozen foods which were then being developed in Britain.

It is not proposed to trace the implementation and modification of this plan for post-war expansion in detail: the main trends can be deduced from Table 3.11, which can be compared with Table 3.4 on Australia. The simple fact is that South Africa followed a very similar pattern to Australia, and this was also the standard growth path for most Unilever companies after 1945 in countries which put no physical restrictions on the range of products any enterprise might make and sell. By 1965 the obvious limitations on this process were that LB(SA) had still not gone into frozen or canned foods, apart from ice-cream, and that its sales of margarine were still very small. The first was due to limitations of the market, the second to the fact that for margarine South Africa was not then an 'open economy'. The interesting question is, therefore, what constraints or stimuli proved most important in influencing Unilever's decisions on questions relating to expansion and diversification; and it is proposed briefly to describe developments in four new or marginal product groups after 1945: margarine, ice-cream, convenience foods and animal compound feeds.

For Unilever margarine was, of course, as basic as soap; and the main defect of LB(SA) as a subsidiary was that at no time before 1965 was the manufacture and sale of margarine in South Africa free from controls. The story falls into three phases. Until 1944 manufacture of margarine was forbidden because it competed with butter, a staple of the South African dairy farmers. But late in 1944, because butter was in short supply and inflation was affecting the nutritional standards of African workers, the government announced that it would permit margarine manufacture, imposing no restrictions on colour or quality. On the other hand the quantity produced was controlled by the Dairy Board, which allocated quotas to all would-be manufacturers: and margarine had to be sold exclusively to Africans and by the government, which subsidised the price and distributed it by a fleet of vans. This made the concession intrinsically unattractive, but Unilever decided that any opportunity to establish their brand was better than none and they installed plant at Durban. The first week's production (30 tons) was sold to Africans in July 1947 and hopes were raised four months later when the authorities allowed Europeans also to buy margarine, provided it was from the

Table 3.11   South Africa: Product Sales and Market Shares, 1946—64

Year	A Soap '000 (tons)	5 of market	B Edible oils & fats '000 (tons)	% of market	C Margarine '000 (tons)	% of market
1946	33	63	7	n/a	n/a	n/a
1947	33	58	n/a	n/a	n/a	n/a
1948	50	66	7	n/a	n/a	n/a
1949	50	67	n/a	n/a	n/a	n/a
1950	52	63	n/a	n/a	n/a	n/a
1951	56	64	10	33	n/a	n/a
1952	55	63	n/a	n/a	n/a	n/a
1953	60	66	n/a	n/a	n/a	n/a
1954	62	66	n/a	n/a	n/a	n/a
1955	65	66	10	n/a	n/a	n/a
1956	72	69	13	38	n/a	n/a
1957	68	67	14	n/a	n/a	n/a
1958	74	68	16	n/a	3067	n/a
1959	78	67	20	21	3965	61
1960	83	67	22	22	4270	61
1961	77	66	22	20	4259	61
1962	78	64	22	20	4257	61
1963	81	64	23	20	4145	59
1964	84	62	25	20	4599	62

vans. Some attempt was made to mobilise demand for the lifting of all controls among urban housewifes; but in 1948 the steam was taken out of the agitation by a glut of butter, and LB(SA)'s production was halted for two months due to lack of demand.

It was, in fact, an open question whether even in a free market there was a worthwhile future for Stork margarine in South Africa at that time. Margarine was regarded by most Europeans as a 'native' food and the economic price was too close to that of butter. Resolute

D Ice-cream		E Foods: pkt. soups		F Toilet preps.	G Animal feeds
'000 (gals)	% of market	'000 (cases/ litres)	% of market	NSV (£'000)	'000 (tons)
n/a	n/a	n/a	n/a	n/a	n/a
n/a	n/a	n/a	n/a	n/a	n/a
n/a	n/a	n/a	n/a	n/a	5
n/a	n/a	n/a	n/a	n/a	5
n/a	n/a	n/a	n/a	113	10
n/a	n/a	n/a	n/a	117	8
n/a	n/a	n/a	n/a	176	10
n/a	n/a	17	n/a	243	7
n/a	n/a	60	n/a	197	10
n/a	n/a	92	n/a	204	9
n/a	n/a	110 (cases)	n/a	420	n/a
n/a	n/a	104	n/a	527	n/a
n/a	n/a	96	n/a	n/a	n/a
522	10	191	67	317	9
892	17	128	69	420	11
1133	23	6156 (litres)	72	493	11
1295	20	7146	80	612	11
2105	32	8186	80	702	12
2164	32	9722	70	799	18

advertising coupled with an eventual increase in the price of butter might ultimately have opened the way to profitable production; but the victory of the Nationalist Party in the general election of 1948 destroyed this possibility. The Nationalists were primarily dependent on the Afrikaner vote which traditionally favoured the farming interest, including dairying. Although margarine quotas were increased in 1949, so that LB(SA) were able to increase production to 55 tons a week, a new act was passed in March 1950 which began the third, most depressing phase of the margarine story. The distribution and sale of margarine were for the first time made entirely free; but in future margarine had to be bleached white, whatever its natural colour, and the Minister of Agriculture might impose any other restrictions he saw fit, including production quotas. Bleaching made it impossible to promote Stork as a butter substitute for Europeans, who would never accept a 'white spread', so margarine was condemned to the role of cooking fat and 'native food'; and in allocating quotas the government tended to favour locally-owned enterprises. Stork emerged as market leader, with 60 per cent of actual sales—though less than half the nominal quotas —by the early 1960s; but no one in Unilever could raise much enthusiasm for so emasculated a business and production was kept going mainly by the hope that, if ever a miracle occurred and margarine were set free, Stork would be poised to dominate a worthwhile market. This apocalypse had not come about by 1965 but did come in the 1970s.

Margarine, of course, was a special case, and there was nothing to prevent LB(SA) from diversifying along lines pioneered in Europe and elsewhere through the manufacture of ice-cream, frozen, packet or canned foods. As late as January 1948 the Special Committee held to the view expressed in 1944 that the South African market was inadequate for local production of such things, minuting in reaction to a proposal from Durban for starting the manufacture of ice-cream that 'we should enter this field only in those countries where the population was sufficiently large and concentrated to permit the employment of large mass-production and merchandising methods'. But circumstances alter cases: four months later, in April 1948, Special Committee agreed to consider a proposal coming from the Durban management that they should negotiate to buy a 51 per cent interest in one of the major established South African ice-cream companies, Rondi Brothers, on the ground that all other plans for diversification and expansion in South Africa were held up by technical, governmental or other obstacles. No sooner had Unilever steeled themselves to this gamble—provided there was a satisfactory report from the auditors—than news came that Rondi Brothers had sold their interests to another party and this ended Unilever's interest in ice-cream in South Africa for nine years. When interest revived in 1957 it was not because any existing local firm was up for purchase but, apparently, because LB(SA) still felt frustrated by the limited range of alternative opportunities for diversification. With London's consent, LB(SA) then did something which had been thought impracticable in Australia—they started manufacturing Walls ice-cream on a portion of the new site acquired at Boksburg, without any local goodwill for their brands. This decision was taken in June 1957 following a visit by J. P. Van den Bergh and sales began early in 1959. 522,000 gallons were sold that year and 892,000 gallons in 1960. But the early results were disappointing, possibly because, as J. P. Van den Bergh put it in May 1961, 'I believe in 1961 [ice-cream production] will make a small profit; if it does it will be a very good performance. We know to our cost how long it takes to build up such a business to a profitable level. In South Africa we paid nothing for goodwill; we had to build it. This has been done.'

The Special Committee shared his optimism: in January 1961 they had hoped for a 7 per cent return on ice-cream in 1961 and 10 per cent in 1962. Both were disappointed. Ice-cream made a loss of £20,500 in 1961 and a profit of only £89,000 on a capital of £1,077,000 in 1962. In 1963 the profit was 7.6 per cent. To increase turnover and reduce competition, in November 1962 Unilever bought from Westons, its successful rival of 1948, an 86 per cent holding of ordinary shares in Rondis at a cost of about £700,000, hoping to buy the balance of 14 per cent in due course. This, according to the then Chairman of LB(SA), R. H. Del Mar, should have given Walls plus Rondis 45 per cent of the market and better access to the Cape and Natal markets than was possible from Boksburg. Again the pot of gold proved elusive. In 1964 LB(SA) still had only 35 per cent of the market by volume and 31 per cent by value, and hope for the future lay in a combination of greater efficiency in the federated businesses and the possibility of arranging production quotas with local rivals.

The main difficulty over ice-cream was that Walls was not first in the field and had to fight for every inch of its share in a competitive market. Convenience foods were a different case because here Unilever was in a position to create a new market. Their first thought was frozen foods; but when J. G. Short of Birds Eye was sent to report on possibilities in September 1947, he recommended against establishing a Birds Eye subsidiary in South Africa on the grounds that there was no established market and that distribution would be very difficult in a country where few warehouses or shops had refrigerating equipment. As in Australia, the cost of providing this would be substantial and possibly not worthwhile. He suggested that

Birds Eye might licence their frosting technique to interested third parties and attempt to build up a market with imports; but nothing significant had been done along these lines by 1965.

These technical problems did not, however, apply to convenience foods, which had been added to the Unilever range in England through the purchase of a Chicago firm manufacturing dehydrated soups early in the Second World War and had been developed in America by Liptons under the brand name Royco. There was also a small dried soup market in South Africa pioneered by imports of Betty Crocker products from the USA; but when Unilever began to make Royco packaged soup at Durban in 1953 they were the only local producers. By 1960 they had thirteen varieties on sale, Royco soups were said to be found in the great majority of European households which used dehydrated soups, and Unilever held an estimated 72 per cent of this market. The pre-tax yield on the capital employed in soups was excellent—an average of 33.5 per cent between 1959 and 1963. Yet, although this was a considerable achievement, its actual or potential importance to LB(SA) must not be exaggerated. Table 3.11 shows that the volume of soup sold did not increase between 1956 and 1958 and that after a subsequent 56 per cent increase, it seemed to be levelling off again in the mid-1960s. This, together with the fact that no other convenience foods, dehydrated or frozen, had been introduced into South Africa by then, indicated that this was a strictly limited market. Only a minority of a minority of the population used such things, for the ready availability of domestic labour differentiated South Africa from Europe and North America. In common, therefore, with toilet preparations, convenience foods remained a profitable but very minor adjunct to the main Lever business. In 1963 foods constituted 2.3 per cent of NSV but made 4.8 per cent of total LB(SA) trading profits. The proportions for toilet preparations were 3.9 per cent and 2.9 per cent.

This points to the general proposition that in South Africa, as in Australia, the Unilever business came up against potentially serious obstacles to continued growth in the 1950s and early 1960s. Between 1945 and 1952, a period of eight years, NSV in South Africa doubled, from £4 million to £8 million; but despite inflation, it took eleven years for it to double again, by 1963. Between 1950 and 1956 (ignoring the immediate post-war years when production was artificially held down by government action) sales of soap by volume increased by 20,000 tons (38 per cent); but in the next six years they increased by only 6,000 tons (8.3 per cent). Some slackening of the rate of growth was, of course, to be expected, for the post-war expansion had been fuelled by pent-up demand. But there was no denying that by the later 1950s LB(SA), with nearly 70 per cent of the soap market, as large a share of the margarine market as it was given by the government, and a dominant position in convenience foods, seemed to be reaching the limits of all existing markets. The problem and its timing was almost exactly the same as in Australia; and in essence, though not in detail, LB(SA)'s response was the same: to attempt to diversify within the boundaries of normal Unilever technology and even, if necessary, beyond, ranging into enterprises in which Unilever would provide the capital and skills and initially buy the industrial technology with the plant. In the decade before 1965 LB(SA) considered a wide range of possible businesses, ranging from baby foods through pricked peas to dog foods. Most proposals were rejected out of hand, but five were considered seriously by Unilever House and four new products were either manufactured or an attempt made to buy a company that made them. These were compound feeding stuffs, chemicals, processed cheese, packaging materials and a polyethylene substitute for jute bags. Each of these proposals and negotiations will be described briefly to demonstrate the widening spectrum of LB(SA)'s thinking and to illustrate the criteria on which they and Unilever House decided such questions.

Animal compound feeds, as has been seen, had already been considered several times and finally rejected by 1947. The subject was raised again in 1954 as a direct consequence of the earlier decision to mill groundnuts and sunflower seeds at the new Boksburg factory, which naturally opened the issue of whether to add plant for converting the by-products into feed. The argument against doing so was strong: the market was almost static; price limits imposed in the farmers' favour by the government were ridiculously low; most other manufacturers were unscrupulous about the quality of their product, so it would be difficult to promote a premium product. On these grounds R. H. Payton of British Oil and Cake Mills (BOCM), a Unilever subsidiary in Britain, advised against compound feeds in 1954, and the following year Sir Herbert Davis, a vice-chairman of Unilever, who had strongly opposed going in for animal feeds in 1947, returned from a visit to South Africa convinced that he had been right. Yet in June that year the Special Committee approved a proposal by A. D. Gourley, Chairman of LB(SA), to produce high protein compounds at Boksburg. The reasons for this change of front were not detailed, but the Special Committee minuted that 'it was not the intention to go into compound manufacture on a big scale, but simply to use up surplus meal by mixing it with molasses and minerals'. Thus no large capital outlay was involved, and the intention seems to have been merely to make better use of existing meal. The results were, to say the least, unspectacular and fully justified early caution. The volume of sales remained much as it had been when LB(SA) were merely selling meal; and in the early 1960s the pre-tax trading profit on capital employed averaged only 5.8 per cent of GCE. The fact that in the mid-1960s Unilever was making a serious study of future possibilities was due more to its general policy of making maximum use of the expertise of the UK milling group than because there were hopes of high profits in South Africa.

Industrial chemicals came under consideration almost entirely because of the accident that the manager and majority shareholder of Silicate and Chemical Industries (Pty) Ltd, which had factories at Johannesburg and Durban producing, among other things, chemicals used by LB(SA) in soap manufacture, had links with Crosfields and wanted to sell a 51 per cent holding. The case for buying was put by Del Mar, now Chairman of LB(SA), but the precise grounds for making this investment of £166,000 (or £234,000 if an additional 20 per cent shareholding was acquired) are not clear. The most likely were that ownership would assure LB(SA)'s supply of chemicals and that Silicate had a proven post-tax yield of 7.8 per cent during the previous three years. The Special Committee agreed to buy, but subsequent experience suggested that they may have been misguided: (Sir) E. Woodroofe, who inspected the factories with the expert eye of the research chemist in 1963, thought them 'unimpressive' and suggested that they might eventually have to be replaced by a single factory with three times their then joint capacity.

Both these ventures involved investment in backward or forward production directly connected with LB(SA)'s basic activities. The next acquisition—processed cheese—did not; indeed, cheese seems never to have been a Unilever line except in Germany. Thus the case for LB(SA) acquiring a 51 per cent holding in Robin Cheese Manufacturing (Pty) Ltd (RCM), which Edgar Graham put forward in 1964, had to be made primarily in terms of the need to find new ways of using the management skills, marketing organisation and profits of LB(SA) at a time when expansion along more conventional lines was limited by the market. The Special Committee accepted the proposal. RCM looked a good investment as it had 50 per cent of the wrapped processed cheese market. The price paid was calculated to give a post-tax return of 11.8 per cent on a Unilever investment of £110,000; and initial know-how was provided by retaining the services of the existing manager and majority shareholder.

Processed cheese marks the limit of LB(SA)'s diversification before 1965; but two other propositions that came up and were rejected indicate where Unilever placed the boundary. The first of these, discussed in June 1964, was Amalgamated Packaging Industries Ltd. The case for buying it was that LB(SA) depended entirely on it for their containers, and to that extent the Special Committee was favourably inclined. But the price was high—£2.75 million for a 40 per cent holding, which it was hoped would eventually be increased to 80 per cent by buying out more shareholders. This represented a large premium on both the asset value and the current stock exchange share price; and this was one reason why Special Committee decided in August 1964 not to proceed. Another was that the business seemed to have little growth potential. But the further reason minuted by the Committee is of greater interest because this was possibly the first occasion on which an investment decision taken by Unilever was stated to have been influenced by the growing hostility among the new, recently decolonised states of Black Africa to South Africa. 'It would', the Special Committee commented, 'be undesirable to appear to be expanding our interests in South Africa in view of the attitude to South Africa of other African States . . . .' The rule was not absolute: the Overseas Committee was invited to raise the proposal again if it saw fit in about a year's time. But the Overseas Committee, possibly taken aback by a principle which seemed inconsistent with Unilever's normal policy of doing business in all hospitable states without taking account of political or other local eccentricities, asked for clarification. Did this mean that 'as a general policy, the Company was not prepared to invest further in South Africa at the present time?' For the Special Committee Lord Cole, Chairman of Limited, replied that 'in principle there was no objection to risking more money in South Africa provided this was not done in such a way as to provoke repercussions in other African states and that any new projects were sufficiently remunerative short term for us to see the possibility of getting our money back in about 5–6 years'—a qualification usually applied to proposals for investment in states far less stable than

South Africa. In this case the principle was never put to the test. In November 1964 the Special Committee agreed to reconsider buying Amalgamated Packaging in the light of further investigation of its prospects, but before it could do so the firm was bought by a third party.

That Lord Cole's principle did not necessarily exclude further investment in diversification in South Africa was shown not only by the purchase of Robin Cheese late in 1964 but also by the consideration given to a suggestion that LB(SA) should invest £3.5 million in a new joint venture with Phillip Hill of South Africa for making a new polyethylene material which would substitute for jute bags. This time political factors were not a significant consideration; but the grounds on which the Special Committee decided not to act are interesting because they indicate the boundaries then set to product diversification. Two of the stated objections might have applied to other similar proposals: the owners of the patent might decide to sell manufacturing rights in other countries, so that a Unilever factory in South Africa might find itself barred from exporting to potential overseas markets. In addition Unilever had recently acquired an interest in the British firm, Commercial Plastics Industries Ltd, which made a wide range of plastic packaging materials, and this might lead to a conflict of interests. The third ground for refusal was more general and important:

> Apart from the capital, Unilever would have nothing to contribute, as exploitation of the process would be using someone else's know-how and we would be involved in selling the end product to an unfamiliar set of customers—probably in the first place Marketing Boards.

This was an important principle because it embodied the rule that a subsidiary should not, by way of diversifying, invest in a business which did not make use of either of Unilever's two main strengths— technical know-how and marketing skills; and in this case the latter seemed excluded because the largest buyers of the product would probably be the state marketing boards of Black African states who would buy at a fixed and locally monopsonic price.

Seen as a whole, then, diversification in South Africa was closely similar in timing, motive and character to that in Australia. In each case the local company expanded its investment in production and sale of a relatively narrow range of established lines to the limit of the local market; and until about 1944 there seems in any case to have been little serious thought of broadening the product base. Thereafter, as opportunities for reinvesting profits in conventional lines began to contract, the company began to investigate the viability of other products already manufactured by Unilever in Europe or North America. Some of these were adopted, but the majority were deemed impracticable because of limited local demand, problems of distribution or established competition. Where, however, as in the case of ice-cream and chemicals, an opportunity came up to buy into the market by acquiring established enterprises, Unilever did not hesitate to do so. Finally, when market constraints appeared to hedge these companies in, Unilever was prepared to consider investment in local enterprises whose technology lay outside existing Unilever limits, provided that the business itself seemed promising and there were prospects that the local company could contribute more than merely capital to the proposed venture—itself an interesting extension of William Lever's invariable refusal to consider mere portfolio investment. In all these respects Australia and South Africa were following normal Unilever practice in Europe and North America; but, by comparison with most of the other subsidiaries to be examined below, these two companies were different. First, because of the relative affluence of the European population in both countries and even of the urban Africans of South Africa, a comparatively wide range of Unilever products were thought to be viable there. Second, there was very limited governmental interference in the process of investment and expansion. In both countries margarine was the only product in which Unilever was interested whose fortunes were determined by state policy. For the rest, once the wartime and post-war system of controls had been dismantled, LB(SA) could operate under free market conditions, apart from price controls on a few products such as animal feeds in South Africa. This fact, more than anything else, differentiated these two subsidiaries from those in the less developed world.

It remains to consider two things: the problem of race in South Africa in its widest context; and the comparative profitability of the South African and Australian businesses after 1945. As to 'race relations' the peculiarity of South African society (though it was not, in fact, unique) was that until the 1950s this term was almost always used of the relationship between those who spoke English and those who spoke primarily Afrikaans. Matters relating to black

Africans, 'coloureds' and Asians, which in other countries would constitute the hub of race relations, were designated 'the native' or 'the coloured' problem. Thus, in coming to terms with its host society after 1945, LB(SA) had to deal with two problems, not one as in most other countries. First it had to recognise the fact of dominant Afrikaner nationhood by replacing at least some of its English-speaking (and in most cases also expatriate) management by indigenous Afrikaners; second it had to decide what attitude to adopt towards non-whites in a society in which convention if not strict law placed tight restrictions on how far these might climb up the political, social and industrial ladders. In addition there was the invariable, though in this case not pressing, question of local participation in the equity of LB(SA) and the still broader issue of what attitude Unilever should adopt to the racial policies of the host government. In no other country studied in this book was 'socialisation' of a Unilever subsidiary so complex a problem.

The key to LB(SA)'s relations with Afrikaner South Africa was that the company was founded by a British entrepreneur at a time when Britons dominated the modern sector of the South African economy without question; that it was for long run by expatriate managers from Britain; and that its headquarters were in English-speaking Durban. Moreover, since the greater part of industry, banking and commerce throughout the Union remained in the hands of English firms until after the Second World War, it was natural for the Lever management to move within the English-speaking world. 1948 was the great watershed when the unexpected defeat of Smuts' Anglo–Afrikaner United Party by the aggressively Afrikaans-speaking Nationalist Party symbolised the eventual reversal of the defeat of Kruger's republic in 1902. Though it was not evident at once, this event affected almost every aspect of life in South Africa; and for a company such as Unilever the consequences were almost as significant as the achievement of independence by India, Ceylon or Pakistan at roughly the same time. In the broadest terms, the concern could no longer act as if it was operating in a British environment. It had to treat Afrikaner sensibilities with the same circumspection as, say, those of Indians; and in no sphere was this more delicate than the employment of Afrikaners in its management.

Awareness of this problem did not, however, begin in 1948: as in many other British colonies and Dominions studied in this book Unilever became aware of the need to recruit indigenous managers some time before local nationalism achieved its formal victory. The first formal mention of the issue in the records is in July 1943 when (Lord) Geoffrey Heyworth reported that he had recently asked Dr Van Eck, of the Industrial Development Board of South Africa,

> whether it would not be a good thing to get Afrikaans-speaking people into our business in South Africa. Mr Van Eck had stated that this would be highly desirable and that there were a number of very good people available, while after the war a number of ex-army people would prove suitable for management positions. [He] had suggested that contact should be established with Stellenbosch and Pretoria Universities and it was agreed that Mr Heyworth should write to Mr Barnish [Chairman of LB(SA)] hereon.

The matter was not allowed to drop: a year later, when C. W. Barnish visited London, it was agreed 'that he should set in motion the policy of recruiting South Africans of high quality when these are released from the services'. They would be trained first in South Africa, then spend a year with Unilever in Britain, after which they might either be sent back to Durban or posted to other parts of the world, 'since it is considered that they should not necessarily be limited to a career in South Africa itself'. In addition to recruiting Afrikaners, efforts were increasingly, and especially after 1948, made to encourage British, English-speaking South African managers to adjust to the character of the new South Africa by learning Afrikaans. In 1950 serious consideration was even given to moving the administrative headquarters of LB(SA) from Durban to Johannesburg to be nearer the centre of government at Pretoria and the heartland of Afrikaner society. In 1955 London took the next step in the localisation of the business by establishing the rule that, with the possible exception of advertising, all future management in South Africa should be recruited locally. A decade later Unilever House accepted the corollary of developing a 'national' management in South Africa by placing that country for the first time in the category of 'foreign' states, along with India, tropical Africa, etc. and in contrast with Australia, New Zealand and North America, which entitled any remaining British nationals working there to overseas educational and other allowances. In the same year the socialisation of the management was symbolically completed by the decision that C. J. van Jaarsveldt, a South African (though from

Rhodesia) of mixed Dutch/English stock, should succeed R. H. Del Mar as Chairman of LB(SA). South Africa thus followed four years after India in having an indigenous chairman.

From the standpoint of the Afrikaner population this represented 'socialisation' if only in name: the only remaining issue that was likely to irritate white nationalist feelings was the fact that the capital of LB(SA) was entirely owned by Unilever. Because this remained an 'open' economy and because South Africa depended so heavily on foreign capital, it was inconceivable that the government should insist on the sale of equity to nationals. But, as in Australia, there was some local feeling on the matter. This was mentioned only once in the available records—in 1960, when J. F. Knight on a visit reported that he had encountered

> a certain amount of curiosity why we do not invite local participation. It hardly amounted to criticism and it was not difficult to convince the questioners that local participation is often a mixed blessing to the economy of the country concerned and that a more sensible solution is to create opportunity for investment in the Parent Company shares.

The issue does not appear to have come up again before 1965; and it was one of the attractions of South Africa, as of Australia, that freedom of foreign investment should still have been accepted without serious question.

But to the outside world, and increasingly to Unilever itself, the real problem of race relations in South Africa turned on the position of Asians and black Africans in the company. On this issue Unilever was in the same impossible situation as all foreign firms operating in countries whose political, social and moral characteristics were incompatible with the norms of the firm's home country: they had to choose between heroic renunciation of potential profit from existing investments, for the most part made before such attitudes became general in Europe, and accepting the facts of the host society and the criticism of liberals overseas. Between these two extremes lay many possible shades of behaviour, ranging from willing and perhaps self-interested endorsement of local practices to open dislike of them and attempts to mitigate their consequences as far as possible. The evidence leaves no doubt where Unilever stood on this issue in South Africa. They continued to operate there because they had a large stake and could see no possible benefit to themselves or non-Europeans in South Africa from withdrawing. On the other hand Unilever men universally disliked racial segregation from every point of view and it is important to summarise the main grounds for this dislike (apart, that is, from personal feelings) and to indicate what steps the company took to mitigate the effects of apartheid.

There were two main commercial grounds for regarding racial segregation and job reservation, with their concommitants of a low paid, physically debilitated and comparatively uneducated labour force, as bad for the business. First, since the majority of the population was black or coloured, they were the largest potential market for Unilever products. Their affluence meant profit for the local manufacturer; and since LB(SA) employed comparatively few non-Europeans—in 1954 2,270 Africans, 132 Indians and 1,232 Europeans, in 1960, 2,630, 199 and 1,494 respectively—any potential saving in the wages paid to non-whites was a drop in the bucket compared with the loss of sales resulting from the low consumer capacity of the 11.5 million Africans, 500,000 Indians and 1,500,000 'coloureds' of South Africa in 1960. Or, to put it another way, the gearing between capital and labour costs in the soap industry was such that a Unilever manufacturing company would always benefit from high wage levels, provided these applied throughout society and not merely to its own employees. In a country such as South Africa, moreover, a foreign company had interests distinct from those of the dominant local white minority. While their main pre-occupation was to safeguard their social and economic status and preserve what they regarded as the values of European civilisation in southern Africa, the international company wanted whatever would maximise its sales and profit margins. And since the amount of soap, cooking fats or ice-cream which a few comparatively affluent whites could or would consume was less than the quantity likely to be bought by the many non-whites if their buying power was increased by greater equality of opportunity and income, Unilever's commercial interests put it in the anti-apartheid camp in South Africa as surely as his desire to sell more soap to the English working class had buttressed William Lever's enthusiasm for social reform in Britain half a century earlier.

The second main ground for Unilever's dislike of racial segregation was the effect it had on the character of the non-white labour force. In theory, as London visitors frequently pointed out, it was legal for LB(SA) to employ Africans and Asians at any level because existing legislation did not extend to the soap industry. But this was unrealistic: as Klijnstra summarised the position in 1960,

> Two things prevent us . . . from moving too fast [towards employing Africans in skilled jobs]:
> First: the Europeans would object strongly—therefore a systematic effort to change the views of the European worker is needed.
> Second: If we should move too fast, we might run the risk that the government would put in some job restriction legislation for our industries.

In practice, therefore, LB(SA) could only employ non-whites in the least skilled and lowest paid posts. The consequences were a very large and relatively expensive European labour force and a disproportionately badly paid non-white labour force. The differentials between each group of hourly paid workers, expressed in average hourly and weekly wages for 1960, were as follows:

Group	Hourly rate	Weekly rate
Europeans	8s 7d	£19 14s 10d
Coloureds	4s 11d.	£9 11s 8d
Asians	3s 9d	£8 12s 6d
Africans	2s 1d	£4 15s 10d

Low wages were, however, only one of the factors contributing to the low calibre of the labour force. From the standpoint of the industrialist government regulations on housing, which forced non-whites to live outside the main urban areas and travel long distances to work and also denied them the right of permanent residence outside their 'homelands', had equally serious consequences. Until the 1950s one result was that most African factory workers were migratory: in 1949 the annual labour turnover among black employees of LB(SA) was nearly 100 per cent, which made it impossible to train an efficient work force and incidentally involved a substantial annual cost, estimated at £20 a head, for recruiting new workers. Moreover segregation of housing meant long journeys to work, which affected the quality of the work done. As the Durban management reported in 1949,

They have to set out very early and, more often than not, without a meal. They work through to the lunch break, when the majority purchase a slice or two of bread with jam and a mineral drink—occasionally milk. They get back to their quarters after dark and have then to set about preparing a meal. Unless they have women-folk, and the majority have not, this is an unappetising meal—maize or bread. It is therefore little wonder that African labour is lackadaisical and inefficient.

These things, coupled with very limited educational opportunities, constituted an effective bar to the evolution of a competent modern industrial work force in South Africa.

These were facts of South African life: Unilever could attempt only amelioration. The 1949 report quoted above also laid down the broad lines of policy which were followed for the rest of this period. Higher wages were not, by themselves, regarded as a solution because they would not necessarily improve the African's standard of living, since a migratory single worker probably could not buy nearer or better housing and might not buy better food: for example, only 120 out of the 450 African workers at the Auckland Park factory were then taking advantage of the heavily subsidised midday meal offered them at the canteen for 4d. The basic need was therefore thought to be to transform the African from a migratory to a settled worker, living with his family in decent modern housing as near as possible to the factories. Once the labour force had been stabilised it could be trained and its wages judiciously raised on the ground of greater worth, though here it would be necessary to avoid annoying the white unions or the government. Careful personnel management on the European pattern was another essential first step, and personnel managers were in fact appointed for the first time in the LB(SA) factories immediately after this report.

Ten years later some results and changes were evident. The labour force had virtually been stabilised, with annual turnover among Africans down to about 5 per cent, though this was due also to the general drift of Africans to the towns in this period. A substantial personnel staff had been built up and, in the words of a brief prepared for a management conference in 1959, 'lines of communication have been established and survived through the Native Affairs Officers and the Native Advisory Committees. We have thus been in a position to be kept informed of employee opinion and to influence it to some extent.' This was a poor substitute for the trade unions South African law denied blacks and 'coloureds'. There had also been some progress in promoting Africans to posts previously reserved for Europeans, for example as glycerine plant operators and heavy vehicle drivers. On the other hand, although there had been some upward mobility among blacks, company policy had come up against strong conventions protecting white employment, policed by the white unions; and they were held back by fear that the government would invoke powers granted by the 1944 Customs Tariff Act to withdraw protection from those industries which did not employ a satisfactory proportion of Europeans. Moreover, although average wages paid to Africans in private industry as a whole in South Africa (which were well below those paid in Unilever factories) had risen by 32 per cent between 1954 and 1961, which was slightly more than the rise in the retail price index for this period, average white wages had risen by 46 per cent. The Special Committee, noting these facts in 1963, summarised its attitude as follows:

It was important to proceed slowly in the replacement of Europeans by Africans. The reason for this in South Africa is different from that elsewhere, where the problem was primarily one of shortage of suitable nationals: in South Africa we had to take care not to upset the white community.

It is, in fact, clear that by the mid-1960s LB(SA) was finding it very difficult to sustain a policy of ameliorating the conditions of their African labour force. They had done something by way of providing recreational and other facilities at work, but on all fundamentals they were held back by fear of union or official intervention. A. F. H. Blaauw summed up the situation in June 1964 after a visit:

Africanization. This is going on very slowly in all factories, partly because apartheid reserves certain activities for white employees, partly owing to lack of suitable people. I do not think much progress will be made in South Africa as long as apartheid legislation prescribes, for instance, four separate canteens and cloakrooms for European, Indian, African and coloured personnel, even in small factories employing only about 100 people altogether, like Commercial Chemicals.

Unilever thus had Hobson's choice. If it operated at all in South Africa it had to accept the morally and commercially obnoxious tenets of apartheid. If it did so, it laid itself open to criticism from liberals and, more seriously, from governments in the many other African states in which it operated. This account is intended neither to defend nor to blame. The historian can only remark that a multi-national company with large fixed assets and an immense investment in commercial goodwill could not afford to sacrifice its investment in every country with whose system of government or social structure it found itself out of sympathy.

(d) Profits in Australia and South Africa, 1945–65

There remains the question of the profitability of LB(SA) in the twenty years after 1945, which will be compared with that of the Australian business in order to highlight common and contrasting factors. Once again, as before 1945, LB(SA) was remarkable not for making particularly high or low returns but for the consistency of its performance. Apart from the immediate post-war years, ending in 1952, when government policies restricted output or imposed price restrictions and so kept profits low, and, at the other extreme, the exceptionally good results of 1960, nett accounting profit of LB(SA) moved between 8.2 per cent and 13.8 per cent of GCE. The average for the whole period was 9.9 per cent. This was very satisfactory and substantially better than for Australia in the same period. For example, in the decade 1956–65 for which identical data is available, the average return to capital after payment of statistical tax in Australia was 6.5 per cent compared with 11.0 per cent in South Africa. What explains this margin?

Lower South African production costs can be ruled out at the start: factory expenses, including labour, were identical as a percentage of NSV for every year except 1956 and 1957, when South African costs were 1 per cent higher. The important facts are that the average pre-tax trading profit made by LB(SA) as a percentage of average gross capital employed was 16.3 per cent in South African and 10.4 per cent in Australia; and that this initial margin was increased by higher taxes in Australia, which averaged 38.3 per cent compared with 31.8 per cent in South Africa. But taxation explains only about 1.3 per cent of the post-tax margin of 4.5 per cent for which we have to account. It is, therefore, necessary to look back into the components of the pre-tax trading profit to find

Table 3.12   South Africa: Trading Summary, 1946—65 (£'000)

Year	A Nett Sales value	B Gross profit	C Advert- ising as a % of A	D Factory & gen. costs % of A	E Trading profit before tax	F Acco'ng profit after tax	G Nett prof after stat.
1946	n/a	n/a	n/a	n/a	n/a	260	n/a
1947	n/a	n/a	n/a	n/a	n/a	512	n/a
1948	6,017	n/a	2	n/a	404	110	n/a
1949	6,091	n/a	3	n/a	452	161	n/a
1950	6,296	n/a	3	n/a	757	510	n/a
1951	7,757	n/a	3	n/a	353	154	n/a
1952	8,075	n/a	4	n/a	661	371	n/a
1953	7,589	n/a	5	n/a	875	576	n/a
1954	8,742	n/a	5	n/a	1,070	795	n/a
1955	9,536	n/a	5	n/a	1,100	824	n/a
1956	10,500	29	5	8	1,107	827	77
1957	11,346	29	6	8	1,120	830	78
1958	12,030	29	6	7	1,357	954	94
1959	13,216	32	7	7	1,817	1,334	1,25
1960	14,871	36	8	7	2,314	1,729	1,62
1961	14,859	36	12	7	1,552	1,129	1,01
1962	15,855	37	12	7	1,823	1,442	1,21
1963	18,495	36	13	7	1,671	1,275	1,11
1964	20,822	35	13	7	2,037	1,440	1,36
1965	24,249	34	14	7	2,000	1,255	1,32

the answer. Starting with the nett sales value, the ratio between turnover and capital employed was 1:49 in South Africa and 1:39 in Australia. We start, therefore, with a slightly more productive use of capital in South Africa. Thereafter South Africa continued to have a slight edge all along the line. Advertising there averaged 9.8 per cent of NSV compared with 11.3 per cent in Australia, though this advantage was built up before 1960, after which South African advertising cost proportionately about the same as in Australia because of increasing competition from Colgate–Palmolive and very

Rands 1961–1965 converted into £s)

CE av. 31 Dec. 1955)	I F/H %	J Dividends (nett)	K Transferred Int'st	L Service fees & roy'ties	M Divi. (nett)	N Stat. tax rate %	O Profit after stat. tax as % of GCE
2,823	9.2	n/a	n/a	n/a	n/a	n/a	n/a
3,645	14.0	n/a	n/a	n/a	n/a	n/a	n/a
4,028	2.7	n/a	n/a	n/a	n/a	25	n/a
3,789	4.2	n/a	n/a	n/a	n/a	n/a	n/a
4,340	11.7	n/a	n/a	n/a	n/a	n/a	n/a
5,407	2.8	n/a	n/a	n/a	n/a	n/a	n/a
6,127	6.1	n/a	n/a	n/a	n/a	n/a	n/a
7,044	8.2	n/a	n/a	n/a	n/a	n/a	n/a
6,674	11.9	n/a	n/a	n/a	n/a	n/a	n/a
7,529	10.9	n/a	n/a	n/a	n/a	30	n/a
8,893	9.3	n/a	n/a	n/a	n/a	30	8.7
9,201	9.0	n/a	n/a	n/a	n/a	30	8.5
9,233	10.3	n/a	(2)	n/a	n/a	30	10.2
9,628	13.9	1,000	(17)	n/a	500	30	13.2
9,573	18.1	1,725	(43)	n/a	1,725	30	16.9
9,926	11.4	2,125	(18)	147	2,125	34.5	10.2
0,430	13.8	1,060	—	146	1,060	33.5	11.6
1,021	11.2	501	—	154	825	33.5	10.1
1,868	12.1	420	—	189	420	33.5	11.5
3,843	9.1	1,000	—	210	1,000	35	9.5

heavy advertising expenditure on foods, running at over 50 per cent of their sales value. Marketing expenses were also consistently higher in Australia, averaging 6.5 per cent of NSV against 4.6 per cent. In themselves none of these differences was very large, but collectively they explain why South African profits were generally rather better. The margin reflects the slightly more favourable position of the South African company in terms of concentration of production facilities and distribution costs; but probably the most important single differentiating factor was the degree of competition, which is reflected in advertising expenditure. Unilever never achieved quite the same dominance of the Australian market that it held, for soap at least, in South Africa; and, as has been seen, attempts to diversify in Australia put a heavy strain on profitability in the decade after 1956. Yet, in the last resort, these contrasts should not be over-stressed: similarities between these two sub-sidiaries were more important than differences. Both typify the evolutionary pattern of Lever/Unilever manufacturing enterprises in newly industrialising countries overseas in which the bulk of the consumers of their products were relatively affluent Europeans.

The primary purpose of this chapter is to lay foundations for the later chapters which examine the history of other Lever/Unilever companies. Australia and South Africa have been described in some detail because these were the models which Lever and his successors had before them when they came to establish manufacturing subsidiaries in the less developed world. In turning to these enterprises, it is important at the outset to put them in their correct chronological context. Australia and South Africa belong to the first phase of Lever Brothers expansion in Britain, Europe, North America and the 'new' countries of white settlement in the British empire; and for Levers that phase was virtually complete by 1914. The second phase, perhaps postponed by the First World War, covers the two decades 1920–40 and marks the beginning of Lever/Unilever manu-facturing enterprises in what are now called less developed countries. By 1940 there were ten of these, established in the following order: during the 1920s in the Belgian Congo, India, Nigeria and Argentina; in the 1930s Brazil, Shanghai, Siam, Indonesia, Palestine and Ceylon (1940). Six of these are examined below. All the many other manu-facturing subsidiaries shown in Figure 3, (p. 53) belong to a third and still continuing phase during which substantially different factors influenced Unilever's investment decisions. It is, therefore, an important initial question why there were so few substantial new industrial ventures in these countries before the 1930s, for those listed above in the 1920s, apart from that in Argentina, were very small indeed, why there were comparatively so few such companies by 1940 and why the number increased so rapidly in the next two decades. This cuts to the root of the problem of direct overseas investment by a multinational and raises the question whether reluctance to invest in local manufacture was connected with colonialism. A second general question is how far the model of early Lever enterprises in the more developed countries was followed elsewhere and whether contrasting conditions resulted in substantially divergent strategies. The ultimate question is whether Unilever benefited more or less from investing in manufacture for local consumption in these tropical countries than in Europe or the 'new' countries where the Lever and Unilever overseas empire began.

4

Unilever in India and Pakistan

Unilever's Indian business, which was divided into two companies in 1947 when Pakistan became a separate state, is the first of nine manufacturing enterprises in less developed countries to be examined in this book. It is given pride of place on three counts. It was the first Lever Brothers manufacturing subsidiary in any LDC whose products replaced the staple imports from the parent companies in Britain: the Congo soap company started in the same year but, as will be seen, had a more limited role. It was founded a quarter of a century before India became independent, and this makes it possible to contrast the situation of a multinational under colonial and post-colonial conditions. Finally Hindustan Lever, the company formed in 1956 to incorporate the several legally distinct Unilever enterprises in India, became the largest, and one of the most autonomous of all Unilever's subsidiaries outside Europe and North America; and for this reason it is the best model against which concern companies in other less developed countries can be compared.

The Origins of Local Manufacture in India, 1917-34

(a) Soap

The history of Lever Brothers' activities in India underlines the truth that a European industrial enterprise is unlikely to give thought to direct productive investment overseas so long as it has a satisfactory and expanding export market in any particular country. Until at least 1917 William Lever seems to have been perfectly satisfied with the conduct of his business in India as an export

148

market. He had registered a Lever Brothers subsidiary, Lever Brothers (India) Ltd as an English company in 1913, but this was only to safeguard his brands. He had no permanent office or distribution centre in India and promotion of Lever products was restricted to occasional visits by Lever sales managers who organised publicity, negotiated with importing agents and attempted to stimulate the larger dealers to order Lever products from the agents. The system was desirable because it did not tie up capital in speculative consignment of goods and no local taxation was paid on profits. Levers simply sold to Indian wholesalers through local agents on a commission basis: as A. C. Knight, a Lever executive, put it in 1924, Levers 'hold no stocks in India, sell for cash against Documents and it is a clear-cut, easily controlled and very satisfactory way of doing business'.

By 1917 Lever had acquired a half interest, extended to full control in 1919, in the two other major British soap companies exporting to India, J. Crosfield and Sons Ltd and W. Gossage and Sons Ltd.[1] Each of these had its own export department which it retained even after 1924 when, as has been seen in Chapter 2, all concern exports were theoretically placed under the control of an Export Trade Board.[2] In India Crosfields used the same system as Levers. By contrast Gossages, who were by far the most important exporter of the three, maintained their own office in India with depots throughout the country to which substantial stocks were consigned from Britain. Resident agents ordered goods from these depots and paid in rupees, whereas all Lever and Crosfield products were paid for in sterling. The advantage of the Gossage system was that goods could be supplied to customers at short notice; the disadvantage that unsaleable stocks might accumulate and that Gossages had to carry the inventories. Even if the question of manufacturing in India had not arisen Levers would still have had to decide sooner or later whether to copy Gossages; and, as will be seen, this became a bone of contention in the later 1920s.

An export market, however, is satisfactory only so long as it works successfully: declining sales may indicate that conditions are no longer suitable or perhaps that different selling methods are needed. There is no doubt that an apparently sustained drop in the volume of soap exported by his three main companies to India in the years 1918–21 was the starting point of Lever's interest in manufacturing in India as a means of protecting his interests there. As Table 4.1 below indicates, exports of British and concern soaps to India remained remarkably steady throughout the war from 1913 to 1917.[3] At most times they constituted between a quarter and a fifth of total British soap exports to all countries, which is a measure of the importance of the Indian market. In 1918 sales in India were halved, but sales to the rest of the world also fell dramatically in that year. In 1919 exports to India remained at the same low level while exports to the rest of the world rose very sharply. This was probably due to 'rehabilitation' exports to Europe after the end of

Table 4.1   India: Soap Exports to India, 1913–22

(a) Shipments of UK Soap to India, Burma and Ceylon, 1913–21

Tons

Year	Total	Gossages	World
1913	18,349	10,399	84,626
1914	19,869	10,945	81,675
1915	19,655	10,958	88,402
1916	18,888	9,822	103,012
1917	20,341	10,300	119,916
1918	10,393	5,657	67,983
1919	10,690	7,079	113,759
1920	18,096	10,694	89,085
1921	10,502	8,179	41,855

Note: The Indian total includes soaps other than those made by Levers, Crosfields, Gossages and associated companies but the proportion was very small, probably not more than 5 per cent. In the absence of a continuous series of figures for Lever and Crosfield exports in this period (the records are lost) the margin between Gossage and total sales may therefore be taken as a rough indication of shipments of Lever and Crosfield soaps, and those of other concern companies such as Pears.

(b) Sales of Soap by Lever Brothers (India) Ltd., 1913, 1921, 1922

Year	Levers	Gossages	Crosfields	Total
1913	3,172	9,851	1,665	14,688
1921	1,810	8,975	677	11,462
1922	2,680	9,110	486	12,276

Note: These figures are taken from a table prepared in 1923 which is headed 'Indian Company, total sales in tons'. There is no indication whether sales include Burma or Ceylon. This, coupled with the fact that these figures are for sales in India, whereas those in Table 4.1 (a) above are for shipments from the UK may explain the difference.

the war, amounting to 60,168 tons; and when exports to India rose in 1920 to the same level as 1913 it might have been thought that the Indian market was no longer in danger. In 1921 another dramatic fall occurred. This might have been due to the impact of the international recession on India but equally it might not; and it was doubt as to the causes that brought Lever to the point at which he began seriously to consider whether he should manufacture locally.

In fact Lever might well have treated these market fluctuations as the transient effect of wartime and immediate post-war conditions, which they probably were, had it not been for the fact that the decline in Lever exports coincided with evidence that for the first time Indian industrialists were becoming interested in vegetable oil and its products. The first evidence he had of this trend was in 1917 when Tatas, the cotton and steel giants, began to consider investment in oil milling and related manufactures, presumably under the stimulus of high wartime prices. Following their usual practice Tatas looked for technical help from established manufacturers and in October 1917 the Policy and Tactics Committee discussed a preliminary proposal for collaboration with Tatas. Lever was away, the committee acted cautiously and in the end nothing came of the suggestion, though contacts with Tatas were kept up. More important, Lever was now alert to the danger that Indian competition might affect his export market and began to probe the situation. In 1918 Levers were negotiating with Ralli Brothers, the large-scale oil dealers, for the purchase of linseed oil and considered that this firm might be a suitable body to advise them on Indian projects. By 1920 Levers had information that, stimulated by wartime shortages, local manufacture of soap had risen to about 20,000 tons a year though most of this was of very low quality, made by artisans for local consumption, and did not compete with imported Sunlight Soap. One of the very few relatively modern soap factories was that owned by the North West Soap Company at Garden Reach, near Calcutta. Its capacity was only about 2,250 tons a year and its plant was already over twenty years old;[4] but it was doing well and its new-found success might well encourage other and larger modern ventures. To cap it all came the non-co-operation and the *Swadeshi* (self-sufficiency) movement, launched by Gandhi in 1919, whose aim was to induce Indians to buy locally made goods rather than imports and in particular to boycott British products. If this was successful Levers might find the Indian market closing against them as surely as if there had been a high protective tariff. The trade in

India seemed thus to have reached the point at which competition from domestic producers threatened a very important Lever export market. The concern reacted in the now conventional way: two experts from Port Sunlight, M. E. Marples and C. E. Tatlow, were sent to India to report on a 'factory proposition'. Their separate reports, both completed in March 1920, mark the starting point of Levers' industrial activities in India.[5]

Both men decided that the time had come for local manufacture, but they recommended different strategies. Marples made out a strong case for building two soap factories in India, at Calcutta and Bombay, on the grounds that inland transport costs were so high that sales might be competitive only within 200–300 miles of a factory. Of the three standard grounds for undertaking local manufacture, local consumer preference was the most significant in India for, in addition to the current *Swadeshi* campaign, the Hindu religion forbad the use of soap made with animal fats, and all British imported soap then contained tallow. The case was strengthened by the fact that local competition in the modern sector was still very weak: 'it cannot be doubted that we can turn out better soap of each class and with a larger production we should be able to under-sell them', he wrote, with particular reference to the North West Soap Company. The main problem, apart from high transport costs and a fragmented market, was that no modern factory could compete with the native 'cottage' producer of cheap soap. But most raw materials were available locally, labour could be obtained through the standard system of sirdars, wages were low and the labour, once trained, efficient. Taxes were 'purely nominal'. There might be a market for by-products, including edible oils and fats, cattle cake and glycerine. Taking everything into account he recommended acquiring a building site at Sinduria, near Calcutta, at once and finding another site near Bombay when land with the necessary services became available there. Tatlow accepted this general argument. He calculated that the total Indian market for laundry soaps such as Sunlight was 40,000 tons a year, half of which was then imported. He therefore recommended that a single factory should be built on the Sinduria site with capacity for 20,000 tons of laundry and 500 tons of toilet soap and a variety of toilet preparations. These figures are important: they show that at the start the idea was to build a factory large enough to replace all imports from Lever factories. The strategy was to be exactly the same as in other more developed countries despite the difference in Indian conditions.

Lever was clearly convinced and the Sinduria site was bought. Had this situation arisen before 1914 it seems likely that a large factory would have been built very soon and Calcutta would have become the base for Levers' production in India. But 1920 was a very bad year to propose capital expenditure on a substantial scale. For reasons explained by Wilson,[6] and in particular because the decision that year to buy the Niger Company for £8 million was followed by the discovery that the company had an overdraft of £2 million, Levers were in acute financial embarrassment. Throughout that year and 1921 the fate of the concern lay in the balance. The worst of the crisis was over by February 1921 but the liquidity position remained serious for several years. These events largely explain the course of events in India: on the one hand why no start was made with building the proposed factory at Sinduria; on the other why Lever attempted to attain the same object by association with Boulton Brothers, using the same technique as had served him well in Australia, South Africa and other countries.[7]

The London bank, Boulton Bros & Co., had interests in India and other countries in the east. During the First World War they had been looking for profitable new investments, for example buying the Colombo Oil Mills in Ceylon in 1917. In 1916 and again in 1918 they unsuccessfully approached Crosfields for co-operation in their prospective acquisition of the North West Soap Company and its related enterprises. By the start of 1921, when they had evidently established close contacts with Lever, they had built up an unstable edifice of interlocking companies, all established since 1916 and all registered in India. The two members of the Boulton family most active were R. G. H. and W. W. Boulton, but they had three leading associates in India, C. M. de Souza, C. F. Treeby and A. D. S. de Mello, who, in turn, had formed a business alliance with the Maharajah of Gwalior. This 'Boulton Group' consisted for the most part of holding companies: the Trust of India Limited (1916), the Development Corporation of India Limited (1917), in which most of the protagonists held shares, and separate holding companies owned by each of the entrepreneurs, Boulton Bros of India Ltd (1921), Delhi Investments Ltd (1920), owned by Treeby and de Mello, and Gerald Don and Company Ltd (1922) run by de Souza. On the sidelines was the Gwalior State Trust Limited, controlled by the Maharajah, and Hopes Limited, a managing agency, whose only asset was a thirty-year licence to buy raw materials and sell the products of all 'Group' companies at 1 per cent commission. Behind all of them lay the Alliance Bank of Simla, controlled by Boultons, which supplied much of the capital.

Impressive though it looked from the outside, the only solid assets possessed by this complex of holding companies were two majority owned subsidiary companies whose purpose was to produce vegetable oils and their products. These were the Premier Oil Company of India Ltd, a holding company which owned Premier Oil Mills Ltd and the other related companies producing vegetable oils together with a factory site at Oyaria on which an Oil Mill was to be built; and the Premier Soap Company of India Ltd, yet another holding company founded in 1919, which owned the North West Soap Company. These enterprises were the reason for Lever's interest in the Boulton empire.

The first contact between the Boultons and Levers seems to have been made in January 1921, when the policy of making soap in India had been accepted in principle. T. H. Boulton approached Lever in London and, according to Lever, wanted 'to get Crosfields, Gossages and Lever Bros interested in the North West Soap Company or Premier Soap Company in India and their various oil mills'. Lever was immediately interested. The main attraction was that association with the Boultons would apparently enable him to launch soap production in India with little or no expenditure of capital. 'I may say', he wrote to Giles Hunt, Chairman of Crosfields, on 15 January 1921,

> that none of us . . . could enter into any undertaking at the present time involving cash payment. If it is an exchange of shares there will be no difficulty, and if the shares were issued shares it could be still more easily handled . . . . I am confident we ought not, any of us, to increase our cash commitments until we know the possibility of making public issues of new capital.

Two days later he expanded this point.

> Unless the interest [in Boultons] to be taken by ourselves and yourselves [Crosfields] . . . is full and complete—I do not say the whole 100% . . . I do not think any of us could look at it. I hear

that Jurgens have been buying up a great many oil interests in the Dutch East Indies. This fact must be borne in mind.

Boultons were agreeable to an exchange of shares and as the depressing quarterly figures for Lever and associated companies' sales in India came in throughout 1921 the attractiveness of manufacturing there increased. By the end of May 1921 Lever was writing to members of the Special Committee that the position was 'very serious'.

Messrs Boulton are quite willing to make a working arrangement on the basis of shares between Crosfields, Gossages and Levers for India. Terms they have quoted have been too vague and it has not appeared attractive, but I rather gather from Mr Hamilton [of Gossages] they are seriously in danger of losing the Indian trade. This, of course, could not apply to specialities, but I assume only to the bread-and-butter business. I cannot imagine how it would affect Messrs Pears, for instance, unless they put on a flagrant imitation which we ought to resist.

Negotiations must have progressed well for in November 1921 de Souza visited London to discuss how the two groups of companies could co-operate. By February 1922 all was arranged, largely, it appears, by Lever himself, who on 3 February 1922 expressed the view that 'in the near future the whole of our soap for India will require to be made in India'. He was still negotiating with Tatas for collaboration in the south of India, but meantime a satisfactory arrangement had been agreed with the Boultons. Briefly, Levers were to set up a new wholly-owned subsidiary, Lever Bros (India) Limited to be registered in Calcutta. Its nominal share capital would be Rs. 12,000,000 (£800,000) and its stated function to take over the management of all the existing Lever Bros (India) Limited interests. The initial assets consisted almost exclusively of the goodwill and trade marks of Levers, Crosfields and Gossages in India, plus the Sinduria site and stocks held by Gossages in India, which together were later valued at £30,062 7s 2d; and its main function was to provide shares which could be exchanged with Boultons to obtain control of the Premier Soap Co. Ltd and its wholly owned subsidiary, the North West Soap Company Limited, without any cash transaction being required. This was done by giving members of the Boulton group 244,889 preference shares, 150,000 ordinary shares and 250,000 deferred ordinary shares, with a total nominal value of £283,332. Levers retained three-quarters of the ordinary shares and full control of Lever Bros (India) Limited. In return they were given shares providing full control of the Premier Soap and North West Soap Companies. Thus, Lever had bought a soap business in India without further straining his over-taxed financial resources by realising the market value of the concern's trading assets there. It was soon to become clear in Port Sunlight that what Levers had acquired with their scrip was worth little more than the paper on which Lever Bros (India) Ltd shares were printed and that the Boulton empire and its assets were largely fictitious; but this was not immediately evident and Levers made enthusiastic arrangements for developing their new India assets. A Consultative Committee was set up in March 1922 in London to control Lever Bros (India) Ltd and to co-operate with the Boultons who, it was at first assumed, would provide the local management to run the Indian soap business. For several months the Committee was energetic and optimistic. Directors of LB(I) Ltd were appointed, technical staff recruited and sent out, samples of North West Co. soap obtained and plans prepared to build an additional factory on land owned by the Premier Soap Company at Asansol, 120 miles north west of Calcutta, in place of the existing Sinduria site.

From October 1922 gloom began to set in as the dismal facts became known. First it became clear that £125,000 in cash would have to be found to complete purchase of equipment for the proposed new factory at Asansol, in addition to the £67,000 the Premier Soap Company had already spent on the plant. It is significant of Levers' reluctance to spend cash in India at this time that their reaction was to ask the Indian Company, which in practice meant Boultons, how to raise this additional money. Late in November the Consultative Committee received a very depressing technical report—the first full investigation by any Lever man of the Boulton enterprises. The North West Soap Company was incapable of making soap of sufficient quality or quantity to replace Lever imports to India and the site of the factory—the one-time palace of an Indian prince—was too small for expansion. Buildings were in bad condition, the plant poor and antiquated. Nearby land was likely to be compulsorily purchased for extension to Calcutta docks. The two alternative inland sites controlled respectively by the Premier Oil and Premier Soap Companies at Oyaria and Asansol were equally unsatisfactory. Although both lay near coalfields they had no other advantages, and were too far from the main markets and sources of raw materials to be economic. If Levers were to manufacture in India on a sufficient scale to substitute for imports they would have to fall back on their own Sinduria site and pay for a new factory. In short, they were back where they had been in 1920.

From October 1922, therefore, the problem was how best to obtain a divorce from the Boultons so that Levers could obtain freedom of action to make something of the North West Soap Company; and beyond that to decide whether soap production on the large scale should after all be undertaken in India. The two problems had to be faced simultaneously but can best be considered in turn.

Lever recognised that his decision to ally with the Boultons was a mistake by November 1922. On 13 November he wrote 'this coy is not going so well as one would have hoped'. On 4 December he wrote 'It seems as if our Indian business was in a stew'. Great efforts were made to salvage something by injecting Lever men and Lever methods. A production expert, R. D. Spencer, was sent out as works manager of the Garden Reach factory and from October 1923 J. P. Cronin became Sales Director of LB(I) Ltd, Premier Soap and North West Soap. Machinery dumped at the Oyaria site was at last protected from the weather. But in April 1923 it was decided, following further reports, that efforts should be concentrated on increasing output at the Garden Reach factory to its potential maximum of 125–150 tons a week. At the same time an important policy decision was taken. Hirst, another Lever expert sent out as director of the various Indian companies, advised that 'under no conditions would I advise you to manufacture "Sunlight" soap or "Empress Pale" soap in India unless the import duty is made prohibitive'. There was a real danger that the goodwill of these imported soaps would suffer unless their price was brought down to that of *Swadeshi* soaps; but 'the bulk of our present buyers will prefer to buy English Soap'. The North West Soap Company factory should therefore continue to make its own, not Lever, brands and at best might be made to do so more efficiently. Its products would be an addition to, not a substitute for, Levers' traditional imports of British soap.

This completely changed the assumptions on which Lever had decided to manufacture in India. But even with this more limited objective success depended on complete detachment of the factory from the Boulton empire, now clearly seen to be ramshackle, and possibly shady. The depressing truth was told in two long reports by C. L. Cole, Secretary of the London Consultative Committee, and A. C. Knight, who was Chairman of this Committee.[8] Cole's report showed that virtually all the Boulton holding companies were financed by loans from the Alliance Bank of Simla which in turn held most of their shares (including shares in LB(I) Ltd exchanged for Boulton stock), and that the Bank itself, in common with the many Indian banks at this time, was on the verge of bankruptcy. The only solid assets Levers had acquired were those belonging to the Premier Soap and North West Soap Companies; and Premier Soap had made a loss in 1921/2 because it had lent large sums to the Development Corporation and Hopes which were both insolvent and had paid no interest. North West Soap was also in a bad way. Sales in 1923 were half those of 1922 and were still declining. The insolvent Hopes Limited, over which Levers held no control, still had a 28-year monopoly as buying and selling agent of the soap companies.

Levers clearly had to extricate themselves and top level investigation was necessary. Therefore A. C. Knight paid visits to India in November 1923 and March 1924 and Lever himself went out with his accountant and chief adviser, D'Arcy Cooper, at the end of 1923. Few records of Lever's reactions survive, but some letters and his marginal comments on Knight's report indicate that he accepted Knight's proposals that Levers must regain freedom of action by breaking off all links with the Boultons and buying full control over Lever Bros (India) Ltd and the North West Soap Co. Ltd. Knight started the process while in India by buying the shares in Lever Bros (India) Ltd held by the Alliance Bank from its liquidators. Levers did not pay cash: the purchase was financed by a loan from the National Bank of India, the interest and debt to be paid from the local earnings of Gossages. The remaining shares were to be bought back from the Boultons and others as soon as possible. By March 1925 Levers held exclusive control of Lever Bros (India) Ltd through its voting shares and all but 41,096 of the 253,335 cumulative preference shares issued. They also held all but 3,173 of the 250,000 shares of the Premier Soap Company and through it had full control over the North West Soap Company. Disengagement from the Boulton group was all but total by 1925, though re-purchase of a few remaining shares in Lever Bros (India) Ltd took a considerable time and disputes over the ownership of the Oyaria site and equipment (between Premier Soap and Premier Oil) continued until 1948. Meanwhile the bankrupt Boulton empire could safely be left to the liquidators of its various companies.

From 1924 the future of Lever Bros in India was again an open question. Two main alternatives were open: to continue the new policy of local manufacturing as a substitute for importing Lever brands from Britain; or to reverse this policy, attempting to expand the market for British imports and retaining the North West Soap Company as a marginal addition to Levers' share of the Indian market. Either way contingent decisions had to be taken. If local manufacture was to be expanded Levers must either develop the North West Soap Company's factory at Garden Reach, or build new factories: if the latter, the problem of the site remained—Calcutta, Bombay, 'up country' or possibly in the south. If the emphasis was to be on imports what was to be done with North West Soap, and should the new Lever Bros (India) Ltd become for the first time the conduit through which all Lever and associated companies operated in India—'scrambled eggs' to use Lever's own favourite phrase—or should each company be left to run its own business, leaving Lever Bros (India) Ltd as a mere holding company for Lever assets? The vital decisions on all these alternatives were taken before or shortly after Lever's death and remained the basis of company policy until 1931.

The first and crucial decision was not to build a new factory in India. Three main considerations seem to have produced this reversal of policy: the upturn in soap imports from 1922, the revived preference shown by Indians for imported soap as the *Swadeshi* movement lost momentum, and disgust with the inadequacy of the industrial base taken over from the Boultons. Of these the first was probably the most important. Within four months of Lever's despondent reaction in February 1922 to the trade figures, the London Consultative Committee learned that the latest sales of imported Lever products in India were up 20 per cent on the same quarter in 1921 and they revised their estimate ('pro forma' in Lever terminology) for 1922. By 1924 it was clear that 1921/2 had been the bottom and that a steady trade revival was now taking place. The recovery of Levers' sales, which, being in the most vulnerable category of laundry soaps, had suffered worst from local competition and the *Swadeshi* movement, was particularly encouraging. Meantime the nett profits made by Levers, Gossages and Crosfields in

India rose faster than turnover, partly because profit margins could be increased as demand expanded, and partly because of movements in the exchange rates between rupee and sterling currency. Whereas during and after the war the rupee had risen from its prewar rate of 1s 4d to 2s 4d in 1919—which improved the competitive position of British imports—it had then floated down by 1921 to 1s 3d sterling, which had severely affected the competitiveness of Lever products. In October 1924, however, it had floated back to 1s 6d sterling, and remained fairly constant at that level until it was finally tied to sterling at the same rate in 1927. Table 4.2 shows the significant rise in nett profits after 1923. Thus, already by 1924/5 favourable conditions for trade with India had returned and the pessimism of 1921 had evaporated.

Table 4.2　India: Sales of Lever Brothers Soap, 1921/2–1928/9 (Tons) (for the twelve months ending in March of each year)

Year	Levers	Gossages	Crosfields	Total	Nett Profit (£)
1922	2,225	8,418	754	11,397	n/a
1923	3,165	9,771	589	13,525	51,071
1924	4,205	10,048	533	14,786	88,514
1925	5,485	10,450	686	16,621	155,638
1926	7,350	10,977	617	18,944	158,827
1927	8,083	10,074	768	18,925	179,888
1928	9,432	10,138	668	20,238	206,046
1929	9,712	9,480	322	19,514	196,900
1930	n/a	n/a	n/a	16,170	178,700
1931	n/a	n/a	n/a	13,291	85,000
1932	n/a	n/a	n/a	11,305	33,700
1933	n/a	n/a	n/a	12,045	61,309

Revived optimism in the penetrating power of British soap exports was supported by evidence that after all foreigners resident in India, and presumably also the minority of Indians who could afford better quality soap, preferred to buy imported rather than locally manufactured brands. This preference, almost universal in the developing world, had momentarily been overlaid by the force of *Swadeshi* but from perhaps 1923, with the decline of the non-importation movement and the suspension of non-co-operation, it emerged again strongly. Simultaneously the sales of soap made at

Garden Reach declined from 926 tons in 1922 to 869 tons in 1923, 642 tons in 1924 and 672 tons in 1925. In 1924 the company made a substantial loss. 'Elysium' and its other brands lacked the established appeal and quality of Lever products and this suggested that local manufacturing was not in itself a recommendation to Indian buyers. On the contrary, as Duraiswami Iyengar, Lever's agent in Madras, put it to A. C. Knight in December 1923:

It would be a mistake to make locally. His argument was that the Soap Trade was divided into two sections—the buyers of good quality imported soap and the buyers of cheap soaps of native make. But the demand was for quality at one end and low price at the other and that there was comparatively little demand for anything in between. If Sunlight were made locally an immediate reduction in price would be expected, the merchant would believe that the only reason for making it locally was that it could be cheaper than in England and therefore ought to be sold to him cheaper. The public at present consider imported soaps of better quality than local made and are willing to pay more for them, but make the same soaps in India and they at once lose their value and even if satisfied of the quality being the same the native would still class them as native soap and expect to buy at a parity of price with native productions.

Such arguments clearly influenced senior Lever executives. In his influential report dated 26 April 1924, A. C. Knight, after summarising the arguments quoted above, continued:

It seems to me that the question of raw material supplies, labour and distribution of the manufactured product, are all against manufacturing in India for our well established brands, and we shall continue to supply these from England, and confine our manufacturing in India to utilizing the plant, such as it is that we have at the North West Soap Company in endeavouring to develop a business in competition with native made soaps.

The experience of running the North West Soap Company's factory underlined the truth of these arguments. Admittedly the factory site was too small, the buildings and plant inadequate and poorly maintained, the management weak and the marketing agents unenterprising. Probably a specially built factory with modern equipment would have done better. But the lesson drawn from the North West Soap Company's poor performance was that, since the market for quality soaps was limited to those who could afford imported soaps and since 'locally made' was not after all a sufficient selling point, it was not worth risking large capital investment on a new project.

Thus, although no formal decision survives in the records, it is clear that the visit paid by Lever and D'Arcy Cooper at the beginning of 1924 marked the end of the project for large-scale local manufacture.[9] Lever's marginal notes on a second report by Knight on his visit to Calcutta in March 1924 indicated that he was convinced that Levers should once again concentrate on exports from Britain. At the same time he was against Knight's proposals for giving up the Garden Reach factory. 'Explain any possible advantages to the three firms if this were done', he wrote. As with most of the other white elephants he acquired over time he preferred to hang on to his possessions, however unpromising, and he or his successors commonly made them pay in the end. Garden Reach was to be retained, prices of existing products raised so that at least they did not sell at a loss, and a new brand of 'dhobi' soap for Indian, not European, consumption developed with the brand name Taj.

So the first phase of the story ended. The great project for establishing Levers as an Indian manufacturing concern had petered out, leaving them with a small inefficient factory in Calcutta, the complex legal problems of extricating themselves from the decaying Boulton empire, and the need to reconstruct the surviving Lever interests to meet the requirements of a predominantly import business.

In relation to the present study of Levers' attitude to manufacturing in India, the seven years after 1924 have a limited interest, for the 'factory proposal' for soap manufacturing was not seriously revived until 1931. The importance of these years lies therefore rather in the way in which Levers' interests in India were reconstructed to meet the needs of an essentially importing business and in the trend of their sales and profits which largely determined whether or not they would ever revive the 'factory proposal'. In 1924 the immediate problem was how to reorganise the component parts of the Lever business in India: the original three British companies, Lever Bros, Gossages and Crosfields; the new and largely notional Indian registered company, Lever Bros (India) Ltd; and the Premier Soap and North West Soap Companies. There were now two options: to incorporate all, or at least the British based interests, into a unitary Lever Bros (India) Ltd; or to leave each of the British firms as an autonomous unit with LB(I) as a holding company for the assets retained from the Boulton companies. The first course was strongly recommended by successive Lever experts in 1923–4; and in 1923 a first step was taken, with Lever's assent, towards consolidation. The general manager of LB(I) became responsible for sales of all concern products. India was divided into five districts, in each of which an LB(I) district manager controlled sales of all concern products. But the largely Indian agents of each of the three British companies remained, so that some competition between concern brands survived; and the different selling methods of each company also continued.

The prospects were, therefore, that LB(I) would gradually become the sole agent of all concern interests in India, buying soap from each parent company. This development was set back by Lever, whose visit to India seems to have strengthened his general belief that each company he acquired should retain its distinct personality. In a vitriolic correspondence in May 1924 with Knight, who had by then lost his confidence, he fulminated against the bad advice he had earlier received on 'making scrambled eggs of the firms in India'. It was vital that native agents should be impressed by the differences between each brand. 'Scrambled eggs would have resulted, in India, in Gossages and Lever Bros trade becoming the outstanding features and Crosfields gradually falling away'. At a meeting held on 20 June 1924—after Knight had resigned—Lever repeated his views. Levers, Gossages and Crosfields would have separate organisations in India 'with somebody at the head of the lot, preferably a Lever man . . .'. All common problems would be dealt with by the new Export Trade Board in London which had just been set up.

The new system came into operation late in 1924 and lasted virtually unchanged until 1933.[10] In effect the three British companies and the two Indian companies, Premier Soap and North West Soap, each continued to sell soap in their own traditional ways. This was perhaps surprising because after Lever's death the constraint on rationalisation was removed and two reports by W. P. Scott after visits in 1927 and 1929, the second with Viscount Leverhulme, argued strongly in favour of some form of unified central control over all aspects of the business. The 1929 report proposed a central Indian holding company which would be responsible for marketing all concern products, including now the imports of vegetable ghee from the Dutch companies newly merged with Levers in Unilever. The Gossage system of depots would be adopted and expanded so that dealers could be supplied rapidly from stock. The wholesalers should be eliminated and replaced by a network of local dealers who would work under the supervision of Lever salesmen. Such a system, Scott and Leverhulme admitted, would take time to establish and overheads would be higher. But in the end Unilever sales, whether of imports or locally-manufactured products, could only be sustained and expanded by an on-the-spot organisation of this kind.

These proposals are important because they formed the basis of the all-Indian sales organisation established by the concern later on, which was perhaps their most important single innovation in India. At the time they were rejected and a quite different restructuring took place. As has been seen in Chapter 2, United Exporters Ltd was set up in England to consolidate the export trade from all Lever factories to all overseas markets. In 1930 LB(I) was wound up, to save paying taxation in India on profits due to be taxed in Britain, and United Exporters took over the whole system of agents and the depots and stocks of Gossages in India, Ceylon and Burma. In 1930, therefore, the conduct of the concern business in India was almost exactly what it had been in 1913, with the difference that United Exporters handled almost the entire import trade and that Levers owned the almost moribund soap factory in Garden Reach, Calcutta. Yet two years later a vegetable ghee factory was in production in Bombay and the decision had been taken to build a large soap factory there. By 1935 India had ceased to be primarily an export market and United Exporters handled only marginal lines not produced by the Indian factories. It is therefore necessary to discover why this dramatic reversal of policy took place.

The reason is simply that by 1931/2, as can be seen in Table 4.2, the coincidence of declining exports and narrowing profit margins had once again forced the concern to assess the potential benefits of large-scale local production and that on this occasion neither liquidity problems nor a trade recovery intervened to block construction of import-substituting factories. That the position was serious, if not desperate, was recognised early in 1931 when three main causes were assigned: the general slump in world trade, though this was assumed to be transitory; the renewed boycott on foreign goods organised by Gandhi as part of his civil disobedience campaign; and the impact of the new India tariff of 1931 which had imposed duties of about 25 per cent *ad valorem* on imported soaps.[11] The London management reacted promptly. On 5 March 1931 the Chairman of Unilever Ltd referred in the Managing Directors' Conference

to the possibility that we should soon have to put up a factory in India to avoid new duties. Hitherto we have thought it cheaper to manufacture in England and pay the shipping freight rather than pay the land freights which in a country the size of India would be very considerable, wherever the factory might be located. The problem would need careful consideration. Mr Greenhalgh gave the profits for 1929 and 1930, which though showing a drop in the last year, were good considering the great difficulties to be contended with in that market. We had a trade of 11,000 tons to deal with, and distribution over the country pointed to a factory at Bombay being a possible proposition. Against the saving of new duties had to be set the putting up of overhead expenses in factories at home if manufacture were transferred to India. He was still looking into the figures, but at present the margin in favour of putting up a factory in India looked like £25,000 a year, which might not be worth the venture.

Caution, however, still prevailed and it was not until June 1932 that the question was fully thrashed out at a joint meeting of the Special Committee, the Overseas Committee and United Exporters Limited. J. H. Hansard pointed out that profits in India, Burma and Ceylon had dropped from £200,000 in 1930 to £100,000 in 1931 and were estimated at £40,000 for 1932. He predicted a continuing decrease in tonnage 'owing . . . to the very strong nationalist feeling which is increasingly anti-British and pro-Indian . . .'. At an earlier meeting it had been decided to postpone consideration of building a soap factory until the Round Table Congress on the Indian constitution had finished its work, the results of establishing a vegetable ghee factory (decided on in 1931 and described below) were known, and nationalist feeling had subsided. It was now decided that further postponement was pointless. The Round Table Conference was clearly failing and vegetable ghee was not in any case a good guide to soap sales. Indian hostility to a British-owned soap factory might be overcome by floating the company in India with 60 per cent of the capital in Indian hands, and with Indians on the board. The proposal was therefore to build a soap factory alongside the new vegetable ghee factory in Bombay, allotting a majority of shares to Levers' Indian agents 'with an option to repurchase their shares at any time, thereby ultimately obtaining a majority'. The home company's goodwill and brand names could be sold to this company by which 'a decent profit could be made'. Thus three objects could be attained: '(i) retain our present and get back our lost trade; (ii) get the consumers on our side; (iii) make a profit on goodwill'. Against this it was argued that such a procedure might merely give the profits of the Indian business to the agents as majority shareholders, that Levers would lose control of their brand names and that if Levers eventually bought a majority of the shares, the whole aura of Indian control would be lost. Eventually it was decided to float a manufacturing company which would make Levers its sole buying and selling agents 'thereby retaining in effect the brands in our control, and also a larger share of the profits'. A proposition along these lines was to be worked out by Hansard and submitted to the Special Committee.

During the later months of 1932 and into 1933 a thorough investigation of the whole situation, and above all of the possible profitability of an Indian factory, was undertaken. A vital stage was reached in September 1932 when Hansard reported that on his estimate of the costs involved soap could be made £2 14s 5d a ton cheaper in Port Sunlight than in a modern Indian factory using Indian labour and Indian raw materials; but that after taking account of freight and the new import duties, which together totalled £13 1s 8d a ton, there was a substantial prospective advantage from manufacturing in India. In the following month the directors were told that 'by erecting a factory we should make a profit of £48,000 as against £30,000 which we were making under present conditions, but which, however, we could not expect to maintain owing to the import duties'. Indeed the emphasis was now increasingly on the significance of the new Indian tariff rather than on the effects of the boycott. Reporting in December on his recent visit to India C. E. Tatlow emphasised that

The general feeling . . . is that in the future increased taxation must be anticipated especially as the tariff increases tend to drive those who previously exported to India to build behind the tariff barrier—as Unilever in Ghee and soon in Soap together with the increasing tendency of the native to buy Indian made goods. The result will be reduced tariff revenue which will have to be made up by taxation in the country.

This militated against local production; but at the same time it is significant that Lever men, having once accepted the need to get inside the tariff barrier, adjusted their thinking accordingly. In the same report, though in a section dealing with the ghee industry, Tatlow emphasised the need to appeal to the Indian government to increase the tariff on imported whale oil—mostly from Japan—on the ground that a factory using local raw materials and labour had a claim to protection against competing imports. On balance he recommended building the new soap factory at Bombay and at the same time either expanding the North West soap factory at Calcutta, or closing it down completely.

Thereafter the momentum of the drive towards full-scale soap manufacturing in India was sustained. There is no record of a formal decision by the Special Committee to adopt the 'factory proposition'; but a firm decision to manufacture in India must have been made by the beginning of 1933. In January 1933 Greenhalgh reported after a visit to India that he was sure 'that the Indian factory will enable us to sell Sunlight Soap at a cheaper price and still make a reasonable margin of profit'. There remained the danger of the Indian boycott, but this had to be accepted. In February 1933 formal application was made for a factory site in Bombay, adjoining the existing vegetable ghee factory site, and in May the Managing Directors' Conference began to consider estimates of capital expenditure. The projected cost of the Bombay factory was stated on 5 May 1933 to be £150,000 plus £25,500 for extending the capacity of the Calcutta factory to 4,000 tons. It was not, however, until mid-July 1933 that this estimate was formally considered; and approval was by no means a formality. There were clearly some directors who distrusted the whole plan. C. W. Barnish thought that the loss of the Indian trade would have a serious effect on production and employment at Port Sunlight and the Chairman, D'Arcy Cooper, agreed that it might be necessary to close down a factory somewhere else in England as a result. Albert Van den Bergh suggested a year's postponement. The total volume of the Indian trade might be increased by importing new lines from Britain without risking a factory in India. This alternative was, however, discounted by Hansard, who had the best knowledge of the position in India.

There was no goodwill line on the market, except those belonging to the concern, and 'we should get a far larger share of the trade by manufacturing on the spot at reduced prices, whereas if we were satisfied merely to export from this country he did not see our share increasing'. This argument carried the day. D'Arcy Cooper 'thought India was too large a gap of the world's surface for us to leave uncovered'. There was danger of a goodwill line with a national distribution being put on the market by some other manufacturer if Unilever did not and he was in favour of going on with the proposal. Finally, after fears about the potential effect on Port Sunlight and the danger of stimulating competition in India had been considered, the financial proposals were approved.

This marked the end of the first phase of the story. A new company, Lever Bros (India) Ltd was incorporated in Bombay in October 1933. The factory was completed in September 1934, and the first soap manufactured the following month. Simultaneously the new company purchased the goodwill and trade marks of all the Lever Bros brands it was to manufacture from the UK company, and the long dormant Indian registered Gossage and Crosfield companies did the same. Lever Bros (India) Ltd rented the expanded Garden Reach factory from the North West Soap Company, and thereafter used it to manufacture Lever and Gossage brands. The effect of these changes was to make the Indian companies fully autonomous in the sense that they did not have to pay royalties on their products to the parent companies in Britain. In one respect, however, the new Lever Bros (India) Ltd was less an Indian concern than had been projected a year earlier for all its nominal capital was entirely owned by Unilever. Why the proposal to give Indians a majority shareholding was not adopted it is impossible to discover from the surviving records. Possibly local advice was that this device would not appease Indian national feeling but would certainly cause problems of control and give much of the profit to Indian share-holders. LB(I) did not, indeed, go public until after Indian independence and there are no grounds for thinking that this in any way affected the company's standing or success.

Two other contingent innovations must be mentioned because they derive from earlier debates on policy. In 1933, even before the factory was decided on, the old sales system was scrapped and the existing agents were replaced by Unilever depots which gradually extended throughout the country. Initially these were run by United Exporters Ltd but in 1934 the new Lever Bros (India) Ltd took over the depots and the marketing of locally made and also some imported Unilever brands. The following year an Indian subsidiary, United Traders Ltd, was set up to market most Unilever imports. At long last all the eggs were scrambled and the concentration of control was completed in 1939 when Lever Bros (India) Ltd bought all Premier Soap Company shares from Unilever and the surviving Indian shareholders and then purchased the Calcutta factory outright.

(b) Vegetable Ghee (Vanaspati)

Unilever's decision to manufacture hydrogenated vegetable oil— alias 'vegetable product', 'vegetable ghee' or 'vanaspati'—in India had much in common with the decision to make soap there. In each case a market had been created by goods exported from Europe which was eventually threatened by Indian competitors and a protective tariff. It is not proposed to describe the origins of the vanaspati business in detail but merely to indicate briefly the grounds on which the decision to invest was taken and to describe the company structure established in the early 1930s.

The export of hydrogenated vegetable oil to India developed only after 1918—much later than for soap—and was a response to Indian demand for an additive to ghee. Natural ghee was made from clarified butter and had a slightly cheesy rancid taste. It was a widely used Indian food, but by the early 1920s demand was outstripping supply and prices rose. Indian traders responded by adulterating ghee with any cheap material that lay to hand and importers recognised that there was now a market for suitable imported additives. The main technical requirements for these were a texture similar to that of ghee and that the taste of the natural product should not be affected. Two internationally available commodities conformed to these specifications—hydrogenated vegetable oil and hardened whale oil, both widely used in the manufacture of margarine and vegetable cooking fats. In the later 1920s the price of imported 'vegetable product', as it was originally called, was about half that of natural ghee and whale oil was still cheaper. The tariff was low: 15 per cent *ad valorem* on all imported edible oils. Conditions were thus favourable to the growth of a substantial import trade; and at first the question was whether vegetable oil processed in Europe or hardened whale oil, which came mostly from Japan, would scoop the market.

Unilever's interest in this trade was brought into the new combine by its Dutch members, Jurgens, Van den Berghs, Hartogs and Verschure Creameries, who had built up a substantial export trade in the early 1920s, the first two through managing agents, Ralli Bros and Brunner Mond, respectively, Hartogs through their own local agent. These Dutch firms almost monopolised the trade and made a quota and price agreement in March 1927: Gossages tried to get a foothold but were unable to compete on price. There is no data in the surviving records of the Dutch companies on the volume, value or profitability of their exports and no statistics of total imports to India are available before 1927, when the Indian authorities first began to distinguish vegetable product from other imported oils; but Table 4.3 shows total imports to India and Burma from 1927/8 to 1930/1, with the percentage share of each exporting country.

Table 4.3   India: Imports of Vegetable Product to India and Burma, 1927/8–1930/1

| Year | Tons | Percentage from each importing country | | |
		Holland	Belgium	Germany
1927/8	22,223	84	13	1.5
1928/9	22,909	87	10	1.5
1929/30	16,056	90	4	4.5
1930/31	14,801	79	9.5	7.5

Until about 1928, therefore, India appeared to offer a satisfactory export market for the Dutch margarine firms but in May of that year a first warning note was sounded by Ralli Bros. There was evidence that the large Indian-owned firm, Ganesh Flour Mills, was looking into the technical possibilities of manufacturing vegetable ghee in India and Herbert Davis, head of Margarine Union in London, took it seriously. 'There is no doubt that this is one of the problems which we shall have to face in the future', he wrote to Paul Rijkens of Van den Berghs in May 1928. 'The duty on GHEE [*sic*] amounts to about £10 a ton so that it is quite evident that if a suitable factory were erected in India, it would be the end of the imported goods.' Davis belonged to Jurgens and Jurgens was the only member of the merger formed in 1927 with any experience of investment in manufacturing overseas (this is described in Chapter 5 below). It was therefore Jurgens, through Davis, who took the initiative during the next three months in investigating the possibility of manufacturing vegetable ghee in India to meet the threat of local competition. An energetic correspondence was carried out with Ralli Bros and other specialists in India and by 10 September Van den Berghs must have been convinced that local manufacture might be necessary for Sidney Van den Bergh then wrote to Davis that 'it has been decided that Mr Royle of Van den Berghs will leave within [a] short [time] for British India to study the question of the erection of a factory and it has also in principle been decided to start a factory there when [*sic*] Mr Royle's reports are favourable in this respect'.

The date of this decision is significant because it took place before the merger between the Dutch companies and Levers was formed. This suggests that under the changing conditions of the later 1920s the margarine companies would probably have found it necessary to break with their tradition and establish a number of overseas factories if they thought it worth while to defend their new markets for vegetable ghee. In 1929, however, Royle did not feel that immediate investment in a factory was justified. The threat was real enough, for three Indian firms were already building factories. But it was by no means clear that these would have any advantage over firms exporting from Holland. Assuming a factory was to be built in Bombay, he demonstrated that manufacturing costs there would be much higher than for the same product made in Holland f.o.b. Amsterdam. The calculations were as follows:

Additional cost per ton of materials and manufacturing
in Bombay as compared with Holland

Raw materials	£6 10s 0d
Manufacturing	£4 8s 0d
Tins	5s 8d
	£11 3s 8d

Raw materials were more expensive because a crushing mill would have to be erected and because of the higher cost of Indian linseed oil which had 15 per cent protection. Manufacturing costs were higher because of the cost of oil, water, coal, etc., and because tins had to be imported. On the other hand there were prospective savings as compared with the landed cost of imported Dutch goods.

Import duty	£9 9s 0d
Cases and freight	£2 14s 10d
	£12 3s 10d

The potential saving was therefore about £1 a ton, but only if these rough estimates proved correct; and in Royle's view this did not provide a margin adequate to justify so large an investment. He therefore concluded that 'a factory in Bombay would not be a practical proposition, unless an assurance could be obtained from a reliable Government source that an increase in duty would be granted, which at the present juncture appears to be quite impossible'.

But by October 1930, when the question seems to have come to the point of decision, conditions had changed. Imports of vanaspati to India continued to decline and under slump conditions the Indian government was clearly moving towards a general protective tariff. A top level meeting was held in London on 29 October 1930. No minutes survive but the conclusion must have been conditionally in favour of local manufacture because on 30 October the Special Committee decided that a Mr Naumann 'should make the full necessary inquiry in connection with the erection of a factory, but that nothing should be decided without the consent of London. Mr Davis is to prepare an estimate of costs of manufacture on this site, as compared with similar estimated costs in India.' Thereafter things moved very fast. There were encouraging reports in December 1930 that the tariff on imported vanaspati would be raised in March 1931, as indeed it was. Negotations to buy an existing oil mill as a factory site fell through but an alternative site at Sewri, five miles from the centre of Bombay, was bought from the Bombay Port Trust and piling operations began by February 1931. It is impossible to date the final decision to go ahead with the factory precisely but it must have been by 20 February 1931 when a meeting was held at Rotterdam to prepare detailed plans for the proposed factory and company structure. Planning and supervision were left to the Dutch companies and were supervised by Rudolph Jurgens. The factory was completed and in production by August 1932. It included an oil refinery and a hydrogenation plant and had a rated capacity of 10,000 tons of vanaspati a year. After further extensions the capital employed in December 1935 was Rs. 2,419,000 (£181,000). To run this enterprise a complicated structure of companies was set up which reflected the fact that Unilever was not yet a fully integrated concern. The factory was run by the Hindustan Vanaspati Manufacturing Co. Ltd (HVM); sales were in the hands of the Hindustan Holland Vanaspati Trading Co. Ltd; and a third company, the Hindustan Holland Vanaspati Handel Maatschappij, was formed to act as a link with Rotterdam. All the nominal capital of these companies, apart from single shares held by directors of the companies in India, was held by members of the family firms which had formed Margarine Union. This company structure proved unnecessarily complicated and in the later 1930s the manufacturing company, HVM, effectively took over the whole operation.

At this point we can compare the grounds on which Lever, Margarine Union and then Unilever decided to invest in local production of soap and edible fats in India. Although there were differences in detail and timing, the underlying motives are remarkably similar. In each case the starting point was a decline or threat of decline in a very important export market coupled with fear or knowledge that Indian entrepreneurs were about to invest in large scale modern manufacture. In each case, also, the first interest was aroused before the Indian tariff provided really effective protection; this partly explains why Lever's first initiative in 1922 proved unnecessary and why in 1929 Royle advised against immediate establishment of a vegetable ghee factory. In the end it was the probability or reality of an adequate tariff that provided the final incentive for both sides of Unilever to take the plunge, though the Dutch companies felt it necessary to commit themselves to action before the tariff was actually raised because for them local competition was already a fact and not merely a threat.

The aim of local production was, therefore, defensive and not aggressive: in India, as in Australia and South Africa, it was not undertaken because production costs were cheaper than in Britain or Holland. Although A. C. Knight had claimed in 1920 that cheaper Indian labour would contribute to profitability, the more sophisticated calculations used a decade later entirely discounted this. Labour constituted a very small component of total production costs—Rs. 0/4/4 per cwt of soap compared with Rs. 9/12/– for raw materials in the Garden Reach factory in 1924; and in any case, as Royle's report put it in 1929, 'labour costs in India are no cheaper than England owing to the small amount of work done by an Indian compared to a European, heavy expense of European supervisory staff and necessary duplication due to holidays and illness'. Nor was there any advantage from using Indian raw materials. In the 1930s vegetable oils were cheaper in Port Sunlight or Rotterdam than in Bombay or Calcutta, for these towns were the focal points of a highly competitive international market, and transport costs from West Africa to Europe were as low as or lower than from the oil-seed producing regions of India to the main industrial regions of the country. All calculations made in the early 1930s predicted lower ex-works costs in Europe than in India, and for this reason India was never regarded as a source of competitive exports.[12]

The grounds on which Unilever decided to manufacture in India were, therefore, remarkably similar to those leading to investment in more developed countries. But this implies an important additional conclusion: that this first major Unilever industrial enterprise in the less developed world was undertaken at the moment and largely on the grounds that India was ceasing to act as a conventional colonial dependency. The threat of serious local competition showed that indigenous capitalism was now willing and able to challenge foreign importers for the home market and the tariff of 1931/2 demonstrated both the new freedom of the Indian government to formulate economic policy in Indian interests rather than those of Britain and also the ability of Indian industrialists to influence public policy. These changes, which were partially reproduced in Ceylon and Indonesia in the 1930s, are significant pointers to the future for they suggest that the main industrial expansion of multi-national firms such as Unilever in the less developed world would not come as a result of advantages provided to metropolitan capital by colonialism but as a consequence of the propensity of autonomous indigenous regimes to provide more than adequate protection for home-based industries. It was because this transformation began to take place in the early 1930s that this decade marks the start of Unilever as a large industrial investor in tropical Africa and in Asia.

Unilever in Imperial India, 1932-40: The Classical Period

From 1932 to 1940 the growth of the Unilever business in India was conditioned by three main things: a tariff which gave local manufacturers effective protection against external competition; the relative of efficiency of HVM and LB(I) as compared with competitors; and limitations of the domestic market for the quality and type of goods they produced. The main facts of their development are summarised in Table 4.4 which shows the growth of capacity and production in the soap, vanaspati and oil milling sides of the business.

Perhaps the most striking aspect of these figures is the spectacular growth of vanaspati production as compared with that of soap. Soap did well but vanaspati did brilliantly; and the rapid increase in vanaspati capacity was clearly a reflection of the relative profitability of the two operations. Table 4.5(a) showing earnings as a percentage of capital employed for the years 1935–8 helps to explain why Unilever thought it desirable to expand its vanaspati production more rapidly than that of soap. But in fact HVM, while continuing to expand, soon lost its dominant market position: by 1943, when the quota system established in the 1930s lapsed, their share of the market was down to 40.9 per cent and by 1949 it had slipped to 23.7 per cent. Wartime shortages of equipment had something to do with this, but there were more fundamental factors at work which suggest that, even before the advent of wartime and post-war regulation of the industry, even the most efficient foreign firm could not sustain its overwhelming predominance in a consumer product such as vanaspati.

The first of these was the nature of the product. Vanaspati began as an additive to ghee and only gradually became a marketable product in its own right after 1939. Vanaspati sold in bulk could not, therefore, be a branded product at this stage. The large market share HVM achieved in the 1930s reflected only the fact that they were one of the first manufacturers in the field and that they expanded their production and sales organisation more rapidly than Indian rivals. So long as demand outran supply any new entrant could sell as much as he produced at almost any price; and unless HVM increased its capacity as fast as all competitors combined, it was bound to lose its initial share of the market.

This it could not do for vanaspati was far too profitable not to attract indigenous entrepreneurs. It was, in fact, one of the striking features of post-1931 Indian industrial history that once the tariff wall was sufficiently high Indian capitalists were very quick to see an industrial opportunity and to invest in it: the sugar refining industry is an obvious example.[13] So long as the vanaspati industry as a whole lacked capacity to satisfy demand, price levels did not

Table 4.4   India: Growth of Capacity and Sales of Unilever Factories, 1931–41

Year	Capacity				Sales	
	Oil milling (Bombay)	Soap (Bombay)	Soap (Calcutta)	Vanaspati (Bombay)	Soap (tons)	Vanaspati (tons)
1931	n/a	n/a	3,000	n/a	n/a	n/a
1932	n/a	n/a	n/a	10,000	n/a	n/a
1933	n/a	n/a	n/a	n/a	n/a	n/a
1934	n/a	12,000	4,000	n/a	n/a	n/a
1935	n/a	n/a	n/a	22,500	9,897	11,222
1936	n/a	n/a	n/a	n/a	11,695	14,444
1937	n/a	n/a	n/a	n/a	12,823	19,875
1938	n/a	n/a	n/a	40,000	14,667	23,694
1939	n/a	n/a	n/a	n/a	18,919	30,222
1940	15,000	n/a	5,500	n/a	10,901	34,790
1941	n/a	25,000	8,000	52,000	20,040	43,065

Table 4.5(a)   India: Earnings as a Percentage of Capital Employed,
Soap and Vanaspati, 1935–8
(Nett accounting profit, after tax but with interest added back)

Year	HVM & Van den Berghs (India) Ltd (Vanaspati) %	LB(I) Ltd & subsidiaries (Soap) %
1935	11.8	9.5
1936	14.2	14.3
1937	50.6	20.6
1938	79.4	11.1

Table 4.5(b)   India: Profit as a Percentage of Capital Employed in Soap
Manufacture, 1935–8

Year	A Capital employed[a] (Rs)	B Turnover (Rs)	C Trading profit[b] (Rs)	D Nett profit[c] (Rs)	C/B %	C/A %	D/A %
1935	6,971,000	6,995,178	749,893	509,790	10.7	10.8	7.3
1936	7,344,000	7,926,035	1,204,096	832,700	15.2	16.4	11.3
1937	7,589,164	8,809,999	1,973,438	1,374,555	22.4	26.0	18.1
1938	7,331,467	8,458,252	1,030,185	636,936	13.8	14.0	8.6

Notes: a. 'Capital employed' excludes bank overdraft, but includes book value of trade
marks and goodwill and a premium on internal shareholding.

b. 'Trading profit' is gross of tax and various adjustments.

c. 'Nett profit' was calculated on the basis of 'trading profit' less interest, adjustments and 'statistical tax' — i.e. the taxes payable in India if all profits had been
distributed as dividends in that year rather than carried over.

matter provided they remained below the cost of natural ghee. The result was that selling prices were fixed by the wholesalers rather than by the manufacturers: if the manufacturer reduced his price to the trade the wholesaler would simply take a higher middle-man profit. This fact ruined HVM's initial strategy. As Sidney Van den Bergh lamented after a visit to India in 1937,

> The policy for this business as laid down . . . in January 1934 . . . has been that vegetable product, not being a proprietary article, should be sold at a [gross] margin of not more than £2 to £3 a ton. By not taking more than this margin we will be able to extend our sales quickly and extend our factories to such a capacity that we should be able to manufacture more cheaply than anybody else in India, and also this policy would not make the article so attractive that many other people would be inclined to enter our industry.

As it was margins had shot up to £4 12s 0d a ton by September 1937 and rose to the fantastic height of £10 a ton by 1939; and this of course explains the extraordinary profits shown in Table 4.5(a). Unilever looked for ways of reducing prices and profits but failed; even market leaders are helpless in conditions such as these.

While vanaspati rocketed to temporary success, soap was plodding steadily upwards: as can be seen from Table 4.4 it was not until 1939 that the symbolically important turnover of 18,000 tons, last achieved in 1929, was regained. This was a substantial achievement; but because local manufacture was undertaken as an alternative to importing, its success must be measured in relative terms. The question is, therefore, whether, so far as can be judged, Unilever might have sold as much soap and as profitably if they had not decided to make it locally. The only basis on which this can be answered is by comparing the volume and profitability of sales of goods made in India with those imported during the 1930s by United Traders Ltd (UTL), This comparison has limited value because the residual products imported by UTL after 1934 consisted of the more expensive or specialised brands of soap and goods such as toothpaste and luxury foods whose market in India may have been affected by different factors from those influencing the laundry and toilet soaps made by LB(I). But for what it is worth Tables 4.5(b) to 4.7 provide a basis for comparison.

Table 4.6   India: Turnover,[a] Trading Results and Nett Profitability of Unilever Sales in India, Burma and Ceylon through United Traders Ltd,[b] 1935–8

Year	A Turnover (Rs)	B Trading profit before selling expenses deducted (Rs)[d]	B as % of A	C Trading profit after selling expenses, depreciation, etc. (Rs)	D Nett profit after Stat. tax (Rs)	C as % of A[c]
1935	1,761,837	314,591	17.8	206,415	168,762	11.7
1936	2,019,500	368,074	18.2	104,761	71,513	5.2
1937	2,278,262	409,511	17.9	110,462	75,057	4.8
1938	2,199,420	402,870	21.3	39,877	9,635	1.8

Notes: a. Turnover is based on depot prices in India.

b. United Traders began operations in 1935 but 1936 was the first full year of operation.

c. The percentage figure in the last column is given in terms of nett profit before tax as a percentage of turnover for comparison with the percentage in Table 4.5(b) Since these goods were all imported a percentage based on nett profits as a proportion of capital employed would have little value.

d. Results in column B include those made by United Traders on goods imported and sold on its own behalf and also profits made by British companies who consigned goods to India to be sold by United Traders Ltd on payment of a service fee.

To consider first sales volume, between 1935 (the first year of full manufacture of soap by LB(I)) and 1939 the volume of Indian made soap rose by 1.91 as compared with an increase of 1.49 in UTL imports. The difference is not in fact very great and suggests that in each case the underlying factor may have been the general economic revival of the mid- and late-1930s: the benefit in terms of sales volume came after 1940, when wartime and post-independence restrictions on imports would virtually have deprived Unilever of a market in India had they not already possessed manufacturing capacity there. In fact the real reward for local manufacture in the 1930s lay in profitability. It is impossible to use the return to capital as the measure, but Tables 4.5(b) and 4.6 show that local manufacture quickly became much more rewarding than importing. It remains to consider why this was so and what general significance the contrast had.

Table 4.7   India: Pre-tax Profits on Soap Imported to India, 1925–9 and Manufactured in India, 1936–8

Year	Tons of soap	Profit (£s)	Profit per ton (£s)
1925	16,621	155,638	9.4
1926	18,944	158,638	8.4
1927	18,925	179,888	9.5
1928	20,238	206,046	10.2
1929	18,830	196,900	10.5
1936	11,695	90,533	7.7
1937	12,823	148,378	11.6
1938	14,667	77,457	5.3

One relevant factor was the relatively high unit cost of fixed selling expenses faced by an importing business, but there were others. Many of UTL's imports faced growing competition from American and Indian brands and few had the established appeal of Sunlight Soap. Promotional difficulties handicapped UTL: it was more difficult with a given advertising budget to push the multiple products of 16 Unilever companies than the 10 separate brands being sold by LB(I) in 1938. But ultimatively the profitability gap seems to have reflected the tariff. UTL was paying 25 per cent on virtually all their imports while LB(I) paid little or no duty on imported raw materials or even intermediates. Whatever their relative importance, the sum of these things clearly gave the local manufacturer a decisive advantage over the importer during the later 1930s. By 1939 it had been recognised that the only future for Unilever in India was gradually to expand the range of its local products until all but the most exotic brands with very small potential markets were made there. In a report written in that year C. W. Barnish summarised the position:

It will . . . be necessary for us to be considering whether we ought not to manufacture in India certain of our Toilet Soaps and Specialities at present sold through United Traders, which will be in obvious danger unless we can meet our competition in India on reasonable and level terms.

He listed the staple imported soaps and toilet preparations, and concluded 'I am afraid that if we do not manufacture these soaps locally it is only a question of time before they will be gradually annihilated by soap made in India'.

Thus the wider significance of the 'classical' period of Unilever in India between 1932 and 1940 was that while local manufacturing may not have been absolutely essential in the short run to save Unilever's existing markets for soap and vanaspati, it was almost certainly necessary to maintain reasonable profit levels once a substantial import tariff had been set up and local entrepreneurs had seen their opportunity. But one important reservation must be made in comparing the profitability of importing and manufacturing in India: on a free trade basis it would still have been more advantageous for Unilever to manufacture in Europe. Table 4.7 compares pre-tax profits per ton on soap imported from Port Sunlight in the 'good' years from 1925 to 1929 with pre-tax profits per ton on soap made in India in the relatively good years from 1936 to 1938. Except in 1937 the difference is striking and reflects the lower price of many inputs and the economics of scale available in Britain. The tariff and other factors discussed above had changed the situation by the 1930s, but Unilever was clearly wise to postpone local manufacture in India and in all other countries as long as possible. Equally there could be no better confirmation of the proposition that local manufacturing was undertaken reluctantly in defence of an established market and was not seen as a way to increase profits so long as conditions remained unchanged.

Unilever in the New India, 1941-65

After about 1940 both the character of the Unilever business in India and its significance for this study changed substantially. Until the Second World War the Lever/Unilever companies in India were special only in the sense that they were among the very first such manufacturing companies in the less developed world: in most other ways they closely resembled other Unilever subsidiaries operating in comparable 'open' economic conditions. But from 1941, and still more after India became independent in 1947, India presented Unilever with two new problems which were to become very common during the following three decades. These were how to operate in an intensively 'managed' economy and how to deal with a newly independent and nationalistic government and society. It was in India that Unilever first had to meet this dual challenge and its experience there affected its attitude and activities throughout the less developed world during the 1950s and beyond. It is, therefore, proposed to examine the Indian story in greater detail than will be possible for other countries. The evidence will be reviewed under the following heads: first, the character of the new economic environment as it evolved from 1941; second, the movement towards localisation of senior management; third, ownership of the equity in the Indian companies; fourth, the growth and diversification of the business after 1940; and finally, the balance of advantage between Unilever and India as the host country.

(a) The Economic Environment

The changes that took place in the Indian environment for industrial activity after the 1930s were so great that it is necessary to emphasise that before 1940 a British-owned corporation in India was in almost exactly the same position as a company in Britain: indeed this was one of the main benefits foreign capital received in any colonial territory. The government was controlled by British officials, even though increasingly from the early 1920s economic policy was influenced by Indian politicians and pressure groups. Despite the adoption of a general tariff in 1931, the economic system was based on nineteenth-century principles and practices. There were no constraints on the movement of capital or profits. Prices were uncontrolled. Government did not attempt to influence or dictate to private companies in matters such as siting factories, volume or type of production. Company taxation was comparatively light: a total of 21.85 per cent nett of double tax relief for a foreign-based company before 1939 plus 6.25 per cent super tax. This was the world Unilever knew from its experience throughout the world and in which the Indian business was built up.

This world changed well before Indian independence in 1947. The Second World War led to a radical increase in state control in many directions; but whereas in most Western countries wartime controls were wound up by the early 1950s, in India they were mostly perpetuated and used as the basis of a new partly socialist economy after 1947. We must therefore start with a short analysis of changes introduced by the British authorities between 1939 and 1945.

The first and immediate consequence of war was higher levels of taxation. Income tax remained constant but a super corporation tax and surcharges on both taxes raised the effective rate of taxation on undistributed profits to 40.62 per cent by 1944 and on distributed profits to 46.87 per cent plus 66.66 per cent excess profits tax. In other respects the war had no significant economic effects on Unilever's business until the entry of Japan in December 1941 but thereafter Unilever had a foretaste of what a siege economy would mean in India. This can be seen in three main spheres: shortage of capital equipment and raw materials; official regulation of production; and the origins of the policy of Indianisation of management.

Shortages were the inevitable result of shipping problems. While demand for soap and vanaspati boomed—driven on by military needs and inflation—production was held back by shortage of inputs. No manufacturing equipment could be imported, so production levelled off after 1941 as full capacity was reached. Imports of raw materials and intermediates were severely limited and it became necessary to use locally-produced substitutes: local in place of American rosin; Indian alkalies produced by the ICI subsidiary in place of Unilever's alkalies from Crosfields; Indian perfumes, Indian wooden boxes, Indian paper, and so on. Use of these substitutes often involved considerable modification in production techniques and some reduction in quality. It also affected profit levels since local materials were in some cases more expensive; but in a period of expanding demand and inflation this was comparatively unimportant.

More significant as a sign of things to come was official regulation of production and prices. Soap remained unregulated, but vanaspati came under official control, both because it was an edible product which affected the cost of living index and also because it was argued that processing oil added little nutritional value. From 1944 the central government controlled selling prices and from 1945, under the Vegetable Oil Products Control orders, not only prices but also quality and manufacturing specifications. From 1944 productive capacity was licensed; firms had to register existing capacity and could not exceed it without official permission. This was seen as a temporary move to limit total production of 'non-essential' commodities; and although their share of the total vanaspati market had dropped from 64 per cent in 1940 to 43 per cent by 1944, due to the growth of Indian competition and their own inability to import new machinery, HVM confidently expected that as soon as the war was over controls would end and large-scale investment would make it possible to regain at least 50 per cent of a rapidly expanding market. This millennium never came. By 1949 HVM had only 23.8 per cent of the market and the licensing system perpetuated by the government of independent India made it very difficult ever to reverse the trend.

Finally the war accelerated, if it did not actually begin, the deliberate movement towards Indianisation of management. Individual Indians had, of course, occasionally been recruited to managerial posts before 1939, Prakash Tandon for one; but such appointments were rare and it was still generally assumed that a British-owned company would continue to have a predominantly expatriate managerial staff. The absence of many British managers and technical staff on military service and the near impossibility of replacing them from home forced a change of attitudes. By July 1942 it was formally accepted as a general principle by the Special Committee that as many Indians as necessary should be recruited 'for junior and senior managerial positions . . .' and that they 'should enjoy equal privileges to the Europeans they substitute, and in addition that they should qualify for the same salary level'. This represented a very important change in Unilever's thinking on the character of subsidiaries in non-European countries. It had vast consequences for the future, and it was never reversed. By 1944 A. D. Gourley reported that 'notwithstanding the moderate degree of success [in getting and keeping able men] the management readily agree that as a matter of policy the training of suitable Indians for managerial positions should be persevered with'.

By 1945, therefore, the environment for foreign industrial enterprise in India had changed significantly. Indeed the government of India, still under British control, published a white paper in 1944 which projected a major state role in post-war industrial development and whose proposals were taken over wholesale by Congress. More significant, it was by then certain that India would become independent soon after the war with Japan ended, so that all non-Indian enterprises would have to face a problem entirely new to that generation: how to plan future operations in the first European dependency (other than the older British Dominions) to achieve sovereign independence during the twentieth century. This transfer of power took place in 1947 and coincided with the division of India into India and Pakistan. Partition necessarily disrupted Unilever's pattern of operation in the north-west and north-east of India and led to the creation of a new subsidiary in Pakistan which is described in the last section of this chapter. For the parent company, however, the prospect of independence raised two novel questions. First, what steps the concern should take in advance; second, what the character of the new environment would be and whether there would still be a place in India for foreign capital.

Judging from the records, Unilever appears to have had remarkably few fears about the effect of Indian independence and took appropriately few precautions. The first surviving mention of the issue is in the major report made by A. D. Gourley in 1944. He admitted that some Indian businessmen were demanding that all 'basic' industries should be Indian owned and that in all fields Indian companies should buy 'technical guidance under some appropriate system of royalties' rather than that foreign companies should be allowed to undertake production on their own account. But he did not think this would result in anything more than a few minor discriminating regulations, 'more irritating than harmful and transitory than permanent'. He assumed, moreover, that India would retain close commercial and monetary links with Britain; and concluded that 'It is hard to picture a state of complete independence for India before the lapse of 15–20 years'.

It is not clear whether this optimistic prediction lulled Unilever House into inaction; but by early 1947 the prospects seemed less rosy. Leading Indian politicians were by then claiming that incipient independence would lead immediately to limitations on all foreign enterprise and ultimately to indigenous ownership of all private foreign companies. Indeed this had been the stated policy of Congress since the early 1930s. Under such threats some British companies liquidated their assets while the going was good but, significantly for its whole future in the post-colonial world, it seems never to have crossed Unilever's collective mind to adopt this policy. The only precautionary steps taken in 1947 were to hedge against the possibility of immediate post-independence devaluation and exchange control by declaring interim and final dividends for 1946 somewhat earlier than usual, capitalising reserves as a bonus issue of shares and remitting surplus cash to Britain. This confidence in the basic moderation of Indian nationalists proved fully justified. For several years Indian businessmen and politicians, including Nehru, continued to make statements that appeared to threaten foreign capital, but gradually the climate of opinion seems to have changed. In April 1949 Nehru announced that Congress welcomed foreign capital provided that it accepted two ultimate objectives—Indian ownership of a proportion of the capital and progressive Indianisation of top management; and during the early 1950s the hostility of Indian private capital gradually evaporated as Indian entrepreneurs took courage from their success and came to regard foreign capital as a useful ally against state socialism. The new state of mind was summarised by a leading Indian entrepreneur in 1957:

> I feel . . . that not only should we allow foreign investment without any restriction, but we should welcome it, provide a climate for it and make the investor feel that the opportunities for profitable utilization of capital here compare favourably with those available anywhere else in the world.[14]

By the mid-1950s, therefore, Unilever could feel reasonably confident that it had a long-term future in India. Security, nevertheless, does not by itself ensure profitable operation: there remains the question of how tight management of a less developed economy such as evolved in India after 1947 would affect Unilever's activities. This makes it necessary briefly to summarise the main features of state control in India as these affect concern companies.

The key to the system was the Planning Commission, set up in 1950. The Prime Minister was Chairman and its members included leading politicians. The Commission was theoretically an advisory body but in practice it was an adjunct of the Cabinet, expressing the intentions of government at the highest level. It was responsible for drawing up the Five-Year Plans for the years 1951–6, 1957–61, and 1962–6, which cover the period of this study. But India was a vast federal country whose interests were anything but uniform. To accommodate special and particularly regional pressures the government set up in 1952 a National Development Council consisting of the Prime Minister, the Chief Minister of each state and the members of the Planning Commission, as a device for sounding regional opinion and for obtaining co-operation from the states. It appears to have exerted considerable influence; and in particular it was able to affect distribution of new productive enterprises so that development was not concentrated in certain already more prosperous areas with significant effects on the pattern of Unilever's growth.

But plans alone had no teeth. Their effect on the economy and on individual concerns was necessarily determined by the administrative agencies through which they were enforced, and the particular economic devices adopted. From the standpoint of private companies a major defect of Indian planning after 1951 was that an increasing proportion of what had previously been normal business decisions now required specific approval by the appropriate ministry under powers delegated by the Lok Sabha—the lower house of the all-Indian parliament; and that to obtain this approval was often a very slow and uncertain business. Under the Industries Act, 1951, all 'scheduled' industries had to be licensed. No new industries could be established or substantial extension undertaken without permission. The same Act gave the government power to continue the control of prices and the volume of production which had begun under the Defence of India Rules during the war. Under the Essential Commodities Act of 1955 and other legislation the range of controls was further extended. Soap, vanaspati and other staple Unilever products came under these regulations. Exchange control began in 1940. It was liberalised in 1945–6, but became very strict after 1947 and a licence was required for any amount of foreign exchange. To ration foreign exchange the government imposed quota restrictions on imported goods of all kinds: to import one also required a licence. Exports might also be controlled or banned, particularly commodities such as vegetable oils and oil seeds (mostly banned entirely from 1952), to ensure availability of vital foodstuffs and to keep down domestic prices. Controls were imposed in many other fields such as the specification of vanaspati and advertising techniques. Thus few aspects of manufacturing or distribution did not in some way require permission or approval by a government agency.

The worst feature of economic management as it affected all private enterprises in India was not, however, the system itself but the way in which it was operated. Bhagwati and Desai, among others, have described the complications of the licensing system and the delays it normally involved. For example, the Estimates Committee of the Lok Sabha found that of 264 applications for foreign collaboration in industrial development, 79 took between six months and a year to decide and 32 more than a year. In January 1964 751 applications for a capital goods import licence from the Capital Goods Committee had been pending for more than a year and 182 for two years or more.[15] Such bureaucratic obstacles made business life complicated; but a still more important feature of economic regulation was its underlying philosophy which seems to have been that in allocating scarce resources, particularly foreign exchange to pay for imports, a more or less constant balance should be kept between each main industry and that, as between competing units within a single industry, licences should be granted on an 'equitable' basis, with a preference for the weaker and less profitable firms. While this approach can be justified on general welfare grounds it was bound to prevent the more efficient and progressive firms such as Unilever from expanding their share of the market and so raising the average standard of efficiency.

The system of import controls was made more complicated in the 1960s by the establishment of import entitlement schemes. Briefly, the government, perturbed by the declining value of Indian exports, attempted to stimulate exporters by giving special import licenses to firms in proportion to the value of their exports. The main principle was that an exporting firm was allowed import licenses of up to 75 per cent, or even more, of the f.o.b. value of its exports, subject to the restriction that the import entitlement should not exceed twice the value of the import content of the goods exported. Although attractive, the scheme raised problems for potential exporters. Given that the resultant import licences commanded a premium because they made it possible to buy raw materials or even capital goods which could command a higher price in India than their overseas cost, was it worthwhile to export at a loss—and if so at how great a loss? This problem was clearly acute for a firm such as Hindustan Lever which had to buy Indian vegetable oils at above world market prices and inevitably sold their products at a loss overseas.

All this meant that after 1947 one could only carry on a profitable business in India by careful study of the regulations and patient and persistent negotiations with the authorities. But even if these administrative hurdles had been surmounted successfully, levels of taxation were certain to reduce the profitability of the business. During the decade 1956–65 the statistical rate of tax, assuming all profits were distributed on dividends, was never less than 61 per cent, and in 1963 it rose to 73 per cent. Under such circumstances it was unlikely that a foreign firm, however, successful it was in dealing with the intricacies of a 'managed' economy, could show after-tax yields comparable with those it had obtained during the period of economic liberalism before 1939.

But there was another side to the picture. If one asks why, given the problems of operating there, India remained an attractive field for investment by large international corporations, one obvious answer was the high level of protection provided for foreign as well as Indian-owned business. Protection could not ensure profits—as will be seen it did not do so in the case of vanaspati—but the system was sufficiently important to the profitability of Unilever's Indian business to require a brief description.

Table 4.8   India: Rates of Effective Protection on Soap and Glycerine, 1961 (per cent).

I Standard tariff	Due to QRs[a]	Due to tariffs	Due to tariffs and QRs.
max.	113.46	285.60	372.06
min.	84.81	193.30	278.10
II British preferential tariff			
max.	113.28	258.85	372.13
min.	84.67	193.47	278.14

Note: a. Quantity restrictions placed on imports.
Source: J. N. Bhagwati and P. Desai, *India: Planning for Industrialization* (OECD, Paris: London 1970), Table 17.1.

Protection had, of course, been fundamental to Unilever's manufacturing activities in India from 1931 and this continued and became more intensive after independence: by the early 1960s the nominal tariff on soap and glycerine had risen to 100 per cent *ad valorem*. High though this was it nevertheless became almost meaningless as a measure of the 'effective protection' received by Indian soap manufacturers because the system of import licensing described above provided much higher levels of protection. It was obvious that if the government banned all imports of a particular commodity, protection against foreign competition would be total whatever the nominal tariff. In that case, limitation on the price at which locally produced commodities could be sold would rise from domestic competition, consumer resistance or government regulation, not from foreign competition. Import quotas imposed after 1947 did not, in fact, totally exclude imports; but in degrees varying with different commodities licensing restricted the volume of imports to levels very substantially lower than they might have been if only a conventional tariff was in operation. The effect was that each item allowed to be imported had a scarcity value, so that it could command a premium over the hypothetical 'free trade' price of that commodity if freely imported. And just as a protective tariff enabled a domestic producer to raise his home selling prices to the level imposed by the tariff on imports, so, under conditions of quantity restrictions, the Indian producer could—assuming the consumers made no distinction between local and imported products and that there were no limits to the protected domestic market—raise his selling price to the extent of this premium fixed by import restrictions. This premium constitutes the rate of 'effective' protection received by the Indian producer of soap, vanaspati and other comparable products. Bhagwati and Desai made complex calculations of the rates of effective protection operating in 1961 on the basis of value added to a wide range of consumer and other goods, taking into account the effect both of quantity restrictions and nominal tariffs, and distinguishing between the effects of standard and commonwealth preferential tariffs. For soap and glycerine the effects of protection as a percentage of value added were as shown in Table 4.8. These figures should not be taken too literally: they indicate orders of magnitude rather than the precise level of protection. But they suggest one important fact: manufacturers in India were, by the 1960s, virtually insulated from the realities of a competitive international market. This was certainly true of the two main Unilever products, soap and vanaspati, though less so of toilet preparations for which the import quotas were relatively generous. Thus, to offset all the difficulties posed by a system of intense economic nationalism, the domestic market was almost exclusively reserved for Indian based firms; and this made it likely that the more efficient of them in each field would be able to make acceptable profits. In this fact lay the main attraction of investment in India and in an increasing number of new post-colonial states to multinational corporations such as Unilever. In a nutshell, the transition by many less developed countries from the 'open' economy of pre-war and colonial days to the 'managed' economy of the modern sovereign state implied loss of freedom by the foreign investor and liability to expropriation in part or whole. But it also gave each enterprise, Indian and foreign alike, once it was established, a place in the economy where it was almost immune to foreign competition.

It remains to see what effects these changes had on Unilever and it is proposed to examine the evidence under three main heads: first, the effects of the government's stated aim that the capital and management of foreign-owned enterprises should be nationalised as fast and as far as possible; second the impact of state regulation and effective protection on the general development of the Unilever enterprises, and in particular on their diversification; finally the profitability of the business and the allocation of profits.

One predictable consequence of Indian independence was that Unilever would be unable, even if it wished, to maintain those two characteristic features of many overseas subsidiaries of international companies—expatriate management and full control of equity in locally registered companies—because both features were anathema to Indian nationalists. A study of how and why Unilever reacted to pressures for change throws light on the likely response of a large international corporation to the challenge of changing circumstances in the post-colonial period.

(b) Localisation of Management

Localisation of management, often referred to by Unilever men as 'Ization', began first in point of time and was probably the more important of these two closely related issues. The concept could have two different interpretations and stages. On the one hand it might mean merely recruitment of some Indians to replace Europeans in a limited number of managerial posts and grades, while leaving top management, and therefore policy formulation, in the hands of expatriates. Alternatively, if Indianisation was to affect the nature of this foreign enterprise, it would be necessary to open the highest posts to Indians not merely on merit, but as an act of deliberate policy; and once the principle was established that only an Indian could be chairman and managing director of Hindustan Lever—as the combined business was called after 1956—then the expatriate company would be 'nationalised' in a sense more real than if Indians merely owned a majority of the equity. In the first sense Indianisation was well advanced by the mid-1950s. The second stage was completed in 1961 when Prakash Tandon became first Indian chairman of Hindustan Lever, heading a board of four Indians and three expatriates which later consisted of six Indians and two others. It is proposed to trace these two stages in the process, emphasising in particular the influences at work and the grounds on which the vital decision was taken in 1955 to move from partial to complete Indianisation.

It is difficult to pinpoint the start of Indianisation simply because there was never any deliberate policy to exclude Indians from managerial positions. When the concern factories were established early in the 1930s it was natural for management to consist of expatriates because these alone, in the absence of a significant Indian-owned vanaspati or soap industry, possessed the skills necessary to run the new business. Yet there was no racial bias against Indians: Tandon was recruited in 1937 without fuss and without raising any issues of principle on the grounds that he was that rare Indian, a graduate willing to enter a business concern other than one owned by his own family. Tandon, indeed, recalls that when he was interviewed for the post the Chairman of LB(I), W. G. I. Shaw, encouraged him by saying 'I don't see why you should not sit in my chair one day'. So long, however, as there was no shortage of European managers, the bias was against large-scale training of Indians since the essence of Unilever's personnel policy was that men were moved from one overseas subsidiary to another as opportunity offered, thus integrating career prospects throughout the whole international concern. Hence, as had been seen above, it was the wartime shortage of trained European managers that really forced the Indian companies to consider long-term needs. By July 1942 a clear decision had been taken:

> Since it is the intention to train Indians to take over junior and senior management positions instead of Europeans, the management consider it desirable that Indians who prove themselves qualified to do so should enjoy equal privileges to the Europeans

they substitute, and in addition that they should qualify for the same salary level.

Although head office had some doubts about the principle of the rate for the job this principle was adopted and thereafter no discrimination was made against Indian employees in this or any other field, except as regards overseas allowances and home leave. By the time of Gourley's visit in 1944 a substantial number of Indians had been recruited; his list of 57 senior managers includes 15 Indian names. Most were at assistant manager level but Tandon was a sales manager for HVM proprietary foods and there were two Indian office managers.

Recruitment thus began at the lower levels of management and its effects became increasingly obvious over time. Predictably, given the tradition of racial discrimination in India, there was some resentment. Some Europeans disliked being subordinate to Indians: others felt that there was no future for them in India if Indianisation continued indefinitely. Conversely Indian managers often felt insecure and looked for evidence of discrimination: Tandon has brilliantly described the embarrassments felt by an Indian manager in this transition period in his book, *Beyond the Punjab*. In view of these and other problems a report of 1947 commented that 'there are still doubts about the course to be followed in the immediate future, the arguments for and against Indianization in the factories being evenly balanced'. Indeed at this stage the prospect was for a long-continuing balance between Indian and expatriate management with no clear view of ultimate objectives. The appointment of Tandon as the first Indian director in 1950 was a milestone, but it was regarded as to some extent a gesture 'to show that we were sincere in our policy of Indianization . . .'. It did not imply a policy of appointing a majority of Indians to the boards of local companies and was only possible because in Tandon there was a candidate well able to do a particular job. There remained one formidable barrier to break—the concept of an Indian chairman and a majority of Indian directors. Unilever was still reluctant to face the risks inherent in deliberately restricting its choice of directors in Indian companies, and still more the chairman, to existing Indian managers. Since the Indian Government was, as Roger Heyworth noted in 1953, still only applying gentle moral pressure on foreign companies to Indianise their management, it was still uncertain when full Indianisation would be adopted.

As far as one can judge from the record the decisive fact was a report made by A. M. Knox after a visit to India during March 1955 whose express purpose was 'to study the problem of the further Indianization of our business . . .'. After tracing the increase of Indians in senior management to 97 out of 149, he noted that all the members of the Senior Management Committee and 8 out of 11 head executives were Europeans. Knox recommended a rapid further reduction in the number of Europeans to below 40—that is, a quarter of the whole—within 18 months: 'This will, I believe, give a sufficiently Indianized set-up to satisfy Indian nationalist sentiment as currently expressed . . .'. But in Knox's view this was not enough, for the business 'would still be essentially what it is today with the real responsibility resting on Europeans . . .'; and this led him to take a decisive intellectual leap to a clear analysis of the fundamental issues involved.

The real problems of Indianization arise in the second phase, when we begin to hand over final responsibility and essential initiative to Indians. When we begin to try to build an Indian business with some European assistance, rather than a European business with some Indian assistance: a business in which an Indian may expect to reach the top and a European can only expect to use his special skill in some specified position.

We must first consider whether we want such a business, and if so, we must consider the short- and long-term problems involved.

Altogether apart from current nationalist sentiments, I believe it to be in our interests, as well as in accord with our declared policy, to Indianize in the true meaning of the word, i.e. the uttermost practical extent. India is probably the most favourable field for an experiment in imaginative foresight such as this and experience in India will help us in tackling similar problems, which are bound to arise elsewhere. We must realize, however, that we add to our risk and our responsibilities. The risk is that our business may lose pace as well as efficiency: we will find Indians with the ability for the top jobs, but they may lack the full capacity for them. Even on the plane of physical energy we may find Indians of mature judgment lacking the capacity of their European counterparts.

Our responsibility is that the business should continue to prosper even though it may lack a full measure of local leadership:

we may have to be a good deal closer to our Indian business with Indian managers than we are at present, or even likely to be under our policy of decentralized responsibilities.

I believe we should face these risks and responsibilities in a sincere attempt to teach and encourage our Indian Management towards ultimate self-reliance.

Here was an unqualified statement of faith in the viability of total Indianisation—the first experiment in transferring full control of a Unilever subsidiary to non-European management and possibly the first such decision reached by any foreign company then operating in India or the developing world. But Knox also saw that, once Indianisation was complete, with Indians in most senior positions and only a few Europeans left to provide contact, one major and still unanswerable question would remain: was it possible for Hindustan Lever to remain an integral part of a European-based concern with all the advantages that implied in terms of experience and standards; or would it become isolated, part of Unilever only in name? Knox saw the problem and suggested the following solution:

Put simply, our task will be to keep our Indian staff loyal to our business in India and 'Concern-minded'. The loyalty will depend basically on our terms and conditions of employment, which will have to be fully as good as those generally on offer in India, having in mind all the time that there will be growing competition for trained Indians . . . Pensions and the whole aura of security are the key factors in terms of employment for Indians.

If our Indianized company is to remain a Unilever company the men and women in it will have to be Unilever people first and foremost, and it is only possible to ensure this by personal contact.

It will be of the utmost importance that our Indian staff should feel as close to Head Office as do our Europeans, and the senior staff will have to be as well known at home as are our senior Europeans now. Regular visits . . . should therefore form part of our understanding with them and it may well be both desirable and necessary that they should bring their wives with them.

For the same reasons, visits by people from the Service Sections at home would have to be even more frequent than in the past . . .

No record of formal discussion of these radical proposals in London survives. One must, however, assume that Knox's arguments were accepted at the highest level for when in July 1956 the first board of Hindustan Lever was appointed, it included three Indians in a board of eight and the salary structure of Indian managers was altered so that no distinction was made between them and Europeans except that Europeans received an overseas allowance. Thereafter the speed of change was made more rapid than Knox had projected by the voluntary retirement of senior Europeans, so that the difficulty now lay more in finding men of sufficient experience on the technical sides of the business rather than in clearing the way to promote Indians to the top. The critical post was that of chairman and managing director; and here it proved impracticable to implement Knox's suggestion that the chairmanship should remain in European hands for a considerable period. In April 1957 it was planned that when the Chairman, Hoskyns-Abrahall, retired in the following year, he should be succeeded for three years by the Vice-Chairman, S. H. Turner, and that he should be followed by D. A. Orr, then a director of Hindustan Lever. But by the time Turner had to retire in 1961 through illness, Orr had left the Indian management to become a member of the Overseas Committee. The next most senior member of the board was P. L. Tandon, and, in view of his distinguished record with the company, it would have been unthinkable to have sent out a new chairman from London over his head. In March 1961, therefore, the Special Committee formally minuted that Turner's future should be discussed when he returned home on sick leave in July; but that 'in the meantime Mr Tandon, Vice-Chairman, would effectively act as Chairman and the intention would be that in due course, subject to his accepting the appointment, Mr J. B. Davies should be made Vice-Chairman'. A month later, after a report by London directors on the visit to India, the Special Committee agreed that 'Mr Tandon should come to London soon to discuss the future organization of the business'. So the last citadel of European control was evacuated. Hindustan Lever was now controlled by an Indian chairman with a board of six directors of whom two only were expatriates; and of the 205 managers in India only 14 were Europeans.

The genesis of Indian management of Hindustan Lever has been described in some detail because this was arguably one of the most important steps ever taken by a multinational in the less developed world. General comment on the significance of this development will be made in the concluding chapter, but one very important point to emerge from the Indian story is the relevance of the transfer of political sovereignty. The replacement of Europeans by Indians had begun under colonial conditions and would presumably have proceeded steadily because local management is always cheaper than foreign. But once India was independent the psychological environment changed dramatically. The onus was now less on Indian managers to prove their ability to replace Europeans than on the company to demonstrate that they had no Indian employee capable of filling each senior post as it became vacant. Localisation of management was able to proceed fast in India after 1947 because Hindustan Lever had a wealth of able men. It was necessarily slower in some other countries where Unilever companies were smaller and had more limited managerial talent. But everywhere political independence came to have the same implication, that local nationals would be promoted to the highest posts as quickly as was consistent with business efficiency; and conversely that once senior management had been localised expatriates should only be used in small numbers and for special reasons. It was this principle, rather than the mere fact of using local men, that tended thereafter to differentiate practice in Unilever subsidiaries in non-European societies from those in countries such as Australia where the nationality of the management was of far smaller significance.

(c) Local Participation in Ownership

Localisation of management was, nevertheless, compatible with Unilever retaining ultimate control over its subsidiaries: local ownership of the capital beyond a certain point was not. In 1945 all Unilever subsidiaries in all countries were entirely owned by the concern except where it had bought into an existing company. India was the first country in which the concern was obliged by official pressure to sell part of its equity and to do so against its will on terms which it found unsatisfactory. The circumstances are clearly important and must be described in some detail.

It has been seen that in 1947 the Indian Congress was threatening to force all foreign enterprises to sell a majority shareholding, either to the government or the Indian public. It was not, however, until 1954 that the Indian authorities began to exert any pressure on Unilever and other foreign-owned companies to sell part of their equity; and it seems that the impulsion then came from the Finance Minister, T. T. Krishnamachari, who had once been a marketing agent for Unilever. According to a later oral source Krishnamachari thought that Unilever was a progressive organisation which would voluntarily set a good example to other foreign firms; and in 1954 he asked his Permanent Secretary to talk informally to the Chairman of LB(I), J. Hoskyns-Abrahall, about offering shares to the public. Unfortunately the negotiations turned sour. Hoskyns-Abrahall apparently replied inflexibly that international companies did not sell equity in their subsidiaries. He then reported to London that the issue was one of 'national prestige rather than business economics' and was told to contact other foreign-owned firms in India to organise a common front. This response suggests that, as was to be expected, Unilever did not yet understand the attitudes of newly independent states on issues of this kind or accept the need to make at least a symbolic concession to Indian sovereignty. Conversely it would have been impossible for Krishnamachari to accept a flat rejection of the government's suggestion, and the scene was therefore set for a symbolic trial of strength between Unilever and the Republic of India.

The key to what followed was that, in India at least, the government held all the cards and the moral is that a multinational is likely to suffer if it refuses to accept official policy. By January 1955 Unilever had been forced to accept that something had to be done but still hoped to evade the central issue of control by selling non-voting preference shares. A month later it was clear that this tactic would not serve, for the government was determined as a matter of principle that Indians must have a share in the equity. It remained only to try to limit the proportion of the shares to be sold and to obtain the best possible terms for selling them. A Contact Director was therefore sent to investigate and he advised that all concern companies in India should be amalgamated into a single company, part of whose equity could then be sold to the public. Encouraged by a 'firm assurance' from the government that 'there would be no difficulty in remitting the sterling proceeds to England' the Special Committee decided to sell up to 20 per cent of the shares in the new 'Hindustan Lever'. L. G. Norton, a tax expert, was sent out to negotiate, particularly on tax questions, and reported back in May 1955. He thought the main problem was that in establishing Hindustan Lever it would be necessary to revalue the assets and capital reserves of the existing companies, with the danger that the government might insist on taxing capital appreciation. London therefore decided to rely on the argument that they were 'only making the proposals at all in order to meet the wishes of the Government . . .' to obtain two special concessions: exemption from taxation on capitalisation of assets and freedom to repatriate the cash price of all shares sold. In addition they expected to sell shares at a market valuation.

This special pleading proved unsuccessful. First, the government insisted that shares should be priced on an official assessment of the asset value of the business after amalgamation. This was Rs. 91.9 million, or Rs. 10 a share. The concern was allowed to sell at a premium of only Rs. 6/8/- a share, and as a result decided to offer only 557,000 shares, 10 per cent rather than 20 per cent of the equity. For the buyers this meant a windfall gain: in 1962, after shareholders had received a bonus issue of 12 for 25, the market value was still Rs. 47/5/- a share; but Unilever had had to forego part of the capital value accumulated during the past two decades. Second, when Krishnamachari introduced his 1956 budget—a year after negotiations for the sale of shares had begun and after the conditions of the market issue had been agreed with the government —he announced a new tax on bonus share issues which represented undistributed profits. Unilever claimed that they should be exempt from this tax, which would cost them some Rs. 2 million (£150,000), on the grounds that it would have an unfair retrospective effect. This plea was rejected by Krishnamachari, possibly (it has been suggested by those who knew him) because he regarded the tax as a just penalty on the company for dragging its feet. In the end, there-fore, Unilever succeeded only in obtaining permission to repatriate the value of the bonus issue after tax, that is some Rs. 13.7 million.

In the context of a multinational's relations with a host society this compulsory sale of shares in the new Hindustan Lever and the conditions imposed on the concern are an important symbolic landmark for they demonstrated, as Krishnamachari no doubt intended, that the government was the master. But in practical terms disinvestment on this scale had limited significance. So far as control of the Indian business was concerned, Unilever was in no danger because only 10 per cent of the equity had been distributed among some 16,000 separate shareholders. The immediate effect was that these private shareholders had a legitimate expectation of dividends and bonus shares, so that the concern had to use its profits as dividends and to capitalise undistributed profits as bonus shares more regularly than they might otherwise have chosen to do. The larger significance of these events lay in two problems they created for the future. First, whether the government would sooner or later insist on extending the 10 per cent public shareholding to the 20 per cent projected in 1956 or even beyond; second, how Unilever could increase its investment in Hindustan Lever without at the same time changing the 90:10 ratio of shareholding.

It was not until 1961 that the Indian government raised the question of a further sale of Hindustan Lever shares; and on this occasion the proposal was connected with Hindustan Lever's desire to raise new capital for expansion and diversification. In June Tandon, now Chairman-elect, reported, after a visit to Delhi, that it had been put to him that co-operation by the government on various questions—mostly relating to import licences and the supply of foreign exchange to pay for capital goods—would be easier if Indian shareholding was further increased. This suggestion was backed by a veiled threat by the Secretary to the Ministry of Commerce and Industry, who was reported to have said:

> I have a long nose for political feelings because I meet people on that plane, and my advice is that it would be in everybody's interest if there were greater identification of the Indian public with Hindustan Lever. I can't press you to do it because government will not raise it as an issue, nor will it discriminate, but it will greatly strengthen your position if you were to take in more Indian capital . . . . I gave similar advice to the Oil Companies 10 years ago but they were then not interested in Indian participation. Their position today might have been different had they identified themselves with the Indian capital even by offering capital to Government.

The Special Committee took this seriously. It discussed the problem in August 1961 but decided that 'it was essential that we received remittable value for any shares offered; non-transferrable rupees would not be acceptable'. Meantime Tandon had already decided that another bonus issue was necessary to capitalise profits and reserves. The 1956 valuation of assets had clearly been too low and in a period of good earnings Hindustan Lever was having to pay a dividend of 26 per cent on its nominal capital, which shocked

Indian opinion accustomed to about 10 per cent. At this point the question became tied up with providing non-rupee finance for the large expansion projects then impending which are described below. As the Secretary to the Ministry had hinted, one concession required another. In December 1961 London heard that the Commonwealth Development Finance Corporation and the Industrial Credit and Investment Corporation of India (ICICI) might be prepared to help finance this planned development on condition that the concern would finance the balance of capital expenditure requiring foreign exchange through a sterling loan convertible into equity shares—a condition Unilever had hoped to avoid—which in turn would mean 'an increase in our holding [or equity] and facilitate extension of the amount issued on the local market'. In January 1962 the implications were further considered. ICICI had insisted that, as a condition of making a loan, they should be able to appoint a director and be consulted before Hindustan Lever could sell and/or raise loans—a standard practice in the USA which provided most of ICICI's foreign exchange. The Special Committee would not accept these conditions and in the event Tandon was able to persuade ICICI not to insist on them. Meantime it was agreed that Unilever would provide Rs. 7,500,000 of foreign exchange which would be capitalised and thus increase their shareholding; and that 'to keep the local participation at 10 per cent a significant number of additional shares would be issued to the Indian public'. An issue large enough to bring Indian participation to 12½ per cent was considered but rejected because there was no prospect of being allowed to repatriate their proceeds and 'it has always been made clear that this would be a condition for further disinvestment'.

The final stage in this complex negotiation began in July 1962. Again the crucial fact was Indian official insistence on an increase of local participation—this time to 15 per cent—and the lever the government used was its agreement to license the various projects for diversification of the business then pending. Again the government insisted on conditions that made little commercial sense. New shares were to be issued to existing shareholders to capitalise the new investment and a further 5 per cent of the total equity was to be placed on the market. The main point at issue was the offering price for shares. The government, through the Secretary to the Ministry of Commerce and Industry, proposed Rs. 35 on the basis of their valuation of the company's assets. Tandon, now Chairman, felt that this was about Rs. 6 or Rs. 7 below a market price, but eventually agreed on the ground that Indian shareholders normally expected some capital appreciation when buying a rights issue. London, however, disapproved. A Contact Director, supported by an accountant from Cooper Brothers, was sent to negotiate for a higher price, making this the condition of proceeding with the concern's projected investment of some Rs. 10 million in sterling to pay for new equipment from overseas. The mission proved fruitless and in the event costly. The Indian authorities refused to make any concessions and in October 1962 Tandon was authorised by Unilever House to sell at Rs. 35. By then the new issue could not be made before March 1963; and by that time the outbreak of war with China had been followed by a draconian finance bill which proposed a 50 per cent super tax on profits above 6 per cent on capital and reserves nett of income and profits tax, rising to 60 per cent on profits above 10 per cent. The Indian Stock Market closed and the rights issue was postponed indefinitely. Hindustan Lever's expansion projects went ahead and their foreign exchange costs were met largely by Unilever Ltd.

The proposed share issue was not revived until July 1964, and then under quite different circumstances. This time the impetus to sell Hindustan shares came not from Indian government ideology but from practical business considerations. Under the 1963 Finance Act supertax was calculated on capital employed. Hindustan Lever was comparatively under-capitalised but had a large overdraft, incurred during the expansion programme, which did not count as capital for tax purposes. A rights issue would thus improve the tax position, reduce the overdraft and raise Hindustan Lever's credit standing and at the same time please the government by increasing Indian participation. But in other respects circumstances were far less propitious. The Stock Market was generally less strong than in 1962; the yield after statistical tax on Hindustan Lever shares was down from 9.8 per cent in 1962 to 7.0 per cent; and the market price of Hindustan Lever shares stood at Rs. 32 in July as compared with Rs. 45 in 1962. The government did not attempt to dictate the terms of the proposed rights issue, but even the Rs. 35 permitted in 1962 was now too high: Rs. 27 was the highest price thought possible and it was agreed to accept Rs. 25 if this could be obtained. But by the time arrangements had been made in 1965 continuing adverse factors had pushed Hindustan Lever shares down to Rs. 23/8/-. In August 1965 Tandon had to launch the new issue at Rs. 18—just over half the officially approved figure of 1962—and the shares were not fully subscribed.

By the end of 1965 issued capital had therefore increased from Rs. 33,700,000 to Rs. 91,413,000, and Indian participation had risen to about 14 per cent. The significance of these developments for Hindustan Lever and for Unilever's interest in India was considerable. First, in terms of the effect on running the business and for reasons already considered, Indian shareholding on this scale made little practical difference. But a more subtle effect could, as Lord Cole noted in December 1965, be seen in the attitude of top Indian management to the company's role.

There is no doubt in my mind that the fact of having a public participation has produced in the minds of our top Indians, not excluding the Chairman, the feeling that they are a public company and as such their attitude of mind on a number of points is rather different from that of a 100% subsidiary . . . . It is interesting, for instance, that Tandon himself said that the soap business which, as I have mentioned, is the complete back-bone of the company, is in his eyes looked upon by government and the public as something quite simple which anybody can do: in fact, a rather exaggerated view of the cosy grocer's shop not contributing very much to the economy. This is really the actuating motive which has sent them into their management studies and their business techniques and their desire for expansion in other products so that they may be seen as making a contribution at the level of management development and training and to the community. In this they have undoubtedly succeeded.

This was not, of course, entirely due to the sale of Hindustan Lever shares. It was the coincidence of Indianisation of management and partial Indianisation of ownership that encouraged the management of Hindustan Lever to feel that their responsibility for furthering the economic development of India was as important as their duty to pursue the interests of Unilever. But there is no doubt that the change occurred or that it was immensely significant for Hindustan Lever's relations with the host country.

The most important aspect of the sale of Hindustan Lever shares between 1956 and 1965 was, in fact, what it implied for the future. By the mid-1960s the attitude of the Indian government, which had seemed outrageous a decade earlier because there was no law in India against 100 per cent foreign ownership of a local company, now seemed very moderate when measured against the actions and attitudes of governments in Indonesia and elsewhere. Few in the concern would by then have disputed the power of a host country to insist on local participation, even though this was still disliked for the same reasons as in the past; and 14 per cent seemed a comparatively modest proportion to be held by Indian citizens. Nevertheless two major problems could be foreseen if, as was to be expected, the Indian government eventually pressed for a larger local shareholding. First, there was the technical difficulty that it seemed impracticable to use the sale of shares in India to finance expansion if this required imported equipment. Indians bought shares for rupees, which could not be converted into hard currency; and if Unilever provided the foreign currency required and this was converted into shares, the balance of shareholding would be affected. It was not until after 1965 that a solution was worked out with the government whereby the company would increase its total share capital and sell all the new shares to Indians. The government would then provide sufficient hard currency to pay for approved imports of capital goods and accepted rupees as payment. By the later 1970s it was therefore open to the company to finance expansion and diversification by increasing its equity and at the same time conform to the government's objectives.

There remained the problem of ultimate control. At some point the dilution of Unilever's shareholding in Hindustan Lever would presumably reach the point at which the centre could no longer effectively control the Indian company. That point had not been reached by 1977; but if and when it came the concern would have to decide whether it was prepared, as a minority shareholder, to take full responsibility for management. If it decided it could not do so it might either retain its shares as a portfolio investment or sell out. Either way Hindustan Lever would stand to lose whatever benefits it received as part of a multinational company; and to the extent that these were regarded as important, the Indian government would presumably pause before insisting on the last stage of disinvestment. This, in fact, is the only weapon of last resort that a multinational can wield against the overwhelming power of a sovereign state.

(d) Growth and Diversification, 1941–65

In examining the industrial and commercial evolution of Unilever's Indian business from 1941 to 1947 the central question is what impact, if any, Indian independence in 1947 and the consequential introduction of moderate state socialism and intensive economic management had on the character and fortunes of the concern companies. The general trends can be summarised very briefly. Unilever went to India to manufacture soap and vanaspati. By 1939 it was accepted that the tariff would make it necessary also to manufacture toilet preparations there. This was the extent of the concern's ambitions—to specialise in those fields in which it was most competent. Yet by 1965, while the bulk of Hindustan Lever's production still consisted of soap, vanaspati and toilet preparations, it was also heavily committed to milk products, dehydrated peas and possibly other vegetables, and animal feeding stuffs. It was making razor blades through an *à façon* arrangement, had toyed with a large range of other possible products, including fish, and, in the words of the then Chairman, the managers 'were confident that they will get the new projects firmly on their feet and then turn their talents and abundant energy to new pastures'. Clearly the trend was from specialisation towards diversification in fields far from the initial industrial base. The question is how much of this resulted from normal corporate preference and how much from environmental factors peculiar to a developing country such as India.

The story falls into two periods: the years of wartime and immediate post-war constraints from 1941 to 1947; and the period from 1947 to 1965 when Unilever gradually turned from its attempt to evolve along traditional lines to search for new opportunities. It is proposed to examine each of these two periods in turn, laying greater stress on the second of them.

It is clear from Tables 4.9 and 4.10 that the years from 1941 to 1947 were a watershed in the early growth of the Indian business. Ignoring 1947, which was abnormal because of raw material shortages, strikes and the disruption caused by partition, two features stand out. First, the growth of vanaspati sales was checked for the first time since 1931 and this was accompanied by what proved to be a sustained downturn in profitability and HVM's share of the

Table 4.9   India: Sales of Unilever Soap and Vanaspati, 1941–8 (Tons)

Year	Soap	Vanaspati
1941	20,040	43,065
1942	24,095	31,211
1943	22,598	37,647
1944	22,044	41,669
1945	26,188	46,827
1946	27,410	44,533
1947	21,645	24,055
1948	30,654	38,393

market. Conversely the volume and value of soap sales rose steadily, leading to parity with vanaspati by the early 1950s. These trends were to be typical of the two decades after 1947; and, since they began before Indian independence, it is important to discover their cause.

The relative decline of the vanaspati business had four evident causes, two affecting the volume of sales, two its profitability. As the first large manufacturer HVM could only safeguard its share of the market if it kept increasing its capacity. By 1942 capacity had been increased to 52,000 tons; but, presumably because raw material

Table 4.10   India: Profit (before tax) as a Percentage of Turnover, HVM and LB(I) 1945–55 (Rs. million)

Year	Turnover	HVM Profit before tax	%	Turnover	LB(I) Profit before tax	%
1945	71.76	9.86	13.7	40.45	3.17	7.9
1946	80.02	7.85	9.8	42.10	3.20	7.6
1947	57.85	5.16	8.9	40.50	4.90	12.1
1948	90.74	6.32	7.0	61.15	7.50	12.2
1949	98.74	5.12	5.2	77.65	9.05	11.6
1950	126.16	5.35	4.2	90.03	9.43	10.5
1951	146.32	2.18	1.5	115.68	13.59	11.7
1952	135.06	(0.10)[a]	–	115.46	18.38	15.9
1953	135.13	7.44	5.5	111.39	15.01	13.5
1954	119.86	(4.64)[a]	–	111.33	18.34	16.5
1955	121.32	6.40	5.3	121.11	19.49	16.1

Note: a. Figures in brackets indicate losses.

shortages made it impossible to utilise this to the full, the momentum of growth then lapsed. It was not until 1944 that a plan was worked out to build additional factories at Delhi and Madras and to expand the Bombay oil mills; and by that time it was too late, for in 1945 the government, rightly foreseeing the development of gross excess capacity in the industry as a whole, imposed licensing on all new productive investment, allocating licences on the basis of existing capacity. Thereafter HVM could only expand by buying existing factories and their quotas; and, although attempts to do this began in 1946, they came to nothing before 1951, partly because the government gave preference to Indian producers. In retrospect it can be seen that Unilever had missed the bus and it was never again to control more than about a quarter of the vanaspati industry.

Table 4.11   India: Profits and Turnover of HVM/Edibles Division of Hindustan Lever, 1951–65

Year	Turnover (Rs. million)	Profit (loss) before tax (Rs. million)	Gross profit as % of turnover
1951	146.32	2.18	1.5
1952	135.06	(0.10)	–
1953	135.13	7.44	5.5
1954	119.86	(4.64)	–
1955	121.32	6.40	5.3
1956	133.01	4.4	3.3
1957	165.09	5.3	3.2
1958	177.10	7.3	4.1
1959	204.52	15.2	7.4
1960	223.31	11.8	5.3
1961	230.21	5.0	2.2
1962	246.56	7.3	3.0
1963	256.86	6.3	2.5
1964	253.93	5.8	2.3
1965	290.26	8.2	2.8

It is, however, highly questionable whether, irrespective of state intervention, it would have been profitable to expand HVM's capacity in an industry whose production was rapidly overhauling demand. HVM's profits in relation to turnover were declining in the mid-1940s and, as can be seen from Table 4.11, they remained very low during the decade 1945–55, when pre-tax profits on soap rose substantially. Although it would have been impossible to predict this trend in 1945, two factors of long-term significance were already in operation. First, raw material costs rose sharply due to wartime shortages, squeezing margins in an increasingly competitive market. Second, from 1947, and even before independence, the government began to control prices. For a terrible period in February and March 1947 groundnut oil prices were fixed so low that producers and middlemen refused to sell and the whole vanaspati

Table 4.12   India: Unilever's Share in Vanaspati Production, 1948–65 (metric tons)

Year	Unilever	Others	Total industry	% Share of Unilever
1948	38,393	91,313	129,706	29.6
1949	37,365	120,036	157,401	23.7
1950	46,870	127,287	174,157	26.9
1951	50,297	123,027	173,324	29.0
1952	55,747	137,748	193,495	28.8
1953	54,035	158,624	212,659	25.4
1954	62,327	171,599	233,926	26.6
1955	62,056	202,439	264,495	23.5
1956	61,273	197,954	259,227	23.6
1957	72,690	233,067	305,757	23.7
1958	75,886	222,595	298,481	25.4
1959	77,311	243,271	320,582	24.1
1960	80,318	256,258	336,576	23.9
1961	72,313	257,838	330,151	21.9
1962	80,747	288,168	368,915	21.9
1963	77,173	305,652	382,825	20.1
1964	67,994	289,981	357,975	18.9
1965	77,164	351,598	428,762	18.0

industry closed down. Then, after oil prices had been freed, retail selling prices were controlled and again the industry, held in an intolerable vice, closed down. In June 1947 price increases were permitted but they were deliberately restricted and thereafter, though conditions varied from time to time, vanaspati—because it was a foodstuff—was subject to price regulation. This is not to say that the industry was now unprofitable: merely that the high profits characteristic of the previous decade were never to return. And, as factory capacity reached and passed the limits of the market and raw material prices generally tended to rise due to chronic shortages, commercial factors reinforced official controls to keep profit margins low.

The early 1940s were also the years in which soap came from behind and became Unilever's main profit-maker in India, and this needs to be explained. To some extent soap production was affected by the same problems as vanaspati—high raw material prices, wartime shortages of imported inputs, government regulations. But there were three specific reasons why detergents did well in this

Table 4.13   India: Detergent Sales and Profits, 1947—65

Year	A M. tons	B Turnover (Rs. million)	C Profit before tax (Rs. million)	Profit as % of turnover
1947	21,625	40.50	4.90	12.1
1948	28,910	61.15	7.50	12.2
1949	35,651	77.65	9.08	11.7
1950	40,287	90.03	9.43	10.5
1951	45,552	115.68	13.59	11.7
1952	49,841	115.46	18.38	15.9
1953	50,136	111.39	15.01	13.5
1954	52,662	111.33	18.30	16.4
1955	57,319	121.11	19.49	16.1
1956	61,902	125.7	16.3	13.0
1957	65,811	143.1	16.69	11.7
1958	72,028	162.4	24.23	14.9
1959	75,072	178.3	27.95	15.7
1960	83,027	199.5	30.50	15.3
1961	87,937	228.9	32.53	14.2
1962	86,245	238.670	31.40	13.2
1963	91,665	267.460	34.07	12.7
1964	92,429	283.096	33.90	12.0
1965	103,177	337.276	32.85	9.7

period. First, the government did not impose price controls. Second, soap sold far more on quality and brand name than vanaspati, even when smaller tins and the brand name Dalda had been launched. Third, it was possible to cover markets throughout India from the two soap factories in Bombay and Calcutta, whereas the markets for vanaspati were much more localised. Thus, while HVM had little significant advantage over its many rivals in terms of established quality and brand names and was at a positive disadvantage in the bulk trade through producing only in Bombay, LB(I) retained all the advantages it had possessed in the 1930s. The main restraint on expanding production was, in fact, the limited size of the market for quality detergents. The size of the total market cannot be known precisely because there was a large and virtually uncharted production outside the modern sector of the economy. But if Unilever estimates were correct, LB(I) had roughly 20 per cent of the total soap market in 1938 and about 26 per cent in 1954. More significant, perhaps, was Unilever's predominance in the field of high-class soaps. In 1944 they had 35 per cent of the package soap trade; in 1950, 34.2 per cent of hard soaps and 57 per cent of soap tablets.

By about 1947, therefore, it seemed likely that the future of Unilever would depend largely on expansion in detergents and that, with wartime restrictions ended, LB(I) would continue to expand its share of an ever growing detergents market. It will, therefore, be necessary to find out why after 1947 Unilever found itself partially blocked in this field as well as in the production of vanaspati and therefore had to look to diversification in other fields as the only way of maintaining the momentum of its growth.

Table 4.14   India: UTL Turnover and Profits after Tax, 1937–44[a]

Year	Turnover (Rs. million)	Profit after tax (Rs.)	Profit as % of turnover
1937	1.8	100,486	5.5
1938	2.4	127,856	5.0
1939	2.6	165,395	6.3
1940	2.3	176,850	7.6
1941	3.2	6,735	0.2
1942	2.9	70,900	2.4
1943	3.3	168,328	5.0
1944	4.8	588,100	12.2

Note: a. Until 1943 all goods were imported; from 1943 they were made in Calcutta.

In 1947, however, Unilever had a third major interest in India which appeared to show considerable promise, toilet preparations, which included a wide variety of goods ranging from toothpaste to hair oil. In the 1930s these commodities had been imported from the concern's UK factories and distributed in India by UTL. But increasingly the tariff, wartime shipping controls and post-1947 import licensing made it necessary, or more profitable, to manufacture staple lines in India. A special factory was built in Calcutta in 1943 and thereafter an increasing proportion of concern brands handled by UTL were manufactured there. Table 4.14 shows the growth in UTL's turnover and variations in profits from 1937 to 1944, though the figures include products other than toilet preparations. The most striking feature of this table is the rapid growth of turnover and profitability after the building of the local factory. Another feature not indicated in these figures is the growth in the sale of toothpaste. Between 1943 and 1945 sales of Gibbs dentifrice rose from 107.6 gross to 6,632 gross and of Gibbs SR toothpaste from 293 gross to 5,735 gross. There was strong growth also in talcum and toilet preparations. On the evidence available in the mid-1940s this seemed a field for further investment and growth in which the concern's technical expertise, brand names and national marketing facilities might give Unilever a dominant market position. Since, moreover, Unilever's chief pre-war rivals in the field of dental preparations—notably Colgates—did not yet manufacture in India and therefore faced both tariffs and import restrictions, the opportunities seemed good. This promise was never fulfilled. Although later reorganisation of the business and the incorporation of UTL with Hindustan Lever in 1956 make it impossible to provide a continuous statistical series after 1944 covering the range of goods previously dealt in by UTL, it is clear that in toilet preparations Unilever failed to find a field for profitable expansion. Again the question must be why this was so.

Thus, at the moment of Indian independence and the partition of the subcontinent in 1947, a reasonable forecast of the pattern of future development in India would have been continued expansion with lower profit margins in vanaspati, but indefinite growth with improving profits in detergents and toilet preparations. By 1965 these predictions had proved partly false. Growth in all these fields had slowed to a crawl and the main drive of Hindustan Lever was towards diversification into comparatively remote fields. The problem is to discover why this was and whether it was due to market forces or the new 'managed' economy. It is proposed to survey briefly the course of development in each of these three basic lines in turn—edibles, detergents and toilet preparations—and then to trace the rise of the movement towards diversification.

(1) Vanaspati, 1947–65. It has been seen that by 1947 HVM faced two major problems: a declining share of the total market due to its limited capacity and declining pre-tax profits. There was, however, a third and then apparently critical problem—the danger that manufacture of vanaspati, like margarine in South Africa, might be completely banned or so regulated that it became unprofitable. Hostility to vanaspati had arisen early in the 1930s and came from two main interest groups: the farming community which feared its effects on the demand for natural ghee and thus for milk; and some followers of Gandhi who distrusted it as a modern, large-scale, factory-based industry, incompatible with their ideal of the village and rural society as the focus for economic activity. Wardha, Gandhi's base, was the centre of a publicity drive against vanaspati and an organisation called Gow-Sewa-Sangh (GSS) acted as a pressure group to disseminate propaganda and influence the government. Before 1947 the main danger to vanaspati was that provincial governments—which were already under Indian control —might pass legislation making it obligatory to colour vanaspati so that its presence as an additive to ghee was obvious. Some legislation was passed but was neither stringent nor effectively policed. Independence changed the situation. Under pressure of the anti-vanaspati lobby the central government set up a research committee to investigate whether vanaspati was harmful or nutritionally deficient. The committee reported in 1949 vindicating vanaspati, but by this time the question had become politically acute and there was danger of legislation by central and provincial governments alike. While it lasted the crisis was serious and the public debate carried on between GSS and the Vanaspati Manufacturers' Association spanned the gap between the eighteenth-century physiocrats and contemporary business economics. In the end a compromise was reached. The central government had no wish to destroy a major industry which produced cheap food nor to alienate manufacturers who included Tatas; but it had to buy off its own GSS supporters. In 1949 Delhi therefore passed legislation first banning the use of the terms 'vanaspati' or 'vegetable product' and then restricting these to letters one-eighth of an inch high on tins of vanaspati; and in due course further legislation, central and local, made it illegal to flavour vanaspati so as to make it resemble natural ghee. No dealer might sell ghee from the same premises as vanaspati. Selling prices were strictly controlled. The result was that vanaspati survived but it was condemned to perpetual

inferiority, branded as mere 'hydrogenated groundnut oil'. This had an important bearing on the future of HVM. Since the concern could not use its superior research and technical resources to raise the quality of its own product to compete directly with ghee—as margarine had been improved to rival butter in Europe—it was impossible to increase market shares or obtain a premium price on the basis of superior quality. This in turn meant that expanded sales depended on superior marketing of a virtually identical product and also that profit margins were likely to remain low, despite the wide appeal of the brand name Dalda. These two facts dominate the history of HVM and after 1956 of the Edibles Division of Hindustan Lever.

Nevertheless, once the immediate crisis of 1948/9 was over, HVM optimistically set about expanding its productive capacity. Two needs had to be met. First, because the government refused to give licences to so large an expatriate firm to expand its own capacity or to import new capital equipment, expansion depended on acquiring other factories with existing production quotas. Second, to reduce transport costs and to win local markets, it was necessary to establish production in several parts of India rather than expand the existing factory in Bombay. As a result, and despite the poor prospects resulting from high raw material prices and the threat of excessive capacity in the industry as a whole, HVM started a search for additional capacity late in 1949. By the end of 1951 three factories had been acquired in Ghaziabad (UP), Trichinopoly (south of Madras) and in Calcutta. By the beginning of 1952 HVM's total capacity had been raised to a prospective total of 74,000 tons a year—that is by about 50 per cent; and this investment in 1951 constituted a once and for all attempt to re-establish HVM as a major manufacturer of vanaspati with factories geographically sited to serve four main areas—Bombay, Delhi, Calcutta and Madras. The question was whether time would reverse the earlier trend, making vanaspati once again the leading product of Unilever in India.

In 1952 the omens seemed reasonably favourable. The government removed all price controls in June and in October the long controversy over quality control effectively ended with a government decision to insist on a standard vitamin and sesame content, which happened to conform closely to HVM's existing specification. During this decade therefore the performance of HVM and of the edibles business depended almost entirely on market factors, with two reservations. First, further expansion of capacity, should it be wanted, and technical improvements in methods of manufacture were both blocked by official control over licences to import the necessary capital equipment. Second, HVM was restricted for its raw materials to locally produced groundnut, cotton seed and sesame oil, which was critical for profits because it meant that the concern had to buy its raw materials at local prices which were increasingly above those prevailing on the international vegetable oil markets. This left HVM very little room for manoeuvre. As G. D. A. Klijnstra commented in 1954,

> It is difficult for us to find ways and means of working sub- stantially cheaper or to produce such a superior product that we can command a substantial premium over competition, especially as nowadays ground-nut, sesame and cotton oil are the only oils allowed to be used in the manufacture of domestic market products.

This indeed proved the great obstacle to satisfactory development in the field of edibles. HVM had increased its share of the market, but, with total capacity still far too large, profitability remained depressingly low. Table 4.12 presents the depressing story. The gamble on expanding vanaspati production largely failed. Although additional plant was bought from a rival factory in 1959 to increase capacity still further, this was virtually the end of the road by 1965. In a major report made by D. J. Mann and R. H. Siddons in 1961, emphasis was laid on the large excess capacity in the industry as a whole—effectively 482,000 tons as compared with current pro- duction running at 336,000 tons—which resulted in vicious price cutting. Hindustan Lever might well increase sales of bulk vanaspati of which it then only had 13.2 per cent: the trouble was that profit margins were extremely small. Conversely, although the branded small pack trade was more profitable, Hindustan Lever already had 82.5 per cent of this market and Dalda sales were tending to fall off. The prospects therefore were extremely gloomy: Unilever found itself in the early 1960s committed to vanaspati production by its very large capital investment—Rs. 51,900,000 (£3,000,000) in 1962— but with little prospect that this would make any substantial contri- bution to the profits of Hindustan Lever. This was the starting point of the search for new fields of activity.

What was the relative importance of the fact of Indian independence and the policies adopted by the government after 1947 in producing this dead end? Clearly government policy was not the main cause of vanaspati entering the doldrums: as has been seen, the high pre-1945 profit levels resulted in serious over-investment by competitors which was certain to reduce profits. Yet the government contributed to the problems of HVM in two main respects. First, by regulating imports of raw materials, it kept vegetable oil prices artificially high and so reduced the relative cheapness of vanaspati as compared with ghee. Second, by banning technical improvements, it made it impossible for Unilever to introduce more advanced brands of vanaspati, which, on the analogy of margarine in Europe, would probably have made them firm market leaders and thus provided a satisfactory premium. In short, by preventing vanaspati from developing into anything more than basic hydrogenated vegetable oil, Delhi condemned it to remaining a standardised product which offered little scope for the enterprising manufacturer. Under such conditions the superior skills and inter-national facilities which Unilever possessed could do nothing to provide reasonable rates of return in India.

(2) Soap and NSDs. The case with soap and other detergents was entirely different. Without building or acquiring new factories LB(I), and later Hindustan Lever, expanded its production from 21,625 tons in 1947 to 103,177 tons in 1965, while turnover increased from Rs. 40.5 million to Rs. 337.3 million. In 1947 pre-tax profits were 12.2 per cent of turnover: in 1965 they were 9.7 per cent. Mean-time, Unilever had more or less retained its share of the total market with some 20.9 per cent in 1948 and 19 per cent in 1961, with about 60 per cent of the 'organised' market at the later date. These figures do not, of course, imply continuous progress. There had been periods of comparatively low profits and static sales. But overall the detergent business was clearly a successful one on which the whole profitability of Unilever's Indian business came to depend. In 1962 it provided Rs. 31,400,000 out of total pre-tax trading profits of Rs. 42,810,000. These figures raise two questions: first, why Unilever was so much more successful in detergents than in edibles; second, given that this was so, why the concern did not make this their main area of new investment and expansion to an even greater extent.

The answer to the first question is simply that Unilever remained market leader in the high-class detergent market and its brand names commanded a premium over all rival products. Until about 1960 Hindustan Lever had little difficulty in getting permits for importing those raw materials not produced in India; but from 1962 import licences became harder to obtain and the company was forced to export refined oils at a loss in order to earn import licences. Nevertheless, as Table 4.15 shows, the concern was able to increase its profits on detergents while keeping the selling prices in line with the cost of living index; though since the indices for edible oils rose faster than the cost of living index for most of this period, the price of Dalda necessarily rose faster than the cost of living. This not only helps to explain why concern sales of detergents could expand as fast as they did but also indicates that LB(I) and later Hindustan Lever did not use their quasi-monopolistic position in certain fields to raise prices and profits unreasonably. This fact was recognised and valued by politicians and officials in New Delhi who saw that, so long as Hindustan Lever (the market leader) kept its prices at reasonable levels, no formal control on soap prices was necessary. In short, Unilever benefited from its relative efficiency in a comparatively free detergents market.

Table 4.15   India: Price Indices for Hindustan Lever Detergents and Edibles, 1953–61

Indices (Base 1952: 100)	1953	1954	1955	1956	1957	1958	1959	1960	1961
Selling price — per ton									
Sunlight	97	94	91	97	103	106	109	109	118
Lifebuoy	94	94	94	100	106	111	117	117	125
Lux Toilet	95	100	100	103	108	108	113	116	125
Dalda	118	99	88	107	119	111	124	138	158
Cost of living indices	103	98	93	102	108	113	117	120	121
Edible oils indices	119	99	79	115	125	121	124	141	159

But why did Unilever not decide to put more of its drive and the capital released by obligatory sale of its equity into still greater expansion in the field of detergents? Two obstacles stood in the way. The first was that the government was not prepared to allow

Hindustan Lever to obtain a larger share of the detergents market. Throughout the post-war period the company's success had excited jealousy among Indian manufacturers, who could exert considerable political pressures, and in the later 1950s expansion was blocked by official opposition which was only partially removed in 1961 when registered capacity was increased from 77,000 to 91,000 tons. Again, an obvious growing point was non-soapy detergents (NSDs) which were new to India in the 1950s and in which Unilever had a great initial advantage since it could import the technology ready-made from Europe and America. But although the government allowed importation of limited capital equipment for about 3,500 tons in the mid-1950s it was reluctant to provide further foreign currency and the lack of raw materials, particularly alkalies, also acted as a constraint. Thus there was no possibility in the late 1950s of a large-scale expansion in this potentially very profitable field.

Limitation of the market was probably equally important. Even without official control of any kind the market for high quality detergents was restricted. Unilever could never compete on price with the small producer of low quality soaps: it could only sell to those Indians who could afford to pay for a better product and the number of these rose comparatively slowly. But, if the domestic market was limited, why not obtain economies of scale by large-scale exports? There are two main reasons. First, it was a characteristic of the concern, as of many international corporations, that, while they did not forbid exports by subsidiaries, in practice all overseas markets of any size were already served by their own local subsidiary and made the same brands within substantial tariff barriers. Second, even if there had been no other Unilever subsidiaries in the region, Indian factories could not have competed on price with identical products from Port Sunlight. This had always been the case, for relatively low wage levels in India did not offset the advantage of economics of scale at Port Sunlight; but after 1947 the margin was increased because of higher vegetable oil prices in India. This was not true of all oils throughout this period: thus in 1956 groundnut oil actually cost £109 in India when the average price for the year in the UK was £132 a ton.[16] But by 1961 the Indian price had risen to £141.5 while the UK price had dropped to £126; and in the following years the gap widened further. Taking into account the need for other raw materials, such as palm oil, which had to be imported to India on licence, it is clear that Port Sunlight could always out-sell Bombay in third markets. Unless

Unilever therefore deliberately cut back on exports from its British factories to help its Indian subsidiaries there was little hope for expansion of LB(I) as an exporter of detergents.

(3) Toilet Preparations. The conclusion must be that Hindustan Lever expanded its very profitable detergents business as fast as it was permitted by the government and the market. But it was not permitted to increase its share of the total market and it was therefore not possible for the concern to plough back into this business more than a limited proportion of its profits, still less the large sums it was forced to realise through the sale of equity in 1956 and 1965. While detergents remained the backbone of the Indian business it was necessary to look to other fields for large-scale expansion; and in the late 1940s there were good grounds for hoping that toilet preparations might provide the answer. With a factory at Calcutta Unilever had an advantage over their main rivals, Colgates, who had either to import over the tariff barrier or manufacture locally *à façon* through a local company. Although difficulties were likely to be created by government restrictions on capital investment and imported raw materials, at least prices were not controlled since these were not foodstuffs. Finally, and most important, the market for European-style toilet preparations, initially very small, might be expected to expand rapidly with the growth of the economy. In fact turnover did increase very much faster than that of soaps or vanaspati, as is shown in Table 4.16. The nett sales value of toilet preparations doubled between 1946 and 1953 and doubled again by 1960. But this did not imply progress along the whole front. Analysis of the performance of six main lines indicates that, whereas toilet powders and shaving soap had followed the pattern of growth in NSV, toothpaste had not; indeed, turnover hardly grew at all between 1947 and 1960. And finally it is important to keep a sense of scale. In 1947 the sales value of toilet preparations at about Rs. 3 million was roughly 8 per cent of that of detergents at Rs. 40.5 million and 5.3 per cent of edibles at Rs. 57 million. By 1962 the turnover of toilet preparations was still under Rs. 10,000,000 whereas turnover of detergents was Rs. 238,000,000 and of edibles Rs. 246,000,000. Thus, far from taking over as Unilever's growth point, toilet preparations had actually declined rapidly as a proportion of total concern sales in India during this period and their profitability was consistently low. These things must be explained.

The reasons appear to have been entirely commercial and had little to do with the character and policies of the government of independent India. In these fields Unilever had no significant technical advantage over its main rivals and was never able to achieve the position of market leader, except possibly in shaving soaps. Competition came from two main sources. In hair oils there was a large number of Indian manufacturers and in toothpaste there was very strong competition from American firms, such as Colgates. Success for any one firm meant hitting on a brand name and a product which happened to catch the fashion or, in the case of toothpaste, appealed to the local palate. Unilever had little luck in either respect, and could therefore increase the volume of sales

Table 4.16   India: Turnover and Profitability of Toilet Preparations, 1953–65 (figures in brackets indicate losses)

Year	A NSV (Rs. '000)	B Trading profit before tax (Rs. '000)	B/A %
1953	4,868	n/a	—
1954	4,794	n/a	—
1955	4,758	n/a	—
1956	5,400	454	8.4
1957	6,363	551	8.6
1958	7,309	546	7.5
1959	8,580	897	10.4
1960	9,660	1,100	11.4
1961	8,532	(490)	—
1962	9,812	252	2.57
1963	15,605	(865)	—
1964	18,794	(500)	—
1965	23,015	470	2.0

only at the cost of profitability. Large sums were spent on advertising to establish brand superiority. In 1956 advertising was 14.2 per cent of NSV as compared with 4.7 per cent on detergents and in 1961 it reached 24.2 per cent of NSV as compared with 5.2 per cent for detergents and 1.2 per cent for edibles. Probably such large advertising expenditure was essential but it certainly affected profits and at various times London showed concern. The only other way to achieve larger sales and greater market shares was by underselling

rivals: indeed profit margins were always very low as the performance of UTL before 1955 and of the Toilet Preparations Division
of Hindustan Lever after 1956 indicates. It is significant that in 1963,
when NSV was increased by a major effort to Rs. 15,665,000, the
Division made a loss of Rs. 865,000. Once again in the early 1960s
the effort was made—large investment, market research, determined
advertising—and again success eluded them. The search for profitability through growth continued, but in 1965 this El Dorado
seemed as far away as ever.

The logic of the argument should now be clear. Unilever went
into manufacturing in India in order to maintain and expand
established markets previously supplied by imports. So long as it
was profitable to do so they concentrated their efforts on three main
groups of products: hydrogenated edible oils (vanaspati), detergents
and toilet preparations. Under 'open market' conditions it is
arguable that they would, through superior technology and research
facilities, have retained a dominant position in detergents, moving
increasingly into NSDs as they came up against the limits in demand
for conventional soap. In the case of vanaspati the concern would
probably have pioneered new branded products once the market for
vanaspati had been swamped by indigenous producers. In each case
these predictable lines of development after 1947 were to some
degree blocked by the action of the Indian government. Detergents
remained profitable but output, particularly production of NSDs,
was restricted by the licensing system. Vanaspati ceased to be really
profitable, due both to excess capacity and legislation forbidding
sale of superior products which might compete with natural ghee.
Toilet preparations were a different case. Despite restrictions
imposed by the government on the importation of raw materials
and capital equipment, the factor restricting Unilever's expansion
and success was straightforward competition. In this field at least
Indian political independence made very little difference.

These were the roots of the policy of diversification adopted by
Unilever in the mid-1950s. On the assumption that the business
must expand or decay it was obviously crucial by about 1956 to find
new opportunities. The search was to lead Unilever into comparatively strange and possibly unprofitable directions.

It is not quite true, however, to say that interest in horizontal
diversification within the limits of Unilever's traditional activities

began only in the mid-1950s for there had been spasmodic attempts to look for new openings a decade earlier. For example, in his comprehensive report on the Indian business in 1944, Gourley, while concentrating on established lines, thought that there might be openings in two new fields. First, the growth of an opulent middle class appeared to offer openings for foodstuffs of the sort Unilever already sold in Europe: sausages, frozen vegetables and fruit, ice-cream, biscuits, infant foods, etc. Initially these could all be imported to establish markets but thereafter local manufacture would have to be considered. Second, as an adjunct to the existing oil mills, he thought it might be profitable to utilise the by-products of groundnuts as flour to be mixed with wheat and rice-flour as a contribution to India's notorious protein deficiency. But nothing came of these proposals. UTL continued to import small quantities of high-class canned goods, but restricted demand and, in the 1950s, import licensing, combined to prevent the creation of a large-scale market. All that survived was the general proposition that at some future time it might be profitable to exploit in India Unilever's vast know-how in the field of processed foodstuffs.

If horizontal diversification seemed for the moment impracticable there was a strong *a priori* case for vertical development, using the by-products of the oil-milling business to better effect. Groundnut flour for human consumption was ruled out by consumer resistance; but why not develop compound feeding stuffs for cattle, a field in which Unilever was already well established in Europe? LB(I) had its own oil· mill in Bombay, which by 1949 was producing some 20,000 tons of cattle cake. All this was sold in bulk to third parties at low prices: indeed, the product did not even merit a separate entry in the accounts. The reason was important because specific to less developed countries such as India: it was then impossible to sell processed compound feeding stuffs to Indian farmers who assumed that their livestock lived off whatever they could find. Since, moreover, Hindus did not eat beef, compounds would only become profitable if farmers could be persuaded to go in for more intensive milk production or improve the quality of their poultry. Meantime, a potentially very valuable input to Indian agriculture from the country's many oil mills was virtually wasted.

The first serious proposal for LB(I) to manufacture cattle compounds came in 1949 when the government of Bombay city and province (as it then was) asked the company whether they would be prepared to co-operate in manufacturing compound cake for the

15,000 buffaloes of Bombay city who were being transferred to a state farm. London was attracted by the idea but felt it unwise to invest the £280,000 of initial capital required if there was to be only this one outlet. In order 'to show willingness to co-operate in any venture where the Company's skill could advance the health and welfare of the nation' they would give advice and if invited run a publicly owned factory on a 'cost only basis'. They would reconsider the question of investment if the use of compound cake became widespread. Similar problems blocked a number of proposals for using the by-products of milling in other ways. In short, vertical expansion of the company's activities seemed blocked by the realities of the Indian economy.

It was because of difficulties of this type in expanding traditional concern products that Unilever turned seriously to horizontal diversification in 1956. It was now recognised that if the government was to insist on progressive sale of Hindustan Lever's equity some profitable use of the capital compulsorily realised would have to be found. At the same time it was obviously desirable to discover openings which would appeal to the government for this was the key to getting licences to import capital equipment and other inputs. This fact pointed towards enterprises which, while making use of the concern's special skills, would in some way generate or stimulate 'basic' improvement in the Indian economy, perhaps by stimulating the agricultural sector to produce raw materials for processing. So began a search which was still continuing in 1965.

The search had begun in 1956 with a visit to India by Dr H. Dickson of Technical Division to investigate markets for processed foods. His report was in most ways discouraging. Many products of concern factories in Europe would be unsaleable and unprofitable in India: frozen foods, except ice-cream, because there were insufficient refrigerating facilities throughout the country; canned goods because the cost of containers was too high for Indian consumers; meat and fish because markets were too localised; cereals and fruits because the cost of processing would make them too dear. In the end he could see only two serious prospects: milk products, including the Indian type of ice-cream *(kula)*, natural ghee and *dahi* (curds) in which Hindustan Lever would have a potential advantage in quality over indigenous products; and dried peas and possibly other dehydrated vegetables. A marginal third possibility was synthetic fruit juices. In addition it might be possible, if Indian prices remained low, to process vegetables and fruit for export to Europe.

Dickson's report created interest in Unilever House and in January 1957 it was agreed to undertake further investigation into the possibility of producing and marketing dehydrated peas and dried milk curd and also of producing dried onions for use in manufacturing dried soups in Europe. Closely connected with this was another and perhaps ultimately more important decision to establish an autonomous Research Unit in Bombay. This proposal was made by Dr (later Sir) Ernest Woodroofe, then a director and subsequently Chairman of Unilever Ltd from 1970 to 1974, who had experience of the concern's research institutes throughout the world. Woodroofe supported this proposal on the grounds that he thought that Hindustan Lever had a big future and that, although 'the immediate future may not promise a generous return on capital . . . research is concerned with a longer term and the Indian Management feels confident about the long-term commercial prospects'. He proposed an initial unit of 15 staff under Hindustan Lever's chief chemist. It would work primarily on the proposed new fruit pro-cessing enterprises, but also on problems relating to other Hindustan Lever products. The Special Committee accepted the proposal, at an initial capital cost estimated at between £25,000 and £35,000, in February 1957, and approved increased expenditure of £56,000 in October 1958.

1957 therefore marked the start of the new era. Instead of merely manufacturing traditional concern products pioneered in Europe and whose technology was largely imported, Hindustan Lever was to venture into new fields which related almost exclusively to the Indian market and have its own research institute to provide the know-how. Seen in terms of the general debate concerning the role of international corporations, this was conceptually an important departure—a clear demonstration that Hindustan Lever was to be 'Indianised' in more ways than the nationality of its management and the partial sale of its equity.

It proved more difficult to launch these new ventures than to plan them. For the first time in India Unilever was groping for answers to technical problems of which they had no experience at home and on which Indians could give little help. How did one accumulate enough peas of adequate quality at a single processing factory when there was no indigenous buying or marketing mechanism on the scale required such as existed in most developed countries? Equally, how could one get enough high quality milk for manufacturing natural ghee when Indian farmers produced only for a very local market and there was no transport? Answers to these and similar problems were gradually worked on between 1958 and 1960. As regards raw materials—peas and milk—Hindustan Lever would have to produce, or at least to organise production of, its own supplies: the market could not supply them. In 1959 a pilot project for growing peas on contract was begun, based on Ghaziabad; and Dickson recommended that a new factory for milk products should be built at Etah (UP) which would be surrounded by a large number of milk-collecting stations and a still larger number of milking centres. Hindustan Lever would make contracts with local farmers to bring their cattle to the milking centres and would then transfer the milk to collecting centres and thence to the central factory for processing. The capital cost of such a large scheme would be some £1,071,000 for the Etah factory and collecting centres. Would the project be profitable? In 1959 Dickson was optimistic: he estimated the yield before tax at a possible 36 per cent. Another director visiting India with Dickson in 1959 agreed with him. Of the pea project he wrote 'I believe we may now have found our first food line'. He was equally keen about the milk project which he thought might yield $12\frac{1}{2}$ per cent after tax on capital after four years. He predicted 150 milking centres employing 19,000 villagers and 27,000 buffaloes, producing 24,500 tons of milk from which 1,000 tons of tinned ghee and 2,000 tons of milk powder might be manufactured.

Others were less optimistic, but in the face of such enthusiasm the Special Committee decided in April 1959 to start a trial milk-collecting project with five milking centres and one collecting centre—the milk to be taken by road and sold without profit to dairies in New Delhi. Meanwhile a suitable site for the processing factory was looked for. By this time the first pilot scheme for dried peas was also under way, but it would be at least a year before the results were available. The search for other openings continued, though without great success. A detailed report prepared by Mr Ramaswami of the Bombay management on his own initiative (he still thinks it might have been successful because of exports to the American market) on the potential profitability of going into fisheries in the Bombay area was reasonably optimistic. *A priori*, it was thought, there might be an opportunity to pioneer the catching, processing and sale of fish by modern methods since the Indian industry was very small in scale and pre-modern in techniques. Per capita consumption of fish in India was only 5.8 lbs a year as compared with 155 lbs in Japan and 55 lbs in the United Kingdom. There was only one modern firm engaged in large-scale fisheries— a Japanese concern. This was thought to make reasonable profits, but it was under-capitalised. If Unilever entered this field it would need to invest about Rs. 5,740,000 (£430,000) to provide trawlers, port facilities, inland transport and retail outlets. Even an optimistic estimate of some 50 per cent pre-tax profits on capital employed could not tempt Unilever into so obviously speculative a venture.

In 1960 a third new venture took shape; though in this case its origins lay, not in the need to find new or more profitable openings, but in a desire to please the Indian government. In June the Special Committee heard the Indian government was putting increasing pressure on Hindustan Lever to go into cotton-seed processing, both to expand the supply of vegetable oil and to provide a market for Indian farmers. An investment of about £1,000,000 was involved. The Committee felt that 'from the commercial point of view the venture into oil milling was not attractive, but to continue to resist the government's wishes could result in a serious loss of good-will and thus affect the standing of our basic business'. On these grounds it was thought wise to agree, but 'if we had to go into cotton-seed extraction it might be more profitable to combine it with compound animal feeding stuffs. This it was estimated, would add another £250,000 to the cost.' Thus was born another important new enterprise, not from hope of profit but from anxiety to please a host government.[17]

From the autumn of 1960 attention in London turned from the search for new projects to the problems of how to finance them. The total projected capital costs were huge.

Milk	£1,250,000
Peas	350,000
Cotton seed	1,000,000
Cattle food	350,000
Catalyst	100,000
	£3,050,000

At that time the total capital employed in India was some £9,470,000, so Unilever were considering an immediate increase of one-third of the capital assets built up in India over some 30 years. Of this two-thirds, it was thought, could be raised in India from profits, reserves, further sale of equity and borrowing; but about £860,000 of foreign exchange was necessary to pay for machinery not available in India. The concern could, of course, find this sum: but, if Unilever injected this amount and increased its holding of the equity accordingly, it would either reduce the 10 per cent equity held by Indians since 1956 or, if the balance was redressed by selling concern shares, leave Unilever with a large rupee balance which it could neither use in India nor repatriate. This was a basic obstacle to new foreign investment, created by the government's policy on Indianisation of equity and repatriation of foreign capital. In the last resort Unilever might have to accept these disadvantages as part of the price of earning good-will in New Delhi; but first attempts were to be made to finance the foreign exchange element in the new investment from third-party loans repayable in rupees—perhaps from ICICI. Once again, however, Unilever found that the final decisions were taken by the Indian government. After long negotiations ICICI was allowed to provide only £200,000 of foreign exchange on condition that Unilever provided the rest—£600,000 in the first instance. London tried to insist that this sum should constitute a sterling loan repayable in sterling over a period of years, but was eventually forced to agree that the money should be converted into an increase in the concern's equity holding.

Between 1960 and 1965 the first generation of new projects matured very slowly: it took six years before the Etah ghee factory was in operation—in 1964—and seven years before pricked peas were on sale in 1965. Cattle foods took four years to reach a production figure of 7,500 tons. In each case, and particularly in that of ghee and pricked peas, delays were caused by two main factors: first, the time consumed in obtaining licences and official approval; second, and more important, the immense technical difficulties that had to be overcome when launching new forms of sophisticated production in a less developed country. As a result it is impossible to assess the commercial success of these new developments by the time this study ends in 1965. In December 1965, when Tandon, as Chairman of Hindustan Lever, reported to the Special Committee, he had still to talk of future prospects. He thought that, if daily collection of milk was increased to an average of 100 tons in 1966,

'We should definitely be in the black'. Lord Cole was less optimistic: 'We certainly will not get any dividends before 1970.' Pricked peas, now centred on Etah, also went into commercial sale in 1965, when some 200 tons were marketed: Tandon hoped they would be making money on these in 1966. Sales of animal feeding stuffs were up to 26,000 tons by 1965, though 18,000 tons of this was for poultry—evidence of the continuing difficulty of creating new consumer habits among milk producers. At least this was a profit-making line. Thus in 1965 it was still reasonable to take an optimistic view of the future. Ten years later it was clear that difficulties in both the supply and demand side of the milk and pea projects made it impossible for either to make reasonable profits: only animal feeds could be regarded as a success. The first major attempt by Hindustan Lever to diversify in India failed to solve its underlying problems.

In the early 1960s, however, the mood both in Bombay and London remained one of optimistic expansion. The question was what to do next. Andrew Knox was clear that Unilever must be constructive: it must take a positive hand in the economic develop- ment of India. 'We should be public-spirited even if we remain in the Private Sector. There should be plenty of scope for us . . . . Surf sells best in Jamshedpur, the great Tata steel town.' If necessary Unilever should drop its normal policy of total control over all its enterprises: Hindustan Lever should be 'flexible in the matter of possible partnership with others. We should not necessarily seek exclusivity.' But even with so open-minded an approach it proved very difficult to find further openings. Several minor projects were considered or experimented with in the early 1960s, most of which had some connection with Hindustan Lever's main business, but none proved promising.

In 1965, therefore, the prospects of Hindustan Lever were full of paradoxes. Opinion in Unilever House was divided about its future. All were agreed that this was one of the Unilever's finest overseas subsidiaries. Andrew Knox and A. H. Smith had been profoundly impressed by their visit in 1962. 'Outside the United States, Hindustan Lever is our biggest overseas company . . . . In 1961 it was also the one with the biggest profit . . . . It is certainly one of the most interesting and . . . it is reasonable to claim that in some respects it is the best.' All were agreed that Indianisation of management had been a great success. 'Right down the line there is a high measure of competence, a commercial knowledge and realism and a dedication to the interests of the business which are outstanding . . .'. The factories were well equipped and efficient, the Research Unit a great success. Perhaps above all the marketing and distribution were outstanding, providing access to most parts of India at comparatively low cost. In short, Hindustan Lever was a first-class industrial concern which had surmounted the earlier problems of operating in independent India triumphantly.

All this constituted solid ground for optimism. But by 1965 there were also two bad omens. First, as will be seen below, profits were falling: nett yield after tax in relation to GCE had dropped from 13.2 per cent in 1960 to around 7.0 per cent in 1963–5, and seemed likely to decline still further. Perhaps more serious, the problem of diversification had not yet been resolved. In 1965 soap amounted to 50 per cent of turnover but provided 94 per cent of profits. Vanaspati remained a very unprofitable product, toilet preparations were still struggling, and it was uncertain how the new ventures in foodstuffs would turn out. In short, there was a danger that Hindustan Lever might find itself in a dead end, unable either to expand its own most profitable lines or to find suitable alternatives, a superb industrial machine lacking full scope for its energies. The danger was certain: the question is what caused it, and at this point it is necessary to revert to the effects of decolonisation and the adoption of a 'managed' economy on a manufacturing subsidiary of a multi-national company. Put simply, it is necessary to decide whether the problems facing Hindustan Lever were primarily due to official controls or the limitations inherent in the market for consumer products in a less developed country.

The evidence in this chapter suggests that both factors were significant, but that the second was probably more important. There is no doubt that governmental regulations, particularly restriction on investment in productive capacity and recurrent controls on vanaspati prices, had a retarding effect on Hindustan Lever's natural propensity to enlarge its share of the market and expand its product range; and to that extent the company was in a more difficult position than Unilever subsidiaries in 'open' economies such as Australia. It is also true that the problem of diversifying into new lines was complicated by official reluctance to allow resources to be used for manufacturing 'unnecessary' products: NSDs, for example, were not allowed to be made in India before 1965, though permission was given subsequently. But when all allowances have been made, the conclusion must be that the underlying problem facing Unilever in India stemmed from the nature of the country and not from government policy. Even under 'open market' conditions they would have faced many of the same difficulties in the 1960s: the market for quality soap and for vanaspati was limited; severe competition made toilet preparations a highly speculative affair. These problems were met in many more developed countries. What made India, as an LDC, different, was that there was very limited scope there for diversification into other typical Unilever lines which had been evolved to meet conditions in Europe and North America. As has been seen, the management of Hindustan Lever inspected, as it were, the whole range of goods on display in the concern's shop window in the 1950s and 1960s and found that almost none of them was wanted or could be afforded by the mass of Indians. In the 1950s Bombay chose three projects which they thought fulfilled the three essential conditions—availability of know-how within Unilever, profit potential and Indian official approval; and of these the last was probably the least influential. In the event their calculations proved inaccurate, for two of these three projects turned out to be unprofitable for various reasons and the third, animal compound feeds, took a long time to develop. In the 1970s the company was therefore still in search of its future role in India.

(e) Profitability and the Balance of Advantage

The final issues to be considered are the most difficult: how profitable Unilever's Indian business was to the concern and to the country. So far as Unilever was concerned, the profits it made in India, as in all overseas countries, were thought of in relative terms—how they changed over time and how they compared with profits made in other parts of the world. For India and all the overseas manufacturing companies described in subsequent chapters the time factor is dominated by the transformation of these countries from colonial status to full sovereignty and, consequentially, from 'open' to 'managed' economies. The first main question must therefore be what effect these changes had on the profitability of Unilever's Indian business.

The data is summarised in Tables 4.17(a) and 4.17(b); and at first sight it would seem that independence in 1947 was a decisive turning point. In so far as estimates of capital employed are consistent (and in fact the changing methods of calculating this probably

Table 4.17(a):   India: Return to Capital 1935–65 (all Concern
Companies in India to 1956, thereafter Hindustan Lever[a])
(nett profit after tax as a percentage of capital employed[b]) (Rs. '000)

Year	A Capital employed	B Nett profit after statistical tax	C Nett accounting profit	Yield after tax B/A	Yield after tax C/A
1935	10,883	736	n/a	6.8	n/a
1936	10,967	1,060	n/a	9.7	n/a
1937	11,407	2,345	n/a	20.6	n/a
1938	11,535	2,902	n/a	25.2	n/a
1939	14,168	3,489	n/a	24.6	n/a
1940	17,985	1,169	n/a	6.5	n/a
1941	20,615	3,382	n/a	16.4	n/a
1942	25,377	4,535	n/a	17.9	n/a
1943	31,470	7,170	n/a	22.8	n/a
1944	32,372	6,472	n/a	20.0	n/a
1945	29,107	8,650	4,090	29.7	14.0
1946	25,358	6,396	4,210	25.2	16.6
1947	28,181	n/a	4,680	n/a	16.6
1948	37,923	n/a	5,550	n/a	14.6
1949	41,090	n/a	7,430	n/a	18.1
1950	45,801	n/a	7,820	n/a	17.1
1951	55,842	n/a	8,130	n/a	14.6
1952	70,713	n/a	9,130	n/a	12.9
1953	75,068	n/a	9,450	n/a	12.6
1954	88,968	n/a	5,670	n/a	6.4
1955	98,565	n/a	12,060	n/a	12.2
1956	93,579	7,409	10,508	7.9	11.2
1957	106,273	8,779	7,375	8.3	6.9
1958	125,823	11,717	12,863	9.3	10.2
1959	125,700	16,928	20,825	13.5	16.6
1960	126,100	16,634	24,951	13.2	19.8
1961	148,900	15,043	22,551	10.1	15.1
1962	152,200	14,983	18,817	9.8	12.4
1963	163,000	11,788	14,109	7.2	8.7
1964	167,900	11,767	16,977	7.0	10.1
1965	179,800	12,015	17,400	6.7	9.7

Notes: a. There is no single continuous record of profits made by the Indian
business throughout the whole period of local manufacture on the
same basis. In this table, columns B and C are divided into three
sections. From 1935–44 and 1956–65 nett profits are after statistical
tax; from 1945–55 they are after actual tax. Comparable figures are
given for 1956–65.

b. 'Capital employed' was calculated differently at different times: in the
earlier period fixed assets were put in at book value after depreciation
at 31 December; but during 1956–65 they are the average for the year
at 60 per cent of replacement value. The result is probably to
exaggerate profits as a percentage of capital in the earlier period.

exaggerate the percentage profit figures in early years), the best years were 1938 and 1939, with post-tax returns of 25.2 and 24.6 per cent; whereas in most years after 1956 the return, calculated on the same basis, was under 10 per cent. One possible explanation might be the effect of various forms of government control on basic profit margins; but closer examination shows that this was not so. Table 4.17(b), which compares the years 1935–8 with 1962–5, indicates that the difference lay not in the pre-tax but in the post-tax yields. In the first period average pre-tax profit as a percentage of

Table 4.17(b)   India: Profits made by Unilever in India, 1935–8 and 1962–5 (Rs. '000)

Year	A Capital employed	B Trading profit before tax	B as % of A	C Nett profit after stat. tax	C as % of A
1935	10,883.0	892.2	8.2	736.0	6.8
1936	10,967.6	1,376.6	12.5	1,060.0	9.7
1937	11,407.7	2,987.6	26.2	2,345.3	20.6
1938	11,525.9	3,697.7	32.1	2,902.7	25.2
Average	11,196.0	2,238.4	20.0	1,761.0	15.7
1962	152,200.0	42,810.0	28.1	14,983.0	9.8
1963	163,000.0	43,660.0	26.8	11,788.0	7.2
1964	167,900.0	32,062.0	19.1	11,767.0	7.0
1965	179,800.0	35,972.0	20.0	12,015.0	6.7
Average	165,725.0	38,626.0	23.3	12,638.0	7.6

Note: The data for 1935–8 relate to the various Unilever companies operating in India: those for 1962–5 to Hindustan Lever into which these companies were amalgamated in 1956. The latter figures exclude the area which became Pakistan in 1947.

capital employed was 20.0 per cent and for 1962–5 it was 23.3 per cent. The contrast lies in the post-tax yield and is the result of a dramatic rise in the statistical tax rate on dividends from around 21 per cent to about 67 per cent of trading profit. Within these figures there are, of course, many concealed variables. The relative importance of different costs, such as advertising and distribution, varied considerably, as did the profitability of different products. In the 1930s much of the profit came from vanaspati, while in the 1960s it came from soap. But taking the business as a whole the evidence suggests that, while post-independence governmental policies may have reduced potential profit-margins in some ways, effective protection of the home market just about cancelled these out, so that efficient private enterprises in India were able to obtain a substantial pre-tax return to investment. It was only high levels of corporate taxation, inflated further by the tax on distributed profits, that dramatically reduced the nett return to the investor.

The second standard by which Indian profits were judged in London was in comparison with profits made by Unilever companies elsewhere. Table 10.1 in the concluding chapter sets out the percentage return to capital after statistical tax in 13 Unilever manufacturing companies and all companies in Europe for the decade 1956–65. Hindustan Lever comes fifth in this league table (though not necessarily in the whole of the Unilever overseas system) and the unweighted average for this decade was slightly above the average for Europe, 9.3 per cent as against 9.0 per cent. This is extremely important. As will be seen later, Unilever tended in the 1960s to assume that a manufacturing company should give a post-tax return of around 10 per cent. Hindustan Lever, one of its largest subsidiaries, operating in a less developed country whose government proclaimed socialist objectives, came nearer to this than either Australia or New Zealand and did much better than either the Latin American or the African countries except for South Africa and Kenya. It is not, therefore, surprising that Unilever regarded India as a rewarding place in which to operate.

The third measure of Hindustan Lever's profitability is its performance in comparison with that of other companies operating in India, whether Indian or foreign owned. This is an important question because one of the arguments commonly put forward both for and against the manufacturing subsidiaries of multinationals in LDCs is that on the one hand they can make more efficient use of real resources than local enterprises, which is shown by their high profitability; and on the other that they do better than local competitors because they have an unfair advantage stemming from their ability to call on ready made technologies. It is unfortunately impossible to provide meaningful comparisons before the mid-1940s because data on the profitability of most Indian companies— other than for dividends in relation to nominal capital—is not available, but Tables 4.18(a) and 4.18(b) provide comparisons between the Unilever companies and a wide range of other companies from 1960 to 1964, and between the Edibles Division of

Table 4.18(a)   India: Gross Profit as a Percentage of Capital
Employed in Select Private Sector Companies, 1960—4

Indian companies only	1960	1961	1962	1963	1964
Edible vegetable and hydrogenated					
oil	8.6	7.3	7.3	6.8	10.4
Sugar	8.6	7.3	7.4	11.1	10.7
Tobacco	13.4	11.7	14.5	11.4	15.5
Cotton textiles	12.2	13.1	8.1	8.9	8.7
Jute textiles	8.0	3.8	17.0	11.1	5.5
Silk and rayon	15.8	13.2	9.7	10.5	12.6
Woollen textiles	19.4	10.1	17.4	16.4	13.1
Iron and steel	7.3	8.3	10.1	12.5	11.7
Non-ferrous metals	12.8	10.9	10.0	9.9	12.3
Transport equipment	9.8	10.1	10.6	10.2	11.3
Electrical appliances, etc.	12.5	11.5	13.9	15.5	15.0
Medical and pharmaceutical					
preparations	14.6	13.6	13.7	15.6	17.2
Other chemical products	11.6	11.3	13.6	12.3	10.1
Matches	16.1	16.2	17.6	15.0	10.8
Cement	8.3	8.7	11.4	10.2	10.0
Paper and paper products	9.5	8.4	8.4	7.9	6.6
Total (including others)	10.2	10.1	10.2	10.6	10.3
Hindustan Lever	34.2	24.9	28.1	26.7	19.1

Source: Bhagwati & Desai, *India: Planning for Industrialization*, Table 9.5,
p. 151. 'Gross profits' are gross of tax and interest. 'Gross capital
employed' represents gross fixed assets minus depreciation plus working
capital. The basis for the Unilever figures is slightly different, so that the
significance of the contrast lies in orders of magnitude.

Hindustan Lever and the hydrogenated vegetable oil industry as a
whole in the single year 1962.

The general implication of these tables, without putting too much
weight on precise figures which may not be strictly comparable, is
uncontestable. Taken as a whole, or even in relation to its less
successful component parts, the Unilever enterprise was substantially

Table 4.18(b)   India: Gross Profit as a Percentage of Capital
Employed in the Edible Oils Industry, 1962

(1) Edible vegetable and hydrogenated oil industry	7.3%
(2) Edibles division of Hindustan Lever	16.1%

Source: for (1) Bhagwati & Desai, *India: Planning for Industrialization*, Table 9.5,
p. 151.

more profitable than any one Indian industry or than the average of all Indian industries covered. This is not, of course, to say that Hindustan Lever or its concern predecessors were more profitable than any individual Indian company; this is unlikely but the data does not make it possible to judge. All that can be certain is that Unilever obtained a gross return on its investments in India which

Table 4.18(c)   India: Average Post-tax Profits of Hindustan Lever as a Percentage of GCE Compared with Average Post-tax Profits of the Subsidiaries of other UK Companies Overseas as a Percentage of Nett Operating Assets, 9 year average, 1956–64

	%
(1) All UK manufacturing subsidiaries overseas	8.1
(2) All UK subsidiaries (excluding oil)	8.7
(3) All UK subsidiaries in India (excluding oil)	7.7
(4) All UK subsidiaries in food, drink, tobacco and household goods	8.8
(5) Hindustan Lever	9.4

Note: All UK subsidiaries includes all those UK companies, in addition to Unilever, who provided data for the Reddaway Report.

Source: (1) & (2) W. B. Reddaway, *The Effects of UK Direct Investment Overseas: Final Report* (London, 1968). Table IV, 2, p. 356.
    (3) Ibid., Table IV, 5, p. 358.
    (4) Ibid., Table IV, 2, p. 356.

was well above the average for Indian industry as a whole. Since the concern was operating within the same economic environment as other Indian companies and because, as has been seen, Unilever's internal accounting arrangements did not distort the performance figures of individual units, it must be assumed that this comparative success was due to the concern's relative efficiency.

One other comparison must be made. Unilever may have performed better than the great majority of other Indian-based companies, but as part of an international enterprise an equally significant general question is how the nett profitability of the Indian companies compares with that of other British subsidiaries overseas. Table 4.18(c) shows the nett profitability of Hindustan Lever from 1956 to 1964 compared with some of the overseas subsidiaries of a number of other British companies (including Unilever subsidiaries) in the field of mining, plantations and manufacturing; and finally, the average profitability of Hindustan Lever compared with that of British subsidiaries (excluding oil) in a number of countries.

These comparisons put Hindustan Lever in quite a different perspective. In comparison with UK subsidiaries as a whole, Hindustan Lever was fairly typical. It did no better than the average of UK mining, plantation and manufacturing groups, and only marginally better—9.4 per cent as against 8.8 per cent—than all UK subsidiaries in the field of drinks, tobacco and household goods. As against all UK subsidiaries in India, Unilever admittedly was more profitable; but UK subsidiaries in Germany, Malaysia, Italy, Ghana and South Africa did significantly better. In short, while Hindustan Lever was by no means one of the most profitable of British overseas manufacturing subsidiaries, it shone as one of the brightest jewels in the Indian industrial scene where comparatively low profits were the norm. Or, to put it another way, the Indian company, while operating in the same environment and under the same constraints as local enterprises, was able to make more efficient use of resources than local enterprises. This fact is of great import- ance when considering the benefits of subsidiaries to less developed countries and will be reviewed under this heading in the concluding chapter.

India, therefore, provided Unilever with a good, though not exceptional, opportunity to use its special skills and broaden its total market. The other and more important side of the question is what contribution Unilever made to Indian economic develop- ment. In view of the intense controversy over the economic role of multinationals and in particular the common accusation that they are partly responsible for generating and maintaining 'under- development' in the Third World, this question has to be handled with great caution; but since Hindustan Lever is the largest Unilever manufacturing subsidiary in any less developed country, the question must be faced, even if no conclusive answer is possible. It is proposed to survey the evidence in terms of a primitive profit and loss account, using the broad criteria defined by Reuber which will also be used in the concluding chapter to assess the contribution made by Unilever subsidiaries as a whole to the prosperity of host countries. Three main issues are involved: first, the financial consequences for India of entertaining Hindustan Lever; second, the effects on Indian production and trade; third, externalities or side effects.

The standard measure of the financial consequences for an LDC of private direct foreign investment is to treat taxes paid locally as benefits received by the host society which might not otherwise have been available and profits transferred overseas in the form of dividends as part of the price the recipient country must pay. Much emphasis is also laid by some on the amount of foreign capital invested by the multinational to establish its business. Some of the evidence for Hindustan Lever under these heads is set out in the concluding chapter and will not be reproduced here, but Tables 4.19,

Table 4.19   India: Hindustan Lever's Sources of Finance, 1957–65 (Rs. million)

Increase in capital employed (Rs. 212.1 − 82.0)   130.1

	Internal	Other	Ex-3rd party shares	Ex-concern	Total
Equity	26.7		4.5	4.5	35.7
Capital reserve			3.6	3.6	7.2
Profits	168.9 (26.7)		(10.7)	(93.0)	38.5
Loans + local borrowing		42.7			42.7
Other		6.0			6.0
	168.9	48.7	(2.6)	(84.9)	130.1
Distribution tax				24.3	
Nett profit transferred to UK				60.6	

4.20 and 4.21 provide detailed information on important issues. The main point, which is true of all the companies studied in this book, is that the amount of foreign capital invested in an overseas company by a multinational such as Unilever was comparatively small. At the start, in 1922, local manufacture was financed mainly by capitalising the goodwill and other assets built up by the import business which were realised in the creation of Lever Brothers (India) Ltd and whose shares were exchanged for a majority holding in the Boulton companies. A decade later large-scale manufacture at Bombay was financed by a direct sterling investment of about Rs. 6.9 million (£518,000) and this was the largest single permanent

Table 4.20 India: Unilever Companies' (Including UTL) Allocation of Income, 1945—65 (Rs. million)

Year	A NSV	B Profit before tax	C Taxation	D Nett accounting profit after tax	E Dividend (nett)	F Income retained in India	C/A %	C/B %	E/A %	F/A %
1945	126.1	13.0	8.9	4.1	3.0	123.1	7.1	68.5	2.4	97.6
1946	141.1	11.1	6.8	4.2	3.7	137.4	4.8	61.3	2.6	97.4
1947	115.3	10.1	8.1	4.7	3.1	112.7	7.0	80.2	2.7	97.3
1948	172.8	13.8	8.3	5.5	5.5	167.3	4.8	60.1	3.2	96.8
1949	200.4	14.2	6.7	7.4	—	200.4	3.3	47.2	—	100.0
1950	240.8	14.8	6.9	7.8	—	240.8	2.9	46.6	—	100.0
1951	297.7	15.8	7.6	8.1	—	297.7	2.5	48.1	—	100.0
1952	275.6	18.3	9.1	9.1	—	275.6	3.3	49.7	—	100.0
1953	274.1	22.5	13.0	9.5	5.0	269.1	4.7	57.8	1.8	98.2
1954	275.8	13.7	8.0	5.7	15.0	260.8	2.9	58.4	5.4	94.6
1955	282.7	25.9	13.8	12.1	7.5	275.2	4.9	53.3	2.6	97.4
1956	264.2	21.2	12.1	10.5	4.7	259.5	4.6	57.1	1.8	98.2
1957	314.6	22.5	10.3	8.8	5.9	308.7	3.3	45.8	1.9	98.1
1958	345.8	32.1	17.4	11.7	6.4	339.4	5.0	54.2	1.8	98.2
1959	391.4	43.9	20.9	15.9	8.4	383.0	5.3	47.6	2.1	97.9
1960	432.6	43.2	20.8	16.3	9.1	423.5	4.8	48.1	2.1	97.9
1961	468.4	39.1	19.3	15.0	9.1	459.3	4.1	49.4	1.9	98.1
1962	497.7	42.8	24.0	11.9	6.2	491.5	4.8	56.1	1.2	98.8
1963	544.5	43.7	28.9	11.8	7.7	536.8	5.3	66.1	1.4	98.6
1964	565.4	32.1	20.5	11.8	7.8	557.6	3.6	63.9	1.4	98.6
1965	678.2	35.9	26.1	12.0	8.1	623.3	3.8	72.7	1.2	91.9
Total	6,905.7	592.7	297.5	203.9	116.2	6,742.7	4.3	56.2	1.7	97.6

investment made by Unilever in this subsidiary. Thereafter new capital was provided by retained profits made in India. If capital reserves were insufficient to meet the cost of a new development the funds might be lent by Unilever Ltd, borrowed locally or, after 1956, realised by sale of shares. Table 4.19 indicates the source of new finance for Hindustan Lever from 1957-65 to show how the system worked. The point is, of course, that Unilever expected that subsidiaries, like any other business enterprise, should be able to pay for their own expansion. British capital was critical at the start and

Table 4.21   India: Hindustan Lever's Balance of Payments
Effects, 1956—65
(Rs. '00,000)

	Inflow		Outflow	
Year	Dividend remittance (nett)	Actual user imports	Exports	Import substitution through R & D
1956	47.42	n/a	73	n/a
1957	59.94	n/a	76	n/a
1958	64.22	55.30	73	n/a
1959	84.22	52.37	87.5	n/a
1960	91.24	45.25	77	n/a
1961	91.24	40.50	74	n/a
1962	62.32	44.94	201	13.19
1963	76.71	40.04	512	18.65
1964	77.90	66.64	345	22.42
1965	80.57	60.84	137	51.05

made it possible for the Indian and other overseas manufacturing enterprises to start production on an efficient scale. But between 1933 and 1965 the original sterling investment had grown to a capital value of over £15 million (at current prices) without any further nett capital inflow.

This is a purely negative point which says nothing about the economic effects of the presence of a Unilever subsidiary in India except that it did not result in recurrent injections of new foreign capital. The important question is how the rewards of this venture were divided as between Unilever and India. Table 4.20 shows the allocation of the income received by the Indian companies/Hindustan Lever during the twenty years 1945–65 into trading profit, taxation and dividends. Statistics can lie and there are some factors which are not reflected in this table: for example it does not indicate that in 1956/7 some Rs. 10 million were transferred to London as a unique result of the compulsory sale of shares. But these things do not, in fact, significantly affect the pattern indicated by this table. During these twenty years some 97 per cent of the total income generated by the Unilever companies in India remained there. Most of it was absorbed by payments for goods and services, leaving only Rs. 529.7 million as trading profit, or 7.7 per cent of NSV. This profit was divided between the government and the business in the ratio 56.2:43.8. Of the company's share a substantial part was put to revenue reserve and ultimately re-invested in return for bonus shares; another part, after 1956, went to Indian shareholders; and, after a further deduction of 30 per cent distribution tax, the remainder, 1.7 per cent of NSV, was transferred to London as dividends. These figures leave no doubt that, at least from the mid-1940s, the Indian government was the prime beneficiary of the profits made by Hindustan Lever. This had not always been so. Between 1935 and 1938, when Indian corporate taxation was comparatively low, the total trading profit of Rs. 4.9 million made by LB(I) on soap was divided with the government in the proportion Rs. 3.3 million profit (nett of statistical tax) to Unilever and Rs. 1.6 million due in taxes. The change between the 1930s and the decades after 1945 marks the triumph of the state in India, first as a result of war, then of Indian independence.

These calculations ignore the effect of Hindustan Lever's operations on the Indian balance of payments. It will be argued in the concluding chapter that this is not, in fact, an important measure of the economic impact of a multinational on an LDC; but since it is often argued that a subsidiary 'costs' its host country a great deal in foreign exchange because it not only repatriates its dividends but also may tend to use an 'excessive' proportion of imported raw materials and intermediates, the point must be investigated. Unfortunately no data on the foreign exchange aspect of the Unilever business in India survives for the period before 1956, but Table 4.21 sets out data provided by Hindustan Lever for the decade 1956–65. Two comments are necessary. First, from 1962 the value of the concern's exports alone is greater in every year except 1965 than the combined costs of dividend remittances and imports. This had clearly not been so in earlier years and the favourable balance achieved in the 1960s was the result of great efforts made by the concern to export its products, even at a loss, under the stimulus provided by the government's import entitlement scheme under which an Indian enterprise could earn the right to use foreign exchange up to 75 per cent or more of the f.o.b. value of its exports. Hindustan Lever was also anxious to earn official goodwill by setting an example in export promotion. Second, while the figures given for import substitution are necessarily somewhat speculative, they reflect the reality that the concern research laboratories in Bombay, set up in the early 1960s, were the only facilities of their kind in India and were able to do fundamental research on a wide range of Indian commodities both for the company and for the government. Whatever the precise figures, it seems clear that by the mid-1960s Hindustan Lever was not a drain on the country's foreign exchange reserves.

The second general measure of the utility of a multinational relates to production, employment and productivity; and if Reuber's basic tests are applied to the evidence on Hindustan Lever it is clear that the company passed them without difficulty. First, it was fully integrated into the Indian economy in that most of its raw materials and intermediates were produced there; its market was almost exclusively within India except in so far as it exported to earn imports; it was largely independent of the parent company for its new technology; its management was almost entirely Indian by 1965; and, although more than 85 per cent of the share capital was still foreign-owned, the character of the business and its forward planning were strongly influenced by official Indian objectives. Second, although Hindustan Lever could make no significant contribution to the problem of industrial unemployment in India (being capital intensive it had only about 8,000 employees in the early 1970s), it could and did make a very valuable contribution to the country's need for technical and managerial skills. Indeed, this may well be the concern's most important single contribution to Indian economic development. In a country where most private businesses were run by members of the families which owned them and the concept of professional corporate management was relatively new, the very high standards set by Unilever had an important demonstration effect. In addition the training of Indian managers and technicians in India and overseas increased the stock of men available to run both public and private industry. Such benefits are impossible to measure; but the government's appreciation of the quality of Hindustan Lever management is shown by the fact that the first Indian Chairman of the company went on to become Chairman of the State Trading Corporation and one of the first Indian Directors, K. T. Chandy, became Chairman of Hindustan Steel Ltd, the largest government corporation in India. The company was constantly being asked to provide experts to sit on official committees and the first three sessions of the first Business School in the country were run by Hindustan Lever. On the technical side the Research and Development laboratories were frequently asked to undertake work for the government; and on the commercial side the company's all-Indian system of marketing and sales was generally regarded as a model for public and private enterprise.

The third test to apply to Hindustan Lever is its productivity— that is, its efficiency in employing Indian resources. Two things suggest that the company may have been the most efficient producer within its product range in India. First, from the start its branded soap products and later Dalda vanaspati (the first vanaspati to be sold in small tins with a brand name) were always market leaders, able, except where there were government price controls, to command a premium over all competing goods. Second, the limited evidence available on relative profitability suggests that the company was well above the average for Indian companies in its main fields, even though it had limited success in other areas, such as toilet preparations and foods. A reasonable conclusion might be that no competing local or foreign-owned company made better use of real resources in producing soap and edible fats.

Finally there is the question of 'externalities', potentially beneficial side effects, of which the most important was likely to be the transfer of technology. To a host government of an LDC the basic question when assessing the utility of a foreign-owned enterprise is commonly what that enterprise can bring in that the host country needs. It has been seen that Unilever's main economic contribution was efficiency rather than capital; but it remains to consider how important a contribution it made or was likely to make to India's stock of industrial technology.

The danger with all business enterprises is, of course, that, while at some time they may be regarded as 'new' capital employing the latest skills, over time they may lose their technical primacy and become 'old' capital living on their reputation and brand loyalties. In a LDC such as India, foreign (predominantly British) capital has tended in the past to lose its innovatory character, to be overtaken and eventually taken over by Indian entrepreneurs. Thus the tea plantations, coal mines, textile manufacturers and managing agencies established in the nineteenth and early twentieth centuries had almost all been taken over by Indians by 1947.[18] These, admittedly, were mostly owned by people resident in India; but a multinational is not exempt from this law of nature, and Hindustan Lever was vulnerable to the charge that by the 1960s it was still mainly dependent on soap and vanaspati which it had made there for the previous 30 years. The company was very conscious of this and knew that it could only survive if it kept ahead of local rivals and could offer new inputs of 'high technology' or something else unique to the Indian economy. By the 1950s Hindustan Lever no longer had a technical lead in vanaspati production, mainly because regulations prevented technical improvement which would make Dalda more nearly identical with natural ghee. Their technical advantage in soap lay in quality control and their ability to use local substitutes for local raw materials as a result of work done by their laboratories rather than in methods of manufacture. The concern made great efforts in the 1950s and early 1960s to innovate by importing technologies and products recently developed in Europe and America, but found that most of these were inapplicable to India either because there was no market or because the government regarded such products as an undesirable luxury. NSDs, for example, were not allowed to be made in India until after 1965. Conversely the two main new ventures undertaken before 1965—milk products and split peas, both of which employed technologies which were comparatively new in India and which pleased the government because they had backward linkages to the agricultural base of the economy—both proved commercially unsuccessful. Thus at the end of the period covered Hindustan Lever were still searching for ways in which they could play an innovatory role; and by 1977 it seemed that they might find this not in a conventional Unilever product but in the field of industrial chemicals which would involve buying technology from some other major producer outside India. If this came to fruition the company would have demonstrated that a multinational can make a contribution to a LDC by its readiness and ability to maintain its initial role as a conduit for new technology, even if the limitations of the local economy made it necessary to search the world for something worth doing there.

In putting forward these arguments it is important not to over-state the case. Hindustan Lever was no more essential to the Indian economy than India was to the survival of Unilever; and this means that the debate over the role of a subsidiary of a multinational whose function is to manufacture goods for local consumption in an LDC turns on whether or not marginal benefits are available to both parties. In the case of India the evidence suggests that such benefits existed. For Unilever, India constituted a significant and reasonably profitable enlargement of its total market: for India, Unilever was a source of certain inputs whose perceived value outweighed 'costs' such as the basic inconvenience that this was a foreign-owned enterprise. These are unheroic conclusions but they are probably a reasonable reflection of how both parties saw the situation in the 1970s.

It was said at the start of this chapter that it was intended to cast the Indian company in the role of a model for Unilever's activities in the less developed world; and it is therefore necessary briefly to summarise those features of the story which seemed to distinguish this from concern enterprises in more developed countries such as Australia. Many points could be underlined, but three seem of potentially general significance.

First, although Lever/Unilever's assessment of the desirability of local manufacture in India was based on the same criteria as in Australia, etc., the barriers to local production here were greater than in the more developed world. On the one hand poverty meant that per capita consumption of concern products was low; on the other the historical fact that under colonial rule European dependencies were normally not allowed to protect their domestic market against products from the metropolis excluded a common incentive to establish subsidiary factories there. India was exceptional among LDCs because its market for modern factory products was comparatively large and because it was the first European dependency that established a right to tariff protection for local industry. Even so, Unilever undertook large-scale manufacture of soap and vanaspati in India some 30 years after Levers had begun to make soap in Australia and Canada; and the time-lag was likely to be still larger in smaller and poorer tropical dependencies which were forced to maintain an 'open door' to overseas competition until the time of decolonisation.

There was therefore nothing in colonialism as such to attract direct foreign investment in manufacturing for local consumption. Conversely, once foreign capital was established in a colonial dependency behind an adequate tariff, it would probably find conditions there peculiarly conducive to success: in particular, it might benefit from low taxation and the comparative weakness of local competition and so make above average post-tax profits. Thus the process of decolonisation was certain to have traumatic consequences which had no equivalent in more developed countries. In India the transfer of power meant a radical adjustment of Unilever's attitudes and methods of operation, involving, above all, recognition that in a newly independent state a foreign firm is unwise to stand on its legal rights. The events of 1954–6 in India may perhaps be seen as Unilever's apprenticeship in the art of dealing with newly sovereign governments of this type and the lessons it learnt are evident in its treatment of all similar problems later on.

Finally, however, Unilever's experience in India after about 1956 suggests that a wisely conducted foreign-owned business may be able to operate as successfully and profitably in a newly sovereign LDC, even though it has an intensively 'managed' economy and is more sensitive to the presence of foreign enterprises, as in a country of a European type such as Australia. The problems facing the multinational are much greater and the future more uncertain; but Hindustan Lever demonstrated that the problems could be solved and that the rewards might balance the risks.

Unilever in Pakistan, 1947-65

The experience of Unilever in Pakistan after the partition of the subcontinent in 1947 differs in almost every possible respect from that of the concern companies in India. The Indian business had been built up over a long period from an import system based on Bombay and Calcutta, and the concern factories in those towns had been in operation for some 15 years before political independence. Although 1947 marked an important watershed for these subsidiaries, it did not fundamentally affect the character of their activities within the areas which were included in the new state of India. Pakistan was different. The regions that came to form East and West Pakistan had always been peripheral to Unilever's business. There were no concern factories in these areas and the sales system for goods manufactured in Bombay or Calcutta and for imports from Britain had its roots in India rather than in the new Pakistan.

Hence, the partition of India posed a major problem for Unilever: how best to maintain and expand markets in these two regions which had been an integral part of the Indian business. Given the large population of Pakistan—77.6 millions in 1949 rising to 112.4 millions in 1963/4—the issue was an important one; and the main function of this short study is to see how Unilever dealt with the situation: whether they treated Pakistan as a marginal export market from their Indian subsidiaries, or established new factories there; and if they manufactured in Pakistan, what special problems and opportunities they encountered in this new political unit, and how profitable their operations proved to be.

The basic facts of Unilever's enterprise in Pakistan are that they established a factory for the production of both vanaspati and soap at Rahim Yar Khan in Bahawalpur State, and that they did so as partners with others. Both facts are surprising: the site because it was not in Karachi, which became by far the most important industrial centre and market in West Pakistan, and the partnership, because it was not normal concern practice to share ownership or control of its subsidiaries with third parties. A further question needs consideration: why Unilever did not serve Pakistan markets from its existing established Indian industrial bases—West Pakistan from Bombay, and East Pakistan from Calcutta.

This last question presents no difficulties. The concern had been looking for possible sites for manufacturing vanaspati in those Indian provinces which later became Pakistan before 1947, partly to make it easier to penetrate local markets, partly to add to its licensed productive capacity. It would almost certainly have established one or more factories in these regions irrespective of partition. But partition made local manufacture imperative. Imports to Pakistan from India were relatively free until 1949, but then the refusal of Pakistan to devalue her rupee along with that of India led to a virtual cessation of trade between the two countries; and, as industrial capacity built up in Pakistan, so import licences for typical Unilever goods became more difficult to obtain. In the long run, therefore, Unilever could only maintain and expand its market in Pakistan by producing inside that country; and the important questions therefore become why they chose to manufacture in Rahim Yar Khan and why they did so in partnership with other local interests.

The explanation for both is that during 1946 the search for licensed capacity for sale in north-west India led to contacts with a

Muslim family collectively known as the Ali Group, which had licences to produce vanaspati and was projecting factories in Bahawalpur state and at Bhopal. This family business was run by the three sons of Wazir Ali, Amjad, Wajid and Babar, of whom Amjad played the most important part in early dealings with Unilever. Their business had evolved from government contracting to manufacture and after partition they became one of the leading industrial companies in Pakistan. Vanaspati was only one of their many interests and they had decided to build a factory at Rahim Yar Khan (RYK) in Bahawalpur because this town offered special advantages. It was in a cotton-growing area which would provide cotton-seed as a basic raw material. It was on the main railway from Karachi to Lahore and so might serve both markets. Most important, the Nawab of Bahawalpur, which, as a princely state, then had considerable autonomy, offered substantial inducements to attract industry to his state. Under the promoter's agreement the Nawab was to assist the Alis in obtaining licences, import permits, sanction for the issue of shares and the highest priority for the import of machinery, plant, etc. The state government would provide land and canal water and for ten years the company would have tax remissions: 50 per cent of state income and corporation tax for the first five and 25 per cent for the next five years. The state also bound itself not to levy any other taxes or excises unless compelled to do so by the Indian—later the Pakistan—government.

It is not clear precisely when Unilever contacted the Ali Group, but by January 1947 the Special Committee had agreed in principle to take a minority shareholding in the Group's two projected vanaspati factories at RYK and Bhopal. It must be emphasised that at this stage the concern did not see the Bahawalpur venture as providing a single main factory to serve a sovereign Pakistan. As late as August 1947 it was uncertain whether the Nawab would choose to join India or Pakistan and even when the lines of the partition were drawn it was assumed that reasonably free trade between India and Pakistan would enable existing concern factories to serve those parts of Pakistan nearest to Bombay and Calcutta. It was only after December 1947 that the proposed Bahawalpur factory began to be seen in the context of a Pakistan with a potentially high protective tariff against goods from India. By this time the Bhopal proposal had been dropped since the Alis had moved to Pakistan; and in 1948 the growing alienation between the two countries was underlined when the Indian government temporarily banned exports of vanaspati to Pakistan. This ban was lifted in 1949 but the exchange crisis of October 1949, when India devalued the rupee and Pakistan refused to follow suit, led to a total stoppage of trade between the two countries. From that time Unilever had to see Pakistan as an autonomous market in which it must acquire adequate productive facilities for both vanaspati and soap; and in this new context the earlier strategy was clearly unsatisfactory.

The fact was that, while RYK might have been satisfactory as the site for a subsidiary vanaspati factory to serve parts of Sind and the north-west which were not easily reached from Bombay, it had serious limitations if it had to serve the whole of West Pakistan not only with vanaspati but also with soap and other Unilever products. Apart from cotton-seed oil, which was used in the production of vanaspati, the region provided no other useful raw materials. This meant that tallow, coconut and other oils used for soap had to be imported via Karachi and the rail freight to RYK, together with the return freight on goods for the rapidly expanding Karachi market, was bound to affect profitability. If Unilever was to have a single factory in West Pakistan it should either have been at Karachi or Lahore. Moreover RYK had other defects. The town was small and primitive, so that there was no adequate supply of labour or housing. To manufacture there Unilever had to import labour and build a complete housing estate and a power house at great cost. In short, the only real benefit lay in the tax and other concessions offered by the Nawab; and it was primarily because of these, though also because no alternative seemed available at the start, that Unilever decided to go ahead with building the factory at RYK. Ironically, by the time it came into production in 1952/3, Bahawalpur state had been absorbed into West Pakistan and lost its autonomy, so the company never received the promised tax concessions.

These facts are of critical importance for the long-term performance of Unilever in Pakistan and, as will be seen, largely explain the company's poor performance. The dangers were, however, perceived by the start of 1948 and the concern attempted to avoid dependence on a single factory at RYK and at the same time to get into production before the new factory could be built there by buying into one or more licensed vanaspati enterprises in more satisfactory locations. Between 1948 and 1950 they negotiated to acquire the

Ganesh Flour Mills factory at Lyallpur, which was owned by a Hindu who was said to want to sell up and move to India. By the spring of 1949 it was unlikely that satisfactory terms could be agreed, although negotiations continued until 1950. Unilever then negotiated with the Ali Group to collaborate in building another vanaspati plant on the site the Group already owned in Hyderabad (in Sind), part of the Hyderabad Vegetable Oils and Allied Industries. The project was killed by the sudden and short-lived suspension in 1949 of the Indian government's ban on the export of vanaspati to Pakistan which momentarily caused a glut on the market and made local production seem unprofitable. The Alis eventually built a vanaspati plant there on their own.

Failure to find an alternative meant that Unilever felt bound to go ahead with the RYK project. Building began there in 1949 and, after interminable delays, the vanaspati plant came into operation in 1952, soap in 1953. Nevertheless the search for additional productive capacity continued. Unilever decided not to buy or lease the Kosil Company factory in Karachi in 1962 on the grounds that it was too cramped and it was not until December 1965 that agreement was reached for them to buy A & B Oil Industries, a complete vanaspati factory in Karachi. In the same year a Unilever factory was opened at Chittagong designed to serve the large East Pakistan market. Thus for the whole of the period covered by this study RYK was the only factory operated by Unilever in Pakistan. This fact to some extent limits the value of Unilever's experience in Pakistan as evidence of the problems and opportunities facing expatriate concerns in that country for a Unilever enterprise based from the first on Karachi or Lahore might have been far more successful. Yet the story of Rahim Yar Khan does throw considerable light on many of the typical problems facing an international firm operating in a 'new' state of this kind; in particular those relating to the inauguration of a sophisticated modern business and the effects of rigorous state control of the economy. It is proposed to consider the evidence very briefly under four main heads: the structure of the companies in which the concern was involved, emphasising in particular the system of collaboration with indigenous partners; the special problems of Rahim Yar Khan leading to the decision to attempt to diversify the range of products and to establish additional factories in other parts of Pakistan; relations with the government, in particular the question of regionalisation of capital and management; and finally the profitability of the business.

(a) Relations with Local Partners

The peculiar interest of Unilever's position in Pakistan was that, in contrast with its normal policy overseas, the concern was at first a minority shareholder in a manufacturing business. The partners with whom Unilever found itself collaborating in the late 1940s bear a superficial resemblance to those involved in the Boulton Brothers' empire in India during the early 1920s, which were described above, except that the leading entrepreneur was not an expatriate but a Muslim and that in this case the partners were able and dynamic. Amjad Ali, the effective head of the family business, was a leading Muslim industrialist who saw the opportunity created by partition and used his family wealth and political influence to build up an extensive industrial and commercial empire in West Pakistan in the later 1940s. To establish an oil-milling business in Rahim Yar Khan he had already recruited two allies: the ruler of Bahawalpur State (who thus equates with the one-time Boulton ally, the Maharajah of Gwalior) and an Englishman, Sir William Roberts, who had large cotton-growing interests in Bahawalpur. At the start the main asset of this group was possession of licences to manufacture vegetable ghee; but after partition and the decision that Bahawalpur should be included in Pakistan rather than in India, they also possessed invaluable political contacts. What the group needed was additional capital, particularly from abroad, and the skills which a great international company, such as Unilever, could bring. Unilever had these assets in abundance but needed a licence to enable it to manufacture, first in the north-west of India and then in Pakistan. It also needed the political know-how and leverage in Pakistan which a man such as Amjad Ali could provide. This is essentially why Unilever was prepared to accept a minority holding in the first instance and then to perpetuate participation with local interests throughout the period with which we are concerned.

The result was that until the mid-1950s there was a very complicated structure of companies with varied concern participation. At Karachi Unilever had two wholly owned subsidiaries—HVM and Lever Brothers Ltd—both established in 1947 to carry on the marketing of Unilever products in Pakistan after partition. Vanaspati was manufactured by the Sadiq Vegetable Oil and Allied Industries Limited, in which the equity was distributed as follows:

Unilever (Commonwealth Holdings) Ltd	45.33%
Bahawalpur State	36.66%
Amjad Ali	15%
Sir William Roberts	3%

Soap was manufactured by a separate company on the same site, the Sadiq Soap Co. Ltd, in which the shareholding was as follows:

Unilever (Commonwealth Holdings) Ltd	70%
Bahawalpur State	20%
Amjad Ali	5%
Sir William Roberts	5%

To ensure effective management by Unilever yet another company, the Bahawalpur Agency Limited, was set up whose nominal capital was allocated as follows:

Unilever (Commonwealth Holdings) Ltd	51%
Amjad Ali	39%
Sir William Roberts	10%

And to strengthen this control all marketing was to be undertaken by the two concern companies in Karachi.

In all essentials these were Unilever enterprises in which even the partners holding between them a majority of the equity were happy to be dormant. The difficulties began only when it became necessary to increase the share capital, first to meet higher construction costs and then to expand production. The initial capital of the two Sadiq Companies was Rs. 20 million. But by early 1952 and even before production began it became evident that more working capital would be required than had originally been expected, mainly because the licensing system forced manufacturers to carry large stocks as a cover against delays. In March 1952 London was advised that the capital employed by the Sadiq Companies should be increased to Rs. 30 million. The Special Committee recognised that the concern must put up more money whenever necessary but felt that there was a danger that their partners might refuse to invest a share proportionate to their equity holding. Conversely, if the concern invested unilaterally, this would change the balance of the equity holding and risk incurring disfavour with the Pakistan authorities. By April 1952 these fears had been realised. The Bahawalpur State Government was prepared to increase their investment but the Ali family, which had so far received no return whatever on their capital, was reluctant to do so. As a result the concern seemed likely, when its new capital investment had been converted into shares, to hold 50 per cent of equity in the edibles company and 74 per cent in the soap company.

By 1954 it was obvious that a major reconstruction of the whole Pakistan business was essential. Due to the divorce between un-profitable manufacturing and profitable import and marketing, the concern by then owned some 70 per cent of the £2 million capital employed, but was entitled to some 88 per cent of the profits. Hansard summed up the position in December 1954. 'If one did have partners it was important that they should be co-operative and satisfied.' As if this was not enough, additional difficulties arose from the fact that Bahawalpur State had now been merged into West Pakistan as part of a restructuring of the Pakistan constitution, so that one virtually private partner had become a public organisation. The solution adopted was to unify all the concern's activities in Pakistan in order to allocate profits equitably as between each shareholding interest. Pakistan official regulations insisted on a minimum of 30 per cent local participation in joint ventures, but this did not necessarily imply 30 per cent of the equity. Thus the concern could hold 80 per cent of the equity and the other parties— the Alis, Roberts and the West Pakistan government—a mixture of ordinary and preference shares, so that just under 40 per cent of the total nominal capital would be in the hands of third parties. The reorganisation was completed in 1955. Unilever now held 61.0 per cent of total nominal capital, 80.1 per cent of equity and 69.3 per cent of voting rights and this seemed satisfactory until 1960, when plans for substantial new developments in West and East Pakistan were prepared. R. H. Siddons summarised the problem in a report made in March 1960. There was a strong case for several major new projects for which much of the capital equipment would have to be imported. To provide foreign exchange for this equipment would constitute Unilever's contribution to the increased capital of the Sadiq companies which were united as Lever Brothers (Pakistan) Ltd (LB(P)) in 1957: but to meet local costs and, more important, to avoid changes in the structure of shareholding, a proportionate amount of new capital would have to be raised in Pakistan. Sir William Roberts and the government of West Pakistan were under-stood not to want to increase their investment; so the only alter-natives were to depend on the Alis or to offer shares to the general public. The difficulty in following this last course was that new shares could not, due to government regulations, be issued at a premium: so public sale would not produce a return related to the concern's commercial prospects. In March 1961 D. J. Mann and R. H. Siddons therefore proposed a rights issue of ordinary shares to existing shareholders sufficient to raise the nominal capital from around Rs. 200 million to about Rs. 300 million. The problem was how to persuade the existing minority shareholders to take up their proposed rights; and for this reason the rights issue should consist entirely of ordinary shares which then earned a dividend of about $10\frac{1}{2}$ per cent before tax as compared with the 5 per cent paid on preference shares. Even so, Mann and Siddons favoured public sale of the balance of shares in order to create a market for Unilever stock in Pakistan for the first time.

The Special Committee agreed to proceed along these lines but negotiations were prolonged. A rights issue of two shares for five existing shares was arranged and by July 1963 all existing partners, except the West Pakistan government, had subscribed the first call for 20 per cent. It looked as if the concern would be forced to sell the balance of shares not taken up under the rights issue to the general public since the government forbad them to take up more than 60 per cent of the rights issue themselves. In the end the problem was solved without the concern going public in Pakistan by the surplus shares being sold at par to the National Investment Trust, set up by the Pakistan government, whose function was to enable the public to have some experience of shareholding without having to speculate on the stock exchange. The result was that the concern's share of the nominal capital in Lever Brothers Pakistan Ltd remained roughly as before:

Unilever (Commonwealth Holdings) Ltd	60.7%
West Pakistan Government	17.9%
Ali/Roberts/Amir Group	14.0%
National Investment Trust	7.4%

Unilever now had 73.2 per cent of ordinary shares and 60.4 per cent of voting power. Subsequent calls for new capital were met successfully in the same way without increasing Unilever's share of the Pakistan business. Thus in October 1964 a rights issue of 1 for 32 was agreed to pay for a new glycerine distillation plant for Rahim Yar Khan; and in May 1965 a rights issue of 1 for 5 was made to pay for the purchase of the A & B Oil Company at Karachi.

Unilever's experience in Pakistan demonstrates some of the benefits and problems associated with collaboration between an expatriate concern and indigenous capital. For Unilever the benefits of collaboration were mostly political. The Alis and other local participants in the business lacked technical know-how and could not provide marketing outlets. The concern did not need the capital its partners provided and had to find the foreign exchange element each time new investment took place. But at every stage local participation was politically crucial. Initially the Sadiq Company possessed a licence for manufacturing vanaspati. After partition the Ali family seemed—though this is impossible to demonstrate from the records—to have provided valuable contacts with the government and clothed the otherwise naked foreignness of this British company. Although it is impossible to document the point, such a partner was almost certainly a valuable ally during the difficult early days of the Pakistan Republic.

(b) *Commercial Problems*

In many ways Pakistan offered exceptionally favourable conditions for foreign entrepreneurs during the first two decades of its independence. Yet as late as 1953 the manufacturing enterprise in Rahim Yar Khan made no profits; and it will be shown later that even during the following decade profits were comparatively low—never rising above a nett yield on GCE of 5.1 per cent and averaging 3.6 per cent over the decade 1956–65. Clearly Pakistan had not provided a quick kill or profitable bonanza for Unilever. Why was this and what light do the reasons throw on the problems facing an international corporation in a less developed country? The problem falls chronologically into two main periods: the years 1946–53 when the factory was being built: and the years 1953–65 when other difficulties arose.

The first major setback was that it took over four years to get into production at Rahim Yar Khan, delays being caused by post-war supply difficulties, disruption of the port and transport, and the total lack of heavy lifting and moving equipment at Rahim Yar Khan. But late completion was the least important reason why Rahim Yar Khan subsequently proved less profitable than had been anticipated. The causes fall under two main heads: the basic unsuitability of this site and restrictions imposed by the government. The first of these has already been explained; as Hansard summed it up in January 1955, 'We have built the wrong sort of factory, too expensively, taking too long, in the wrong place, with the wrong partners for wrong reasons.' But this is not in fact the only reason for the low profitability of the Pakistan business and we must now turn to the effects of government control of the economy on the concern's performance.

The fact is that, however well disposed the government of Pakistan might be to expatriate enterprises, it had its own severe problems, and in particular those relating to foreign exchange. As soon as Rahim Yar Khan was in full production—that is, by 1954—it was

Table 4.22   Pakistan: Volume of Sales 1948–65

Year	Edibles (m.tons)	Concern share of Vanaspati market %	Detergents (m.tons)	Concern share of soap market %	Toilets Rs. '000	All products Rs. '000
1948	2,194	n/a	2,173	n/a	672	n/a
1949	6,268	n/a	2,043	n/a	350	12,528
1950	102	1	2,743	10.9	348	6,454
1951	204	n/a	3,675	n/a	416	n/a
1952	n/a	n/a	4,013	n/a	n/a	n/a
1953	3,710	n/a	769	n/a	n/a	8,027
1954	3,307	n/a	3,030	n/a	100	16,944
1955	2,477	n/a	3,927	n/a	215	16,806
1956	2,458	15	4,246	10	59	18,632
1957	2,545	15	4,463	10	50	21,117
1958	3,097	16	4,971	11	51	26,199
1959	4,350	16	6,587	17	57	32,694
1960	7,615	23	7,493	18	543	45,759
1961	9,161	22	7,354	18	392	48,804
1962	11,164	19	9,260	21	266	58,024
1963	10,090	14	10,503	21	387	57,433
1964	11,287	13	11,531	19	555	68,334
1965	10,897	11	11,592	16	1,050	96,313

Note: To 1953 all products were imported; thereafter they were locally made.

held up by a shortage of oil supplies for which the government could only apologise. Similar raw material shortages occurred throughout the rest of the period due variously to a short-fall in local oil production, the ban on trade with India and the need to ration foreign exchange. Such unavoidable shortages were accentuated by a system of economic controls which closely resembled those in India.[19] In 1954 it was reported that it took between 8 and 17 months from the date of applying for a licence for imported goods of any kind before they became available; and if anything went wrong production had to be held up. Furthermore licences to use imported oils were related to the licensed capacity of a particular enterprise. Thus, because the concern had a licensed vanaspati capacity of only 6,000 tons in 1961, as compared with actual production of over 9,000 tons, it received only 5,000 tons of American oils imported under PL 480. While Unilever was in no worse position than most of its competitors, the combination of

Table 4.23 Pakistan: Comparative Profitability of Edibles and Detergents, 1953–65 (Rs. '000)

	Edibles			Detergents		
	A	B	C	D	E	F
Year	GCE	Trading profit after tax	Yield %	GCE	Trading profit after tax	Yield %
1953	n/a	(328)	n/a	n/a	116	n/a
1954	n/a	229	n/a	n/a	247	n/a
1955	n/a	19	n/a	n/a	801	n/a
1956	7,354	179	2.4	18,223	902	4.9
1957	9,979	142	1.4	17,547	366	2.1
1958	13,618	238	1.7	20,129	405	2.0
1959	10,978	416	3.8	22,047	868	3.9
1960	19,282	802	4.2	22,614	813	3.6
1961	20,040	625	3.1	24,519	1,348	5.5
1962	17,840	904	5.1	24,740	1,219	4.9
1963	16,780	928	5.5	24,335	1,224	5.0
1964	18,430	1,354	7.3	28,379	917	3.2
1965	17,166	401	2.3	35,118	329	0.9

recurrent shortages and a fundamentally unsatisfactory site served to condemn the enterprise to very modest results.

What was the solution? Different remedies were required for diverse problems. The concern could do little about discontinuity in supplies nor could it significantly increase its allocation of foreign exchange by means of the export bonus scheme because there was little that it could export. But two problems it could attempt to solve. Disadvantages stemming from the inadequacy of Rahim Yar Khan could be mitigated by acquiring additional capacity in other and more suitable places, such as Karachi, and eventually moving the centre of the Pakistan business to such a place. This would also mitigate the effects of the restriction on production of vanaspati imposed by the Pakistan Government, and the limit on detergents resulting from inadequate capacity at Rahim Yar Khan. In addition. the concern could, as in India, look for opportunities to diversify into other fields in the hope that this would earn official approval and might eventually provide an escape from the restrictions placed on vanaspati and soap. The attempt to buy or build additional factories has already been summarised, and by the end of this period Unilever had greatly widened its industrial base in Pakistan.

Table 4.24　Pakistan: Nett Profit after Statistical Tax as a Percentage of Average Gross Capital Employed, 1953—65 (RS. '000)

Year	A GCE	B Profit after tax	C Yield (B as % of A)
1953	n/a	(207)	n/a
1954	n/a	483	n/a
1955	n/a	834	n/a
1956	25,577	1,084	4.3
1957	27,526	510	1.9
1958	33,747	646	1.9
1959	33,226	1,287	3.9
1960	43,065	1,610	4.0
1961	46,354	1,709	3.7
1962	44,580	2,297	5.1
1963	42,997	2,024	4.7
1964	49,620	2,423	4.9
1965	55,477	966	1.7

In addition to one badly sited factory at Rahim Yar Khan they had new factories at Karachi and Chittagong which were well placed to serve major centres of population. In course of time Karachi might well replace Rahim Yar Khan as the centre of the enterprise in West Pakistan; and by foresight Unilever had established its East Pakistan base before that region achieved autonomy as Bangladesh. But these developments did not solve the basic problem of how the concern could keep up the momentum of expansion and solve the problem of low profits. In West Pakistan their vanaspati production was limited by the licensing system and soap sales by restricted

Table 4.25 Pakistan: Profits and Costs in Relation to NSV, 1953–65 (Rs. '000)

	A	B		C		D		E		F	
Year	NSV	Gross profit	B/A %	Adver-tising	C/A %	Marketing expenses	D/A %	Factory and general expenses	E/A %	Trading profit before tax	F/A %
1953	8,027	179	2	n/a	n/a	1,125	14	n/a	n/a	n/a	n/a
1954	16,944	4,440	26	n/a	n/a	961	6	n/a	n/a	n/a	n/a
1955	16,806	6,245	37	n/a	n/a	876	5	n/a	n/a	n/a	n/a
1956	18,632	6,540	35	519	2	551	3	1,638	9	3,497	18.8
1957	21,117	6,276	30	890	4	742	4	2,466	12	2,123	10.0
1958	26,199	6,807	26	749	3	778	3	2,878	11	2,690	10.3
1959	32,694	8,746	27	889	3	789	2	3,123	10	3,784	11.6
1960	45,759	9,360	20	1,529	3	1,034	2	3,361	7	3,445	7.5
1961	48,804	10,939	22	2,036	4	1,651	3	3,763	8	3,452	7.1
1962	58,024	13,225	23	1,915	3	1,956	3	4,087	7	4,640	8.0
1963	57,433	14,527	25	2,505	4	2,081	4	4,851	8	4,497	7.8
1964	68,934	17,272	25	3,149	5	2,225	3	5,778	8	5,385	7.8
1965	81,288	15,998	20	3,231	4	2,926	4	7,080	9	1,952	2.4

imports of raw materials and a limited market for quality detergents. As in India, therefore, Unilever turned to diversification as a possible means not only to break through these limitations but also to earn the goodwill of a host government on whose readiness to provide licences of all sorts the prosperity of the enterprise depended.

The campaign to diversify had begun as early as 1956—three years after the Rahim Yar Khan factory came into full production and at a time when the bottlenecks caused by shortages of imports were acute. R. H. Siddons argued in June 1956, after a visit to Pakistan:

> The main problem . . . continued to be that of supply. Everything was subject to import licences; machinery for new developments were virtually debarred and spares and raw materials were very difficult to obtain. As a result of the shortage of tallow, we were using hardened cotton oil for soap which meant that less was available for vanaspati . . . We were overcapitalized and we had a surplus of unremittable cash of about Rs. 50 lakhs . . . Our best course might be to extend our activities into other fields, again subject to the availability of raw materials and machinery.

He might have added that small profits from the existing products was an inhibiting factor; even so it was not easy to find alternative lines. Toothpastes were an obvious possibility but by 1956 two other companies had been given import licences for capital equipment and a third application had already been refused. As in India there was therefore a case for investigating fields in which there was no existing enterprise and which might at the same time provide some stimulus to Pakistan agriculture—that is, milk products, compound cattle feeding stuffs, dried vegetables and so on. Many such alternatives were investigated during the next decade but animal feeding stuffs emerged as the only potentially viable proposition: after a visit by experts from British Oil and Cake Mills (BOCM) in 1958 (an example incidentally of the special skills a large international firm can utilise in a developing country), London decided in principle to go ahead with trial production of compound cattle cake at Rahim Yar Khan. A moderately optimistic assessment of the project was made by R. P. Tripp of BOCM late in 1960, provided the price of cattle compound was not above what West Pakistan farmers were accustomed to pay for oil cake. Rahim Yar Khan might produce 40,000 tons a year and additional mills could be built at Lahore or other major population centres. But, as in India, the project had to be justified mainly on non-commercial grounds. 'Although it might prove difficult to justify such a venture commercially there can be no question that a flourishing compound trade would be of great value to the country and would be much appreciated by those concerned with animal nutrition and by the government.' In short, this would be a contribution to Pakistan's economic development rather than a profit-maximising commercial enterprise.

Experience substantiated this prediction. In 1961 Mann and Siddons had to report that the selling price of compound cake was determined by the current price of undecorticated cotton-seed cake. This normally fluctuated seasonally between £30.6 and £36.7 a ton and at the present price of £32.2 the concern could break even only if 10,000 tons of cattle compound were sold. Already, as in India, hope centred on poultry feed, which LB(P) had started making at Rahim Yar Khan in 1960, as a potentially more viable proposition if only commercial production of poultry could be stimulated and Unilever was able to attract two international poultry breeders to Pakistan to encourage local enterprise. In May 1965 G. M. Brock, Chairman of the Pakistan company, reported that production estimates for 1965 included 6,500 tons of feeding stuffs, of which 5,550 were poultry feed, 'the only one on which we make a margin'. There was no local competition in poultry feeds, but equally there was no certainty of sufficient demand to make the enterprise profitable on a large scale and RYK was far too far from Karachi for profitable production. In December 1965 it was decided to buy a poultry feed plant then at Karachi for £100,000, which would be placed on the newly acquired A & B Oils site to serve the growing poultry industry in that city; but this came to nothing because the government insisted that payment should be made in foreign exchange.

The evidence to the end of 1965 suggests one clear conclusion. With all the will in the world it was difficult in the short term for even a major company such as Unilever to diversify its industrial base in an economy as undeveloped as that of Pakistan. The licensing system made it impossible to manufacture goods such as toilet preparations for which there was a proven market, but also existing licensed producers. On the other hand market limitations made it unprofitable to show enterprise in fields such as cattle compounds, even with governmental support. This is why, some 30 years after the partition of India and Pakistan, Unilever was still dependent on manufacturing the two basic products with which it started in Pakistan—vanaspati and detergents (including NSDs made to Unilever specification *à façon* by a local firm but packed and marketed by LB(P))—and had not yet found an answer to the basic problem of how and in what direction it should develop in the future.

(c) Unilever and the Government of Pakistan

As far as one can judge from the records, relations between Unilever and the Pakistan government were generally cordial. As early as April 1949 R. H. Muir was impressed by 'the spirit of friendliness prevailing' and, although anti-British feeling rose from time to time, due mainly to Britain's alleged lack of sympathy over issues such as Kashmir and later the struggle with India, the company never seems to have been subjected to hostile discrimination. For its part, concern reaction to the political system and changes in the regime was muted: the criterion was not legitimacy but stability, and it was recognised that, despite recurrent shortages, the tedium of the licensing system and limitations placed on the extent of development, successive regimes throughout the period 1947–65 were genuinely attempting to improve economic conditions in Pakistan and were at the same time dealing fairly with foreign companies. But on two matters the government did impose constraints: on the proportion of Pakistan participation in joint ventures of this kind, and on the gradual transfer of management to Pakistanis.

The question of local participation in the equity of concern companies in Pakistan has already been considered. The government insisted that where collaboration existed Pakistanis should hold not less than 30 per cent of the total capital; but it showed no interest in forcing Unilever to dis-invest or to 'go public'. In 1965, therefore, the concern was still collaborating with a small group of private and state investors and no share dealings took place on the stock exchanges. Nor did localisation of management cause any serious problems in Pakistan. The basic conceptual issue had been faced in India in 1955 and it was natural that in Pakistan Unilever should follow the course mapped out there, though with a different time-table. From the start there were very practical reasons for reducing the number of expatriate staff to a minimum. European managers disliked working at Rahim Yar Khan because of its remoteness; and, although many Pakistanis shared their repugnance, the only solution was to recruit and train local men. By May 1956 40 per cent of senior managers and managers (eight) were Pakistanis and it was proposed to fill a directorship with a Pakistani as soon as possible. By 1958 there were two Pakistanis in a board of six, and this proportion remained constant until 1965, not because the concern wished to retain a majority of European directors but because it had not managed to recruit and retain men of sufficient ability to replace them who would live at Rahim Yar Khan. In 1965 a problem arose which, for the first time, produced official intervention. The concern decided that a European would have to succeed Brock as Chairman of the local company, and one of the two Pakistani directors, who, it was said, had hoped for the reversion of this post, resigned in protest at a man being brought in from outside. Since no other Pakistani manager was thought suitable to replace him, Unilever proposed to send someone from London and the government refused an entry permit on the ground that the Pakistani element on the Board would be reduced to one. A simple solution was found: two additional Pakistanis were raised to the Board, making three out of seven, and the government gave the desired entry permit. Localisation was not complete at the end of our period but it was then only a matter of time before the Chairman and the majority of the Board were Pakistanis.

(d) Investment, Production and Profits

Unilever's total investment in the Pakistan business to 1965 (including short-term indebtedness to the parent company) was about Rs. 27.6 million (£2.1 million). In the same period remittances to Europe (consisting of dividends, Rs. 5.7 million and service fees and royalties, Rs. 2.8 million) amounted to Rs. 8.5 million (£640,000), leaving a nett input of about Rs. 19.1 million (£1.4 million). It is significant that, by contrast with India, most of the concern's capital in Pakistan came from London and relatively little was generated by the local company. This was not the outcome of concern altruism: there were comparatively few profits to invest and the fact that in Pakistan the minority shareholders expected that most profits would be distributed as dividends further limited capital accumulation. But it did mean that Unilever made a substantial contribution to Pakistan's stock of capital at the start and that during the first 20 years the concern put no strain on the country's foreign exchange position.

Low profitability was, in fact, a basic feature of the Pakistan business from the start, as is clear from Tables 4.23 and 4.25. This is in some ways surprising for Unilever products were well-established before 1947 and Pakistan provided conditions in which many other companies were able to thrive. One possible cause of low profitability can be eliminated to start with: it was not primarily due to tight margins between the price of raw materials and selling prices. Table 4.25 shows that gross profit never fell below 20 per cent of NSV after 1954. This was substantially higher than the profit margins current in India and higher even than those on soap sales there. Nor was the low nett profit due to uniquely high corporate taxes: again the rate of statistical tax paid in India was substantially higher than in Pakistan, except during the three years 1956–8. The basic fact, which follows from what has already been said about Rahim Yar Khan as an industrial base, is simply that overheads were far too high. If one takes a fairly 'normal' year— 1963—advertising, marketing and factory and general expenses together amounted to 17 per cent of NSV; whereas in India they were only 10 per cent that year. But more important still, the capital tied up in fixed assets at Rahim Yar Khan (inflated by the cost of an oil mill closed because it was uncompetitive with small low-overhead millers) and the working capital employed were an intolerable burden for a small new enterprise to carry. In 1961, for example, gross capital employed in Pakistan, Rs. 46,354,000, was almost as large as nett sales value, Rs. 48,804,000; whereas in the same year in India GCE was less than a third of NSV. It is true that after 1961 the ratio changed for the better: in 1965 GCE was Rs. 55,477,000 as compared with NSV of Rs. 81,288,000; but this was still much less favourable than the Indian ratio of GCE Rs. 179,800,000 to NSV Rs. 678,156,000.

Why were these ratios so comparatively unfavourable? There are of course different answers for overheads and the high proportion of capital to NSV. Advertising was relatively expensive because these were new markets to develop. Marketing expenses were on the high side because of the high cost of transport and distribution. Factory and general expenses were inflated by the very large cost of providing and maintaining a complete social unit rather than merely maintaining a factory in an existing town. Recurrent shortages of raw materials reduced the volume of production and increased the burden of overheads. But in the last resort the reason was simply that Rahim Yar Khan had absorbed too much capital and was too expensive to run.

The time period covered by this study is too short to justify any firm conclusions. By 1965 Unilever was potentially in a much more favourable position than ever before in Pakistan for it had acquired or bought additional capacity in Karachi and Chittagong which had for the moment inflated the GCE without contributing profits but might be expected in future to improve the return very considerably. Nevertheless the Pakistan experience suggests the general conclusion that even a highly efficient international firm which establishes a manufacturing subsidiary in a 'new' developing country at its very birth and is able to take advantage of the first phase of import substitution does not necessarily make a large profit from its operations.

5

Unilever in Indonesia and Ceylon (Sri Lanka)

Indonesia

There are several reasons why the Netherlands Indies (NEI) and
its successor state, Indonesia, are included in this study. This was
a Dutch rather than a British colonial possession and until 1957
the Unilever enterprise there was more closely related to the Dutch
side of Unilever than most other overseas companies studied in
this book. Second, this was an important Unilever subsidiary.
It was one of the first to be established in a less developed country
during the second wave of Lever/Unilever industrial expansion
overseas; and the country's size and population made it a valuable
market. In 1930 the population was over 60 million; and although
this was spread over many islands and there were problems with
freight costs, distribution and sales promotion, two-thirds of the
population was in Java. In the 1950s Indonesia's per capita income
was estimated at US $127, compared with $122 in Ceylon and
$72 in India, which put it well up the league table of LDCs.[1] This
made it an attractive site for direct foreign investment, more
particularly because it also possessed many of the raw materials
required for typical Unilever products. But above all Indonesia is
important for this study because the Unilever companies there
experienced more political hazards during the 30 years after 1935
than any others included in this book. After a quiet birth in the
1930s, the local business was seized by the Japanese in 1942.
Returned to Unilever in 1946, it had to survive the next four years
when the Dutch were attempting to reassert political control over
the Netherlands Indies. Having then come to terms with the
successor Republic of Indonesia, Unilever suffered as the modern

264

sector of the economy decayed after the mid-1950s and the business was effectively taken over in 1964, only to be returned in 1967. No other Unilever subsidiary provides better evidence on how the company faced these characteristic problems of the early post-decolonisation era, nor on the relative power of a multinational and a sovereign successor state in South Asia.

(a) The Origins of Local Manufacture to 1941

(1) *Lever Brothers: Soap Imports.* Until about 1928 NEI was merely one of many export markets for the three soap-making firms which were part of Lever Brothers. Although data for the early years are defective, Tables 5.1 and 5.2 give an impression of the size of soap exports to NEI between 1910 and 1934, when local manufacture began. What proportion of total soap sales in NEI this represented is impossible to calculate since the great majority was made by very small enterprises, mostly Chinese, from whom no statistics were collected: but Levers undoubtedly dominated the import market: in the mid-1920s they were thought to hold well over 70 per cent of total hard soap imports. It was only in and after 1930 that competition from overseas, particularly from Japan, became strong, and this had an influence on the decision to build a local Lever factory. There are difficulties also in estimating the profits made on exports; but pre-tax profits for 1929–32, set out in Table 5.2, suggest that until the economic crisis NEI sales provided a reasonable return as well as contributing to Lever overheads. This is one probable reason why little interest was shown in local manufacture before the drop in profits in 1931/2; another was the tariff. Import duties were low, even after they were increased in 1931. In the 1920s the duty on common soap was 6 per cent and was only 9 per cent (18 per cent on carbolic and toilet soap) after two increases in June 1932. The implications for local manufacture are obvious.

As in all less developed countries during the 1920s and 1930s Levers relied on local agents to handle their products; and the problems of distribution in NEI were so great that even Gossages did not maintain their own depots there. So long as the relatively small volume of goods had to be distributed over so wide an area, it was not worth while for an overseas company to maintain a sufficiently large sales force or enough wholesale depots to undertake their own distribution. Nestlés had tried direct selling to retailers in NEI before 1928 and had failed because they could not estimate the credit worthiness of wholesalers and retailers. Only with local manufacture and greatly increased turnover did this' become practicable; and, as will be seen, even in 1965 Unilever Indonesia still relied on agents for some of its distribution. In NEI before 1941 there were five big firms who between them more or less monopolised the import–export trade and a number of smaller firms with less widescale activities. The 'big five' were George Wehry

Table 5.1   NEI: Total and Gossage Shipments from United Kingdom of Household and Fancy Soap to Borneo, Sumatra and Netherlands East Indies, 1910–21 (in tons)

Date	Total	Gossage	Gossage %
1910	2,755	2,222	81
1911	2,162	1,311	61
1912	2,581	1,367	53
1913	3,370	1,621	48
1914	4,260	2,097	49
1915	6,272	3,483	56
1916	7,736	4,078	53
1917	7,306	2,735	37
1918	4,128	1,745	42
1919	3,160	1,713	54
1920	5,303	2,001	38
1921	4,713	2,828	60

Note: This table, which is also used for exports of soap to India, was found in the Lever Bros records in London. It is not clear whether 'Total' is for the whole of UK exports of soap or for all exports by what eventually became Lever Bros firms. It is possible that the document was prepared by Gossages and that 'Total' includes all UK firms. Nevertheless, since by 1911 Levers, Crosfields and Gossages together dominated the UK soap market and even more UK exports, these 'Totals' are probably fairly close to the exports of these three firms.

and Co., Borsumy, Reiss and Co., Schnitzler and Co., and Internationale Credeit HV Rotterdam. In the 1920s Levers used several of these agents, each of whom bought Lever goods (with a few exceptions) for cash against documents and earned a commission of 3 to 5 per cent and a bonus of 1 to 3 per cent for payment to wholesalers. Crosfields had a special agreement with Borsumy and shipped goods to them at 7.5 per cent; while Gossages used only one agent, Reiss and Co., on the same commission. Thus Levers took no risks, leaving the agent to buy his goods outright, while Gossages and Crosfields both sold on their own account through their agents.

It would be wrong to give the impression that Levers took no part in promoting their goods in NEI: as in India, they employed their own representatives whose business it was to survey the market and stimulate demand among wholesalers and retailers—who were predominantly Chinese—and to a limited extent also among the consuming public. The degree of supervision and market research was, however, slight. In the 1920s Levers employed a single sales

Table 5.2   NEI: Soap Exports by Lever Bros Ltd and Associated Companies from (1) UK and (2) Australia to Netherlands East Indies, 1923–34[a] (in tons)

Year	(1) From the UK	Nett Profit (£)	Profit per ton (£)	(2) From Australia
1923	n/a	n/a	n/a	957.5
1924	n/a	n/a	n/a	695.7
1925	9,150	n/a	n/a	614.8
1926	9,629	n/a	n/a	415.2
1927	9,744	n/a	n/a	501.2
1928	[10,000] [b]	n/a	n/a	533.4
1929	8,350	65,469 [c]	7.8	413.5
1930	6,295	47,152	7.5	253.3
1931	5,275	29,518	6.8	164.5
1932	4,225	4,757	1.1	n/a
1933	3,718	n/a	n/a	n/a
1934	2,846	n/a	n/a	n/a

Note: a.   UK exports include Levers, Gossages and Crosfields. Australian exports were from Kitchens and Burfords.

b.   The figure for UK exports in 1928 is approximate.

c.   Nett profit on UK exports from 1929–32 (the only figures available) relate to profit made by the home companies on exports to Indonesia.

representative who spent perhaps eight months of the year in Indonesia and whose business it was to advise the export departments and then UEL on products, prices and advertising. This was clearly beyond his capacity to do effectively and it was a common complaint that the agents often raised the selling prices laid down by UEL. Advertising was also difficult in a country where in 1928 there was said to be only about 1.5 million out of a total population of 51.5 million who could read. Press advertising was largely a waste of money, yet other types of promotion, such as lorries, required considerable organisation. As a result, even though administrative charges and advertising were expensive, Levers could exert very little influence on the sale of their products. They were dependent on their agents and the state of the market. While this was acceptable in good years it was not in the bad years after 1931. Efforts were made after 1928 to improve the effectiveness of UEL supervision, but ultimately only a locally-based industry with detailed knowledge of the market and its own promotional agencies could take a real grip on the situation. This was one of the most important changes resulting from local manufacture after 1934.

(2) Jurgens and Van den Berghs: Margarine Imports. Since NEI was a Dutch possession it might have been expected that Jurgens and Van den Berghs, the two main Dutch companies which, as Margarine Unie, merged with Levers in 1929, would have pioneered the Indonesian market. In fact this was not so. Levers had established a large export market for soap there well before the Dutch possessed a comparable market for margarine. Thus in 1926 Levers' soap exports to NEI were 9,629 tons, whereas Jurgens and Van den Berghs and their subsidiaries exported only 413.4 tons of margarine there. On the other hand, the first attempt by a member firm of the future Unilever to undertake any form of industrial production in NEI was made by Jurgens from 1917; and although this oil-milling venture was a disaster it at least entitles Jurgens to pride of place in this account.

The attempts made by Anton Jurgens to take a leading role in the vegetable oil commodity market and also to invest in the initial processing of vegetable oil must be seen as the Dutch companies' equivalent to Lever's more successful attempts at vertical integration of the soap business before 1925.[2] Both policies sprang from a common belief in the actual and potential shortfall in world supplies which would leave the unprotected buyer in a dangerously vulnerable position. Lever felt this well before 1914 and the plantations in the Solomon Islands and the Congo, both of which are described elsewhere in this book, were the outcome. Anton Jurgens' initiative came later—in and after 1916—and lasted only about five years: by 1921 he had admitted failure and had returned to the traditional Dutch method of buying raw materials on the open market, which the Van den Berghs never dropped. With two of these ventures—large-scale purchase of palm oil and palm kernels in Nigeria and the purchase and milling of linseed in Argentina—we are not concerned in this account: they are described in outline by Wilson.[3] Nevertheless Jurgens' venture in NEI must be seen in the wider context of an attempt both to safeguard essential raw materials and to deal in the world commodity market. If successful, he would have laid the foundations of Unilever's industrial activities in Indonesia and provided the starting point for an evolutionary process of growth from commodity purchase to oil milling and ultimately manufacture of edible oils, fats and soaps. It did not, however, work out that way. The chain of events was broken in 1921, and when Unilever eventually undertook manufacture in Indonesia it was for reasons quite unconnected with oil milling.

Jurgens' activities in NEI began in 1916 as an attempt first to avoid paying extortionate prices for copra, then to speculate in the wartime and projected post-war boom in vegetable oils by accumulating large stocks of copra. One of his main buying agents was the firm of Manders, Seemann & Co., which was renamed in 1916 N. V. Manders, Seemann & Co., Handel Maatschappij; and in 1917 Jurgens paid Fl. 1,500,000 for shares in this company, plus Fl. 1,000,000 as Jurgens' share in the increase of its capital. On the trading side this investment produced good returns in 1919, but there was a loss in 1920 of Fl. 1,600,000 and of Fl. 6,000,000 in 1921. In January 1922 Jurgens decided to write off their investment. They sold their holdings of ordinary shares to the Nederland Indische Escompto Mij at 30 per cent of their par value and withdrew from commodity speculation in the East Indies.

Meantime, however, this association had led Jurgens into oil milling in NEI. The first modern oil mill in the country had been built in 1909 and by 1913 there were a number of small-scale mills, one at Macassar being owned by Manders, Seemann & Co. This had been established as a subsidiary company, EMO, in which Jurgens automatically acquired an interest when they bought the Manders, Seemann shares in 1917. Other oil-milling companies included N. V. Olifabrieken Insulinde, with mills at Batavia; and United Java Oil Mills owned by Ross, Taylor & Co. Once interested in oil milling, Anton Jurgens took stock of these rivals. To combat the expansion of Insulinde, which was tending to push up the price of copra. Jurgens in June 1917 bought the freehold of an oil mill in Macassar, in which Manders, Seemann & Co. already had an interest through the controlling company EMO. Two months later Jurgens bought yet another mill, this one at Jacatra. He paid Fl. 420,000 for it and set up a new company, N. V. Oliefabriek 'Jacatra', with Fl. 1 million nominal capital, to run it. In 1918 his stake was further increased by decisions taken to build a new plant for EMO, and also to create a fourth company, NIOF, with a capital of Fl. 2 million in order to establish a plant at Padang. Neither of these came into operation until 1920.

Jurgens' enterprises, together with the considerable number of other oil mills built during the First World War (there were 20 modern mills in Java alone in 1918 with a capacity of over 135,000 tons a year) were potentially of considerable importance to the Indonesian economy. On the general hypothesis that processing of a locally produced primary commodity is a desirable first step towards economic development, leading perhaps to secondary industrial processing, this might have had important long-term consequences. Conversely, it is often held that the more developed countries deliberately refuse to undertake such processing in the country of origin in order to obtain the benefit for their own economy. It is therefore of some interest to establish why it was that the Indonesian oil-milling industry in general and Jurgens' mills in particular proved so unprofitable in peace-time that neither he nor any other member of Unilever again indulged in oil milling in Indonesia except to meet their own local industrial needs.

The standard economic case for extracting oil from copra in Indonesia rather than exporting the copra to Europe or North America can be summarised under two main heads: quality and price. In principle coconut oil (hereafter CNO) might, though this is debated, retain its quality better after transport overseas than copra, which is liable to become mouldy and rancid. More important, by cutting out the middlemen in the copra trade, using local labour in the mills and achieving a 40 per cent saving in the space required in ships, the cost of the oil when sold in Europe or America should be substantially lower, enabling it to compete with other vegetable oils, such as palm oil and palm kernel oil from West Africa. As against these potential benefits, however, there are many potential or actual disadvantages in local processing. The freight advantage depends on the charging policy adopted by the shipping companies; and if these decide to discount the bulk factor, the advantage of local milling might disappear. This indeed happened in 1931, when freight rates dropped to one-fifth of the 1919 level, so reducing the relative significance of the differential freight charges; and the shipping conference so arranged freights that it actually became cheaper to transport copra than oil.

There were, however, more general considerations. Oil milling is a capital intensive industry, and the relatively low cost of local labour is of little importance as compared with the high cost of transporting and maintaining capital equipment and paying the salaries of expatriate managers, foremen, etc. Most important is the problem of selling the by-products. Except in periods of acute shortage—as during both world wars—it has never been very profitable to sell vegetable oil in the world market without obtaining a good market for the by-product, oil cake. Equally, the comparatively high freight costs of transporting oil cake in relation to its market value makes it almost essential that it be consumed locally, which in turn postulates a market for compound animal feeding stuffs. It is at this point that economic conditions typical of less developed countries become critical for local oil milling. Use of compound animal feeding stuffs is virtually restricted to the richer countries of Europe, North America and Australasia, for the great mass of farmers in the less developed world cannot afford processed animal food. If, therefore, an oil miller in Java who has no market for his main by-product has to compete in the international oil market with oil millers in Europe or America who regard the income from the sale of oil as only part of the return they look for, the Javanese miller cannot survive on the return he receives for his oil. This, more than any other single factor, has tended to perpetuate the milling of vegetable oils in the more developed countries. It is not the malevolence of international capital but the facts of oil marketing that determine distribution of industrial activity.

In the case of the Jurgens' oil mills after 1917, these two adverse factors quickly proved decisive. The problem was intensified by the comparatively high price he had paid during the wartime boom period for the factories and other assets acquired. By 1920 the Jurgens' investment was roughly as follows:

	Fl.	
EMO (Macassar)	1,500,000	(shares)
	1,000,000	(additional capital)
	2,500,000	
Oliefabriek 'Jacatra'	5,000,000	(paid up capital)
NIOF (Padang)	2,000,000	

Of these only EMO made any profit—Fl. 1,283,000 in 1919. In 1920 a loss of Fl. 1,600,000 was made which rose to a loss of Fl. 6,000,000 and also exhaustion of the reserves of Fl. 2,000,000 in

1921; and heavy losses were made on stocks of copra bought by this company. Neither the Jacatra nor Padang plant was in operation until 1920 and neither ever made a trading profit. In 1921 the whole group of enterprises was clearly floundering; and as a last hope an appeal was made to William Lever to establish a buyers' consortium in Indonesia. The object was to force the market price of copra down to a level at which the oil factories could operate profitably and supply both Levers and Jurgens with CNO at cost. Lever, however, said he regarded the whole project as too small-scale. If the combination included his main rivals—Maypole, Van den Berghs and Jurgens—and took over the Insulinde Oliefabriek as well, the scheme might be worth considering. In the end it came to nothing. Jurgens was forced to give up his whole copra buying and oil-milling project and write off his losses. The shares held in Manders, Seemann & Co. were written off because by January 1922 that company was in liquidation. As for the three oil mills, they were simply locked up in 1922 and in later years most of the machinery was removed to Europe. The mills remained in the possession of Jurgens and so passed in due course to Margarine Unie and thus to Unilever. In 1929, when a report was prepared for the newly estab-lished Unilever on these properties in the context of the possibility of building a soap factory, it was found that they were quite unsuit-able. The Batavia site—Jacatra—was less than an acre; the others, though relatively large, were of no use for a factory because they were not in Java where the main market for soap existed. Thus, the Jurgens enterprises ended in total disaster. Ironically, when it was decided in the 1930s to acquire an oil mill to supply the new Batavia soap factory, Unilever chose to buy an oil mill there rather than reactivate these existing properties.

For the history of Unilever in Indonesia the significance of all this was that manufacturing operations there did not, as they might well have done, grow from an already established oil-milling business; and, although Van den Berghs thought seriously in 1920/1 of buying an interest in the Javanese oil mills to secure their own supply of copra, from 1922 to the mid-1930s both Jurgens and Van den Berghs treated NEI merely as an export market for edible fats manufactured in Europe and the decision to manufacture margarine and other edible fats there in the 1930s grew from problems arising from this established export market. Before examining the origins of this decision to manufacture we must therefore look briefly at the character and vicissitudes of the Jurgens and Van den Berghs export market in NEI in the 1920s and early 1930s.

Although NEI was a Dutch possession, the stake of the Dutch margarine firms there was very small. The market for edible fats in NEI was restricted and Dutch exports were minute compared with Levers' soap sales. Even at the peak of Dutch margarine exports—before the slump in 1929—the volume of 793.6 metric tons was less than a tenth of Levers' soap sales at 8,350 tons from Britain plus 413.5 tons from the Australian subsidiaries. Until after 1926 margarine exports to NEI were mainly the products of Van de Griendt of Utrecht and Haarlem, a relatively small firm, which specialised in the manufacture of cheap second-grade margarine for export to the tropics. The firm was acquired in 1919/20, on the initiative of Griendts, because it possessed a highly effective process for making and canning margarine for these markets; so in buying Griendts, Van den Berghs were buying also an established export market and a new dimension to their European business. Once involved in the export of margarine, VDB changed its character. Leaving export of second-grade margarine to Griendts, it concentrated on creating a market for their own high-grade Blue Band and Table 5.3 shows that they were reasonably successful: exports to NEI rose from 450 kg in 1923 to 393 tons in 1929. This was an achievement but must be seen in proportion. NEI was then the largest single export market for Margarine Unie outside Europe and North America; even so, it represented only about 7.7 per cent of total exports and in the early 1930s, when imported butter from Australia became very cheap, margarine exports fell away rapidly. By 1935, the last full year of importing, sales were below the 1925 level and it seems certain that the subsequent expansion was only made possible by the introduction of local manufacturing.

(3) Soap Manufacture. It is not clear why the possibility of local manufacture of soap in NEI first came up, as the records suggest, in 1928. Sales of imported Lever soap had been increasing during the 1920s and in 1927 reached 9,744 tons, which was not reached again until 1940, and there had been no change in the tariff or other relevant considerations. In any case, C. E. Tatlow, who was sent to investigate, did not recommend local manufacture. He admitted that the coincidence of ample raw materials, cheap labour and a

Table 5.3   NEI: Margarine Union/Unie and Unilever Exports of Margarine to NEI, 1923–38, and Shares of Each Component Company, 1923–9 (in kilograms)

			(From English A/C)		Griendt			
Year	VDB Rotterdam	Jurgens Oss	VDB Rotterdam	Jurgens Oss	Utrecht	Haarlem	Others	Total
1923	450	—	—	—	166,283		76,429	243,162
1924	11,136	—	—	—	153,282	100,497	6,709	271,624
1925	24,378	—	—	—	154,488	142,577	9,680	331,123
1926	72,196	—	—	—	154,714	141,532	45,000	413,442
1927	112,792	3,163	—	42,494	182,535	145,817	26,152	512,953
1928	203,343		50,844		148,202	100,564	4,491	516,083
1929	392,684		31,437		195,840	128,288	16,122	793,607
1930	n/a		n/a		n/a	n/a	n/a	282,234
1931	n/a		n/a		n/a	n/a	n/a	228,990
1932	n/a		n/a		n/a	n/a	n/a	204,918
1933	n/a		n/a		n/a	n/a	n/a	253,000
1934	n/a		n/a		n/a	n/a	n/a	358,000
1935	n/a		n/a		n/a	n/a	n/a	370,000
1936	(local manufacturing begins: total includes imports)				n/a	n/a	n/a	[512,400]
1937	ditto				n/a	n/a	n/a	[852,000]
1938	ditto				n/a	n/a	n/a	[1,412,400]

Notes: a. From 1928 the figures are shown differently in the records; in particular there is an entry 'from England', i.e. probably from the VDB factory. This is small and is excluded here; but as a result the sum of the individual figures does not tally with the total.

b. Import figures from 1930–32 inclusive slightly understate total concern imports since these relate only to the main Unilever agent in Indonesia.

c. It has proved impossible to isolate imports as distinct from locally manufactured products from 1936–8, but imports clearly dropped quickly and in 1938 were only 34,000 kg.

large established market was 'attractive'; but this was offset by the fact that the bulk of imports consisted of cheap soap which was in direct and increasing competition with soap made by local Chinese manufacturers. The market for quality wrapped soaps was only about 2,700 tons, and this did not justify a local factory: efforts should therefore be made to build up this market. Lever House accepted this view and improved its marketing system in 1929. The merger with Margarine Unie that year suggested the possibility of using the Jurgens oil mills as sites for soap factories and a Lever man was sent to investigate. His report was unfavourable, mainly because the only site in Java (in Batavia) was too small; but by 1932 new and much more compelling arguments were coming into play. Unilever soap sales plummeted from 8,350 in 1929 to 5,275 tons in 1931. Declining sales in an established export market of sufficient size constituted a standard incitement to local manufacture; and from 1931 the Special Committee had this constantly in view.

Yet it was not until September 1933 that the decision to invest in a factory was taken. In March 1931 it was decided to fight for the NEI market by supplying UEL with bar soaps and cubes at cost to compete with locally made lines. In July 1932 news came that raw material prices were rising and that the NEI had imposed a surcharge on import duties, increasing the *ad valorem* duty on laundry soap to 9 per cent and on toilet and carbolic soap to 18 per cent. This made a 'factory proposition' much more attractive, and the Special Committee asked for calculations based on building a factory in Java with an output of 15,000 tons to supply Malaya and British Borneo as well as NEI. In July the answer came that there was a favourable margin of £35,029; but a decision was deferred until a report could be received from Tatlow, who was on tour in the Far East. Tatlow again recommended inaction:

> To lock up Sterling Capital on a falling market against Guilders could very considerably vitiate any original estimate of capital cost and unduly handicap the investment from the interest standpoint in perpetuity. Taxation as an unknown factor 'running wild' might play havoc with margins already too narrow to allow of undue depletion to meet Budget deficiencies.

But by September 1933 the exchange position was more stable, taxes had risen in NEI and the future of import duties was known.

From 1934 toilet soaps would pay between 18 per cent and 30 per cent, other soaps between 9 per cent and 18 per cent according to size and quality. Margarine and other edible vegetable fats would be charged 18 per cent. Under these conditions Unilever hesitated no longer. On 27 September the Special Committee noted that the increased import duties, coupled with currency depreciation, would result in a trading loss on the basis of imports from England, whereas local manufacture might produce a saving of about £40,000 once the higher import duties came into effect. Unilever's Chairman, D'Arcy Cooper, took the decision to invest in local production reluctantly because, as he told the Directors' Conference, he was 'very chary of putting up new factories anywhere, as it was not to be supposed that the present high tariffs would be permanent'. But action followed quickly. Tatlow was told to form a locally registered company, Levers Zeep Fabrieken NV (LZF), with an authorised capital of 2 million Guilders, the shares to be held by Unilever NV. He rejected Surabaya as a factory site because it was the centre of a sugar growing area which was then in a depressed state and because municipal taxes were relatively high. He also rejected a proposal from the German firm of Georg Dralle at Surabaya to manufacture soap for Unilever *à façon*. Instead he bought a site at Angke, Batavia. The cost of the factory he financed by retaining remittances due to UEL from local agents for imported soap and the factory came into operation in October 1934.

(4) Margarine Manufacture. Manufacture of margarine at Batavia was made feasible by the existence of a soap factory and desirable by declining margarine imports. The established import market was being lost to imports from the Philippines Manufacturing Co., Manilla (PMC), a subsidiary of Procter and Gamble built in 1931, which then broke into the NEI market with their Palmboter, using an efficient and dynamic agent, Borsumij. This new competition, coupled with a drastic reduction in the price of Australian butter (the main competitor with margarine among the European population of NEI) brought down Dutch margarine exports from 793 tons in 1929 to about 229 tons in 1931 and other Unilever NV products, such as Calvé Delft's Delfia (cooking oil) were also badly affected. The obvious solution was to take advantage of the new tariff and to use the 18 per cent margin to compete both with Australian butter and the misleadingly named Palmboter (palm butter); and Tatlow advised in 1932 that, if a soap factory was built, provision should be

made in it for manufacturing edible fats and oils. This was not done and as late as 1935 J. H. Hansard advised against local manufacture of these products after visiting Batavia. Yet sometime within the next year this advice was rejected in Europe: the decision to manufacture margarine at Angke is mentioned as a fact in a report made by Sidney Van den Bergh in November 1936. Unfortunately there is no record of when and on what grounds this decision was taken; but, reading between the lines of his report, it seems probable that the following factors proved decisive. First, while total imports of margarine to NEI increased from 266 tons in 1933 to 765 tons in 1935, the Dutch share increased only from 253 tons to 370 tons. Since the balance came mostly from Manilla, this suggested that the market was promising, provided Unilever could compete on price with the Procter and Gamble product, now renamed Palmboom (palm tree instead of palm butter) following legal action taken by Unilever in NEI. Second, calculations indicated that the low cost of NEI coconut oil in the mid-1930s coupled with the import duty would provide a profit margin of Fl. 28.83 per 100 kilos on locally made margarine as against Fl. 0.14 on Blue Band made in Holland; and this margin could be used to fight Palmboom on price. Finally it was thought that local manufacture could be exploited in promoting Blue Band: the initial publicity campaign stressed that 'Blue Band was daily churned in Batavia'.

Local manufacture of Unilever margarine was therefore undertaken as the only means of salvaging a decayed import market: as Sidney Van den Bergh put it in 1937, 'if we had not started local manufacture it would have been impossible to hold our trade against these imports from neighbouring countries'. Two separate companies, Van den Berghs Fabrieken (NI) NV (VDB) for margarine and Oliefabrieken Calvé Delft (NI) NV for vegetable salad oils, were registered in Batavia in 1936, the first as an active, the second as a dormant trade mark company; and, like LZF, both were owned by Unilever NV. Their success was immediate and must have surprised those who doubted.

(b) Unilever in NEI, 1934–41: the 'Classical Period'

The 'classical' period of local manufacture in NEI was short—only seven years for soap and five for edible oils; but it was long enough to demonstrate one important fact about subsidiary companies manufacturing for local consumption in a LDC—that they are more vulnerable to domestic than foreign competition, even if the former comes from competitors who do not possess comparable production facilities and operate in a much less sophisticated way.

This point is clear from Tables 5.4 and 5.5 which summarise the performance of the soap and edible fats companies. LZF did well in that by 1940 the volume of Unilever soap sales in NEI had risen to over 9,000 tons, the level of imports in 1927, after falling to

Table 5.4   NEI: Sales and Profitability of the Batavia Soap Factory, 1935—40

(a) Sales, actual profit after tax, profit as % of NSV and profit per ton

Year	A (Metric tons)	B NSV (FL)	C Nett accounting profit (FL)	D C/B%	E C/A (FL)
1935	3,870	n/a	26,054	n/a	n/a
1936	5,203	1,325,069	104,713	7.9	20.1
1937	7,149	1,836,400	159,815	8.7	22.3
1938	7,063	1,773,764	108,896	6.1	15.4
1939	8,489	n/a	179,740	n/a	21.2
1940	9,713	n/a	127,828	n/a	13.2

(b) Actual post-tax profit in relation to capital employed, 1935—40

Year	A Nett accounting profit (FL)	B CE (FL)	C A/B%
1935	26,054	n/a	n/a
1936	104,713	1,876,671	5.6
1937	159,815	2,120,345	7.5
1938	109,896	2,024,355	5.4
1939	179,740	1,944,053	9.2
1940	127,828	2,284,854	5.6

(c) Profit after statistical tax in relation to capital employed, 1935—9

Year	A Nett profit (FL)	B CE (FL)	C A/B%
1935	39,569	n/a	n/a
1936	108,627	1,876,671	5.8
1937	144,525	2,120,345	6.8
1938	106,619	2,024,355	5.3
1939	[225,408] [a]	1,944,053	[5.9] [a]

Note: [a] The nett profit after statistical tax for 1939 includes the estimated profit of one quarter as I have been unable to find the final figure.

2,800 tons in 1934. This was an achievement, but it did not result in high profits: although capital employed was kept low by depreciating goodwill, nett profit after statistical tax remained under 7 per cent. Moreover nett profit per ton showed no sign of rising and was substantially down in 1940. The explanation clearly lies in the strength of the competition. Most of LZF's sales volume consisted

Table 5.5   NEI: Sales and Profitability of Edible Products, 1936—40.

(a) Sales volume of all edible products and accounting profit after tax

Year	A Metric tons	B Nett accounting profit (FL)	C Profit per ton (FL)
1936[a]	808	n/a	n/a
1937	1,343	76,144	56.7
1938	2,302	151,527	65.8
1939	4,296	227,054	52.8
1940	5,045	173,349	34.4

Notes: a. Manufacture started in the September quarter 1936. The 1936 figures therefore consist largely of imports: thereafter there was a small and declining element of imported products.

b. Sales include exports to Malaya and other parts of SE Asia.

(b) Actual profit after tax in relation to capital employed, 1937—40

Year	A Nett accounting profit (FL)	B CE (FL)	C A/B%
1937	76,144	488,968	15.6
1938	151,520	500,785	30.3
1939	227,054	1,340,177	16.9
1940	173,349	1,381,898	12.5

(c) Nett profit after statistical tax in relation to capital employed, 1937—8

Year	A Nett profit (FL)	B CE (FL)	A/B%
1937	79,689	488,968	16.3
1938	152,339	500,785	30.4

Note: Profits for 1937 and 1938 are inflated by the fact that part of the stocks used by VDB appeared in the balance sheet of LZP and also by an unrealistic apportionment of fixed assets between the two companies. This was corrected in 1939.

of cheap, unbranded bar soaps, sold to Indonesians. These were in direct competition with a large number of small Chinese makers who had the double advantage of low overheads and savings on freight, since they were made from local raw materials for a local market. Such soap made a contribution to LZF's overheads but would never provide large profit margins. These depended on branded toilet soap, branded laundry soap, such as Sunlight, and soap powders, of which the first was critical for profits. In 1941 the total market was reckoned to be about 4,350 tons and LZF had about a third, with Lux Toilet Soap, holding 22 per cent of total sales and making a trading profit of Fl. 212 a ton, as market leader. But competition was intense. The main rivals were Camay, imported from the USA (220 tons), Palmolive, made locally by Dralle (225 tons), various other Dralle lines (1,025 tons) and other brands totalling 1,500 tons. Thus, although the import tariff coupled with import quotas (adopted in the mid-1930s) had eliminated the Japanese threat and handicapped foreign competitors, Unilever faced sufficiently strong internal competition at all levels of the market to keep profit margins low.

The contrast with the edible fats business is striking: its success is written across the statistics summarised in Table 5.5. Two main features stand out: rapidly increased sales volume and market shares coupled with very good profits. Sales volume grew from 808 tons in 1936 to 5,045 tons in 1940, including margarine, which increased from 339 tons (imported) in 1935 to 2,429 tons in 1940. This increased Unilever's share of the local butter and margarine market from 7 per cent to 47 per cent and was achieved both by expanding the total market and also at the expense of rivals. In 1935 PMC had 52.2 per cent of the total margarine market to VDB's 47.8 per cent (ignoring the small portion held by others). In June 1939 the market was estimated to be divided in the proportion VDB 60 per cent, PMC 28 per cent, Archa 5 per cent, others 7 per cent. Meantime margarine was defeating butter. Total consumption of butter and margarine remained remarkably consistent between 1935 (5,089 tons) and 1940 (4,997 tons); and, since the volume of PMC's sales also remained steady, it is clear that Unilever expanded at the expense of Australian butter imports. It could do so for the same reason that it could seize market leadership from PMC: it benefitted from low commodity prices coupled with the 18 per cent import duty on edible fats. By 1940 butter had risen from its very low price level of the early 1930s and was selling at about Fl. 1.50

per kilo, whereas Blue Band sold at about 65 cents a kilo. This produced a major swing away from butter, accentuated by the fact that in 1938 Blue Band replaced butter in the diet of the Dutch army in NEI. Price, however, does not explain the victory over PMC since the two companies adopted identical prices and in 1938 made a price agreement; nor was there any significant difference in quality or in distribution. The explanation probably lies in the greater amount VDB could afford to spend on advertising, using some of the margin provided by the protective duty. In 1937 it was estimated that PMC was spending about Fl. 40,000 to 50,000 on advertising, against Blue Band's Fl. 24,000. In 1938 VDB spent Fl. 134,915 advertising Blue Band and made Fl. 149,580 profit on it. In 1940 advertising cost them Fl. 224,500 and was clearly winning the war. The result, however, was that Procter and Gamble decided to build a PMC subsidiary at Surabaya to compete on equal terms and only the coming of war prevented cut-throat competition.

Heavy promotional expenditure did not, however, exclude good profits. The reasons are that raw material costs were low and as against foreign competition were further reduced by the devaluation of the Florin/Guilder in 1936. As butter prices rose, the potential profit margin on margarine widened; and so long as PMC, the only local competitor was outside the tariff wall, VDB had a large margin to play with. As in India in the same period, this was too good to last; but here also a new local manufacturer was able for a limited period to exploit uniquely favourable conditions.

In 1940/1 Unilever seemed well set in NEI and plans were prepared for expansion. In 1940 expenditure of Fl. 630,000 was authorised to increase soap capacity to 15,000 tons. By November 1941 it had been decided also to buy the Dralle factory at Surabaya which, being owned by Germans, had been sequestrated in 1940. Unilever paid more for it than they had expected, due to the ingenuity of the Custodian of Enemy Properties: they did so partly to prevent it falling into the hands of Procter and Gamble but also because they saw Dralle as a means of diversifying into perfumes, toothpastes, cosmetics, etc. Finally it had been decided by the end of 1941 that VDB should aim to expand the margarine market by about 2,500 tons, recruiting 'the better class of natives' to 'the spreading habit'. Factory extensions had been approved and in 1940 a small fat-hardening plant had been installed in Jakarta. It was at this moment that the Japanese brought the first phase of Unilever's industrial activities in NEI to an abrupt end.

(c) Rehabilitation and Growth, 1945–57

Probably no other Unilever subsidiary has had so discontinuous a history as that in Indonesia since 1941. The Japanese invasion in 1942 cut Indonesian companies off entirely, and they were not handed back until March 1946. During the following ten years the enterprise had a conventional history by the standards of the new ex-colonial world of the post-war period; but in 1957 a major crisis occurred in which all Dutch employees had to be removed and ownership of this subsidiary transferred from Rotterdam to London. In 1963 this transfer had to be reversed as Confrontation with Britain over the Malaysian issue developed; and in 1965 Unilever completely lost control over its subsidiary, although it remained legally the owner. This might well have been the end of the story; but in 1967, following political changes in Indonesia, the enterprise was handed back and a new and still continuing phase of redevelopment began. Behind these obvious discontinuities there were also important underlying changes in the conditions affecting company activity in Indonesia, with the main division in 1956/7. It is therefore necessary to tell the story of Unilever in post-war Indonesia in two parts, dividing at 1957. The theme of the first period will be reconstruction and growth, and the plan will follow that for other subsidiaries described in this book. The final section will be primarily concerned with the uncertainty and economic decline caused by political changes in Indonesia, and the main theme will be the reactions of the company to political instability, hyper-inflation and hostility to foreign enterprises.

(1) Political Change. It is ironic that in many ways the most dynamic and successful years for the Unilever companies in NEI after 1945 were from 1946 to 1950. This was a period of political uncertainty and intermittent fighting; yet by 1949 sales of soap and edible fats were some three times the volume of 1940. Space makes it impossible to describe the political events of this period, but it is important at least to establish Unilever's attitude towards the process of decolonisation and its aftermath.[4]

From 15 August 1945, when the Japanese finally surrendered, to 27 December 1949, when the Dutch formally transferred sovereignty over NEI to the government of the short-lived United States of Indonesia (excluding West Irian), the key issue was whether the

Dutch, anxious not to lose control of valuable sources of raw materials and still not aware of the psychological change the Japanese occupation had brought about in Asia, could set up a loose federation formally under the Dutch Crown; or whether Indonesian nationalists, who had been active since the 1920s and had greatly increased in importance during the Japanese occupation, would succeed in establishing an independent republic. In 1945 the Indonesians appeared to have everything on their side. Many of their leaders had collaborated with the Japanese and were in a position to seize political control before the Dutch could return. On 17 August 1945 two leading republicans, Sukarno and Hatta, signed and promulgated a declaration of Indonesian independence and then set up a government in Batavia. Thus, when British troops, the first allied force, arrived at the end of September 1945 to take over from the Japanese Army, the British commander recognised the 'Indonesian Government' as *de facto* administering all areas outside those actually occupied by British troops. It seemed that Dutch colonial rule was at an end, but the Dutch did not accept this. Their troops began to arrive in October 1945, gradually replacing British forces in the main coastal towns of Java and Sumatra. The Republican leaders withdrew to Jogjakarta and for the next four years of negotiation and fighting it seemed likely that the Dutch would succeed in creating a client Indonesian federation. They were eventually thwarted by the USA acting through the United Nations; and after a series of meetings that culminated in the Round Table Conference at The Hague in August–November 1949 the Dutch were forced to transfer sovereignty by 1 January 1950.

It is clear, both from the records and from the recollections of Unilever men who were involved with Indonesia at that time, that Unilever took a much more realistic and less dogmatic view of the political situation after 1946 than The Hague or Dutch officials in Jakarta. This was not surprising. Although traditionally most Unilever managers in Indonesia were Dutch rather than British, they did not share the typical Dutch settler's determination to preserve his privileged position in Indonesia, the paternalism of the conventional Dutch colonial administrator, or the neo-mercantilism of Dutch metropolitan governments and officials, with their post-1945 preoccupation with raw materials and balance of payments. Thus, while they were not entirely right in how they predicted the future pattern of Indonesian development after 1945, they were at least consistent in regretting the excesses of Dutch policy, particularly in and after 1947; and it came as no surprise or disappointment to them that Dutch policies eventually failed.

Until about March 1947, when the Dutch took the first steps towards their subsequent 'police action' by landing troops at Modjokerto (East Java), Unilever men seem to have taken it as axiomatic that Indonesia would become 'an independent state within the framework of the Dutch empire . . .' and accepted that this would result in a planned economy 'and possibly a gradual nationalization or state control of such industries as railways, shipping, electricity and other services . . . combined with a system of price regulations, wage policies and the like'. That comment was written in March 1947. In the same month Sidney Van den Bergh gave a critical account of the conditions he had seen on a visit between December 1946 and January 1947. He thought it ridiculous that the Netherlands should maintain an army of 100,000 in the country at great cost to Holland and Indonesia, while conditions in the republican areas were alleged to be terrible. 'In his view the Netherlands Government were faced with the alternatives of marching in or marching out, and that the time for negotiations and parleying was over.' His view was clearly that the Dutch should 'march out'.

In fact, however, they marched in. There is no indication in the records of Unilever's reaction to this, but personal information suggests that behind the scenes the Rotterdam management was attempting to persuade the Dutch government that their military action was based on the false assumption that the majority of Indonesians were hostile to Sukarno. This was certainly the view of Unilever management in Jakarta, who, in retrospect, say that they took an unduly favourable view of Sukarno and the consequences of Indonesian independence. The strongest evidence of their optimism is the fact that in May 1949 it was planned to increase total investment (with fixed assets calculated on a replacement basis) to about 52,000,000 Guilders. There was more to this investment than mere calculation of profitability: 'Unilever had a certain moral obligation to show confidence in . . . the future [of Indonesia] . . .'.

Four years later, long before the sudden expropriation of Dutch property and the expulsion of Dutch nationals, this confidence had substantially diminished. During 1952 and 1953, as the fall in commodity prices after the Korean war boom affected the Indonesian balance of payments, the government introduced a number of new restrictions on profit transfers, raw material, imports, etc. These were not in themselves unusual in the less developed world and Unilever accepted them without complaint. But they were straws in a wind that was clearly blowing Indonesia towards insolvency; and in a long, considered report made after a visit in October 1953 Sidney Van den Bergh explained why he was beginning to lose confidence in the future of Indonesia. The root of the problem lay in a combination of financial difficulties and political inability to cope with them. Exogenous factors had increased the difficulty, notably the drop in the export price of rubber. In the previous 'good' years of the Korean war commodity boom, successive governments had frittered away their foreign exchange holdings, and between December 1951 and September 1953 total gold and foreign exchange holdings of the Bank of Indonesia had fallen from Rp. 4,247 million to Rp. 1,187 million at the official rate of Rp. 3 = Fl. 1. As a result, the black market rate for Dutch currency had risen to Rp. 6–10 = Fl. 1 and was still deteriorating. Coalition governments, and particularly the current PNI ministry founded in April 1953, which excluded the conservative Masjumi Party for the first time since independence, seemed to have no firm policy, and above all were unable to reduce government expenditure, the key to inflation, except to cut imports. Rumours of official corruption were growing, especially in the sale of import licences and the increase of patronage of all kinds; and there were strong dissident movements in the outlying provinces. In Van den Bergh's view the key to the problem was political. He remained optimistic in the long term, but feared instability and possibly violence during the next years of weak government, which might result either in a new and more efficient government, or, conversely, in a military takeover or a communist coup—though the last seemed unlikely at that stage. Whatever happened, Unilever would be wise to act cautiously for the time being.

In retrospect it can be seen that the problems pinpointed by Sidney Van den Bergh were to become endemic during the next fourteen years, and to end in virtual bankruptcy in 1965–6. Between 1948 and 1960 total money supply rose at an average annual rate of 26 per cent and price levels rose more or less in proportion.[5] Between 1950 and 1954 consumer prices doubled; they more than doubled between 1954 and 1958 and again between 1958 and 1961. From 1961 to 1964 prices increased 14 times, 7 times in the single year 1964/5.[6] Simultaneously export earnings continued to fall. Non-oil exports fell from US $900 millions in 1951 to $755 millions in 1955, and to an annual average of $562 millions in 1956–61, and $434 millions in 1962–5. Oil exports fluctuated between $195 millions and $280 millions between 1956 and 1965. The balance of payments suffered accordingly. There was a favourable balance of US $99 millions in 1955 but an annual average deficit of $74 millions in 1956–60 and an annual average deficit of $293 millions in 1961–5.[7] Useful estimates of national per capita income are not available before 1958; but for 1958–62 the index of national income at constant prices rose only from 100 to 109.2 while per capita income declined slightly from 100 to 99.8 in the same period.[8] These downward trends probably did not affect the bulk of Indonesians very markedly, since agricultural production increased at about 4 per cent a year from 1958 to 1962. The real decline was in the modern, and above all manufacturing, sector, hit by shortage of foreign exchange and therefore restrictions on the import of raw materials, intermediates and capital equipment. At the same time the capitalist sector of agriculture, producing mostly for export, fell off as investment was curtailed and labour productivity declined. Behind it all was increasing government expenditure, most of it on non-productive areas such as the armed forces (first for the West Irian campaign and then confrontation with Malaysia), for the civil service and also prestige building and other projects. During 1955–65 97.8 per cent of total new money supply was on government account.[9]

It does not require hindsight to see this pattern of decline. In its annual review of the economy in the year 1954/5, the Bank of Indonesia pinpointed the basic cause of weakness in the economy as deficit government financing. In 1954 there had been a deficit of Rp. 3,500 millions in a budget of Rp. 11,558.6 millions, mostly financed by unbacked credit from the Bank, which in turn was the main cause of an increase of 46.7 per cent in the money supply in 1953/4. The report analysed the probable consequences of continued deficit financing on this scale, including hyperinflation, decline in foreign currency reserves and a drop in production in the modern sector; and recommended orthodox financial and fiscal remedies. It also suggested that, given the urgent need for foreign exchange, it was unwise to press on too fast with the stated policy of nationalising foreign enterprises. There was thus no lack of expert local advice; but, except for the year 1955/6, when the caretaker government dominated by the Masjumi Party almost eliminated the budget deficit, it seems to have been politically impossible for any govern-

ment to impose effective control on the big spenders—the armed forces, the civil service and regional governments; and after 1957 Sukarno, as active head of the government under 'guided democracy', showed no interest in economics.

It was not until 1956 that Unilever became seriously worried by these trends, for until then it was always hoped that a new government might adopt more orthodox economic policies. Indeed, in retrospect, it is clear that the company was unduly optimistic. There seems to have been no grasp of how little economics mattered to Sukarno as compared with preserving what he called 'the continuing revolution' at all costs. [10] The management appears also not to have recognised until about 1956 that the unions had changed from being shop-floor negotiating bodies to professionally run political organisations whose main objective was to support the communist party, PKI. As a result Unilever was to some extent caught unprepared by the constitutional change of March 1957 which lead to 'guided democracy' and growing economic and political disorder.

(2) Investment and Growth. The most impressive feature of post-war development was that, after more than four years of Japanese occupation during which soap production at Jakarta stopped entirely and much of the plant became useless, there was a very rapid rise of output despite limited new investment. When the two main company factories, at Jakarta and Surabaya, were formally handed back in March 1946 they were intact but in very poor condition. The Jakarta factory had been used by the Japanese for manufacturing soap, margarine, tooth-powder and dried egg powder. It had been run by Mitsubishi, but very little maintenance had been done. No refined vegetable oil was available, there was no transport and one boiler was broken. The managers sent from London were a very strong team, led by A. W. J. Caron, H. G. W. Van Aardenne and Klijnstra, two of whom were later to become directors of Unilever. They had to improvise; and here ability to call on the resources of a multinational company at a time of general world shortage was critical. Second-hand equipment was obtained from London and other Unilever centres. To meet the shortage of electricity ex-American Army generators were bought. There was an acute shortage of raw materials, but the newly returned Dutch authorities were co-operative in providing licences, since much of the production was for the Dutch Army. Price controls restricted profits, but there was ample labour and insatiable demand for all

products. Since the Special Committee felt that the political situation was too uncertain to justify the investment of new capital from Europe, the company had to rely on a small loan from the Batavian government and its own undistributed profits to pay for rehabilitation and expansion. An additional problem was that the company depended for its refined oils on a ring of Chinese-owned oil mills in and around Jakarta; and Sidney Van den Bergh therefore recommended buying the Archa Oil Mill, near the Jakarta factory, which was up for sale, primarily as a means of breaking this ring. The mill was bought and paid for itself within nine months by reducing the market price for refined oil. Thus, by the beginning of 1947, Unilever was effectively back in business, and in its first full year of operation not only exceeded pre-war turnover, but even the targets set for soap and margarine production for that year. Toilet preparations were held up for lack of imported raw materials, and in fact did not get fully into production until 1949.

The key to Unilever's success in the decade 1947–56 is that at the start they saw and exploited the opportunities offered. They were, for the moment, the only large-scale manufacturers of soap and one of the two large producers of edible fats. Monopoly was out of the question since there were a large number of local manufacturers of soap and one large maker of margarine in 1950. But now that Unilever had bought Dralle and competition from American or Filipino imports was temporarily removed, they could become market leaders in both fields, provided they could expand fast enough while the going was good.

At the start the company seriously considered the possibility of building additional capacity outside Java to use local raw materials and serve local markets and thus save freight both ways to Jakarta. In 1948 the Special Committee adopted in principle a proposal to build an oil mill and soap factory at Macassar since there were obvious economic benefits in processing and using copra produced in the Celebes to serve the eastern market. But there was also a political aspect: at that time the Celebes seemed likely to be cut off from Java; and, although the stated reason for dropping this project in May 1950 was that the 10,000 tons of soap required for the Celebes 'could be provided more cheaply by extending the factory at Djakarta', since the cost of additional machinery there would be less than a fifth of the total cost predicted for Macassar, it is likely that Unilever was influenced by the fact that by that time the Celebes had been integrated with Java into a unitary Republic of

Indonesia. Thereafter the concern showed no further interest in dispersing its productive facilities and the main investment was in expanding the capacity and replacing old equipment in Jakarta and Surabaya. Until 1949 the management had to make do, squeezing maximum production out of antiquated and patched up machinery by working the factories 24 hours a day on two or three shifts. By May 1949 the Special Committee had approved proposals that would bring total investment, including assets at replacement value, to approximately 52 million Guilders.

Table 5.6(a)   Indonesia: Soap Sales, 1947–65. (metric tons)

Year	Laundry soap (Sunlight, Cube, Flag)	Toilet soap (Lux Toilet, Lifebuoy, Colibrita, Bris, Vinolia)	Soap powders	Total
1947	n/a	n/a	n/a	12,133
1948	19,221	1,570	142	22,959
1949	22,201	2,781	132	30,455
1950	24,108	4,552	35	31,087
1951	30,808	5,065	29	38,777
1952	24,986	5,550	82	32,819
1953	35,341	7,908	117	46,914
1954	41,263	9,186	195	54,548
1955	46,669	11,690	342	63,811
1956	51,670	7,202	364	63,317
1957	48,459	9,141	322	64,171
1958	24,656	3,605	96	30,682
1959	38,687	7,760	182	50,538
1960	42,224	7,073	267	54,179
1961	38,753	7,755	356	51,199
1962	25,430	6,418	732	35,577
1963	18,055	6,250	546	26,469
1964	22,574	5,381	305	30,882
1965	19,062	2,895	286	24,020

Notes: a. The total includes other soaps and by-products.

   b. Before 1949 the bulk of soap sales consisted of 'interim' brands discontinued once normal production of branded soaps was possible.

This first post-war effort to modernise and expand the productive capacity of the soap and margarine factories began in 1950 and was virtually completed in 1952/3. As can be seen from Table 5.6(a), soap sales rose rapidly from 32,819 tons in 1952 to a post-war peak of 64,171 tons in 1957. Edible oils and fats reached their pre-1957 peak of 12,555 tons in 1955. These sales volumes were well above the total capacity planned in 1949/50. Expansion was paid for by using local profits and whatever currency allocation the Indonesian government provided from time to time. At the end of 1953 the Unilever companies were still in an expansionist mood and talking about further developments. But from that point a growing sense of insecurity becomes evident in the records. By the spring of 1955 the foreign exchange position had become so serious that there were doubts whether the government would allow transfer of dividends and the company's liquidity position was so precarious that the

Table 5.6(b)   Indonesia: Distribution of Laundry Soap Sales in Indonesia 1955–6

	% of population	% Unilever sales	% Share of local market
Java	70	42	22
Sumatra	15	37	58
Borneo	5	11	80
Celebes, etc.	10	10	10

Indonesian management proposed, for the first time since the war, that factory extensions should either be financed from new capital from Europe or from transferable profits. Since the effective exchange rate for new investment was Rp. 3.75 = Fl. 1 as against Rp. 5 = Fl. 1 for transferable profits, it seemed logical to adopt the first alternative, but this was rejected by the Special Committee on the grounds that the future of Indonesia was uncertain. Since 1956 proved the last year before 1965 in which dividends were allowed to be remitted, their judgement was clearly correct: Unilever Indonesia had to soldier on, using their own resources.

1955 thus marked the end of investment in expansion of the Indonesian business before 1967 and the post-Sukarno era. It also marked the end of proposals to diversify the business. The main thrust of the expansionist policy adopted in 1949/50 was in soap and edible fats, but there were also proposals to diversify. The search for new products began in about 1950. The first decision was negative: 'Not to proceed with the suggestion to produce ice-cream in Indonesia', the likely reason being that there was insufficient refrigeration capacity in the shops. Two years later the proposal was to experiment in selling Royco noodle soup, by then a standard product in Europe. This was conceived by the Jakarta management; but they had to admit that the capacity of the Indonesian food industry was so limited that it would be necessary to import all the materials for this packet soup, even the noodles. It was, therefore, decided to import the finished product 'for the purpose of a practical sales test' on a cost plus 5 per cent basis. The results must have been disappointing: nothing more was heard of packet soups. In the same year Dr Dickson of Technical Division visited Jakarta to investigate the possibility of manufacturing filled milk. Sidney Van

Table 5.7   Indonesia: Sales of Edible Fats and Oil Products, 1947–65 (metric tons)

Year	Blue Band margarine	Vitello margarine	Delfia cooking oil	Total edible fats and oils
1947	n/a	n/a	n/a	7,773
1948	328	5,840	n/a	9,453
1949	4,260	2,673	1,593	10,321
1950	3,599	2,201	2,093	9,245
1951	2,640	1,573	2,934	7,422
1952	2,062	1,842	2,385	7,003
1953	2,242	2,542	2,699	8,902
1954	3,178	1,743	2,891	10,055
1955	3,479	2,218	3,719	12,555
1956	3,509	2,020	4,839	13,150
1957	4,398	2,110	2,578	12,472
1958	1,707	1,814	1,811	6,803
1959	3,590	2,361	1,422	10,071
1960	3,964	2,879	2,060	13,932
1961	3,341	2,605	1,138	16,213
1962	2,333	1,629	298	11,500
1963	1,921	441	119	8,470
1964	2,914	308	725	8,300
1965	1,706	356	309	5,266

Notes: a. In the early post-war years the bulk of sales consisted of 'interim' brands, discontinued once normal production was possible.
b. The total includes other products than Blue Band, Vitello and Delfia.

den Bergh was impressed by the project and the Special Committee gave its approval in September 1956. The stated ground was that imports of condensed milk had reached 30,000 tons a year, so that a proven market existed; the trial sale of Fortimel, the chosen brand name, had been a success; the use of locally available fats plus avoidance of import duty should ensure a reasonable profit; and the estimate of Rp. 4.8 million could be met out of the 40 per cent of profits then blocked in Indonesia which had to be reinvested locally. But Fortimel was overwhelmed by the financial and political crisis of 1956/7: in 1957 total sales of foodstuffs, including Fortimel, were only 27 tons; and thereafter it disappeared altogether, a casualty of Guided Democracy. This also proved the end of diversification until after 1967, for from 1956 onwards it was clear that neither of the two conditions normally justifying diversification was present in Indonesia: existing production fell increasingly below factory capacity, due to shortage of raw materials and trade union action; and there was no enthusiasm for new investment in so uncertain a political and economic climate. For the time being the Indonesian business had been demoted from a dynamic to a static holding operation.

Before this happened Unilever had enjoyed nearly a decade of rapid growth and reasonable profits. This is clearly reflected in the tables and it is unnecessary to describe commercial developments here. But there were two aspects of the business that are not evident from the statistics and need comment and explanation because they resulted from and typified the peculiarities of Indonesian economic life in this period. First, by the mid-1950s both soap and edible fats and oils, normally the pillars of any Unilever subsidiary, had virtually ceased to make a profit. In each case there were two reasons. On the one hand the government consistently controlled selling prices of soap and edible fats; on the other the price of local raw materials rose with inflation while that of imported raw materials was inflated by government regulations on exchange rates which acted both as an additional import duty and as a substitute for devaluation.[11] Unilever was thus caught in a squeeze. Frequent approaches were made to the government to allow increased selling prices and some increases were made from time to time, but never enough to match inflation. For a large and necessarily respectable foreign company there was no other solution. In the case of soap products Unilever could not, like its Chinese competitors, reduce overheads by cutting the labour force (because of strong trade union resistance supported by the government), nor evade price regulations. As for margarine, profits were eroded by stiff competition with Procter and Gamble in Surabaya. By the mid-1950s soap and

Table 5.8   Indonesia: Sales of Toilet Preparations, 1947—65

(a) Nett Sales value (Ind. Florins to 1949; Rupiahs, 1950—)

Year	(Rp. '000)
1947	n/a
1948	306
1949	1,405
1950	8,404
1951	15,709
1952	21,539
1953	39,817
1954	47,782
1955	79,948
1956	64,007
1957	83,826
1958	66,968
1959	96,796
1960	147,600
1961	263,700
1962	263,248
1963	1,020,000
1964	2,241,224
1965	2,811,910

(b) Toothpaste sales, 1949—65 (grosses, various sizes)

Year	Pepsodent	Gibbs Dentifrice	Mentasol	Total
1949	n/a	4,361	n/a	4,361
1950	13,063	11,510	n/a	24,573
1951	30,911	22,970	n/a	53,881
1952	28,808	13,277	n/a	42,085
1953	47,134	13,567	805	61,506
1954	58,635	13,448	3,820	75,903
1955	70,958	28,605	2,582	102,145
1956	76,456	7,819	3,576	87,851
1957	80,979	5,580	3,578	90,137
1958	48,425	1,816	1,995	52,236
1959	38,853	2,384	908	42,145
1960	44,481	4,658	1,812	50,951
1961	50,537	353	1,018	51,908
1962	46,398	5	851	47,254
1963	38,390	2	1,181	39,573
1964	16,895	947	275	18,117
1965	17,638	560	547	18,745

edibles made a contribution to overheads but did not provide a respectable profit. Table 5.9 shows that profits did, indeed, slide fast after 1955/6; yet the fact that there were any profits at all is largely due to the fortuitous and (as is clear from most other countries studied in this book) unusual fact that in Indonesia the concern made good profits on its toilet preparations. There seem to have been two main reasons for this fortunate fact: limited competition and no price controls. The first resulted from Unilever having bought the Dralle factory at Surabaya in 1941, re-equipping it after 1947 as Colibri Fabrieken NV. After 1950 the government virtually banned imports of toilet preparations while allowing importation of most relevant raw materials and intermediates; and the only foreign-owned company of comparable size or efficiency was Prodent which specialised in toothpaste. Colibri therefore acquired a substantial share of the considerable market for toothpaste (50 per cent in 1956), face powders (about 20 per cent), etc., and held about 32 per cent of the total market for toilet preparations in 1957. In the following decade it was this side of the business that kept it solvent and provided modest profits.

The other main development of the 1950s, which continued after 1957, was that political pressures greatly speeded up the transition from selling through the 'big five' agents, as in the pre-war period, to the system of direct sales through Unilever depots to Indonesian wholesalers, which had already been established in other countries, such as India. By 1949 a still nascent organisation was selling all soaps in West Java and also the new toilet preparations throughout Java; but in other places and for all other products, such as margarine, Unilever continued to sell to the agents. By 1956 the government was applying strong informal pressure for the company to switch to direct sales to Indonesian middlemen on the grounds that the agents were foreign; and in 1957 a first step was taken by giving the distribution of Sunlight Soap in Bali to an indigenous local firm. The transition in the business as a whole might, however, have been slow on account of the complexities and costs involved in direct sales from depots in a country as large and under-developed as Indonesia. Ironically action was stimulated by government policies designed to have the opposite effect. As part of the anti-Dutch measures adopted by Sukarno in 1957, the 'big five' agents were nationalised. The government was anxious to maintain distribution through these agencies, now increased from five to eight and re-named Depot Keepers, but the old system soon became almost

Table 5.9   Indonesia: Results, 1946—65 (losses in brackets). (Million NEI Guilders to 1948; Indonesian Guilders, 1949; Indonesian Rupiahs, 1950—65)

Year	A Sales volume all products M. tons	B NSV	C Trading profit before tax	D Trading profit after stat. tax	E Nett accounting profit	F GCE	G D/F %	H C/B %	I E/B %
1946	n/a	n/a	n/a	n/a	(0.8)	2	n/a	n/a	n/a
1947	n/a	50	n/a	n/a	8	3	n/a	n/a	16.0
1948	30,488	71	16	12	6	8	150.0	22.0	8.0
1949	35,620	83	21	15	10	16	93.7	25.0	12.0
1950	38,092	161	31	8	18	41	19.5	19.0	11.0
1951	44,052	277	44	26	16	76	34.2	16.0	6.0
1952	41,318	222	26	15	17	106	14.1	12.0	8.0
1953	59,002	330	55	28	28	140	20.0	17.0	8.0
1954	67,882	403	89	45	34	165	27.3	22.0	8.0
1955	81,130	476	123	64	58	209	30.6	26.0	12.0
1956	81,839	470	68	32	36	282	11.3	14.0	8.0
1957	78,588	550	63	30	26	465	6.4	11.0	5.0
1958	41,368	524	54	26	38	647	4.0	10.0	7.0
1959	64,645	918	135	56	41	767	7.3	15.0	4.0
1960	73,649	1,225	136	27	34	791	3.4	11.0	3.0
1961	74,759	1,434	208	79	64	971	8.1	14.0	4.0
1962	48,913	2,891	718	93	75	1,021	9.1	25.0	3.0
1963	36,152	7,741	1,843	62	80	2,444	2.5	24.0	1.0
1964	41,282	14,633	(741)	(3,078)	16	6,223	—	(5.0)	0.1
1965	29,775	44,313	354	(8,331)	28	4,548	—	0.8	0.06

Notes: a. This statement was produced by Unilever Indonesia. The figures differ in some respect from those available in Unilever House, particularly for the years 1961 to 1965. The figures for NSV are the same but post-tax results and GCE are substantially different. It is not clear why this is so, but the most likely cause is that London adopted different accounting procedures in the period of hyperinflation.

b. The extraordinarily high percentage profit figures in Column G for 1948—55 result mainly from the fact that the fixed assets had been written off during the war and revaluation of assets was irregular until 1958. For these years a better indication of profitability is in Columns H and I.

c. The large increase in GCE for 1957 was due to revaluation of fixed assets at the current effective exchange rate (Rp. 7.65 = Fl.1).

unworkable. In 1962 Unilever took the step they had regarded as impracticable: in Java they stopped selling to the Depot Keepers and went over to direct selling. The island was divided into ten big areas, each under an Area Manager, who became responsible for sales promotion and payments and had his own team of sales managers. They either hired godowns (stores) from the Depot Keepers or acquired their own, and dealt in all concern products, as individual agents had often not done. Goods were sold for cash to Indonesian or Chinese wholesalers. The new system had the double advantage that it facilitated penetration of the market and was much cheaper: distribution costs dropped from over 10 per cent of NSV to 4 per cent. Outside Java direct selling was not yet practicable, so 'stockists' were appointed. They were new men, not the Depot Keepers, and they were backed up by Unilever marketing teams.

Table 5.10   Indonesia: Remittances to Holland and Total Profits, 1948–65 (million Rupiahs/Florins)

Year	Rupiah = A	Florin B
1948	3	3
1949	3	3
1950	7	2.4
1951	11	3.6
1952	9	3.1
1953	13	4.4
1954	23	4.7
1955	23	4.6
1956	13	2.5
1957	18	3.6
1958–65	No dividends were remitted	
TOTAL	123	36.8

Note: The data indicates the year in which the transfer was actually made. The last year in respect of which profits were transferred was 1955, the profits being remitted during 1956 and 1957.

(3) Localisation of Management. Although by 1946 the principle of recruiting and training non-Europeans for the highest managerial posts had already been put into practice in India and Ceylon, the idea was new in Indonesia and there were obstacles to its realisation there which did not exist in other parts of South Asia. In pre-war

Indonesia, the authorities had not, as in India, adopted an official policy of training Indonesians for the higher levels of the civil service. Universities were less developed; and, although there was by then a substantial local middle class, it was stronger in the professions and education than in business: indeed, Indonesian culture was hostile to business and was not 'achievement oriented' in a Western sense. Conversely, the presence of a large Dutch population, foreign business firms and Chinese entrepreneurs had tended to exclude the Indonesian population from both official and commercial activities. It was not, therefore, surprising that the Unilever companies contained no university-trained Indonesians in managerial positions before 1941. Even the clerical staff were mostly Chinese and it was inevitable in the years after 1946, when it was essential to use men of experience, that a large number of foreign managers and technicians should have been sent to Indonesia.

After 1946 the younger Unilever men who took over the business took a different view of these matters from their pre-war predecessors and also from the traditional Dutch civil service. Seeing independence approaching and aware of the changes taking place in other parts of Asia, the new senior managers in Jakarta quickly accepted the need to recruit able young men in Java and Sumatra. Their views were supported on business grounds by Unilever House when, in January 1947, the Special Committee suggested that the local management should aim at 'an ultimate structure based on the minimum of high-level Europeans . . .'. The first intake of local management trainees—mostly Indonesians of good backgrounds, the sons of doctors, civil servants, etc.—was made in 1950 and most of them were sent to Holland for long periods of training. Yet by the later 1950s there were still only two Indonesians on the boards of the local companies and an unusually large number of Europeans at lower levels of management. This was certainly not due to lack of will on the part of management, since there were recurrent complaints from London that the cost of expatriate managers was too high and every effort must be made to replace them. On the other hand, those general factors which had held back Indonesian entry into corporate business and the public service in the past still operated. As two visiting directors reported in March 1952,

Although we endeavour to train Indonesians for more responsible positions, the level of education and feeling of responsibility has not yet reached the standard which would enable us to replace Europeans by Indonesians for these [senior staff] positions.

Another Unilever director who visited Jakarta at the same time thought that

Another reason for the large [European] staff lies in the fact that for many years now the factories have been working at top capacity with plant that was in many cases worn out and requiring more attention than usual, while production was more important than cost.

The outcome of these efforts and disappointments was that in 1956 there were five Indonesian senior managers and 53 junior managers; and in 1957 there were still 68 European staff there, though 20 of these were local Dutch settlers, locally recruited. Of the senior managers, two were reported to be first-class: H. Bustami, the Sales Manager, and R. Machribie, Manager of the personnel department at Surabaya, whom Klijnstra described as 'an outstanding man'. It was indeed fortunate for Unilever as the crisis hit them in and after 1957 that they had got so far with training and promoting Indonesians: the survival of the business to 1965, and its recovery after 1967, was largely due to having a corps of trained, indigenous management. To carry the story briefly down to 1965, Unilever's first reaction when the anti-Dutch measures were taken by the government in 1957 was to appoint Bustami and Machribie as Directors (though their appointments were delayed so as not to give the impression that it was done under duress), so that they could, if necessary, constitute a legal board if all Dutchmen were ejected. Although in the event the immediate problem was met by replacing the senior Dutchmen by Britons, Germans and other expatriates, Bustami became a Director in May 1958; and in February London decided that it was 'advisable to make the maximum use of Indonesians, even if this involved taking a certain amount of risk'. By April 1964 there were only six expatriates left in the whole business, four of them on the board of five, out of a total staff and labour force of 3,800; and visiting directors commented that the survival of the business under extreme duress 'shows that we have a great number of competent Indonesians'. The intense official campaign of these years, first against the Dutch, then against the British, and finally against all foreigners in positions of power or profit, placed a great strain on the loyalty of indigenous company servants. A few in the middle management joined the trade union demand for nationalisation, using the Managers' Social Club as an agency; but the majority appear to have remained either neutral or firmly loyal to Unilever. By 1964 this made little difference to the conduct of the business, which, as will be seen, was under government supervision and trade union control; but by then Unilever's considered view was that there should be only about three Europeans in the Indonesian business, all of them members of the board. No clear decision had been taken about appointing an Indonesian as chairman: probably this step would have taken longer in Jakarta than in Bombay because of the relatively short experience of even the most senior Indonesian managers—a mere thirteen years at that time. The takeover of 1965–7 and the subsequent need for rebuilding the business postponed further development and in 1976 there were still three expatriates, including the chairman, in a board of six.

(d) Guided Democracy and Business Decay, 1957–65

For both Indonesia and the Unilever companies there 1957 was the most important turning point after the achievement of full independence in 1949. From March 1957, when the PMI ministry under Ali Sastroamidjojo resigned, Indonesia became a quasi-dictatorship ruled by Sukarno through successive non-party cabinets appointed by himself, which were not responsible to an elected parliament. The last normal cabinet declared a state of national emergency in March 1957, and on this basis Sukarno was able to establish a National Council of 42 members and thereafter to rule by presidential decree. On the same grounds the Army took administrative control over the provinces. But, to balance the increased power of the military, Sukarno now gave the Communist Party, PKI, a substantial share of official positions; and in Java the Communist-dominated trade unions became an important factor in local affairs. In fact, far from having absolute power, Sukarno was attempting to hold a balance between conflicting political and social forces, of which the Army and the Communists were now the most important. The result was endless compromise and inability to deal with the country's urgent problems, of which rampant inflation and regional separatism were probably the two most serious. Partly as a means of papering over these cracks, Sukarno adopted an aggressive foreign policy which might distract domestic attention and increase national unity. He was remarkably successful in that he held his position for some eight years after 1957; but in the end the intensifying struggle between the PKI and the Army, coupled with hyperinflation and growing disorder, pulled him down. His effective loss of power in 1965—though he did not formally resign until March 1967—coincides with the end of this study; but it will be necessary to look briefly at the consequences of the end of 'guided democracy' for Unilever's subsequent activities in Indonesia.

Guided democracy, dictatorship, or whatever Sukarno's regime is called, was not, of course, necessarily bad for foreign enterprises such as Unilever. But there were developments in Indonseia which seriously affected Unilever's activities and eventually made it impossible for them to operate there; and the rest of this chapter is a study of how a multinational company attempted to survive in such circumstances and how it eventually accepted defeat.

The four main developments that affected Unilever after 1957 were the successive anti-Dutch and anti-British policies adopted by Sukarno in 1957 and 1963 respectively; acute inflation coupled with very tight curbs on business activities; and finally the increasing and uncontrolled power of the Communist-led trade unions, resulting in the fall of the business.

(1) The Anti-Dutch Policy, 1957–63. The anti-Dutch policy was announced very soon after Sukarno took effective power in 1957. A convincing ground for breaking off relations with Holland and ridding the country of the large number of Dutch nationals and enterprises which still dominated many parts of the economy was the unresolved dispute over control of Western New Guinea—West Irian. In 1957 the UNO General Assembly voted in favour of calling on Holland to resume negotiations on this issue, but failed to do so by the requisite two-thirds majority. Sukarno then acted unilaterally. In November 1957 there were government-inspired riots against the Dutch in Java; on 30 November an attempt was made to assassinate Sukarno; on 5 December the remaining 45,000 Dutch residents were told to leave and it was announced that all Dutch property would be expropriated. In 1958 a law nationalising all Dutch companies was passed and in 1960 Sukarno broke off diplomatic relations with Holland. The following year Indonesia bought US $1,000 million of arms from Russia and in March 1962 Indonesian military units landed in West Irian. In August the Dutch

accepted a face-saving USA plan to transfer West Irian to the UNO which in turn would place it under Indonesian administration from April 1963 until a plebiscite could be held to determine its ultimate future. Thereafter Indonesia dropped its anti-Dutch policy, though the effects were in many cases irreversible.

For Unilever the critical aspect of this anti-Dutch policy was that, because the Indonesian companies were run by Dutchmen, were regarded as Dutch enterprises in Indonesia, and were owned by Unilever NV in Rotterdam, they were extremely vulnerable to a take-over of all Dutch assets. Unilever had one possible line of defence: it was an international company and more than half of the capital of Unilever as a holding company was owned outside Holland, mainly in Britain and America. In 1959 the portions were said to be 32 per cent Dutch and 68 per cent non-Dutch. This was a convenient technicality; but Unilever had a more useful asset: the Indonesian government had no animus against them and indeed favoured them for many reasons. Thus, if Unilever could find technical grounds for justifying the claim that they should not be treated like all undeniably Dutch enterprises, there was a fair chance that they might be allowed to get away with it. This point is, however, critical. Only the goodwill of the Jakarta government made it feasible for Unilever to play their cards as they did; and this was fully appreciated in London and Rotterdam.

The reaction of Unilever House to the news of the projected nationalisation of all Dutch property, which was learnt in November 1957, was immediately to send a director to emphasise Unilever's international character, with authority to transfer the shares to London. The transfer took time and was not completed until July 1958; but meantime—as early as 30 December 1957—it was known in London that the Indonesian government had accepted the case for international ownership and that the local companies would not be nationalised on the grounds that they were Dutch. That left the problem of the local management and legal responsibility, since the great majority of the boards of Indonesian companies and many of the lower management consisted of Dutch nationals, who were obliged to leave Indonesia. On 2 January 1958 it was decided to evacuate all Dutch employees, to appoint a new board consisting of two English (one the chairman), one German and two Indonesian managers, and to replace Dutch staff by Britons, Germans and Scandinavians. By mid-March 1958 this had been done. All Dutch staff were evacuated by June and thereafter the business ran reasonably well, though at greatly reduced output due to other factors, until the Confrontation with Malaysia began in 1963.

(2) The Effects of Confrontation, 1963–5. 1963 was in many ways a mirror image of 1957/8. Trouble over the projected federation of Malaya, Singapore and the British possession of Sarawak and North Borneo (Sabah) was always predictable from its inception in 1961 because it would include part of Borneo of which the major part was within Indonesia. Jakarta damned the project from the start and although negotiations and conferences between Sukarno and Tunku Abdul Rahman, the Prime Minister of Malaya, produced agreement in August 1963 that the future of British Borneo should be decided by referendum, both Indonesia and the Philippines rejected the verdict of this referendum when it proved favourable to incorporation with Malaya. Malaysia formally came into existence in September 1963 and there were violent reactions in Indonesia where the prospect of what Sukarno called Confrontation pleased many groups with specific objectives. The Army saw the opportunity to maintain its size, which had been inflated to 280,000 men for the West Irian campaign, and to use its new Russian equipment, rather than be employed on public works or be partially demobilised; the Communists saw the chance to take over British-owned enterprises and to widen their power base by supporting a generally popular nationalist policy; while Sukarno welcomed a cause which would help to damp down separatism and magnify his own role. Confrontation began late in 1963 and continued until August 1966. Indonesia had little military success in Borneo and received almost no international support except from China; but at home the enterprise had important consequences, not least for Unilever.

It was, of course, fortunate for Unilever that Confrontation with Malaysia began only after normal relations with the Dutch were resumed. This made it possible, once again with the connivance of the Indonesian government, for the concern to play its 'international' card. Indeed it was Subandrio, the Prime Minister, himself who told a Unilever deputation on 20 April 1964 that he wished to regard Unilever as an example of co-operation between the Netherlands and Indonesia. All British managers must be withdrawn; and as regards the shares, which had been moved to London, he said 'I advise you to transfer them back to Rotterdam without any noise'.

So, once again, in May 1964, the Indonesian shares crossed the North Sea to Rotterdam; and once again the European management was changed round, Dutch nationals replacing the British; though by this time the total number of expatriates had in any case been much reduced through continuing localisation and the slowing down of business activity. And on this basis, as a non-British enterprise, Unilever at least formally retained its identity in Indonesia to the end of the period of 'guided democracy'.

(3) Hyperinflation and Economic Management. But if the concern was able to change its skin twice in this way, thus demonstrating the Protean characteristics of a multinational and infuriating the British Ambassador at Jakarta (who expected all British firms to stand together in adversity and complained bitterly in April 1964 when the Unilever companies refused to join a protest signed by several British firms) there was no guarantee of economic survival. The basic fact in the economic situation throughout this period, and more especially after 1957, was Sukarno's lack of interest in economic and fiscal matters. Earlier cabinets had failed to combat inflation effectively, but at least they had tried. After 1957 inflation became virtually unchecked. From an average of 10 per cent in 1950–5 the rate adopted in 1952 of US $1 = Rp. 11.4 to US $1 = Rp. 45.0 March 1966 the consumer price index for Jakarta rose from 100 to 152,200, the most dramatic rise being from 330 in 1960 to 61,400 in 1965.[12] The most important single cause was the increase in government spending, mostly on military and non-productive enterprises. Inevitably the foreign exchange position deteriorated rapidly. The Rupiah was devalued in August 1959 from the original exchange rate adopted in 1952 of US $1 = Rp. 11.4 to US $1 = Rp. 45.0 and thereafter, despite devices such as simultaneous reduction of the value of all notes of Rp. 500 and Rp. 1,000 denomination and blocking 90 per cent of all bank credits amounting to Rp. 25,000 or more (the blocked balances being regarded as a long-term loan to the government), and many physical controls, the Rupiah continued to lose its international value very fast. While the previous exchange rate remained unchanged until May 1963, the black market rate declined from $1 = Rp. 220 in 1960 to $1 = Rp. 300 in 1961, $1 = Rp. 1,100 in 1962 to $1 = Rp. 1,500 in 1963. The official exchange rate was again altered to $1 = Rp. 315 in May 1963, but this was well behind the black market rate. In that year foreign

debts were US $2,500 million and foreign exchange reserves had virtually disappeared. By normal standards Indonesia was a bankrupt state.

In one sense this hyperinflation had a limited effect on the economy, for the index of the per capita national product at constant prices (1958 = 100) never dropped below 93.1 (in 1963) and stood at 95.8 in 1965.[13] This was mainly because more than half the national product came from agriculture and this was not greatly affected by domestic inflation and foreign indebtedness, though nationalisation of the Dutch-owned plantations of Sumatra in the late 1950s reduced production substantially. The main effects of economic decline therefore fell mainly on the relatively small modern sector of the economy. As they affected Unilever the most important were the following: reduction in the purchasing power of those sections of society which could normally afford to buy industrial products due to price inflation and comparative stability of money incomes; acute shortage of raw materials due both to disorganisation of inter-island communications and also limitations on foreign imports due to currency shortage; a partial breakdown of the marketing system due to the take-over of the former Dutch agents and the ejection of Chinese wholesalers and middlemen; and, above all, the squeeze on profits caused by rising raw material costs and tight government control of selling prices. The effects can be seen in Tables 5.6 to 5.10.

Bearing these tables in mind, perhaps the most surprising feature of this period is that, despite declining production and the squeeze on profits, profits nevertheless continued to be made until Unilever lost control of the business in 1964/5. The main explanation is that there were no price controls on toilet preparations and for some years these provided the bulk of profits. Even so, by the middle 1960s the business was experiencing acute cash-flow problems and was on the verge of bankruptcy. But, from the point of view of Unilever as a multinational company, the most significant feature of these years was that it was not allowed to remit any dividends overseas. Until 1956, as can be seen from Table 5.10, the government allowed a fairly consistent amount (when expressed in Florins) to be transferred each year. This was never a matter of right and year by year the local management had to negotiate with the government over remittance of part of the profits of the previous year as dividends. From 1953 the rules became stricter as Indonesian currency reserves came under increasing strain. In that year the

Currency Institute restricted transfer of profits to a maximum of 40 per cent of profits on 'active new investment' and banned transfer of money representing capital appreciation. In 1956 it laid down that remittances were to be calculated at the export certificate rate of exchange or the current official exchange value, whichever was higher. But the last profits actually remitted were those made in 1955. Thereafter all transfers were stopped and from 1959 the government blocked a large proportion of the company's liquid assets. Thus from 1957 to 1965 the picture is of a Unilever subsidiary unable to fulfil its first duty—to remit dividends to its owners.

(4) The Decline and Fall of Unilever Indonesia, 1963–5. It is important that the public control of the business imposed in 1965 seems not to have been intended by the government, at least before 1964, and that at no stage was the business formally nationalised. The reason appears to be that Sukarno himself and the rest of his ministers regarded Unilever as a comparatively desirable enterprise. They knew that it was 'honest' in the sense that its accounts represented the facts; that it did not attempt to evade taxation or the controls on imports and exports; and that it did not use artificially high internal transfer prices. The business provided demonstrable benefits for the Indonesian economy. It produced quality goods at reasonable prices for which there was a substantial demand and which might otherwise have had to be imported. It used mostly local raw materials providing valuable backward linkages to the agricultural base and to producers of intermediates such as containers. The company trained Indonesian managers overseas, thus contributing to the country's very limited stock of indigenous managerial skills. It was also a comparatively large employer of urban labour since it was not, by normal Unilever standards, capital intensive; it took some 40 man hours to produce one ton of soap in Indonesia as compared with ten man hours in the UK or Germany. Moreover, in most product areas, Unilever was competing not with the Indonesians but with other European and Chinese manufacturers; and, as has been seen, the government recognised the convenience of using the largest single enterprise in the country as a way of controlling the price of a range of basic consumer products. In short, and rather to the surprise of successive Unilever directors who visited Jakarta and talked to Sukarno and his associates, they found goodwill and willingness to connive at the delicate process

whereby the Unilever leopard twice changes his spots during this period from Dutch to British and back to Dutch.

Why, then, did the business eventually come under public control, though not under formal public ownership?[14] The main reasons were that SERBUNI (Serikat Buruh Unilever), the largest of the four unions in the Jakarta and Surabaya factories, was Communist-led; that the PKI was determined to use the unions to gain worker control over foreign and possibly also indigenous capitalist organisations; and that Sukarno, in pursuit of his stated object of national unity and synthesis (expressed in many words and acronyms such as Gotongroyong, PANTJA SILA, MAKOSOS and NEFO), was unwilling to oppose this important element in society. Another way of putting the same argument is to say that, once he had broken the parliamentary system in 1957, Sukarno depended increasingly on support from PKI to offset the danger of military preponderance and that he had therefore to accept the syndicalist methods adopted by the unions. In any case, it was union action which led to the loss of executive control over the Unilever factories. By 1956 the unions were extremely active in the concern factories and were demanding a share in Unilever's profits. Moreover, government regulations made it impossible to get rid of militants: in 1958 the labour force at the three factories amounted to 4,500, even though only 1,200 were needed for production then running at 30 per cent of capacity. Under these conditions management could exert very little control; in 1959 the German manager of the Surabaya factory had to reinstate a man dismissed for refusing to act as a relief lorry driver after threats of physical violence. In 1960 David Orr reported a slight improvement in labour relations, with no major incidents at Jakarta but very low production at Surabaya; but this improvement was reversed the next year. In January 1961 there was trouble at the Surabaya factory over the transfer of a supervisor from one department to another. Unilever House learned that

the Army authorities came to the factory of their own accord, arrested seven union leaders and held them in custody without trial until May. On Army advice we issued dismissal notices when these people had been absent from duty for three months. A few months later we learnt that the seven had been released and shortly after we were asked by the Army to 'suspend' our dismissal notices and let them return to work.

This episode reflects the fundamental political fact of these years —the growing conflict between the Army and the PKI for political power. This became critical for Unilever in 1963/4 when confrontation gave SERBUNI the excuse for more extreme action. What held SERBUNI back from formal occupation of the factories was thought to be that under presidential decrees any foreign enterprises taken over by the unions automatically became state enterprises, and all their workers would have to join the special union for state enterprise, SOKSI, which was not Communist controlled. Paradoxically, therefore, in December 1963 at the start of Confrontation SERBUNI picketed the Unilever factories, nominally to prevent damage during the anti-British riots, but actually to preserve them for their own union and PKI. In this situation the Army, which under the emergency had control of law and order, decided to intervene. Late in 1963 the Governor of East Java set up 'committees for help' in the Surabaya area to safeguard industries which were British owned or involved British interests. The apparent object was to prevent trade union take-overs, and may have been stimulated by an unsuccessful attempt by the unions to take over Unilever's Jakarta head office and factories. But under the conditions of the following two years such precautionary measures were quite ineffective and, starting in January 1964, the Unilever business lost its independence in three main stages.

The first stage began on 18 January 1964 when SERBUNI leaders, probably inspired by recent attacks on the British Embassy and British companies such as Shell, announced to the management of the Unilever factory at Angke, Jakarta, that they had taken it over. The management appealed to the police (a director in fact walking to the police station for fear of attacks on a rickshaw if he used one) and the local police authorities formally assumed control of the factory, ejecting the SERBUNI members who had occupied it. On 25 January the police set up a joint supervisory committee under a police chairman which included representatives of the judiciary, the army, the local civil service, the management, the Managers' Club (representing middle management and now aligned with SERBUNI) and the union. In Surabaya SERBUNI attempted to take over the Colibri factory on 24 January. Again the local police undertook general supervision but there the management carried on without a supervisory committee in an uneasy partnership with the union.

These arrangements were only stop-gap measures taken by the local police authorities to implement the President's decree of 1963 that British property was not to be attacked. Given continuing union pressure, a second more formal and uniform system of control was necessary and in March 1964 the Jakarta government set up a central controlling organisation for all British businesses under the Minister of Light Industry. The Minister appointed a chief chargé d'affaires, Kapala Kuasa Usaha (KKU), generally known in the Unilever records as Chief Supervisor, and a Deputy KU to supervise the whole business from the head office in Jakarta. Subordinate KUs were appointed to each Unilever factory. While this phase lasted, from March to November, the Unilever management was still technically responsible for the business, though expatriates such as the German general manager of the Angke factory and others who were obnoxious to the unions were excluded from the factories. The remaining middle management continued to run the factories, though almost all of them thought it wise to join the Staff Association (the one-time Managers' Social Club) to safeguard their position and to influence policy through the representative committees set up in each factory and in the Archa oil mill to advise management and the KU and which were dominated by the labour unions.

The worst feature of this situation was that it left Unilever responsible as legal owners for a business which neither London nor the Jakarta board of directors could now control. In April 1964 two Directors, Tempel and Klijnstra, therefore flew to Jakarta and attempted to regain effective control by going to the highest level, the Prime Minister, Subandrio. The interview was apparently friendly and encouraging. Subandrio is reported to have opened the conversation by saying: 'Mr Tempel, I have studied your case and I inform you that my decision is "hands off Unilever". I have also informed the SOBSI [the umbrella Communist-run trade union of which SERBUNI was a part] of this policy.' This sounded hopeful and Tempel asked that, although full management control would thus revert to the company, the KUs should remain as advisers to provide some security. This was agreed: but few things were what they seemed to be in Indonesia in the mid-1960s and in practice this agreement seems to have had no effect. In a subsequent meeting with the Minister of Light Industry and the Deputy KU for the Unilever business, and others, the Minister said that it would be most unwise to withdraw the order concerning supervision of Unilever factories since this would produce violent reactions from the unions which maintained that the business had been nationalised by their action. Subsequent events showed how difficult the position then was. SERBUNI organised demonstrations when Klijnstra visited the Jakarta factory at Angke, and only four of the 40 managers dared attend the special lunch in his honour. At a later entertainment a third of the managers braved union displeasure and attended a farewell buffet supper.

In fact, from this point and despite continuing official assurances of goodwill, Unilever in London effectively lost control of their business in Indonesia because no communication was allowed, even though the local management ran the business much as before. In August 1964 Klijnstra told the Special Committee that no Europeans were now allowed by the union to enter the Surabaya factory, nor to contact the Indonesian managers, except by letter. He therefore recommended taking an extreme step: offering 40 per cent of the equity of the Indonesian business to the Indonesian government at a very low estimate of its value (£2 million as compared with £4 million placed on the assets of 1958 when the business was transferred to Limited). This proposal was agreed in principle by Unilever House and negotiations continued for some time. In September 1964 the unions persuaded the government to withhold permission for three Dutch managers to enter Indonesia, demanding formal confiscation of the three-quarters of the capital of the business allegedly held in Britain and America, and nationalisation of the remaining Dutch quarter. The Chairman of the Indonesian companies, I. E. B. Quarles van Ufford, was physically prevented from visiting any of his factories and even services at his office were curtailed.

The third stage began on 11 November 1964 when Sukarno issued a decree placing all British-owned companies under the central government as from 1 May 1965: a schedule included the Unilever factories, despite the government's acceptance that they were nominally Dutch. These were now the responsibility of the Department of People's Industry, and its supervising committee for British companies, BAPPIRA, which in turn placed their management under the Chief Industrial Controller, still called KKU. The Controller was given exclusive power over all financial matters and all the companies' books were closed on 30 November for an investigation. The Industrial Controller then took over all management functions at all levels. These changes were largely terminological. Technically the KU in each factory was in sole control of all aspects of production and marketing and the remaining Unilever management was supposed to have no responsibility or direct access to the work force. In practice, however, these officials were civil servants or army officers without commercial experience and they had to rely on the management for expertise. As a result Unilever managers continued to manage, but did so through the KU; and how this was done depended largely on personal factors. From November 1964, for example, J. Hussan, the senior surviving manager at the Colibri factory, was on bad terms with his KU and corresponded with him by letter from adjacent rooms in the factory. A new KU who took over early in 1965 was more realistic. He ran only the personnel and political side and let Hussan run the factory. A similar situation existed in the Angke factory where the new general works manager came from a top military family and had some political weight.

On this basis the business staggered on from late 1964 to 1967. Until late in 1965 SERBUNI kept up constant pressure for greater control as the PKI built up towards the attempted political *coup* of 1 October 1965. There were regular demonstrations at the factories; a 'voluntary corps', which everyone under 40 was forced to join, was formed at each factory and did training in working hours; and political rallies were held on the seventeenth of each month. The company was, in fact, bleeding to death, There was little maintenance, no imported spares were available, prices were fixed while costs rose and raw materials were paid for only by using all revenue as it came in. In 1964 production was down to two-thirds of the 1957 level for oils and fats, to half for soaps and a quarter for toilet preparations. By 1965 it was only a matter of time before production came to a halt due to mechanical failure and financial bankruptcy.

From the standpoint of Unilever House the situation was in some ways more difficult than if the business had been nationalised outright. They had no way of controlling the company and the local directors were confined, powerless, to the head office in Jakarta, deprived even of air conditioning by order of the union. Yet Unilever still owned the business and was responsible for its mounting debts. The Special Committee was frankly non-plussed. In March 1965 they debated whether it would be better to press the Indonesian government for clarification of their intentions or whether this was likely to precipitate overt nationalisation. In June Quarles van Ufford reported in person. On his advice it was decided to press the Indonesian government for renewal of work permits for himself and the only remaining expatriate, the technical director, and if these were granted, make his return conditional on his having full authority. If these requests were refused Unilever would formally disown responsibility and would take the existing value of its assets in Indonesia as the basis for any future claim for compensation. This seemed a critical decision, since it might mean final abandonment of the business without any assurance of compensation; but the outcome was an anti-climax: there was no answer by August. It was then decided, as a last gesture, to make another approach for a permit for a new chairman. If this failed Quarles van Ufford would leave a letter reserving the company's rights and basing its position on a claim that they had effectively been nationalised. This was the position at the end of September 1965 when Indonesian politics suddenly changed dramatically with the attempted Communist *coup* of 1 October and the counter *coup* led by General Suharto.

It should perhaps, in view of the benefits to Unilever resulting from the establishment of a new regime, be stated categorically that the company (and for that matter the other few remaining foreign companies in Indonesia) had no hand whatever in these events, which clearly took them entirely by surprise. Indeed, when Quarles van Ufford reported at Unilever House on 13 October 1965, he had the impression that nothing substantial had or would change; Sukarno seemed to have survived and 'in the general atmosphere of compromise which was traditional in Indonesia' the PKI seemed likely to avoid any formal responsibility for the attempted *coup* of 1 October and was too strong for the Army to suppress. Indeed early in October SERBUNI attempted to take over the Surabaya factory and was stopped only by military intervention. Yet the *coup* had one immediate effect: Quarles van Ufford decided not to hand over the letter in which Unilever would abdicate all responsibility in Indonesia because, in view of present uncertainties, this might have got into the wrong hands and the future was no less uncertain. He therefore proposed to return to Jakarta and keep an eye on events. In November he reported that the KKU of the Unilever business had dismissed 36 employees, including 8 managers, and suspended 73 others (including 11 managers) on half pay because they were sympathisers with the 30 September Movement. This was allegedly done on Sukarno's instructions, though, of course, under strong Army pressure and it showed that the tide was beginning to turn.

Yet, at the end of 1965 Unilever had no means of predicting

whether it would ever regain control of its Indonesian business or whether this substantial asset would have to be written off completely. At that time it might even have been a relief for the government formally to nationalise the business since at least that would have provided a clear basis for future action. As it was, all the company could do was to watch the enterprise gradually dying. The closing cash balance at the end of September 1965 was Rp. 1,645,657; and at current levels of expenditure and receipts there was a predicted cash deficit of Rp. 7 million by the end of the year. Thereafter the business could only survive if the government was willing to subsidise it; and without proper supervision, maintenance or new investment; the whole enterprise was grinding to a halt.

The present study, in so far as it uses confidential material, stops in December 1965; but it would be misleading to leave the story there without a brief note of what happened later. For reasons entirely related to the domestic history of Indonesia, the business was in fact saved and reverted to Unilever control in 1967. In that year the new government which succeeded that of President Sukarno passed a Foreign Investment Law which secured foreign investments against nationalisation except 'in the national interest' and then with full compensation. The same law guaranteed foreign enterprises full authority and freedom to transfer profits (including depreciation) made on capital invested from overseas, but not specifically on profits resulting from the investment of local profits. In return, certain conditions were laid down, of which some of the more important were that investment permits were limited to thirty years, foreign companies had to incorporate under Indonesian law, indigenous manpower had to be used (though not exclusively) and local capital allowed to participate in the enterprise. On these terms agreement was reached with the Indonesian Department of Basic, Light and Power Industries whereby Unilever regained control of their factories on the condition that they accepted them in the state in which they found them and waived any claim for losses suffered during 1964 and 1965, calculated at US $2 million. Unilever agreed to invest $1.5 million; $1.0 million on rehabilitation and $500,000 on expansion and reorganisation. Unilever took over full control on 1 April 1967. Once again it had to rebuild its business in Indonesia, but between 1967 and 1973 production rose from 15 per cent of its 1956 level to just above that level and expansion could begin once again.

The story of Unilever in Indonesia thus had a happy ending by the 1970s. But this should not obscure one fact which relates to the company's position in any developing independent country. At every stage from 1946 to 1965 and thereafter Unilever had depended entirely on the goodwill of the Indonesian regime, accepting without question the right of successive governments, Dutch, democratic and dictatorial, to set the conditions within which it had to operate. As a manufacturer of goods for local consumption it had very little bargaining power. Nothing it made or sold was 'essential' in the sense that the Indonesian economy would have been seriously affected if the business had been closed down: there were plenty of alternative manufacturers of soap, edible fats and toilet preparations, and very little which the company made was or could economically be exported. Nor did the company possess any political leverage. It made no attempt to use either the Dutch or British government to bring pressure to bear on Sukarno; and when it took political initiatives, it was always direct to an Indonesian minister in its own right and on the merits of its case. Unilever survived as long as it did only because it was generally trusted by successive Indonesian governments and ministers; and even when its commercial death seemed imminent, Unilever was ready to die quietly. To say this is not to imply any particular virtue. As in all other countries studied in this book, Unilever recognised that its well-being depended entirely on the benevolence of a host government and that this could be solicited but not extorted by threat or force.

Ceylon (Sri Lanka)

Lever Brothers (Ceylon) Ltd, renamed Ceylon Unilever Ltd in 1959, has two particularly interesting features. When it was founded in 1939 as a local manufacturing company Ceylon had a smaller population than any other less developed country in which Unilever had started import-substituting production. This makes the economic background important as a possible explanation for this investment decision. Second, although successive post-independence governments after 1956 were to the left of political centre and threatened foreign capital, in practice Unilever got on very well with all of them; and, down to 1965 at least, Ceylon Unilever remained one of the most consistently profitable of all Unilever's overseas subsidiaries.

(a) The Economic Background[15]

In the 1930s and indeed throughout the period to 1965 Ceylon was a graphic example of the export-oriented primary producing country. The economy was geared to large-scale export of a limited range of tropical commodities, most of them developed by European settlers or stimulated by foreign commercial houses. Tea, a plantation crop, was by far the most important, normally providing more than 50 per cent of total export value. It was followed by rubber—also predominantly a large plantation crop—and coconuts—partly a peasant crop—each of which accounted for some 15 to 20 per cent of export receipts. Other less important exports were cinnamon oil, citronella oil and cocoa. Specialisation in commodity exports naturally resulted in heavy dependence on imports. Before 1939 and still in 1951 foodstuffs accounted for some 44 per cent of total imports, raw materials for 10 to 15 per cent and manufactures, mostly consumer goods, for the balance.[16] This was, indeed, the classic pattern of an 'open' economy based on the principle of comparative advantage; and although it left Ceylon vulnerable to fluctuations in world commodity markets—the terms of trade moved strongly against Ceylon from 1938 to 1949—it also produced a per capita national income which was high by the standards of developing countries. Gross per capita income in the mid-1950s was US $122, which put Ceylon in the same category as Egypt ($133) and Indonesia ($127) and well above many others including India ($72), China ($56) and Ethiopia ($54).[17] And since the terms of trade for Ceylon improved markedly from 1950 there was a strong case for thinking that this specialisation in the export of tea, rubber and coconut products was, as the mission sent by the International Bank for Reconstruction and Development (IBRD) in 1952 reported, the best economic policy Ceylon could pursue.

The obverse of this heavy commitment to commodity exports was limited industrialisation. Almost all consumer goods were imported during the 1930s and there was, of course, no heavy industry. It is true that, by comparison with many other developing countries, Ceylon did possess considerable industrial capacity of a sort. Whereas commodity exports from other countries, notably West Africa, were often unprocessed, the nature of Ceylon's products required that they should be processed on the spot. There were some 950 tea factories by 1952, and many rubber mills and coconut oil mills, which employed hundreds of thousands of workers: in

1946, 286,500—11 per cent of those in gainful employment—were in industry and mining.[18] By this time, also, there were a number of small factories, the typical first industrial enterprises of a less developed country, producing matches, textiles, shoes, beer and soft drinks. During the Second World War, and largely due to restricted imports, the Ceylon government set up a dozen small industries making plywood, paper, drugs, glassware, etc. Though the only one of these of any importance to survive into the 1950s was the plywood industry, which made tea chests, the government of post-independence Ceylon then set up a new generation of import-substituting factories, which again had limited economic success. Fundamentally, therefore, Ceylon remained throughout this period what it had been in the 1930s—an agricultural economy in which most capital and enterprise were necessarily absorbed by the commodity export industries and the improvement of local food production.

By this time, nevertheless, Ceylon had ceased to be the 'open' economy of colonial days. Three successive changes had taken place which affected an overseas business such as Unilever: the adoption of a protective import tariff; relatively high company taxation; and state regulation of many aspects of the economy.

In the early 1930s Ceylon had a low revenue producing tariff which provided virtually no protection for local products. For example, in 1931 the duty on common soap was 7.5 per cent and on toilet soap 10 per cent *ad valorem*, both lower than Indian import duties during the 1920s. These duties were raised to 10 per cent and 15 per cent respectively in 1932; and in October 1935 the British preferential duty was raised to 20 per cent on laundry soaps and 15 per cent on toilet soaps, the foreign duties being 40 per cent and 35 per cent respectively. Thus, like India, Ceylon became a protected economy before 1939 and this necessarily affected Unilever's attitude towards it.

The Second World War had two main effects on the economic environment. First, the level of company taxation rose considerably. In 1940 the rate of tax on non-resident companies was 15 per cent and on resident companies 12 per cent plus 3 per cent on dividends. By 1946 it amounted to 52.2 per cent. It then declined to 36.8 per cent in 1948 but by 1956 had risen to 57 per cent in profits tax plus 17 per cent dividend tax based on total nett profits. By the early 1960s the total statistical tax on concern profits, assuming that all profits were distributed as dividends, had risen to 74 per cent. Thus in a short period Ceylon had changed from being a country with low corporate rates of taxation to one with exceptionally high taxes which also encouraged re-investment of profits rather than distribution of dividends. Second, Ceylon ceased to be an 'open' economy during the war. Foreign exchange controls were imposed in 1939 and were carried on by the Central Bank of Ceylon when it was established in 1950. Quantitative controls on imports and exports of all kinds were also imposed in 1939 and after 1948 were used to ration imports of all kinds. From 1949 the Industrial Products Act enabled the government to name 'regulated products' whose import was permitted only with specific licences from the Controller of Industrial Products, who might oblige the importer to purchase local products in a specified proportion to imports—the aim being to stimulate local manufacture. In practice import controls were liberalised from 1951 to 1961 by giving Open General Licences to importers of many things: but from January 1961 49 items were brought under individual import licensing; and thereafter controls began to be severe as Ceylon's balance of payments situation worsened.

The newly independent Ceylon therefore inherited from the British colonial authorities the basic tools of a state regulated economy. But it also took over from economic theorists and the example of totalitarian states elsewhere the ideal of planned economic development, which had been quite alien to pre-war British practice. Six-year plans were inaugurated in 1947 and the government began to take a lead in stimulating economic growth. A Planning Secretariat was set up, together with an Institute of Scientific Industrial Research, a Development Finance Corporation and a Development Advisory Board. The attitude adopted by successive governments from 1948 to the private sector of industry and in particular to foreign enterprises varied. In the early 1950s the emphasis was on state enterprise and against foreign investment. It changed somewhat after the publication of the report of the IBRD mission of 1952 which strongly criticised uneconomic government enterprises, but shifted back after the People's United Front replaced the United National Party as the government in 1956; and for the rest of our period government policy was, in principle at least, to restrict foreign enterprise and stimulate state-sponsored industrial development.

If these various changes in the fiscal and political background are considered in relation to the position of Unilever in Ceylon, a pattern immediately becomes obvious. Before 1935 Ceylon was a good export market for concern factories in Britain. From the later 1930s rising tariffs, wartime quantity restrictions and official encouragement of local industry provided opportunities for profitable local manufacturing, even though rising taxation and raw material shortages might affect the scale of production and the level of profits. But from about 1960 onwards, although tariffs and import restrictions tended to favour the concern as a local manufacturer, government controls on imports, particularly of raw materials and intermediates, together with increasingly severe company taxation, were likely eventually to affect profitability. One would therefore expect the 'golden age' of importing to end in the mid-1930s and for the best years for local manufacturing to last from about 1939 to the mid- or later 1950s, with a subsequent decline in profitability and prospects as high taxation and adverse government policies began to bite. Was this in fact the curriculum vitae of Unilever in Ceylon?

(b) From Trading to Manufacture, 1914–39

Until the later 1930s Ceylon constituted a typical and valuable export market for Lever Brothers and then Unilever. The statistics are hard to establish in detail because for most of the period Ceylon was merged with India and Burma in the accounts kept at Port Sunlight. Tables 5.11(a), (b), (c) and (d) present the available evidence, and suggest three conclusions. First, Ceylon had grown into a valuable export market for British soap manufacturers well before 1930, and Unilever already had by far the largest share of the market, with 82.1 per cent of total imports. Second, per capita consumption of imported soap in Ceylon was remarkably high. In 1931/2 the ratio of soap imports to population in India was 1 cwt to 1,138 people: in Ceylon it was 1 cwt to 95 people. These contrasts reflect the higher average income of Ceylon and imply that, so long as local manufacturing did not develop, Ceylon was an exceptionally valuable market in proportion to its size. Finally, Tables 5.11(b) and (c) show that, by contrast with India, the slump of the 1930s had remarkably little effect on either the volume or profitability of concern soap imports to Ceylon. On all these grounds Ceylon clearly still offered a good export market in the 1930s, and there therefore seemed no need to establish a local manufacturing subsidiary.

Table 5.11   Ceylon: Lever Bros/Unilever Exports of Soap to Ceylon, 1910–35

(a) 1910–1921. Total UK and Gossages exports of soap to Ceylon (Tons)

Year	Total UK	Gossages
1910	453	126
1911	595	135
1912	548	88
1913	649	91
1914	716	139
1915	623	86
1916	894	33
1917	522	61
1918	326	79
1919	226	7
1920	455	63
1921	417	48

(b) United Exporters Ltd exports of soap to Ceylon, 1930–2 (£)

Year	A Gross sales value	B Pre-tax profit	B as % of A
1930 (9 months)	87,937	5,884	6.7%
1931	134,737	34,654	25.7%
1932	113,175	19,464	17.2%
1933	78,623	15,363	19.5%

(c) Concern sales of imported soap and toilet preparations in Ceylon 1929–39 (tons)
     (To 1935 all exports were from UK through United Exporters Ltd; from 1936–9 the total includes small imports from India through United Traders)

Year	Soap (tons)	Toilet preparations (Rs.)
1929	2,442	n/a
1930	1,932	n/a
1931	2,266	n/a
1932	2,208	n/a
1933	2,113	n/a
1934	2,015	n/a
1935	2,114	n/a
1936	2,586	60,527
1937	2,928	58,061
1938	2,690	54,380
1939	2,765	61,308

(d) Imports of laundry and toilet soaps to Ceylon, 1931–4. Volume of UK and Unilever's imports and shares of total imports

Year	From UK (tons)	Total (tons)	UK % volume	Unilever (tons)	Unilever % total imports
1931	2,437	2,759	88.3	2,266	82.1
1932	2,265	2,434	93.1	2,208	90.7
1933	2,292	2,534	90.4	2,113	83.4
1934	2,264	2,527	89.6	2,015	79.7

Until the mid-1930s there was, in fact, no serious possibility that Unilever would do so, and it was not until major tariff changes occurred that Unilever seriously considered building a factory in Ceylon. The higher duties established in 1932 were ignored because they could be absorbed by higher selling prices without reducing sales; but the revised tariff of 1935 was another matter. Pressure for higher duties came, according to Hansard, from the small local soap-makers backed up by the coconut-oil producers, who looked for a better market for coconut oil. They were supported by nationalists on the Ceylon State Council and apparently by the Financial Secretary, Huxham, who was said to be 'impressed by the claims of local soap makers that they were being kept down by Sunlight Soap and . . . represented that they were not all making cheap soaps, but that some were selling at nearly the price of Sunlight'. In response to these demands import duties were raised in October 1935 to 20 per cent *ad valorem* on British and 40 per cent on foreign laundry soaps and to 15 per cent and 50 per cent respectively on toilet soaps. But this was only a first step: there were demands for still higher duties, and this at least Unilever tried to prevent. Hansard visited Ceylon in November 1935 and, in conjunction with Sankar Iyer, their importing agents, who continued to distribute Unilever products until the company adopted its own marketing and distribution system in 1957/8, made out the case against still higher duties in a letter to the Financial Secretary. The question turned on laundry rather than toilet soaps. In 1934 2,018 tons of laundry soaps were imported from the UK and a rough estimate of local production was 2,000 tons. But there was virtually no competition between the two categories. Before October 1935 Sunlight Soap was selling at Rs. 23.04 a case, nett of commission, and would sell at Rs. 25.65 after the new duties. Only 1 per cent of local soap sold at above Rs. 16.00 a case and even the most expensive was 10 per cent cheaper than Sunlight. This suggested that a higher duty would raise the price of Sunlight without increasing the sales of its competitors. Behind this public statement lay fear that, if the import tariff continued to rise, the selling price of concern laundry soaps would have to rise to the point at which even the discriminating Ceylon buyer would have to settle for a cheaper and inferior local product. Where this point lay no one could then estimate; but once it was reached the concern would obviously have to consider building a local factory. The interesting fact is that in 1935 Unilever was anxious not to have to do this on two grounds. First, the profitability of a local factory would depend on raw material prices. The only local oils available were coconut and mee oil, and it was expected that other imported oils would soon face a substantial protective duty. It was therefore too soon to calculate the possible advantage of local manufacture as compared with importing from Britain. Second, there was talk of passing an act insisting that locally registered manufacturing companies should have a majority of local capital, which was contrary to contemporary Unilever practice. Hansard concluded that the concern should fight against higher import duties on soap rather than contemplate using the tariff barrier to protect local manufacture.

It is impossible to know what weight, if any, these arguments carried with the Ceylon government and politicians; the basic rates of duty on British soap were not then increased and the rate on imported foreign toilet soap was reduced to 35 per cent *ad valorem*, or Rs. 40.00 cwt. Nevertheless, the duties already imposed in 1935 proved high enough without further increases to persuade Unilever to build a factory at Colombo, though the grounds for this decision, which was taken in June 1938, are not entirely clear. The only surviving evidence is contained in a minute of the Directors' Conference for 30 June 1938:

> Mr Albert Van den Bergh reported that we were faced with import duties on soap imports in Ceylon, which put us at a grave disadvantage with local factories, and therefore it was proposed to erect a soap factory in Colombo with a capacity of 3,900 tons of soap per annum . . . . Although part of the profits derivable from local manufacture would be at the expense of exporting Companies in this country, the nett benefit to the Concern through local manufacture should be between £4,000 and £5,000 per annum.

The same point was made in a brief prepared in London for J. L. Heyworth's visit to Ceylon in 1940: 'the continued rise in import duty decided us to erect a soap factory inside the tariff barrier . . .'. The tariff did not, in fact, rise between October 1935 and June 1938, though the actual duty paid, based as it was on a percentage of the assessed value of the product, may have increased as import prices rose. The probable explanation is that, while the volume of exports to Ceylon remained satisfactory, the margin of profit to Port Sunlight fell as a result of the tariff. It is impossible to demonstrate this satisfactorily because profit figures for the export trade to Ceylon, which was then being handled through United Traders Limited in India, are not available. But in November 1938 the Special Committee noted that margins on 'Umbrella'—one of the concern's cheaper soaps—had disappeared due to local competition, and that once local manufacture started the premium of £3 18s 0d a ton could be re-established. It seems likely, therefore, that the decision to manufacture was intended primarily to maintain profit margins rather than to defend a threatened volume of sales.

(c) Local Manufacture, 1940–65

(1) The War, 1941–5. It is unfortunate from the standpoint of the present study that the Colombo soap factory only came into production during 1940 and the vanaspati factory in 1941. Wartime conditions largely determined the development and future of these enterprises until late in 1945 and three years later Ceylon achieved political independence. The concern factories in Ceylon do not therefore, offer much useful evidence on the effect of the change from colonialism to independence for a foreign subsidiary. Yet these first five years were, in fact, critical for the future of Unilever in Ceylon for it was during the Second World War, when American competition was entirely shut out by official controls, that the concern established, willy-nilly, the predominant share of the Ceylon soap market which it never again lost.

The war had paradoxical effects on the success of the new manufacturing venture. Unilever was lucky that it had got its factory built before the eastern crisis of 1941/2 virtually stopped imports of capital equipment and consumer goods from Europe and America. But the fact that no action was taken on building the factory until after war had broken out in September 1939 had one adverse result. The building, a Jurgens copra warehouse which was already 23 years old, was used because it was available and cheap. Most of the plant was secondhand because there was no alternative. This meant that the new company had a small capital which enhanced its profitability; but the site was unsatisfactory in many ways and there was a price for this to be paid later. Nevertheless Unilever were wise to get into production when they did. As one of the few 'modern' soap manufacturers in Ceylon, the concern could exploit a market which grew rapidly as inflation and the needs of the armed forces increased demand and there was almost no limit to how much it could have sold given sufficient productive capacity and raw materials. Table 5.12 shows the rising trend of detergent sales from 1938 to 1948, with 1941 the first complete year of local production.

Table 5.12   Ceylon: Unilever Sales of Soap Products, 1938–48, (tons)

Year	Sales
1938	2,686
1939	2,765
1940	2,682
1941	2,932
1942	2,609
1943	3,613
1944	4,935
1945	4,502
1946	4,455
1947	6,031
1948	6,397

Clearly 1943–5 were critical years and wartime boom conditions had undoubtedly helped this growth. As A. D. Gourley said after his visit in 1944,

> With their earnings at a high level the people of Ceylon are now able, within limits, to indulge their natural inclination to spend generously on amenities. Whether it is soap, cigarettes or any other consumer article in common every-day use price considerations provide little deterrent to the purchase of the best available, and we, in common with all other manufacturers possessing production facilities locally, are benefitting from this period of prosperity.

The only real inconvenience caused by the war was government price controls which were imposed on soap late in 1940 on the basis of high existing prices. Since demand for quality soap exceeded supply, this meant that Unilever's three main local rivals—British Ceylon Corporation, Swadeshi Industrial Works and Fernando and Brothers—could sell inferior products at the same fixed prices as higher quality Unilever soaps. Nevertheless, on the eve of Ceylon's independence, all reports by Contact Directors and others optimistically recommended substantial new investment and expansion. In November 1947 Sidney Van den Bergh reported on his visit there with (Lord) Geoffrey Heyworth. Local production had virtually eliminated imports. The market had grown to 11,500 tons and would expand further. Unilever was market leader in laundry and toilet soaps and had more than half the total market. The concern should aim at a productive capacity of 11,000 tons and reduce prices to meet competition. The edibles trade also offered good opportunities. Compound lard sales should be increased to 2,000 tons and margarine to 500 tons. Finally there were great possibilities in the field of toilet preparations. Import prices could be substantially reduced by local manufacture of certain lines and the sale of other imported products could be increased by improved quality and packaging. In short, the prospects were excellent 'if political conditions remain favourable'.

But of course the unknown factor was the trend of politics and governmental policies in the newly independent Ceylon; and the effect of independence is crucial to the present study. It is proposed briefly to examine subsequent developments under the following heads: expansion and diversification, 1948–65; relations between the company and the local government; the question of local participation in the equity; localisation of management; and, finally, the profitability of the Ceylon business and its economic significance for the Ceylonese economy.

(2) Expansion and Diversification, 1948–65. The broad lines of the concern's development are indicated in Tables 5.13 (a), (b) and (c), and it is proposed to comment briefly on each major product in turn.

The fact which determined the history of Unilever in Ceylon was that by 1948, and largely because the concern had built its factory before the eastern war restricted imports, Lever Bros (Ceylon) Ltd

Table 5.13(a)   Ceylon: Sales of Soap, 1949—65 and Share of Market

Year	Est. total consumption (tons)	Lever sales (metric tons)	Lever share %
1948	11,209	6,397	57.0
1949	n/a	7,207	n/a
1950	9,991	8,068	81.0
1951	n/a	8,411	n/a
1952	n/a	9,583	n/a
1953	n/a	9,193	n/a
1954	n/a	9,818	n/a
1955	n/a	10,256	n/a
1956	14,623	12,306	84.0
1957	14,730	12,352	84.0
1958	15,326	13,348	87.0
1959	17,055	13,998	82.0
1960	17,652	13,977	79.0
1961	19,000	14,863	78.0
1962	19,462	15,222	78.0
1963	19,086	14,519	76.0
1964	19,529	15,551	80.0
1965	20,788	15,891	76.0

Table 5.13(b)   Ceylon: Sales of Toilet Preparations and Share of Market

Year	Sales turnover (Rs. '000)	Share of total market	Share of market for Dental preps.	Skin and toilet preps.	Hair preps.
1948	254	n/a	n/a	n/a	n/a
1949	471	n/a	n/a	n/a	n/a
1950	425	n/a	n/a	n/a	n/a
1951	588	n/a	n/a	n/a	n/a
1952	751	n/a	n/a	n/a	n/a
1953	797	n/a	n/a	n/a	n/a
1954	743	n/a	n/a	n/a	n/a
1955	742	n/a	n/a	n/a	n/a
1956	1,305	n/a	n/a	n/a	n/a
1957	1,439	17	17	21	8
1958	1,772	18	16	26	5
1959	1,861	13	18	18	3
1960	2,140	15	20	21	4
1961	2,950	19	28	27	5
1962	3,567	26	34	46	1
1963	4,898	35	56	50	13
1964	5,127	51	63	49	18
1965	4,489	50	62	49	14

Table 5.13(c) Ceylon: Sales of Edibles and Share of Market
(including Imports) (tons)

Year	Total Market	LB(C)	% share	Margarine and Vanaspati LB(C)	% share	Compounds, etc. LB(C)	%share
1948	22,911	464	2.0	63[b]	61.8	226	100
1949	n/a	533	n/a	41[b]	n/a	319	n/a
1950	24,076	677	2.8	51[b]	55.4	453	100
1951	n/a	770	n/a	137[b]	n/a	601	n/a
1952	n/a	997	n/a	n/a	n/a	n/a	n/a
1953	n/a	1,222	n/a	n/a	n/a	n/a	n/a
1954	n/a	1,127	n/a	n/a	n/a	n/a	n/a
1955	n/a	1,212	n/a	n/a	n/a	n/a	n/a
1956	35,970	1,489	4.0	n/a	n/a	n/a	n/a
1957	43,700	1,604	4.0	101.2	44	1,440	90
1958	47,120	1,594	3.0	136.3	48	1,449	90
1959	52,015	1,680	3.0	205.8	49	1,479	87
1960	53,550	1,801	3.0	229.5	51	1,522	87
1961	54,975	2,177	4.0	492.1	74	1,674	92
1962	57,696	2,337	4.0	527.1[c]	65	1,748	92
1963	59,231	2,555	4.0	531.1[c]	68	1,861	94
1964	61,386	2,971	5.0	776	95	2,153	96
1965	62,501	3,257	5.0	1,041	100	2,216	83

Notes: a. Includes crude vegetable oils and other commodities not produced by Lever Bros (Ceylon) Ltd.

b. Imported margarine and share of margarine market only.

c. Excludes vanaspati.

had a dominant share of the detergents market and that Sunlight laundry soap and Lux toilet soap were market leaders and sold at a premium over local competitors. Initially the main limit on concern sales was productive capacity; and Unilever was planning a great increase in capacity before the end of the war. Early in 1949 the Special Committee agreed to buy a site of three-quarters of an acre adjacent to the existing factory and in January 1951 the Committee noted that on his forthcoming visit Muir would study the long-term possibilities. 'As the business was very profitable it was important to keep pace with the demand. Expansion already approved was expected to bring the present 8,000 tons capacity up to 11,000 tons in a few years, but possible requirements beyond this would have to be considered.' And so it went on almost to the end of the 1950s; each successive increase in productive capacity seemed unable to satisfy an ever expanding market.

But by 1957 the great growth in the soap market was virtually over. The reason was not the success of rivals but simply limitations of the market and an economy which was beginning to falter. As early as 1950 Unilever had some 80.7 per cent of the total soap market. By 1957 this had increased to 84 per cent and the concern also held 90 per cent of the 'family wash business and 60 per cent in personal use field'. These shares were embarrassingly large, as Lord Heyworth commented after his visit late in 1957; and in considering the annual estimates for 1959 the Special Committee minuted that 'there was little prospect of further expansion in Ceylon as we already had a very large share of the market'. But 1958 proved the peak of the concern's share of the market at 87 per cent. It dropped to 82 per cent in 1959 and was down to 76 per cent in 1963, though sales reached a new peak of 15,222 tons in 1962. From this point on further growth depended either on expanding other lines, such as toilet preparations or edibles, or on diversification into new fields such as NSDs.

The development of local manufacture of toilet preparations in Ceylon provides a typical example of the combined effects of tariffs and local shortages on an importing enterprise. Until 1950 Unilever continued to import its whole basic range of shaving soaps, toilet powders, toothpastes, hair preparations and perfumes; and, apart from 1942–4 when imports were restricted by wartime conditions, importing continued to seem satisfactory for it was a small market and the import duties imposed in 1940—15 per cent on British and 25 per cent on foreign goods—were too low to stimulate local manufacture. Even the 30 per cent tariff imposed by 1944 was not enough. Then in November 1947 the import duty on toilet preparations was raised from 30 per cent to 90 per cent and in the same month Sidney Van den Bergh, reporting on his visit to Ceylon with Lord Heyworth, wrote that imports suggested that a large market was available.

There are very great possibilities for our products if we can produce some of them locally, and others can be imported in improved qualities and packs . . . . We can reduce [the] price materially through local production and conquer a much larger share of this important market. Also talcum powder and hair oils might be produced locally.

By December 1949 London had approved capital proposals for manufacturing shaving soap, talcum powder, toothpaste and hair oil in Ceylon and the machinery had been ordered. Production of toothpaste began in July 1951, talcum powder in November, and other lines during the following year.

By that time, however, the situation had again altered, for in July 1950, when London was committed to local manufacture but before production actually started, the Ceylon government reduced import duties on toilet preparations to the previous level of 30 per cent. This was raised to 33 per cent in July 1952; but it remained dubious whether a level of protection deemed inadequate before 1947 would now prove sufficient. Reporting early in 1953 Andrew Knox was, however, optimistic, and Table 5.13(b) shows that he was right. After a period of virtual stagnation from 1952–5 sales climbed rapidly; and, more significant, the concern share of the total market, which did not increase significantly until 1960, shot up to 35 per cent in 1963. The major obstacle had been competition from imported Colgate products, which held 60 per cent of the toothpaste market in 1961. After 1956 import licensing had gradually affected these and other imported brands; and in 1962 it was reported that Colgates were likely to lose their import licence which would give Unilever its opportunity. By May 1963 J. D. Mould, Chairman of Ceylon Unilever, could report that 'two years ago Colgate had 60 per cent of the toothpaste market, while our share was 20 per cent; now the shares were exactly reversed'. The position was at that moment clouded by the fact that Colgates were said to 'be setting up locally' but the threat never materialised. As Mould reported in May 1965, 'Colgate, on the brink of local manufacture, backed out and there is a complete protection and in that field we have virtually got a monopoly spread between three brands. The difficulty is the procurement of imported materials for toilet preparations, as they take a fairly low priority.'

Clearly local manufacture of toilet preparations, even though undertaken under a misapprehension, paid off handsomely. Not only did it enable Unilever to increase their sales and share of the market but, as will be seen later, to earn a significantly higher profit than on either detergents or edibles.

Before the Second World War Unilever had a very small stake in the Ceylon food market. A limited quantity of specialised foodstuffs —canned fish, sausages, fruit and other luxuries—was imported to serve a small market consisting mostly of expatriates; but in the basic Unilever field of edible oils the concern had virtually no share. Most Ceylonese used only coconut oil, but there was a small market for vegetable product, mostly to serve the immigrant Tamil population, which amounted to some 400 tons before 1939. There was apparently no demand for margarine since the limited demand by Europeans was satisfied by Australian butter. Before 1941 Unilever's only interest in this market was a small import of vegetable product (vanaspati) from Unilever NV under the brand name Nemco, but this was very small, always less than 150 tons a year. There was, therefore, no significant import market for Unilever to defend or expand; so that the decision taken in 1940—'In view of the high import duty . . . to take advantage of the erection of a soap factory in Colombo to construct an edible plant also to take over the supply of Nemco . . .'—really implied a new departure. The original intention was merely to manufacture bulk vanaspati of the type used as an additive to pure ghee. In 1941, however, Gourley suggested that in addition a compound consisting entirely of CNO should be made for use by bakers, and this proposal was adopted in principle. Production began, but in 1943 the electrolyser essential to the fat hardening process exploded and could not be replaced or repaired; so for the rest of the Second World War the Colombo factory manufactured refined coconut oil. It was not until 1947 that the hardening plant was in action again; and then it was decided to concentrate on vegetable oil compounds for the baking and cooking trade—Nemco and a new product Covo—rather than to return to vanaspati.

This was the foundation of the concern's post-war edible business in Ceylon, whose strategy was finalised late in 1947. It was then decided to concentrate on vegetable compounds but also to try to expand margarine sales. These policies were adhered to for the rest of our period. As Table 5.13(c) shows, until about 1960 almost all expansion took place in the two compounds—Nemco and Covo. These continued to expand to 1965, but from 1961 a significant increase also took place in margarine. In 1965 J. D. Mould was still optimistic about their future prospects.

Our future lies with edibles, where we have doubled our refining capacity, got protection for margarine, and some restriction on the imports of butter, so that our margarine business is making good progress this year. In terms of new products, we are test marketing at this moment Good Luck, the new flavoured spread, but it is too early to say whether this will prove a success. This year we expect to sell nearly 4,000 tons of edible products, whereas three years ago we were at 600 tons.

To this point the story of Lever Bros (Ceylon) Ltd has been one of success. Yet the success achieved in the 1950s posed the inevitable problem: where to go next. The problem first became obvious in soaps since concern sales levelled off from 1958/9 with some 80 per cent of the market and was unlikely to expand further except as population and wealth grew. Cooking compounds also were relatively static by the late 1950s and only toilet preparations showed much scope for expansion through increasing the concern's market share. On the analogy of India one would expect to find that this was the moment at which Unilever began to consider diversification outside these three traditional fields; and the search for new opportunities did indeed begin at this time. The significant fact is that by 1965 no new lines had been firmly established. Why was this and what light does it throw on the position of Unilever in Ceylon?

Serious efforts were in fact made after 1957 to discover new fields for profitable expansion and a wide range of possible Unilever lines, ranging from filled milk to NSDs, was considered. But by 1965 the search had proved fruitless: either there was no market or prospective profit margins were too low. The two main reasons appear to have been lack of encouragement by the Ceylon government and Unilever's lack of confidence in official policy. By the later 1950s Ceylon had a quasi-Marxist government, first elected in 1956, which, as will be seen below, initially inspired little confidence among foreign enterprises. From 1956 the nett yield on capital employed declined on all concern products except toilet preparations; controls on investment and repatriation of funds became more intense; there were supply shortages of many kinds; and in 1964–5 the government was forced by shortages of foreign exchange to place a moratorium on overseas remittances. Under such conditions it seems to have been tacitly understood that the local company must do the best it could with its existing lines and productive capacity, making modest experiments in new enterprises which could be paid for from local profits. No major new initiative involving imported capital was possible until and unless the market grew substantially and political and economic conditions improved.

(3) Lever Bros (Ceylon) Ltd and the Economy of Ceylon. So far LB(C) has been treated simply as a business enterprise. We must now in conclusion consider it in relation to the government and economic life of the host country. The questions will be those asked for other countries: the concern's attitude towards and relations with the Ceylon government; localisation of management; local participation in the equity; and the broader questions of profitability, both for the company and the Ceylon economy.

The most significant feature of the concern's early relations with the government of independent Ceylon is that between 1948 and 1957 there are very few references indeed to government policy or actions in the records. The reason is that until 1956 successive governments of Ceylon were in practice moderate and conservative, whatever their stated intentions, and were in no apparent hurry to alter the conditions on which a foreign firm such as Unilever operated there. The general election of 1956, and the coming to power of Mr Bandaranaike, marked the turning point. The concern, as always, reserved judgement: it was accustomed to dealing with political regimes of all kinds. But by July 1957 London had to recognise that conditions were likely to change for the worse. In February of that year A. D. Bonham-Carter had reported after a visit to Ceylon that

> The situation in Ceylon was dominated by the inability of the Government, which had come into power in last year's elections, to carry out their strongly nationalistic promises. Although they realized the need for encouragement to foreign capital, they were making things difficult for industry by applying strict regulations in respect of permits and licences.

Things did not improve: a year later, in July 1958, the Directors' Conference was told that 'a definite conclusion had been reached that in view of the present political and economic situation in Ceylon, the amount of new capital invested would need to be carefully restricted'; and these opinions and policies were never thereafter substantially changed. The general view taken by London was not that the Ceylon government posed any immediate danger to Unilever, for the threat of nationalisation seemed to have passed and, as will be seen below, even pressure to allow local participation in the equity had been checked by 1961. Rather the trouble was weak and confused government which could not provide conditions encouraging to business enterprise. Thus (Sir) Ernest Woodroofe commented, after a visit in 1962, that

The political and economic situation is depressing, with a general atmosphere of a mixture of vicious self-seeking and indolence. They realize this themselves and even . . . the Prime Minister seems to accept the fact that the administration is ineffective in pushing new legislation through. The only legislation likely is a further restriction on imports which could lead to inflation and make raw materials procurement more difficult, but on the other hand it might involve a ban on the import of butter.

This became the refrain of most subsequent reports by Unilever executives visiting Ceylon. By 1965 there was no optimism left. Unilever could only hang on and keep the business going. Nevertheless, one point stands out from the documents: Unilever executives were sorry for the Ceylonese rather than resentful at their own lost opportunities. Basically they blamed the politicians for taking the easy road to electoral victory—promising more welfare payments, particularly rice subsidies, than the country could afford. As Mould said in 1965, 'someone has got to reverse that trend, but politically that task is very difficult'. Unilever could only sit and watch as the country struggled with its self-imposed problems.

Because of its comparatively small size and late start Lever Bros (Ceylon) Ltd was not a pioneering company in any field, and certainly not in terms of replacing expatriate staff by indigenous management. The local company had, as usual, been set up with exclusively European directors, senior management and technical staff. This was to be expected: but it is more surprising that by 1965 'ization' was still far from complete. This was certainly not due to racial attitudes or distrust of the ability of the Ceylonese. The problem was summed up by R. H. Muir after a visit early in 1950.

The Ceylonese are intelligent but have not the application and determination of the Indian worker. Also higher education facilities are not so easily available and the better-class Ceylonese have not the habit of going into commerce, so to get somebody of the trainee class may take a long time. However, Mr Lloyd [the Chairman] has this in mind and will keep looking around.

From this time progress was slow but definite. By 1961 only 7 out of 24 managers were expatriate and there were then 21 Ceylonese managerial assistants. Two years later the ratio was 6 to 25 and, although the number of Ceylonese managers continued to grow, the final stages of localisation of management had not been reached by 1965. There were still six expatriate managers in that year and, as Mould reported, 'we have not really got one genuine Ceylonese on the Board'. Obviously complete 'ization' was then only a matter of time and personality; and there were three Ceylonese on the board by 1966. But they were up against the problem facing other companies in Ceylon, expatriate and local alike, that a business career was not part of the tradition of Ceylon life and it was therefore necessary within a single generation to recruit and train men capable of taking complete responsibility for large and complex enterprises. Mould summed up the situation and prospects in his report of May 1965.

Nationalism will take the form of Ceylonization in various aspects—in terms of staff and sooner or later in terms of capital. The point will not be reached where they say we cannot have any expatriates any more: I do not see how they can hope for foreign aid and say that in the same breath. We are a long way ahead of most firms in Ceylon and when they say Ceylonization there is plenty of room to tighten control on nationals before it affects us, because in our own company apart from the Chairman and Marketing Director all our other expatriates are technical people and there has been a shortage of technical people in Ceylon. We have good contacts in the United Kingdom, and when they qualify we grab them. Even on the technical side, given another three/four years I do not think the Ceylonization programme will worry us. We have six expatriates at the moment including the Chairman.

When the Ceylon factories were built the concern followed normal practice in that the Unilever companies were wholly-owned subsidiaries of Unilever Limited through Unilever (Commonwealth Holdings) Limited. As in India, however, political independence in

1948 and the coming to power of the various political groups, all of whom were, in varying degrees, pledged to nationalist and socialist ideals, made it likely that the concern would sooner or later have to sell some or even all of the equity in Lever Bros (Ceylon) Ltd; and the surprising thing is that the first mention in the records of either possibility is Lord Heyworth's reference to possible nationalisation late in 1957. In fact complete nationalisation never became a serious danger, possibly because various state-owned enterprises, including the Oils and Fats Corporation and Paritan Chemicals, built and run by the government, proved in the 1950s to be financial failures. Indeed the government at various times pressed Unilever to take a share in the ownership and management of these enterprises. But the possibility of compulsory sale of part of the equity remained and between 1958 and 1963 Unilever had to take this seriously. The question was first raised as an immediate possibility by A. D. Bonham-Carter in July 1958 after a visit to Ceylon. Reporting to the Special Committee he said: 'It was difficult to assess whether local participation in the capital of the Company would be to our advantage. Although the Government were interested in this possibility, it was believed they were mainly influenced by the fact that local participation had been arranged in India.' The Special Committee's view was clear and remained consistent throughout the rest of the period: 'unless there were definitely political advantages to be gained, this should be avoided'. A year later the question still seemed academic but in April 1959 Lord Cole thought the concern would 'encounter pressure to allow local capital participation and, since as at present constituted the company was much under-capitalized, particularly in relation to profits, this would need careful study'. During the next three years, therefore, the concern made preparations for going public if this became necessary or tactically desirable.

As in India, the main need was to revalue the assets so that the increase in the capital value of the company could be fully reflected in its capital structure if and when shares were sold to the public. In December 1959 Lever Brothers (Ceylon) Ltd and the three dormant trademark owning companies registered there became subsidiaries of a new locally-registered holding company, Ceylon Unilever Ltd. At the same time the nominal capital was increased from Rs. 5.1 million to Rs. 17 million. Everything was done to make a first sale of equity in the holding company attractive to Ceylonese buyers, but no sale came and no shares had been sold by

1965. The main reason was that the government failed, as it were, to chop off Unilever's outstretched neck. The reason for this must be speculative, but the most likely explanation is that disinvestment by a multinational normally results in a substantial transfer of funds overseas and this would have imposed an unacceptable strain on the country's then precarious foreign exchange position. Thus in 1965 (and indeed still in 1977) Ceylon Unilever remained a wholly owned Unilever subsidiary.

Two related questions remain: why Unilever was able to make such comparatively large profits in Ceylon down to at least the early 1960s; and what advantages the country received from Unilever's presence there.

Profitability is, of course, relative; and the profits shown in Table 5.14 are high as a percentage of capital employed down to about 1958 mainly because the initial capital investment was small (old buildings, second-hand plant) and because a conservative policy has been followed in revaluing fixed assets. A more useful guide to profitability is, therefore, trading profits in relation to NSV which were not particularly high. Nevertheless, even after the capital had been revalued in 1959 and with effective tax rates on dividends of over 70 per cent, Ceylon Unilever was one of the most consistent profit-makers in the Unilever system, and this needs to be explained.

The answer lies not in one but in a medley of favourable factors, some of which have already been mentioned. Most important was the fact that Unilever was the clear market leader in soaps, with around 80 per cent of the market from the late 1940s. It would be wrong to say that there was no local competition. The British Ceylon Corporation, for example, were keen competitors with advanced soap-making equipment; their weakness lay in marketing skills. Until the early 1960s, moreover, when import licences were relatively easy to acquire, there was a struggle with Colgates and Procter and Gamble in several fields, particularly the nascent NSD market which each firm was trying to build up with imports. It was only the withdrawal of import licences in 1961 that ended this battle for the NSD and toilet preparations market, leaving Unilever in command of the field. Market dominance, however, did not by itself ensure high profits or encourage industrial lethargy. High taxation, liquidity problems, Unilever's insistence that development should be financed from local profits and the residual possibility that other enterprises might be stimulated by excessive profit margins were all incentives to efficiency. Even so profits ultimately depended on governmental acquiescence, since the authorities could have imposed price controls had they chosen. In fact, despite their socialist professions, they did not do so. The government expected the company to show reasonable restraint and the company would not have made a significant increase in the price of widely used products such as Sunlight Soap if there was any indication of informal official displeasure. But the evidence suggests that through-out this period there was a tacit understanding between government and company that pre-tax margins should be relatively high so that the government could take a substantial share of the profit in taxes. Behind this strategy lay the government's dilemma that, while it was committed to very large expenditure on various forms of welfare, income taxes were unpopular and only about half the total tax due from individuals could be collected. Large companies which could not evade payment of corporate taxes were therefore a convenient means of raising revenue; and if the public complained at high prices, the blame could be put on the companies. Or, to put it another way, the government used high levels of corporate taxation on generous profits as an alternative to excise duties on consumer products.

There remains the standard question of the costs and benefits to the Ceylon economy resulting from Unilever's activities there. Both to save space and because Ceylon's experience was similar, on a very much smaller scale, to that of India, it is not proposed to examine these questions in detail. First, the financial consequences for Ceylon were comparable with those in India. There was little new capital inflow after the initial investment of about Rs. 1.7 million, so most of the capital employed in 1965—Rs. 27.5 million —must have been accumulated by ploughing back profits. Figures for transfers are not available before 1956, but a crude estimate would put the amount available for transfer as dividends at about Rs. 20 million for the 25 years 1941–65. During the same period taxes paid in Ceylon (estimating taxes for the six years for which no data survives conservatively at Rs. 500,000 a year) may have amounted to some Rs. 51 million—more than the total increase in the capital value of the business plus dividends. On this basis Ceylon was the main beneficiary of Unilever's activities there. There is no direct evidence on the balance of payments effects but this is likely to have been small. Unilever did import tallow and other raw materials and remitted dividends; but they exported glycerine, coconut oil, tea and citronella; and the importation of tallow, which

Table 5.14 Ceylon: Trading Summary, 1941–65 (Rs. '000)

Year	A NSV	B Trading profit	C B/A %	D Nett accounting profit	E Capital employed at 31 Dec	F Dividend Gross	F Dividend Nett	G Yield D/E %	H Profit after stat. tax[a]	I Profit after stat. tax as % of av. gross capital employed[b]	J Remitted to London Fees	J Remitted to London Dividend
1941	2,361	n/a	n/a	206	1,723 (est.)	n/a	n/a	10.07 (est.)	n/a	n/a	n/a	n/a
1942	2,711	n/a	n/a	199	n/a	n/a	n/a	n/a	n/a	n/a	n/a	n/a
1943	4,053	857	21.1	408	2,644	n/a	n/a	15.4	n/a	n/a	n/a	n/a
1944	n/a	n/a	n/a	n/a	n/a	n/a	n/a	n/a	n/a	n/a	n/a	n/a
1945	n/a	1,396	n/a	577	n/a	n/a	n/a	n/a	n/a	n/a	n/a	n/a
1946	n/a	n/a	n/a	1,255	n/a	600	n/a	n/a	1,074	n/a	n/a	n/a
1947	n/a	2,064	n/a	726	n/a	–	n/a	19.2	n/a	n/a	n/a	n/a
1948	n/a	1,149	n/a	916	3,773	600	n/a	n/a	n/a	n/a	n/a	n/a
1949	11,539	n/a	n/a	n/a	n/a	–	n/a	n/a	n/a	n/a	n/a	n/a
1950	14,355	n/a	n/a	1,560	n/a	850	n/a	n/a	n/a	n/a	n/a	1,859

Year												
1951	18,225	3,671	20.1	1,892	4,392	1,750	n/a	43.1	n/a	n/a	n/a	n/a
1952	18,885	4,310	22.8	2,188	4,820	2,400	n/a	45.4	n/a	n/a	n/a	n/a
1953	18,202	4,263	23.4	2,005	4,001	1,900	n/a	50.1	n/a	n/a	n/a	n/a
1954	18,712	4,118	22.0	2,049	4,154	1,900	n/a	49.3	n/a	n/a	n/a	n/a
1955	19,615	4,405	22.4	2,157	5,137	2,000	1,937	42.0	n/a	n/a	—	—
1956	24,206	5,139	21.2	2,136	9,648	2,141	1,560	22.1	2,210	22.7	—	—
1957	25,013	3,958	15.8	1,751	11,145	1,730	1,397	15.7	1,582	13.6	—	—
1958	28,355	4,261	15.0	1,773	10,503	1,550	1,213	16.9	1,380	11.3	—	—
1959	32,368	4,776	14.7	2,111	17,382	2,000	1,238	12.1	1,576	10.9	—	—
1960	33,013	6,775	20.5	1,669	19,023	2,040	1,517	8.8	1,829	11.0	—	—
1961	35,970	7,346	20.4	3,001	22,039	2,500	1,577	13.6	1,983	10.6	—	—
1962	37,080	8,031	21.7	2,576	22,959	2,500	1,638	11.2	2,088	10.5	365	1,517
1963	38,179	7,996	20.9	2,813	25,519	2,600	1,965	11.0	2,079	9.4	370	1,517
1964	42,743	7,571	17.7	2,911	24,589	2,700	n/a	11.8	1,968	8.2	185	1,222
1965	48,986	8,320	17.0	4,478	27,566	3,500	n/a	16.2	2,496	9.7	425	—

Notes: a. Nett of profits tax plus dividends tax where applicable.

b. For reasons of space, average GCE is not shown in this table.

c. Figures for GCE and in consequence, profits as a percentage of GCE, change dramatically in 1959 because Unilver belatedly revalued the fixed assets of Lever Bros (Ceylon) Ltd in that year as a preliminary to going public.

d. There is no record of remittances to London before 1956; but it can be assumed that all dividends were transferred. No fees were charged before 1962.

was relatively cheap, released a proportionate amount of dearer CNO, which otherwise would have been used in local manufacture, for export.

Under the second conventional heading, production and productivity, the Unilever business was fully integrated into the local economy, increasingly used indigenous management as well as labour and was almost certainly the most efficient firm in its field in the country. The company actively encouraged and advised on the establishment of such local ancillary industries as tube making (for toothpaste), tin making, and biscuit manufacture; it encouraged production of new oil-bearing crops as an alternative to coconuts and provided agricultural advice. It set high standards of employment and training, and on average one technical manager in ten trained by them was lost to other public and private enterprises. Finally, under the heading of externalities, transfer of technology was limited by the restricted opportunities for introducing new products; but the company made efforts to develop management skills beyond its own needs by running university seminars and study groups in the factory.

Ceylon Unilever was not one of the concern's more important subsidiaries. It was handicapped by a restricted site, poor buildings, a limited market and, by the 1960s, a host economy in serious difficulties. Yet in many ways this company was more typical of the majority of Unilever subsidiaries in the less developed world than, say, Hindustan Lever, which was exceptionally large yet remained a small fish in a very big pool. Ceylon Unilever was a Leviathan in Ceylon, one of its country's largest and most efficient manufacturing enterprises. This made the company vulnerable to criticism on any of the standard arguments used against foreign enterprise; and from the mid-1950s all Ceylon governments were left of centre. Yet the company was able to get on very well with all of them and to sustain a good public image by being seen to be responsible, progressive and responsive to governmental wishes. Their reward was to receive generally helpful treatment; and it is said that when President Allende came to power in Chile, where there was also a Unilever subsidiary, and his government enquired of their fellow Marxist government in Ceylon how they found Unilever, the answer was 'sympathetic'.

6

Unilever in Black Africa

By the 1970s Unilever had a very large number of commercial and industrial interests in Black Africa, defined as those parts of the continent north of South Africa and south of the Sahara. These interests divide into three: manufacturing companies in Kenya, Ghana, Malawi, Nigeria, Rhodesia (though this was no longer controlled by Unilever in the 1970s) and Zaire, all of which were under the control of the Overseas Committee; plantation companies in Cameroun, Nigeria and Zaire, which were the responsibility of Plantation Group; and UAC (International) Ltd. Before the 1960s UAC's interests were primarily commercial, though they had for long included plantations and timber extraction; but from the 1960s UAC gradually turned from trading to industry and by 1973, as can be seen in Figure 4, they owned, part owned or acted as agents for a very large number of strictly industrial enterprises. Measured either by the size of the investment or the range of its activities UAC was by far the most important of these Unilever enterprises: in Nigeria, for example, UAC employed a capital of £26.7 million in 1958 as against Lever Brothers (Nigeria) Ltd (LB(N)) with some £2 million; and UAC's timber mill at Sapele employed some 3,000 men to LB(N)'s 900. For reasons already explained UAC is excluded from this study; but the two remaining Unilever interests are of considerable interest in their own right. Of the plantation companies the largest, Huileries du Congo Belge (HCB), is studied in some detail in Chapter 9 below. Of the manufacturing companies under the Overseas Committee those in Nigeria and the Belgian Congo (Zaire) are of importance because these were among the first factories set up by Lever Brothers or the Dutch margarine companies in the less developed world. The other Unilever manufacturing companies began much later, starting with Rhodesia in the early 1940s and culminating with Ghana in 1963. All these companies were studied in preparing this book and it was originally intended to include detailed accounts of all of them. It was, however, eventually found that space could not be spared for this and it was decided to provide a cursory history of four—Nigeria, the Congo, Kenya and Ghana— giving Nigeria pride of place and the longest treatment because it was one of the first to be set up, became the largest in terms of capital employed and turnover and provides the clearest evidence on the special problems of manufacturing for local consumption in Black Africa.

Lever Brothers (Nigeria) Ltd

(a) Origins of Local Manufacture to 1923

The Unilever manufacturing business in Nigeria, together with that in the Belgian Congo (Zaire), has two features which are important for the present study. Along with Lever Brothers (India) these formed the first generation of Lever Bros manufacturing subsidiaries established in countries which did not have a sub- stantial European population. They were contemporary with the first Latin American subsidiary in Argentina, and it was more than a decade before the next companies were established in South and South-east Asia in the 1930s. Moreover, when they were created the colonial dependencies in which they were situated were all free trading, with low revenue tariffs and no preferences. This in itself is a surprising and almost unique phenomenon for, as becomes obvious throughout the present study, the existence of a substantial import tariff or other import controls was normally essential for establishing a Lever subsidiary. There were special reasons for this in India: it will be necessary to discover what these were in Nigeria and the Congo.

Indeed, the paradox underlying the creaticn of Lever Brothers (West Africa) Ltd in April 1923 is that none of the conventional grounds for establishing a subsidiary seemed relevant. There were no protective or preferential tariffs in British West Africa and no import controls. There was a revenue tariff of £4 per metric ton on imported hard soap and the cost of sea freight from Britain was about £2 10s 0d—a total of £6 10s 0d per ton. This was by no means insignificant, amounting to perhaps a quarter of the price commonly

paid by importing merchant firms such as UAC to foreign manufacturers; yet in the first quarter of the twentieth century such costs
seemed to constitute no bar to imports nor to provide an incentive
to local manufacturers. West Africa remained a model market for
the European exporter. In 1910, for example, total UK imports of
'household and fancy soap' to West Africa as a whole were 9,369
tons, as compared with 13,560 tons to India, Burma and Ceylon
together with their immensely larger combined population, and
8,913 tons to China. Indeed the very existence of this trade reflects
a minor social revolution in West Africa, indicating that Africans
adopted European attitudes to personal cleanliness as soon as
supplies of soap at a reasonable price were available. Of this export
trade the vast majority was the product of Lever Bros, Gossages and
Crosfields, not yet amalgamated in 1910, but part of Lever Bros
by 1919. Although the volume of exports declined during the First
World War from a pre-war peak of 12,295 tons in 1913, they were
up to 9,209 tons in 1920 and there was no reason in the early 1920s
to think that this valuable market was endangered either by foreign
competition or by local manufacture. On what grounds, then, could
the building of a local soap factory in Nigeria be justified?

The answer is that it was initially a by-product of William Lever's
preoccupation with supplies of vegetable oil for his soap factories
and his belief in the advantages of crushing palm oil kernels where
they were grown rather than in Europe. The story has been told by
Wilson, Pedler and others and need not be repeated here.[1] So far
as the Nigerian soap business is concerned the relevant facts are as
follows. In 1910 Lever bought W. MacIver and Co., a Nigerian
trading company, among whose assets were saw-mills at Apapa,
near Lagos, and at Opobo. Lever renamed MacIvers the West
African Oil Company (WAOC) and set up kernel-crushing mills with
oil storage tanks, etc. at each of these places. This proved ill-judged.
For reasons already discussed in Chapter 5 in relation to Anton
Jurgens' oil-milling ventures in Indonesia, it was almost invariably
unprofitable to crush palm kernels in less developed countries at
that time and it was the failure of Lever's attempt to do this profitably
in Nigeria that led ultimately to soap manufacture as an alternative
way of utilising the same facilities. As early as June 1912 the Policy
and Tactics Committee noted that a loss was expected before the
Lagos and Opobo mills even started working; and in the last 12
months before these were closed in March 1913 they made a loss of
£25,448 and £25,210 respectively. In the normal course of things

this might well have been the end of local milling by Levers; but the outbreak of war in August 1914, and the exclusion of the hitherto dominant German kernel-crushing industry at Hamburg from the world market, led by 1916 to a rise in palm kernel oil prices and the WAOC mills were therefore reopened. They continued to operate until 1920, when the post-war slump in oil prices again made them entirely unprofitable: indeed losses were then about £60,000 a year and, according to Greenhalgh, the mills had only been kept going 'on account of the possibility of our commencing soap-making at Lagos . . .'. As this idea was then again postponed the mills finally closed in 1920.

This was the background to a debate that lasted within Lever Bros for ten years from 1913 to 1923 about the possible advantages of making soap at Apapa. The broad case for doing so was that Lagos was one of the main centres of the oil export trade, so that ample supplies of palm oil were available there; that Levers, through MacIvers, already had a substantial share in this trade with a managerial organisation in Lagos; that the oil mills at Apapa could be used to house soap-making equipment; that the railway system from Lagos would help distribution of soap up-country; and finally that there was no other large-scale local manufacture of the cheap 'filled' soap (i.e. with a relatively low proportion of fatty acid) in Nigeria. Throughout this decade it was William Lever more than anyone else who appears to have been enthusiastic about the project. His case was consistent; as he put it to the PTC in late November 1915, given the availability of the otherwise useless Apapa mill, the capital cost of making soap would be very small. To make a cheap soap only caustic soda, resin and a few other un-important materials would have to be imported; the product, although inferior by European standards, would be better than anything made in Nigeria; oil cost £7 a ton less at Lagos than at Port Sunlight; and this might be the best way of securing Levers' West African soap trade against stiff overseas competition.

These propositions were first considered seriously in June 1913 and a cost-benefit calculation was made, based on a capital cost of £13,000 and production of 500 tons of Sunlight soap and 4,000 tons of filled soap a year. No action was taken, though the reasons are not clear. A year later Levers heard that Crosfields, still a rival, were considering soap manufacture in West Africa and 'Sir William said that this matter must be taken up'. The outcome was a thorough reconsideration of the issue in November 1915. The initiative was that of Lever, though he was not personally present at the main meeting of the PTC held on 22 November. The Committee had to consider a specific question put to it by him, 'whether a soap works would affect our previous decision to dispose of the oil mills'. Greenhalgh therefore reviewed changes in the situation since the pro forma (estimate) for a factory had been prepared in 1913. He argued first that the soap issue should be entirely divorced from that of reopening the oil mills, since to make soap cheap enough to be competitive in West Africa only palm oil, then costing about £28 a ton in Lagos, and not palm kernel oil, which cost £38, could be used. Taking the soap proposal in isolation, it still did not look profitable. Soap imports to the whole of British West Africa were then about 10,000 tons a year, of which only about half entered through Lagos: hence to serve other markets in the area from Apapa would involve substantial freight costs which would reduce the margin of advantage over imports from Europe. Africans in any case had a strong prejudice in favour of imported goods; and there would be technical difficulties to overcome. The African might be educated to buy more expensive, but also more economical, bar soap of the type made in Europe; but that would take time. Another difficulty was that there was a pooling arrangement with Brunner Mond in respect of Gossages and Crosfields to standardise qualities of soap sold in West Africa: to introduce a new, cheaper locally-made soap would break that agreement. Finally profit margins would be tight because of fierce competition. Some imported filled soaps sold at £18 a ton and Sunlight made in Lagos would cost £22 12s 0d to make and would have to be sold at £25 a ton, though he did not calculate the production and selling costs of a cheaper bar soap. On this argument the Committee clearly felt that there was no case for soap manufacture at Apapa and recommended that the oil mills be closed.

But Lever was not convinced. When he saw the minutes of this meeting on 25 November he immediately pinpointed the fact that Greenhalgh had talked in terms of making Sunlight Soap, whereas his own idea was to make only cheaper, filled soap at Apapa. The soap proposal was, nevertheless, shelved for the moment. The oil mills were reopened in March 1916—again mainly on Lever's personal insistence, backed by the suggestion that the mills might make palm kernel oil for his own margarine manufacture—and additional warehousing was built at Apapa. The soap proposition did not come up again until February 1918 when it was decided to obtain estimates of the cost of machinery, but no action had been taken by 26 July 1920, when the now renamed Policy Committee decided that as the oil mills were losing £15,000 a quarter—even more than before 1914—they should again be closed. It was noted that 'the only reason the mills had been continued was on account of the possibility of our commencing soap-making at Lagos but it had now been decided to defer the soap factory for Lagos'—so that there was no point in continuing to run the mills at a loss. The mills were therefore closed for the last time; but the concept of soap making survived them, presumably because Lever himself remained convinced that this was a sound proposition. When, therefore, his son, W. H. Lever, visited Nigeria in July 1921 he reported, possibly on instructions from his father, that

> the shell of the mills buildings is in pretty good condition and could easily be converted into the frame room and packing room. There are also good oil storage tanks there which could be used and an engine and boiler. But we must study conditions over Nigeria as a whole, also the neighbouring colonies before we can express an opinion.

At this point, unfortunately, the surviving evidence on the Apapa soap project and factory becomes exceedingly thin until after 1930. There is no record of the final decision to instal soap-making equipment in the Apapa buildings in 1923; but it is a reasonable guess that the drive still came from Lever and that his ideas had not changed significantly during the previous decade. Essentially then, this subsidiary must have been established because, on the one hand Levers happened to own an unprofitable kernel crushing mill which could be transformed quite cheaply into a small soap works; and, more important, because Lever believed that by using local raw materials he could produce a low quality soap for the local Nigerian market at a lower price than soap made in Port Sunlight or in other European factories could be landed at a Nigerian port. The important point is that this was not a decision to substitute local manufacture for imports in the full sense, as occurred in all overseas companies so far examined. As J. L. Heyworth pointed out in 1934 in the first report on Apapa written by a member of the Overseas Committee, no arrangement had ever been made for the three British soap-exporting companies—Lever Bros, Gossages and Crosfields—to leave even the cheap bar soap market in Nigeria to the local company, as was normal in other countries where Lever trademarks were transferred or leased to a subsidiary. On the contrary, presumably in line with Lever's policy of encouraging competition within the 'family', the home companies continued to export cheap bar soaps to Nigeria as well as their 'specialities' which were not manufactured there. In short, Lever seems to have intended simply to make cheap soap from local raw materials on the assumption that the effective protection provided by the revenue tariff and freight costs should provide a higher profit than could be made on exports from Britain; but had nevertheless hedged his bets by allowing free export of competing soaps made by his own British companies. This policy, which was common also to the Congo soap enterprise, puts these two African soap companies in a special category of overseas manufacturing subsidiaries, where they remained until each was allowed to become fully import-substituting after 1945.

(b) WASCO, 1923–40

Lever Brothers (West Africa) Ltd was incorporated in April 1923 at Lagos, but was renamed the West African Soap Company (WASCO) a year later, possibly for fear that local consumers would associate the word Lever with the relatively inferior products to be made at the Apapa factory and so lose faith in genuine Lever products from Port Sunlight. The company's share capital was at first only £20,000 in ordinary shares, held by the four home soap companies within the Lever empire whose trademarks were to be used—Lever Bros, Gossages, Crosfields and also T. H. Harris—in the ratio 2:1:1:1. In 1926 the share capital was increased to £30,000 by capitalising loans made to WASCO by Lever Bros on capital account and in 1930 it was again increased to £60,000 by capitalising £30,000 from the general reserve. Although technically an autonomous company incorporated in West Africa, in practice WASCO was little more than a factory. Its board of directors was in Britain; the local management consisted of a works manager—who was also the managing director—a European accountant, and two European travelling salesmen. Effective supervision was in the hands of the Niger Co., and later UAC, and it was not until after 1930, when the company was transferred to the Overseas Committee, that anyone in London seems to have taken a critical look at WASCO and its future.

The first Overseas Committee visitor was J. L. Heyworth; and by the time he visited Nigeria in 1934 the property appeared to be a wasting asset. Mainly because the company lacked senior managerial staff who might have been able to think constructively and react to changing conditions in Nigeria, the company had clearly lost what had once been an excellent position as market leader in cheap soaps. Its fortunes are clearly reflected in Tables 6.1, 6.2 and 6.3. At the start Lever's estimate of the market possibilities had clearly been

Table 6.1   Nigeria: Sales of Soap made at Apapa, 1924–40 (metric tons)

Year	In Nigeria and Cameroons	In other West African Colonies	Total
1924			264
1925	641	118	759
1926	959	180	1,139
1927	1,462	235	1,697
1928	2,146	216	2,362
1929	2,840	303	3,143
1930	2,760	290	3,050
1931	1,864	82	1,946
1932	2,102	96	2,198
1933	1,712	56	1,768
1934	1,127	–	1,127
1935	2,275	11	2,286
1936	3,537	20	3,557
1937	4,386	14	4,400
1938	3,441	4	3,445
1939	3,351	–	3,351
1940	2,989	83	3,072

correct: the sales record demonstrated that there had been a demand for a locally-made cheap soap which, because of the effective protection provided by the tariff and freight charges on imports, could undersell imported soap of the same quality. After a slow start with a pale bar soap, which proved unpopular, the company had concentrated production on an equally cheap red carbolic soap with 52 per cent fatty acid content, made from 85 per cent palm oil and 15 per cent resin. Sold at just below the price of imported pale soaps of similar quality, it virtually captured the Nigerian market. In 1929, its peak year before 1940, it had about half the Nigerian market for all factory-made soap, selling 2,840 tons there and 303 tons in neighbouring British colonies. Together with the Lever imports handled by WASCO (for which at this time it obtained the profit) the 'family' then held some 79 per cent of the total Nigerian market for factory-made soaps. These achievements fully justified Lever's decision to undertake local manufacture in Nigeria.

What really shocked Heyworth in 1934 was that this dominant position had been squandered. In 1934 sales of WASCO soap were down to 1,036 tons; and, with an even more dramatic decline in the

Table 6.2   Nigeria: WASCO's Share of Total Soap Sales in Nigeria, 1929–43 (metric tons)

	Imports			Local			
Year	UEL	Other UK	Other foreign	Total import	Apapa sales	Other local	Total	WASCO's share of total %
1929	1,603	272	866	2,741	2,600	n/a	5,341	48.7
1930	1,037	564	886	2,487	2,541	n/a	5,028	50.5
1931	224	990	348	1,562	1,741	n/a	3,303	52.7
1932	55	992	73	1,120	1,982	n/a	3,102	63.9
1933	40	936	87	1,063	1,643	n/a	2,706	60.7
1934	186	827	90	1,103	1,036	n/a	2,139	48.4
1935	94	919	128	1,141	2,275	n/a	3,416	66.6
1936	n/a	n/a	n/a	1,598	3,537	n/a	5,135	68.8
1937	n/a	n/a	n/a	1,959	4,386	50	6,395	68.6
1938	n/a	n/a	n/a	1,500	3,441	100	5,041	68.3
1939	n/a	n/a	n/a	1,020	3,351	150	4,521	74.1
1940	n/a	n/a	n/a	491	2,989	170	3,650	81.9
1941	n/a	n/a	n/a	89	4,756	300	5,145	92.4
1942	n/a	n/a	n/a	10	5,064	450	5,524	91.7
1943	n/a	n/a	n/a	—	5,026	600	5,626	89.3

sale of Lever exports from England, Unilever now held only about 56 per cent of a much smaller total soap market. What or who was to blame? For the decline in the absolute volume of sales the slump in commodity prices and greatly reduced African buying power were clearly responsible; but this did not account for the decline in WASCO's share of the market: it should have been able to maintain or even increase its sales by reducing its previously excessive profit margin of £10 a ton to maintain a competitive edge over all imported soaps. It had not done so, said Heyworth, because in the good days WASCO had committed the unforgiveable sin of a market leader in any country—that of greed. It had over-exploited its largely fortuitous position by maintaining a profit margin greater than was justified by its natural advantage (£6 10s 0d a ton) and so made the trade too attractive to potential rivals. In this case the main rival was not a local manufacturer at all, but a Liverpool oil-milling firm, Bibbys, who started soap manufacture in the early 1920s. From 1930 Bibbys began to offer a comparable red carbolic soap made in England from a nut oil base with a higher soap content (58 per cent) and better heat resistant qualities. They were helped in establishing a market in Nigeria by co-operation from John Holt, the main surviving rival to UAC as a merchant firm in Nigeria, who were apparently glad to find a soap which would reduce their dependence on WASCO as a source of supply and would also provide freight for their ships on the West African run. Bibbys were helped by the dramatic decline in ocean freights during the slump, since Holts were apparently willing to carry their soap at very low rates, so that WASCO's effective protection was substantially reduced. As a result, and partly because WASCO was slow to see the danger and did not sufficiently reduce its selling price, Bibbys were able to penetrate deep into the Nigerian market. By 1933 they were selling some 900 tons against WASCO's 1,643 tons, and in 1934 over 800 tons as compared with WASCO's 1,036 tons. Seldom had so apparently secure a market position been lost so quickly.

Clearly the main cause of this failure to adjust to changes in the market was the inadequacy of WASCO's small local management and the absence of effective supervision from London. Behind this failure lay a fundamental fact of West African life—the commercial dominance of the big merchant houses and the consequential absence of any proper sales organisation specific to WASCO or Lever imported products. This is not the place to describe these commercial organisations and a substantial literature now exists on this question.[2] But to understand WASCO's problems in the 1930s it is necessary to emphasise two special features of the commercial system in West Africa which made it very difficult, even for a local manufacturer, to influence the fortunes of his own products in the market.

First, it was a peculiarity of the merchant firms in West Africa, that, by contrast with the comparable managing agencies common throughout the Middle East, India, South-east Asia and China in this period, firms such as UAC or Holts made no attempt to push products of one company against those of another and were happy to deal impartially in any product that seemed to promise profits. Thus, whereas in Indonesia any one of the 'big five' trading companies would not sell more than one competing brand in the same area (though it might well do so in some other part of the country),

Table 6.3   Nigeria: WASCO Profits (Losses) in Relation to Capital Employed, 1924–40[a]

Year	A Profits after tax (£)	B Capital employed (£)	A/B %
1923	–	20,000*	–
1924	(5,249)	25,000*	–
1925	(4,565)	31,000*	–
1926	2,512	37,000*	6.8*
1927	11,408	43,000*	26.5*
1928	22,157	49,000*	45.2*
1929	32,162	55,000*	58.4*
1930	42,127	61,000*	69.1*
1931	13,406	67,000*	20.0*
1932	6,000	73,000*	8.2*
1933	5,487	79,000*	6.9*
1934	248	85,869	0.3
1935	(1,367)	82,427	–
1936[b]	10,826	88,000*	9.8
1937	21,056	96,000*	21.9
1938	468	103,000*	0.4
1939	934	110,000*	0.8
1940	(5,335)	118,000*	–

Notes: a. All figures for capital employed shown in Column B are starred, except those for 1934 and 1935, to indicate that these are rough estimates based on plotting a linear graph between the initial capital investment of £20,000 in 1923 and the known 1934 capital employed, and from the known 1935 capital employed to the next known capital employed in 1949. This assumes a consistent growth in capital employed, which may not have happened; but it provides some indication of the relative profitability of the business over time.

b. Until 1935 the accounting years covered the 12 months ending on 30 September, so each previous year should strictly be indicated as 1934/5, etc. From 1936 the accounting year ended on 31 December and the profits for 1936 cover the 15 months from 1 October 1935 to 31 December 1936. In calculating the return on capital for that year allowance was made for this.

in West Africa Holts sold both WASCO and Bibby soap, leaving the consumer to choose between them; and in 1935 UAC sold 65 per cent of WASCO's soap, Ollivant 18 per cent, and other firms the rest. The corollary was that there was virtually no sales promotion by any merchant firm, and a product had to depend on its reputation among the African 'market women' who bought soap from a merchant firm's distributing point for resale in the market. Like other commodities soap sold on its appearance, smell, reputation and above all its price. Thus, once sales of WASCO soap began to slip, it was extremely difficult to take countervailing measures.

Second, and for the same reasons, there was no direct link between WASCO as the manufacturer and the ultimate African consumer; and in a prolonged chain of distribution both prices and consumer preference became obscured. In particular, that fundamental tool of sales promotion in Europe—the manufacturers' ability to alter prices to the consumer to meet commercial competition—was not available to WASCO. The key to the system lay in a set of conventions which originally related to the sale of goods by manufacturers in Europe to merchants operating in West Africa. The manufacturer fixed a price for his product c.i.f. any port in Nigeria or other parts of West Africa. He paid the British headquarters of the appropriate merchant firm 5 per cent on this price, which was known as the 'home commission'. The merchant firm then took delivery of the product at a West African port at the agreed price and made whatever profit it could on resale to the 'market women' through its depots. This was known as the 'coast profit'. Thus the final stages of the sales and distribution system were entirely in the hands of the merchant houses who organised distribution throughout a West African country, provided credit to the African middleman, ran the risk of loss and in return had the opportunity to make a speculative profit. The only guidelines the manufacturer had were the orders he received from the merchant and any information he might receive about the products and their prices available from his rivals.

Rational and perhaps essential though the system may have been for British-based firms exporting to West Africa, it was clearly irrelevant to a local-based enterprise such as WASCO. Yet, although Overseas Committee visitors speculated for a decade after 1934 on what could be done to get WASCO a better sales and promotional system, there seemed no feasible alternative in the economic and social conditions of West Africa in this period. Had there existed a group of professional traders with some capital, fulfilling the role of Indians in East Africa or Chinese in South-east Asia, it might have been possible to build up an alternative system of direct sales and distribution based on company depots selling to a large number of local wholesalers on a cash basis, as was eventually done in the

1950s and 1960s. But this was only made possible by the later growth of a class of small-scale Nigerian wholesalers who did not exist in the 1930s and 1940s and whom Unilever eventually helped to bring into existence. The Nigerian was, of course, a willing and keen trader but he lacked both capital and warehousing facilities. The trade therefore continued to depend on credit and storage facilities provided by expatriates; and only a merchant house, trading in a very wide range of commodities, could afford the cost of maintaining such premises throughout the country.

Thus it was that WASCO, for all that it was only a few miles from Lagos, had to trade as if it was at Port Sunlight: even the conventional 5 per cent commission was paid to the merchant firms' home companies. Insulated from the African consumers, they had little idea of what quality would appeal and at what price to sell. This more than any other single factor seems to have been responsible for the disastrous errors made in the early 1930s and for the failure of WASCO to regain its overwhelming dominance before 1940.

But, in accounting for the relatively poor performance of WASCO in the 1930s in terms of its weakened competitive position, there was one other factor which was not perceived at the time but which was emphasised by Roger Heyworth in 1944. This was the price paid by WASCO to UAC for its oil supplies which, in Heyworth's view, was unreasonably high and seriously reduced WASCO's potential advantage over a British firm such as Bibby. Since this issue throws some light on transfer pricing between WASCO and UAC, and therefore between two parts of a single multinational, it is worth a brief discussion.

It was natural that WASCO, as a by-product and former protégé of the Niger Co., should buy its raw materials from UAC, which was a major palm oil and kernel exporter and had bulk tank installations next to the soap factory. But the basis of payment for the oil or kernels was more difficult to determine. If WASCO had been an autonomous company, it would presumably have bought oil from whichever of the exporting firms offered the lowest price. But WASCO was tied to UAC; and it was fundamental to Unilever practice that, as was laid down in a formal agreement between Unilever and UAC in 1932, 'all trading transactions between Unilever or Lever's or their subsidiaries and the [UA] Company shall as in the past be carried out at prices not below market prices'. To realise this principle in West Africa the rule laid down in the 1920s and 1930s was that oil was sold to Apapa by UAC 'at the Liverpool price less the actual cash savings involved in delivering oil locally as compared with shipping to the UK, less half the estimated UAC profit on oil sales'. This meant that WASCO paid the Liverpool price less £2 8s a ton on freight and 7s a ton representing half UAC's profit—a total of £2 15s a ton—provided the oil came from the Lagos area. But if, as was increasingly the case, oil had to be brought from other areas to Lagos, WASCO paid the local freight of about 13s 6d a ton, so reducing its nett advantage over the British manufacturer to £2 1s 6d.

On the face of it this formula seemed immaculate; but in practice during the 1930s it forced WASCO to pay far more for its oil than an independent company in West Africa would have done. Table 6.4(a) sets out the available data from 1935 to 1946. It is clear from comparing Column D with Column B that at all times Apapa was paying substantially more for oil than the current export price; so manufacturing costs would have been substantially lower had it been allowed to buy oil at that price rather than the price paid to UAC. And in practice UAC could legitimately have sold oil to WASCO for less than the average official export values without breaking the rule on internal transfer prices and still leave UAC with a reasonable margin. That is, UAC could reasonably have given WASCO the benefit of its own successful buying policies.

In one respect it was of little importance within a multinational such as Unilever whether profits were taken by UAC or WASCO. But it had always been a basic principle of Lever Bros, clearly laid down by Lever on many occasions, that no one part of his business should make a profit out of dealings with another; and it is therefore surprising that it was not until 1944 that any member of the Overseas Committee seriously questioned this system of internal accounting in West Africa. Possibly this was because another and potentially incompatible principle had been established as early as 1924 by Lever himself as a promise to a meeting of Niger Co.'s shareholders at a time when the future of that company was at risk. He then stated that interest paid by the Niger Co. to Lever Bros for loans, overdraft, etc. would always be lower than could be paid to any bank or alternative source of finance; and that 'with reference to the price of palm oil . . . the price paid by Lever Bros and Associated Companies is the full market price but that the Niger Co. saves payment of brokerage on all produce sold to Lever Bros or Associated Companies'. Thus oil-consuming Lever companies were

Table 6.4(a)   Nigeria: Cost of Palm Oil to WASCO, 1935—46

	A	B	C	D
Year	Tons exported from Lagos	Average value per ton (official) (£)	UAC maximum buying price (£)	Average cost to WASCO per ton (£)
1935	n/a	n/a	11.0.0	12. 7.8
1936	18,731	13.11.7	12.0.0	15. 3.6
1937	9,290	15.16.4	13.5.0	19. 2.2
1938	735	9.13.10	6.5.0	12.18.10
1939	2,311	8.18.6	5.4.3	10.16.9
1940	5,216	7.12.1	7.7.6	12. 2.6
1941	13,928	7. 4.0	n/a	11.15.2
1942	27,539	9.19.0	n/a	14. 4.0
1943	36,810	11.14.10	n/a	14. 1.7
1944	21,356	16. 2.1	n/a	19. 1.11
1945	12,731	15.16.11	n/a	19.13.5
1946	17,731	20. 5.5	n/a	22. 9.9

Note: The average price paid by WASCO varies slightly in different Unilever documents, but is always substantially above both the official average value and UAC's maximum buying price. From 1941 the buying price was fixed by the West African Produce Control Board.

Table 6.4(b)   Nigeria: WASCO Fixed Expenses and Profits of Soap, per Ton of Soap, 1935—47

Year	Sales volume (metric tons)	Total fixed expenses per ton (£)	Nett accounting profit per ton after tax (£)
1935	2,286	7.2	(—)
1936	3,557	4.9	3.04
1937	4,400	4.275	4.78
1938	3,445	6.45	0.14
1939	3,351	n/a	0.38
1940	3,072	n/a	(—)
1941	4,834	n/a	2.68
1942	6,867	3.75	3.20
1943	6,843	4.12	2.19
1944	8,033	n/a	0.99
1945	10,643	3.075	2.92
1946	10,836	3.40	3.41

to pay a full world market price to UAC, who would obtain a built-in profit from them. This constituted an interesting inversion of roles between UAC, which had originally been built up in order to provide cheap or at least reasonably priced oil for Lever's factories, and his manufacturing interests which, far from receiving raw materials at the lowest available prices, were to be forced to pay more for their raw materials than they might otherwise have had to do.

In Europe this probably did not matter very much since Lever factories paid the same price for oil as other European competitors. Moreover, the consumer capacity of the European market was not directly connected with vegetable oil prices. But in West Africa, and also in the Belgian Congo, rival local manufacturers (mostly 'cottage' soap-makers) could and did pay far less than WASCO; so, by tying WASCO to UAC on a particular formula, Unilever was handicapping the soap factory. More important, West African demand for soap depended to a very large extent on the selling price of palm oil and kernels and in the North on groundnut prices. If the local price of these primary products went down, then the price at which Nigerians could afford to buy soap went down also. Thus it should have been a first principle of business policy in Nigeria that the price to be paid by WASCO to UAC should be tied to the index of local prices and not to those of the world market.

Surprisingly this fact seems to have been seen and stated for the first time by R. H. Heyworth in 1944. In his view, the low profits made by WASCO in the 1930s were to a large extent due to their having what he called 'the dirty end of the stick'. There was 'a real clash of family interests, and one that must be resolved if we are to put our soap manufacturing business in Nigeria onto a firm and progressive basis for the future'. Essentially, he thought, a choice had to be made.

Either our policy is to encourage the production and consumption of locally made factory soap in Nigeria, or to make our first aim that of making profits on the export of produce from Nigeria. If the former, we must attempt to diminish the margin between the price paid to the grower, and the consuming price for soap making; if the latter is our aim, then we should never have erected a soap factory in Nigeria at all, but continue to export from home as successfully as Bibbys did until the export prohibition in the UK [from 1940] made it impossible for them to continue.

Two main reasons for WASCO's poor performance in the 1930s were, therefore, the price it had to pay for its raw materials and the reduction in Nigerian incomes. But there were two more, both pinpointed by Heyworth in 1944 and closely related. On the one hand the fixed expenses of a factory as small as that at Apapa were too high in relation to its turnover and profit margins. Apapa could not make profits in the later 1930s when margins were very low unless it could sell over 4,000 tons of soap; and it could not sell that amount unless it held a dominant share of the restricted market left by the 'cottage' manufacturers. The trouble was that, as can be seen in Table 6.2, although imports of Unilever products virtually stopped due to lack of demand, imports from rival manufacturers rose and remained high throughout the 1930s. These imports consisted almost entirely of the cheap carbolic soap made by Bibbys, which achieved great popularity in certain parts of Nigeria, especially the Port Harcourt region. Thus in 1937, the best year of the decade, Bibbys sold 1,767 tons in Nigeria as against WASCO's 4,386 tons, and had 28.7 per cent of total factory made soap sales.

That a British exporter should be able to take over nearly a third of the Nigerian market in competition with a Unilever subsidiary, which had been manufacturing there for six years before Bibbys entered the market and had the benefit of substantial effective protection provided by import duties and freights from Europe, seemed to run contrary to all the economic principles which favoured local manufacturing. Price was not at all a factor, since the two firms had quickly established price agreements and, contrary to most West African experience, these agreements survived into and after the Second World War. Quality was obviously important, for Bibby's soap was better made and could command a premium in the market. But how could Bibbys overcome the disadvantage resulting from manufacturing in Britain? Many calculations were made by Unilever men to solve this riddle and to see how great the advantage was. In 1937 J. H. Hansard calculated that, so long as WASCO's profit margin did not exceed £7 13s 6d a ton, there would be no profit in the trade for Bibbys and therefore no incentive for them to compete. In 1944 retrospective calculations suggested that in 1937 Bibbys cost ex-factory in England was £16 1s 3d, including

£2 16s 4d for fixed expenses, or £13 4s 11d for fluctuating expenses only; and that at the same time the fluctuating cost of soap manufactured at Apapa was £13 19s 2d—significantly just above that calculated for Bibbys. Thus, if Bibbys chose to ignore their own overheads to balance the higher cost to them of West African raw materials and freight, they could get their soap to Lagos at approximately the same price as WASCO could deliver it to their factory gates. Yet WASCO still possessed a potential profit margin of £4 15s 4d, representing largely the import duties Bibbys had to pay on landing of their soap. How was it, then, that WASCO, with this margin in hand, made only £934 profit in 1939 and that Bibbys were able and willing to compete with them?

The answer must be a double one. On the one hand, on this costing, Bibbys could expect to break even if they included British overheads in their costings and to make a small profit if they did not; but in any case their strategy was presumably to build up their market to the point that they might hope to drive WASCO out of business. Alternatively they might have been content to use the West African market to spread overheads on their British production. Either way, the reason why WASCO could not capitalise on the margin provided by freight and import duties and drive Bibbys out of the Nigerian market altogether—that is, by reducing their prices to the point at which Bibbys were making an unacceptable loss on their imports—was precisely that WASCO's own overheads absorbed virtually the whole margin between local and British production costs. Unfortunately the figure for WASCO overheads in 1939 is not available; but assuming roughly the same per ton as in 1938 (reasonable, since the sales tonnage was approximately the same) Apapa's overheads at £6 9s 4d would have been roughly equal to Bibby's overheads plus freight (£1) and duty (£4 7s 9d).

It is, therefore, clear that the main reasons why WASCO was still at the end of the 1930s a small and relatively unprofitable enterprise relate to the general character of the West African economy. Without formal tariff protection, facing competition from African producers and a limited market for quality soap, any factory making goods for local consumption was exposed to hazards seldom found in so acute a form in more developed countries. Profits depended on the margin between raw material costs and selling prices. The former were fixed too high by a rule intended to prevent profit-making by one Unilever enterprise at the expense of another, while selling prices were held down both by consumer poverty and by a type of cut-throat competition from overseas that had always been characteristic of the 'open' economy of West Africa. With profits of only £934 on a capital of perhaps £100,000 in 1939 Unilever might well have wondered whether there was any point in continuing so unrewarding an enterprise; and what dismayed them may well have deterred other foreign firms from investing in manufacturing in Nigeria and, for that matter, all other countries in West Africa.

(c) Expansion and the Effects of Decolonisation, 1940–65

It is evident from Tables 6.1, 6.2, 6.3, 6.5(a) and 6.5(b) that between 1940 and 1965 WASCO (renamed Lever Brothers (Nigeria) Limited in 1956, hereafter LB(N)) changed fundamentally. In the 1930s factory capacity was about 7,000 tons (which was never used), capital employed was under £100,000 and only cheap soaps, which did not include any of the main Lever Brothers international brands, were made. By 1965 total soap capacity was well over 30,000 tons, there was a second factory at Aba (Eastern Region), total production was running at over 20,000 tons and the range of products had widened to include several Unilever international brands of soap, margarine, edible oils and some toilet preparations. Capital employed had risen to £2,577,000 and in 1965 (a good year, as it happened) the nett result after tax was £214,000. There had been other developments which radically affected the nature of the business. Although there was still no local participation in the equity, by 1965 there were 39 African to 16 European managers and one African director. The system of sales had at last broken free from the grasp of the European merchant firms: in 1965 51 per cent of the company's turnover was sold to Nigerian distributors and LB(N) possessed a network of depots throughout the country which enabled it at last to control sales and prices.

By the 1960s LB(N) thus appeared to have broken out of its chrysalis, changing from a mere factory into a dynamic, industrial enterprise, and so become comparable with progressive Unilever subsidiaries in other countries. Yet there is another side to the picture. The most impressive period of growth had in fact been between 1940 and the early 1950s: total soap manufacture reached 17,235 tons in 1953 and dropped well below that figure in several later years. More serious, while capital employed rose rapidly,

Table 6.5(a)   Nigeria: WASCO Soap Sales, 1941—60 (metric tons)

Year	A Bar soaps	B Sunlight	C Lifebuoy	D Lux TS	E Total	A/E %	B/E %
1941	n/a	n/a	n/a	n/a	4,834	n/a	n/a
1942	n/a	n/a	n/a	n/a	6,867	n/a	n/a
1943	n/a	n/a	n/a	n/a	6,843	n/a	n/a
1944	n/a	n/a	n/a	n/a	8,033	n/a	n/a
1945	n/a	n/a	n/a	n/a	10,643	n/a	n/a
1946	n/a	n/a	n/a	n/a	10,836	n/a	n/a
1947	n/a	n/a	n/a	n/a	9,454	n/a	n/a
1948	n/a	n/a	n/a	n/a	n/a	n/a	n/a
1949	9,398	503	757	n/a	10,672	88	5
1950	10,224	496	709	n/a	11,444	89	4
1951	9,676	766	867	137	11,407	85	7
1952	11,730	1,277	1,092	276	14,374	82	9
1953	13,415	2,301	1,222	290	17,235	78	13
1954	n/a	n/a	n/a	n/a	n/a	n/a	n/a
1955	n/a	n/a	n/a	n/a	n/a	n/a	n/a
1956	15,100	5,400	n/a	284	n/a	n/a	n/a
1957	16,200	3,400	n/a	445	n/a	n/a	n/a
1958	10,876	3,789	n/a	377	15,674	69	24
1959	9,507	3,221	n/a	435	13,840	69	23
1960	12,646	4,572	n/a	512	18,516	68	25

Table 6.5(b)   Nigeria: Sales of Non-soapy Detergents, 1954—60 (metric tons)

Year	Omo	Surf	(Fab)	Total	Unilever share %
1954	n/a	33	n/a	n/a	n/a
1955	n/a	45	n/a	n/a	n/a
1956	66	143	n/a	235	88.9
1957	129	n/a	n/a	450	n/a
1958	246	n/a	n/a	700	n/a
1959	305	482	110	950	82.8
1960	472	n/a	n/a	n/a	n/a

Note: Until 1963 Omo was imported in bulk from UEL and packed and
distributed by LB(N) Ltd. Surf was originally imported in cartons and
distributed by Hazlehursts for UEL. Fab was the main competitor, made
and imported by Colgates.

doubling between 1956 and 1965, profitability became as low and
volatile as in the 1930s. The arithmetic average of nett profits in
Table 6.6(a) as a percentage of capital employed was only 4.26 per

Table 6.6(a)   Nigeria: Actual Post-tax Profits in Relation to Capital
Employed, 1941—65

Year	A Nett accounting profit (£ '000)	B Nominal capital (£ '000)	C A/B %	D Capital employed (£ '000)	E A/D %
1941	12	n/a	n/a	125*	9.6*
1942	22	n/a	n/a	132*	16.6*
1943	15	n/a	n/a	139*	10.8*
1944	8	n/a	n/a	146*	5.5*
1945	29	n/a	n/a	153*	18.9*
1946	37	n/a	n/a	161*	23.0*
1947	49	n/a	n/a	169*	29.0*
1948	n/a	n/a	n/a	n/a	n/a
1949	37	160	23.1	186	19.9
1950	54	160	33.7	232	23.2
1951	104	200	52.0	364	28.6
1952	140	310	45.2	416*	33.6*
1953	177	n/a	n/a	n/a	n/a
1954	n/a	n/a	n/a	n/a	n/a
1955	n/a	n/a	n/a	n/a	n/a
1956	154	710	21.7	1,200	12.8
1957	85	810	10.5	1,687	5.0
1958	(4)	810	—	2,065	—
1959	(48)	810	—	2,281	—
1960	210	810	25.9	2,245	9.3
1961	(11)	1,000	—	2,450	—
1962	(18)	1,000	—	2,325	—
1963	60	1,000	6.0	2,505	2.4
1964	93	1,000	9.3	2,456	3.8
1965	214	1,000	21.4	2,577	8.3

Note: Figures for capital employed in column D and percentages in column E
which are starred are hypothetical. Since data for CE is missing for these
years, the CE has been calculated by plotting a linear graph between the
previous known figure, for 1935, and the next known figure, for 1949.
Although very approximate, this probably gives a reasonably reliable
indication of the profitability of the business in these years. For 1956—
65 figures in this column show the average gross capital employed during
each year.

cent and even this was buoyed up by good years at the beginning
and end—1956 and 1965. Moreover, while by the standards of
many other Unilever subsidiaries the product base of LB(N) remained

very narrow, a surprisingly wide range of goods were still imported
by UEL and sold through its local subsidiary, Hazlehurst (Nigeria)
Ltd. Unstable profitability, discontinuous growth in sales volume
and a restricted product range suggests that there were still many
factors at work in Nigeria to check the growth of a manufacturing
subsidiary of this kind. It is proposed to begin with a short survey
of the more important political and economic changes in Nigeria
which may have affected the operation of this and other foreign
enterprises, then to consider the Unilever company under the
following heads: local participation and Africanisation of management; production, diversification and distribution; profitability; and
finally the effects on the Nigerian economy.

Table 6.6(b)   Nigeria: Return to Capital, 1955–65 (£ '000)

Year	A Trading profit before tax	B Nett profit after statistical tax	C Statistical tax rate %	D Gross capital employed	E Yield after tax B/D %
1956	226	125	45	1,200	10.4
1957	133	83	40	1,687	4.9
1958	21	13	40	2,065	0.6
1959	(16)	(16)	40	2,281	—
1960	234	140	40	2,245	6.2
1961	23	14	40	2,450	0.6
1962	91	55	40	2,325	2.4
1963	131	79	40	2,505	3.2
1964	176	106	40	2,456	4.3
1965	440	264	40	2,557	10.3

(1) The Political and Economic Environment. Between 1940 and
1965 fundamental changes occurred which necessarily altered the
position and affected the fortunes of WASCO and all other foreign
enterprises in Nigeria. The outbreak of war in 1939 marked the
beginnings of an economic revolution. The British and local
governments together imposed wide ranging commercial regulations
which included export and import licensing, selective price controls
and a state monopoly of commodity exports by the West African
Produce Control Board (WAPCB). Taxes were increased. In 1939
for the first time a company tax was introduced, initially at 2s 6d in
the pound, increased in 1940 to 4s and in 1941 to 5s. For WASCO

the consequences of war were mixed but generally very favourable. From 1940 the British government banned the export of soap (among other goods) to West Africa to save shipping. This gave WASCO a virtual monopoly of the market for factory-made soap, not only in Nigeria, but also in other British West African territories which, so to speak, it inherited from United Exporters Ltd. The result was an immense increase in demand, which is reflected in the production data in Table 6.2. Since, moreover, overseas competition (notably from Bibbys) was suddenly cut off, the tight constraint on prices was relaxed and the profitability of soap manufacture increased. Paradoxically, the establishment of state marketing of produce increased profit margins, since it was official policy to keep palm oil prices down (in the interests of the British consumer and the balance of payments), and local consumers bought their supplies at the price fixed by the WAPCB. The composite result of these two factors was greatly increased production and profitability. Hence the war years were the best WASCO had known since 1929/30 and they enabled the company to break through some of the barriers which had held them back since then.

From 1946, however, there were far more radical changes. During the next fourteen years a very rapid and quite unpredicted political evolution occurred which ended with full Nigerian independence in 1960 as a federal republic. Thus, for the first time in Nigeria, Unilever men had to begin to think in political terms. They had still to deal with British colonial governments until 1960; but in practice the shift to indigenous political control began long before that time. In 1946 Nigeria was for the first time given a legislative council, with authority over the whole country, which had a majority of Nigerian members—though some of these were still nominated and so not politically active. During the next few years African political parties grew fast, partly as a response to the mere existence of an electoral system. Simultaneously the old regions were reorganised to meet new political needs and in 1954 three states—West, North and East—were formed with local assemblies and power over most domestic matters, including economic policies. From that moment the environment in which foreign enterprises had to work changed fundamentally, far more than it was to do in 1960 when Nigeria became formally independent, for this was the birth of politics, government by party and the transfer of effective power to political ministers. The first mention of politics and indigenous Nigerian opinion which survives in the company records is in 1953; and thereafter political considerations become a predominant theme in Unilever calculations.

By the 1950s, of course, the senior Unilever men with experience in Asia were familiar with the concept and the process of decolonisation and, once the new regional governments were set up in 1954 the one consistent theme in all reports, correspondence and minutes is that the company must adapt flexibly to the new situation. The first evidence of this was recognition that regionalisation must affect the pattern of the business. For some years before 1954 there had been recurrent talk of building a second soap factory, possibly at Port Harcourt, to take advantage of the large eastern market and ample supplies of palm oil and palm kernel oil. Formal proposals for this had been prepared in 1946; but in 1948 calculations showed that the high cost of duplicating overheads would outweigh other possible benefits, the proposal was dropped, and the Apapa factory was expanded to provide additional capacity. But in 1954 the transfer of control of economic development to the new regions and the creation there of elected assemblies and indigenous governments put the issue onto a wholly new footing. As Beausire of Marketing Division wrote after a visit, the danger was now that the new government of the Eastern Region would set up or subsidise its own factory if Unilever did not do so. His conclusion was that there were now 'overwhelming political reasons' for building a factory in the East. Indeed 'the new form of government might be more co-operative [than the British Colonial authorities had been between 1946 and 1948] and more anxious to attract industrial capital and encourage industrial products, and we should be well advised to take exploratory steps now'. Unilever did, indeed, act quickly. On 23 December 1954 the Special Committee decided in principle to build a factory at Aba, north of Port Harcourt. The recorded argument is instructive:

In considering the whole project it was necessary to take account of the probable future political development of the country. Although it was possible to have doubts in this respect, having regard to the rapid transition from colonial status to self-government as elsewhere within the Commonwealth, there seemed no reason to have any special doubts about Nigeria in particular. It was therefore decided, as the proposition was considered commercially sound, to recommend to the Board the expansion of the WASCO business on the basis outlined in the memorandum.

So a new factory was built at Aba primarily to ensure that, if the new region became autonomous, Unilever was well placed in this highly populous area. Within a few years it was recognised that the decision had been commercially unwise—total demand in Nigeria did not warrant two factories and Aba's overheads were excessive. By 1963 Aba was losing £80,000 a year, but the same political considerations forbad its closure: as Daniel, now Managing Director of the business, said in 1965, 'it would be extremely dangerous from a political point of view' to close it, whatever the losses made. On the same argument, when the Special Committee decided in 1961 not to buy additional land adjacent to the Apapa factory for expansion, they commented that if further capacity was required in Nigeria it should be in the Northern Region, again for political reasons.

Thus perhaps the most important single feature of political change in Nigeria after 1954 was that Unilever had for the first time had to take account of political factors—which now meant the attitudes and aspirations of Nigerians rather than expatriate administrators—and also to think of regions rather than of Nigeria as a whole. That is, business criteria were no longer conclusive. As in other countries included in the present study, this marked the essential difference between colonialism and independence. But in other respects also the Nigeria in which Unilever operated after 1940 was changing rapidly. The statistics reflect rapid growth: population rose to some 55 million at the 1963 census, though there was great suspicion that this was exaggerated. During the 1960s the economy grew at an annual average rate of 4.5 per cent, industrial production at 8.5 per cent. Petroleum was developed in the Eastern Region from the mid-1950s and provided valuable foreign exchange for investment. From 1959 there was a Central Bank to regulate an autonomous Nigerian currency, though this for the time being remained at par with the pound sterling. By the mid-1960s there was a nascent stock exchange at Lagos. Here, apparently, was a society expanding rapidly which might provide exciting opportunities for foreign firms.

But not all was new; and many features of the old Nigeria, and in particular those which favoured foreign business enterprise, survived at least until the civil war in 1967–70. Most important, Nigeria remained until then essentially an 'open' economy. There were virtually no restrictions on imports, remittances, investments or business enterprises. Taxation remained comparatively low, though much higher than in the past; in the early 1960s the statistical tax rate on company profits distributed as dividends was only 40 per cent. All this was favourable to WASCO and later LB(N); but with much that was favourable from the past two important factors survived to limit the company's growth and profitability. First, Nigeria remained a relatively very poor country: in 1960 the estimated per capita income was only $88 million. Second, buying power was heavily dependent on world prices for vegetable oils and cocoa, though by 1966 petroleum oil had reduced their importance. In that year groundnuts provided 15 per cent of export earnings, cocoa 10 per cent, palm kernels 8 per cent, rubber 4 per cent, palm oil 4 per cent, and groundnut oil 4 per cent. In the two decades 1950–70 world production of non-mineral fats and oils increased by some 73 per cent while world population increased by 44 per cent; and the rapid growth of palm oil production in South-east Asia put considerable pressure on the less efficient producers of West and West Central Africa. As in the 1930s, the prosperity of Nigeria and above all the purchasing power of the mass of the population was closely related to commodity prices; and, although these were generally good in the post-1945 period, prolonged by the Korean war boom, they were low for most of the decade before 1965.

The impact of the commodity market on Nigerian purchasing power was, however, complicated by an institution carried over from the Second World War to the post-war and post-independence period—the Marketing Boards.[3] These were established from 1947 in each British West African territory to take over the functions of the old WAPCB. The stated object of maintaining the system of controls, though with separate Marketing Boards for each main commodity and each of the colonies from 1947, was to prevent wide fluctuations in the return to the producer as a result of changes in world commodity prices, and so to reduce one of the more serious economic weaknesses of the West African economy as it had been before 1939. In practice, however, the Boards tended to make the accumulation of reserve funds an end in itself rather than to use them as a buffer against cyclical depressions. Thus between 1947 and 1956 a total of 29 per cent of the export value of palm kernels and 17 per cent of palm oil was withheld by the authorities in the form either of retained Marketing Boards surpluses or of the much smaller export and produce taxes. For cocoa the figures were 39 per cent and groundnuts 40 per cent. By 1956 the reserves accumulating in the hands of the Marketing Boards as a whole were £119,914,700 and of this only £6.9 million had been distributed as subsidies to palm oil exporters in 1953/4. The general effect was that the Nigerian producers' personal terms of trade with the rest of the world were significantly affected; in 1951 they were worse in relation to imported cotton piece goods (a major article of consumption) than they had been in 1935–7. This inevitably reduced the ability of the Nigerian peasants to buy consumer goods such as soap.

A further change occurred after 1954 when the Marketing Boards were handed over to the new Regions and also to the African politicians who now controlled regional governments. In the next few years until 1961 both the West and East Regions continued to build up surpluses—only the Northern Board did not do so; and these two regions were withholding some 25 per cent of total producers' incomes. The palm oil and palm kernel producers were worst hit because of the reduced world commodity prices; they suffered an actual decline in real income in these years. Moreover, in the first years of regional self-government, the purpose of price control changed from building up reserves against a possible recession. Increasingly the system was seen as a means of taxing peasant producers to provide funds for economic and social development— that is, as a means of capital accumulation in the public sector in a country with a relatively very small propensity to save. The calls potentially made on these funds were endless and not all can easily be related to economic or social development. But it was at least clear that the system of commodity price control had come to stay.

For LB(N) this system was significant in two main respects. First, unless they bought illegally in the unofficial vegetable oil market, they had to buy their raw materials from the authorities at whatever price these authorities chose to fix. In the early days of the WAPCB this was beneficial, since the price was that paid to producers and not the higher world price; so the effective protection on locally manufactured soap was increased. Later, the regional Marketing Boards changed this policy and fixed prices to local industrial consumers at world market prices; so LB(N) had lost their advantage over foreign competitors except for the cost of freight. Since, moreover, local 'cottage' producers could buy their oil much more cheaply from the producers, LB(N) found it more difficult to compete profitably at the lower end of their product range. Equally important, the Marketing Boards' policy of withholding a substantial part of the purchasing power of the Nigerian peasant producer had a generally deflationary affect on the consumer goods industry because an investment in, say, road construction, new universities, or an African-owned bank did not necessarily increase the market for Sunlight Soap.

(2) Local Participation and Africanisation of Management. In form at least WASCO changed remarkably little between 1940 and 1965. At the start it was a wholly-owned locally registered company with a nominal capital of £60,000. In 1965 its nominal capital was £1,000,000 and in 1956 the name had been changed to Lever Brothers (Nigeria) Limited; but it was still a wholly-owned Unilever subsidiary. There is, therefore, little to say about the evolution of the company as an organisation; but two aspects require comment: first, the total absence of any local participation in the equity; second, the extent to which the company was staffed by Nigerians in 1965.

It has been seen that Unilever never chose to share ownership of a subsidiary once it had been established; and in Nigeria this was a particularly sensitive matter because, as Andrew Knox pointed out in 1954 when investigating the proposed factory at Aba, 'any participation by the Eastern Region in our Aba venture would inevitably raise far wider issues even than participation in WASCO as a whole'. By this Knox presumably meant participation in UAC, which had for decades been a matter of controversy among nationalist politicians in West Africa; but in the event the Eastern Region government agreed to the Aba venture without raising the question of local participation. It was not until Nigeria's final independence in 1960 that this became an issue; and then David Orr, reading the now familiar signs of a newly independent state, warned that sale of part of the equity might soon become necessary. He could see no commercial advantage in this unless it was necessary on political grounds to buy 'goodwill or interest in the company'; but he advised London to make preparations in case participation should be forced on them. These precautions included the merging of Van den Berghs (Nigeria) Ltd with LB(N); establishing a service fee agreement with Unilever; and examining existing agreements with other concern companies, such as UEL, putting them on 'an arm's length basis'— that is, ensuring that, if the Nigerian govern-should acquire a share in LB(N) Ltd, it did not thereby acquire legal title to any of the trademarks used by UEL or other Unilever companies. Late in 1961 the Special Committee agreed on these measures, 'in case it should ever be necessary to offer to the public in Nigeria some of the capital of Lever Brothers (Nigeria) Ltd . . .'.

By that time the local stock exchange had got under way in Lagos and some local shares were being quoted, such as government securities, John Holt and Nigerian Tobacco; but there was still no official pressure for sale of Lever Brothers' shares and in 1965 the company was still a wholly-owned subsidiary of Unilever.

This was not, in fact, surprising. Although politicians might feel strongly about the dominance of expatriate companies in the Nigerian economy, neither the central nor the regional governments, and still less the public as a whole, yet possessed sufficient capital to buy out foreign enterprises or even to participate largely in them. Nigeria was beginning to experience a serious balance of payments problem in the early 1960s and was dependent on public and private investment from overseas; and to insist on local participation might deter new investment. But in any case, as has been suggested in earlier chapters, the character of a foreign subsidiary and its relationship with the host society may be more affected by localisation of management and its control of policy than by local participation in the equity. To what extent was the management of LB(N) 'Nigerianised' by 1965 and what influence on this process had the rapid evolution of Nigerian independence?

Localisation of management came late in West Africa: it was not until 1954 that the possibility of a significant African role in higher management became accepted. Behind this lay a long history of European belief in the inability or unwillingness of Africans to take responsibility, which was shared by the management of WASCO and Unilever. Thus J. H. Hansard commented after his visit in 1938 that

The amount of European supervision in Nigeria is necessarily higher than in most native countries. In the factory the native labour is not mechanically minded, and in the office a low standard of education is combined with a doubtful standard of integrity. Without serious loss of efficiency I do not think our European staff can be reduced, even if our tonnage falls.

Ten years later even A. M. Knox, perhaps the main proponent of localisation in all non-European countries, took rather the same view of Nigeria. To some extent the facts supported their hesitation. There were then very few Africans with university or even secondary education; and of this very small élite most preferred to go into government service rather than into industry or commerce. There were only two ways in which this deadlock could be broken: either the 'number of Africans with technical or other qualifications must be increased or the company must make strenuous efforts to train able but unqualified junior African staff'. This was Knox's view; and in 1954, with the decision taken to build a factory at Aba, he wrote to Ealey, the Managing Director, emphasising that 'It is our policy to try to train Africans for management positions, but this is a long process and we would hope this Government [of the Eastern Region] would trust our bona fides in this matter.' In November he again emphasised in a report that 'our job is not only to develop a business but also to develop useful participation by Africans in management'.

From 1954 to 1965 these objectives were pursued diligently under the dual stimulus of the high cost of European management and awareness of the implications of Nigerian self-government. By 1965 there were 39 African managers and 16 expatriates; and in his annual report to the Special Committee that year Daniel, as Managing Director, made an optimistic survey of Africanisation. It was still difficult to recruit university trained Africans, but

> Despite these difficulties I think we, in Nigeria, are more izated than any other company of our size. Soaps have been completely izated for three years, NSDs should be by this autumn; and edibles by next year. The Planning Department also should be by next year and the Aba factory has this summer been under Nigerian management, although on a temporary basis. Our most difficult area in this respect is marketing and the problems in the north [i.e., the friction between Hausa and Ibo] do not make it any easier.

Moreover a major barrier had been breached: Dr M. O. Omalayole had been appointed as first Nigerian Director of LB(N). Thereafter it would be a matter of time before the company became as completely 'isated' at the top as Unilever companies in other countries and Omalayole eventually became Chairman and Managing Director of a board which in 1977 included two Nigerians out of six.

(3) Production, Diversification and Distribution. Three aspects of WASCO's commercial performance and development after 1940 require special comment and explanation. First, why there was such

an astonishing increase in the volume of soap sales from 1940 to the mid-1950s and why this expansion subsequently tended to level off. Second, why, despite this growth, the range of products made and sold in Nigeria by the local company was still so narrow by 1965—effectively only bar and toilet soaps, small quantities of margarine and a limited range of toilet preparations. Third, why and how it was possible for WASCO after the 1950s to break free from that most difficult of all West Coast commercial constraints—monopoly of distribution and sales by the big merchant firms.

1940 marked as decisive a turning point in the history of WASCO as had the slump of 1930/1. Suddenly this apparently weak little company which could not compete even with imported British bar soaps began to use its full capacity; so that within the next five years sales had increased more than three times, from 3,072 tons in 1940 to 10,643 tons in 1945. In the same period the £5,335 loss of 1940 was converted into a profit of £29,596 in 1945; and by 1944 Unilever was planning large post-war expansion and diversification in Nigeria. This sudden reversal of fortunes was almost entirely an accidental bonus of the war. Because exports of soap from Britain were banned, Bibbys could no longer compete in Nigeria; and other parts of West Africa, notably the Gold Coast, its richest area, which were previously supplied by UEL and other British exporters, came to depend entirely on Apapa for their soap supply. So for five years the normal laws of economics were suspended. To anyone who remembered the gloomy predictions of the later 1930s WASCO seemed to have undergone a miraculous transformation.

But those who understood the business best and the special problems of West Africa knew that all this was built on sand. Once the war was over and imports to West Africa resumed, the old problems would certainly come back. Moreover, the main increase in sales consisted of cheap pale bar soap, which was most vulnerable to local 'cottage' competition and also provided the smallest profit margins. A good start had been made with the two previously imported branded bar soaps of higher quality—Sunlight and Lifebuoy—which might provide more substantial profit margins; but these constituted only about a tenth of total output and would presumably face severe market limitations in Nigeria once the more affluent Gold Coast market reverted to UEL products. Thus the problem facing WASCO and Unilever in 1944/45 was how they could consolidate wartime achievements after the war.

The first considered analysis of the situation and future needs was made, as has been seen, in 1944 by Roger Heyworth. Heyworth regarded the present favourable position as basically transitory. The essential need was to reduce the cost of soap production and so increase WASCO's competitiveness and profitability. One means of doing so was to build a new factory at Aba, in the Niger Delta region, where there were better oil supplies and a large local market. Costs could be further reduced by arranging more realistic terms with UAC for providing raw materials and also by cutting down the profit margins allowed to the merchant firms for distribution and sales. Sales volume must be held above 8,000 tons a year—the level reached for the first time in 1944—to offset relatively high overheads. Heyworth's recommendations on marketing policy were essentially conservative: the business must still be based on cheap soaps and he was against attempting to build up Sunlight and Lifebuoy sales on the grounds that the cheaper Magnet brand had better goodwill. This reflected a pessimistic view of the Nigerian consumer's future ability to buy relatively high quality soap. But in other respects Heyworth was an optimist and proposed the first significant diversification of the Apapa business since 1923. His suggestion was for toilet soaps to be made in limited quantities, plus pomades and other toilet preparations; expansion of palm kernel milling provided the export duty on this oil was reduced and a market could be found for oil cake; cotton-seed crushing; manufacture of protein flour bread from groundnuts, possibly in the form of 'cabin bread' (i.e. biscuit); and possibly limited amounts of edible oils and fats, including margarine. More remote possibilities were, he thought, a protein flour made from biltong and groundnut flour, and proprietary mineral drinks.

Roger Heyworth's report was the most thorough-going analysis of the productive possibilities of the Nigerian business made by anyone from Unilever before then or until the early 1960s; and it was not until 1963 that proposals for further diversification were made. How far were his suggestions put into practice?

First, the concept of building a new factory in the Eastern Region, as it was to become, was taken up at once and a careful examination was made of various possible sites. In November 1946 the Special Committee agreed to a Port Harcourt factory with a capacity of 3,000 tons of fully boiled soap, a palm kernel mill able to process 600 tons, and an estimated total cost of £98,000. This project fell through due to failure to find a suitable factory site, reflecting lack of co-operation from colonial government officials; and in 1949 it was decided instead to increase the soap capacity of the Apapa factory from 10,000 to 14,000 tons at a cost of £75,000. But the idea of an Eastern factory persisted and received impetus from the new regional structure. In June 1954 Knox suggested to Ealey, Managing Director at Apapa, that the case for expanding in the East rather than at Apapa had two aspects: political, in that it was desirable to please Eastern politicians; practical, in that Apapa had reached the optimal size in which it could be 'managed in the personal way necessary in dealing with a large African staff and labour force', and that there was a large consumer public around Port Harcourt. The Apapa management, therefore, made another survey of possible factory sites in the East and eventually came back to Roger Heyworth's proposal for Aba. In December 1954 the Special Committee approved a capital proposal of £620,000 for a site and factory at Aba with a capacity of 10,000 tons; but in fact the total capital required, including working capital, rose to £1,000,000. The new factory came into operation in 1958. By then, unfortunately, the great boom was nearly over: there was no more talk, as there had been in 1954, of a need for 50,000 tons capacity by 1966; and in 1960 Lord Cole pointed out that the two factories were running at only a third of their combined capacities. As will be seen, the Aba factory contributed significantly to the low profitability of the Nigerian business in the decade before 1965.

Thus, one of Roger Heyworth's 1944 proposals, though carried out, proved unsuccessful in the context of the 1960s. For different reasons, his claim that essential savings could be made by changing the terms on which WASCO bought its raw materials from UAC became irrelevant. The reason was, of course, that the Marketing Boards rather than UAC now decided commodity prices, and this had important consequences. WASCO had no complaints about the price, quality or quantity of the oil provided, but they had now lost two commercial advantages: as against overseas competitors, because from now on they were paying approximately the same price for their oil; and against the local 'cottage' manufacturer, who could continue to buy his oil in small quantities well below the Marketing Boards' price and so compete very effectively with WASCO at the cheaper end of the market. Thus, while WASCO was in no worse position than before the war, by the mid-1950s it had lost most of the artificial advantages it had enjoyed during the previous decade.

More important, by the 1960s it was clear that Heyworth's

projected plan for diversification had been too optimistic and many of his proposals were never adopted. On the soap side, the core of the business continued to be pale bar soaps, not carbolics; and from the latter 1940s Sunlight at last began to constitute a significant proportion of total sales. Lux Toilet Soap was manufactured at Apapa from 1951: but although it did reasonably well the market was clearly a limited one. By the latter 1950s the main growth point in the detergent field was in NSDs—which could not, of course, have been foreseen in 1944. Omo was imported in bulk and packed and distributed by WASCO (Surf was simultaneously imported in packed form by UEL and distributed through their own network). By the early 1960s a sufficient local market for NSDs had been established for both products to be made locally, and by 1965 Apapa had its own sulphonation plant and was in a strong position to compete with Fab, which was imported by Colgate. Thus, while the sales volume of soap and other detergents had increased substantially, the range of products remained relatively narrow and by the 1960s the volume of sales appeared to have levelled off. The fundamental fact was that the Nigerian market was too limited to support local manufacture of a wide range of products, and the continued import of luxury lines in small quantities by UEL and its foreign rivals reflected this fact.

Of Heyworth's other proposals for diversification several were tried out but in most cases limitations of the market proved an insuperable barrier. Cheap pomades were made for some years for distribution by UEL, but were discontinued in 1962. 1963 saw new enterprises. Toothpastes and branded edible oils had just been started, shampoos and face creams were due to start production in 1964; and by 1965 a still wider range was under consideration, including Vim, Domestos, liquid detergents and toilet soap flakes. But by far the most important, and perhaps surprising, post-war innovation was the introduction of margarine and other edible fat products. Very small quantities of Blue Band margarine had been imported into Nigeria and other parts of West Africa for a long time, but these were primarily for the very limited European market as represented by patrons of UAC's Kingsway Stores. On three counts there seemed little chance that demand would be large enough to justify local manufacture: first, the 'spreading habit' was alien to the West Coast; second, as a cooking medium, margarine and other processed oils were too expensive for most Nigerians; finally, the heat was bound to present technical problems and there was virtually no refrigerated capacity. Nevertheless, after a visit in 1950, Sidney Van den Bergh argued that the demand for limited amounts of imported butter of poor quality suggested that there was a potential market for margarine. UAC was asked its opinion and agreed; and in April 1951 the Special Committee accepted a proposal for plant with a capacity for 1,000 tons of margarine. Production began in February 1954 at Apapa. Progress of sales was slow but by the mid-1960s margarine seemed to be firmly established as an important Unilever product in Nigeria.

Yet, taken as a whole, it is difficult to deny that diversification had not proceeded very far or very fast in Nigeria in the 1960s; and probably the greatest single achievement of WASCO in this period, following the lines projected by Roger Heyworth in 1944, was the establishment of direct sales throughout the country. Since this constituted a radical change in the Nigerian commercial system as well as laying foundations for more profitable expansion for LB(N), the story must be summarised.

It has been seen that, while UAC was the largest of the European-owned trading companies that dominated the import/export trade and internal distribution system of Nigeria, this fact gave WASCO almost no advantages in selling its products. It was clear to Heyworth in 1944 and to most Unilever men later that WASCO's success depended ultimately on its ability to follow the example of concern subsidiaries elsewhere in establishing its own selling organisation with direct links to as large a number of distributors and retailers as possible, and by this means to promote its brands and widen its sales. The difficulty in West Africa was that, by contrast with Asian countries, there were very few credit-worthy indigenous wholesalers with adequate storage and distributive facilities; and to introduce direct selling from WASCO depots would constitute a minor commercial revolution in the Nigeria of the 1940s. Yet by 1965 this had been achieved and it is important to see how it was done.

The first stage, beginning before the Second World War and intensified after 1945, was to build up the brand image of Unilever products by a small sales force, using lorries to reach as far as possible into the countryside and to make contact with individual consumers and the market women or store-holders. At the same time, pressure was brought on the merchant firms to maintain recommended prices and to regulate deliveries to their depots in such a way as to keep demand firm. This was the limit of achievement by 1958, when R. H. Horsley, a UAC man, made a report recommending more fundamental changes. The timing of the report was influenced by two important new factors: on the one hand the shortage of soap, which was endemic from 1940, was ending with the addition of the Aba factory and competition from another soap factory at Aba owned by Paterson Zochonis. Thereafter it was clear that it would be a buyer's, not a seller's, market. Second, the prospect of full Nigerian independence in 1960 and the growing demand by Africans for a larger share in all forms of business enterprise made it politically wise to open up the sales system. Horsley therefore suggested that LB(N) should immediately create the nucleus of a system of direct sales to African wholesalers. At the start this would involve establishing a number of depots throughout the country, using existing UAC facilities, such as depots, which would be stocked by LB(N) on its own account and from which sales would be made to African distributors. These depots would initially stock only bar soap which would be sold on a cash down basis. This was inconsistent with the long-established tradition of providing credit in West African trade, but Horsley argued that the small African middlemen and distributors would be happy to give up the credit in return for obtaining the profit margin previously retained by the big merchant firm, for this would more than offset the loss to them of short-term credits. At the start these depots would be concentrated in 15 main centres and about 40 African distributors should be taken on. Hence the great bulk of sales would continue to be through the big European merchants. But Horsley projected some 90 or more depots with 5,000–7,000 distributors in the near future, which would be grouped into five or six main sales areas, each with two sales managers and teams of about fifteen salesmen, which between them would cover the whole country. When that was achieved Nigeria would have a nationwide sales force organised on conventional Unilever lines for the first time in its history. This project was accepted and carried out with remarkable and unforeseen speed. The Special Committee noted the new policy in January 1959. By June 1960 David Orr could report that although some 85 per cent of LB(N) sales was still through the big merchants, there were already 100 African dealers buying direct from the new LB(N) depots. In 1963 Daniel reported that 60 per cent of sales were now through 500 direct African distributors; and in 1965 the porportion had risen to about 70 per cent. Experiments were being made with providing one week's credit, which would imply a 5 per cent increase in the firm's working capital, in order to increase the distributors' working capital. By that time UAC had entirely ceased to distribute LB(N) products except through their Kingsway Stores. In the early months of 1965 Ollivants (also a Unilever trading company) were still taking 17.8 per cent of LB(N) bar soap, 14.5 per cent of tablet soap, and 12.2 per cent of toilet soap for resale; and 15.8 per cent of all LB(N) products by value were being sold through these two outlets. A further 9.8 per cent were being sold through John Holt, the only other merchant firm still operating in a traditional way; while 61 per cent were sold through Nigerian distributors and the rest through LB(N) vans, Syrian merchants and other very small firms.

Two years later civil war affected this newly established marketing system, but in the context of Nigerian economic development its importance was considerable. Although British American Tobacco may just have beaten Unilever to the post, LB(N) now had established one of the first systems of depots selling direct from a local manufacturer to African distributors and retailers in Nigerian history. They were helped by the existence of UAC, which in effect turned over many of their depot facilities as they withdrew from general trading; but this in itself constituted an economic revolution since it meant that the largest single expatriate merchant firm was abandoning a role built up by Europeans over perhaps two centuries.

(4) Profitability. It was suggested at the beginning of this section that one of the obvious facts of LB(N)'s history after 1940 was the continued volatility of its profits, and this is clearly reflected in Tables 6.6(a) and 6.6(b). In the period before 1940 the main determinants of WASCO's profitability were raw material prices, consumer demand, turnover and the amount of capital employed. It was the same after 1940, but now the underlying forces were changing. The good years lasted from 1941 to 1956. They were good because turnover expanded very fast while capital employed did not: there was little new investment and the book value of the original investment had by then been heavily written down. They were good also because after 1940 there was very little overseas competition; because until about 1954 the cost to local industrial users of vegetable oil was fixed by the public authorities in relation to what was paid to producers; and finally because Nigerian incomes were generally increasing. It was not, therefore, surprising that in

the mid-1950s Unilever became enthusiastic for investment in expanding productive capacity.

But from this moment conditions became much less favourable. The price of commodities fell after the Korean War and, although the Marketing Boards to some extent reduced the impact of this on the producer in that they had not paid the highest price in the boom, the peasant farmer felt a significant decline in income at a time when the prices of manufactured goods were generally rising. Thus the Marketing Boards' policy of siphoning off income attributable to the peasant producer significantly deflated the market for consumer goods, including soap. Simultaneously, increased taxation in the form of an excise duty on soap (later replaced by import duties on caustic soda) increased prices and further reduced consumer capacity. Together these largely explain the flattening out of soap sales in the decade after 1956, which made nonsense of an investment strategy that included establishment of the Aba factory and which was based on the belief that the soap market would continue to expand at the same rate as during the previous decade.

To make matters worse, while sales volume was virtually static after 1956, profits were squeezed between rising raw material costs and selling prices kept down by increasing competition and limited consumer demand. Raw material prices were, of course, set by the Marketing Boards; and by the mid-1950s these sold to local industrial users at world prices rather than at the price they paid to local producers. Thus the advantage previously held by LB(N) over foreign manufacturers disappeared. Perhaps more important, large enterprises of this kind found it difficult not to buy from the Marketing Boards at their fixed prices, whereas the small 'cottage' manufacturers could still get their oil much cheaper from other suppliers; and this accentuated their built-in price advantage. By 1965 raw material prices had become critical for LB(N)'s profitability; in that year its chairman estimated that if he had to buy all his oil from the Marketing Boards (some was imported), the additional cost would be some £200,000 a year—equivalent to the total nett profit predicted for 1965.

This might not have mattered so much if the market itself had not been so price elastic and if there had still been no local factory competition. But by the mid-1950s Paterson Zochonis, one of the surviving independent merchant firms, possibly attracted by the large profits known to be made by LB(N) in the 1940s and early 1950s, had built a rival soap factory at Aba owned by a subsidiary called Alagbon. This made cheap bar soap called Duck of very similar quality and price to the LB(N) Key brand. Here, at last, was effective local competition which might not take any large share of the market but which, like Bibby's soap in the 1930s, set an upper limit to Lever prices and forced them to maintain quality. Indeed, when, for technical reasons, Lever soap quality temporarily dropped in 1959/60, this had a very striking effect on sales volume, to the advantage of Duck. There was other competition also: three or four small local factories producing for the lower end of the price and quality range, importers of toilet soap, toilet preparations, etc., such as Colegate–Palmolive and Procter and Gamble, at the higher end.

But there can be no doubt that it was the building of the Aba factory that really brought down profits. NSV rose fairly consistently after 1960, reflecting higher selling prices as well as increasing sales volume; and gross profits remained about 25 per cent of NSV. The striking new fact was the rise of overheads in proportion to sales and capital employed. As can be seen from Table 6.6(c), in which overheads are expressed as a percentage of gross profit (incidentally not a calculation conventionally made by Unilever), there were major increases in the proportionate cost of marketing, advertising, factory and general expenses. Of these costs marketing expenses are misleading since the higher figures reflect the new direct sales system and are balanced by savings on commissions no longer paid to the merchant firms. The really significant items are the cost of factory and general expenses and interest charges. As a percentage of gross profit these reached their peak in 1959 when together they amounted to 88.3 per cent of gross profit; by 1964 the combined total was down to 36.9 per cent. This improvement was due partly to an absolute reduction in factory expenses resulting from more efficient organisation, but still more to increased turnover. Clearly the disastrous years between 1957 and 1964 were caused by a combination of new investment in capacity and a simultaneous check to expansion of the domestic market. LB(N) was thus left with a new under-utilised factory to maintain on whose capital cost they had to pay interest.

(5) Unilever and the Nigerian Economy. Finally what contribution did Unilever through WASCO make to the economic development of Nigeria? It is not proposed to make a formal analysis of costs and benefits for in most respects the Nigerian experience seems to have been similar to that of other LDCs. There was comparatively little

Table 6.6(c)   Nigeria: Costs in Relation to Gross Profit, 1956–65

Year	A NSV £'000	B Gross profit £'000	C Advert. % of B	D Marketing expenses % of B	E Factory and general expenses as % of B	F Other trading items as % of B	G Concern interest as % of B	H Service fees as % of B	I Total costs C–H as % of B	J Profit before tax (£'000)
1956	1,816	428	6.3	4.7	31.7	4.7	—	—	48.1	222
1957	1,974	385	9.8	6.5	43.1	5.9	—	—	65.4	133
1958	1,626	335	13.1	9.5	65.7	7.5	—	—	93.7	21
1959	1,574	342	19.2	11.1	75.1	1.2	13.2	—	119.8	(16)
1960	2,095	606	9.9	8.9	40.6	1.9	6.9	—	68.3	234
1961	1,888	473	19.0	20.5	52.4	3.2	7.4	—	102.5	23
1962	2,350	565	18.0	24.7	40.7	0.3	10.7	3.7	98.4	91
1963	2,535	636	18.4	22.7	36.9	1.3	8.9	3.6	91.9	131
1964	2,712	710	17.3	18.6	26.6	11.8	10.3	3.5	89	176
1965	3,274	993	19.5	37.8		—	4.0	4.0	63.7	440

capital inflow, for most of the capital employed was built up from local profits. Conversely it is unfortunately impossible to compare the financial benefits received by Nigeria and Unilever because there are no surviving records of taxes actually paid by WASCO before 1956 and in the following decade profits were so low that no dividends were remitted and taxes were paid in only three years. The sums involved were in any case too small to have had much effect either way on Nigerian economic development.

The real importance of WASCO was, in fact, its pioneering role at two stages of Nigerian industrial and commercial development. According to Kilby, the 'list of sizeable private industrial ventures there before 1940 consisted only of four cotton ginneries, half a dozen saw mills, the WASCO factory, two palm-oil bulking plants, a cigarette factory and a metal drum plant, the last two set up only in 1937 and 1939 respectively'. [4] WASCO was thus in select company. In its early days it demonstrated that even in an unprotected market it was feasible to make consumer goods from local raw materials and it must have made a small contribution to the creation of an industrial labour force. After the Second World War WASCO's relative importance declined as the number of import-substituting industries grew. Yet it remained one of the larger Nigerian manu-facturing enterprises and leader in its own field. It set an example by training Africans for management and in building a factory in the Eastern Region. But its main post-war achievement was to set up a single system of distribution covering the whole of Nigeria and at the same time to help a substantial number of Africans to establish themselves as independent distributors. Within the limits of what a single company can do these were significant contributions to the industrial and commercial development of Nigeria.

The Belgian Congo (Zaire): SAVCO/MARSAVCO

As the Niger Company/UAC was to WASCO, so HCB and its sister trading company, SEDEC (which became part of the UAC organisation in 1929) were to the Lever soap business in the Belgian Congo. In Nigeria WASCO was established largely because Lever Brothers already owned suitable buildings at Apapa and because the trading companies, MacIvers and then the Niger Company, could provide palm oil and managerial oversight. In much the same way the Unilever soap company at Leopoldville came into existence because Levers possessed both a plantation business—HCB—and a trading company—SEDEC—in the Congo. HCB, which is studied below in Chapter 9, came first in 1911, a vast and partially romantic project for exploiting and developing the raw materials of Equatorial Africa. SEDEC followed quickly. It was formed in 1913 and started trading in the Congo in 1916. Its original purpose was to buy and export palm oil and palm kernels but it soon evolved into a general trading company of the same type as the Niger Company with which it was amalgamated after 1929 as part of UAC. Both these were very large enterprises, SAVCO (Société Anonyme des Savonneries Congolaises) followed a decade later, a small, unambitious and unromatic enterprise intended to make a limited amount of low-quality soap for local consumption from oil stored by HCB and SEDEC in their oil tanks at Kinshasa (Leopoldville). It would be easy to ignore the significance of SAVCO and many have done so. It is mentioned neither in the unpublished account of the first years of HCB written by its early organiser, Sidney Edkins, nor in Wilson's *History of Unilever*. Yet, though its origins were humble, SAVCO is of considerable interest in its own right as one of the very few Unilever manufacturing subsidiaries that were never very successful, and it will be studied from this angle.

The origins of SAVCO remain obscure. The first reference in the surviving records to a soap manufacturing project in the Congo is on 27 July 1920, when Harold Greenhalgh told the Policy Committee that 'the Chairman [Leverhulme] had expressed his opinion that we should proceed with these works'. The estimated capital cost was £15,000 if glycerine extraction was not provided for, but a more realistic estimate would be £20,000 to £30,000. 'The best place for these works would be Kinshasa as we already had an engineering shop there. It was proposed to manufacture pale bar, blue mottled and cheap toilet soaps . . . . The council decided that Mr Greenhalgh should be authorized to proceed with this scheme.'

Clearly the idea of manufacturing soap in the Congo had been in the air for some time before this, and it is virtually certain that it was conceived by Lever. Indeed, on his last visit to the Congo in 1924, he claimed that the very existence of a market for soap among the Congolese was 'entirely due to the missionary efforts made twelve years ago on the Lusanga [a river steamer on the Congo] when we took some blue mottled on board with us and tried the natives with it. Blue mottled is always the pioneer in starting the soap habit.' The genesis of SAVCO is thus to be found in the same combination of elements as generated the soap factory in Nigeria at almost precisely the same time: ample supplies of local raw materials, an existing Lever trading enterprise to provide managerial control and to distribute the product, and, most important, an untapped local market for soap. There were then no rival soap factories and, in marked contrast with Nigeria, virtually no 'cottage' manufacture. In such a situation the great entrepreneur clearly scented commercial opportunity at minimum cost and little apparent risk. SAVCO was a characteristic product of his nose for an entirely new market.

The company was founded in 1922 and registered as a Belgian company. The share capital was F. 2.5 million divided into 25,000 shares, all but seven of them owned by Levers. At the exchange rate current in the early 1920s this represented about £50,000, which makes it closely comparable as an investment with the Nigerian company; and, since there was much else common between them, it would have been reasonable to expect similar patterns of development. But in fact SAVCO's early history was depressingly different. At the end of the decade, in 1929, WASCO sold 2,600 tons of soap, SAVCO only 714 tons. Even 20 years after their establishment, when SAVCO was selling a more respectable 3,000 tons to WASCO's 5,000 tons, these were still the lowest quality bar and tablet soaps, selling by weight, price and smell rather than by brand: 'blue mottled', the lowest quality soap made in any Lever factory, along with 'special yellow' and other pale soaps with very low fatty acid contents. SAVCO did not manufacture any of the standard international Lever brands and had not begun to diversify out of soaps. Clearly a factory which made so little soap of such low quality could not be regarded as a success in its early years; and it is not surprising that, after visiting Leopoldville in 1930, Greenhalgh described it as 'the Cinderella of the Congo'.

The reasons for this depressing performance are to some extent speculative and different Unilever analysts provided different explanations, all of which may be relevant. First, for all its large size and population (over 10 million in 1947) and the presence of some 34,000 relatively affluent Europeans, the Congo was a difficult market. Distances were vast, freights high despite governmental attempts to keep them down.[5] There were few large towns and sales depended on general trading companies such as SEDEC and its Belgian-owned rivals. Congo Africans were much less sophisticated than those in Nigeria and incomes were generally very low. But these environmental problems were made worse by poor management of SAVCO. When Lever visited the factory in 1924 he praised the production side but remarked that 'the commercial side we regret we cannot speak well of'. After his death in 1925 it seems likely that Lever Brothers' interest in the company declined. It was the

Table 6.7   Congo: SAVCO Soap Sales (Including Exports) and Profits, 1923–45

Year	Sales volume (metric tons)	Trading profit (loss) before tax (F. '000)	Sterling equivalent (£)	Profit (loss) per ton (£)
1923	156	n/a	n/a	n/a
1924	322	n/a	n/a	n/a
1925	482	178	1,647	3.4
1926	557	313	1,953	3.5
1927	662	966	5,525	8.3
1928	698	1,221	6,989	10.0
1929	714	1,095	6,276	8.8
1930	1,185	2,003	11,475	9.7
1931	655	512	3,169	4.8
1932	765	(1,490)	(11,840)	(2.4)
1933	871	(438)	(3,690)	(4.2)
1934	567	(290)	(2,685)	(4.7)
1935	975	19	145	0.1
1936	1,671	212	1,428	0.8
1937	2,375	312	2,137	0.9
1938	2,377	452	3,222	1.3
1939	2,663	591	4,255	1.6
1940	2,827	622	3,843	1.4
1941	3,326	1,139	6,403	1.9
1942	3,278	1,265	7,164	2.2
1943	3,754	958	5,596	1.5
1944	3,867	1,267	7,412	1.9
1945	4,806	2,466	14,223	3.0

Notes: a. To 30 June 1929 accounting years ran from July to June of the year for which the profit is given. Profits shown for 1930 are for the 18 months from July 1929 to December 1930. From January 1931 accounts are for the calendar year.

b. The data for 1923–7 is taken from sources different from those for later years and may not be precisely comparable.

responsibility of HCB and was run as part of that business from Brussels until 1932. It traded entirely through SEDEC, who in turn considered the 5 per cent commission they received on SAVCO products inadequate and failed to push its sales. From 1932 to 1934 SAVCO passed under direct control of the Overseas Committee, who showed considerable interest and might have given the company the attention it needed. But by 1934 economic conditions in the Congo were so bad and SAVCO's losses so large that Unilever House decided that it could only survive as an ancillary to HCB and SEDEC, a mere factory using HCB oil and providing trade goods for SEDEC. In that year SAVCO was therefore transferred to UAC (of which SEDEC was now a part) and supervision returned from London to Brussels; though technical matters, including appointment of factory management and quality control, was still under Technical Division in London. To reduce overheads the factory management was reduced to one European, Len Hollington, who had been in charge from 1922 and had earned Lever's praise in 1924. For another decade the factory remained much as it had been at the start. There was very little new investment or even replacement of old and primitive machinery. As late as 1945 it was capable of producing 5,000 tons only by ingenious reduction of normal processing time. Meantime, as SAVCO stagnated, local rivals emerged. Société Général established a soap works at Coquilhatville and others followed. To meet this challenge would have required considerable investment and marketing effort. Hollington repeatedly pressed this point but was always refused; and his assistant as Factory Manager from 1937, A. E. Chadwick, later commented, 'it was only after leaving Leopoldville [in 1946] that I learned the expression "capital investment" '.

During the 1930s, therefore, SAVCO lost its primacy as the first modern soap business in the Congo. The great increase in demand caused by the Second World War gave it a second chance; and when Roger Heyworth visited the Congo in 1944 he proposed major changes. SAVCO should be transferred back to the Overseas Committee. Investment was necessary to increase soap production and allow for some diversification into edible fats. A start should be made on developing a sales organisation ancillary to SEDEC. It might even be desirable to establish factories in other parts of the Congo to reduce freight costs and compete more effectively with local rivals.

Heyworth's optimism—though his proposed capital expenditure of only £74,000 suggests that even he had limited faith—provides the only glimmer of hope in SAVCO's history to 1960. One at least of his recommendations—transfer to Overseas Committee—was immediately carried out; but this had disappointing results. One senior Unilever executive has suggested that the main reason was that to the majority of OSC visitors in the late 40s and mid-50s the Congo was an alien land compared with Lagos. In Lagos they might have differences but could get themselves across to UAC. But in Leo it was Brussels and HCB which was much more difficult and so the effort was not made. This atmosphere was also reflected in London even at the highest level.

This analysis is fully supported by contemporary comments by Overseas Committee visitors: SAVCO (renamed MARSAVCO in 1953 when margarine production started) was outside the experience of Overseas Committee and this may well have been partly responsible for the company's depressing performance. There were, it is true, some successes, notably in the creation of a market for margarine, but the real failure lay in the company's inability to take advantage of the boom conditions of the 1950s and in its original role of the Congo's premier maker of soap.

The ironic fact is that every economic indicator shows that the decade before 1959 offered unprecedented opportunities in the Congo. The index of nominal wages rose from 100 in 1950 to 251 in 1959. The real cost of inland freight declined. Urban growth offered a better market.[6] The average post-tax profit made by Congolese industry as a whole between 1949 and 1959 was 13.8 per cent of capital employed.[7] Average consumption of soap rose to 1.5 kilos a head by 1964, giving a total market of around 20,400 tons. Yet MARSAVCO missed all these opportunities. Soap sales increased to over 9,000 tons, but SAVCO could not get even half the market it had pioneered and in the late 1950s it still relied mainly on the market for cheap tablet and bar soaps. It made post-tax profits in only five years between 1949 and 1960 and its average accounting profit for this period was only 0.5 per cent of capital employed. Fundamentally the explanation seems to be inadequate investment to make the most of opportunities and to meet growing competition, coupled with unimaginative management in the broadest sense. No significant new investment was made until 1950. The additional soap capacity then planned did not come into use until 1956, and by then the original scheme had been pared to reduce costs, so that the new plant was technically inferior to that used by some local competitors even before it came into operation. The result was that MARSAVCO soap was of comparatively low quality and this inhibited sales promotion based on Unilever brand names. Tables 6.8, 6.9 and 6.10 summarise the depressing story.

1960 was, of course, a major watershed in the Congo for independence that year led to a crisis that lasted until about 1965. Paradoxically these were also the best years in the history of MARSAVCO, particularly allowing for the fact that during this period markets in the provinces furthest from Leopoldville were cut off for considerable periods. The explanation probably lies in a number of favourable, but also transient, factors: demand from the UNO peace-keeping force (20,000 at its peak); efficient allocation of resources by the UNO administrators and their success in keeping the state-owned transport system going; the high spending propensity among Congolese who had inherited Belgian jobs; the

Table 6.8   Congo: MARSAVCO Sales of Soap, 1946–62 (metric tons)

Year	Tablet and bar soaps	Sunlight soap	Toilet soap	Soap powders	Total
1946	4,349	n/a	n/a	n/a	4,349
1947	5,723	n/a	n/a	n/a	5,723
1948	4,982	n/a	n/a	n/a	4,982
1949	3,988	n/a	n/a	n/a	4,001
1950	4,276	n/a	n/a	n/a	4,295
1951	4,348	n/a	101	n/a	4,462
1952	4,485	104	222	n/a	4,845
1953	3,719	119	189	n/a	4,077
1954	3,611	143	197	n/a	4,061
1955	4,901	236	176	n/a	5,405
1956	7,911	376	236	n/a	8,308
1957	7,850	396	268	n/a	8,717
1958	n/a	n/a	n/a	n/a	n/a
1959	n/a	669	445	510	9,160
1960	n/a	454	510	380	7,315
1961	n/a	790	720	290	8,550
1962	n/a	n/a	1,410	350	9,600

Note: The total includes sales of products not listed individually.

disappearance of a number of competing small European competitors; and finally the suspension of the credit previously given to distributors, which reduced MARSAVCO's working capital and improved profit as a percentage of capital employed.

It would, however, be misleading to suggest that decolonisation in the Congo was likely to lead to permanent affluence on the part of MARSAVCO. By 1965 inflation was becoming a serious threat to profit margins instead of a mild stimulus. Tax levels were rising steeply. Repatriation of profits was banned. The political future was extremely uncertain and it seemed likely that, in a country where so exceptionally large a proportion of the economy was controlled by foreign-owned capital, almost any government was likely sooner

Table 6.9   Congo: MARSAVCO Sales of Edible Fats and Oils, 1950–62 (metric tons)

Year	Blue Band margarine	Huildor (cooking oil)	Planta margarine	Total
1950	220	n/a	n/a	220
1951	225	n/a	n/a	225
1952	220	n/a	n/a	230
1953	201	5	n/a	238
1954	243	263	n/a	585
1955	312	344	n/a	744
1956	445	661	n/a	1,266
1957	637	777	n/a	1,725
1958	n/a	n/a	n/a	n/a
1959	770	877	198	2,156
1960	835	825	170	1,979
1961	1,250	1,120	43	3,030
1962	1,910	2,740	n/a	5,015

Notes: a. Blue Band margarine was imported until early in 1953.

b. The total includes sales of products not listed individually.

c. Planta margarine was imported.

or later to nationalise foreign companies or at least demand a major Congolese share in their equity. Union Minière, which owned the Katanga copper mines, was nationalised without immediate compensation in 1965 and this seemed a likely pointer to future trends. Events after 1965 lie beyond the scope of this book, but a summary of events in the following decade will underline the point that any short-run benefits foreign capital receive from decolonisation may be transient. In November 1973 President Mobutu announced that all Unilever properties in the Congo, along with many other foreign investments, would be nationalised and un-specified compensation paid in due course. A month later he singled out Unilever in a press conference he gave in London as 'a model foreign company', mainly because of its good record on 'Zaireanisation'.⁸ In January 1975 all Unilever companies were, nevertheless, nationalised; but in September 1977 they were returned to full Unilever ownership and management on the understanding that 40 per cent of the shareholding should be sold to Zaïrois interests within the medium-term future. The parallel with events in Indonesia is close; but the outcome lies beyond the date when this account was written.

East African Industries Ltd, Nairobi

(a) The Background to 1953

It is important for the main argument of this book that after the establishment of Lever Brothers (Nigeria) Ltd in 1923 it was 20 years before Unilever undertook any further manufacturing activities in Black Africa. The next enterprises set up were in Southern and Northern Rhodesia (Zambia) and Nyasaland (Malawi). In Southern Rhodesia Unilever began local manufacture of a sort in 1943 when it bought out the existing soap business of the Rhodesian Milling and Mining Co. Ltd (RMM), a part-owned British South Africa Company subsidiary with a factory in Salisbury, and also bought RMM's shares in the Progress Soap, Oil and Chemical Co. Ltd (PSOC) in Bulawayo. Through a newly established subsidiary, Lever Brothers (Rhodesia) Ltd, these purchases gave Unilever the lease of RMM's soap works at Salisbury and Bulawayo, PSOC's soap works at Bulawayo, and also a half share in yet another small soap factory at Ndola in Northern Rhodesia, owned by Northern Rhodesian Industries Ltd which had been part-owned by RMM. For four years RMM continued to manage all these enterprises, making and selling Unilever brands of soap as well as the brands owned by these companies. Then in 1947 Unilever bought the Express Nut, Oil and Soap Co. Ltd, which had a modern soap factory on the outskirts of Salisbury. Unilever extended and modernised this factory and in 1953 all production for Southern Rhodesia was concentrated there and the other properties disposed of. The Ndola business was kept on and in 1947 Unilever had bought the Citrona Soap Company at Blantyre, Nyasaland. In 1951 a new factory was built at Limbe to serve Nyasaland and the Blantyre factory sold.

Space makes it impossible to include these enterprises in the present study; but it is significant that the first and only new Unilever manufacturing subsidiaries established in Africa between 1923 and

Year											
1954	n/a	138,000	—	78,207	(12,610)	(7,259)	(12,610)	(—)	(—)	(—)	n/a
1955	n/a	142,032	—	90,372	(10,803)	(5,924)	(10,803)	(—)	(—)	(—)	(—)
1956	209,236	170,407	151,850	136,891	(5,090)	9,030	(5,090)	(—)	5.3	(—)	(—)
1957	207,763	188,459	157,356	164,565	(1,724)	9,704	(1,724)	(—)	5.1	0.3	(—)
1958	200,224	184,512	148,836	186,738	3,010	7,175	1,236	2,107	1.6	3.9	1
1959	202,950	167,371	124,515	194,371	7,064	6,203	1,000	4,450	3.6	3.7	2
1960	199,876	129,319	108,813	170,942	(844)	3,195	(844)	(844)	(—)	(—)	(—)
1961	196,982	139,697	91,120	254,843	43,679	5,689	23,682	23,587	17.1	16.9	12
1962	224,919	192,275	107,839	469,889	122,576	27,721	62,609	50,256	26.1	32.6	22
1963	320,000	270,141	146,259	629,844	153,888	19,070	44,694	79,293	24.4	26.1	25
1964	669,000	971,032	222,866	1,076,161	170,698	75,738	82,861	56,330	16.5	15.8	8
1965	714,000	1,034,945	261,951	1,354,920	204,481	40,000	112,177	67,479	10.8	15.1	9

Notes: a. The tax paid in 1960 relates to previous years.

b. The figures in column H show the nett profit that would have resulted if all profits had been distributed as dividends and paid tax proportionately.

c. Until 1957 the 'nett accounting profit' included one-third of the profit made by the HCB oil mill at Leopoldville.

d. All data for 1952 is taken from an estimate made late in the year. The final results are not available.

Table 6.10   Congo: MARSAVCO Trading Summary, 1945–65 ('000 Belgian/Congo Francs)

	A	B	C	D	E	F	G	H	I	J	K
Year	Average GCE for year	Capital employed on 31 December	Current A/C indebtedness within concern (nett)	NSV	Trading profit	Taxation	Nett accounting profit	Nett profit after statistical tax	E/D %	G/B %	H/A %
1945	n/a	n/a	n/a	20,466	2,466	n/a	n/a	n/a	12.1	—	n/a
1946	n/a	n/a	n/a	21,291	2,088	n/a	n/a	n/a	9.8	—	n/a
1947	n/a	n/a	n/a	38,847	4,515	n/a	n/a	n/a	11.6	—	n/a
1948	n/a	n/a	n/a	42,088	3,529	n/a	n/a	n/a	8.4	—	n/a
1949	n/a	25,815	1,660	31,253	543.5	2.4	618	n/a	1.7	2.4	n/a
1950	n/a	35,399	7,000	37,373	3,927.6	431.0	4,244	n/a	10.5	12.0	n/a
1951	n/a	51,303	21,898	64,826	255.4	28.3	1,006	n/a	0.39	2.0	n/a
1952	n/a	77,883	21,271	73,509	(4,219.7)	—	(2,792.7)	(4,219.7)	(—)	(—)	n/a
1953	n/a	n/a	51,271	62,316	(12,438)	—	n/a	(12,438)	(—)	n/a	n/a

1953 should have been in Central Africa. Conditions there were a stimulant to local manufacture on two main counts. First, there was a substantial and affluent European population—223,000 in Southern Rhodesia, 76,000 in Northern Rhodesia and 10,000 in Nyasaland in 1960. Second, from 1935 the customs agreement between South Africa and Southern Rhodesia was ended, with the result that local manufacturers there, protected by high inland freights and the new import duties, were for the first time in a position to threaten the market previously supplied by Unilever factories in South Africa. Unilever's subsequent decision to manufacture there followed the same imperatives as in other countries that have already been examined—effective protection for local rivals and a threat to established Unilever exports in a valued market. The change came when and because the relevant conditions were first fulfilled, though delayed by adverse economic conditions in the 1930s and then by the Second World War. Comparable factors resulted in additional factories to serve Northern Rhodesia and Nyasaland.

These conditions were specific to Central Africa: they did not necessarily imply any general policy of extending Unilever's manufacturing commitments in other parts of Black Africa. At first sight the fact that the next industrial venture to be undertaken there was in Nairobi in 1953 might suggest that once again the attraction was a sizeable white settler population and a protective tariff. In fact this was not the main reason for the concern's investment in Kenya and even in abbreviated form the story of how this happened and its commercial consequences is of considerable interest.

The surprising thing is that Unilever did not become involved in manufacturing in East Africa earlier than 1953 for British East Africa, consisting of Uganda, Kenya, Tanganyika and Zanzibar, formed one of the largest common markets in Africa. The total population of the three territories was about 12 million in the 1930s, rising to 16.7 million (7.4 million in Tanganyika, 3.9 million in Uganda, 5.4 million in Kenya) in 1948 and 24.4 million in 1960. Since this was a single free trading area from the early 1920s, a factory sited in any of these territories had duty free access to a unit containing the second largest number of potential consumers of any country in sub-Saharan Africa. It is true that their estimated per capita incomes were not very high—$67 in Tanganyika, $79 in Kenya, $87 in Uganda in 1960, as contrasted with $88 in Nigeria and $222 in the affluent Gold Coast; but these were all above those for the Belgian Congo and a number of other African countries, and the presence of a substantial number of Europeans and Indians with much higher than average incomes should have provided a good market for the more expensive and profitable products. Nor was East Africa dangerously open to foreign competition. The tariff system was affected by international treaties relating to the conventional Congo Basin, and also by League of Nations and United Nations rules concerning Tanganyika as a Mandate and then Trust Territory, to the extent that British preferential duties were forbidden and the tariff was supposed to be revenue-producing and not protective. But, as in the Congo, this did not mean a low tariff. By the 1930s duties on all types of imported soap were 5s per 100 lbs or 20 per cent *ad valorem*, whichever was the higher; and in the 1950s the duty on imported margarine was 22 per cent *ad valorem*. Taken together with the high cost of ocean freight to East Africa, these duties provided potentially very effective protection to local manufacturers on all but the most expensive goods.

The raw material position also seemed favourable. British East Africa was a large-scale producer of copra, exporting more than 5,000 tons a year in the early 1940s, with ample capacity to increase output. Exports of simsim seed in 1938 were 8,600 tons; and in that year 122,718 tons of cotton seed were exported as a by-product of Uganda's main staple. There was, therefore, no obvious practical reason why Levers should not have made soap in East Africa at almost any time in the early twentieth century; and their reluctance to do so cannot have been due to the possession of a satisfactory export market. In 1913 Gossages, then the most dynamic exporter among the firms which in 1919 coalesced with Lever Brothers, sent only 365 tons to East Africa out of total British exports there of 1,151 tons, compared with 5,929 out of total British exports of 10,268 tons to West Africa. Data on later Lever Brothers' exports are incomplete; but the evidence set out in Table 6.11 suggests that they were always small; and even in 1949, when the population of East Africa was substantially larger, total Lever sales were about the same as they had been in the late 1920s.

All this points back to the initial problem: why Unilever did not invest in a soap factory in this region until 1958, and then only in partnership with two public corporations. The explanation, which was put forward by W. P. Scott of Unilever Export in 1930 but held good until the 1950s, was that local Indian manufacturers, who made mostly blue mottled and other unwrapped bar soaps, held some

4,750 out of a total soap market of about 5,500 tons. Their production costs were low because soap-making was usually ancillary to some other enterprise and their transport costs were small because they sold in local markets; and for the next 20 years the basic question facing Unilever was whether it would be possible to build up a market for a higher quality but more expensive type of soap if they built a factory in any part of British East Africa.

Table 6.11   East Africa: Exports of Soap by Unilever to East Africa, 1929–39 and 1949–52

Year	Tons	Nett sales value £
1929	980*	53,867[a]
1930	900*	49,482
1931	588*	32,375
1932	385*	21,173
1933	373*	20,511
1934	429*	23,585
1935	370*	20,314[a]
1936	432	25,636
1937	464	25,917
1938	494	24,875
1939	454	n/a
1949	932	n/a
1950	555	n/a
1951	1,154	n/a
1952	1,155	n/a

Notes: a. The nett sales values for 1929 and 1935 are partly estimated since the value of one-quarter's sales is missing in the records for each of these years.

b. The figures for the volume of sales for 1929–35 are starred because these are rough estimates based on dividing the known sales value for these years by the average price per ton for 1936–8, which was about £55 a ton. In fact the tonnage in 1929–35 may have been higher than shown if average soap prices were lower than this or if the mix of products was different.

Underlying this question was the cost of raw materials. If a Unilever factory could use cheaper materials than the Indians, this might offset its higher overheads and transport costs and enable it to expand its sales at the upper end of the market. Scott grasped that this was the determinant of policy in 1930 and thereafter all analyses made by Unilever reporters turned on where raw materials would be cheapest and therefore where a factory should be built. From the start there were two alternative strategies: on the coast, because imported raw materials were cheaper there than at Nairobi; or in Uganda, because it was a large producer of cotton seed and could also produce other suitable vegetable oils. In 1930 Scott supported Mombasa as a port to which raw materials could be brought and from which the whole of East Africa could be served with soap. Immediately afterwards F. M. Dyke, an HCB man who naturally thought in terms of vegetable oil production, proposed Jinja in Uganda as the site on the ground that if an oil mill was built there it could mill the cotton seed that was then being exported for processing in Europe and possibly other oil-bearing seeds or nuts such as simsim, shea nuts or groundnuts, which were then exported unprocessed. It might even be feasible to establish palm oil plantations, though further investigation showed this to be impracticable. In this way, by pioneering the processing of local oil-bearing products, Unilever might obtain a substantial cost advantage over Indian soap manufacturers which would hold good at least for markets served by the line of rail from Mombasa to Uganda.

Between them Scott and Dyke had, at the very start, defined the issues and alternative lines of action on which the debate over manufacturing in East Africa was to turn for nearly a quarter of a century: should a factory be geared primarily to processing local raw materials, in which case it should probably be placed in Uganda; or should it be seen in terms of the communications system, in which case access to imported raw materials and markets was critical and Mombasa or possibly Nairobi were better sites? But the question had no sooner been posed than it seems to have been forgotten: there is no record of any further proposal for local manufacture in East Africa until 1944, and Scott himself did not refer to it in another report he made on this area in 1935. The reason is almost certainly that the dramatic decline in Lever soap imports between 1929 and any time from 1931 to 1939 was taken as evidence that under slump conditions the soap market had contracted to the point that even the most ingeniously situated mill and factory could not operate at a profit. It was not, therefore, until 1943 that Unilever House again showed any interest in the question, and this seems to have been stimulated by reports that the Kenyan government, faced with a dual shortage of imports and a market for raw materials, had made unprecedented efforts to develop local manufacture of a wide range of goods, including hydrogenated vegetable oil, the basis of margarine and other edible fats. Whether or not this was the only reason, it was decided that Roger Heyworth should visit East Africa in 1944 in the course of his visit to China, the Congo and West Africa on which, as has been seen, he made detailed surveys of post-war industrial possibilities. The story of Unilever's interest in East African manufacture dates from that visit.

Heyworth's analysis was very detailed, but essentially he adopted Dyke's position and elaborated it. Unilever should build an industrial complex at Kampala, in Uganda, to contain mills capable of processing up to 42,000 tons of cotton seed and plant to manufacture 5,140 tons of soap, 2,962 tons of refined oil and possibly also some vegetable ghee. This would serve Uganda, western Kenya as far as Nairobi ('the edge' of the market, providing very small profit margins because of high freight costs) and the Lake Victoria region of Tanganyika as far as Tabora. To serve other markets Unilever would need to build three other factories: one at Mwanza, on Lake Victoria in Tanganyika, consisting of a cotton-seed mill and a small plant to make cheap semi-boiled soaps; a second at Dar es Salaam making about 2,200 tons of soap, mainly from coconut oil and therefore including a small copra mill; and a third at Tanga, in northern Tanganyika, which would incorporate oil palm plantations and produce some 1,000 to 1,500 tons of oil from which soap could be made for the Tanga–Mombasa region. The total capital cost, at pre-war prices, was calculated at around £400,000, which Heyworth thought might provide a profit of between £36,400 and £60,600 a year before tax, according to the current price of cotton seed and other raw materials.

This was certainly a grandiose project in a region which had hitherto proved unattractive to Unilever; and Heyworth admitted that he had been influenced by the Governors of Kenya, Uganda and Tanganyika, all of whom seemed anxious to see industrial investment and greater local utilisation of raw materials, and in addition appeared to welcome the prospect of some counterweight to Indian preponderance in industry. In his conclusions he pointed to possible interlocking advantages:

I am sure this territory presents a field where we can undertake a useful task, with profit both to it and to ourselves, and believe, that once we made a beginning we shall find greater prospects than can be reckoned out in advance. A manufacturing business of the kind we have in view complements the UAC produce business to a great degree; the more vegetable ghee we sell, the more butter ghee we may free for export, and the [more] cotton-seed oil we put into the market, the more groundnuts and simsim seed can be shipped abroad. The Management of the two enter-prises must be closely co-ordinated, not only in East Africa, but also with the raw material buying in London, and will call for the exercise of good judgment and commercial ability. I believe too that good technical efficiency will make selling prices possible that may bring really astonishing increases in consumption, and reveal latent wants on the part of the African population, the satisfaction of which can only be to the benefit of the country as a whole.

Yet, the project eventually came to nothing: or rather, in place of Heyworth's ambitious plan for a large Uganda-based complex and three other factories, all linked to local raw material supplies, Unilever eventually became a partner in a relatively small factory in Nairobi which depended almost entirely on the market for its raw materials. The story is long and complicated and cannot be told in detail here, but the salient points must be mentioned because they reflect the influences which may determine where a multi-national decides to place its investment and at the same time throw some light on the peculiarities of British planning for development in the colonies in the last two decades of the colonial period.

By 1945 Roger Heyworth had obtained agreement in principle to go ahead with his Kampala project, whose first stage alone was estimated to cost up to £400,000, in marked contrast with the contemporary proposals for Leopoldville; and he visited East Africa to negotiate with the British colonial authorities whose assent would be essential. Sir Charles Lockhart, Governor of Kenya and Chair-man of the East African War Production Board which had general control over economic policy throughout the area, gave the project his blessing and offered to harden oil milled at Kampala at the Nairobi plant owned by the East African Industrial Management Board (EAIMB) until Unilever obtained their own plant. But when Heyworth met the Governor of Uganda, Sir John Hall, in what he described as 'the ethereal seclusion of Entebbe' the capital, he came up against serious difficulties. Despite his alleged enthusiasm for industrialisation,[9] Sir John Hall's reaction to Unilever's proposal was strictly non-economic and conventionally paternalistic. As Heyworth reported, 'his immediate reaction to the scheme was that "big business" was entering a territory in which the safeguarding and promotion of native interests was government policy and that we should not be well received . . .'. Hall went on to say that 'he had hoped to develop the oil milling industry on the basis of African co-operative enterprise (under European supervision) and could we help at that?' When Heyworth answered that cotton-seed milling required expensive capital equipment and technical skills (as the Uganda Cotton Commission of 1938 had already pointed out), so that it would be necessary for Africans to get previous experience from milling easier products such as groundnuts and sesame, Hall seemed reluctantly to acquiesce; but he then shifted to that other staple of Ugandan government policy, maintenance of artificial prices for local raw materials. Would Unilever be prepared to pay 'more than previously' for cotton seed: that is, more than the export parity based on current world oil-seed prices which UAC and other firms paid for the cotton seed they exported? He was naturally disappointed that Heyworth again refused, on the ground that this would make the project uneconomic; but he seemed to accept, and pressed for the factory and mill to be sited at Jinja rather than Kampala, mainly because there were then political problems in Uganda relating to land utilisation. Heyworth said Jinja was ruled out for economic reasons and in the end Hall, after referring the matter to his Control of Industries Committee, said that the project could go forward provided the Colonial Office gave its approval.

On this basis Unilever drew up detailed and ever more expensive plans which by 1949 had risen to £1 million for the Kampala project alone, plus the cost of a factory at Dar es Salaam. These rising costs were one of the reasons why in the end the project came to nothing; but a much more important reason was that the Colonial Office sat on the project from 1946 to 1948 when Unilever was most enthusiastic about it, and then announced that a decision would be further postponed until a Special Commissioner had reviewed all outstanding plans for capital investment in Uganda. This appears to have been the last straw, or perhaps a welcome release, for by then Unilever was becoming frightened by escalating costs and the Special Committee immediately decided to inform the Colonial Office that Unilever 'was withdrawing for the present until circumstances were more suitable'. That time never came. By 1948, and still more by 1950, there were strong reasons other than capital costs for dropping the Kampala project. First, until about 1950 the supply of cotton seed was greatly reduced because African cotton growers responded to the government's policy of paying them substantially less than a market price by reducing production: in 1948 cotton exports were less than half the 1938 level and less than they had been in 1925. Had this trend persisted Unilever would certainly have had to drop the proposal to mill cotton seed. An upturn in cotton production came in 1950 and thereafter supply was no obstacle. But by that time a third and decisive deterrent to the Kampala milling project had developed. Attracted by high vegetable oil prices and encouraged by a British firm which made and exported expellers, Indians in Uganda had built up capacity to mill some 80,000 tons of cotton seed a year, which later rose to over 200,000 tons capacity. Since at best there was only about 100,000 tons of cotton seed available, it would thereafter have been pointless to enter this field and Unilever might well feel glad that official procrastination, whether deliberate or accidental, had prevented them from committing a very large investment to so unrewarding an activity.

This fiasco might well have meant that Unilever kept out of manufacturing in East Africa for an indefinite period. Yet four years after its final decision to drop the Kampala project the concern was committed to running an oil mill, refinery and fat hardening plant and to the eventual manufacture of soap and edible fats and oils in Nairobi. The explanation is not that Unilever had decided that Kenya offered better prospects than Uganda, but that a British public corporation, the Colonial Development Corporation (CDC), asked Unilever to help salvage something from the complex of industrial enterprises which had been built up by the Kenyan government during the Second World War under a government body, the East African Industrial Management Board. When CDC was formed it asked all colonial governments to suggest enterprises in which it might become involved; and the Kenyan government, embarrassed by EAIMB, proposed that CDC should take a majority shareholding and management control of this conglomerate enterprise.[10] CDC acquired a two-thirds share in what was now called East Africa Industries Ltd (EAI) and for two years EAI did reasonably well. But in 1951 the company fell on hard times. Most of the wide range of industrial activities built up during and after the war in a period of intense shortages were uneconomic under peace-time conditions and the business was losing about £150,000 a year. The only viable enterprises carried on in its 25-acre site in Nairobi were the manufacture of fire bricks, oil-refining and oil-hardening. By 1951 the oil refinery was unable to sell sufficient refined oil to use all the cotton-seed oil it had contracted to buy at inflated prices from Uganda under conditions of shortage and the hardening plant was running at a loss because of the high price of vegetable oil. Clearly EAI needed to close down its unprofitable activities, improve its managerial skills and expand on the basis of refined and hardened oils. To do so efficiently the company needed expert advice, and no one was better qualified to give it than Unilever which had already shown an interest in EAI's hardening plant. In July 1952 Lord Reith, who had become Chairman of CDC after leaving the British Broadcasting Corporation, asked Unilever to provide a general assessment of EAI's commercial potential and a month later to advise on the possibility of margarine manufacture in Nairobi.

It is of some importance, in case it might be thought that Unilever eagerly exploited EAI's need, that the concern's first reactions were anything but enthusiastic. Nevertheless J. H. Hansard was sent to Nairobi in September 1952 and discussed EAI's problems and possibilities on the spot with Lord Reith and Roger Norton, head of CDC's operations in East Africa. The three of them agreed that the oil-refining and fat-hardening plant should be kept going for another year to get it into good condition, after which it would be sold to the highest bidder as a going concern on about five acres of land. The fire-brick works would be moved elsewhere, and the remaining 15 acres and other assets would be sold as soon as possible. This might well have been the end of Unilever's association with CDC and EAI, though the concern might have put in a bid for the oil-refining and fat-hardening plant later on. But at this point Lord Reith took an initiative which led eventually to the business partnership between CDC and Unilever by remarking to Hansard that 'it was their policy to try and interest commercial firms as partners in their activities, thus giving the Colonial Development Corporation the benefit of skilled management and know-how'. Presumably he was fishing for continued Unilever co-operation; and Hansard responded by asking 'whether he would be interested in a project by which we leased the oil-refinery and hardening plant from them and operated it under our own management'. According to Hansard, Reith and Norton 'jumped at the idea with enthusiasm' and both sides then began to elaborate proposals.

This was the start of a negotiation which proceeded fast and amicably. In April 1953 the Special Committee agreed in principle to collaborate with CDC and the Kenyan government[11] through its Industrial Development Corporation (IDC), owners of the remaining 33.5 per cent of EAI shares, provided a satisfactory relationship could be agreed. After further negotiation the capital structure was arranged as follows. Unilever was to have 50 per cent of the ordinary capital of the reorganised company in return for a cash investment of £37,500 plus use of its trademarks, management and know-how, leaving CDC with one-third of the ordinary capital and the Kenyan government one-sixth. Unilever appointed two of the four directors, but one of these would be chairman of the board of EAI and his casting vote would, if necessary, give Unilever effective control of policy. In addition to the ordinary shares, CDC and the government held B and C shares representing existing assets of EAI not initially brought into the new business; so that overall Unilever was a minority shareholder. Development would be in two stages. In the first EAI would make and sell only cooking compound, refined oil and margarine. Stage two would follow only if the business prospered and circumstances seemed propitious for soap manufacture. EAI would continue to buy its raw materials on the open market and would not undertake oil milling. On this basis the final agreement was signed early in October 1953 and Unilever undertook full responsibility for running EAI.

(b) Performance, 1953–65

The history of EAI after it came under Unilever management in 1953 is of considerable interest. It provides evidence on the relations between Unilever and the two public corporations, CDC and IDC, which were its partners; it covers the period of the Mau Mau crisis and decolonisation; and in recent literature on 'under-development' the company has achieved a certain significance as allegedly an example of how foreign capital may ally with an indigenous bourgeoisie at the expense of the local producer and consumer.[12] Unfortunately space prevents treatment of these themes, and it is proposed merely to comment on one salient aspect of EAI's performance, its comparatively high profitability.

Seen in contrast with the various ambitious schemes for East Africa which had been in the air since 1944 the fact that in the end Unilever had settled for a 50 per cent holding plus management control of a small existing business in Nairobi may seem an anticlimax. Yet in its context it was the logical outcome of earlier failures and far more in line with the economic realities of the 1950s.

A similar venture would have been impracticable in the 1930s or earlier because margarine was banned in Kenya, demand for other edible fats limited, and the market for soap too small to accommodate both Unilever and the Indian manufacturers. During the 1940s a factory not related to an oil mill which exploited new sources of vegetable oil would have been starved of raw materials. But by 1953 these pre- and post-war impediments had been removed and in an expanding East African economy the demand for edible oils and fats and for quality soap was capable of supporting a substantial modern enterprise. Unilever was, perhaps, fortunate that it was not tied to a vast milling and manufacturing complex in Kampala and that in the end chance provided what the concern had needed all along—a convenient industrial base from which to supply Kenya and Uganda with a limited range of quality products.

Table 6.12   East Africa: Sales of Unilever Soap in East Africa, 1954—6! (tons)

Date	Sunlight	Lifebuoy	Bar soaps	Lux T.S.	Lifebuoy T.S.	Total
1954	856	n/a	235	280	288	1,659
1955	455	89	705	370	371	1,990
1956	855	91	712	211	443	2,312
1957	647	100	816	235	565	2,363
1958	935	130	1,100	265	610	3,060
1959	1,249	174	1,458	307	675	3,863
1960	2,403	198	2,445	293	696	6,035
1961	4,104	301	2,583	360	736	8,084
1962	5,007	456	2,641	437	760	9,301
1963	5,342	585	3,093	428	859	10,307
1964	5,124	425	3,547	423	955	10,474
1965	4,888	287	3,151	493	1,053	9,872

It is immediately clear from Tables 6.12 to 6.14 that, as a simple business proposition, Unilever's involvement in EAI proved a resounding success for all three parties. Partly by getting rid of the unprofitable parts of the earlier business and partly by reorganising the residual elements, the earlier loss was turned into a consistent, though not outstanding, profit from 1953 to 1958: the low profit in relation to Gross Capital Employed for 1958 was due to the fact that the new plant for soap manufacture had been bought and had to pay interest some time before actual soap production could begin.

But it was from 1959 with, and largely because of, the spectacular expansion of soap sales that the large profits were made; and since soap, apart from margarine, represented Unilever's main contribution to EAI, this must be seen as the direct consequence of their joining the company.

It is, however, important to ask precisely why EAI should have done so well out of soap, bearing in mind the pessimistic estimates made in the 1930s and again in 1944 of the commercial prospects of a single soap factory attempting to serve the whole of East Africa's fragmented market. The key fact, which itself requires explanation, is that EAI was able to build up the volume of its sales of quality soap—Sunlight, Lifebuoy and, to a lesser extent, Lux Toilet and Lifebuoy Toilet Soap—far beyond the volume of imports in the early 1950s and still further beyond all earlier Unilever predictions.

Table 6.13   East Africa: Sales of Unilever Edible Fats and Oils in East Africa, 1955—65 (tons)

Year	Blue Band	Kimbo	Veg. ghee	Other edibles	Total
1955	53	835	218	647	1,753
1956	184	875	439	810	2,308
1957	235	866	707	748	2,556
1958	255	840	900	600	2,595
1959	280	829	1,025	570	2,704
1960	670	948	1,300	360	3,278
1961	835	1,113	1,612	466	4,026
1962	881	1,254	1,383	314	3,832
1963	871	1,490	1,672	273	4,306
1964	920	1,865	2,036	184	5,005
1965	1,071	2,719	1,496	158	5,444

These products were critical for profits because they alone, by contrast with blue mottled and pale bar soaps, provided satisfactory profit margins and were not in direct competition with Indian-made soaps. Moreover only a quality product providing a substantial profit margin could have surmounted the hurdle of high freight costs inevitable for any firm which tried to serve the whole East African market from Nairobi.

Successful extension of the market for quality soaps still begs the question of how this was achieved. Any answer must be partly speculative; but if the composite analysis provided by a number of

Table 6.14 East Africa: EAI Capital, Turnover and Profits, 1954–65 (£'000)

Year	A NSV	B Trading profit before tax	C Trading profit after statistical tax	B Nominal capital	E GCE	B/A %	C/E %
1954	278	34	n/a	207 (67)	n/a	12.2	n/a
1955	316	30	23	207 (67)	331	9.5	6.9
1956	417	53	39	207 (67)	380	12.7	10.3
1957	474	56	42	207 (67)	575	11.8	7.3
1958	505	43	31	575 (252)	874	8.5	3.5
1959	998	166	120	575 (252)	1,030	16.6	11.6
1960	1,331	258	187	575 (252)	1,080	19.4	17.3
1961	1,786	338	211	750 (339)	1,002	18.9	21.1
1962	2,052	417	261	750 (339)	1,039	20.3	25.1
1963	2,286	491	307	750 (339)	1,115	21.5	27.5
1964	2,516	382	239	750 (339)	1,209	15.2	19.8
1965	3,096	488	305	750 (339)	1,459	15.8	20.9

Notes: a. Figures for nominal capital are for the whole of EAI, including 'A' and 'B' preferred shares. Figures in brackets are Unilever's holding.

b. Unilever's share of ordinary capital was 50 per cent to 31 December 1962, thereafter 54.8 per cent.

Unilever men is correct, success flowed from quality, price and marketing. Quality was important because of the growing sophistication of the expanding African population, which would buy good soap if it could afford it. EAI produced the best hard soap made in the region and the only good toilet soap until Colgate-Palmolive built their Nairobi factory in the early 1960s. But preference for quality is conditioned by price: and it was more than anything else EAI's ability to sell Sunlight at an acceptable price and still make a good profit that gave them this expanded market. In this they were helped by two factors outside their control. On the one hand they were now able to buy in Kenya the most suitable raw materials, from whatever source, at declining world market prices plus cost of freight, which they could not have done in East Africa between 1939 and about 1952 and could not do at any time after about 1950 in many other countries, such as India or Pakistan. Second, they had a substantial price advantage over importers, provided by an import duty of 20 per cent (rising to 37.5 per cent after 1963) and the cost of freight to Mombasa and up the railway to inland markets: indeed Hansard calculated in 1953 that Sunlight manufactured in Nairobi could be sold there at £22 a ton less than Sunlight imported from Port Sunlight.

To these fortunate circumstances Unilever executives added another for which they could claim no credit—the absence of effective local competition in the quality market which 'allowed us to make sales progress without any substantial price cutting'. But there were some things on which they could congratulate the concern: 'good organisation', 'shrewd buying' of raw materials and, possibly more important, radically improved marketing arrangements.

When local manufacture through EAI developed in the early 1950s, its products were sold through the existing distributive agents on commission, commonly about 5 per cent. But as early as 1954 Unilever marketing specialists recommended that EAI should establish their own distributive and selling organisation, as soon as sales volume justified this, in order to reduce costs and ensure effective promotion. By 1960, with soap providing the necessary sales volume at last, EAI replaced their main agents, Hamiltons, by their own depots in Uganda (at Kampala and M'Bale), selling direct to local middlemen and retailers on a cash basis. Despite the need for more working capital, this cost less than the previous agents' commission and provided much more dynamic promotion. By 1962

Kenya and the Arusha and Moshi regions of Tanganyika were also served by EAI depots and sales teams, the rest of Tanganyika being covered by the firm of Smith Mackenzie. By that time teams of van salesmen were covering all three territories and advertising was carried on with mobile cinemas. Thus, by the early 1960s, EAI was using standard Unilever sales and marketing methods which gave maximum penetration of the East African market at relatively low cost: in 1965 advertising and marketing together cost only 8 per cent of nett sales value.

These factors, coupled with East Africa's relatively low rates of corporate taxation, are sufficient to account for the substantial profits made by EAI in the decade after 1953. Their continuance after these territories became independent in the early 1960s was, of course, contingent on other and mostly political factors. But it is at least worth emphasising that here, as in South Africa, there was one dog that did not bark: the use of 'cheap' African labour was not a significant cause of high profits. Industrial labour costs have two main components: management and semi-skilled or unskilled workers. In East Africa Unilever's by then conventional policy of replacing European staff with local staff as quickly as possible to save money and improve relations with the host society moved slowly, held back by the very small number of adequately educated Africans who were prepared to enter business and also by the political difficulty, which became worse as independence drew nearer, of using Asians. In 1965 management of EAI was still entirely in European and Asian hands; and the very high cost of expatriate management in a country which was not (in view of political developments) treated like South Africa or Australia so far as European managers were concerned, continued to disappoint and embarrass Unilever.

Management was therefore expensive; but it might be expected that the relatively low wages paid to African semi-skilled and unskilled workers would more than offset these managerial costs and so contribute to high profits. African wages were indeed low. They were negotiated annually with the union; but the union was weak, the labour pool vast and in 1962 the lowest monthly wage rate in the factory was a mere £6 5s, though actual incomes were considerably swollen by overtime. Yet there is no case for attributing high company profits to these low wage rates. It has been seen in studies of other Unilever subsidiaries in less developed countries that in this capital-intensive industry wages never significantly affected profits; and in the case of EAI an independent study of the Kenyan soap industry (along with other industries there) by Reichelt fully supports this view.[13] His analysis showed that in 1966/7, when wage rates had risen substantially above those paid in 1962, labour costs amounted to only about 5 per cent of total production costs in the Kenyan soap industry (consisting largely of EAI and Colgate-Palmolive) as compared with 80–90 per cent for raw materials. He commented that, although labour was paid only about 30–50 per cent of wages common in Europe at the time for similar work, output was proportionately lower. This he attributed mainly to the fact that, due largely to their 'non-industrialised sociological back-ground, unskilled workers frequently lacked a sense of time and efficiency which was the basis of any organised industrial activity' and were also 'generally lacking a minimum of general technical experience, which in industrialised countries is considered almost natural and part of the modern way of life'. Moreover, some 'semi-skilled' African workers lacked 'even a superficial knowledge about the way in which the machine works'; 'they required more super-vision by expensive European staff', so that the total effect was that 'the labour cost per unit of production is in general higher than it would be in Europe'. This was true not only of EAI but of all modern industries in Kenya.

Ghana: the Genesis of Lever Brothers (Ghana) Ltd

The interest of Lever Brothers (Ghana) Ltd (LB(G)) does not lie in its age—it began production only in 1963—its size, profitability or other exceptional features, but in the dual problem of why no Unilever soap factory was built there earlier and why it came to exist in the end. The arguments against a manufacturing subsidiary in the Gold Coast—which became Ghana in 1957—were always formid-able. Three such arguments were always deemed conclusive before the 1950s and explain the long postponement of a decision to set up a Lever factory there.

First, although, because of its highly developed cocoa production, the Gold Coast was comparatively wealthy by African standards, with an estimated per capita income of $222 in 1960 as compared with $88 in Nigeria, its population was small: 1.5 million in 1901, 2.9 million in 1934, 4.1 million in 1948 and 6.9 million in 1960; and this was a small market for any modern consumer industry. Second, by contrast with Nigeria, the Gold Coast was not a large producer or exporter of vegetable oils or other potential raw materials for soap or margarine manufacture. The colonial government had initially forbidden Lever Brothers to establish oil palm plantations and later narrowly restricted their extent. No palm oil was exported between the 1930s and 1950s and local supplies were used for cooking. The export of palm kernels was only 5,300 tons in 1938 and 9,200 tons in 1958. Thus most raw materials for manufacturing would have to be imported; and this was what made the tariff structure of British West Africa the really conclusive obstacle to manufacturing.

The third adverse factor was the Gold Coast tariff. Paradoxically, although it is conventional to describe this tariff as 'free-trading' and 'revenue-producing' because there were no protective nor preferential import duties in any of the British West African colonies, in practice it might well have provided effective protection for a local soap industry. Duties of £4 a ton before 1939, and £6 a ton from the 1940s on hard soap and £14 rising to £16 16s 0d a ton on toilet soaps provided protection amounting to between 15 per cent and 20 per cent *ad valorem*, varying with the current price of soap. By most criteria this constituted reasonably effective protection, especially when freight charges on oil despatched to Europe and freight and handling charges on soap exported from Europe to West Africa are taken into consideration. What really made the tariff system of British West Africa pleasing to dogmatic free traders and discouraging to would-be local manufacturers was the fact that there was a duty on imported oils and other industrial raw materials which, on an *ad valorem* basis, more or less balanced the import duties on products such as soap. This meant there was absolutely no tariff advantage in local manufacture of this or any other product dependent on imported materials: indeed the colonial government was so preoccupied with its customs revenue—the basis of local government finance—that any suggestions of establishing a local manufacture to replace imports were likely to lead to talk of a countervailing excise on the domestic product.

Nature and British free trade orthodoxy seemed thus to combine to exclude all incentives to large-scale local manufacture of soap on the Gold Coast so long as the colonial economic system survived. Decolonisation, which could be expected to result in a radical change of tariff policy, was likely to remove one impediment. But it still remained uncertain whether it would be to the economic advantage of the Gold Coast to attract large-scale modern industries such as a Unilever soap factory so long as raw materials had to be imported. This, indeed, seems to have been the conclusion reached by Professor W. A. Lewis in his *Report on Industrialization and the Gold Coast*,[14] made in 1953 for the Gold Coast government. Lewis's criteria for local industry on the Gold Coast (or elsewhere) were three-fold: local availability of raw materials or use of inputs which did not lose weight substantially in processing; average requirements of capital, skills and fuel; and a sufficiently large market. For soap the raw materials would have to be imported to the Gold Coast, but it would lose no weight in processing. The requirement in terms of capital, skill and fuel was not outrageous; and the market, which Lewis put conservatively at 5,774.5 tons for common soap and 359.8 tons for toilet soap, was, he thought, adequate to support 'a large modern factory'. Thus soap manufacture, while not in the same 'favourable' category as, say, timber products, salt, beer, bricks and tiles, cement, glass, plywood, lime, some chemicals, canned fruit and vegetables and industrial alcohol (his complete list), was at least 'marginal' and therefore possible.

But this did not mean that it was necessarily advantageous to the Ghanaian economy under all conditions. It would, in Lewis's terms, be worthwhile only if, once the imported raw materials were free of all duties, the soap factory did not need protection or subsidy for more than a short initial period and could thereafter rely on the cost of freight on competing imports for protection. Such conditions never seemed satisfactory to Unilever and, one must assume, to other foreign manufacturers. When they came to consider the criteria for local manufacture in the Gold Coast in 1953, it was thought that import duties on hard soap must be at least 15 per cent *ad valorem* (raised to 20 per cent in 1959) and on toilet soap 25 per cent; that these must be permanent; and that the government should commit itself to exclude imports of artificially cheap soap. In short, because the Gold Coast possessed no natural advantages for soap manufacture, the only potential economic advantage of local production would be the value added by local labour; and if sufficient protection was provided to attract a big company such as Unilever, the nett result might very well be negative value added. There might, of course, be secondary economic advantages to offset this: the demonstration effect, backward and forward linkages, some foreign exchange saving; but on balance such a factory was likely to provide a return in prestige rather than national wealth.

The reason for establishing LB(G), which eventually went into soap production at Tema, the newly developed port and industrial zone on the coast near Accra, in 1963, lies, therefore, in the consequences of the transition from colonialism to independence and still more in the character of the successor regime in Ghana. Under British colonial rule the iron laws of free trade economics survived in West Africa even after they had been eroded or discarded in Britain. Professor Lewis's report marks the watershed between old and new thinking. When he was asked to make this study in 1952, the Gold Coast had just been given a form of home rule under the constitution of 1951. There was a responsible cabinet under Kwame Nkrumah, the first Prime Minister. Reacting to the new developing science of growth economics, the government was beginning to plan economic development and was projecting a managed economy. But it was not until full independence in 1957, and still more after about 1960, when Nkrumah began to discard many of the orthodoxies inherited from the British, that the economic environment really became propitious for large-scale industrial investment; and it was only in the radically changed conditions provided by the new regime that Unilever seriously considered local manufacture. Thus a major interest of the story lies in examining the consequences of political independence in this West African state for a multinational corporation and in the light this throws on the wider problems of foreign investment in developing countries. It is therefore proposed to divide this story at 1953, briefly surveying Unilever's attitudes to the Gold Coast during the previous half century, to explain why no factory was set up in this period; and then, after sketching the changing character of the Ghanaian government and its economic policy in the decade before 1965, to examine in more detail the considerations which led Unilever to invest in manufacturing in the early 1960s.

It is significant that, although William Lever was interested in soap manufacturing in Nigeria before the First World War, the possibility of doing the same in the Gold Coast is never mentioned in the surviving Lever papers or in any available Lever Brothers records before 1934. Throughout the 1920s the Gold Coast remained entirely an export market for Port Sunlight; and although UEL accounts do not distinguish Lever exports to this colony from those to other parts of West Africa, it seems likely that they were above 2,000 tons a year and constituted the bulk of the concern's trade in West Africa once Nigeria made its own bar soap at Apapa.

The first serious consideration of local manufacture in the Gold Coast seems to have been made in 1934 when J. L. Heyworth visited the colony. His main concern was then whether WASCO should be allowed to continue to sell its carbolic soap there in competition with the pale bar soaps imported by United Exporters Ltd (UEL) and distributed by UAC; and his conclusion was that, while WASCO products should not be excluded, it was financially un- profitable to promote Nigerian soap in the Gold Coast. A secondary issue was the possible consequences of the establishment of the first significant modern soap factory in Ghana, set up by a Syrian named Bardoweel at Accra, called the Accra Chemical Works. Using coconut oil, Bardoweel was apparently able to undersell the cheapest UEL soap and had good distribution in the coastal area and the three main towns. This at least raised the possibility that if he went on expanding Unilever might be forced to manufacture locally to protect its own market against him. Heyworth made no firm recom- mendations on this point, but emphasised that if soap was to be made there it must be 'on the cheapest possible scale by making it a subsidiary department of the palm oil mill [at Sese, run by UAC], provided raw materials are available in sufficient quantity. Only in this way . . . could we hope to compete with the Syrian production, otherwise we should be killed by overheads.'

But nascent local competition was not the only problem facing Unilever in the Gold Coast; and in the same year W. P. Scott visited the Gold Coast to consider the implications of a decline in soap imports resulting from the slump. The decline, he concluded, was due to reduced local purchasing power, itself the result of declining cocoa prices: foreign competition was not as serious as in Nigeria since Bibby's carbolic soaps were not popular in the Gold Coast. Bardoweel was potentially dangerous due to his low prices; but Scott rejected a casual suggestion made to him by a customs officer at Accra that an excise might be imposed on locally-made soap. From the customs point of view this would offset revenue loss on import duties and he had obviously thought that this would also please Unilever. But Scott thought the suggestion embarrassing since it might be applied to WASCO's soap products in Nigeria. Thus Unilever stuck to its old course. Throughout the 1930s UEL battled for its share of the Gold Coast market, using traditional West Coast methods such as a price agreement with Bibbys covering the whole coast, fine tuning of selling prices, and periodical modification of produce to meet market preferences. In the event nothing catastrophic happened. Bardoweel failed to exploit his potential advantage while maintaining his business; and UEL held about 80 per cent of the total market for factory-made soap. Sales volume rose and fell with the profitability of cocoa production, reaching a peak of over 4,000 tons in 1937, but dropping the next year due to a slump in market prices and the famous boycott staged by the cocoa producers. In short, no new factors which might have made local manufacture worth consideration came into play before the Second World War. Symbolically the Overseas Committee records at Unilever House on the Gold Coast are a blank from 1936 to 1944.

By 1944, when Roger Heyworth visited the colony, much had changed. Wartime restrictions had eliminated imports from Britain, so the Gold Coast had to be satisfied with a limited quota of WASCO soap, amounting to about half the volume of pre-war imports. This meant that the Unilever market would in any case have to be rebuilt after the war; and the question was now whether, under changed circumstances, this could best be done with imports or by local manufacture. There were, moreover, certain new factors which now appeared more favourable to local manufacture. The higher wartime specific import duties would, if retained, have a more protective effect when prices of soap declined; local manufacturers —particularly Bardoweel's Accra Chemical Works—would probably re-equip and improve their quality; the government might, in the already changing climate of opinion on colonial development, abolish the import duties on raw materials. In such circumstances Unilever might be forced into local manufacture as a means of regaining their pre-war market share or any large part of it; so Heyworth felt it wise to look once again into the economics of local production.

His analysis concentrated on the future of the import duties on raw materials, which he regarded as the one critical factor. Since freight and other transport charges on palm oil brought from Port Harcourt (Nigeria) to Accra were, paradoxically, higher than those from Nigeria to Port Sunlight, a local factory would not have any advantage over Britain in respect of raw material costs. If, therefore, the duty on imported oils and caustic soda continued to be roughly equivalent to the duty on imported hard soap, a Gold Coast manufacturer would have no advantage whatever over his British competitor. Under such circumstances local manufacture would be prohibitively uneconomic. Heyworth therefore tried to discover official intentions on the import tariff after the war, but could get no indication—let alone a commitment—from anyone on anything. His general conclusion was that the traditional preoccupation with import duties as a source of revenue was likely to bar their removal, which meant that imported raw materials would continue to be prohibitively expensive. The only alternative was to use, and if necessary stimulate the production of, the limited supply of Gold Coast palm kernel oil; though whether sufficient could be obtained even for 5,000 tons of soap was problematical. If it could, and if the manufacture was technically efficient, Heyworth thought there might be a nett margin of £2 10s 0d over imports. This involved many hypotheses, including the level of duties on imported soap: but he concluded that

if the present separate customs administrations of the British West African territories remained [i.e. if there continued to be duties on WASCO soap], and . . . if the present Gold Coast tariff policy is not altered, we shall be compelled to erect a factory in defence of our trade, in spite of the fact that an adequate raw material basis is not present and that the factory would not, under less onerous tariff barriers, be an economic proposition.

These were agnostic conclusions because everything depended on post-war tariff policy, which in turn would be determined by more fundamental policy decisions on economic priorities in British West Africa. Such decisions were not taken quickly even after 1945. The Gold Coast therefore remained an import market until the 1950s, by which time Lever soaps were again being sent from Port Sunlight rather than Apapa. The main post-war novelty was that, due largely to higher cocoa prices and increasing population, Unilever sales grew rapidly, rising to 5,979 tons of soap in 1950, 10,313 tons in 1953, and 19,950 tons in 1959. Profits also rose substantially: UEL's pre-tax profit in 1953 was £150,000. Thus, by 1953, Unilever had a very much more valuable import market to protect than before the war; and, since 1952/3 turned out to be a critical year in the history of Ghana's political and economic development, it will be convenient at this point to summarise the facts as they affected Unilever.

The basic chronology of the Gold Coast's post-war political history is as follows. The legislative council was liberalised in 1946 and in 1951 was expanded to a proto-parliament, half of whose members were elected from conventional constituencies, the rest from traditional councils. In this parliament the Convention People's Party (CPP) emerged as the largest group and Kwame Nkrumah, its dominant member, became Leader of Government Business in an Executive Council which was evolving into a cabinet. In 1952 Nkrumah became Prime Minister and effective political power passed to a conventional cabinet consisting entirely of CPP members. Two years later a new constitution provided for a fully elected parliament of 104 members in which the CPP had 72 seats—reduced to 70 in 1956 at the last general election held before independence. The moderation shown by Nkrumah in the years after 1952 undoubtedly speeded up the transfer of sovereignty in 1957 and for about three years thereafter many observers felt that Ghana—as the Gold Coast was now called—demonstrated the universal benefits of rapid decolonisation. Certainly this was how it seemed to many potential foreign investors, such as Unilever.

But during the six years after 1960 the character of the regime in Ghana and its economic policies became more unpredictable. In 1960 a plebiscite confirmed Nkrumah as president for life and made Ghana a one-party state. British traditions in politics and administration were gradually discarded and state control of all aspects of the economy became intense. By 1960, also, the economic climate had deteriorated. There was an accelerating adverse balance of trade, due both to reduced cocoa prices and to government spending; and this resulted in a leftward shift in economic policy from 1961 to about 1963 which included a brief attempt to reduce Ghana's dependence on the commodity market by bartering cocoa for capital and consumer goods from eastern Europe. This policy was not sustained, but by 1966, when Nkrumah was deposed, Ghana was in a very serious economic and financial position and had ceased to be either an 'open' economy or a parliamentary democracy.

These developments provide the key to why Unilever found it necessary to reverse its earlier assumption that local manufacture on the Gold Coast was undesirable. In retrospect it is clear that 1953, the year in which Lewis's *Report* was published, was the turning point, not only for Unilever but for the future industrial development of Ghana. The very fact that the *Report* had been commissioned reflected Nkrumah's belief that large-scale investment was necessary both in the infrastructure and in industry. Although he believed in state socialism, he also accepted that rapid development in the consumer goods sector depended on direct foreign investment, and he seemed willing to attract such investment by providing tariff protection, tax concessions in the earlier years, guarantees for the safety of foreign property and state action to provide essential services. These were the carrots which were likely to attract Unilever and other foreign companies. But there was also a latent stick. Given the Ghana government's commitment to import substitution, foreign firms such as Unilever with a large established import market might be forced to invest in local production as a defensive measure in case they lost their market to others who set up local factories. Thus hope of profit and fear of loss combined to persuade Unilever after 1953 to calculate the costs and benefits of building a soap factory in Ghana.

The difficulty was that for some years after 1953 there was a great deal of talk in Ghana but no legislation or action on which firm decisions could be based. In 1953, for example, the Accra Chemical Works came up for sale, but it was rejected on the grounds that its output—585 tons—was unprofitable; that the short lease on the site made it uneconomic to invest in greater capacity; and above all that the import duties on oil remained and that Tema, when eventually developed, would make a much better site for any factory than Accra. Obviously, however, the underlying feeling was that Unilever should wait and see what happened and this marked the start of ten years of negotiation and planning. The first positive step was taken in November 1954 when Andrew Knox visited Accra and offered the Governor, Sir C. N. Arden-Clarke, a large investment of not less than £500,000 in a factory which, he said, would not increase profits but might protect the goodwill of Lever products. There were, however, three essential conditions for making this investment: import duties on soap must be increased from their then level of 5 per cent to 15 per cent or more *ad valorem* on hard soaps and to 25 per cent on toilet soaps; there must be no import duties on raw materials; and there must be adequate facilities for a factory at Tema. But, although many officials showed interest, Knox could get no promises from anyone. The Special Committee therefore decided that while 'Mr Knox had confirmed our willingness in principle to build a soap factory in the Gold Coast . . . under present circumstances it was not felt to be either commercially or economically sound to do so'. And there the matter rested until after Ghana had become formally independent in 1957, the only steps taken in the meantime being to apply for a site in the industrial zone being developed at Tema (in December 1956) and to make preliminary plans for a sales organisation.

In 1958, however, Unilever decided that a new initiative must be made and in April 1959 the Special Committee approved a new proposal to the Ghanaian government. The initial capital to be invested would now be much larger to provide greater capacity: £1,050,000 for fixed assets and £400,000 for working capital. Government participation could be discussed; but still the two essential conditions laid down in 1954 remained: an official commitment to the waiving of import duties on imported raw materials and the import duty on imported hard soaps to be at least 20 per cent *ad valorem* or its equivalent in specific duty. A modest return of 8 per cent was hoped for.

This marked the beginning of the final stage; but the passage was not smooth. For the first year all seemed to go well. In a letter of 23 July 1959 the Permanent Secretary of the Ministry of Trade and Industries in Ghana gave what seemed to be favourable assurances on key issues—'pioneer status' (i.e. postponement of tax liability from year to year), amendment to the duties on hard soap and exemption from import duties on raw materials. Initial confusion over the extent of government participation in the equity seemed to have been cleared up by October 1959, when it was heard that the government did not want a public holding at the start but would like 10 per cent of the shares to be available for private investors to buy later on at a reasonable valuation. On this basis planning went ahead; and by October 1960 it had been decided that the investment might amount to £1.3 million for fixed assets and £500,000 for working capital. Taylor Woodrow, in whose local subsidiary UAC had an interest, would be the building contractors and would begin to clear the site in November. Meantime, the government had duly increased import duties on soap as part of a major shift to a protectionist tariff.

But at this point serious difficulties began; in retrospect it can be seen that these reflected the turning point in Ghana's political and economic history which has already been mentioned. Unilever felt the impact of this new orientation of domestic and foreign policies very quickly. Official enthusiasm in Accra for Unilever's propositions clearly waned early in 1961 and this was reflected in obstructiveness, which Unilever could only meet by holding up or slowing down its investment programme. The Special Committee nevertheless decided to proceed with its construction work on the grounds that:

1. Withdrawal would indicate complete lack of confidence on the part of Unilever.
2. As long as we were proceeding with this project UAC were able to resist other investment invitations . . . .
3. The effect on the morale of UAC staff. Withdrawal would suggest to our expatriate and local employees that the concern did not offer a good future in Ghana.

So construction work went on. In September 1961 it was decided to appoint M. C. Hagan, a Director of UAC (Ghana) Ltd and a native Ghanaian, to be the first Chairman and Managing Director of the proposed new LB(G)—the first time a non-European had ever become the founding chairman of a local Unilever subsidiary. But still the vital assurances originally required by Knox in 1954 as the condition of the Unilever investment were not forthcoming. There had been verbal promises by Gbedemah and other ministers and the 1961 budget had doubled the specific duty on soap to £12 a ton; but there was still no written assurance of the 20 per cent *ad valorem* duty demanded, that import duties would be waived or of tax concessions, freedom to remit profits, etc. In the summer of 1961 it was therefore decided once again, as a precaution, to hold up shipments of factory machinery until definite and written promises had been received on the tax position, import duties, raw materials and import duties on soap.

The suspense continued until May 1962 when the first Ghanaian seven-year plan had been published. In April Hagan was told the government would not after all want to participate in the equity. Since this seemed to imply increasing lack of interest, Unilever decided to arrange a meeting between Sir F. Pedler as Managing Director of UAC and Nkrumah. Meantime Hagan should reiterate that the minimum condition for undertaking the full investment was a written assurance from the government that (1) no other local factory would receive better treatment than LB(G); (2) that they would be given protection against cheap imports—i.e. a 25 per cent import duty in place of the present 17 per cent or removal of the 30 per cent on imported tallow. If these were not forthcoming Unilever would sell the still empty factory building, which had so far cost £300,000. This, in fact, proved the final turning point. By May

1962 the Ghanaian government had accepted a report by Professor Bogner advising the government to accept capitalist as well as socialist investment. Thus, when Pedler saw Nkrumah on 2 May and told him that no decision had yet been given by his Ministers, the President charged Ayeh-Kumi, the new Minister of Industries, to look into the matter: eight days later the Unilever men were told that they would be given satisfactory answers on their two main points. On this basis David Orr of the Overseas Committee recommended completion of the factory, pointing out that once LB(G) was in full production it was much less likely that the government would wish a Czech enterprise or other domestic rival to set up the country's first large soap factory.

Unilever accepted this recommendation. The factory came into production by May 1963 and President Nkrumah formally opened it in August, giving it a Presidential warrant, equivalent to appointment to the monarch in England, six months later. The government stood by their promises: indeed imports of hard soaps were totally banned, so that LB(G) could increase its projected volume of sales to 27,000 tons in 1964 and 32,500 tons in 1967. There remained only the question of government participation and associated technicalities. Again the main difficulty was that by 1963/4 the Ghanaian government was so heavily in debt and so short of money that its instinct was to barter rather than pay cash for a shareholding. In March 1964 Unilever heard a suggestion that it should exchange 49 per cent of the LB(G) shares for 49 per cent of the equity in a textile printing factory partly owned by the government. This did not appeal to the concern; but after long negotiations a deal along these lines was arranged. The equity capital was kept down to £500,000—an exceptionally low proportion of the total capital employed of £2,207,000 at the end of 1965. The Ghanaian government acquired 49 per cent of the equity, partly for cash and partly by exchange of shares.

It is not proposed to discuss the early operations of LB(G) for the evidence available for the two years of operation (1964–5) would not support any valid generalisations. It is, however, necessary to summarise the evidence on why Unilever eventually built an expensive soap factory in Ghana and to assess the larger implications of this action.

The evidence shows that Unilever only decided to manufacture in Ghana in response to new developments there which compelled it to do so. It was perfectly happy with an export market that provided as much as £150,000 pre-tax profits in the 1950s and there is no indication in the records of hope that local production would provide a better return. But by the later 1950s the concern was faced with a stark choice: invest or probably lose an established import market to whichever enterprise, public or private, was allowed to set up the one large soap factory the Ghanaian market could support. Unilever chose to invest and was able to obtain what appeared to be very favourable conditions. Such a commitment was inevitably a gamble, since governments might change and conditions might be altered; but uncertain profit was at least preferable to certain loss.

The record of these four Unilever manufacturing companies in Black Africa suggests several general conclusions about the position of this and other multinational companies in that continent. First, this was clearly one of the least attractive regions in the world for any multinational whose overseas subsidiaries made goods for local consumption. The basic problem was poverty which inhibited demand. Very few of the vast range of Unilever products were within the capacity of most Africans to buy. Soap was the only thing in universal demand, and most of the soap sold in Africa had to be of the cheapest type that offered very low profit margins. But poverty was compounded by political and economic structures. Apart from Nigeria and Zaire, most political units formed by the colonial powers, though large by comparison with the preceding indigenous units, were far too small in population and resources to constitute viable markets for modern consumer industries unless these were given heavy protection. Decolonisation made this still worse because three relatively large common markets—French West and Equatorial Africa and British East Africa—subsequently broke up into their component parts. One typical consequence was that in 1964 Unilever decided not to build a large plant to make NSDs at Dar es Salaam (Tanganyika) on the ground that that newly independent country seemed likely to isolate itself from Kenya and Uganda on whose markets the profitability of such an enterprise partly depended. Among other deterrents to direct foreign investment were bad and expensive internal communications, fluctuations in purchasing power resulting from excessive dependence on the commodity market and, during the colonial period, tariff policies which did nothing to stimulate the growth of import-substituting industries. Given such deterrents, the surprising thing is not that

Unilever had so few African manufacturing subsidiaries during the colonial period but that it had any at all; and, as has been suggested, the companies in Nigeria and the Congo might never have come into existence had it not been for the personal initiative of William Lever.

The second point is that changes after 1940 had a limited effect on Unilever's basic assumption about Black Africa. The war and post-war boom in commodity prices, coupled with a large post-war influx of public and private investment, greatly increased buying power in many places; and these stimulated the first significant European and American investment in import-substituting industries in a number of countries. More important, official enthusiasm for industrial development, both in the last stages of colonial rule down to the early 1960s and still more after decolonisation, resulted in radical changes in the economic environment which greatly increased the attraction of Black Africa to foreign capital. It is, nevertheless, significant that Unilever founded only two new African manufacturing subsidiaries (other than those in which UAC had interests) between 1947 and 1965. Only one more, in Uganda, was set up before 1977, and this was a response to the weakening of the East African Common Market. Thus, while the economic policies adopted by most post-independence African states might in principle be expected to tempt a company such as Unilever, in practice it seems that the underlying socio-economic limitations that had inhibited direct investment before decolonisation retained much of their deterrent effect. For Unilever, at least, Black Africa remained one of the least attractive regions of the world in which to undertake local production for local consumption.

7

Unilever in Turkey[1]

Sheila Fieldhouse

The Genesis of Unilever-Is, 1939-50

The first surviving mention of Turkey as the site for a Unilever manufacturing subsidiary is a report made in 1939 by Sidney Van den Bergh, a member of the Overseas Committee until 1938 and then of the NV Continental and Overseas Committee, and G. F. Ferwerda. There is nothing to indicate why they were sent and the oral tradition, that they made a survey of the Turkish market when stranded in Istanbul on a flight from the Far East, seems likely to be a garbled version of the events that led Van den Bergh and J. J. Clerk to make a second report on Turkey in 1949. The 1939 report, in fact, was probably a deliberate investigation of a hitherto virtually unexploited market. It was comprehensive and constitutes an admirable starting point for this account even though, as will be seen, it did not lead to immediate action.

The main theme of the report was that Turkey was a large country, with a population of between 16 million and 17 million, which was in process of modernisation under a liberal government that encouraged private enterprise and foreign capital. Historically Unilever's interests in Turkey stemmed from three sources: the soap import trade established by Levers from Port Sunlight, margarine imported by Van den Berghs from Holland, and a trading firm, G. and A. Baker. By 1939 none of these was important. The earliest import figures for margarine now available are for 1923, when a mere 900 kg was imported. In 1924 this was down to 588 kg and thereafter Turkey disappears from the export figures. Earlier imports of edible fats had been larger, as much as 1,000 tons in one

419

year, consisting mainly of vegetable ghee; but in the 1920s the Turkish government under Kemal Ataturk imposed heavy duties and the import trade in edible fats had virtually been destroyed. It is impossible to determine just how big Lever Brothers' soap imports had been because the statistics group Turkey with Bulgaria and Greece, but they were certainly not large: the value of soap imports to these three countries for the three years 1930, 1933 and 1937 was £13,902, £9,608 and £10,168 respectively. Bakers was the most important Unilever interest in the 1930s. This was primarily an import business established during the nineteenth century in Istanbul and was one of the foreign businesses whose rights, including freedom to remit profits overseas, were secured under the Treaty of Lausanne of 1923, which had abolished most privileges previously held by foreigners under the Capitulations. Bakers owned a 60 per cent share in a small oil mill at Bakirkoy, near Istanbul, called the Yag Ticareti Co., the balance being held by the family firm of Messrs Isaac Modiano Frères et Fils of Istanbul. The mill was managed by Moise Rafael, Modiano's nephew, on a commission, but it was actually run by a Turk, Selim Bey, who had previously owned the mill. It was very small, in poor condition and operated for only part of each year. At most it offered a site for a factory should Unilever ever decide to build one in Turkey, though in 1939 the Bakirkoy mill was also being used to produce 32 tons of Vim a year with materials sent from Port Sunlight.

The significance of all this is that in 1939—and indeed a decade later—Turkey was unlike most of the other countries included in this study in that Unilever did not possess an established import market of any size from which local manufacture might grow. At most it represented a lost market for soap and edible fats which provided a challenge. This was how Van den Bergh and Ferwerda treated it. Had they been Lever men from Port Sunlight they might well have concentrated on the soap trade; but with a Van den Bergh reporting to the NV Continental and Overseas Committee it was not surprising that margarine and vegetable fats were given priority. The report noted that there might be an important market for 'a cheap and wholesome substitute of Butter and Clarified Butter as both these articles are outside the reach of the large majority of the population. We feel that a market can be created for these products additional to the existing market for Butter and Ghee.' They estimated this market at about 1,500 tons of margarine and 1,000 tons of ghee substitute, with the possibility of considerable further expansion after three or four years. They were encouraged in this by J. J. Hochstrasser, a Swiss national, who ran the sales side of Turyag, a subsidiary of Eastova Ltd of London with whom Unilever were partners in another industrial venture in the Middle East. Turyag owned an oil mill, refinery, hardening plant, margarine factory and soap factory at Izmir (Smyrna) and claimed to control 75 per cent of organised oil sales in Turkey. Hochstrasser admitted that Turyag had been unable to make margarine from the plant they had installed several years earlier, but said that if they could master their technical problems they could sell margarine to their capacity of 3,500 tons.

Van den Bergh and Ferwerda therefore decided that there was scope for Unilever to establish local manufacture of margarine and vegetable ghee in Turkey. They admitted that there were technical difficulties. The unstable currency was a problem and official permission would be required to remit profits. The latter problem could, however, probably be solved. The government already permitted royalty payments on Vim made at the Bakirkoy factory, Turyag was allowed to pay a management fee to Eastova in London, and as the government seemed keen to have margarine manufactured it might also permit the transfer of dividends. If the capital could be raised locally this could be paid off out of profits made in Turkey. There remained two alternative investment strategies. The first was to buy into Turyag by setting up a new company, in which Unilever would hold not less than 52 per cent of the shares. This company would buy out the existing hardening plant and margarine factory but would buy its oil from Turyag on a cost plus basis, leaving Turyag with their refined oil and soap business. This proposal had the advantage of eliminating competition since Turyag would agree not to manufacture or sell margarine or edible fats and it would also avoid delay while a new factory was built. If Turyag refused, the alternative plan was to build a margarine complex on the land adjacent to the Bakirkoy mill which would include hydrogenation plant for 2,500 tons and a margarine factory with 1,500 tons capacity and was estimated to cost about £25,000.

On either basis Van den Bergh and Ferwerda were reasonably confident: 'We believe that a market can be created for our Substitutes in addition to the existing market for Butter and Ghee and that we have a reasonable chance of having the market to ourselves for some years, or at least until we have been able to build up a strong position through the creation of a goodwill for our advertised proprietary brands.' On the prospects for soap they were more reserved. The market was 'in its infancy'; present soap sales were estimated at only $1\frac{1}{2}$ kilos a head, though the government was educating school children to use soap and a considerable extension of the trade was expected. Apart from Turyag, who only made 500–600 tons of mostly cheap laundry soaps, there was no modern competition, but a large number of small soap-makers. Indications were therefore that there were 'favourable prospects in the Soap trade which as yet have not been developed'. But they made no positive recommendations about soap and this reticence symbolises the order of Unilever's priorities in Turkey.

This report might well have been the starting point of a Unilever manufacturing subsidiary in Turkey. Unilever House accepted Van den Bergh's proposals and by June 1939 the concern was exchanging letters and documents with Eastova. But negotiations dragged on because Eastovas were not satisfied with the proposed allocation of shares and in March 1940 Unilever decided to shelve the whole project because of the Second World War. After that silence descends: there is no further mention of the factory proposal until 1948; and the only significant change that occurred before then was that Unilever acquired the balance of shares in the Bakirkoy oil mill as a result of the financial difficulties the Modiano family experienced when Italy entered the war. It is, therefore, difficult to determine whether there was any continuity of thinking in Unilever on the question of manufacture in Turkey. The possibility that Unilever House had not forgotten about the project is suggested by the fact that in 1948 the Special Committee asked the Contact Directors to discuss with Professor Mitrany, Unilever's adviser on international affairs, the prospects for forming a company in Turkey to manufacture margarine and ghee substitute. On the other hand J. J. Clerk, who was to be the first Managing Director of the Unilever business there, states that the original proposal was 'dropped entirely when war broke out and not revived as such later on'. In his account the revival of the project in a different form was the result of a chance visit to Turkey by himelf and Sidney Van den Bergh in 1949 when they had several days to wait in Istanbul for flights to and from Cyprus.

It was during those few days when walking around Istanbul that we made a mental note on matters like soap, butter, etc. and left it at that. Since . . . we had to go back the same way and with delays, Sidney and I agreed . . . to have a closer look at Turkey which we did. We spent a few more days there and visited Istanbul, Izmir and Ankara.

It was only then that the 1949 report was prepared, in fact I wrote it myself and we later on discussed it with both Overseas and Special Committees. Sidney did, in the process, mention that he had been there before the war but that report [of 1939] was never again referred to and was therefore no basis for further development. A merger or even taking over Turyag were discussed but almost immediately dropped.

The report made by Van den Bergh and Clerk was undoubtedly the immediate starting point of the Turkish business. In many respects they found conditions little changed since 1939. There was still no margarine manufactured in Turkey, despite the government's wartime intention of starting the industry, though shortly after the 1949 report was written a small factory in Istanbul started to make what it called margarine but was really a ghee substitute. Its maximum capacity was only three tons a day and it was clearly not a serious competitor. For their part Turyag had still not learned how to make margarine, though they were said to have spent a great deal on new equipment. Most important the government was very eager to see a margarine and vegetable ghee industry established in view of the shortage of butter and ghee. Van den Bergh and Clerk therefore recommended that Unilever should investigate the possibility of local production of edible oils and fats. They suggested that production should be at Bakirkoy. The existing oil mill should be enlarged so as to produce 2,000 tons of oil and hardening and margarine plant should be installed to produce 2,000 tons of hardened fat and ghee and 1,000 tons of margarine. In addition 1,000 tons of edible oil would be sold. These capacities were smaller than those proposed by Van den Bergh and Ferwerda in 1939 for the same Bakirkoy site. The novel and very important element in the new scheme was that the raw material would be sunflower oil whose production in Thrace had increased immensely in the past few years. This development was quite important for Turkish agriculture and the stimulus of the demand later created by the Unilever factory, together with the considerable technical assistance the concern could provide to the growers, constituted a significant contribution to the country's economic development.

This report was made in July 1949 and Unilever acted with remarkable speed. In September Clerk and two specialists from

Technical Division visited Istanbul to report on 'the minimum capital expenditure required' and to investigate other problems, including how best to approach the Turkish government. Their estimate of the capital cost was about £220,000 and there was reason to hope that the Turkish authorities would favour the project. This was accepted in London as a reasonable basis for further investigation and from October 1949 to December 1950 intensive negotiations took place. The main problem was how to provide the capital. Normally this would have presented few difficulties: Unilever would have borrowed part of the money in Turkey and provided the rest, particularly the currency needed to pay for imported equipment, in Netherland guilders. But in 1949/50 neither seemed possible. In Turkey credit and capital were in very short supply and the Netherlands were so short of foreign currency during this period of post-war rehabilitation that it was by no means certain that the government would provide foreign currency for the investment. Unilever had thus to search for funds at home and in Turkey and it was not until December 1950 that the problem was finally solved. The story can only be told briefly, but it is important because it resulted in the partnership between Unilever and the Is-Bank in Turkey that was to be central to the success of the business.

In Turkey the search for capital began with the Ottoman Bank and the Istanbul branch of the Hollandsche Bank-Unie. The former offered TL 2 million, but only as a short-term loan, the latter TL 400,000 as a short-term credit. Neither met the need. The next possibility considered was the Economic Co-operation Administration (ECA) which was giving Turkey considerable help at this stage. The ECA counterpart funds were jointly administered by the Turkish and USA governments and Unilever men discussed the project with both. The American mission was favourably impressed because Unilever were proposing to bring in TL 4 million and only wanted a loan of TL 2 million. But the Turkish authorities thought otherwise. They had refused several of their own nationals use of these ECA funds and did not wish to appear to favour a big foreign company. They made it clear that they hoped that, if they were denied ECA funds, Unilever would ultimately have to provide them in much wanted currency. Alternatively, as they impressed on J. J. Clerk and the two other Unilever executives who were negotiating on this issue, they would welcome participation by Turkish nationals as shareholders in the proposed Unilever company. The Minister of Finance therefore suggested that Unilever might like to get in touch with Mecit Duruiz, the General Director of the Is-Bank.

At this period Clerk was in touch with a number of possible sources of finance in Turkey, including the Gulek brothers, who were large landowners and had other financial and commercial interests. They were initially prepared to put up TL 2 million, but lost interest when they were offered only a 15 per cent share in the proposed company. The Is-Bank proved more rewarding. Unlike most other banks the Is-Bank did not confine itself to providing short-term credits and was prepared to take up and hold shares in industrial enterprises. Indeed, it had just gone into partnership with the General Electric Co. of New York and Vehbi Koc[2] to form the General Electric Turk Anonim Ortakligi, in which General Electric had 60 per cent of the shares, the Is-Bank 25 per cent and Vehbi Koc 15 per cent. The Is-Bank was therefore prepared to be co-operative. Assuming that Unilever's Turkish enterprise would have a share capital of TL 5 million, they suggested that Unilever should provide TL 4 million and the Is-Bank TL 1 million. The bank would then provide additional funds of TL 3 million to cover working capital, of which TL 2 million would be fixed and TL 1 million fluctuating. This seemed eminently satisfactory and the Is-Bank could be expected to provide political as well as financial support.

Before partnership with the Is-Bank was finally decided the ghost of the original project for collaborating with Eastova and Turyag had to be laid. Eastova had discovered that Unilever intended to manufacture margarine and vegetable ghee in Turkey and got in touch with Unilever House to suggest new terms of partnership. Unilever was attracted by the fact that Turyag possessed hardening plant; but, when Turyag decided to withdraw this plant from the projected joint margarine plant and to use it for soap making, Unilever called off the negotiations. In the event this proved wise since the Is-Bank feared the effect on public opinion if the new company obtained a virtual monopoly by eliminating the potential competition of Turyag and the Turkish Under-Minister of Commerce said his department would have had to lay down rules to prevent Unilever from abusing its monopoly position if they had become partners with Turyag.

This meant that the Is-Bank would be Unilever's only partners and from February 1950 detailed estimates of production costs and profit margins and of capital costs began to be made. A critical point was the time schedule for the provision of Unilever's TL

4 million share of the nominal capital, which was arranged as follows.

1. By 31 December 1950, TL 1.5 million, consisting of:

TL 650,000   land, and erection costs for building.

TL 250,000   purchase of Baker's assets (the oil mill and land).

TL 600,000   payment on formation of the new company, so that when the Is-Bank paid their TL 1 million half the share capital would be paid up in accordance with Turkish company law.

2. By June 1951, TL 2.5 million, consisting of:

TL 1,300,000   balance of working capital provided by Unilever.

TL 1,200,000   equivalent amount required for purchase of the plant.

It remained to get formal governmental approval of the project so that dividends and other transfers could be approved under Turkish Law 6224, which controlled foreign investments. At the same time Unilever defined, in the form of a credo, the prospective benefits of the business to Turkey, which they intended for submission to the government.

We believe that the enterprise will be beneficial to the Turkish Economy mainly for the following reasons:

(a) By using almost entirely indigenous raw materials, it will create a new outlet for agricultural products.

(b) By making available products of a high nutritive value, it will increase the general standard of health in this country.

(c) By a policy of reasonable selling prices, it will assist the Government in their aim of reducing the cost of living.

(d) It will, once the products have been accepted by a large part of the population, including the armed forces, free considerable quantities of oils, such as olive oil, for export.

(e) It can, particularly if exports could be arranged under Turkey's trade agreements with other countries, play a certain part in the Government's export drive.

The government in any case welcomed the proposal. On 8 June 1950 the Minister of Finance wrote a letter to Unilever which said: 'I am pleased to inform you that the transfer of nett earnings on the foreign capital invested in Turkey by your firm in order to establish a vegetable oil plant has been agreed in principle.' It seemed that the last hurdle had been cleared. On 22 July Clerk received a letter from Mecit Duruiz summarising the four main points on which agreement had been reached: the Is-Bank and Unilever would jointly form a company to manufacture margarine and edible fats; the company would have a share capital of TL 5 million, to which the Is-Bank would subscribe 20 per cent and Unilever 80 per cent; the Is-Bank preferred that Unilever should take full responsibility for the technical and commercial side of the business; and finally,

> The Is-Bank appreciates that should, against expectations, no satisfactory solution be found for creating the funds in Turkey required by Unilever, or should no satisfactory guarantee be obtained, Unilever reserve complete freedom to reconsider the principle of their proposed investment in Turkey.

On this basis detailed plans for the new factory went ahead and it was decided to call the company Unilever-Is Turk Ltd Sirketi.

But it was by no means certain that the currency problem would be solved by the first deadline of 31 December. When Sidney Van den Bergh had first discussed the Turkish project with the Director of the Netherlands Bank in February 1950, stating that they would need foreign currency amounting to TL 2.65 million, the Bank had agreed to make this available in sterling. Subsequently, however, under pressure of acute foreign exchange difficulties, the Dutch government had changed its position and attempted to force Unilever to earn the necessary foreign exchange by exporting Dutch goods to Turkey. This was rejected by the Turkish authorities and Unilever was forced to investigate a number of other ways of acquiring Turkish currency. None proved viable and by December 1950 the situation was becoming critical. Sir Herbert Davis, the Vice-Chairman of Unilever, who had been against the Turkish venture throughout, could now point to the serious legal consequences if the Netherlands Bank continued to be obdurate and prevented Unilever from fulfilling its commitments; but Sidney Van den Bergh remained unperturbed. He understood unofficially that the Netherlands Bank were unlikely to persist in their refusal to allow the investment in Dutch currency if all possible alternatives had been tried and he was right. On 28 December 1950, three days before the completion date agreed with the Is-Bank, the Dutch authorities gave formal permission to transfer Fl. 5.4 million, partly in cash and partly in machinery. The first tranche of Fl. 2.75 million (TL 2 million) would be transferred in January 1951 to fulfil Unilever's commitments.

Unilever-Is, 1951-65

This marked the effective birth of Unilever's Turkish enterprise and the next stage in the story concerns the process of company building and the problems a multinational company may experience in establishing a new overseas venture. The first team of managers was appointed late in 1950. J. J. Clerk, who had been involved since his visit in 1949, became Managing Director, Dr Kac Sales Director, Roodhuyzen Technical Director and F. Van den Hoven (later to become Chairman of NV) Chief Accountant. Mr Muammer Eris, a brother-in-law of the President, was appointed by the Is-Bank as political adviser. At this stage the full value of a multinational company became obvious in the flow of experts who arrived in Istanbul to advise and help the nascent company. Bicker Caarten, an expert on marketing margarine, spent 18 days in the autumn of 1951 investigating distribution problems. His visit overlapped with one by J. C. A. Faure who came to discuss the purchase of raw materials. After discussions with Suphi Argon, an advisory director of Unilever-Is who was on the board of the Industrial Bank and knew a great deal about the oils and seeds market, Faure agreed with Clerk that cotton, sunflower and sesame seeds should be bought direct from the farmers because of the shortcomings of the facilities and service provided by local middlemen. Eight days after Caarten's visit R. B. Ratcliffe, who was to be in charge of advertising, arrived and analysed promotional possibilities. His conclusion was that the budget should be divided in the ratio press 67 per cent, radio 14 per cent, shop demonstrations 5 per cent, exhibitions 9 per cent, display material 4 per cent and printed matter 1 per cent. The emphasis on the press was a tribute to the increase in literacy. The radio budget was relatively small partly because Turks without a mains electricity supply saved their batteries by turning them off during advertisements. Late in 1952, as the opening date for the factory approached, technical experts came from Rotterdam to deal with teething problems. Everything was in order by December 1952.

Long before that stage Unilever-Is ran into an obstacle which exemplifies the difficulty a multinational may face when using its standard production methods and product formulae overseas. During the summer of 1950 a draft law intended to define margarine was remitted for consideration to a committee of three senior Turkish scientists. Their conclusion, that margarine must be made by 'shaking fat with cream', surprised and disturbed Unilever men because the standard European method of making margarine was with water rather than milk. They had considerable difficulty in persuading the committee of the better preservative qualities of margarine made by the European method but in the end the formula defining methods of manufacture was dropped from the draft regulation. The Turkish scientists also accepted the use of a preservative and the addition of vitamins, together with proposals to reduce the minimum fat content from 86 per cent to 80 per cent and to fix 36 °C as a maximum melting point of each fat used rather than restrict it, as originally proposed, to a lower than human body temperature. Professor Ural, the Chairman, promised to give favourable consideration to the use of carotene, butyric acid and ethyl butyrate as colouring and flavouring matter and the committee was provided with Danish and Swedish government regulations on margarine manufacture. The company promised to send samples of margarine with and without a milk content for analysis and the question of adding a percentage of water was shelved for the time being.

Even the efficiency of a Unilever team could not ensure punctual completion of the factory. The official opening was postponed from June to August to October 1952 and it was finally opened with a flourish on 5 January 1953, attended by many eminent men including the President of the Turkish Republic and, very appropriately, by Paul Rijkens, Chairman of Unilever NV and Sidney Van den Bergh who between them had carried the project through the difficulties of the previous three years. But once the factory was in production efficient planning immediately paid off. There was a weekly turnover of 50 tons of Vita vegetable ghee and 20 tons of Sana margarine. What was more, the Quartermaster General ordered 300 tons of vegetable ghee for the First Army Corps and 20 tons of table margarine for army hospitals, prisons, etc. Sidney Van den Bergh exulted: 'Our brand name on all packets and tins will get known through the soldiers to every hamlet in Turkey.' He was right. The Vita tins, which were used for many purposes including (after being flattened) roofing houses, were the means by which publicity spread to many parts of Turkey which could not have been penetrated by normal advertising for a very long time. It was, in fact, Vita vegetable ghee rather than Sana margarine that ensured the initial success of Unilever's manufacturing enterprise in Turkey in the first stage because ghee was a product already in general use and Vita, as a much cheaper substitute, was almost certain to sell well as soon as the public became aware of its quality and price.

Yet ultimately good profits in Turkey depended on establishing a substantial market for margarine; and in achieving this Unilever faced two problems characteristic of LDCs: it had to surmount legal and technical difficulties relating to the nature of the product and, more important, it had to create a market. In 1953 Clerk had to deal with one technical and two legal problems. The outcome of the earlier government committee on the nature of margarine was that the authorities finally decided on 37 °C as the legal melting point for margarine and alleged that the melting point of Sana was 42 °C. Clerk was not satisfied by their methods and hastily invited a leading German scientist in that field, Professor Kaufman, to visit Turkey and discuss the question with the Turkish scientists. Fortunately he was able to convince them that Sana complied with the new regulations. Another outcome of the same official investigation was that margarine was classed as a manufactured product on the grounds that it contained added vitamins, flavouring and colouring, and this made it liable to a 15 per cent tax. This was serious since Turyag, Unilever's main competitor, paid no tax on their butter and hardened fats. Sidney Van den Bergh therefore saw the Minister of Finance during a visit in April 1953 and obtained a document exempting Unilever-Is from this tax. This made a difference of TL 40,000 to the results for the first three months and Clerk therefore reduced the price of Sana to pass the saving on to the public. Finally the company had to face a technical difficulty that resulted from using sunflower oil. At the start the sunflower oil when hydrogenated became brittle and wet and this caused the margarine to fall to pieces. Stocks of poor quality had to be taken back twice and this so unnerved the technical director that he resigned. A temporary solution was found by using cotton-seed oil rather than sunflower oil but in course of time the technical difficulties associated with sunflower oil were resolved.

With these initial problems out of the way it remained to persuade Turks to use Sana and Vita in place of butter and ghee. Table 7.1 shows that they did so very readily and that the original estimates of the market proved very pessimistic. It is, however, less easy to explain this astonishing volume of sales. It was certainly not due to intensive promotion since advertising expenditure shown in Table 7.2 was exceptionally low. Probably the two main reasons were rising demand and the relatively low price of Unilever products. Demand for edible fats was swollen by the incoming tide as the population of Turkey rose from 21 million in 1950 to 31 million in 1965. Production of butter and natural ghee could not keep pace with this surge, partly because cattle were being replaced by tractors and pasture by arable; this created an expanding market for good quality substitutes in margarine and vegetable ghee. A closely related factor was that prices of these natural foods rose as demand outran supply. Unilever-Is, by contrast, was able to keep the price of its margarine and vegetable ghee well below that of butter and natural ghee because the price of its raw materials did not rise as fast. This was the composite result of efficient buying of domestic raw materials such as sunflower seed and of the good fortune that imported oil from the USA was available under PL 480 at relatively low prices. This oil was used with the agreement of the Turkish government, although it was resented by local oil producers, because they knew that the cost of living would increase if cheap oil imports ceased. As a result, to take January 1962 as an example, fresh salted butter of the Trabizon type cost TL 13 a kilo as compared with Sana margarine at TL 6 a kilo. Even the superior quality Supra margarine, sold only in Ankara, was a mere TL 7 a kilo. Melted butter (urfa) then cost TL 11–13 and olive oil TL 8 a kilo, while Unilever-Is sold Vita at TL 5.50–5.75 a kilo and sunflower oil at TL 5.50–6.00 a kilo. These margins were very important in Turkey where the average income was then estimated at TL 1,625. As J. P. Somerville wrote in a marketing survey in 1962, 'women want butter but can only afford Vita'. In that year Unilever estimated that out of a total market for edible fats and oils of 166,370 tons, only 18,000 were butter and natural ghee. It was these conditions that provided Unilever-Is with so satisfactory a market.

It would, however, be wrong to give the impression that once the

Table 7.1   Turkey: Unilever-Is Sales (by Brand), 1953—65

Year	Sana (table margarine) Tons	TL'000	Vita (ghee) Tons	TL'000	Marga (ghee) Tons	TL'000	Bakery fats Tons	TL'000	Sundry Tons	TL'000	Total Tons	TL'000
1953	770	2,339	5,264	14,499	200	435	30	92	n/a	n/a	6,264	17,365
1954	1,835	5,496	9,874	26,683	1,246	2,788	47	141	n/a	n/a	13,002	35,108
1955	2,609	8,624	14,121	42,884	90	256	83	276	n/a	n/a	16,903	52,040
1956	4,033	14,853	18,262	61,666	n/a	n/a	174	658	n/a	n/a	22,469	77,177
1957	6,699	26,437	21,043	76,704	n/a	n/a	372	1,519	n/a	n/a	28,114	104,660
1958	9,372	43,923	25,295	109,504	n/a	n/a	541	2,644	n/a	n/a	35,208	156,071
1959	9,165	46,716	30,746	147,778	n/a	n/a	510	2,558	n/a	n/a	40,421	197,052
1960	10,299	54,031	33,901	165,052	391	1,789	603	3,075	n/a	n/a	45,194	223,947
1961	12,013	64,635	39,088	193,495	476	2,163	628	3,273	n/a	n/a	52,205	263,566
1962	13,831	74,257	45,628	225,874	529	2,416	817	4,246	16	105	60,821	306,898
1963	16,097	92,417	45,400	229,662	2,420	11,100	1,883	10,095	121	758	65,921	344,032
1964	15,951	90,608	56,217	286,983	3,674	16,791	1,906	10,236	107	572	77,855	405,190
1965	16,534	92,295	46,123	236,214	2,764	12,493	2,069	11,025	190	1,016	67,680	353,043

initial teething problems were over Unilever-Is had no further difficulties. Turkey, in fact, was typical of many LDCs in that, while it offered an excellent market to the enterprising firm that took advantage of latent opportunities, it also presented problems seldom found in more affluent countries with 'open' economies. Between 1953 and 1965 the company in fact faced two main obstacles: recurrent difficulties in obtaining sufficient raw materials and official restrictions on the range of its products.

The supply problem was summed up by (Sir) Ernest Woodroofe in the Directors' Conference of Unilever in May 1964:

> one of our major problems is getting raw materials. I get the picture of our business always tottering on the brink of running out of materials but nevertheless always managing to carry on, although this involves a good deal of Government contacts and lobbying ministers and others.

This had been true from the start. Not only had the management to know about producing and selling their products, they had to negotiate to obtain permits and licences to get raw materials and to use foreign currency to pay for other things. To take one example, Klijnstra, visiting Istanbul in June 1958, reported that

> Stocks of packing materials and chemicals are exhausted at the factory, but at the customs cover for 4–5 weeks is awaiting release. The release can take place as soon as a licence document is signed by five ministers; those of Finance, Commerce, Industry, Customs and the Minister of State, plus a President of the Bank of Turkey. This document was promised us several months ago, but only at the time of writing these notes did the last Minister sign. It meant that our factory was idle for about two weeks. Muammer Eris, Smit and Van den Hoven spent half their time in Ankara chasing Ministers.

J. J. Clerk recalls that he often spent whole days from 5 a.m. sitting near the lift in the Hilton Hotel, Istanbul, or some other place, hoping to catch a minister and get him to sign a vital document.

The reason for these delays lay in the chronic balance of payments problems experienced by most LDCs. The government delayed mainly because the foreign currency to pay for imports was simply not available and they hoped to gain time until the autumn when the

Table 7.2   Turkey: Unilever-Is Trading Summary, 1956–65 (Turkish £'000)

Year	Net sales value	Gross profit	% NSV	Advertising	% NSV	Marketing expenses	% NSV	Factory and gen. expenses	% NSV
1956	77,917	11,354	15	1,013	1	1,815	2	2,043	3
1957	105,957	16,939	16	671	1	2,420	2	3,275	3
1958	158,718	25,839	16	672	1	3,378	2	4,234	3
1959	200,759	31,161	16	1,616	1	5,073	3	6,169	3
1960	228,448	35,647	15	2,998	1	6,309	3	7,933	3
1961	268,889	39,185	15	3,891	1	7,748	3	9,156	3
1962[c]	315,315	50,388	16	5,023	2	8,640	3	11,271	4
1963	355,539	57,163	16	6,354	2	8,784	2	12,801	4
1964	424,070	68,871	16	8,679	2	10,110	2	13,984	3
1965	376,242	61,281	16	8,852	2	10,564	3	14,660	4

Notes: a. Includes HO charge 1963 onwards.

b. Including tax gifts 1964 onwards.

c. Includes as from 1 July 1962 the detergents and toilet preparations business which G & A Baker took over from McNamara.

export of new crops brought in more foreign exchange. This often affected payment of overseas debts. Unilever men reported on one occasion that 'The mineral oil companies leave their tankers just outside the three mile limit, where they actually wait until payment for that ship has been given'. In the same way Unilever-Is' outstanding debts for chemicals imported in 1956 had not been repaid in 1958; and although in August that year the company was granted a licence for the transfer of £80,000 for this purpose, at the last moment the State Bank imposed a 'moratorium'. This meant that allocations of foreign currency could be used only for importing new materials, not to pay old debts, and the management had to try to get this decision reversed. Dependence on foreign economic aid caused similar supply problems. Scarcity of oils and fats in Turkey led to the import of foreign vegetable oil and the Americans began to supply cotton-seed oil under their aid scheme, PL 480. By 1962, partly due to the orobanche disease, which had ruined most of the Turkish sunflower crop, Unilever found itself relying on American

Other trading items[a]	Trading profit before tax	Nett profit after stat. tax	Stat. tax rate[b]	Gross capital employed	
					% yield after tax
575	6,508	4,978	23.5	25,505	19.5
947	9,626	7,364	23.5	42,622	17.3
512	17,043	13,038	23.5	49,469	26.4
158	18,145	13,881	23.5	73,154	19.0
384	18,023	11,534	36.0	85,157	13.5
426	17,964	11,497	36.0	99,108	11.6
1,545	23,909	15,302	36.0	106,874	14.3
4,483	24,741	15,834	36.0	104,073	15.2
5,071	31,027	19,857	36.0	133,697	14.8
5,543	21,662	13,864	36.0	149,868	9.3

imports for 70 per cent of its oil. Klijnstra summed up the consequences in that year.

> The drawback of having to rely on P.L. 480 is that contracts are concluded by Government officials who are not sufficiently aware of the need for continuous supply. Consequently we are at present heading towards a crisis, as it looks as if we may have to close the factory in February or March for some weeks.

The most significant limitation imposed by government policy on Unilever-Is, which is again characteristic of the 'managed' economies found in many of the LDCs studied in this book, was that diversification was strictly limited. The most important aspect of this was soap, which will be described below. On the edibles side the natural line of development, once the edible fats business was fully launched, was to go into convenience foods. This had been planned in 1954 but by 1965 the company had still not obtained a licence to manufacture chicken noodle soup, mayonnaise or any similar product. Other projects were throttled by the refusal of licences to import raw materials, again due to the desperate shortage of foreign exchange. In Unilever House there are pages of recipes for and pictures of Turkish cakes and sweetmeats; yet Unilever-Is never had a sufficient flow of raw materials to make as much shortening and cooking fats as could have been sold to the manufacturers of these popular products.

Lever Brothers (Turkey) Ltd and the Soap Problem

The most surprising feature of the Unilever business in Turkey before 1965 was that it made and sold so little soap. It is evident throughout this book that soap was historically the basis of Unilever's expansion outside Europe and that a Unilever subsidiary that did not make substantial quantities of soap (and later NSDs) was almost a contradiction in terms. Yet in Turkey they sold only 3,647 tons of soap and detergents in 1965, consisting of 964 tons of Lux Toilet Soap, 2,416 tons of Vim scourer and 243 tons of Omo, an NSD. In the same year they sold 67,680 tons of edibles. There was no local manufacture of any other Lever Brothers' soaps, nor were these imported; and the only other product Unilever made in Turkey was TL 23,199 worth of toilet preparations. Yet in 1962 total sales of soap and detergents in Turkey was 83,235 tons, of which 72,360 tons were hard soaps. The question must therefore be why one of the world's largest manufacturers of soap made virtually none in Turkey; and, alternatively, why, if there were insuperable obstacles, Unilever bothered with such relatively very small quantities of toilet soaps and scourers.

The answer to the first part of the question is simple but important for the study of limitations on the power of a multinational: Unilever could never obtain a licence under Law 6224 to manufacture laundry soap or NSDs and remit the profits. It has been seen that the concern received permission under this law in June 1950 to make margarine and vegetable ghee. In 1954 a licence was also granted to make toilet soap and scouring powder, but critically this did not include laundry soaps or NSDs. At the time this did not seem to matter much because Unilever was preoccupied with the early stages of the margarine and vegetable ghee enterprise and they therefore used their licence to make toilet soap and Vim on a small scale in conjunction with a small local manufacturer called Couteaux whose business will be described below. But by 1958 circumstances again made it desirable to attempt to obtain permission to make laundry soaps and NSDs. Competition in toilet soaps was coming from a local firm, Puro, who had also obtained permission to erect an NSD tower. Another local firm was expanding its sales of soap powders. Couteaux's Bell factory was too small to enable Unilever, through its new soap-making subsidiary, Lever Brothers (Turkey) Ltd Sirketi (LB(T)), formed in 1952, to expand production of Lux Toilet Soap and Vim to compete effectively. By 1958, therefore, it seemed evident that, if Unilever could not start large-scale production of soap and detergents, it might lose all chance of becoming leader in this market. Alternatively, if it built a new factory that made only toilet soap and scourers, this would suffer from diseconomies of scale. Thus success now seemed to depend on obtaining permission to make laundry soaps and NSDs.

This, at least, appears to have been the analysis made by the local Unilever management in 1958, supported by visiting experts from London. By 1960 plans had been drawn up for a new venture in which both the Is-Bank and Couteaux would participate and negotiations began with the government over application for a licence under the Foreign Investment Law 6224. It was at this point that a serious obstacle became evident: the Turkish soap-makers, mostly operating on small scale but numerous and well-entrenched, made it clear to the government that they would strongly object to Unilever as a powerful outsider being given a licence to make laundry soap, which was their stock in trade. Possibly because of their complaints the government advised Unilever to drop laundry soap from their application and this was done. On this basis the application was successful: in the summer of 1960 the government issued a licence for importing plant to make NSDs and orders were placed. But this proved a false dawn. There was a change of government in Turkey, the local soap-makers protested against the NSD licence on the grounds that it would affect their sales of soap and the new Minister of Industry informed Van den Hoven, now Managing Director of both Unilever-Is and LB(T), that he could only proceed with the venture if the entire product was exported. Unilever cancelled its orders for equipment. A year later another chance for Unilever to take part in NSD production seemed to have arisen. Puro were unable to operate their NSD tower and invited Unilever's participation in a joint venture. By the beginning of 1962 plans for a new enterprise, involving Puro as well as Unilever, the

Is-Bank and Couteaux, had been prepared; but while these were being got ready the Turkish soap-makers heard about the project and again organised protest meetings. Unilever decided to test the climate of opinion before making formal application to the government and its representatives were present at two of these meetings.

They found that opposition was extremely strong. The tone was summed up in one statement which Eris, who represented Unilever-Is at the soap-makers' meeting held in Istanbul, reported as follows:

> We do not want a foreigner to come to the country and carry on the business of soap. Because we are afraid. If a rich company such as Unilever starts this business it means we are all ruined. Now I would like to tell you something; we are capable of manufacturing soap, we know this business. We Turks can make soap and detergent.

The parallel conference held at Izmir felt equally strongly and decided 'to go as high as the Prime Minister to kill the Unilever soap project'. Two manufacturers said that if they failed they might as well take the keys of their factories and leave them with the Prime Minister. These protests had the desired effect: Puro decided to withdraw from the proposed partnership and Unilever had lost the last opportunity it had, at least before this book ends in 1965, to enter the soap and detergents field on a substantial scale.

There remains the question of why they failed in Turkey where they succeeded in so many other places. Explanations must be speculative but the most likely are as follows. First, Lever Brothers had not undertaken local manufacture in Turkey before the establishment of the Republic and so was not covered by the terms of the Treaty of Lausanne. Then, during the 1920s and 1930s what had been a substantial import market for Lever soaps was virtually destroyed by the high import tariffs and import restrictions imposed by the new government and these in turn stimulated the growth of a large number of small local manufacturers whose products were not comparable in quality with those of a company such as Levers but which were acceptable to the mass of Turkish consumers. After 1945 conditions changed in some respects. Most post-war Turkish governments were anxious to stimulate industrialisation and welcomed foreign capital where no local enterprise could fill a particular need. A Lever soap factory would certainly have been more efficient and would probably have produced better and cheaper soap than the local makers. On the other hand the chronic balance of payments difficulty made all governments reluctant to bring in foreign enterprises which might, on balance, cost more in foreign exchange through repatriation of profits than they saved by substituting for imports; and in the case of laundry soap and NSDs, though not of toilet soaps, it was not clear that a Lever soap and NSD plant would produce any savings on imports. Finally, to add emotion to economic logic, many Turks appear to have been prone to recurrent waves of xenophobia, which were a product of their history. Since the sixteenth century the Ottoman empire had been forced to concede foreigners extensive legal and commercial privileges under the Capitulations. In 1919, after five years of almost continuous fighting, the empire had been completely over-run and seemed about to be finally dismembered. Only the astonishing efforts of Mustapha Kemal rescued Anatolia and a small area north of the Bosphorus and forged it into a new, modern Turkish state. In the early 1960s the Republic was only 40 years old and determined never again to be dominated by foreigners in any respect. In its own way the response of the soap-makers to Unilever's soap project and the government's reaction to it typified the ambivalence of Turkish reactions in the later twentieth century to contacts with the outside world.

For all these reasons it seemed unlikely in 1965 that Unilever would ever manufacture soap or NSDs in Turkey on a large scale. The fact nevertheless remains that when Unilever received a licence to make toilet soap and scourers in 1954 they manufactured these things in a small factory in Istanbul on what was perhaps the smallest scale and under the most unusual commercial circumstances in the history of the Lever/Unilever business. This can only be explained in terms of historical accident; and, although it is of little importance for the present study, the story is worth telling briefly as an example of how a partnership might evolve between a multinational and a comparatively small local business firm which, in other circumstances, might well have led both parties into co-operation in large-scale soap production.

The story began in 1920 when Lever Brothers started to sell Sunlight Soap and other Port Sunlight products to a general import company in Istanbul called McNamara. This had been bought by a Belgian family resident in Turkey called Couteaux in 1918 and after 1922 the youngest of three brothers, Gabriel Couteaux, ran the McNamara business. He established close contacts with Levers when he visited Port Sunlight in 1922 and by 1930 he had started to manufacture Gibbs dentifrice *à façon* for Thibaud Gibbs, a Lever subsidiary in France, on a royalty basis. The Second World War was really responsible for Couteaux's eventual position as a local partner with Unilever in a manufacturing enterprise. Until 1939 Vim had been mixed and packed at the Unilever oil mill at Bakirkoy but during the war Unilever could no longer deliver raw materials to Istanbul and this gave Couteaux the idea of making Vim out of local materials. He and two Turkish employees searched until they found silex on the shores of the Black Sea. He got millstones to grind the silex and faced them with granite to keep the powder as white as possible. In a short time he was manufacturing Vim *à façon* and paying royalties. But other Port Sunlight products were cut off by the war and soap was in short supply in Turkey. Couteaux therefore bought a very old private house in the heart of Istanbul called the Bell House. He converted it into a primitive factory, made his own Bell Soap there, and then obtained permission to make Lux Soap Flakes, again on a royalty basis. After the war he sent his son-in-law to Port Sunlight to learn how to boil soap in the Lever manner. By 1951, when (Lord) Geoffrey Heyworth and Sidney Van den Bergh visited Istanbul to take stock of conditions, they found that Couteaux was ambitious to extend his Lever range and make Lux Toilet Soap; and at this point Unilever had seriously to consider future policy. Should they continue to entrust one after another of their premium brands to a small independent firm operating under relatively primitive conditions in old Istanbul or reserve their attack on the Turkish market in the hope that sooner or later they might be in a position to manufacture there on a satisfactory scale?

Heyworth and Van den Bergh seem to have decided to trust their fortunes to Couteaux. Their decision may have been influenced by the fact that at about the same time the Turkish firm Puro, which already sold toothpaste and aspirin, had started to sell toilet soap, and this threat of competition with imported Lux Toilet Soap from within the Turkish import tariff may have induced them to use Couteaux to defend their established market. The only alternative seemed to be to build a Unilever soap factory and, as has been seen, it was by no means certain that the Turkish authorities would give a licence for this. Since the market for toilet soap was small, a Lever factory making only toilet soap would probably not have been viable even if it was permitted. It was for these reasons that Unilever decided to enter the Turkish soap market in as limited and inconspicuous a way as possible and therefore decided that this was best done in partnership with Couteaux.

The outcome was that Unilever set up LB(T) in 1952 with the share capital divided in the proportion 75 per cent Unilever and 25 per cent Couteaux. Two years later the government gave LB(T) a licence which entitled them to repatriate profits arising from their share in this company and permitted LB(T) to manufacture Lux Toilet Soap and Vim. But, although Unilever now had a soap company in Istanbul, they had no factory: the new company had therefore to operate from Couteaux's Bell House. This caused major problems and led ultimately to the attempt already noted to get permission to expand the soap business to the point at which it would justify building a new and much larger factory. From 1952 Unilever experts attempted to improve the technical efficiency of the Bell factory but there were limits to how far they could go. In 1954, after five months of production, Klijnstra was horrified by the quality of Lux Toilet Soap made there: it discoloured with age, was wasteful in consumption and the perfume deteriorated or disappeared. People were prepared to pay more for Port Sunlight Lux Toilet Soap smuggled from Cyprus than for the local product. Quality was thereafter improved but there was a strict limit to the quantity that could be made. In 1955 Klijnstra predicted that the Bell factory might eventually produce 400 tons of Lux, but there it would have to stop: 'That is the maximum capacity of the Bell factory, which will always be an inefficient production unit'. 1957 proved the psychological turning point. LB(T) was making only about 15 tons of Lux Toilet Soap a month, due to the difficulty of obtaining licences for imported raw materials, and production was estimated to be 30–50 per cent below demand. In April Klijnstra reported after a visit that it was time to review the whole set of arrangements by which Couteaux made Lux Toilet Soap for LB(T) and Vim for McNamara, still on a royalty basis. Sooner or later Unilever would have to take responsibility for making and selling its own soap products in Turkey. Two years later Van den Hoven, pursuing this theme, estimated that LB(T) could sell 1,000 tons of Lux Toilet Soap in 1960/1 if they could produce it, rising to perhaps 2,000 tons, half the total market for toilet soap, by 1964. The result was the attempt to obtain a licence to build a factory to make not only toilet soap and Vim but also laundry soap and NSDs in order to ensure a large enough turnover to carry overheads.

This attempt, as has already been seen, failed; and failure left

Unilever to pick up the pieces and decide what to do with LB(T) and its continued dependence on the Bell factory. By 1962 a move was imperative: as Klijnstra reported in December, under the heading 'Emergency Move', an Istanbul University professor had investigated the Bell factory and concluded that it was so dangerous that a slight tremor or vibration would cause the whole place to collapse. Klijnstra had tried to delay the move until they knew whether they could get a licence to make NSDs and could then build a new complex for all their soap and detergent activities but now they could no longer risk staying on. All the LB(T) moveable equipment was taken out of the Bell factory and stored at Unilever's tin-making plant at Gungoren. It was later moved again to a small rented factory at Eyup and from there in 1965 they sold 964 tons of toilet soap, 2,416 tons of Vim and 24 tons of Gibbs shaving sticks. This, in the words of a Unilever Technical Division report, was 'a good short-term method of economically manufacturing products pending a decision on a longer-term plan for expanding our share of the soaps, detergents and toilet preparations market in Turkey'.

These words could easily have been written about Couteaux's Bell factory in 1955 and it might seem that the wheel had merely gone full circle. Unilever was still waiting for an opportunity to deploy its resources. But there had been movement. Collaboration with Couteaux had at least given Unilever a toehold in the Turkish soap market at small cost and very little risk. As a by-product of their unsuccessful application for a licence in 1960 the concern now owned a factory site near Bakirkoy; and if the wheel of fortune ever happened to turn their way Unilever would be poised to take advantage of it. This was from the start and remained in 1965 the main explanation and justification for their policy of making such apparently ridiculously small quantities of soap products in Turkey.

Rewards and Results

Three questions remain: the light this story throws on the position of a multinational in a developing country; the rewards Unilever obtained from its Turkish enterprises; and the significance of their activities for the Turkish economy. On the first point the evidence of Unilever's relations with the Turkish government fully supports the general proposition that is repeated throughout this book that, however powerful a multinational company may appear to be from the outside, it is virtually powerless in the face of the government of a country in which it wishes to make goods for local consumption. At every stage Unilever had to operate on conditions laid down by the Turkish authorities. They had local partners in both Unilever-Is and LB(T) because this was essential to satisfy local requirements of different kinds. To manufacture at all and be free to remit profits to Europe they had to have a licence. Once granted this could be revoked; and even if it was not, permission had to be obtained before any dividends were remitted. The concern had to apply for permission to import all raw materials or machinery, even if no foreign currency was required and the imports were a gift from Unilever. When Turkey was in difficult financial circumstances the government could and did discontinue all royalty payments abroad. At any time the authorities could have closed down the two Unilever businesses merely by cutting off the permits for raw materials on which the two factories depended: like all other foreign-owned enterprises Unilever's only security was the fact that such action was likely to make it difficult for Turkey to attract foreign capital in the future. In few overseas countries was Unilever more aware that it existed by grace and favour of its hosts.

Nevertheless, though living dangerously, Unilever lived well in Turkey during this period. The financial results are summarised in Table 7.2. Between 1951 and 1965 issued share capital rose from TL 5 million to TL 41.8 million, of which 75 per cent belonged to Unilever, the rest to the Is-Bank. In the same period Unilever transferred TL 49.2 million in dividends and the Is-Bank received TL 12.3 million. No payments were made to Unilever in the form of service fees or royalties. The dividends paid by Unilever-Is were, however, only about a third of the total pre-tax trading profits made: they were kept at this level partly because the business needed funds for expansion, partly because the government were happy to allow that proportion of profits to be transferred. If the trading profit for the decade 1956–65, for which full financial information is available—a total of TL 188.6 million—is broken down according to how it was applied, TL 58.5 million went in taxation, TL 52.4 million was retained in the business, TL 11.9 million went to the Is-Bank and TL 47.6 million was transferred as dividends to Rotterdam. Thus only about a quarter of the total profits made by the business was withdrawn from the Turkish economy and the Turkish government benefited more than Unilever from its activities.

Nevertheless the return to capital in Unilever-Is was consistently very good and among the highest of any Unilever subsidiary, fully justifying the remark made by Woodroofe in 1964 that this was 'one of the gems of the Overseas Committee's Crown'. We must therefore consider why the return was so satisfactory and in particular whether it was due to the ability of Unilever-Is as the sole local manufacturer of margarine and vegetable ghee on any scale to exploit the Turkish consumer. Examination of the composition of the nett profit and comparison with another successful Unilever subsidiary shows that this was not so. Gross profit as a percentage of nett sales value was remarkably low—never more than 16 per cent in the decade after 1956 compared with a maximum of 38 per cent in South Africa; and this was lower than for any other company surveyed in the course of this study. Clearly the Turkish consumer was not paying a high monopoly price. But this leaves the question of why, with so small a mark up, Unilever-Is could still produce such high nett profits as a percentage of gross capital employed. By tracing costs across the lines on Table 7.2 the explanation emerges: this company had remarkably small overheads. Advertising was 1 or 2 per cent of NSV compared with 5 per cent rising to 14 per cent in South Africa; marketing expenses 2 to 3 per cent, compared with 4 or 5; and 3 to 4 per cent on 'factory and general expenses' as against 7 to 8. The result, to take the single year 1960, was a total expenditure of 7 per cent of NSV on these things in Turkey compared with 20 per cent in South Africa. The other main item was taxation and there the difference was not so great. The statistical tax rate in Turkey was low at 23.5 per cent from 1956 to 1959 and then rose to 36 per cent. In South Africa it was 30 per cent to 1960, then between 32.8 per cent and 34.5 per cent.

Thus the basic reason why Unilever-Is could combine low profit margins with high profits was that it was able to keep its costs remarkably low, notwithstanding high distribution costs in Anatolia due to large distances and lack of roads. This in turn was possible because of exceptionally favourable all-round conditions. Apart from soaps, which were not important, all production was carried out in a single new, highly mechanised and efficient factory. The greater part of the production consisted of two things, margarine and vegetable ghee: there were no losing marginal lines. Unilever-Is was the only large-scale firm during this period that made either of these products with vegetable oil and water without using animal fats and they had no effective competitor in either field. This meant that, apart from the need to 'educate' the Turkish public to accept substitutes for butter and ghee, which seems to have been done very quickly, there was no need to spend large sums on advertising: there was no brand rivalry. Finally, through efficient buying in Turkey and the good fortune of oil being available at relatively low prices from the USA under PL 480, it was possible to keep raw material costs to reasonable levels. The paradoxical result was that in Turkey the monopoly held by a foreign multinational resulted in high profits without high prices.

There remains the question of what benefits Turkey received from the margarine and ghee business. The financial benefits have already been mentioned: they were considerable even though at that time corporate taxation in Turkey was light by the standards of some other LDCs. But the government's main aim in encouraging Unilever to come in at the start had been to have a cheap and wholesome substitute for butter and natural ghee to feed the rising population. This Unilever provided. If the price index for Vita, Sana and the general cost of living in Turkey are taken to be 100 in 1953, by 1963 Vita had risen to 180, Sana to 184 and the cost of living to 270. Or, to take another example, if the price index of Vita, Sana, sugar, rice, bread, olive oil, animal ghee, beef, white cheese and dry beans was 100 in 1958, by February 1963 Vita was 112, Sana 118, sugar 129, rice 170, bread 182, olive oil 200, animal ghee 200, white cheese 207 and dry beans 313. Turkey was thus getting relatively cheap foods from Unilever, helped by the ability of Unilever-Is to make use of comparatively cheap imported raw materials; and it did not follow that any other firm could necessarily have provided the same benefits since these depended on mass production, experience in hardened fats and a wide range of technical and other skills which relatively small Turkish firms did not possess. The point, that Unilever-Is justified its position by making the most efficient use of Turkish resources, can be illustrated anecdotally. Muammer Eris took a visitor from the Board of Managers of the Chamber of Commerce to see Unilever-Is the day after he had visited another local factory; and after seeing the technical department, refinery, production department and laboratory of Vita, he said in front of the company's chief chemist that he wished he had not seen the other factory 'because I feel as if I came down to New York from a village in a remote spot'.

This was the main benefit Turkey looked for and received from Unilever, but there were others. From the start Unilever-Is aimed to replace Europeans by Turks as soon as possible for all the reasons already examined in earlier chapters. By June 1958, five years after the start of production, there were only ten expatriates out of 534 employees: by 1976 only the Chairman of Unilever-Is was an expatriate. The company, of course, offered a career open to local talent: an able Turk could rise to become a director and this was seldom possible for any but the family in the typical Turkish family business. For the work force as a whole Unilever-Is was an exceptionally good employer, setting high standards in a country only just experiencing large-scale industrialisation. Wages were relatively good: in 1961, for example, a government clerk in the bottom grade earned TL 3,600 a year while an unskilled factory hand in Unilever-Is earned TL 5,000. Working conditions and other facilities were well above normal Turkish standards: for example, the company supported a co-operative housing development for members of the staff.

In more general terms Turkey illustrates the point that a large multinational can be of service to an LDC in many ways and a few concrete examples can be given. It was to Unilever that the government turned in 1951 when an American who was responsible for developing the Turkish fishing fleet with ECA dollars disappeared, and Unilever was able to put them in touch with the Nordsee management in Bremerhafen. Unilever participated in the government's groundnut scheme in 1955; and when in 1962 Turkey's sunflower crop was ruined by orobanche disease, the company supplied Turkish farmers with an orobanche-resistant strain of sunflower seed with a higher oil yield which they obtained from Russia via France. In 1964/5 Unilever started a venture in exporting jasmin to increase foreign exchange earnings, though this had little commercial advantage for the concern. Unilever-Is was the first company in Turkey to sign a collective agreement with a trade union, which they did as soon as collective bargaining had been legalised. Unilever managers played an instrumental role in a variety of public activities, for example in founding and supporting the Management Association, the Social Conference Board, etc., which were new and needed support as Turkey developed into a modern society. Unilever-Is was one of the first Turkish companies to sell their products at the same price and quality in all parts of the country. Turks were apt to comment that this enabled them to travel in Turkey from the Greek to the Russian border without getting indigestion from using different fats in each place they visited; and this was made possible by the establishment of a standard Unilever system of depots and links with distributors throughout the country.

In more formal terms, the factory at Bakirkoy had valuable backward and forward links into the Turkish economy. It was largely responsible, through the stimulus of demand and by providing seed with higher oil content, for increasing the local sunflower crop from 50,000 to 150,000 tons. This benefited farmers and helped to end Turkey's dependence on imports of vegetable oil under PL 480. Forward linkages included stimulus to can and box makers and the transport industry. In sum, while to many Turks the presence of Unilever constituted a regrettable invasion, the evidence suggests that the government successfully restricted Unilever's range of activities and was able to extract maximum benefit for the country at minimum cost.

8

Lever's Pacific Plantations Ltd.

Plantations and Business Strategy

In the Unilever overseas empire plantations occupy a peculiar and somewhat uncertain position. Why, after all, should a business built on manufacturing soap and margarine concern itself also with the production of palm oil, palm kernel oil and coconut oil, not to mention cocoa, coffee, tea, rubber and other tropical commodities? In principle there might be two different reasons for doing so—horizontal diversification and vertical integration—and these must be defined.

Horizontal diversification might well be undertaken by any large international business with a fund of knowledge of those countries in which tropical commodities such as vegetable oils could be produced, simply as a means of spreading risks and using resources. What the plantation actually produced would not be important since it would be sold on the world market and would not be for consumption by the parent manufacturing company. Thus Unilever invested on a limited scale in tea plantations at Mweso, in Zaire, not because of its association with Liptons but partly because the Belgian colonial authorities were anxious to develop Kivu, which had the lowest wage rates in the Congo, and partly because in their own judgement tea would prove profitable in that part of Africa. Again, the large-scale timber operations undertaken by United Africa Company in West Africa and the Pacific were a form of horizontal diversification and even plantations producing vegetable oil, with which this study is primarily concerned, might well have been acquired in the same way.

In principle at least vertical integration has a different function, which may be either defensive or offensive. The basic aim is to undertake production and possibly intermediate processing of the raw materials required by the parent manufacturing company. If the object is defensive, the aim will be to ensure a supply of materials against the danger of world shortage and market-rigging operations by other producers or middlemen. Conversely, if production and processing are undertaken on a sufficiently large scale, these might provide an offensive commercial weapon, for the plantation owners might drive down the general market price and so reduce their own manufacturing costs. Alternatively, they can adjust production in order to supply their own industrial needs, fixing the internal transfer price so as to enable them to undersell industrial competitors, selling any surplus on the market at a substantially higher price. It must, however, be said that, because of the variety of areas in which vegetable oils are produced, the scale of the world market and, most important, the possibility of substitution between oils, it has never been possible for any one producer or even a cartel to harness market forces in these ways.

If the Lever/Unilever plantations in Africa, the Pacific and Southeast Asia are seen in terms of these two categories, it is clear that their intended function changed over time and that in the end they do not exactly fit either model. The first copra and palm oil plantations set up before 1914 by William Lever were clearly part of a defensive policy of vertical integration, designed both to safeguard his soap business against a predicted secular shortage of vegetable oils, and also to give him freedom to make his own arrangements, and formed part of the same strategy as the acquisition of West African trading companies. To complete this defensive strategy, Lever after 1916 built up his own merchant shipping fleet for the West African trade as a defence against the alleged machinations of the West African shipping conference, then led by Elder Dempster.

This was undoubtedly Lever's original concept. Yet by the 1920s it had been substantially modified; and the reasons will become clear from these studies of his experience of the Solomon Islands and Congo plantations. In essence, once his plantations began to produce copra and palm oil on a substantial scale, Lever realised that, as both producer and consumer, he was in a schizophrenic state. If world prices were well above plantation production costs, he might, as manufacturer, benefit from selling his vegetable oil at market prices and where possible use cheaper substitutes, such as whale oil, in his factories. If, on the other hand, world prices were below plantation production costs, there was no benefit to him as a manufacturer in paying himself as vegetable oil producer an artificially high price for his own plantations' product. Moreover, if he chose to fix internal transfer prices arbitrarily, so that, for example, the oil was always below market price, he was merely reducing the profitability of his plantation companies; and if he tried to help the plantations by adopting some formula which ensured their profitability, he was handicapping his soap factories. Such problems have already been noticed from the standpoint of Lever manufacturing companies in Australia, Nigeria and the Congo. These were on a small scale; but, if artificial internal transfer pricing had been a general feature of the Unilever system, the economic dislocation would have been serious.

Thus from about 1920 the existing Lever plantations in the Solomons and the Congo, together with the later plantations in Nigeria, the Cameroons, Malaya and Sabah, must be regarded as a form of horizontal diversification. From the standpoint of the men who had run the Lever empire after his death in 1925, the existing plantations were in many ways an embarrassment. But they, along with much else in the Lever conglomerate of the 1920s, were an integral part of a business which had long outgrown logic. The plantations existed; it was unlikely they could have been sold at a price reflecting the substantial investment made in them; and there was no reason why under normal conditions they should not be made to yield reasonable profits. Indeed, once commodity prices recovered from the slump of the early 1930s, new, smaller and more sophisticated plantations were set up by UAC at Calabar in Nigeria and at N'dian in the Cameroons; and after the Second World War new and very successful plantations were bought or built in Malaya and Sabah. Thus in the end the Unilever plantations must be seen in terms of horizontal diversification rather than of vertical integration.

All this is well known. The purpose of Chapters 8 and 9 is not to demonstrate the obvious but to examine the history of two Lever/Unilever plantations from this standpoint. Those chosen are the first to be established: Lever's Pacific Plantations Ltd (LPPL) in the Solomon Islands and Huileries du Congo Belge (HCB). It is proposed in each case to show in greater detail why and how these were established by William Lever; how well they fulfilled his original expectations down to 1920; when and why they ceased to be regarded as directly relevant to his industrial activities; how they were organised once they had become autonomous enterprises, and their relations with other concern companies; and finally how they performed as profit-making enterprises. Although in relation to Unilever as a whole these plantations have limited importance, the story will be told in some detail because it throws light on the motives of those Europeans who invested in tropical plantations early in the twentieth century and because these developments are of considerable importance for the domestic history of the territories concerned.

Origins of the Solomon Islands Plantations

It is impossible to document precisely when and why William Lever decided to extend his industrial activities into commodity production. His son stated in his biography that his father 'had first given consideration to the question of producing his own raw materials in the Tropics in 1896' when he was offered, and refused 'a large tract of land in New Guinea'. [1] No mention of the idea has survived in his correspondence or in the formal records of Lever Brothers between then and 1901. Thereafter he showed consistent enthusiasm for commodity production until his death: indeed the Congo enterprise ranked with his schemes for the Hebrides in his later years. The first question must therefore be whether the decisions he took between 1901 and 1914, which committed Lever Brothers to very large investments in the Solomon Islands and the Belgian Congo, stemmed from a rational assessment of the market or from a more general and possibly romantic enthusiasm for the idea of developing the tropics.

A reasonable case can be made out either way. First, the trend of prices in the oils and fats market would support the argument that it was only after the early 1900s, and more specifically from 1906, that there was any marked and sustained upward trend in prices. According to Hopkins, West African palm oil prices reached £45 a ton in 1854–61, but then declined to an average of £20 a ton in 1886–90 and did not regain their earlier level until after 1906. Palm kernels also dropped from about £15 a ton in the 1860s to around £10 in 1886–90. Senegal groundnut prices followed a similar pattern. [2] Wilson's data, though differing slightly, also indicates that prices of cotton seed, tallow, copra and palm oil were all fairly consistent and low during the twenty years after 1885. Copra began what proved to be a sustained (though fluctuating) increase from about 1903, palm oil from 1905 and tallow, although also fluctuating wildly, from the same period. From then until 1920 the price of all fats and oils remained high, reaching peaks between 1915 and 1920. They then collapsed abruptly and in the 1930s dropped to well below even the level of the 1890s. Meantime the retail price of Sunlight Soap remained constant from 1896 to 1913, apart from a small and short-lived increase from 1906 to 1908.[3]

This makes it unlikely that Lever saw any serious threat to the profitability of his soap business resulting from a secular increase in raw material prices until after 1905; and this would explain why his major initiatives—restructuring the Pacific business, the purchase of MacIvers to get a foothold in the West African commodity trade, and the negotiations for the Congo concession of 1911—all came after that date. But it is still possible that, even before 1905/6, Lever foresaw or feared that the steadily increasing consumption of oils and fats, particularly by the expanding margarine-makers of Europe, would eventually force prices up and create shortages. If so, while he may not have felt any great urgency, he was quite likely (given his forward-looking and speculative bent of mind) to have become interested in plans for increasing the world supply and to some extent insuring himself against a future rising market. The available evidence certainly supports this hypothesis and helps to explain his readiness to respond to proposals put to him for an initial investment in the Pacific islands. The story of how this first venture began has been told before; but it is necessary to recapitulate it both as a basis for what followed and also because there are inconsistencies between previous accounts. Moreover Lever's activities in the Solomon Islands constitute an interesting footnote to the last stage of the partition of the South Pacific, and the account will be somewhat more detailed than that given of the manufacturing companies already described.

There seems little doubt that it was Lever's visit to his copra oil mill and soap factory at Balmain, Sydney, in 1901 and his subsequent voyage across the Pacific in the company of J. T. Arundel that started him off on the Solomon Islands venture. The oil mill depended on Pacific copra and its profitability varied with copra prices, since coconut oil was to some extent competing with tallow in Australia. Lever may, therefore, have been receptive to any proposition that would provide Balmain with cheaper raw materials. Nevertheless in J. T. Arundel Lever met a promoter who had been selling commercial projects in the Pacific to more or less susceptible investors for many years and had recently persuaded men with much better knowledge of the area than Lever had that production and trade in copra and phosphates was not only a profitable investment but would also be good for the islanders. His own trading firm was J. T. Arundel Ltd; and in 1897 he had bought out another trading company, Hendersons, to form the Pacific Islands Company (PIC). More surprising, he had persuaded Lord Stanmore, Sir Robert Herbert and Sir John Bramston to be shareholders and directors. Since Stanmore, as Sir Arthur Gordon, had made his reputation when, as the first Governor of Fiji from 1875 to 1882 and as High Commissioner for the Western Pacific, he had resolutely defended 'native' interests in the islands against rapacious Europeans; and as Herbert and Bramston had each spent an official lifetime as Permanent Under-Secretary and Assistant Under-Secretary respectively of the Colonial Office, it was reasonable to assume that Arundel's company would not only be honest but also equipped with expert knowledge of the area.

In retrospect the PIC can best be seen as one of the last of those private commercial ventures which had taken a leading role in the establishment of British, German or French political and economic control in countries ranging from Africa to the Pacific. But by 1901 it was an anachronism. The political map of the Pacific was fixed as it was to remain until the First World War; and, although imperial control over those territories allocated to Britain, and therefore open to the company's trade, was still weak, the official mind now rejected administration by private companies. Thus the PIC was forced back onto the more limited role of trading and acquiring land in islands already under British control to obtain copra and phosphate. Arundel's wide knowledge and trading contacts made it easy to acquire land, plantations or concessions and by 1902 PIC had properties or trading interests in many islands. These were mostly in the eastern Pacific but Stanmore believed the best prospects were in the Solomons, which had only become a British protectorate in 1893 and where there was still ample land not acquired by Europeans or occupied by islanders. Moreover the Deputy Commissioner in charge of the Solomons, C. M. Woodford, was concerned that he could only ensure continued British rule by raising revenue to pay for his administration; and that in turn depended on 'attracting a big company prepared to invest large sums in opening copra plantations'.[4] In 1899 Woodford took a PIC agent round the Solomons and offered him occupation leases for 99 years. There were outstanding claims by the German company, Deutsche Handels-und Plantagen-Gesellschaft (DHPG), but when these had been bought out in 1902 the PIC acquired something over 200,000 acres on 99-year leases for low rents.

In about 1899, therefore, it seemed likely that the PIC would develop along lines similar to the DHPG, as a trading enterprise which also owned land and plantations in a number of islands. But by the time Arundel met Lever in 1901 the company's attitude had been changed by the discovery of phosphate deposits on Nauru Island, in the Marshall Group, and on Ocean Island, near the Gilbert and Ellice Islands. Nauru was a German protectorate and the German trading company, Jaluit Gesellschaft (JG) had claims there. It was not until 1900 that PIC, in alliance with JG, obtained a mining concession from the German authorities that was to last until the year 2000. Ocean Island was within the British sphere of influence, though not technically part of the Gilbert and Ellice Islands Protectorate, and in 1900 the Colonial Office issued a licence enabling the PIC to export phosphates from the island for 21 years at a rent of £50 a year. In 1901 this was revised to give the company the exclusive right to work the deposits for 99 years at a royalty of 6d a ton from 1 July 1906. Phosphate was not gold but it was one of the most valuable organic minerals, in great demand in Europe and North America where agriculture had increasingly depended on the importation of additional fertilisers, such as Pacific guano. Like many other concessionary companies, the PIC, once it had discovered easily exploitable minerals, quickly lost interest in copra plantations, which required infinitely more administrative effort and were a far more speculative investment. Stanmore, it is true, continued to believe in the possibilities offered by the Solomon Island concessions, but from 1901 there was no doubt that the PIC would put its main effort into exploiting its one special asset, phosphate.

It was at this point that Arundel had the opportunity to talk to Lever about investments in the Pacific; and as a company promoter in need of money for his phosphate venture, Lever must have been a godsend. Arundel's immediate need was for a new cash investment in PIC. He had had to accept the JG's demand that a separate company be formed to exploit the Nauru phosphate deposits, which would be jointly owned by PIC and JG. Its nominal capital would be £250,000, of which £50,000 would be working capital; and JG would be given £25,000 in shares in payment for the rights it conveyed to the new company. To raise money to exploit Nauru and Ocean

Island PIC had therefore two alternatives: it could capitalise the prospective value of its new phosphate concessions by selling shares in the PIC; or it could sell off some of its existing properties elsewhere. The first could be done without difficulty provided the investing public was convinced of the potential profitability of the Phosphate Co.; but to find a buyer for widely dispersed trading stations and barely established copra plantations was more difficult. Lever, as a rich man who was already interested in production of copra, was an ideal candidate.

Yet, although this might seem to resemble the classical situation in which the wealthy amateur falls victim to the wily company promoter with his bogus prospectus and misleading statistics, and even though Lever later described the islands he bought from the PIC as 'practically a gold brick', he also stated categorically that it was he, rather than Arundel, who took the lead on the voyage to San Francisco.

> When Mr. Arundel mentioned to myself on the voyage across the Pacific from Sydney to San Francisco the financial difficulties the Pacific Islands Company were in I advised Mr. Arundel the best lines to take to preserve the interests of the original Shareholders in the Pacific Islands Company. Mr. Cayford agreed that my advice had been acted upon, that it had saved the interests of the original Shareholders in the Pacific Islands Company, and that Shares that were practically valueless are now saleable, £1 Shares at 52/- each, but holders are not willing to accept this price for them.

There is, then, no suggestion that Lever was deluded into investing in a moribund venture. On the contrary, he probably saw the double opportunity to acquire coconut islands cheaply, because PIC needed the money urgently, and at the same time to make a potentially profitable investment in the phosphate venture. As will be seen, he made a very careful investigation into PIC before committing his money to it; and the only thing he did not examine carefully was the actual island properties he was to buy.

The proposal that emerged was that Lever should buy £25,000 of shares at par in a new PIC, to be called Pacific Islands Company (1902) Ltd, and also to buy the old PIC's interests in a number of the smaller islands, leaving PIC(1902) with its phosphate claims and leases in the Solomon and other islands. This seemed favourable to both parties. PIC(1902) would get £50,000 cash towards the cost of establishing the phosphate company, while Lever, who had no experience in Pacific island enterprises, could buy the results of years of work by Arundel. Nevertheless Lever was not a novice in company promotion. Soon after he arrived back in England, which could not have been much before December 1901, he looked into the finer points of Arundel's offer. His first discovery was that most of the island properties he was offered were held on short leases, which, as he pointed out to Arundel in a letter of 20 December 1901, offered little chance of profitable investment in plantations:

> The cost of planting cocoanuts [sic] is exceptionally heavy. I believe heavier than almost any other planting, and in addition thirteen years has to elapse before the plants are in full yield.
>
> Bearing these facts in mind and the heavy cost of maintenance during the unproductive period, I do not see what your company has to offer to its Shareholders for investments [sic] of capital in cocoanut planting. If land can only be had on short leases . . . such business has no interest for myself and those associated with me. Can you not acquire the freehold or 99 years lease of such islands for cocoanut planting?

Lever was, of course, quite right, and this is probably the first time he came up against Colonial Office policy on land tenures in areas such as the South Pacific and West Africa which was to thwart him during the next ten years. On this occasion, however, Stanmore was able to persuade the Colonial Office to offer new leases of 99 years on the ten islands to be transferred to Levers, though they insisted on a low rent plus a royalty of 5s a ton on copra exported during the first five years and $2\frac{1}{2}$ per cent *ad valorem* thereafter. Lever protested that 5s was too high and Arundel managed to persuade the Colonial Office to reduce it to 2s with the promise that if this still proved too high it could be reconsidered.

Lever also found cause to doubt PIC's financial position and profit record, for in February 1902 he asked his accountants, Cooper Brothers, to investigate. He seems to have been satisfied, for, when PIC issued the prospectus for the new PIC(1902) on 18 March 1902, it was stated that Lever Brothers had agreed 'to purchase the cocoanut interests . . . for £25,000 in cash, and to invest at par value a further £25,000 in the reconstructed Pacific Island Company . . . '.

By June Lever's intentions were sufficiently well known for Sir Henry Jackson, Governor of Fiji and High Commissioner for the Western Pacific, to approach him and ask if he would undertake to mill the copra which was paid to the government in lieu of tax by Fijians. Lever agreed, but in return asked for various forms of government help in making the proposed oil mill profitable, including free delivery of government copra, freedom from taxes on imported goods needed by the mill, use of the government wharf, a free site for the mill on government land, etc. Nevertheless, although by now committed, Lever, perhaps scenting that the only real asset PIC(1902) would have was the phosphate company, insisted that his £25,000 investment in PIC(1902) should entitle him to that value of shares in the phosphate company, and that these should stand in his name rather than, as was intended for all other phosphate company shares, in that of PIC(1902) and the Jaluit Gesellschaft. He got his way, presumably because his cash was critical: PIC had to sell £60,000 debentures at a discount of 5 per cent that year to meet their liabilities. But Stanmore sent him an agonised letter begging him not to sell any of the phosphate shares to third parties until the company was in production for fear of giving the impression that its prospects were poor.

From that point the history of Pacific Phosphates has little direct connection with Lever's plantation interests and his later association with it can be summarised briefly. The company did very well, especially after doubts about its Nauru concession were cleared up in 1905. It paid some large dividends and its authorised capital was increased successively from £250,000 to £875,000 by 1910. Lever felt it was too good to be true: in 1908 he wrote 'the prospects are so bright that one almost feels nervous in these days of sudden slumps and surprises, earthquakes and convulsions that the reports are too good to be realized'.[5] He hung onto his shares, and transferred them to LPPL in 1904 as part of their capital assets. Additional shares were taken up as the capital expanded, and in 1910, when LPPL needed cash, Lever bought them back with his private fortune at the market price. In 1918 he sold them to Lever Brothers, who in turn were paid £700,000 cash plus shares in a subsidiary, the French Phosphate Company, when the Pacific Phosphates Commission compulsorily acquired the Nauru and Ocean Island phosphate deposits in 1920. The shares had turned out to be one of Lever's best investments; and, although he normally refused to make portfolio investments, he used this as the text for a lecture he gave to a colleague in 1920 on the virtues of not selling assets when the price became temptingly high or frighteningly low. That ended Lever Brothers' connection with Pacific Phosphates; but twenty years later the fortunes of Ocean Island were again linked with those of LPPL. By then phosphate extraction had made the island virtually unin-habitable and the Phosphates Commission looked around for a suitable island on which to resettle the inhabitants, the Banabans. By that time LPPL had decided to sell Rabi Island, off Vita Levu in the Fiji Group, one of the properties it had bought from PIC in 1902. The Commission bought Rabi in 1942 and moved the Banabans there, lock, stock and barrel, three years later. More than thirty years later still the Banabans were engaged in a law suit in which they claimed immense damages for the value of the phosphate taken from their island.

In 1902, therefore, Lever had acquired island leases from the original PIC for which he paid £25,000; and this, together with the investment in Pacific Phosphates, was the patrimony of LPPL, founded the same year, with a nominal capital of £50,000. Through-out the later part of the year he remained enthusiastic about the new venture. He had hoped to visit the island properties himself, but pressure of work made it necessary to send Harold Greenhalgh, who thus began a long connection with Lever Brothers' plantations there and also in the Congo. But bit by bit the difficulties became apparent. The first part of the original scheme to be jettisoned was the proposed Fiji oil mill, which fell through because the Fiji government refused to commit itself to a long-term contract for the quantity and price of government copra to be milled there. As Lever commented to Arundel in November, 'It was quite bad enough under our own proposal to have the quantity indefinite, but to have both quantity and price indefinite makes it an impossible proposition'. This made it pointless to make Fiji the centre of the intended copra business, and it was decided that instead copra would be shipped direct to the copra mill at Balmain. Doubt then arose whether there would, in fact, be any significant quantity of copra to send. The new LPPL properties produced only 337 tons in 1902; the trading stations provided negligible quantities; and, to make matters worse, the market price of copra fell dramatically later in the year. Lever ascribed the last to 'two important factors, one the large corn crop in America . . . the other the opening up of the West Coast of Africa by railways, which have brought enormous quantities of palm oil and palm kernels to the coast'. This was, of course, good for Lever Brothers as a whole, but it called into question the future of LPPL.

Lever was determined to persist. In 1903 he was considering buying the Fanning and Washington Islands and told the Balmain management to buy a £10,000 vessel to carry his island trade. Yet 1903 proved in many ways a year of disillusionment. In February he wrote to Arundel of the difficulty of getting a coconut business onto a sound footing since all the accounts were showing a loss; and in April he ruefully commented that

there is not the profit in the copra business that people imagine. Our figures for the properties we took over from the Pacific Islands Company prepared for 1903 from estimates, show that we cannot possibly avoid a loss during 1903. The profit made during 1902 was made on abnormal market conditions, and these have long since ceased. The existing copra is valued at £4 per ton lower than 1902 and the prospects are of it being lower still before the end of the year.

Arundel tried to reassure him; but already Lever was evolving a more sophisticated attitude to copra, and indeed to commodity production as a whole, which was to become the basis of his later policies both in the Pacific and Africa.

During 1903/4 Lever seems to have reached three conclusions. First, that to be profitable, commodity production must be on the largest possible scale: 'the Pacific is not a field of operations where small profits can prevail. The many contingencies I think to be faced necessitates large profits . . . . In my opinion with their present rate of production of copra these islands must result in a loss for many years to come.' Second, that the profitability of plantations must be taken one year with another, and seen as the obverse of his manufacturing activities: 'The inducement to Lever Bros. has been that in times of scarcity when copra is high, the Islands may make a profit, and it is just at such times that such profit will be welcome. I only hope that the balance of lean years and fat years will mean that we shall hold our own.' But the third principle was much more important for his future actions: the overall objective of creating vegetable oil plantations from the standpoint of the industrialist who used them must be to increase the total supply so as to tilt the balance in his favour, rather than to supply his own factories direct from the plantations. This argument emerged from an exchange of letters with R. Barrie, a Port Sunlight executive who, expressing the characteristic attitude of most British and European industrialists, argued that vegetable oil production was outside the proper limits of the soap business and must therefore be seen merely as an investment. This stimulated Lever in August 1904 into writing out a considered statement of his evolving assumptions.

For many years now this [Nut Oils] market has been becoming a more and more difficult one. It was for this reason I felt we ought to be doing some pioneer work, with regard to increasing the supply of Coprah [*sic*]. You may depend upon it that if Coprah growing is an industry that cannot be brought onto a systematic basis of cultivation and production, we are not likely to get much relief in increasing the supply of this class of Nut Oils. The recent use of Coprah Oil for edible purposes increases our difficulties. There is no corresponding increase in production. To leave the production of Coprah in the hands of natives, who stop producing as soon as they have supplied their own limited wants, will not give the world the Coprah it wants. We want the market as much over-done as the Tea-Market is over-done with Tea. Since the failure of Coffee in Ceylon, planters have been turning their attention to Tea, both in Ceylon and India. Coffee in other parts of the world has recovered, and Tea is being produced in enormous quantities in Ceylon and India. The result is, that Tea and Coffee to-day are extremely unprofitable to the grower but extremely profitable to the consumer. We want the same position with regard to Coprah and Palm Kernels, and nothing is being done, as far as I know, in a systematic fashion, in any part of the world to give us this result . . . We are the most interested in this question of any firm in the world, and we have got to make some attempt to relieve the position. Otherwise, what may be represented by 100,000 pounds expenditure now, might cost us many hundreds of thousands a year in the future. It is all a question of whether the supply should be 10% below the requirements or 5% above them. If 10% below the requirements, prices will rule high. If 5% above the requirements, prices will rule reasonably in our favour. It is not a question of the money to be put in the Cocoanut properties that would be the difficulty, but the difficulty is that neither ourselves, nor (as far as I know) our predecessors, who had islands in the Pacific for 30 years, nor any available source of information—Governmental or other—know anything at all practically upon the subject of systematic growing of Cocoanuts. Under these circumstances we shall have to pay for our experience, and we must go as slowly and as gently as we can until we see our way more clearly, but on the general principle that we ought to be doing some pioneer work, I think there can be not the slightest doubt whatever.

Barrie nevertheless did doubt:

pioneer work may be all right for us, but the difficulty always seems to me to be, that no appreciable quantity of product can be produced by any one concern, and if an appreciable quantity was produced, the undertaking, with its allied industries, would be much greater than the making and disposing of Soap from such material, while we can always depend on the economic force of high prices encouraging production and curtailing consumption, thereby producing an equilibrium in due time . . . . In any case, the market value will always govern the position, no matter who produces the stuff, and if Oils from these products remain very high compared with other Soap making materials, less would have to be used, or a higher price obtained for Cocoanut and Kernel Oil Soap.

Records of the debate stop at this point but it is clear that the difference between them lay in Barrie's assumption that no one commodity producer could put enough into the market to affect the world price, whereas Lever still believed that he could do so with sufficient effort. There is no doubt that from then onward his primary aim, both in the Pacific and in Africa, was to operate on a scale sufficient both to produce profit by economies of scale and, more important still, to exert a measurable influence on the world commodity market for oils.

In the Pacific this policy was quickly reflected in Lever's conclusion that the islands bought from PIC were far too small: he must acquire more and very much larger plantations and get rid of those he already had. That it would not be easy to find enough suitable land there to operate on a sufficiently large scale became clear, however, from Greenhalgh's report on his visit in 1903 and thereafter first West and then Equatorial Africa became the focal point of Lever's search. In 1904 Joseph Meek, now in charge of the Balmain factory, got the impression that 'Lever's Pacific Plantations Limited was to be practically abandoned entirely, the oil mill [at Sydney] closed down except for soapery requirements' and he himself transferred to the Lever soap works at Boston.[6] Thus the genesis of the LPPL plantations in the Solomon Islands was somewhat fortuitous and can be traced to problems being experienced by PIC (1902).

This company had not, as has been assumed by some writers, died in 1902 at the moment of giving birth to Pacific Phosphates. It survived, not only as a holding company for Pacific Phosphates but also holding interests in the Solomon Islands which Stanmore for one regarded as very promising for plantations. In 1902 he formed a syndicate of PIC(1902) shareholders for developing these estates. They bought out the claims of DHPG in the group, probably for £5,000, and the value of their interests was greatly increased in 1903 when they persuaded the High Commissioner to give them a certificate of occupation for 193,490 acres in the Solomons for 99 years. The rent was low, rising to £1,000 a year for the last 70 years, and in addition the company had to pay for the cost of a general survey and spend not less than 2s an acre on improvements within ten years. Unoccupied land could be resumed without compensation by the government, but the certificate provided reasonable incentive to invest in plantations, oil mills and transport facilities.

Stanmore could not meet these conditions because neither PIC(1902) nor his syndicate could raise additional capital, and by December 1904 he had turned to Lever as a potential buyer of the company's rights. Lever was interested, but negotiations lasted for two years, turning mainly on the price. In 1904 Lever offered £5,000, Stanmore held out for £6,000 plus an advance of £1,000 to cover the syndicate's costs to date. There the matter might have rested, for Lever by now felt that he had been duped by the PIC in 1902. But at this point Meek, a convinced enthusiast for Pacific plantations, took a hand. When in England in 1904 he had tried to persuade Lever that there was a good future for plantations in the islands. Lever had great confidence in Meek's judgement and must have authorised him to prospect for and buy suitable land if he could find it. On his way back to Australia Meek visited the Straits Settlements and Malaya to investigate the possibility of coconut plantations there; and later in the year, with Lever's permission, he visited the Solomons, which he had regarded as the most promising area ever since he had gone to Sydney in 1900. He found that low copra prices had forced land values down and he was able to buy 51,000 acres of allegedly freehold land which a Captain Svenson had bought from islanders in the days before the Protectorate government had stopped land alienation in perpetuity. These properties included much land suitable for plantations, including the island of Gavatu, three miles from the Protectorate capital at Tulagi, and a number of trading stations at which native produced copra could be bought. Meek also bought 28,870 acres from islanders, subject to confirmation by government lease, and a further 12,000 acres for which occupancy certificates had already been granted.

Thus by the beginning of 1906 the centre of LPPL's interests had shifted from the islands inherited from PIC(1902) to the Solomons, and this may have encouraged both sides to come to terms over PIC(1902)'s leases there: late in 1906, after further haggling, Lever bought the lease for the £5,000 he had originally offered. Two things remained to do before LPPL took the form it was to retain until 1941: to convert the 99-year occupancy certificate obtained by PIC(1902) into a certificate for 999 years so as to satisfy Lever's instinct for perpetual possession; and to get rid of the unwanted relics of the islands purchased in 1902. The first was done in 1907 and this reflected the relief felt by everyone on the official side, from Woodford (now Deputy Commissioner in charge of the Solomons) to Lord Ripon, Secretary of State at the Colonial Office who, in a well-known minute, remarked: 'It is not every day that we find a millionaire tenant in the Solomon Islands, and I think we may assume that the rental he pays is the lesser part of the advantage the Protectorate will derive from him.'[7]

The 999-year lease dated from 1 January 1904, as before, but the rent was adjusted so that it would indeed make little contribution to Solomon Islands public finances. According to a later Lever document, no rent was to be paid to 1930, £484 11s 6d from 1931 to 1933, £1,051 14s 11d from 1934 to 2101 and £1,651 19s 2d from then until 2903. In fact, of course, the real benefit to the Protectorate would result from LPPL's investment, the trade it generated, the duties it paid on imports, the stimulus it would provide to the cash economy through payment of wages and the encouragement its entry might give to other potential investors and traders, such as Burns Philp. Protectorate revenues did, in fact, rise from £1,994 in 1904/5 to £7,430 in 1907/8 and continued to increase. Woodford later expressed disappointment at the limited scale of LPPL's investment and the fact that most of it had gone on the most accessible lands in Guadalcanal, the Russell Islands and Rendova, which were the estates bought in freehold from Svenson, leaving the vast leasehold territories virtually undeveloped. He and his subordinates were also critical of the type of manager LPPL employed and their sometimes high-handed dealings with islanders. But in view of PIC(1902)'s inability to attract any other investors before 1906 it seems unlikely that there was any alternative to LPPL if the Protectorate had to rely on foreign capital to undertake economic development.

It remained for LPPL to get rid of the incubus of the other island properties. The decision to do so was taken in principle in 1905, but the process was slow because buyers were few. The Mbua and St Heliers estates in Fiji were the easiest to move and were sold in 1906 and 1908 respectively. The Flint, Carolina and Vostock Islands were sold to S. R. Maxwell & Co. of Auckland in 1911, and they also bought Suwarrow Island, by then attached politically to New Zealand, the following year. In 1914 properties in Christmas Island were sold to a Father E. Reugier and those in the Hull, Sydney, Canton, Gardner, Phoenix and Birnie Islands to the Samoan Trading Company. That left only Rabi Island, held on lease from one Josiah Smale. The freehold was bought from him in 1923 and, as has been seen, it was finally sold to the government of the Gilbert and Ellice Islands Protectorate in 1942 for the inhabitants of Ocean Island.

For all practical purposes, then, LPPL's plantation business after 1907 was concentrated in the Solomons, and the following account will deal almost entirely with these islands, though a property in Papua, New Guinea, was in fact transferred to LPPL from Kitchens of Australia in 1924. Although the details are interesting, space makes it necessary to concentrate on the main themes and their relevance to the larger issues relating to plantation production within Unilever as a whole. It is proposed to divide the narrative at the time of the Japanese occupation in January 1942, since this constituted a major watershed in the history of the enterprise.

LPPL, 1907-42

The whole history of LPPL (which became Lever's Pacific Plantation Proprietary Ltd in 1928, but will be referred to throughout as LPPL) is an anti-climax. As has been seen, Lever conceived the project as part of a vast scheme to increase the world supply of vegetable oils and fats and so keep down raw material costs to manufacturers such as himself. In 1907 he owned or had leases for around 300,000 acres in the Solomons, together with land in Fiji and elsewhere, and this area might well have been extended over time if the project was successful. It was obvious that the actual area that could profitably be planted in the Solomons would be very much less than 300,000 acres, since much of this, particularly in Kulambangra, was unsuitable for palm trees; but even if half this acreage had been used and had produced the average amount of copra per acre the existing LPPL estates did produce in the 1930s—just under 8 cwt per acre—the total would have been around 60,000 tons of copra a year. In 1930 world trade in copra was around one million tons, so LPPL would in any case have supplied only some 6 per cent of the total. But it would have been one of the largest single suppliers and even 6 per cent might have had some marginal effect on world prices. Taken in conjunction with the Lever estates projected in West and Equatorial Africa, which were likely to be far larger, Lever's plantations might well have filled their intended role in the grand design.

The outcome was very different. By the late 1920s the total area of the Solomons concession had been considerably reduced as a result of investigations made by a Protectorate Land Commission into the validity of the PIC(1902) occupation lease, which was reduced from 280,000 acres to about 150,000 acres. Far more important, however, was the fact that so little of the residue was in use. By the early 1920s there were a mere 20,000 acres of coconuts, and this proved to be the maximum area ever effectively used by LPPL. As can be seen from Table 8.2(b), copra production steadily increased after 1920 as palms grew to maturity, but never rose above the peak of 7,850 tons reached in 1937 and had declined to 6,218 tons in 1941. The mountain had indeed given birth to a mouse: LPPL could not even supply all the copra milled by Balmain, let alone contribute significantly to the needs of Lever Brothers as a whole. Nor, looking at the venture in terms of horizontal diversification, were profits particularly high. During the decade 1920–29, when oil prices were relatively good, LPPL made a total accounting profit of £350,000, giving an average return to about $5\frac{1}{2}$ per cent on the capital employed: but this was barely enough to cover payments due to the holders of Lever Brothers' 5 per cent preference shares which had been issued to pay for the establishment of the plantations. In the 1930s, LPPL managed to break even only with the help of a subsidy paid on copra by Lever Brothers, Sydney.

Twenty thousand acres of plantations providing about half the total copra exported from the Solomons was, of course, a substantial and potentially profitable enterprise, larger than any of the plantations Unilever was to establish later on in Nigeria, the Cameroons, Malaya and Sabah. But this is to apply a quite different and *ex post* standard of measurement. Historically the correct question is why LPPL came to so much less than Lever had intended, and also why it was so different in scale from his Congo venture, HCB. There are four main reasons, two of which will be elaborated below. First, the volume of copra LPPL could export depended entirely on how much its plantations could produce, for the Pacific copra trade had by this

Table 8.1   LPPL: Native Labour on The Solomon Islands Plantations, 1923–37

Year	Total number (average for year)	Annual output per worker (tons)	Annual cost of each worker to nearest £1 (including recruitment, food, wages) (£)
1923	1,125	17.9	37
1924	1,049	18.4	40
1925	1,282	18.4	36
1926	962	17.6	41
1927	882	17.6	43
1928	982	16.7	40
1929	889	16.1	41
1930	1,200	n/a	n/a
1931	1,040	n/a	n/a
1932	750	n/a	37
1933	750	n/a	n/a
1934	750	n/a	n/a
1935	749	n/a	27
1936	733	n/a	n/a
1937	679	n/a	21

time dwindled. By contrast, until the 1930s HCB depended almost entirely on the considerable amount of palm oil and kernels it could obtain from natural palmeries or buy from Africans, and this alone enabled it to carry the overheads of communications, mills, storage facilities, hospitals, schools, etc. it was obliged to provide even before it had any plantations in bearing. Second, for reasons to be discussed, LPPL never had enough labour to plant and maintain more than about 20,000 acres. This, more than anything else, set the limit to its size. Third, from 1930 until after 1945 copra prices were unprofitably low and made extension of the total area under production pointless. Finally, from 1929 the very survival of the plantations was put at risk by the activities of a pest, Amblypelta Cocophaga, which had destroyed coconuts over large areas of the Solomons. Thereafter the successive Japanese and American occupations of the Second World War, which destroyed many plantations, were merely the *coup de grâce* to Lever's original project.

Table 8.2(a)   LPPL: Profits and Losses, 1902—10

Year	Nett accounting profit/(loss) £'000
1902	1.3
1903	(4.5)
1904	(9.3)
1905	(10.3)
1906	(2.2)
1907	28.1
1908	53.3
1909	16.2
1910	168.2

Note: The profits and losses shown in this table are those shown in the balance sheets of Lever's Pacific Plantations Ltd and do not represent the actual results of its operations in the Pacific. The company must have been making a loss on its copra business since the volume of trade was very low and large amounts were being spent on establishing new plantations, none of which began to come into bearing until 1911. LPPL's only significant source of income was the dividends it received from its shares in Pacific Phosphates; and it is virtually certain that the very large profit shown for 1910 represents the capital gain credited to LPPL when Lever bought out their shareholding in Phosphates.

(a) The Business Structure

1928 marks a formal watershed in the history of LPPL in that it was then transformed from being a British company wholly owned by Lever Brothers to being an Australian company wholly owned by J. Kitchen and Sons Pty Ltd and was fused with Kitchen's Commonwealth Copra Company Ltd, which ran a copra plantation and produced dessicated coconut for the Australian market at Milne Bay, Papua. By this time LPPL has its own subsidiary companies which had been set up by Lever before 1914 to run three estates—Vila, Stanmore and Somata—as joint enterprises with their managers. But these were mere technicalities. In practice the plantations were run from the Lever headquarters at Balmain. Until 1928 the Chairman and Managing Director of LPPL was George Fulton, who lived in Sydney and acted as the link between the plantations, the Sydney management and London. Lever was often very critical of him and used Meek, as Chairman of Lever Brothers, Sydney, to keep an eye on him. From 1928, with the reconstruction of LPPL, Fulton ceased to be Chairman, surviving as Managing Director until

Table 8.2(b)   LPPL: Production and Profitability, 1911—42, Excluding Commonwealth Copra

Year	A Copra (tons)	B Acreage cultivated	C Capital employed (£'000)	D Nett accounting profit (£'000)	E D/A £	F D/C %
1911	514	n/a	n/a	2.4	4.6	n/a
1912	765	n/a	n/a	4.9	6.4	n/a
1913	1,121	n/a	n/a	6.9	6.2	n/a
1914	1,507	n/a	n/a	(4.9)	3.2	n/a
1915	1,823	n/a	n/a	(11.1)	6.1	n/a
1916	2,539	n/a	n/a	9.5	3.7	n/a
1917	2,925	n/a	n/a	22.4	7.7	n/a
1918	3,442	n/a	n/a	35.7	10.4	n/a
1919	3,838	n/a	n/a	60.9	15.9	n/a
1920	4,311	n/a	n/a	60.5	14.0	n/a
1921	5,059	n/a	n/a	4.8	0.9	n/a
1922	5,497	n/a	n/a	(15.6)	2.8	n/a
1923	5,470	n/a	n/a	36.9	6.7	n/a
1924	5,528	n/a	n/a	36.0	6.5	n/a
1925	5,917	20,109	n/a	21.8	3.7	n/a
1926	6,284	20,445	n/a	23.9	3.8	n/a
1927	6,637	20,480	713	93.5	14.1	13.1
1928	7,142	20,433	n/a	43.3	6.1	n/a
1929	7,042	20,387	719	14.6	2.1	2.3
1930	6,991	n/a	n/a	3.8	0.5	n/a
1931	7,120	n/a	n/a	1.2	0.2	n/a
1932	7,455	20,728	n/a	32.7	4.4	n/a
1933	7,695	n/a	n/a	(7.3)	(—)	n/a
1934	7,387	n/a	n/a	(27.5)	(—)	n/a
1935	7,448	20,575	n/a	14.7	2.0	n/a
1936	7,506	20,000	n/a	n/a	n/a	n/a
1937	7,850	20,063	n/a	n/a	n/a	n/a
1938	7,538	20,000	656	2.5	0.3	0.4
1939	6,952	n/a	n/a	n/a	n/a	n/a
1940	6,997	n/a	n/a	n/a	n/a	n/a
1941	6,218	22,800	n/a	n/a	n/a	n/a

his retirement in 1934; and thereafter the chairman of LPPL was normally the chairman of the main Australian holding company. The plantation business was thus reduced to being a subsidiary activity of the Lever soap business in Australia.

Fulton and his successors as managing directors of LPPL visited the Solomons from time to time, but communications were poor and for the most part the plantations were run by the company's manager

Table 8.2(c)   LPPL: Production and Profitability 1928–39, including Commonwealth Copra Co.

Year	A Nett accounting profit £A'000	B Capital employed £A'000	C A/B %	D Apportionment of profit General reserve A£'000	E Dividends
1927	46.8	n/a	n/a	–	–
1928	43.3	n/a	n/a	40.0	–
1929	18.9	n/a	n/a	–	–
1930	0.7	n/a	n/a	–	–
1931	8.8	n/a	n/a	–	–
1932	40.1	n/a	n/a	–	–
1933	2.0	n/a	n/a	–	–
1934	25.6	n/a	n/a	74.2	–
1935	17.8	725	2.5	–	–
1936	60.9	790	7.7	–	–
1937	79.1	650	12.1	84.4	–
1938	0.4	653	0.06	81.0	–
1939	n/a	757	n/a	–	–

at Gavatu and by the individual estate managers. By the early 1920s the pattern of the plantations was established as it was to remain. There were just over 20 estates, varying in size but mostly ranging from 600 to 1,000 acres. They were dispersed in many islands over some 360 miles, but most were clustered in three areas: the western estates in Kulambangra, Gizo, New Georgia and Rendova; the central estates in the Russell Islands; and the eastern estates in Guadalcanal and the Three Sisters, north of San Christobel. Communications between the estates was maintained by a small fleet of steamers, which carried copra to the central storehouse at Gavatu and distributed stores and labourers. From Gavatu the copra was originally taken to Sydney by a Lever steamship, the *Kulambangra*, but just before the First World War Lever transferred it to West Africa and instead made a contract with Burns Philp, who thereafter carried all goods and men between the islands and Australia. The terms they offered were favourable because they were very anxious for return cargoes to Sydney and this was one main reason why Solomons copra was always sent there rather than to Europe, as was done with Fiji copra. By far the most productive of the individual estates were those in the Russells, the first area to be developed. These amounted to 8,450 acres in 1938 and their average production was 12.35 cwt per acre. The eastern estates, totalling 6,950 acres, had an average yield of only 4.28 cwt and the western estates, of 4,600 acres, averaged 5.03 cwt an acre.

At the start Lever had to decide how to manage properties dispersed over areas so large that close supervision was impracticable. Essentially he had three choices: to lease the estates; to provide capital and labour but to give the manager a share in the profits; or to have a conventional salaried management and hope that they would do their best. He seems to have started with the assumption that leases for life to the managers of individual plantations would be best since 'a capable manager would have a splendid opportunity, and he would have every inducement to keep down expenses of planting, otherwise he would be unable to make the undertaking sufficiently profitable'. Meek disagreed and got his way. Lever tried two other profit-sharing ideas. First, he set up four separate companies to plant and work part of his leases in Kulambangra, giving half the capital to their managers. There is nothing in the records to show how this experiment worked, but the probability is that it was unsatisfactory because, although three of these companies survived on paper until 1931, this experiment in profit-sharing was not extended. Another experiment, tried in 1913, was to engage Australian bushmen on contract (as was common in Australia) to clear a timbered estate for planting. Eight men were recruited in Sydney to clear Stanmore estate; but within a month they had decided that the climate and conditions were intolerable and returned home.

In the end, therefore, Lever had to fall back on the conventional plantation system of employing salaried European managers and a non-European work force. Almost all estate managers were recruited in Australia among what Lever called 'Backwoodsmen or Bushmen'. The Protectorate administrators, by this time mostly British born and of gentle origin, tended to complain that these men were rough, tough and apt to bring with them the conventional Australian attitude to 'abos'. Mahaffy, for instance, complained in 1908 that conditions on some plantations would 'horrify the proprietor of the model town of Port Sunlight' and one Lever manager was deported in 1909 for alleged shooting and assault.[8] But the proprietor of Port Sunlight did not react with horror when he visited his estates in 1913: on the contrary, he eulogised his managers as ingenious at solving technical problems and more enterprising than the Port Sunlight men he used in HCB.

(b) LPPL and Lever Brothers (Australia)

Despite its autonomy, LPPL relied heavily on Lever Brothers at Balmain. The soap company provided the head office services the plantations needed and this reduced LPPL's overheads. More important, LB(A) bought all the copra LPPL exported from the Solomons and this raises two questions: why it did so and what internal transfer prices were paid. The main reason why LPPL copra went to Sydney rather than to Europe (as did Fiji copra) was that Burns Philp, the Australian shipowners and merchants, were prepared to carry it there cheaply and because there was a sufficient demand in Australia. LB(A) did not, in fact, need LPPL copra in the sense that otherwise the oil mill and factory would have been short of it. Balmain had ample supplies before LPPL came into production; Lever never specifically said that the Solomon plantations would supply Balmain; and LB(A) always bought additional copra on the Sydney market. Thus the case for direct sale of the whole LPPL production of some 7,000 tons to Balmain was that this saved the soap business the middleman profit that they would have paid if they bought in the Sydney market.

Direct transfer raised the question of internal transfer pricing. Broadly three strategies were open: for Balmain to pay an artificial price which would subsidise LPPL and minimise taxes paid by both Lever enterprises; to use a formula based on the world market price of copra; or to charge at prices current in the local Sydney market. The basic Lever/Unilever rule on internal transfer pricing was that no part of the business must make a profit out of another; so the first strategy was never formally adopted. Conversely the Sydney copra market was too small to provide a reasonable guide to price levels; so the normal principle was the second. Balmain paid LPPL a price based on the price of Ceylon copra f.o.b. London (or, from 1928 to

1930 on Fiji copra f.o.b. London because this gave a better return to LPPL), with allowances for difference in quality, freight, etc. This worked well until 1930/1, when the catastrophic drop in commodity prices reduced that of copra to the point at which LPPL would make a loss of £3,664 in that year while LB(A) made a profit. To keep LPPL solvent and to reduce taxable profits made by the soap company Balmain paid LPPL a premium of 15s a ton for that year. This was a stop-gap measure and with the prolonged depression of the commodity market something more permanent was needed. In 1931/2 the pre-1928 formula based on Ceylon copra would give LPPL £11 11s 6d a ton f.o.b. Gavatu and would cost LB(A) £14 17s 3d c.i.f. Balmain. At this price LPPL might make a small profit on which they would pay no tax; but at the same time LB(A) could buy copra in Sydney from Burns Philp at £11 17s 3d a ton. This raised the question of which market price the Lever rule obliged LB(A) to pay and also what view the Australian tax authorities would take if Levers paid the higher price. Legal counsel assured Balmain that in using the Ceylon formula they would be acting properly and the Australian tax authorities accepted this. Throughout the 1930s Balmain therefore paid LPPL substantially above the market price of copra on the Sydney market and by 1941 the system had been so far conventionalised that one visitor from London commented that 'as our Sydney mill pays the plantations a premium of £2/5/- a ton for high quality and regularity of supply, the Plantations accounts can show a small profit'. The sums involved were small and the sin a very little one because Unilever were maintaining a principle which had previously operated to ensure a fair balance between the interests of two parts of the business. Yet the deliberate choice of one pricing formula rather than another between 1931 and 1941 is a good example of the complexities of internal price fixing within an international business. It is interesting that the only other example discovered in the course of research for this book was that between SAVCO, SEDEC and HCB in the Congo at the same time, and there the financial relationship between soap factory and oil producer and trader was exactly the reverse of that in the Pacific: the plantation and trading companies subsidised the soap business. The common denominator was that these manipulations were a response to the slump of the early 1930s and were not characteristic of Lever or Unilever practice before 1929 or after 1941.

An enterprise dependent for its profits on co-operative accounting by a sister company does not inspire confidence, and low profitability was partly responsible for the failure to expand the plantations after 1930. But profits had not always been dependent on charity and they do not themselves explain why LPPL failed to expand to the size Lever had intended. The explanation lies in two other factors—an insufficient supply of labour and the ravages of Cocophaga—which must now be described.

(c) Labour Supply

It is no exaggeration to say that the success of all plantations in the tropics depends from first to last on a satisfactory labour supply; and it is equally certain that the growth of LPPL was eventually throttled by shortage of labour rather than by low prices or disease. Labour might in principle have been obtained from any one or more of three sources: from the Solomons, notably Malaita Island, which contained about half the total Protectorate population; from other Pacific islands under British control; or from further afield in India, Indonesia or China. The problem throughout was that the first two of these sources of supply proved totally inadequate. The Solomons population was too small to provide enough labour for plantations on the scale Lever had envisaged, and LPPL were not the only planters in the group. If one worker to about 20 acres—roughly the proportion working for LPPL in the early 1920s—is taken as the norm, the company would have needed more than 5,000 men to maintain even 100,000 of Lever's original 300,000 acres, and more would have been required while the initial process of clearing and planting was in progress. But 5,000 seems to have been the largest number of Solomon Islanders willing to take paid employment of any sort at any one time before 1941; and since this number could apparently not be increased whatever payment or other incentives were offered, it was inconceivable that LPPL should monopolise the entire labour supply. It was therefore very soon clear that concentration of the means of production in plantations depended on recruiting a labour force from much further afield.

Fifty years earlier a solution might have been found by recruitment in other Pacific islands; but by the 1900s 'black-birding' (quasi-slaving) had been outlawed by the European states which controlled the islands, and each of these in any case monopolised its own labour supply. LPPL would therefore have to look still further afield, as the Fiji planters had done since the 1870s, to the 'teeming millions' of Asia; and on this issue the attitude of the Solomon Islands Protectorate government and the Colonial Office was critical.

LPPL had many grievances against the Protectorate government at Tulagi—labelled by one Lever man 'the seat of misgovernment'; but on the importation of Asian labour at least they were in agreement. The Fiji High Commission had believed since the early days when Sir Arthur Gordon had established the government of Fiji that the island peoples were predestined gradually to die out from disease and inability (or lack of will) to cope with the impact of Europeans. Government had a moral duty to help them to enjoy the declining years of their culture, which could best be done by, in effect, pensioning them off in their own areas, protected against liquor, firearms and European land grabbers. But someone had to make the islands productive so that taxes could be levied to pay for the government; and the only possible agent of development seemed to be European capital coupled with imported Asian labour. The formula was thought to have succeeded in many other parts of the world. As an alternative to slavery it had enabled the British sugar islands of the Caribbean and Indian Ocean to maintain production after the abolition of slavery in the 1830s, and more recently it was fructifying Ceylon, Malaya and Fiji. It seemed obvious to Lever and successive High Commissioners of the Western Pacific that the same combination would have to be used in the Solomon Islands.

If plantation production was to succeed on a scale comparable with that in Fiji they were certainly right: but time and changing attitudes were against LPPL and they were never able to import a single Asian worker on contract. Their official allies and opponents on this issue varied over time. When the first request for Asian labour was made in 1909 both the High Commission and the Colonial Office supported it but the Australian government objected, presumably because this might give the Solomons an advantage over Papua, where Asian immigration was blocked by the 'white Australia' policy. Levers were therefore told by the Colonial Office that they could use Asians as free but not as indentured labour.[9] This qualification proved fatal because Lever and all later concern executives took the view that, if they paid to recruit and transport Indians, they must have some assurance that they would work for LPPL for a specified time. Yet even if the Colonial Office (CO) had agreed to indentures the Indian government would not have done so. Faced with strong hostility among nationalists to this trade in human muscle, it automatically rejected any schemes after 1910 that involved contractual periods of work overseas.[10] Lever took this hard and his son later suggested that official obstruction in the Solomons was partly responsible for his active interest in the Belgian Congo plantations, where the labour supply caused much less difficulty.[11] Yet he never gave up the struggle. By September 1918 he was again negotiating with the CO over Asian indentured labour, only to be told in 1919 that the Office had changed its policy and was now opposed to the introduction of coolies to Pacific islands. He tried again in 1923/4 when he visited India; and by that time LPPL were negotiating with the High Commission over bringing families from China or any other Asian country. In 1924 the CO closed that door also. Lever died in 1925 but the concern continued to press inter- mittently. The only moment when the authorities seemed likely to concede any ground was in 1937 when a new High Commissioner, Sir Arthur Richards, seemed willing to consider a scheme for Indian immigration with suitable safeguards; and ironically LPPL decided not to pursue the matter on the ground that the copra market was depressed and disease rampant.

1937 was, in any case, 30 years too late: the failure of LPPL to fulfil Lever's objects had been sealed before 1914 by shortage of labour when enthusiasm for plantation production was at the flood. Even in 1902 it was becoming anachronistic to establish plantations dependent on imported indentured labour in view of the intense criticism this was already creating in India and elsewhere. Lever may have been ignorant of this or treated it as a transient phenomenon; yet he could still have given up his Solomon Islands project in 1910, when he received his first rebuff, before he had made a large invest- ment there. Thus, while it is undeniable that the limited achievement of LPPL was primarily due to official refusal to allow imported Asian labour, it is legitimate to argue that this failure was inherent in any attempt to establish so labour-intensive an enterprise in any country which could not provide sufficient labour. One great advantage possessed by the Unilever plantations later established in Malaysia was that there the capital was taken to where the labour already existed.

(d) Disease

The last factor holding back expansion and reducing the profitability of LPPL was disease. The plantations suffered from a number of diseases and insect pests in the early years, notably the Frogatti beetle which attacked the budding leaves. Mina birds imported to deal with Frogatti 'in no sense distinguished themselves'. But none of these was as serious as 'nutfall', the name given to an unknown pest which caused nuts to fall before they were ripe. Two estates in the eastern group were affected in 1929 and by 1937 their annual yield had declined from 1,368 to 489 tons. The disease spread to the plantations in the central and western groups and threatened the future of the whole enterprise. The local government entomologist could not explain it and it was not until Unilever sent out an English entomologist, Dr Phillipps, in 1935 that the guilt was pinned onto a sap-sucking insect, Amblypelta Cocophaga (AC). In 1939 another entomologist employed by Unilever, Leach, advised that the yellow ant Oecophylla was the most effective antidote; but little was known about this creature or what environmental factors were needed to stimulate its activities. In 1941 the future of LPPL largely depended on solving this riddle.

Rehabilitation, 1945–61

The first main era in the history of LPPL, which was abruptly terminated by the arrival of the Japanese in the Solomons in January 1942, thus ended ingloriously. The plantations had not expanded for a decade. They had been unprofitable since 1929. The labour force was inadequate and possibly declining. A fatal disease was spreading unchecked. It would not, therefore, have been surprising if the Pacific war had been the *coup de grace*. The Japanese were not in the Solomons for long, for they had been occupied by the Americans by the end of 1942 and at first LPPL hoped that this would enable them to get some of their plantations into production again. But the Americans needed to use the Solomons as a military and air force base and plantation production was quite impossible until after 1945. When the managers returned in 1946 to take stock they found that almost nothing survived. Most buildings had been destroyed during the fighting or by the Japanese as part of their scorched earth policy. Many plantations had been bulldozed by the Americans to build airstrips, camps, etc. The herds of cattle which had been used to keep down the undergrowth had been partly destroyed because they exacerbated the fly problem, though the survivors and a number of estate horses were roaming wild. There were two small consolations:

the Americans had built many roads which would be useful for plantation work; and in some areas the uninhibited growth of vines had helped the yellow ants to get Cocophaga under control and incidentally indicated how this could be done in future.

Thus, when Unilever came to consider the prospects late in 1945, the future of the plantations was an open question. Early estimates for replanting and rebuilding put the cost at not less than £350,000, and it was found that no war damage compensation would be paid, which effectively ruined many of the smaller pre-war planters. There was, therefore, a real possibility that Unilever would wind up LPPL. On the other hand there were some incentives to continue, though possibly on a more limited scale and not necessarily in coconut plantations alone. Post-war shortages produced high copra prices, even though all Solomon Islands copra had to be sold through the local Copra Board at a price determined by the British Ministry of Food. If plantations were to be re-established, there seemed at first to be possibilities other than palm trees. Among the alternatives considered in 1945/6 were hevea rubber, oil palms, cocoa, bananas and a wide range of other tropical fruit. Money was not an immediate constraint. The book value of the plantations had been written off during the war and there was £250,000 depreciation reserve available. In conjunction these factors made it likely that Unilever would attempt to re-establish some form of plantation production in the Solomons, though it might be on a much smaller scale and along new lines.

In the event no heroic new ventures were undertaken. To summarise developments from 1945 to 1965, LPPL found that the continued labour shortage, together with climatic and soil characteristics, inhibited the introduction of most alternative tropical plantation crops. With copra prices buoyant until after 1953 and the British government anxious to stimulate production of vegetable oils throughout the empire, it was natural to drift back into copra. The remaining question was on what scale; and as early as 31 October 1945, when no survey of conditions had been made, the Special Committee minuted tersely: 'Future plans, not yet finally decided upon, envisaged concentrating in the central area [sc. the Russell Islands] which were comparatively free of pests, and leasing or selling the Western and Guadalcanal areas whose yields in the past had been low as a result of pests, etc.' By 1965 LPPL had done precisely that. As can be seen from Table 8.3 some 10,000 acres, almost all in the Russells, had been rehabilitated by the early 1950s. In 1957 some

2,000 acres had been bought, also in the Russells, from the Fairy-mead Sugar Corporation; and by 1965 3,000 acres of new plantations had been established, making a total of over 15,000 acres. Copra production per acre of bearing trees was back to the pre-war average of about 8 cwt (0.4 tons). By this time most of the other LPPL properties had been sold or leased. Rabi, as has been seen, was handed over for the Ocean Islanders in 1945. The Commonwealth Copra Corporation estate at Giligili, Papua, was first leased and

Table 8.3   LPPL: Acreage under Cultivation, Labour Force and Copra Production, 1948–65

Year	Average acreage cultivated	Output (tons)	Average number of workers
1948	n/a	n/a	140
1949	n/a	897	560
1950	n/a	2,282	610
1951	n/a	3,214	763
1952	n/a	3,140	814
1953	10,790	3,767	782
1954	10,040	4,691	820
1955	10,040	4,696	933
1956	10,040	4,811	828
1957	13,323	4,567	1,159
1958	13,323	5,602	1,160
1959	13,710	5,068	1,215
1960	13,710	5,171	1,363
1961	14,250	5,373	1,393
1962	14,703	5,517	1,237
1963	15,205	5,769	1,309
1964	15,485	5,960	963
1965	15,485	5,924	1,093

Notes: a. Fairymead Sugar Estates were acquired on 18 October 1957, so later totals include their production.

   b. The bonus system was introduced in the second quarter of 1950.

   c. The number of workers given for 1949 is at the end of the year, not the average.

then sold in 1957 for £15,000, well below its book value. Of the remaining Solomon Island estates, most of those in Kulambangra and Gizo were leased or abandoned, leaving the balance of productive plantations in 1965 69 per cent in the Russells to 24 per cent in Guadalcanal and 7 per cent in the Three Sisters. This proved a wise

Table 8.4   LPPL: Trading Summary, 1956—65 (£ sterling '000)

Year	Planted area acres	Production copra M. ton	Trading results				Fixed assets	Working capital	Gross capital employed	Yield %
			Sales	Before tax	After stat. tax	Nett accounting profit				
1956	10,040	4,811	278	69	64	62	323	35	358	17.9
1957	13,323	4,567	243	42	39	38	326	55	381	10.2
1958	13,323	5,602	322	48	45	52	514	76	590	7.6
1959	13,710	5,068	378	88	82	114	507	66	573	14.3
1960	13,710	5,171	312	32	29	31	488	69	557	5.2
1961	14,250	5,373	268	(15)	(15)	(15)	448	69	517	(—)
1962	14,703	5,517	229	(2)	(2)	(13)	825	53	878	(—)
1963	15,205	5,769	271	49	45	47	859	63	922	4.9
1964	15,485	5,960	289	87	81	85	922	73	995	8.1
1965	15,485	5,924	343	128	119	121	1,046	77	1,123	10.6

Notes: a. Rate of exchange £1 = A £1.25 all years.
b. Statistical tax rate 7½ per cent all years.
c. Change in fixed asset definition from 1962.
d. Only dividend paid — A£600,000 in December 1960 ex profits retained.

policy, for the estates chosen for rehabilitation were those with the best record, and the result was high profits in good years: about 29 per cent on capital employed in 1954, 25.8 per cent in 1955, 17.9 per cent in 1956.

But this achievement should not obscure the price at which it was bought. The LPPL estates had been made efficient by reducing the scale of the operation to that of the relatively small plantations Unilever possessed in West Africa, Malaya and Sabah. These had from the start been planned as limited operations but LPPL had not. At its post-war peak, reached in 1957 but not maintained, LPPL was using only 16,898 acres out of the 200,000 acres remaining of its original concession; and at some point in the early 1960s it was decided not to proceed with plans for using the balance of the concession for copra or other tropical crops and to hand the greater part of the leasehold land back to the government after extracting as much timber as possible. Clearly at this stage the impulse to exploit LPPL's potential evaporated; and, without examining the evidence in detail, it is important to establish when and why this happened.

The evidence suggests that the year of decision was 1960/1. By then the conditions which had encouraged expansion and diversification were dissipating, most important high copra prices and good profit margins. Between 1945 and 1957 the price of all Solomon Islands copra was fixed by the local Copra Board, which resembled the West African Marketing Boards in that it had a monopoly of handling all copra, which it sold to the British Ministry of Food at a price fixed in advance for each year. But there were differences. The Solomon Islands Board did not accumulate reserves in a stabilisation fund but paid producers the full amount it received from the Ministry, less a fee to cover administrative costs. On the whole this system seems to have been satisfactory to LPPL and in the mid-1950s there was even some concern that the end of bulk buying might leave the producers exposed to a falling market after the end of the Korean War. Moreover, from about 1949 LPPL was allowed to send up to 4,500 tons of copra a year (the limit set by Australian import quotas intended to protect Papuan production) direct to Balmain, provided the f.o.b. price was that set by the Copra Board and that its levy was paid. LPPL had a double motive for reviving this pre-war system: it enabled them to avoid an irritating commission of £4 15s 0d charged by the Fairymead Sugar Company as the government's buying agents in the Russell Islands for what were, in the case of a much larger producer such as LPPL, purely notional services; and it also reduced the price paid by Balmain for a proportion of their consumption as compared with the price of other locally available copra. Moreover, since the prospect was that, after the Ministry of Food contract ran out in 1957, the Solomons might set up a marketing board on the West African pattern, LPPL felt that change might be for the worse. In the event, however, the government announced that, although the Copra Board would continue, producers could sell on an open market provided they paid the Board a levy. No stabilisation fund would be established. This was very satisfactory. From 1957 LPPL re-established its pre-war system, sending all its copra (except that from the Fairymead estates) to Balmain at a price based on the average European copra price for the previous year, nett of transport from the Solomons to Europe and less the 15 per cent duty, the 3s 1d Copra Board levy and 5s a ton for loss of weight.

In 1957 optimism had encouraged Unilever to undertake substantial new investments in the Solomons. By 1961 four years of low copra prices in an open-market situation had dissipated this optimism and low profitability was once again, as in 1929/30, the most important single reason for decisions taken in 1960/1 which changed the future history of LPPL. But there were other factors; and, as before the war, the most important of these was labour.

At the start, in the late 1940s, the main difficulty was that the established links with the labour recruiting areas in Malaita had been severed and also that previous plantation workers there were aggrieved that, in the crisis of January 1942, many of them had neither received the pay owing to them nor been transported back home when European employees of LPPL were evacuated. In time this distrust was overcome, but pre-war standards of work were never re-established. According to D. L. Martin, cutters had averaged 750 lbs of fresh copra a day before the war, so that five man-days were needed to produce the equivalent of one ton of dried copra. In 1949 the daily task, set by the government, was 450 lbs of fresh copra, but the average output was only 300 lbs and it took twelve man-days to produce one ton of dried copra. In 1949 this was still partly due to bad working conditions when the estates had still not been cleared of undergrowth; but in fact the pre-war task was never re-established, and LPPL men tended to provide two alternative explanations. The first was that the government now insisted that men be repatriated at the end of each one-year contract, which meant that they never achieved reasonable levels of efficiency. The other was the argument, very commonly used by Europeans in the tropics, that the natives had no work ethic or impulse. A quarterly report by LPPL in March 1950 put it as follows.

> An important factor making for inefficiency is the lack of need for the Solomon Islands native to work. . . . His relatives, if any, are self-supporting and not dependent on him for subsistence. Thus there is no real need for him to work, and in most cases he does not want work. When he does, the job must be easy and of short duration. We have so far sought in vain for some incentive to stimulate the workers to further effort, but with little success. The offer of increased wages is no inducement. In fact, it would tend to make the situation worse, since the worker could accumulate what he considered to be sufficient savings in a shorter period. The one inducement that could attract more labour would be a reduction in the task performed, but this would be disastrous, as the return for the wage would become increasingly less.

This explanation is not entirely satisfactory. Later in 1950 a bonus system was introduced which resulted in 60 per cent of all cutters earning a bonus. Admittedly the bonus was based on a task of only 300 lbs a day, well below the government standard; yet over time output per worker rose substantially, from 3.74 tons a year in 1950 to 5.74 tons in 1954 and 6.2 tons in 1964, reflecting improved conditions on the rehabilitated estates as well as greater productive effort.

LPPL had no doubt as to the best solution of its labour problems: they must build up a permanent and therefore potentially professional and efficient work force in place of the migrant labour on which they had always depended. Except for one passing thought about the possibility of importing Javanese workers in 1949, stimulated by a rumour that North Borneo planters were negotiating with Indonesia for Javanese immigrants, there was no return to the old demand for Asian labour. Management instead constantly pressed the government for two concessions: two-year rather than one-year contracts for unmarried workers and permission to establish permanent settlements on the Russells. They were unsuccessful on the first count because the government insisted that contract labour must not lose its contacts with the villages and also because the workers preferred to go home after one year. They had very limited success on the second because it was only under very special circumstances that islanders could be persuaded to migrate permanently. One hope was to attract Gilbertese families because their islands had been badly affected by the war. In 1947 LPPL aimed to recruit about 190 families there who would be given two acres each for subsistence in addition to wages and would be repatriated after two years if they became unhappy. Nothing came of this, but in 1952 LPPL was able to establish settlers from Tikopea Island, which had been affected by salt spray, in West Bay, Russells Island. Average production on that estate rose well above the average, and recruitment continued, though the numbers were too small to have much effect on the labour problem as a whole. In 1956 the government refused to allow Fiji Indians to be brought in, but in 1959 they allowed head workers from other Solomon Islands to be established permanently on LPPL estates if they brought their wives. In 1960 the government agreed that permanent settlement was best in principle, but the high capital cost of providing housing to the official specification at a time of low copra prices made it impossible for LPPL to move fast in this direction. In 1964 80 per cent of the plantation labour force was still on yearly contract and the general level of skill remained low. To make matters worse from the company's standpoint, a union was established in 1963. The first wage agreement of that year increased basic wages by 20 per cent to £7 16s 0d a month for cutters, giving them average earnings (including payment for piece work) of £9 10s 0d, and £11 13s 0d for planters. In return the union promised to fire those members who did not fulfil their task of 300 lbs a day. A year later the union demanded a 45 per cent increase, on the ground that copra prices had risen, and also a closed shop. When this was refused a strike was called. It lasted only a week and the union lost the support of most workers, who thereafter refused to allow union officials to act for them. Smaller wage increases were conceded and by 1965 the union had not re-established itself.

The virtual failure of LPPL to establish a stable professional labour force was critical for the future of the Solomon Islands business. No one was to blame. The company could not, given low copra prices in the 1960s, afford significantly higher wages nor elaborate housing and amenities; and for their part most islanders felt no desire to leave their homes and social groups and live on alien islands. But when Unilever undertook a general review of the future of the plantations business in 1960/1, the labour shortage tilted the balance against any large-scale further investment in copra production in the Solomons.

Diversification, 1961–5

The residual question in 1960/1 was whether LPPL should hold onto the very large undeveloped area which it still held from its original concession in the hope that it might eventually be possible to get enough labour to expand the plantations. Plantation Group and Special Committee had to bear four main considerations in mind, three old, and one very new. The three recurrent problems were low copra prices, the failure to discover other and more profitable plantation crops suited to Solomon Islands conditions, and the labour shortage. The new problem was that the Protectorate government was increasingly aware that it was politically undesirable in an age of nascent political consciousness among the islanders that an expatriate company should lock up so much land without making any attempt to develop it. From this conjunction grew the scheme for timber extraction as an alternative to plantation production.

The first suggestion that LPPL should do something with its undeveloped estates or give up its leases seems to have come from the High Commission staff. The Senior Finance Officer was concerned at reduced revenues resulting from declining copra exports and the Commissioner for Labour was anxious about future employment prospects. It was not that the High Commission was hostile to LPPL: on the contrary, it is obvious from the voluminous correspondence between the Protectorate capital at Honiara and LPPL headquarters, now at Gandina, that personal relations were always excellent. From at least 1955 there were regular meetings between senior officials on both sides to sort out any problems and in 1961 the High Commissioner asked Lord Cole whether LPPL's headquarters could be moved to Honiara so that Walton, the Managing Director, could be 'available in order to help him with affairs, such as the running of the Legislative Council'. But affability did not indicate identity of interest. On any matter in which the interests of the islanders seemed to clash with those of LPPL, officialdom became resolute. It had no doubt that its primary obligation was to its subjects rather than to a British multinational; and from 1961 Honiara was increasingly determined that LPPL must use its concession constructively or give up its rights. This was the genesis of Unilever's timber extraction project in the western estates.

Unilever's first reaction to official pressure, expressed at a meeting of Plantation Group in London in April 1961, was that unused land might be leased to third parties for timber extraction, since the Japanese seemed keen on buying Pacific hardwood, and the Chief Financial Office of the Protectorate was to be asked to advise on timber values. But it was Lord Cole, by then Chairman of Unilever, who was primarily responsible for the decision that the concern itself should undertake the exploitation of the timber. He visited the Solomons in July 1961 and discussed the position with the High Commissioner. The High Commissioner emphasised that this was essentially a political problem, for the islanders were at last becoming politically conscious. Cole replied that 'Levers had no wish to sit on the land; they always liked to be a jump ahead in such matters', and promised to get Plantation Group to investigate timber prospects. He reported this to the Directors' Conference in August without expressing any opinion, but it seems likely that, as a one-time UAC man with experience of UAC's timber enterprises in West Africa, he was more keen on the project than anyone else; and his support gave the scheme its best chance of success.

No time was wasted and the project was considered at the highest level. A meeting was held at the Colonial Office later in 1961, attended by H. P. Hall of the CO, C. Swabey of the Department of Technical Co-operation and two UAC(Timber) Ltd (UAC(T)) men. The CO was interested and agreed to send a questionnaire to K. W. Trenaway, the Chief Conservator of Forests in the Solomons. In April 1962, while his report was awaited, LPPL made a goodwill gesture by offering to relinquish its lease of 6,920 acres on Gizo Island once timber extraction there had been completed, asking for no compensation but a reduction in its annual rent. By June 1962 the High Commission was ready to begin the timber survey, and at this point the High Commissioner took the opportunity of a visit to Honiara by G. H. Rushworth, Chairman of Unilever (Australia) and also of LPPL, to raise a problem which was to bedevil negotiations over timber for the next five years. It seemed that the 800 indigenous inhabitants of Kulambangra had strong views on what should happen to LPPL land there after timber extraction had been completed. The High Commissioner suggested that, at that stage, all the land should be handed back to the government and the lease cancelled, after which land could be distributed to the islanders. Rushworth made no promises; but it was thereafter clear that the government aimed to use this opportunity to prise away all of LPPL's leasehold land that was not actually under copra cultivation once the timber had been removed, and in this way to eradicate the long-term political and economic consequences of the concessionary policy adopted by the Colonial Office 60 years earlier.

First omens were favourable. In November 1962 A. D. Melhuish, one of the two UAC(T) men sent to investigate Kulambangra, sent a series of preliminary reports. The timber supply looked promising ('capable of supplying an industry such as we have in Ghana for some 15 years') and the government co-operative. But difficulties loomed. Existing royalties and export duties on timber looked dangerously high on top of high freights to Japan, and the government agreed to review them. More serious, it was not clear where the labour would come from since, characteristically, 'the government wishes to encourage industry but frowns on the importation of labour'. Bougainville seemed a hopeless recruiting ground, but it might be possible to recruit 2,000 or more men from Malaita over five to six years and the government was in favour of resettling family groups from the Gilbert Islands if the Colonial Development Corporation would pay for their transport.

All this suggested that the timber operation might be difficult and not necessarily very profitable; and in 1963 the Protectorate government raised another issue which might well have deterred Unilever altogether. It has been seen that from the start the High Commission had made it clear that they hoped Unilever would give up its leases once the timber extraction was over, but both parties seem to have assumed that this would be the end: LPPL could simply hand over the land on Gizo and Kulambangra as it then stood. But early in 1963 Trenaway pointed out that he had power under the Forest Ordinance to declare the land to be cleared a 'Forest Area', with the implication that Unilever would be responsible for replanting the areas from which they had extracted timber before handing it over. Rightly or wrongly a UAC(T) visitor to the Solomons in 1964 concluded that Trenaway, as a committed conservationist, was the main official enthusiast for obligatory replanting and that, if he had his way, forestry would become the first priority, even to the exclusion of oil palms, coconuts and any other perennial tree crop in so far as new development was concerned. The question was whether he could carry the Honiara government with him and, if he did, whether this would prove an insuperable obstacle to the Kulambangra timber project. The story is, perhaps, of little intrinsic importance, but is worth recounting briefly as a microcosmic study of conflict of interest between a very large multinational and one of the smallest of all colonial governments which ended substantially in victory for the latter.

By March 1963 UAC(T) had assessed the possibilities of Gizo and Kulambangra. They calculated that they could extract some four million cubic feet of logs a year for 15 years or more for export, mainly to Japan. The capital required for fixed assets would be £346,700 over the first five years and £283,800 over the following ten, all of which would be written off after 15 years, plus £144,000 at the peak for working capital. Unilever Ltd should lend the capital to UAC(T) at 3 per cent interest. Profits were estimated at 25 per cent after local tax and 19 per cent after UK tax. Management should be drawn from UAC(T) in West Africa and a labour force of about 280 recruited in the Solomons. During the summer it was decided to establish a subsidiary of UAC(T) to operate in the Solomons, which would be called Lever's Pacific Timber Ltd (LPT) 'in order to identify the company with the owners of the land which will be worked in the first place'. The company would have a nominal capital of £25,000 and three directors, two of them UAC(T) men, the third the Managing Director of LPPL. This left an important domestic matter to decide: what should LPT pay to LPPL as 'owners of the land'? Financial Group in London thought it important that LPT should pay LPPL as much as possible because the latter was expected to make losses on its plantations over the next five years and the Protectorate only allowed losses to be deducted to the extent of 50 per cent of each of the next six years' profits: no profits, no tax rebate. To take advantage of this LPPL would therefore need an income of £300,000 from timber over five years; so LPT should pay £60,000 a year to them, either as a royalty or as a rent. But Financial Group was over-ridden: Plantations Group thought that so large a payment was too obviously a tax dodge and would irritate the Protectorate government. In July 1963 it was decided that LPT should pay a rent of only £20,000 a year and Walton, the Managing Director of LPPL, thought the arrangement 'eminently fair to ourselves. Obviously someone did some pretty hard and effective bargaining on our part. The arrangement will of course have a very worthwhile effect on our efforts to make more than sufficient profit in future years so that we may recoup for Income Tax purposes our heavy expenditure on New Development.'

So far as Unilever was concerned this cleared the way for action. LPT was formally set up late in 1963, Melhuish went to the islands in October and by April 1964 the first 1,000 tons of logs from Gizo were awaiting shipment to Japan. But this left the question of LPT's obligations in Kulambangra; and until this was settled there was no chance of operating there. Indeed the whole operation might have been restricted to Gizo unless satisfactory terms were agreed with the government. In the event it took five years to reach agreement with Honiara, mainly because the government continually introduced new issues which complicated negotiations. The basic question was whether Honiara would declare LPPL's leases a Forest Area and if so what price the company would have to pay to avoid the cost and inconvenience of replanting the land to be cleared by LPT. The first major discussion took place in Honiara on 14 June 1964 between Rushworth, Martin, Walton and others for LPPL and the High Commissioner, the Chief Financial Office and Trenaway. For LPPL Martin said that the company would like to keep about 25,000 acres of land on Kulambangra in case a projected scheme for co-operative coconut planting between LPPL, CDC and the Solomon Islands Protectorate came to fruition, but was ready to hand over the balance of some 95,000 acres progressively as each block was cleared of timber. In reply Trenaway outlined the obligations imposed by the Forest Area Ordinance: if LPPL retained the land after logging, they would have to take responsibility for regeneration, or alternatively pay stumpage on a formula estimated to cost them about £225,000. If the land was returned to the government before regeneration, it would cost the local treasury some £2 an acre to replant; and he clearly thought that this obligation should lie with the company. Martin commented that LPPL would never have considered the timber project if they had been told of these requirements when the scheme was first bruited in 1961, and they might still decide not to proceed if they were insisted on. The High Commissioner took the point and laid down four emollient principles. No regeneration requirement would be imposed on land released to the government; there would be no formal time limit on developing the reserved 25,000 acres, though assurance must be given that this would be done as soon as possible; the government would attempt to acquire, and then release to LPT, the land claimed by islanders within the general area of the LPPL concession on Kulambangra, so that the company would not have to face disputes or be excluded from certain areas; and, finally, referring to another threat previously made by Trenaway, LPPL would have to survey only land to be retained by the company. Defeated on his main points, Trenaway fell back on another Forest Area regulation—that permission to fell might be conditional on erecting a saw mill to process the timber. Martin challenged this, since it had been decided not to mill or make plywood on grounds of unprofitability, and the Chief Financial Officer pointed out in return that the government would have no obligation to allow LPT to extend its operations to New Georgia or other islands if it appeared that the company made no contribution to the industrialisation or employment opportunities in the islands.

Clearly the more junior members of the Honiara government were keen to use the few legal weapons at the government's disposal to obtain maximum benefits for the very poor society for which they felt themselves responsible. But for the moment the rules of the game seemed to have been established, and it is therefore surprising that it was not until 1968 that final agreement was reached on the precise conditions for timber extraction from Kulambangra. One reason for this delay was that it was not until then that LPT had finished with Gizo and was ready to move to Kulambangra, so that Unilever was under no immediate pressure to come to terms. But the main point in dispute which held up agreement did not even emerge until 1965. This was whether, as proposed by LPPL and apparently accepted by the government, LPPL should retain the leasehold of the whole area until it cleared each section, then handing that part of Kulambangra back to the government, or whether the occupation certificate should be surrendered before logging began. The government seems to have decided to demand prior surrender of the whole lease in advance for fear that, during the course of logging, LPPL or LPT might decide it was no longer profitable, stop operations and hold onto those parts of the leasehold land which had not already been cleared. Since the government's main object seems to have been to terminate the concession made to Lever to satisfy growing nationalist criticism of this alienation of the country's endowment, such an ending would have been disastrous. The new demand was launched at LPPL in a letter from the Chief Financial Secretary (as he was now called) on 11 May 1965, explained at a meeting in Honiara on 2 June, and finally set out in a formal letter from the High Commissioner to LPPL on 22 June 1965. The terms offered were that, if the occupation lease for 120,000 acres was returned 'as early as possible', and certainly before logging began, LPT would be allowed 'exclusive rights' to cut timber on the land relinquished, with no obligation to pay stumpage or undertake regeneration, and LPPL could retain

25,000 acres as 'a perpetual estate'. The stated reason for the new proposal was that the government would find it easier to persuade islanders to give up claims to land in the area to be cleared if it had previously been announced that Levers were giving up their concession.

Unilever's reaction was initially very hostile. Walton advised London not to agree on the grounds that, once the government had resumed the leases, it might insist on LPT paying a rent or royalties on the timber. Conversely LPPL could hardly get the proposed rent if it no longer owned the land on which LPT was operating. Plantation Group agreed: a telegram sent in reply to Walton on 2 June 1965 ran 'not prepared comply government proposals . . . but see no objection announcement of principle of eventual repeat eventual release of our holdings with exception 25,000 acres provided this will facilitate timber rights native customary land'. But this was not maintained. Once Plantation Group had seen the minutes of the Honiara meeting of 2 June 1965 they were impressed by the new concession that no time limit would be set on selection of the 25,000 acres to be retained, that there would be no royalty or stump charge and that immediate surrender of the lease might help the government in its negotiations with the islanders. Lancaster concluded that 'there is nothing to lose, and possibly quite a lot to gain in good relations, in accepting the proposals'. LPPL was instructed to negotiate on this basis.

From this moment it was clear that the Honiara government had won its war and the remaining negotiations were over matters of detail. Late in 1968 LPPL surrendered its occupation leases in return for the issue of a permit under the Forest Ordinances entitling them to extract timber without payment of royalty or any obligation to replant the land. The company was to retain 20,000 acres of land in perpetuity for agricultural purposes, but was to return any part of that area without compensation if it had not been developed within 30 years. All other demands on both sides were dropped. Within Unilever it was agreed that LPT would pay LPPL a rent of £20,000 a year, even though the latter no longer owned the land, and a royalty at the same rate per cubic foot as the levy government had by then decided to impose on timber extracted from native customary land, estimated at £20,000 a year. If necessary, LPT would also pay LPPL a service fee of £10,000 a year to help its finances. So, with all parties satisfied, LPT were able to start timber felling on Kulam-bangra late in 1968.

The history of LPPL to the late 1960s thus ends with something resembling a dying fall. The area under cultivation and copra production was very nearly stagnant at about three-quarters of what it had been in 1942. Profitability was very low. After 1968 the total area still held in freehold or on lease was reduced from around 180,000 to some 80,000 acres. Meantime the main Unilever activity in the Solomons had become timber extraction which was a once for all process and not very profitable at that. The concession of the Kulambangra leases was, in effect, an admission that Unilever had at last given up Lever's dream of a really large-scale plantation enterprise in the Solomons. LPPL would never significantly affect the world supply of vegetable oils.

The Profitability of LPPL

There remains the question whether, within its limitations, the Solomons business had proved worthwhile. It was suggested at the start of this chapter that, for a multinational manufacturing company such as Lever/Unilever, two sorts of advantage might be looked for from plantations: the benefit of an assured supply of a potentially scarce raw material, or a financial profit. Seen in relation to Unilever as a whole LPPL had clearly never had any significance on the supply side. Its product was infinitesimally small in proportion to total world production of copra and coconut oil; and, except in wartime, there was never any world shortage. As to the profitability of these plantations seen as a straightforward business investment or as a horizontal diversification, the data is incomplete: there is little firm evidence on capital employed before 1937 and profit figures for 1936–41 and for 1947–53 are missing. But a very rough calculation can be made for two significant and relatively long periods—from the start in 1902 to 1935 and from 1954 to 1965—by taking known post-tax profits as a percentage of estimated capital employed. For the earlier period the capital employed will be taken as £600,000, since the first available figure, for 1927, is £713,000 and most of the investment in new plantations had taken place by 1914. For 1954–65 capital employed is known precisely. The results are as follows:

Profitability of LPPL, 1902–35 and 1954–65

Years	A Average Capital Employed £	B Total Nett Profits £	C Average Nett Profits £	C/A %
1902–35	?600,000	675,844	19,877	3.3
1920–29	?600,000	351,457	35,146	5.8
1954–65	638,333	694,000	57,833	8.3

The earlier figures may understate the average return to capital, since £600,000 may be too high an average figure for the capital employed. Yet on any basis the average yield must have been low since large-scale planting began in 1906 and it was not until after 1920 that the yield of copra reached 5,000 tons, that is, 0.25 tons an acre. In the 1920s profits were reasonable, yet they were low by the standards of most other parts of the Unilever business. To put it another way, by 1935 the total nett profit after 33 years almost exactly equalled total capital employed. Between 1955 and 1965 new capital investment amounted to £782,000 and total nett profits to £584,000. These represent very low rates of return and it is significant that there is no record of any dividends being transferred from LPPL before 1935. Between 1945 and 1965 the only dividend paid was a single lump sum of £480,000 in 1960, which represented profits retained in the business since the war.

Only one conclusion seems possible. Whether considered as a source of vegetable oils or as an investment of capital, LPPL failed to live up to the most modest expectations. The reasons have already been discussed: a generally poor market for copra, relatively high production costs due to adverse conditions and diseconomies of scale resulting from an inadequate labour force. None of this was predictable in 1902 or in 1906 when Lever committed himself to the enterprise: indeed, on the available evidence LPPL might well have turned out to be an admirable investment. More important, the comparative failure of these coconut plantations did not prove that other sorts of plantations in other places where factors were more favourable would be equally unrewarding. It is therefore necessary to examine the history of the Congo plantations in some detail and that of other Lever/Unilever plantations more cursorily before any general conclusions can be drawn on the reward a multinational might reap from undertaking the production of vegetable oils.

9

Huileries du Congo Belge[1]

If Lever's large hopes for the Solomons were disappointed, the project he established in the Belgian Congo in 1911, Huileries du Congo Belge (HCB), came nearer to achieving his ambitions. In 1959 the planted area was 140,868 acres and the product 54,208 tons of palm oil, 25,472 tons of palm kernels, 6,252 tons of hevea rubber, 930 tons of cocoa, 440 tons of coffee and 89 tons of tea. The capital then employed was £14.8 million, turnover £9.6 million and nett profit £1.3 million, giving a yield of 9 per cent. HCB provided 9.2 per cent of the world trade in palm oil and 3.4 per cent of that in palm kernels. Whether or not this could claim to be the world's largest single plantation enterprise, it must surely have satisfied Lever's instinct for operating on the largest possible scale.

So large a venture deserves a full account of its history. Unfortunately there are two reasons why this cannot be provided here. First, an adequate account would require a complete book: HCB must therefore be treated as a case study in certain aspects of plantation production within a multinational company. But even if space was no constraint, it seems unlikely that the source materials for a full history are now available; and to allay suspicions that evidence is concealed this must be explained.

The problem with sources arises from the fact that the structure of HCB was so complicated that no one part of the Lever/Unilever organisation established or preserved a complete archive. From 1911 to 1957 HCB was a Belgian company with its official headquarters in Brussels, after which it became a Congolese registered company with its headquarters in Leopoldville, later Kinshasa. Brussels therefore contained the head office which held certain categories of

494

documents and dealt with matters such as taxation and marketing. But Brussels was never the real decision-making centre for HCB. For the most part it was run by its managing director and staff in Leopoldville, who took their own decisions and sent only such information to Brussels as was necessary. To complicate matters further, ultimate control always lay in England. Until 1925 Lever seems to have taken all important decisions with the advice of a London Committee of the Brussels Board. This committee continued until 1929 when, because of the merger between Levers and Margarine Union, and to escape double taxation in Britain and Belgium, all formal links between Unilever Ltd and HCB were severed. But Special Committee remained the final authority, with Overseas Committee and UAC being involved at various times; and from 1955 the new Plantations Executive/Group in London took responsibility for HCB along with all other plantations. There are, therefore, intermittent materials relating to HCB in Unilever House. Finally, to add to the confusion, from 1931 to 1957 HCB was legally merged with the two other Unilever businesses in Belgium— Savonneries Lever Frères (SLF) and Compagnies Réunies de Raffineries du Congo Belge (CRRCB)—to form a single company, Huilever, whose official accounts do not distinguish between the activities of these three component parts.

The results, so far as they affect historical research, are as follows. There was never a single comprehensive collection of records covering all aspects of the Congo plantations. The material in London survives but is very limited between 1925 and 1955. The Brussels archive was dispersed or destroyed when HCB became a Congolese company in 1957, and there is almost nothing in the present Brussels office of Unilever. There may well be detailed material in the headquarters of the company in Kinshasa (now Plantations Lever au Zaire (PLZ), but if so these were not available when research for this book was done because the company had been nationalised. The surviving evidence makes it possible to provide reasonably confident answers to the questions posed at the start of Chapter 8 about the purpose and character of Lever/ Unilever plantations, but not to tell a continuous story of the evolution of HCB. It is therefore proposed to concentrate on three successive issues at particular times. First, the establishment of the business in 1911 down to the 1930s. The two central themes of this period are Lever's motives and the special character and problems created by a concession of this kind in tropical Africa whose function was to exploit natural resources rather than establish new sources of wealth. In this case the intention was not to set up plantations of oil palms but to collect, mill and export the fruit of natural palms. An enterprise of this kind during the first 40 years of the twentieth century faced problems characteristic of much contemporaneous European economic activity in Africa: physical difficulties, the almost total absence of an infrastructure, the comparative inefficiency of this mode of production and, above all, the moral and practical questions associated with the use of African labour and the use of land claimed by Africans.

These last problems were never satisfactorily solved, but they lost much of their intensity in the later 1930s when HCB began to shift its main effort from culling wild fruit to cultivating oil palm plantations, for these required much less land and were best run by a stabilised labour force. Thus the second main period and theme to be studied runs from about 1938—a convenient but not otherwise significant date when the original Convention of 1911 was renewed in a revised form for a further twenty years—to 1960, when the Congo became independent. The main themes of this period were the rapid extension of oil palm plantations, post-war diversification into other plantation crops, and, in general, the evolution of a sophisticated modern plantation enterprise able to compete with similar plantations in South-east Asia. Yet even during these years ghosts from the past were around, most important the need to extend HCB's monopoly of purchasing natural palm oil and kernels (which they only achieved in the 1920s) within the vicinity of its land holdings. This was the main point at issue when the Convention was revised and reissued yet again in 1958, ironical evidence that even at that late date neither the Belgians nor HCB had any inkling that Belgian authority in the Congo would disappear within two years.

The third and last phase, from 1960–5, was, of course, dominated by the effects of the Congo's independence and the resultant political crisis. 1965 had no significance for these developments and a short summary of later events, notably the nationalisation of HCB along with all European plantations and business enterprises and their subsequent return, will be necessary. At the end of the chapter an attempt will be made to place HCB and the Solomon Island plantations in the context of Unilever's various other plantation enterprises in the 1960s and to reconsider some of the broader themes mentioned at the start of Chapter 8.

The Establishment of HCB, 1911-31

Throughout its life the character of HCB was largely determined by the terms of the Convention made between William Lever and the Belgian government and ratified by the Belgian Parliament in 1911. The Convention, in turn, was the product of traditions deriving from the Congo Free State as it had been developed under Leopold II and, more immediately, of its condition after it had been transferred to Belgium as a full colony in 1908.

(a) The Convention of 1911

Two fundamental features of recent Congolese history gave birth and shape to the concessions made to Lever in 1911: the tradition of making very large concessions of land and other rights to European capitalists, and the virtual absence of any substantial economic development there after some 30 years of European occupation of the Congo. The concession policy was, of course, conceived by Leopold II on the model of the chartered and other trading and colonising companies that had been used by other European states since the sixteenth century to open up land and trade in 'new' lands overseas. The principle was that where an overseas territory was, from a European point of view, so 'undeveloped' that its indigenous inhabitants occupied very little of the land, exploited almost none of its assets and did not generate sufficient products to form the basis of an import/export trade or a tax system, economic activity had to be started by Europeans. If, moreover, the imperial state lacked the means or will to restructure the indigenous economy by public action, it was necessary to invite private capital and enterprise to do so by giving large concessions with or without administrative authority. In its most common form such a concession might give a European company rights to minerals, timber, ivory and other natural products in a relatively large area or areas for a specified period on payment of a royalty on minerals and possibly a proportion of profits or a rent. It would also usually provide that, after a certain period, the company would give up its general rights in return for more limited rights, such as full ownership of such areas of land as it had 'improved'. Such companies were, in effect, regarded as a gamble by government and investor alike: by the government because there was the risk that the company might extract whatever assets they could from their concession as quickly as possible and then withdraw without making any permanent investment; by the company because a great deal of money could easily be spent on surveys, communications, etc. before it was found that the concessionary area offered no readily exploitable sources of wealth.

This is not the place to describe the results of concessions of this type in both the French and Belgian Congo. Many companies were dissolved without making any profit or establishing ̄claims to permanent property and as an engine of economic or social progress most were a disaster. In addition, the methods used in the forcible collection of rubber in the Congo Free State had caused such an outcry in Belgium and other countries that the new Belgian Colonial Ministry set up after the establishment of the colony in 1908 felt bound to ensure that the terms of any future concessions included safeguards for the rights of Africans. Thus the Convention which William Lever signed in 1911 had, if it was to be accepted by the Belgian Parliament, to have two main features: it must ensure that the company fulfilled very precise conditions before it was given any permanent property or rights; and it must protect both the personal freedom and land claims of Africans in the areas in which HCB was to operate.

The first of these features seemed particularly important because by 1908 none of the many Belgian companies set up since 1886 to develop the Congo Free State had made any significant or effective investment in agriculture. Belgians were ready to invest in what they understood—railways and mines—particularly if, as in the former case, the government would guarantee a reasonable return. But they were not attracted by the potentially vast but still unexplored opportunities for developing staple agricultural products or even harnessing natural products such as palm oil, because these required very large investment and gave no security whatever. Yet without private investment there could be no economic development of this sort in the Congo, for the new constitution absolutely ruled out financial assistance by the Belgian government and the Congo government had neither funds nor credit. Someone had to bell this cat; and Jules Renkin, the Colonial Minister, hoped that by enticing a British entrepreneur to invest in an agricultural concession he would achieve two objectives at once: stimulate Belgian capitalists to do the same and offset the fact that the main attack on Leopold II's concessionary policy in the Congo had been organised in Britain.

Clearly the Belgian colonial authorities needed someone like Lever: the surprising thing is that he was prepared to fill the vacant role of pathmaker in the Congo. This becomes still more surprising when the minimum investment laid down by the Belgians, £1 million, is seen in the context of Lever's investment strategy and the size of Lever Brothers' capital at that time. In 1910 the total capital employed by Levers throughout the world was only £6.6 million, and to establish the Congo operation on the scale defined by the Convention, Lever would have to dilute the equity of Lever Brothers by about a sixth and sell some one million pounds worth of preference shares on the market. Hindsight makes the Congo investment seem small in comparison with the purchase of the Niger Company for some £8 millions (also in cash, not shares) in 1920; but the Congo can be seen as the first of Lever's large imaginative or speculative investments, which, during the decade after 1910, increased the total capital employed by Lever Brothers from £6.6 to £47.3 million and radically changed the character of the business. The question is, therefore, why Lever decided to establish a palm oil enterprise in the Congo. The story has been told both by Lever's son and by Wilson and will not be repeated in detail, but two aspects of the original negotiations require emphasis because they are fundamental to later analysis of the fortunes of HCB. These are how much accurate information Lever possessed about the Congo before he signed the Convention in 1911, and the precise terms of the Convention itself.

It is certain that, through no fault of his own, Lever was given an unrealistically favourable view of conditions in the Congo. He was first approached in 1909 by Dr Max Horn, who had been sent to England by Renkin to solicit investment in the Congo. Horn had contacted Sir Alfred Jones, Chairman of the West African shipping firm of Elder Dempster, who had been Consul General in the Congo Free State and was in close business contact with Lever. According to Wilson, Lever was at the time particularly willing to be interested in a large concession in the Congo because of his recent rebuffs in Nigeria and Sierra Leone.[2] He readily began to negotiate with the Belgians; but he was fully aware of the logistical problems of trading in undeveloped and virtually unknown regions of Africa far from the coast, and he therefore took two precautionary steps. First, he sent two successive expeditions to report on the extent and accessibility of natural palm forests and to select the five 'circles' which the Belgian authorities proposed to allocate him. The first mission consisted of Henri de Keyser, an ex-employee of the Congo Free State, and a Lever employee. They were sent off in 1909 and reported in favourable but general terms in 1910. The second embassy was L. H. Moseley, who had served with the Bank of West Africa and was thought to be expert on palm oil production and trade, and an engineer, H. Beckwith, who would report on the technical aspects of building oil mills and establishing communications. Their commission was to investigate the various regions in which there were said to be large concentrations of natural oil palms and to recommend five 'circles' with a radius of 60 kilometres which offered good prospects for harvesting natural fruit and transporting the oil and kernels economically to the coast.

The future success of HCB largely turned on how well these men did their job; and according to Sidney Edkins, who was Manager of Leverville (Lusanga) from the start and whose unpublished account is an essential source for this early period, they did it badly. They visited three of the five regions suggested by the Belgian authorities —Lusanga, Elisabetha and Alberta—but not the other two, Flandria and Brabanta. Even in those they visited, so Edkins claimed, their personal knowledge 'was limited to a walk of a few miles into the interior at two places in the Lusanga circle and at one place in the Elisabetha and Alberta circles, and it was on this evidence and some unreliable information given by the Government Officials and the Agents of Trading Concerns that the positions of the circles to be granted was fixed'. Lusanga was the only area containing sufficient natural palm forest 'to really justify the obligations imposed on Lever Bros. Ltd. by the Convention'. Alberta and Elisabetha could just about feed a mill in each circle processing 1,000 tons of fruit a month; but Brabanta and Flandria, which had not even been brought under Belgian administration at this time, and could therefore not be visited safely, were found later to contain only very small and quite inadequate areas of natural palm forest. Yet Moseley and Beckwith wrote a generally favourable report, recommending acceptance of the five circles proposed by the Belgian authorities. Their main reservations were that social conditions were bad; that Africans, particularly in the Lusanga region, appeared to have been alienated by the harsh treatment they had received during the previous 20 years; and that Belgian officials and private firms were likely to be obstructive because they feared foreign intrusion.

On this basis Lever decided to go ahead; but he must have felt some hesitation because his second precautionary step was to attempt to form a partnership with the Belgian banker, Albert Thys, of the Banque d'Outre Mer, who had founded the first Belgian

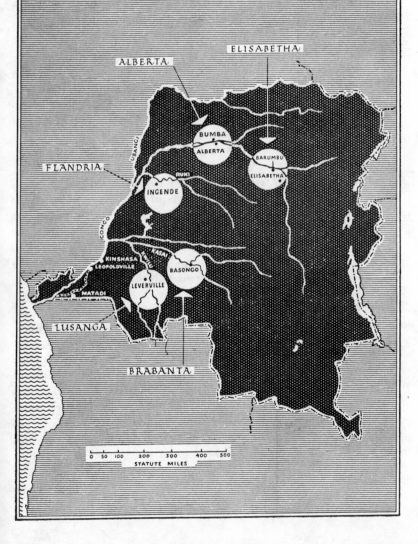

THE
BELGIAN CONGO
*showing the relative situation of
the concession areas of the
1911 convention*

ALBERTA

ELISABETHA

SANGA

FLANDRIA

BUMBA
ALBERTA

BARUMBU
ELISABETHA

RUKI

INGENDE

CONGO

KINSHASA
LEOPOLDVILLE

KASAI

MATADI

BASONGO

LEVERVILLE

LUSANGA

BRABANTA

0 50 100   200   300   400   500
STATUTE MILES

investment company operating in the Congo, the Compagnie du Congo pour le Commerce et l'Industrie (CCCI) in 1886. A partnership with Thys would have had the triple advantage for Lever of spreading his risks, buying expertise and mollifying those many Belgians who were likely to resent his intrusion as a foreigner in Belgium's solitary colonial possession. But Thys would have none of it. According to Edkins, Thys replied

> My dear Sir, form a Company to exploit the wild oil palms in the Upper Congo, hopeless, there aren't any palms there worth mentioning and I know my Congo. If you want to exploit oil palms, you should go to the Mayumbe in the Lower Congo and even there all the available labour is needed for the cocoa plantations and timber concessions which, dealing with more valuable products than palm oil and kernels, can pay higher wages than you can afford.[3]

This, as it turned out, was good advice, though it was later discovered that the Mayumbe region also would have been unsatisfactory, since the oil content of the fruit of palms in that area was substantially less than in the upper Congo where Lever got his concessions. But he rejected it. He may have assumed that Thys was trying to divert him into those parts of the Congo in which he already had interests, or he may have put greater faith in the reports made by his investigators. In any case he must have thought the risks were reasonable, for in April 1911 he signed a Convention with the Belgian government which, after ratification by the Belgian Parliament, became the basis of his rights in the Congo and the establishment of HCB in May 1911. The Convention plays so large a part in the history of HCB that its terms need careful analysis. Its main characteristic is that it attempted to reconcile two incompatible objectives. On the one hand Lever was to be given a reasonable chance to make profits from natural oil palm products; on the other hand there were to be no adverse consequences for the Africans whose labour was essential to his success and whose claims to possess rights to part at least of the land which the Convention allocated to HCB were necessarily over-ridden. Or, to put the position in a broader historical context, the Convention expressed the then evolving notion, which was later given its classical expression in Lugard's *Dual Mandate*, that the happiness and improvement of Africans was fully compatible with profit-making enterprises run by

Europeans.[4] The Convention was a long and complicated document, but its main points can be summarised in the form of three statements, each defining a particular complex of obligations and benefits; the first the benefits to be received by Belgium and the Congo, the second the benefits to be received by Levers, the last the rights and obligations of the Africans.

(1) The Benefits Expected by Belgium and the Congo. Lever promised (articles 1 & 2) that, within three months of the publication of the Belgian decree granting him concessions, he would set up a company with an authorised capital of not less than 25 million francs (£1 million) which must be fully subscribed at the start. Within six years (extended to eleven years because of the First World War, as were all other time limits defined in the original Convention) he would set up oil mills in the five circles defined as his spheres of activity, each capable of processing at least 6,000 tons of fresh fruit a year. HCB would also, at its own expense (article 6), set up a system of road, river and rail transport and telegraphic communications to its circles, which could be used by the colonial authorities for a reasonable charge and which could (article 10) be expropriated with compensation. By article 5 at least one-third of the machinery and plant (other than that made at Port Sunlight) and at least half all other imported goods had to come from Belgium. All company boats must be Belgian registered and at least half of the European staff of HCB must be of Belgian nationality. All this would be pure gain to colony and metropolis because neither undertook any counterbalancing obligations; and if HCB did not maintain a defined time-table of investment and development, it would automatically forfeit the land and other rights which were to be its reward. In this respect the Belgians had clearly learned from the disastrous experience of earlier concessions in tropical Africa.

(2) The Benefits Offered to Levers. Levers' main return for this very considerable commitment would be the right to utilise and eventually to own land in the Congo. Article 8 gave HCB the initial right to collect fruit from 'domainial lands bearing Elais palms, situated around and within a radius of sixty kilometres of each [of five] points'. This, however, was a preliminary stage. HCB's ultimate reward would be to own a maximum of 750,000 hectares of land in freehold, which could lie in any of its five circles, provided no more than 200,000 hectares were in any one circle. But that final stage

would not be reached until 1944, and then only if HCB had complied with an extremely arduous set of regulations. The aim was, very sensibly, to ensure that the promised investment and development should be carried out before any permanent rewards were given. To obtain any land at all, and that only leasehold, HCB had to be capable of processing at least 6,000 tons of fruit a year in any one circle by 1917(1922). It could then mark out 75,000 hectares in that circle and, if the government approved, HCB would hold this land in lease until 1944, when it might, provided other conditions mentioned later were met, be converted into freehold. If, however, HCB could process 15,000 tons a year by 1921(1926), the leaseholds could be extended to 200,000 hectares in any one circle, up to the maximum of 750,000 hectares altogether. At that point HCB would give up its original right to collect or buy natural palm products within the whole area of any one circle and would restrict its operations to its leaseholds. Thereafter, that is from 1921(1926), HCB had to satisfy a further set of conditions in order to transform its leaseholds into freehold. It must demarcate the provisional boundaries of its claims by 1921(1926) and the final boundaries by 1931(1936). From 1932(1937) it must, by article 9, export every year '1,000 kilograms or its equivalent oleaginous products, per fifty hectares held on lease . . .'. If this was done, the final reckoning would come at the end of 1944(1949). By article 12 HCB could in any case transform 40,000 hectares of leasehold into freehold land in each circle, up to a maximum of 150,000 hectares. It could claim additional freehold in the ratio of four hectares for each ton of oil (or its equivalent) exported from a Congo sea port in the course of the preceding five years. Provided HCB kept to this rigorous time-table and had exported an average of 30,000 tons of oil, etc. during the quinquennium 1940–4 (1945–9) it would finally emerge with 750,000 hectares—1,875,000 acres—of freehold land in the Congo.

In retrospect these seem grotesque and impossibly legalistic conditions, inspired, perhaps, by the game of snakes and ladders or the concept of stimulating a donkey with both carrot and stick. In the event two world wars and practical experience made it essential to modify the rules and Unilever emerged with a smaller area— 350,000 hectares—much of it operated in a totally unforeseen way. Yet, if emphasis is laid on broad aims rather than legal niceties, the Convention had one great virtue from the standpoint of the Congo: HCB would have to invest a great deal of hard cash and operate successfully for 35 years before it obtained any permanent rights there. This alone distinguished the HCB Convention from most of the earlier concessions made to Europeans in tropical Africa.

(3) The Rights and Obligations of Africans. The most distinctive feature of the Convention was that it purported to give Africans full protection against those types of exploitation practised then and later in most parts of tropical Africa while at the same time ensuring that HCB obtained the labour force it would need. No aspect of squaring the circle was more difficult. Africans would be involved in HCB's operations in two capacities—as occupiers or occasional users of at least part of the land assigned to HCB and as the only available supply of labour. By 1911 the state of humanitarian opinion in Belgium and Europe made it impossible for the Congo government openly to ignore African land rights, to force Africans to work for HCB, or even to sell the company all their tradable produce. Yet in practice HCB was almost certain to harvest natural oil palm fruit from land used by Africans for cultivation or hunting; and, since a large labour force was essential for collecting and carrying the fruit, some form of pressure would almost certainly have to be exerted on reluctant Africans to take paid employment with the company. Finally the whole HCB operation could be ruined if other trading concerns were able to buy palm produce freely within areas the company had opened up for its own use, so a *de facto* monopoly would have to be imposed within the five circles. All this meant that the Convention would have to steer a devious path. It must appear to provide all the safeguards for African welfare which European humanitarians were demanding, while at the same time it must, specifically or by omission, ensure that HCB had adequate access to the land, labour and palm products it needed.

This the Convention did very skilfully. Heavy emphasis was laid on the duties of HCB as a paternalistic employer: indeed, Lever's son later alleged that the support given by the Belgian socialist leader, Vandervelde, in parliament resulted from his knowledge of workers' conditions at Port Sunlight, which he assumed would be the model for Lever factories in the Congo.[5] By article 4 HCB was to keep 'at least one medical man' and one hospital in each circle, together with schools which would give instruction in 'one of the national languages of Belgium or in a native language'. This was easily fulfilled: the real difficulties were African employment and land rights. Article 3 laid it down that adult African labourers must be paid at least 25 centimes a day (about 2.4d sterling), excluding rations. If they were employed on contract work supplying fruit, the price paid must be calculated so that an adult was 'able to comfortably earn an amount at least equal to the salary fixed above for an eight-hour working day . . .'. All labour contracts could be cancelled by a Belgian colonial official. All this implied that Africans would work for HCB if they chose to do so: nothing was said about what would happen if they refused. The rights conferred upon HCB as prospective leaseholder of land claimed by Africans were left equally vague. Article 10 gave HCB 'the right of gathering, treating and exporting the oleaginous products' from areas held in leasehold, but did not specify whether this excluded Africans. Conversely Africans would be free 'to gather for their own account, india rubber, ivory and copal which may be found on the land held on lease by the Company . . . without, however, injuring its plantations nor hindering the exploitation of the oleaginous products'. Did this mean that the natives could also collect palm fruit in the leasehold areas 'for their own use'? Again, were they free to collect palm products from parts of the circles which were not demarcated as leaseholds for sale to third parties, the rival European merchants? On these vital issues the Convention was silent.

Potentially the most difficult problem of all concerned African land rights, yet this too was virtually ignored in the Convention. Article 8 stated that, until it had chosen its leasehold land, the company could 'establish itself provisionally on lands not burdened with the rights of third parties . . .'; and article 15 expressly stated that all rights given to HCB were 'under the reserve of the rights of third parties, natives or otherwise and according to the terms of the Royal Decree of the 23rd. February 1910 for the sale or the letting of land in the Belgian Congo as far as the present provisions do not detract therefrom'. This could only mean that Africans' claims to effective occupation or use of land would be protected, as they had not been under the Congo Free State: but in 1911 no one had any idea what these claims would be, and it was highly likely that they would prove to be so extensive and undefined that delimitation would take many years, holding up the rigid time-table imposed on HCB.

Seen as a whole, then, the main feature of the Convention was that it cloaked ambiguities in the deceptively precise language of legal obligation and entitlement. From Lever's standpoint his ability to qualify for the benefits held out depended on three quite unpredictable factors: whether there were enough natural palms within the circles he had chosen and in sufficient concentration to allow economic operation of the central factories; uncertainties about native land rights and the availability of African labour; and, more broadly, factors affecting profitability—transport costs, export duties and the market price of palm oil and kernels. These constitute the main themes in the history of HCB during the first period of its development from 1911 to the eve of the Second World War.

(b) Investment and Profits

The most important and surprising fact about the early history of HCB is that it not only survived but met all the targets set by the convention for 1921 by about 1925, allowing for the five-year extension of the various deadlines granted due to the war. When Lever made his final visit in 1924/5 there were seven mills in the five circles, which processed 56,000 tons of fruit and produced 10,000 tons of oil and 4,800 tons of kernels for export. Welfare requirements were more than met: by December 1926 there were 15 hospitals, five schools and more than the required number of doctors, nurses, etc. for the 23,000 African workers and 335 European staff. Some 1,000 kilometres of road and 70 kilometres of light railway had been built and there was a river fleet of 19 steamers and 72 barges. In addition to HCB Lever also ran a trading company, SEDEC, whose function was to buy palm fruit and other natural products outside the concessionary circles in order to increase the volume of fruit available for processing by the factories. And of course there was SAVCO, the small soap factory at Leopoldville started in 1922. On the face of it this was a stupendous achievement and the question is how it was done and at what price.

The basic answer is that Lever and his subordinates showed exceptional determination in overcoming the many physical and psychological problems they encountered. Lever insisted throughout that the venture must not fail and it was this and his readiness to investigate and decide even minute problems that took HCB past the early disasters which wrecked so many contemporary African ventures. Yet in analytical terms the survival and relative success of HCB are explained by two things—the very large and probably disproportionate amount of capital Lever was prepared to sink in the company and the fact that compromise solutions were worked out in the early 1920s to the joint obstacles of land utilisation and labour supply.

The fact that dominated the commercial life of HCB from 1911 to the 1970s was that it cost very much more to create the initial infrastructure and set up the factories than presumably Lever had expected or intended. As had been seen, the authorised and paid up capital of HCB was set at £1 million. Already by June 1914 Lever

Table 9.1   HCB: Production and Export of Palm Oil and Kernels, 1911–31 (Including those Bought by SEDEC) ('000 metric tons)

Year	Fruit processed	Exports		Total Congo exports	
		Oil	Kernels	Oil	Kernels
1911	–	–	–	2.3	6.7
1912	3.0	0.39	0.1	1.9	5.9
1913	5.0	0.65	0.2	1.9	7.2
1914	8.0	1.0	0.3	2.5	8.1
1915	10.0	1.3	0.4	3.4	11.0
1916	20.3	2.4	0.7	3.8	22.4
1917	22.9	3.5	1.6	–	–
1918	27.3	4.6	2.2	n/a	n/a
1919	25.8	4.7	2.1	n/a	n/a
1920	29.3	5.4	2.2	n/a	n/a
1921	31.7	5.7	2.3	n/a	n/a
1922	41.3	7.4	3.0	n/a	n/a
1923	45.3	8.1	3.6	n/a	n/a
1924	54.1	9.7	4.3	n/a	n/a
1925	56.6	10.1	4.8	n/a	n/a
1926	58.3	10.3	5.9	n/a	n/a
1927	64.7	11.8	6.5	n/a	n/a
1928	74.7	13.9	7.8	n/a	n/a
1929	84.2	15.8	8.8	27.0	n/a
1930	96.9	18.0	10.3	37.0	n/a
1931	94.9	17.4	10.1	37.0	n/a

said that £520,000 had been spent and in November 1915 he reported that this had risen to £800,000. In October 1917 the Policy and Tactics Committee was told that capital invested was £840,000. There are no surviving statements for the next twelve years, but in 1930 the share capital was £2,385,857 and total capital employed £3,045,109. No profits were made until the two boom years 1918/19 and 1919/20, and these amounted to a total of £71,413. This was followed by losses amounting to £330,000 in the two years 1920/1 and 1921/2.

Clearly palm oil production in the Congo was a poor way to employ Lever Brothers' capital and in 1915–17 and again in 1921/2 Lever's senior management in Britain seriously challenged his policy of ploughing more and more money into HCB and this criticism, together with the difficulty of exporting capital goods under wartime conditions, had the result that little new investment took place until after 1918. But in the end Lever had his way and by November 1923 the main investment had been made. Lever ruefully told E. Hyslop Bell, an HCB director, that he had by then sunk 'between two and three millions of money in the Belgian Congo [and was] just beginning to reap the reward of our persistency and bull-doggedness in holding on . . . I wish I could say skill in handling but I feel sure that we have made so many blunders all through that I had better say nothing about this'. Nevertheless he remained enthusiastic to the end, and on his last visit of 1924/5 he planned a great deal of additional capital expenditure, most of it non-productive, on accommodation for both Europeans and Africans and on welfare services.

It is, therefore, clear that HCB survived and fulfilled its early targets only because Lever was willing and able to pour far more money into the Congo than was justified by the current or pre-dictable earning potential of the business. As a result HCB was always heavily over-capitalised. It could show reasonable profits only when oil prices were exceptionally good, as in 1918–19 and, to a lesser extent, from 1924 to 1929. Even so the return to capital would not have been acceptable to Lever from his soap factories; and in the 1930s much of the original capital had to be written off. This was the financial price of success in establishing HCB.

(c) *Labour Problems*

The ability of HCB to function at all depended on finding a solution or palliative for the complex problems of African labour and land rights, which became more acute in the early 1920s as the number of oil mills and the consequential demand for fruit increased. By the 1930s answers, or at least temporary solutions, had been found to both, though neither was satisfactory from a commercial and still less from a moral point of view.

The problem of labour supply was common to most parts of Africa and other places where the indigenous population was not accustomed to doing paid work. The desire to work for wages and their reward had to be implanted, and this was made more difficult

Table 9.2 HCB: Profits as Shown in the Accounts, 1911—55
('000 Belgian Francs and £'000 Sterling at official exchange rate)

Date	Gross (Francs)	Tax reserve (Francs)	Nett Francs	Nett £
(To 31 June)				
1911/13	(37)	—	(37)	(1.5)
1914/16	(7,007)	—	(7,007)	(200.3)
1917	(2,435)	—	(2,435)	(96.2)
1918	(380)	—	(380)	(15.0)
1919	1,056	(10)	1,046	34.0
1920	1,801	(10)	1,791	39.3
1921	(11,714)	—	(11,714)	(225.2)
1922	(5,411)	—	(5,411)	(104.0)
1923	1,905	(393)	1,512	3.1
1924	4,086	(86)	4,000	134.5
1925	7,071	(2,860)	4,210	123.3
1926	24,241	(2,144)	22,096	127.5
1927	21,087	373	21,461	122.8
1928	24,332	(195)	24,137	138.2
1929	27,059	294	27,353	156.7
(To December — 18 months)				
1929–30	19,236	43	19,280	82.7
1931	(6,192)	—	(6,192)	n/a
1932	(24,961)	—	(24,961)	n/a
1933	(18,377)	—	(18,377)	n/a

Year	(Reserved in	Tax Issue	Combined	Huilever SA
1934	(10,555)	—	(10,555)	n/a
1935	3,939		3,939	n/a
1936	25,956		25,956	n/a
1937	26,857		26,857	n/a
1938	1,391		1,391	n/a
1939	19,438		19,438	n/a
1940	(1,713)		(1,713)	n/a
1941	38,021	(3,750)	34,271	342
1942	58,802	(10,240)	48,562	277
1943	52,854	(8,868)	43,986	251
1944	37,373	(8,288)	29,139	166
1945	25,575	(1,986)	23,589	134
1946	46,818	(518)	46,300	264
1947	148,581	(18,750)	129,781	741
1948	204,466	(41,000)	163,466	934
1949	258,223	(47,500)	210,723	1,505
1950	216,077	(24,050)	192,027	1,371
1951	326,533	(74,000)	252,533	1,803
1952	231,393	(25,000)	206,393	1,474
1953	179,802	(21,000)	158,802	1,134
1954	225,006	(26,300)	198,706	1,419
1955	257,062	(35,000)	222,062	1,586

Notes: a. These figures are taken from the only surviving continuous statement of profits for the whole period. It is clear from Table 9.3 for 1955 that nett profit is accounting profit; but 'gross profit' is not identical with the 'trading profit' in Table 10.7 below and it is not clear what this represents.

b. No sterling equivalent is given for 1931–40 because the exchange rate varied considerably.

where, as in much of the Congo, commodity production was profitable only so long as the labour cost was very low indeed. For HCB these common problems were intensified by the nature of its activities and the work Africans were required to do. The collection and transportation of natural oil palm products from trees dispersed over vast areas was a highly inefficient means of producing vegetable oil, particularly when the company was competing with palm oil produced under much more suitable circumstances in West Africa and increasingly also with palm oil from plantations in South-east Asia as well as with vegetable oils derived from other sources such as groundnut and coconut oil. High wages would, in fact, have made the whole HCB enterprise totally unprofitable. Further, cutting palm fruit from wild trees was intensely unpopular with most Africans. In many African societies this was slaves' work: few men would do it voluntarily. In the end the solution was to establish plantations which, because the trees could be concentrated into limited areas and the whole process of cutting and transport made more efficient, would also make it possible to recruit and keep a professional and relatively well-paid voluntary labour force. This, as will be seen, was the policy adopted from the later 1930s. But for the first quarter century HCB had to operate under the conditions it found in its five circles; and the question is how it managed to obtain and keep sufficient workers—over 26,000 between the five areas in 1930—to enable it to meet its successive production targets.

The simple answer is that the Belgian government, which had defined the objective, also provided the means. The Convention had stated (article 3) that one of HCB's functions was to stimulate the African population to take paid work and so extend the cash economy. The minimum wage of 25 centimes a day might not be sufficient to attract enough men, so the government stimulated labour recruitment in two ways. First, they imposed capitation and supplementary taxes (the second based on the number of wives a man had and so essentially a luxury tax), both of which had to be paid in cash and not in kind. This forced Africans to sell either goods or their labour. The level of these taxes varied between one province and another, commonly adjusted according to the opportunities available for earning money and local attitudes to taking paid work. In Elisabetha circle, for example, the local commissioner calculated in 1915 that there was a local adult male labour force of about 20,000, and, if these men worked in rotation as cutters for about six weeks at a time, HCB would always have a labour supply of about 2,000. He therefore set the annual tax at F. 12, which could be earned in 48 working days at the minimum rate. Since the company provided rations and accommodation, Africans would pay all they earned to the government; only if they stayed longer than 48 days would they have a surplus to spend in the stores the company was induced to set up and run (at virtually cost prices) in each centre.

The second method used by the Congo authorities was administrative pressure. Local officials would instruct chiefs to allocate men to sign contracts to work as cutters for specified periods, commonly three years: often the chiefs received a proportion of the wages, though, if they sent their slaves, the chiefs took all money earned after payment of tax. Government agents also normally accompanied company recruiters when they toured the villages to give additional support; and pressure was added by Catholic missions who shared the government's general objectives. The result was that the men recruited by HCB (and by most other European enterprises) were conscripts. The system closely resembled that described by modern 'under-development' theorists who have argued that 'pre-capitalist' servile labour was typical of the operation of foreign capitalism in less developed countries.

These methods were not, however, common to all the HCB circles nor were they consistent over time. Flandria and Brabanta, which were not opened until the early 1920s and were found to possess relatively few oil palms, do not seem to have had great difficulty in recruiting a sufficient local labour force, supplemented by recruitment further afield. Africans living in the Brabanta region in particular were said to have been comparatively sophisticated and anxious to work for wages. In Elisabetha, after early dependence on unwilling local labour, HCB built up a permanent labour force largely recruited elsewhere: by 1930 only about 1,000 of the 6,350 working there were locally recruited and 3,000 from other places had become part of a stabilised labour force. Thus it was Lusanga/ Leverville in Kasai province which created the greatest problems and requires the most detailed description.

The basic trouble with the Lever business in Lusanga was that, while this was the first circle to be developed and had the best concentration of natural palms, the local labour force was totally inadequate to meet the needs of the mills. There were several reasons for this: the oil palms were widely dispersed, population in the circle was limited and people were generally reluctant, after earlier experience, to work for a European company. HCB had little difficulty in recruiting men to work in the factories but they never solved the problem of getting volunteer labour to cut and carry fruit from the more distant oil palm concentrations. From the start, according to Edkins, recruitment was impossible 'for the price the Société could afford to pay, 10/- (12.5 francs) a ton'. Moreover the region had been devastated by sickness, under-nourishment and inter-tribal wars, so that the remaining population were in very poor physical condition.[6] Three complementary solutions were adopted. First, HCB relied on local chiefs to provide labour which, as Harold Greenhalgh discovered with disgust in 1915, consisted almost entirely of slaves, many of them children who lacked the strength to act as carriers. The company stopped the allocation of children but could not avoid reliance on slaves who were sent back after the end of each contractual period by their chiefs and so came to form a permanent semi-servile labour force. In 1930 Greenhalgh found that many of the original slaves were still working for HCB and that it was now impossible ever to send them home because their chiefs would not allow them back.

One alternative was to recruit Africans living further afield and some were brought from distant parts of the Congo. The other was to make contracts with men living in areas where there were concentrations of oil palms to cut and carry fruit to the nearest collecting point rather than to leave home and work in company camps. This was generally preferred by Africans and saved the company the cost and inconvenience of building and running camps. In 1930 Greenhalgh claimed that contract cutters of this type were being paid F. 100 a ton for decorticated fruit and that the system was so successful that it had been adopted also in Elisabetha, where it was not uncommon for men to earn as much as F.200 a month by hard work. In Lusanga the result was that 8,000 of the total labour force of 12,000 to 13,000 lived in their own villages and worked round the year, earning far more than the government demanded in taxes so that they could afford 'luxuries' such as bicycles and sewing machines.

But Greenhalgh, presumably depending on information provided by the HCB management, painted too rosy a picture. There were serious defects when he wrote this report and a year later, in 1931, things became worse as the international slump forced down palm oil and kernel prices and so what HCB was prepared to pay to contract cutters. Average prices for palm oil at Liverpool dropped from £37 a ton in 1928 to £20 in 1930, £17 2s 0d in 1931 and £13 12s 0d in 1933. This meant that, while HCB had to pay its regular labour force the minimum 25 centimes a day, it had to extract as much work as possible from them; and also that it was willing to buy oil and kernels from Africans only at derisorily low prices. Meantime long-run defects had been highlighted by two reports made in 1930, the first by a Belgian doctor in government service, Dr Daco, the other by a Belgian Area Manager in the Lusanga circle, C. H. Dupont, who was at odds with the Managing Director at Leopoldville, E. Dusseljie; and some, though not all, their allegations were supported by a subsequent official commission set up at the request of HCB. In particular, the commission, consisting of Belgian colonial officials, criticised three things: the inflexibility of contracts made with independent cutters which took no account of seasonal variations in the amount of fruit available; the continued use of slaves sent by their chiefs; and excessive dependence on action by state officials in matters of discipline. The report made a number of specific proposals for reforming these and other practices, but ended with a tribute to the social, medical and economic improvements HCB had brought about and a statement of faith in Dusseljie's humane views and his ability to play an effective moderating role.

That was in 1930. A year later an event occurred some 200 kilometres to the south of the Lusanga circle which emphasised that under slump conditions already vulnerable aspects of the system of labour recruitment and contract cutting had become so much worse that they were a threat to the peace of the province.[7] HCB, in common with other trading and oil producing enterprises such as the Compagnie du Kasai (CK), had come to rely on using African labour in the Kikwit region, from the Mbunda, Kwese and Pende tribes. From 1924 the local administration had given official support to HCB's recruiters by bringing pressure to bear on the chiefs to produce men to work at Lusanga. These men technically accepted three-year contracts, after which they were roped up and marched off. Quite large numbers were involved—987 in 1930, 300 in the first five months of 1931. The death rate among these men, according to later oral evidence, was sometimes as high as 50 per cent, and when they could no longer work they were simply told to walk home. All this was a continuing grievance among these tribes, but resentment came to a head in 1931 because of another aspect of official policy. The dramatic fall in the international price of oil meant that local European traders were only interested in buying it from the Africans at unacceptably low prices, which had fallen from over F.1 a kilo to 30 centimes a kilo for palm fruit during the previous four years. Under free market conditions the Africans would presumably have refused to fulfil their contracts to supply fruit and nuts at these prices; but Belgian policy was to maintain the volume of commodity exports and to force Africans to work even at this very low return; and to force them to do so the local administration increased and rigorously collected the capitation and supplementary taxes. Since the price of imported consumer goods remained at virtually its previous level, Africans found themselves compelled to work intensively merely to pay their taxes. When the Kwango region failed to pay its quota of taxes, the administration resorted to physical punishment, including whipping and seizing the wives of those who refused to pay. It happened that the refusal of a Pende community at Lilamba in May 1931 to provide cutters for HCB and CK provided the occasion for a rising. The male villagers had fled, so the Belgian officials who accompanied the recruiting agents burned the village and seized several wives as hostages. A chief who complained was whipped. He then joined a revolutionary sect, the Tupelepele and subsequently staged a rising. A Belgian official was killed and his limbs dispersed as a symbol of the weakness of Belgian rule. Eventually the rising was put down by the Force Publique with extraordinary savagery.

The significance for this study of the Pende revolt lies mainly in the light it throws on the Belgian strategy of using fiscal policy backed by physical force to induce Africans to work as labourers and producers against their will. HCB was in some sense a lay figure because it was caught between the government's insistence that it must maintain production and exports of palm products to fulfil the conditions of the Convention and the fact that in Lusanga at least, the largest of its productive units, this could only be done by relying on the state to provide it with semi-servile labour. Clearly the whole system of exploiting the natural palm forests of the Lusanga region was fundamentally unsound, particularly under the economic conditions of the early 1930s. Nor was the Africans' loss Unilever's gain: HCB made very large losses in 1931–4 and made a reasonable profit in only two years between 1931 and 1940. Unfortunately there are no surviving or available records of either the volume of HCB's production between 1930 and the 1950s or their methods of labour recruitment and employment, so it is impossible to know what happened after 1931 and how soon the system described above was replaced. But the limited evidence already considered at least makes it possible to answer the question posed above—how HCB was able to solve or evade the constraint imposed by the shortage of indigenous labour whereas LPPL in the Solomons could not do this. The difference was that, whereas the British protectorate administration would neither force the islanders to work on plantations nor allow indentured immigration, the Belgian authorities allowed and indeed forced HCB to stick to its production targets by compelling Africans to work for them. This, it must be emphasised, was significant mainly in the Lusanga/ Leverville circle; but it nevertheless demonstrates that exploitation of natural palm products in the Congo on the scale required by the Convention was made possible only by using methods of labour recruitment and employment which would not have been tolerated in any British colonial possession by the 1930s. Only the conversion to plantation production and the use of a relatively well paid, permanent and voluntary labour force, which was possible on plantations and developed from the 1930s, could provide a satisfactory solution to this dilemma.

(d) The Tripartite Agreements

The other major problem the Convention had evaded was definition of African rights to land and the broader issue of whether they were free to exploit oil palm and other natural products within and around HCB's circles and later leaseholds. Since the solutions adopted effectively stretched the Convention to meet the company's needs and then became a critical element in the relations between company and government until the Congo became independent, it is necessary to establish how these matters were arranged.

There were, in fact, three problems inherent in this and any land concession made on this scale in tropical Africa. First, if HCB was entitled to claim leases of any 'vacant' land within their circles, provided only that they qualified for them and claimed them within the specified time, it was very unlikely that a severely under-staffed Congo administration could carry out the essential preliminary surveys and investigation of African rights. Second, the Convention had envisaged a rapid transition from collection of natural palm fruit over the whole area of the five concessions to concentration on the maximum of 200,000 h. leasehold which HCB would be entitled to select within any one circle. In practice, however, it was soon found that in some circles, notably Flandria and Brabanta, natural palms were so widely dispersed that there would not have been sufficient palms within any 200,000 h. to feed the oil mills specified by the Convention. The only solution would be for HCB to have the right, whether exclusive or not, to collect fruit outside its leaseholds; and this would require an amendment to the Convention. The final problem was related to this because it turned on whether Africans could sell palm fruit, kernels or oil taken from trees within the original HCB circles to rival traders. By inference (though the Convention was not explicit) it seemed that once HCB had claimed and been awarded the lease of a particular block, it would have a monopoly of the 'oleaginous products' found there, though the Africans explicitly retained their right to 'gather for their own account' non-oleaginous products found in these leasehold areas. Equally it seemed that Africans would have complete freedom to trade in palm products from areas in which they were recognised as having rights and, by negative inference, also from residual parts of the concessionary circles not included in the company's chosen leaseholds. This seemed eminently reasonable: the difficulty was that it would be quite impossible to distinguish fruit taken from HCB's leases from fruit cut on African land and elsewhere. It was therefore predictable that, as soon as the company had invested its capital on opening up these areas, other traders would move in and buy fruit from the Africans who were unlikely to worry whether they collected it from company, African or public land. The result might be a free market in palm products, similar to that in British West Africa where there were virtually no foreign concessions; and this would make nonsense of the whole investment strategy on which the Convention was based.

All these problems arose because the Convention had ignored the realities of conditions in the Congo. By the early 1920s there was only one possible solution, or at least temporary expedient: to ignore the distinction between different sorts of land—company leaseholds, areas to which Africans might eventually establish a claim, the colony's domainial land—and give HCB a *de facto* monopoly of the commercial exploitation of natural oil palm products throughout their concessionary circles until it was feasible to demarcate the rights of each party. This could not be done overtly as an act of state because monopoly was contrary to the colonial charter of 1908 and smacked of the Congo Free State scandals. The essence of the Tripartite agreements was, therefore, that each interested party would waive its precise rights, voluntarily and for a defined period. This would merely postpone the final reckoning, but meantime HCB could get going and could consider its future policy, including the alternative strategy of establishing plantations which would largely solve all these land problems by ending the company's dependence on natural palm products. This alternative was not, in fact, fully grasped until late in the 1920s or acted on for another decade; but it was clearly understood by 1915 that, unless a temporary compromise was worked out, HCB had no hope of success.

The First World War postponed action, but after 1920 a solution of the three issues became pressing because HCB could not expand its investment as the Convention required until the question of native land rights had been solved or shelved. The outcome of prolonged negotiations was the so-called Tripartite agreements. It is not clear who was responsible for these: Edkins claimed that he negotiated them with the then Governor-General, Lippens, while in 1930 Greenhalgh attributed them to Max Horn. Nor is it clear when agreement was reached: Edkins said it was in 1921/2, and so far as the negotiations in the Congo were concerned this may have been so; but as late as November 1923 Lever was writing to E. Hyslop Bell about 'the hitch that has occurred in the ratification of the Tripartite agreement relating to the Belgian Congo'. In the end agreements relating to different areas officially came into force at various times in 1925, but all were due to last in the first instance until 1936. In fact, as will be seen, they were then extended in revised form until 1944, continued yet again until 1956, and finally remodelled and reissued in 1958. It is not too much to say that they largely determined the evolving character of HCB.

They were called Tripartite because in principle three separate agreements were involved, each between two willing negotiators. The first was between the Congo government and the various African social groups living in the concessionary circles. These multiple agreements, negotiated individually by the colonial administration, had the effect of temporarily homogenising as '*indivise*' all land which might ultimately be declared 'company', 'domainial' or 'African' without in any way affecting the legal rights and claims of any party. This made it possible for the colony to make the second agreement, with HCB, by which the company was allowed for ten years to use for the collection of natural palm products not only the area of land which it would eventually be entitled to hold as leases but also land which seemed likely in the end to be classified as 'native land' when proper investigations had taken place. The company would go ahead with demarcating and claiming its lease-holds, the government would investigate possible native rights and, if none were found, the leases would date from May 1936.

But the most important agreements from the company's stand-point were the third set, made directly between HCB and individual African political or social units in each area covered by the Convention. By no means all the groups approached were prepared to make an agreement; but those that did so agreed that all palm fruit growing in the *indivise* land covered by the first and second Tripartite agreements would either be collected by HCB or sold to them by the Africans who collected it on their own account, excepting only what Africans consumed themselves. That is, Africans promised not to sell to third parties or even to mill the fruit gathered for their own consumption (it would be done free at their request by the HCB mills) because this was wasteful of scarce resources. In this way HCB got a monopoly of all oil palm products in their three circles for ten years.

This ingenious system worked very satisfactorily for the first ten years of its intended life. The government got ahead with the demarcation of native rights and simultaneously HCB gradually selected and marked out its prospective leaseholds as it qualified for them by its milling capacity and production. By 1930 543,272 hectares had been chosen and approved by the authorities as not entrenching on native rights: there seemed no reason why the remaining 200,000 hectares should not be fixed by the time the agreements expired in 1936; and meantime the company had a trading monopoly over twice that area—1,027,750 hectares—for which it had made contracts with Africans. 1936 should therefore have marked the dividing line between the old world, in which HCB operated extensively over vast areas which it did not own, and the projected new world, in which it would restrict its activities to its own 750,000 hectares and lose its monopoly of palm products everywhere else.

In fact things worked out very differently. Far from being allowed to expire in 1936 the agreements were renewed in a severely modified form in 1938 and remained central to HCB's activities until they were again revised and renewed in 1958. The predicted new world took an unconscionable time to be born. Why this was so can only be understood in terms of the radical changes that took place in the position and needs of HCB between 1925 and the later 1930s; and it will therefore be necessary, before describing the process of renegotiation of the agreements during 1936–8 and their later consequences, to examine two integrally related developments during the 1930s: declining profitability and the consequential decision to change the whole production strategy from exploitation of natural palm forests to plantations.

Modernisation, 1931-60

The genesis of HCB's decision to establish intensive plantation production not only of palm products but also of other tropical commodities in the Congo lay in the collapse of Lever's original strategy during the slump of the early 1930s. Exploitation of natural palms had been sensible and probably inevitable at the start, but it depended for its viability on three things: an adequate supply of cheap African labour, a satisfactory concentration of natural palms and the absence of more efficient and therefore cheaper palm oil producers in other places. From the early 1920s it was evident that these conditions were not met. Three of the five concessionary areas did not contain sufficient palms to justify intensive production and labour problems had become acute in Leverville, the one area where there were a sufficient number of natural palms. Finally during the 1920s the development of much more efficient oil palm plantations in Sumatra and Malaya had made the Congo system antiquated. From Unilever's standpoint the proof that things had gone wrong was that HCB made very large losses throughout the early 1930s; and, as unprofitability proved, though in a roundabout way, to be the genesis of the new strategy adopted in the later 1930s, the company's profit record must be examined first.

The essential fact about HCB down to 1940 was that, seen as a profit-making enterprise, it was a disastrous failure. Table 9.2 sets out the evidence, which can be summarised as follows. Down to 1930 total post-tax accounting profits were £962,500 and losses £642,200 leaving a credit balance of only £320,300 or an average return of about £16,000 a year on an investment which after 1920 was over £2 million. A large proportion of the profits made to this point were made in the six relatively good years 1925–30, which amounted to £751,200; but in the same period £844,988 was spent on new development, which more than absorbed current profits. Thus HCB had furnished Lever Brothers with not a single dividend after twenty years. The following decade was no better. Total post-tax profits amounted to F. 77.6 million and losses to F. 61.8 million, leaving a nett accounting balance of F. 15.8 million. Given volatile exchange rates during the 1930s this might amount to some £100,000, or about £10,000 a year, almost all of it made in the three years of improved commodity prices, 1935, 1936 and 1939; and again no dividend was declared. Even so, these good years could not be foreseen in the darkest years of the slump before 1935 and it is not surprising that, with losses between 1931 and 1934 amounting to F. 60.1 million (about £400,000), Unilever became extremely pessimistic about the whole Congo venture. It was during these disastrous years that a fundamental reassessment of HCB was undertaken and in retrospect this can be seen to mark the dividing line between HCB as it was originally conceived by Lever and the company as it was to evolve in the following thirty years.

(a) Administrative Reforms, 1931

The first minor change was made in 1931 in response to a dramatic decline in palm oil prices and a prospective loss for the year. To reduce administrative costs and taxes paid by Unilever companies in Belgium, the three existing Brussels companies—HCB, Savonneries Lever Frères (SLF) and Raffineries du Congo Belge (RCB)—were amalgamated into a single Belgian company, Compagnies Réunies du HCB et SLF (Huilever) SA, hereafter Huilever. This lasted until 1958. At the same time all European salaries in the Congo were to be calculated in Belgian francs rather than sterling to take advantage of the falling value of the franc. Other palliatives were adopted as oil prices continued to go down. The Congo government agreed to a reduction in the scale of expenditure on schools, hospitals and housing, though wages remained unchanged. The number of expatriate staff was reduced from 346 in 1929 to 221 in 1933, of whom 178 were working in the circles. The result, taken together with a significant reduction in internal and ocean freights, was that production costs at constant pre-1931 sterling values went down from about £26 0s 9d c.i.f. a ton in 1929 to £17 7s 0d in 1932.

(b) The Origins of Plantations

These were significant savings; but in Unilever eyes success was qualified. The market price of oil remained below HCB production costs from 1930–4, so the company made very large losses; and HCB costs were well above those of plantations in Nigeria, the Cameroons, Sumatra and Malaya. In conjunction these seem to have convinced the London management that HCB was an inefficient high-cost producer which could only be expected to make reasonable profits when commodity prices were high. This was a depressing prospect for a firm in which Levers had invested some £3 million and from which no dividend had so far been received; and the result was a fundamental reappraisal which led to the transformation of HCB from an enterprise which collected and processed natural palm fruit over very wide areas into one which exploited a relatively very small acreage by cultivating oil palms, rubber, cocoa, coffee and tea. The transition did not take place suddenly, nor did Unilever abruptly decide to substitute intensive for extensive methods. The shift began in the early 1930s, became accepted policy in 1935 and was beginning to produce results by 1946. It is proposed briefly to trace this metamorphosis in Unilever thinking before examining the effects it had on the negotiation of the new Convention and Tripartite agreements in 1936–8.

Until at least 1933 the function of planting oil palms was not to replace but to supplement natural palms in areas where the natural supply was insufficient to enable the HCB mills to meet the targets set in the Convention. Thus it was decided in 1915 to plant 8,000 hectares at Alberta (though this was not done) and during the 1920s comparatively small areas were planted in all five circles. By 1928 there were 2,512 hectares altogether, of which 1,007 were at Alberta, 583 at Flandria, 508 at Elisabetha, 333 at Brabanta and only 81 at Lusanga. In 1930 Greenhalgh, reporting that the planted area now totalled 3,170 hectares, proposed that a further 4,300 should be planted 'to entitle us to the full allotment of freehold and to bring certain stations up to the economic level'.

To this point there is no evidence that anyone in Unilever had calculated the relative profitability of natural as against planted palm oil production or seriously considered plantations as an alternative to existing methods. Accumulating losses, however, then forced radical reconsideration; and in 1933 R. H. Muir made a detailed analysis of the causes of HCB's low profitability by comparing the unit cost of producing oil from natural palms in the Congo with that of competing plantations in West Africa (UAC's Cameroons plantations) and South-east Asia (Hallett's Sumatra plantations). His conclusions were shocking. Taking as his yardstick the capacity to produce 24,000 tons of palm oil or its rough equivalent in kernels (48,000 tons), he found that the capital needed to produce one ton of oil was £58 for HCB, £32 for Sumatra and £25 in the Cameroons. This was largely due to the expensive welfare and other services which HCB had had to provide as part of its contractual obligations which, Muir suggested, 'must be taken as an elaboration, which either should show a return by reduction in the cost of production, or represent the surmounting of disadvantages peculiar to HCB'. But, even if this capital was ignored as an historic cost and excluded from the calculations of future profitability, HCB was deplorably non-competitive in current production costs. Labour was a major factor. Halletts and UAC employed less than the equivalent of 24 Europeans to produce 24,000 tons, while HCB, on the most favourable estimate, employed 178. As to local labour, Sumatra employed 6,000 men to produce 24,000 tons of oil to HCB's 16,000, giving ratios of 0.25 and 0.66 men per ton. Thus, even though wage rates in Sumatra were about twice those in the Congo, labour costs there were substantially higher. Freight costs also were against HCB. Total internal and external freight and insurance costs from Leopoldville to northern Europe were then £3 9s 6d as compared with £2 0s 0d from West Africa and £2 11s 6d from Sumatra to North America. Finally plantation palms produced more oil per ton of fruit milled than natural palms in the proportion 3 to 2.

The conclusion was that HCB was a comparatively high cost producer because it was less efficient at every stage from tree to ultimate market. Some of its disadvantages were insuperable, notably high transport costs, so that it would probably never compete with the cheapest producers. But it was obviously essential to change as quickly as possible from extensive to intensive methods of production, planting large areas of improved oil palms on the most favourable sites, within or outside the original concessions, so reducing overheads and increasing the yield per ton of fruit. Muir did not actually propose this in his report, possibly because his brief was to suggest means of reducing costs in the short term. Instead he suggested a number of palliatives, mostly involving concessions by the Congo government: permission for the HCB river fleet to compete with the government-controlled UNATRA boats for third party cargoes; reduction in the freights charged on the railway from Leopoldville to Matadi; modification of some of the more expensive welfare services prescribed by the Convention. Unilever House accepted these proposals, the Congo government proved generally helpful, and by 1937 production costs had been substantially reduced to £13 10s 0d a ton, compared with £12 10s 0d a ton in Sumatra: HCB actually made profits from 1935 to 1939. But by that time Unilever had accepted the underlying logic of Muir's argument: in 1935 HCB began a large-scale planting project which, as D'Arcy Cooper put it in 1937, 'contemplated a production of 48,000 tons of oil per annum by 1945 against 24,000 tons at present'. This marked the birth of a new Congo enterprise.

Since this was a major conceptual innovation it is unfortunate that there is nothing in the surviving records to show precisely when and on what grounds this decision was taken: there is no material available between 1933 and 1937. Even in 1937 D'Arcy Cooper was vague about the grounds for the new policy:

> The wild palm was diminishing, and for this reason two years ago HCB had started a programme of planting, and 11,000 hectares had been planted at a cost of Fcs. 1,000 a hectare. The question now was whether this programme was to be continued. The cost of oil produced from such plantations was £9.7.0d per ton and the opinion was that anyone who could produce at under £10 a ton would not make a loss.

One director, who found this explanation surprising, asked 'whether it was clear whether the natural supply of palm oil was giving out' and was answered obliquely by Greenhalgh that 'it was a very arduous task to gather the fruit from wild trees'. D'Arcy Cooper added that 'there was no doubt that the quantity of native-produced oil was steadily diminishing'. The proposal to continue the programme of planting passed; but it remains uncertain whether the original arguments used for it in 1935 were primarily based on maintaining and increasing the volume of production so as to fulfil the terms of the Convention or on the more rational ground of comparative efficiency.

This may disappoint the historian, but there is no doubt that the new policy was undertaken deliberately and was seen to be the best means of saving HCB. In 1938 W. A. Faure wrote a very pessimistic survey of HCB as a whole, which he regarded as an inefficient and badly run enterprise; but he was enthusiastic about the new plantations, where he found 'the most refreshing enthusiasm' among the staff. He thought management would have to improve standards of mechanisation, work efficiency, living conditions and food supply, but was optimistic about yields, costs and profits. In May 1939 Unilever momentarily decided, following a drop in the Liverpool price of palm oil in 1938 to £13 13s 0d (the lowest since 1933), to slow up the planting programme; but commodity prices rose in 1939 and 1940 (by then controlled by the British government) and the original programme was carried through. Its later history will not be followed at this point for it belongs to the next phase of HCB's history. But it is now possible to examine the renegotiation of the Convention and the Tripartite agreements which took place between 1936 and 1938 in the light of the new investment and production strategy Unilever was evolving at the same time. The revised Convention and agreements of 1938 must be seen in terms of HCB's new needs.

(c) The Tripartite Agreements of 1938

The starting point of the negotiations was that Unilever was no longer primarily concerned with the extent of the land it would ultimately acquire in freehold and wanted to be able to select land outside the original circles which would be suitable for plantations; while the Congo government no longer, as it had done in 1911, saw HCB as a device for opening up virtually unknown regions of the upper Congo and providing services which the state could not afford. There was therefore room for radical revision of the original Convention. On the other hand HCB was still interested in the Tripartite agreements for two reasons. First, they would need to draw palm fruit from a larger area of natural palmeries than the 62,488 hectares so far formally allocated to them on lease at least until the new plantations were in bearing—that is, the mid-1940s—and possibly even beyond. Second, it was thought essential for the indefinite future to prevent the growth of rival oil mills processing fruit from natural palmeries round HCB plantations to stop Africans taking fruit from the plantations to sell to rival European enterprises. Thus what HCB wanted was to renew at least these two rights —ability to draw natural palm fruit from the areas outside their leaseholds by agreement with Africans, and a monopoly of milling in the vicinity of their new plantations; and they were prepared to pay for these by reducing their original entitlement to land under the 1911 Convention.

The Tripartite agreements expired in 1936 but already in 1935 the Belgian Colonial Council had debated at length whether they should be extended. There was considerable feeling that they should not, but in the end it was decided that the Governor-General of the Congo should be authorised at his discretion to extend the agreements to 1944, when the Convention provided for the final demarcation of HCB's properties. Much, therefore, turned on the attitude of the Governor-General, Pierre Ryckmans; and it seems from discussions between him and HCB in Brussels in 1936 that he wanted to end the agreements in 1938. The Congo government had already provisionally delimited 837,373 hectares within the five circles as being free of native rights, so that the original ground for the agreements no longer existed; and, as he argued, it was increasingly difficult, in a changing climate of opinion on the rights of Africans, to justify HCB's monopoly of fruit collection and milling in areas outside their actual leases. But he was also known to be interested in reducing the total area of land to which HCB was entitled, particularly blocks within their 750,000 hectares which they did not use; and this provided the basis for a possible deal.

For their part HCB began to consider the position in detail in June 1937, when F. M. Dyke summarised the company's essential objectives in a letter to Greenhalgh which became the basis of Unilever's approach.

I would suggest that we should, for a while, clear our minds of any final area which we might agree to accept from the Government in replacement of the 750,000 hectares promised by the original Convention; and tabulate, with Mr Dusselje's guidance, the following two classes of land, which in my view are absolutely essential to the existence of the HCB:

(1) Natural palmeries actually exploited at the present.
(2) Forest land needed for plantation extensions.

We need the first, not only as the mainstay of our production for the next 15 years (while plantations are coming to full bearing), but also, after that period, as a protection against theft in the plantations (since, if the natural palmeries fell into other hands, we could not distinguish between plantation and wild palmery fruit). The area of this land is probably of the order of 100–150,000 hectares and its delimitation is likely to present the major part of our land problem (native right question etc.).

The second type of land is generally free from native rights, and need offer no serious difficulty in delimitation. Possibly 100,000 hectares would be an ample reserve in this case.

I think, if we approached the Government and Governor-General on these lines, we should receive real support not only in land delimitations, but in such measures and decrees as would give us reasonable security, perhaps along the lines already discussed informally by Mr Genon with Mr Heyse. Otherwise, I think we are likely to meet obstruction at every turn—the Governor-General practically says so in one of his letters.

On this last point at least Dyke was right. HCB drafted a revised Convention and agreements and when Lord Trenchard, as Chairman of HCB, discussed these with Ryckmans in Leopoldville in March 1938 it was clear that accommodation was possible. Ryckmans said his main concern was that HCB should not eventually sit on land it did not use and it was agreed that the land grant provisions of the Convention should be modified so that HCB would become entitled to 350,000, not 750,000 hectares. All natural palmeries which were to become company freehold must be claimed by 1944, but the balance of land which was intended for plantations could be chosen outside the original circles at any time up to 1958. From 1968 the government could take back blocks which had been neither planted nor improved. In return Ryckmans accepted an extension of the Tripartite agreements for 18 years from 1936 (he had suggested 15 years, HCB had asked for 20 years); but he was adamant that the test of whether land within the *indivise* areas was open for selection by HCB must be African use or need as they stood in 1938, not as they had been in 1911, since the native population and its agriculture had expanded immensely in the meantime. As to the duration of the 'protection' afforded to HCB against rival mills in areas covered by the agreements, Ryckmans did not want this to last longer than the 18 years of the new agreement, whereas HCB asked for it to be guaranteed at least until 1958 and longer if possible. They also asked that this protection should cover the whole of their original circles, whereas at present it operated only in the areas in which HCB had made specific agreements with Africans. This and other matters were left for decision in Brussels.

With most issues thus arranged in Leopoldville, agreement in principle was reached in Brussels in April 1938. The revised Convention was signed by the government on 2 July 1938, then ratified by the Colonial Council and issued as a decree in March 1939. It had come into force on 30 June 1938 and, with minor modifications made in 1942 and 1943, which extended the 1944 deadline for establishing freeholds because of the Second World War, lasted until July 1956. This marks the end of the first 'heroic' period of HCB's history and the following 20 years saw its evolution into a modern plantation enterprise; yet it is typical of the company's history—indeed of the Congo's history also—that historical land-marks did not indicate total change. The essential feature of the agreements made in 1938 was that the old would coexist with the new. HCB continued for the next three decades to rely, though decreasingly, on natural palm products collected from large areas outside their now defined properties and also on a monopoly of processing palm fruit in the regions covered by the multiple agree-ments made with Africans, though not, as had been hoped, through-out the original circles as well. The central themes of the company's history from 1938 to 1960 are, therefore, the gradual increase in plantation production, diversification away from total dependence on oil palm products, and greatly improved profitability; but at no point was there a radical break with past practices. The outcome of these developments was the third and final revision of the Con-vention and Tripartite agreements in 1958 and this provides the best measure of how far the character of the business had changed. The story will not be told in detail, partly because its general features have already been outlined, but also because very little detailed evidence is available between 1938 and 1955. It is proposed first to describe the expansion of the plantation programme, then review the profitability of the company and finally to deal with the re-negotiation of the Convention and agreements in 1958.

(d) Plantations and Profits, 1937-59

The first checkpoint for the plantation programme provided by the existing records is in 1944, when W. A. Faure wrote a detailed report. For the most part the plantations were being established outside the original concessionary circles, where soil and climate were best and there were no problems connected with native land rights. The revised Convention allowed HCB to select 100,000 hectares outside the circles, and by 1944 it had chosen and the government approved 73,000 hectares. Not all of this would actually be planted: Faure predicted that, if the current programme was completed, HCB would have 43,000 hectares of planted palms and 10,000 hectares of planted rubber trees by 1956. These, in addition to the natural palm forests still being exploited, should produce 95,000 tons of oil, 45,000 tons of palm kernels and 22 million lbs of rubber. The capital cost would be considerable. By 1944 the original capital of £3 million had been written down to £750,000—itself a significant comment on the effects of over-capitalisation in the first decade and the consequences of the slump in commodity prices. The existing planting programme would cost £1.8 million, further plantations needed to achieve Faure's target £750,000 and other capital needed during the next ten years £285,000, resulting in a capital employed of about £3,585,000. On this basis HCB might, for the first time, be able to provide the 10 per cent return on capital that Unilever conventionally looked for.

Faure's projection, at least on the size and output of the reborn HCB's plantations, was remarkably accurate. By 1960 HCB had 46,839 hectares of planted oil palms, 6,818 hectares of rubber, 5,008 hectares of cocoa, 741 hectares of coffee and 136 hectares of tea. Some plantations were within the original circles, but one of the most important was at Yaligimba, east of Alberta circle, and another at Oshwe, 160km north of Brabanta, acquired in 1956 because the Congo government was anxious to start commercial operations in that area. To match this change in the location of production HCB's administrative structure had been remodelled. There were now three administrative units in the Congo: the north (Flandria, Alberta, Elisabetha, Yaligimba, Gwaka and Mokaria); the south (Lusanga/Leverville and Brabanta) and the offices, storage facilities and transport organisations at Leopoldville. Each was now largely autonomous, their managing directors being treated as chairmen of Unilever companies. Meantime the headquarters of the company itself had moved from Brussels to Leopoldville in 1958 as a result of the reorganisation of Huilever which will be described later.

Faure was over-optimistic about the volume of production but his projection of a 10 per cent return on capital was nearly realised during the thirteen years from 1947 to 1959; and since this represented a striking improvement over all previous periods, the reasons must be considered. The main cause was obviously the price of palm oil. During 1940–6 Congo oil was sold in Britain where the Ministry of Food controlled prices. These prices were better than before 1939 but were kept artificially low to reduce British food costs and did not keep pace after 1942 with rising production costs in the Congo: hence the declining yield of HCB in 1942–5. In this period, moreover, HCB still relied almost entirely on natural palm products, so no benefit was obtained from the investment already made in plantations. The turning point was 1946/7, when the official price in Britain rose to something near world commodity market levels (though bulk buying by the Ministry did not end until 1954) and also when the new plantations were coming into bearing. From 1947 to 1959 nett profits were never less than 6 per cent or more than 14 per cent on capital employed. This was a triumph for those who had planned and executed the restructuring of the archaic organisation that had seemed in the early 1930s to have been left high and dry by the tide of change.

But 1959 also proved to be the last good year for HCB, at least before 1965. After 1960 the post-independence crisis may be held partly responsible for the decline, but the downturn clearly began before 1960 and it is important to consider why this was so. The explanation lies in the relative deterioration of the profitability of palm oil and kernels as compared with other plantation products in the Congo which in turn was caused by rising production costs. Whereas HCB's average production cost per ton of palm oil rose from £37.8 in 1955 to £62.5 in 1960, and the gross profit margin declined from £29.6 to £3.1, production costs in Nigeria and Malaya showed no comparable upward trend. At various times HCB men provided five explanations. The most significant was the rising cost of Congo African labour. In 1957/8 alone the average daily cost of each full-time African plantation worker, including rations and other overheads, increased by 10 per cent to above F.25 (£0.18) or over £65 a year; and with a labour force of 40,036 in 1958 wage costs were £2.6 million. Total production costs for palm oil that year were £3.8 million; and, although the labour force was also engaged on other plantations and activities, it is clear that in this labour-intensive industry rising costs of this order would press hard on profit margins. Wages continued to rise after 1958 while the price of palm oil and kernels remained virtually static. By the later 1950s it was predictable that, given HCB's special disadvantages, rising wage costs would eventually make HCB once again unprofitable as a palm oil producer.

But this was only one of several downward pressures on profits in the 1950s. The price paid to Africans for palm fruit sold to HCB was, under the Convention, always tied to the daily rate of wages, so that the price of this marginal source of raw material rose at the same rate. By the later 1950s the government was pressing for higher welfare expenditure by all large employers. In 1956 alone the cost of pensions rose by £71,400 and by 1962 the cost of medical services (at 1959 prices) was £206,521. Expenditure on schools, housing and other social services, all of which the government expected private enterprise rather than the state to provide, was rising faster than productivity or commodity prices. Simultaneously the government increased export duties from 7 per cent to 9 per cent in 1956, which cost the company F. 10 million since the cost could not be passed on, and in 1959 the export tax on palm kernel oil was increased from 12 per cent to 15 per cent. In 1956 internal freight rates were increased by 12.5 per cent, a serious threat because, although the Congo government had traditionally kept down internal freights,[8] exports from the upper Congo were still at a disadvantage compared with exports from West Africa.

Clearly, then, HCB as a relatively high cost and therefore marginal producer at all times had, by the later 1950s, reached the second major crisis of its history, apparently unable to compete in an international market where prices were determined by the more efficient producers of South-east Asia and the state-controlled marketing boards of West Africa. Once again HCB was haunted by its origins: by continuing partial dependence on natural palmeries and obligatory welfare provisions. As D. L. Martin of Unilever's Plantation Group remarked in 1962,

> The trouble really lies in the fact that although the first Lord Leverhulme was right in 1911 to make use of the natural palmery areas, we are suffering for this policy today because it is not only a costly fruit to bring in but the yield is lower and we have a crippling burden of expense from the wholesale paternalism. As one small indication of that I found that in the first quarter of this year we had to provide F. 28,000 for coffins.

But the depressing prospects of the later 1950s must not obscure the fact that reasonable profits had at last been made in the previous twenty years. What did Unilever do with these? Lack of information on the period before 1955 makes it difficult to be certain for those years, but in broad terms the answer is clear. Between 1941 and 1955 nett accounting profits totalled £13,401,000. In the same period capital employed increased by an estimated £5.8 million. Assuming that most of the new investment was financed from retained profits, there may have been a balance of £7.6 million available for transfer during these 15 years. It is, however, likely that, if accounting habits in this earlier period were similar to those used in 1955–65, for which full information is available, some part of the new capital investment was financed out of depreciation and other sources. From 1956-9 nett accounting profits totalled £7,000,000, dividends £5,698,000, capital expenditure £4,966,000 and depreciation £2,876,000. This suggests that in these years rather more than half the new capital invested was financed from depreciation. It is therefore a reasonable assumption that the figure of £7.6 million assumed to be available for transfer as dividends between 1941 to 1955 is on the conservative side; and, if this is added to the £5.6 million known to have been transferred as dividends between 1956 and 1959, the total for the period is something over £13 million: £15 million would be a fair guess. Since no dividends were transferred between 1911 and 1940 and again from 1960 to 1965 (or indeed again until 1970), this constitutes the total profit Lever/Unilever obtained from the Congo business over a period of 54 years.

(e) The Last Tripartite Agreements, 1958

Unilever had had to wait a long time for the reward of its pioneering efforts in the Congo and it happened that 1956, the year in which HCB made its highest ever profit as a percentage of capital employed (apart possibly from 1951 for which the capital employed is speculative), was also the year in which the revised Tripartite agreements of 1938 expired and HCB was supposed to become owner of 350,000 hectares in freehold. Given that the company had changed a great deal and that new attitudes to concessions of this kind had by 1956 made many aspects both of the Convention and the agreements unacceptable to Congolese opinion, it might have been assumed that all HCB's special rights would have ended at that point. It would then have been left as a substantial owner of freehold land, burdened with a number of welfare obligations towards its employees, but without those peculiar monopolistic rights which were summed up in June 1957 in a minute written for the Special Committee as giving 'the exclusive rights of harvesting and purchasing fruit and of the establishment of oil plants on the land not susceptible of becoming the private property of the company, within the zones foreseen by the convention'.

It is, therefore, one of the most significant facts about the history of HCB that as late as 1957/8, on the eve (as it later emerged) of the Congo becoming independent, the company did not feel able to bury the past: once again, as in 1936-8, it decided to negotiate with the Belgian government for at least a partial extension of its special privileges. The grounds for doing this were set out in the same note for the Special Committee by J. Jonniaux, the Managing Director of HCB: it is undated, but it must have been written in 1957 before June.

The object of our present talks is the eventual renewal of these rights, in the Company's interest, for a period which the Government proposes to fix at 10 years. Our company is undoubtedly interested in this renewal. Our experience as palm oil producers . . . has led us to opt definitely for the plantation system. Despite the excellent results already obtained in this way, the Company is still not yet able, above all in the South, to feed to capacity its mills exclusively with plantation fruit. The harvesting of fruit from the natural palmeries will remain a necessity for the next 10 years.

The Government realizes that this necessity involves the corollary of maintenance of the Company's exclusive rights to the natural palmery fruit, in the regions which supply its mills. The abrupt change from a regime of tripartite agreements to that of free markets would inevitably cause economic and social difficulties which would trouble the present harmony.

The key to the negotiations of 1957/8 lay in this last point. Paternalistic to the last, the government of the Congo accepted the case for a gradual liberalisation of the commercial system. They might have left HCB to renegotiate agreements with as many African chefferies as were prepared to extend these; but, as in 1936-8, the Congo government shrewdly saw an opportunity to obtain a number of balancing concessions from HCB as a trade off for allowing the Tripartite agreements to continue, and this explains the complexity of the negotiations that took place in 1956-8. These began in 1956 in Leopoldville, and it was obvious that the Governor-General wanted to strike a tough bargain, possibly because of growing nationalistic feeling in the capital which was becoming very critical of this and other concessions made to European capitalists half a century earlier. His basic demands at the start were as follows: the 1911 Convention should be entirely replaced, not, as in 1938, modified by a codicil; the new Convention should be between HCB and the Congo, not Belgium; HCB could use its land only for agriculture and not indulge in speculation in development values; forests should not be used for commercial timber extraction unless under the same rules and taxes as were imposed on timber firms operating on domainial land; HCB should accept all fruit offered by native co-operatives for milling on a jobbing basis; it could be forced to give up land within its holdings for African agriculture; and, most important, the Congo government should be given 5,000 shares in Huilever without payment in return for renewing the Convention. In December 1956 negotiations were on the point of breaking down because HCB thought these demands excessive; but in February 1957 they were taken over by the Colonial Ministry in Brussels who, possibly because Unilever was at the time being very helpful over the Colohuile business (a state-owned margarine company in the Congo which was in serious financial difficulties), were more amenable. By June 1957 a compromise had been reached on the more contentious points. HCB was no longer to be restricted to agricultural use of its land; forestry was to be allowed on payment of a small tax or on condition of replanting; a quarter, not half as the Governor-General had proposed, of the nett proceeds of HCB land sold or let for development would be paid to the government; and, if company land was ceded for African agriculture, HCB would have the right to buy all palm fruit at prices defined by the government in relation to its oil content and the current market price and would also be able to choose domainial land elsewhere in compensation. The government, nevertheless, stood on the principle that there must be a new Convention and that 5,000 shares should be handed over.

In this form all these demands were acceptable to Unilever, but the gift of shares created technical difficulties. As has been seen, in 1931 HCB had been merged with two other Lever subsidiaries in Brussels to form a single holding company, Huilever. If the Congo was given 5,000 shares in this company the Congo government would have a say in the management and dividend distribution of two strictly Belgian companies which had no connection with the Congo. Moreover it was against Congolese official policy to own shares in companies outside the colony. HCB tried to resolve these difficulties by offering the Congo government an annual payment based on the quantity of native fruit offered under the extended Tripartite agreements: F. 5 per tonne would amount about F. 700,000 a year at the current volume of fruit traded; and, if the rent still to be paid on HCB freehold land was taken into account, the government would receive between F. 2 million and F. 2.5 million £14,280–£17,850). It was, nevertheless, appreciated in London that the Congo government's motive for wanting shares was not so much financial as political: as a Special Committee minute put it, 'simply to bring HCB into line with their general policy of seeking participation in colonial ventures . . .'. The Special Committee therefore agreed in principle to the Congo having shares in HCB, but made this contingent on the Belgian government making it feasible to split up Huilever into two separate companies (so that HCB once again became an entirely Congo company in which the government could hold shares) without Unilever having to pay the substantial taxes normally due in Belgium on the realisation of assets of companies being wound up. The negotiations in Brussels that followed on this narrow point were complicated and in October they looked so likely to fail that Jonniaux feared the Convention itself was in jeopardy. But agreement was reached early in December 1957 and on 23 December a new HCB, registered in Leopoldville but with its administrative headquarters still in Brussels, was born. For one day all but six of its 275,000 shares were owned by the still extant Huilever, but they were then transferred to the Niger Company and Unilever Ltd. On 26 December a parallel new Belgian company, S.A. Lever, came into existence in which the non-Congolese components of Huilever were fused with another Unilever subsidiary in Belgium, Savonnerie Pierre Wey. By 1 March 1958 the whole process was complete: HCB had been made an autonomous Congolese company for the first time.

This corporate cosmetic surgery opened the way for agreement on the new Convention, which was dated 16 April 1958 and was to run until 31 December 1967. The draft was debated by the Colonial Council on 23 May 1958, approved unanimously after some stiff probing, and issued as a royal decree the same day. Five months later the Congo got its reward: the shareholders of HCB formally increased the total number of shares by 5,000 to 280,000, representing 'the rights and privileges granted to our Company and defined in the Convention of 16 April 1958', and allotted the 5,000 shares to the Belgian Congo 'in return for their contribution'. Since the balance sheet at the end of 1957 had shown the nett value of HCB to be F. 2,209 million (£15,778,000), these shares represented a capital transfer of about F. 40.2 million (£286,883).

(f) HCB at the End of the Colonial Period, 1959

The new Convention was almost the last formal action affecting HCB taken by the Belgian authorities before the colony became independent in 1960. This is, therefore, a convenient point at which to take stock of the character of HCB at the end of the colonial period. Two main points demand comment: the general character of the business and the degree to which it had begun to meet the challenge of new ideas on the relations between foreign capital and African society.

The character of HCB in the late 1950s is paradoxical because, while in some respects it was new and forward looking, in others it had changed little since the 1920s. The element of continuity is stamped onto the new Convention of 1958. HCB remained a large land concessionary company which had acquired 350,000 hectares in return for injecting capital and providing a wide range of services which the colonial government could not have afforded. Although the original figure of 750,000 hectares had been more than halved, the residue was enormous in relation to the area actually under cultivation as plantations—about 60,000 hectares in 1960: much of the rest was held as a *cordon sanitaire*. Moreover even in the late 1950s a substantial part of the palm fruit processed by HCB, and also by Cultures du Congo Belge, a separate company in which HCB had had a 48 per cent (and controlling) interest since the 1920s but which was run separately, was cut from natural palms within the companies' protected zones and sold to the mills by Africans under the terms of the Tripartite agreements. In 1956, for instance, 22,000 out of a total of 52,000 tons of palm oil was made from 'native fruit'. Hence much of the company's anxiety to get the Convention and agreements renewed. There were sound business reasons for this: yet renewal meant extension for a further decade of obligations which appear archaic: continued provision of medical and educational services even beyond the limits of its labour force, the commitment to buy 'native' palm fruit at prices determined by the government and to process all fruit presented by co-operative societies, limitations on where HCB bought its capital equipment overseas, the nationality of its employees and the registration of its boats. In return HCB retained for ten years its monopoly of buying all palm fruit within its protected zones and of milling palm fruit inside or within 10 km of these zones. To accept such obligations in exchange for such rights in the year that the Gold Coast achieved independence and when Congo Africans were showing strong interest in political advance can only reflect that fact that the winds of change had scarcely yet been noticed by those Belgians who ran the Congo and HCB.

This atavism represents one aspect of HCB in the 1950s. In other respects it was fast developing into a modern enterprise. Most of its activity was now concentrated on its limited area of plantations, which could compete in efficiency, though not necessarily on price once freights were taken into account, with other Unilever plantations elsewhere. Through its plantations, moreover, HCB had broken away from monoculture, diversifying successfully into rubber, cocoa, coffee and tea. There was even a subsidiary enterprise, formed into a separate company in 1952 as Cie. Africaine d'Elevage, which had been building up herds of cattle in Katenga and other suitable places since 1948/9 to supply fresh meat for HCB's employees. Two other signs of modernity were the sale of the company's river fleet to OTRACO in 1949, which symbolised the declining need for HCB to operate as a pioneer and autarkic venture; and the decision taken in 1952 to build a palm kernel crushing mill at Leopoldville at a cost of F. 13 million (£92,857). This indeed was a novelty because it had always been axiomatic that it was uneconomic to extract kernel oil in Africa; and its establishment reflected the growing local demand for kernel oil together with the government's desire to increase local processing of primary commodities as a contribution to industrialisation.

Similar contrasts are reflected in HCB's approach to Africanisation of its staff and the political evolution of the Congo. As was seen above in the context of MARSAVCO, Unilever's Leopoldville management seems to have shown little interest in localisation of management until late in the 1950s: indeed, HCB was probably even more conservative on this than MARSAVCO. In 1957 all responsible posts were still held by the extraordinarily large number of expatriates —230—of whom all but 36 (25 British and 11 other Europeans) were Belgian. But by 1958 two forces were tending to bring HCB into line with long-established Unilever policy: the high cost of European managers measured against declining palm product prices, and the first evident stirrings of Congolese nationalism. In May 1957 Jonniaux reported a 'very successful' conference held at Leopoldville, attended by district managers and heads of HCB departments, which discussed labour policy 'and in particular the development of the African staff'.

The conclusion had been reached that although we were not yet in a position to replace Europeans by Africans there was no doubt that the standard of skill of the Africans was steadily improving and it should not be too many years before some were sufficiently advanced to reach the 'chef de division' level, i.e. to take charge of a 2,000 hectares sector . . . Mr Jonniaux regarded the opinions expressed as a very considerable advance in management thinking.

Two months later, in July 1957, C. F. Black of Plantation Group in London, reporting on a visit to the Congo, spelt out the economic thinking behind this. Commenting on the difficulty of making Brabanta profitable, given its limited area of useful land, he pointed out that the European management of eight constituted a charge of almost £10 a ton on an output of 4,000 tons of oil. He concluded that 'unless it was possible in time to replace Europeans by Africans on a substantial scale, the project did not offer much financial attraction'.

Thereafter action was comparatively swift. Perhaps encouraged by the effective co-operation of senior African workers during the go-slow strike of Bapena cutters in the southern area, when the police had been used in the Leverville district, it was decided to press on with the replacement of Europeans. In April 1959 Jonniaux reported to the Special Committee that

Last year one [African] only had been promoted but the scheme had now been extended to a further 5, mainly in the plantation services but one on the medical side, and shortly it was hoped to add others in the accounts and probably the technical departments. The total number of Africans it was hoped to promote in this way was about 18 and at present only 5 or 6 suitable jobs were available. There would be no displacement of Europeans, the appointments being made as a consequence of normal wastage, although in future special appointments would probably have to be created. The Congolese were given the same privileges as were accorded to the Europeans who had previously held the posts. Mr. Jonniaux was particularly encouraged by the co-operative attitude of the European managers in carrying out this policy, and so far it seemed also to have the approval of the natives who would be working under their own compatriots. The Government of the Congo had been following a similar policy and had been able to appoint 450 Congolese to management positions.

Later that year Lord Heyworth, about to retire as Chairman of Unilever Ltd, made a tour of Unilever's African interests and was most impressed by the progress made by HCB.

The progress made with Africanization since I was last [in Africa] is most impressive. The people who have done best at it are the HCB plantations, who have made a tremendous leap forward. They have now nine 'European' jobs being done by Africans; whereas there were none when I was there before. They start with young men at the age of about 20, give them four years' training in their agricultural school and then give them a junior supervisor's job.

Thus, on the very eve of Congolese independence (although of course no one, and certainly not the HCB management, expected this to happen in the foreseeable future in 1958), HCB was committed to a policy of Africanisation. It seems likely that under existing circumstances the process would have been slow, conditioned partly by the need to train Africans and partly by the policy of not dismissing Belgian plantation managers for whom it was virtually impossible to find alternative posts in other Unilever plantations or industries. But at least the principle had been established and the events of 1960, when many Belgian managers left the Congo, merely speeded up the process.

If, then, one attempts to strike a balance, it is probably fair to say that by the later 1950s HCB had very nearly outgrown its chrysallis and might soon be ready to operate as a specialised plantation and oil-milling enterprise comparable to those Unilever was by then operating in West Africa and South-east Asia, freed from the special obligations and no longer dependent on the peculiar rights imposed and conferred by the Convention in its three forms. Yet the process of change had been remarkably slow and it is difficult to determine how far this was the responsibility of the company or the environment in which it had to work. There is no doubt, judging from the many reports made by Unilever visitors, that the local management tended to become unprogressive through inbreeding and the fact that the majority were living in comparative isolation in some of the least developed parts of the Congo. The fact, also, that HCB was a self-contained organisation within Unilever, oriented towards Brussels rather than to London or Rotterdam, probably limited the flow of new ideas. Equally important was the influence of Belgian colonialism which, at least by the standards of British thinking on West Africa, remained conservative and paternalistic well into the 1950s. It is simply inconceivable that any British colonial government should in 1958 have negotiated a document like the new HCB Convention which extended for a decade a system of commercial monopoly and corporate paternalism which had been strongly criticised by Belgian liberals and humanitarians in the 1930s. Equally it was the Congo government's rigid adherence to the legalism of both the 1911 and 1958 Conventions that forced HCB to maintain many archaic attitudes and practices, especially those relating to making good their title to land. It is reasonable to conclude that most of HCB's peculiar features were a reflection of the environment in which it operated rather than an expression of conscious Unilever policy.

Independence, 1960–5

It would be misleading to use the first five years of Congolese independence from 1960–65 as conclusive evidence of the consequences of decolonisation for a plantation enterprise such as HCB—renamed Plantations Lever au Congo(PLC) in 1960 to mark the change. In fact the data set out in Table 9.3 are full of paradoxes and data for the years 1966–74, which fall outside the limits of this study, are even more contradictory. At first sight the end of Belgian rule appears calamitous. In two of the six years 1960–5 PLC made a loss on trading account and there was a loss on post-tax accounts in every year but one. In sterling currency the value of the fixed assets dropped from £12.7 million in 1959 to £8.2 million in 1965, working capital remained almost unchanged and no dividends were transferred. In 1965 the volume of palm oil was about half that produced in 1959. Such figures suggest that within five years of the end of Belgian rule the foundations of this vast business had crumbled and that there was no future for PLC in the new state.

But this would be a false conclusion, and the tables suggest that other factors must have been at work. In three of these years, 1960, 1962 and 1963 the volume of palm oil produced was greater than in any previous year and low profits were due mainly to a surge in production costs caused by domestic inflation before the major devaluations of 1962 and 1963 took effect, coinciding with a disastrous drop in the c.i.f. selling price of palm oil in Liverpool from £94.00 in 1956 to £78.25 in 1962 and £80.15 in 1963. Inflation was, admittedly, almost entirely due to the political crisis of the early 1960s; but in the six years after 1965, when monetary stability and a realistic exchange rate were established, PLC was able to

Table 9.3 HCB/PLC: Profits 1955–65 (£'000)

PLC	1955	1956	1957	1958	1959	1960	1961	1962	1963	1964	1965
Palm oil and kernels	1,313	1,332	945	291	805	(166)	(813)	(206)	(77)	435	(120)
Rubber	115	592	482	342	730	611	247	340	102	197	21
Cocoa	63	(15)	(8)	81	10	19	(64)	(18)	(18)	—	(47)
Coffee	14	36	32	(10)	(15)	(10)	(44)	(11)	(18)	(28)	—
Tea	—	—	—	—	—	—	—	—	9	—	65
PK crushing (PLC only)	31	43	57	112	165	111	55	41	142	209	(56)
Other activities	123	90	94	132	164	114	(16)	97	(21)	146	113
Trading result	1,659	2,078	1,602	948	1,859	679	(635)	243	119	959	(24)
Exchange difference and extra depreciation	—	—	—	—	—	—	—	—	—	—	—
Nett result per accounts	1,586	1,983	1,719	1,479	1,828	412	(855)	(586)	(208)	(194)	(542)
Trading result less stat. tax[a]	1,205	1,501	1,270	762	1,338	542	(594)	(554)	147	636	(5)
Statistical tax rate	30%	30%	26%	26%	32%	28%	32%	—	—	43%	43%
Gross capital employed	10,134	11,056	11,828	12,684	14,807	15,040	16,948	10,816	11,212	11,502	10,092
Yield (after stat. tax) (%)	11.9	13.6	10.7	6.0	9.0	3.6	—	—	1.3	5.5	—
Dividends transferred (before Congo distribution tax; date refers to year profit made, not year of transfer)	714	1,428	535	2,100	1,635	—	—	—	—	—	—
Capital expenditure	1,085	1,125	1,095	1,488	1,258	1,553	1,030	901	859	441	418
Depreciation	574	632	688	754	802	723	937	949	992	691	704
Official rate of exchange (CF/£1)	140	140	140	140	140	140	184	400	504	504	504

obtain reasonable margins even when (as in 1968/9) commodity prices were low and to make substantial profits on palm oil when, as in 1970–1, prices were better. Moreover, the volume of production in this later period rose to a new peak; and, with the sterling book value of capital reduced by further devaluation, the return to capital was again to be respectable. In short, in the later 1960s PLC once again looked like a 'ten per cent proposition'.

The point, then, is that decolonisation in the Congo did not necessarily prove incompatible with the operation of a plantation business such as PLC. The most important thing in HCB's favour was it did not seem to arouse the hostility associated with other major Belgian companies, such as Union Minière: on the contrary, its provision of medical and educational services on a scale well beyond that laid down in the Convention, the comparatively good housing and other facilities it provided for its permanent work force and its late but definite inauguration of a policy of Africanising the management seem to have given it a relatively good reputation. PLC was a substantial earner of foreign exchange; and, apart from the later 1950s, it had always reinvested a large proportion of its profits. Those Congolese politicians who disliked all foreign capital no doubt wished to nationalise this along with all other foreign-owned businesses; but for the most part the men who controlled government in Leopoldville after the dismissal of Lumumba in September 1960 appeared to have no wish to kill this golden goose.

This was understood by HCB and Unilever and they approached independence without panic. In a key report made in January 1960, well before there seemed any chance of independence in the near future, Jonniaux commented that, despite much labour unrest on certain plantations and political disturbances in the towns, 'Many Belgians felt that the future lay in the Congo. [He] thought that they were probably wise in this opinion provided freedom were given soon; the sooner the better.' This report set the tone of Unilever's approach to the evolving Congo situation: to assimilate as closely as possible to the emergent Congo nation state. In administrative terms this had two immediate consequences. First, although PLC kept an office in Brussels, most of the administrative and technical staff moved to Leopoldville during 1960. Then to co-ordinate the three main Unilever companies, PLC, SEDEC and MARSAVCO, a joint committee was set up in the spring of 1960 which was then formalised into a 'Unilever Congo' executive consisting of a chairman and the managing directors or chairmen of the three companies.

This, however, never worked well and was replaced by less formal arrangements for consultation between the three companies. From 1960 also all European staff of PLC held local appointments: that is, they had no right to employment by Unilever outside the Congo. These changes were paralleled by acceleration of the programme of Africanisation of management. Plans for training Africans at home and in Europe were speeded up. By 1962 there were 80 African and under 100 European managers and thereafter Africanisation continued as fast as possible.

PLC was attempting to move with events, but it was bound to be a relatively passive victim of conditions in the crisis years during 1960–5. It is not proposed to tell the story but briefly to consider what practical effect political change and governmental weakness had on the business in these years. PLC's experience was, in many ways, the opposite of that of MARSAVCO. Whereas the soap business in Leopoldville, despite losing some of its outlying markets and experiencing problems of supply, throve on increased demand and was not badly affected by fighting or insecurity, PLC's properties were certain to suffer from intermittent disorder and inter-tribal fighting. Its experience can best be summed up in the words of C. F. Black after a visit in April 1963:

> Conditions at the centre were orderly, but up-country remained very disturbed. The business was affected by inefficiency of labour, distraction of the management from their normal duties by political difficulties, constant breakdown on the engineering side and still some inefficiency in accounting and administration. Good progress was being made in the districts towards restoring normal conditions . . . .

This was typical of reports made at almost all times from July 1960 to the end of 1965: Leopoldville remained 'normal' but there was likely to be terrorism or fighting at one or more of the plantation areas. By January 1965 it was calculated that damage due to terrorists would cost at least £617,000 to repair. Taking into account the estimated cost of destruction of vehicles and the plantations maintenance that could not be done, the bill already amounted to £1.4 millions and PLC was seriously considering whether to withdraw altogether from the plantation business if the Congo government did not allow sufficient hard currency to pay for the import of essential replacements.

The second phase of the Congo crisis outlasted 1965 and stable conditions were not re-established until 1966/7; but Unilever did not withdraw. The rest of the story lies outside the range of this study, but to round off this account later developments can be summarised briefly. PLC survived the difficulties of the mid-1960s and, while reducing the size of its plantations substantially, actually increased production of most commodities down to the early 1970s. Then, in November 1973, President Mobutu, while singling out Plantations Lever au Zaire (PLZ), as it now was, for praise, nevertheless announced that it would be nationalised along with all other foreign-owned plantations, promising full compensation. Nationalisation took place in January 1975. Unilever men continued to run the plantations under government supervision. In January 1976, however, the Congo government asked Unilever to send a team to discuss the situation and Edgar Graham, as Chairman of the Overseas Committee, went out. Initially agreement was reached in principle that Unilever would be given back 40 per cent of the share capital of all their three companies and would have unrestricted management control. Compensation for the balance of the shares retained by the government would be paid out of future profits. Subsequently, however, the government decided to return all the shares of the three companies and official control was removed on the understanding that 40 per cent of the shareholding would be sold within Zaire within a reasonable period. In September 1977 Unilever took back full control of its Zaire interests and a new period in its history began.

Epilogue: Unilever Plantations in the Later Twentieth Century

This study has concentrated almost entirely on the two earliest and longest lived of the Lever/Unilever plantation projects; but by 1955, when Unilever set up the Plantation Executive (later Group) in London, LPPL and HCB were by no means its only concern. It is not intended to give an account of all these other ventures but briefly to analyse their performance in the decade after 1955 for which reliable evidence is available in order to answer the major general question with which these chapters began: what benefit a multinational obtained from establishing and running plantations.

During the decade after 1955 Unilever owned plantations of different kinds in six countries other than the Solomons and the Congo. Of these the oldest were in Nigeria and Cameroun, initially established in the later 1920s as a posthumous reward for Lever's repeated efforts to induce the colonial authorities in British West Africa to give him long leases of land for the cultivation of oil palms, etc. These formed a single enterprise under the supervision of UAC until 1955 when they passed to the control of the Plantation Executive. In 1961 they were separated into two companies as Pamol (Nigeria) Ltd and Pamol (Cameroons) Ltd when these countries became independent. There was a long interval after the 1920s before Unilever founded any new plantations, not surprising in view of the unprofitability of commodity production during the 1930s. The next venture was in Malaya where UAC took the initiative in 1947 in proposing to use £205,000 due from war damage claims in Malaya to buy a small pre-war plantation in Johore. Initially this covered only 4,000 acres but more adjoining land was added until by 1960 it had some 11,400 planted acres. Three other new plantations were acquired or started after 1955. In that year negotiations began with the government of Gabon (then part of French Equatorial Africa) for a joint venture in palm oil and rubber plantations. The company, Palmeries et Heveas du Gabon, was set up in 1957, Gabon holding 21.4 per cent of the capital. A final venture was begun in Sabah, North Borneo, in 1960 as Pamol (North Borneo) Ltd.

The main and very important feature distinguishing all these later ventures from LPPL and HCB was that they were relatively small in size and were from the start intended simply to make a profit by applying capital and skills already available within the Unilever system. In 1955, when the new Plantation Executive was set up, the Special Committee took the opportunity precisely to define their attitude.

The major criterion to apply when deciding on an investment of any kind was the return expected from it, and it was generally felt that the return throughout the concern should be 10%. Some operations, however, were inherently likely to be more profitable than others, and the working of plantations was a type of activity which, they felt, should be capable of commanding a return higher than the average. Another important consideration was the political atmosphere in which the investment was to be undertaken. This could not be taken into account in formulating overall policy, but should not be overlooked in considering individual proposals.

This was a long way from Lever's stated objectives in the early 1900s and the way Plantations interpreted their brief resulted in very different types of enterprise. First, the object was now above-average profitability: 10 to 15 per cent was not a 'bread and butter' rate of return and it was a long way above the historical return on LPPL and HCB to that date. Second, plantations of the size established after 1955 (and also those already in West Africa) were far too small to have any effect on the world supply and therefore on price levels. Third, in the modern period Unilever did not go in for large-scale pioneer work or social engineering in running plantations. To some extent this was because conditions in most less developed countries were less primitive than they had been in the decade after 1900, but also because the modern Unilever management would never have considered undertaking the vast commitments which Lever, the entrepreneur, readily undertook as the price of starting his ventures in the Pacific and Equatorial Africa. This is not to make invidious comparisons: it was simply not open to Lever in the early years to invest in ready-made or easily developed plantations as he might have done in British farmlands: he had to take on the role of paternalistic ruler of the jungle as a necessary precondition of becoming a bourgeois capitalist owner of a few thousand acres of productive palm forest or coconut groves. By the 1950s, however, one did not take on concessions with a radius of 60 kilometres in the hope of finding suitable land within it. One bought an existing Malayan plantation or, to be more venturesome, one might, as the Special Committee agreed to do in 1960, 'negotiate for an area of 10,000 acres of undeveloped forest [in North Borneo]. The price was about $50 an acre and the land was ideally situated, with extensive frontage on a river which was navigable to the coast.' This was a gamble but a limited one. It is significant that the only suggestion in the records of the decade after 1955 which bears any resemblance to Lever's ideas for opening up the wilderness, a proposal for establishing oil palm plantations in the Amazon valley using imported plantation labour which came up in 1960, was rejected at once. Nor did Unilever respond when the United Fruit Co. in the same year dangled the bait of redeveloping plantations in Costa Rica, Colombia, Honduras, Guatemala and Ecuador.

The test of this more circumscribed approach to commodity production was its profitability. Table 9.4(a) sets out the essential data for all the plantation companies for the eleven years 1955–65, which may be taken as a fairly typical post-1945 period because it

Table 9.4(a)   Comparative Yield on Gross Capital Employed: All Unilever Plantations, 1955–65 (£'000)[a]

	1955	1956	1957	1958[b]	1959	1960	1961	1962[c]	1963	1964	1965
PLC Capital	10,134	11,056	11,828	12,684	14,807	15,040	16,948	10,816	11,212	11,502	10,092
Profit after tax	1,205	1,501	1,270	762	1,338	542	(594)	(305)	147	636	(5)
Yield (%)	11.9	13.6	10.7	6.0	9.0	3.6	(–)	(–)	1.3	5.5	(–)
TPS Capital	n/a	n/a	n/a	n/a	n/a	–	–	Included in PLC			
Profit after tax	n/a	n/a	n/a	n/a	n/a	(19)	8				
Yield (%)	n/a	n/a	n/a	n/a	n/a	–	–				
Elevage Capital	205	228	251	330	623	708	669	163	168	174	Included in PLC
Profit after tax				(3)	(3)	(3)	–	(3)	11		
Yield (%)								(–)	6.5		
Pamol Nigeria Capital	3,137	3,154	3,132	2,771	2,639	2,737	2,000	2,326	2,368	2,481	2,367
Profit after tax	132	152	112	147	297	344	285	187	163	87	153
Yield (%)	4.2	4.8	3.6	5.3	11.3	12.6	14.3	8.0	6.9	3.5	6.5
Pamol (Cameroons) Capital	n/a	n/a	n/a	n/a	n/a	n/a	900	2,498	2,521	2,905	3,373
Profit after tax	n/a	n/a	n/a	n/a	n/a	n/a	6	(59)	4	17	154
Yield (%)	n/a	n/a	n/a	n/a	n/a	n/a	0.7	(–)	0.2	0.6	4.6

								Pamol (Sabah)			
Pamol (Ghana)											
Capital	76	68	76	84	91	86	n/a	228	458	870	1,436
Profit after tax	9	10	5	5	7	(7)	n/a	–	–	–	–
Yield (%)	11.8	14.7	6.6	5.9	7.7	–	n/a	–	–	–	–
Pamol (Malaya)											
Capital	264	277	395	542	424	453	586	1,450	2,060	2,057	1,898
Profit after Tax	56	65	16	39	63	96	88	52	64	(31)	246
Yield (%)	21.2	23.5	4.1	7.2	14.9	21.2	15.0	3.6	3.1	–	13.0
Palmeveas											
Capital	n/a	n/a	n/a	n/a	n/a	n/a	n/a	334	403	446	461
Profit after tax	n/a	n/a	n/a	n/a	n/a	n/a	n/a	(5)	(26)	(45)	(46)
Yield (%)	n/a	n/a	n/a	n/a	n/a	n/a	n/a	(–)	(–)	(–)	(–)
LPP											
Capital	376	358	381	590	573	557	517	878	922	995	1,123
Profit after tax	97	64	39	45	82	29	(10)	(2)	45	81	119
Yield (%)	25.8	17.9	10.2	7.6	14.3	5.2	–	–	4.9	8.1	10.6
Grand total											
Capital	14,192	15,141	16,063	17,001	19,157	19,581	21,620	18,693	20,112	21,430	20,750
Profit after tax	1,499	1,792	1,442	995	1,784	982	(217)	(135)	408	745	621
Yield (%)	10.6	11.8	9.0	5.8	9.3	5.0	(–)	(–)	2.0	3.5	3.0

Notes: a. Including Sedec and Marsavco share of Leopoldville Crushing.

b. Basis of calculating fixed assets revised to include notional interest on plantation development and to exclude assets not yet productive.

c. Immature areas now included and Brabanta and Lusanga valued at the nett book value per the accounts.

d. Pamol (Ghana) was wound up after 1960.

Table 9.4(b)   Average Return to GCE of the Plantation
Companies 1955—65 (Arithmetical average of nett profit after
statistical tax as a percentage of the arithmetical average of capital
employed)

Company	A Average nett profit (£'000)	B Average GCE (£'000)	A/B %
PLC	590	12,204	4.8
Pamol (Nigeria) [a]	198	3,755	5.3
Pamol (Malaya)	68	705	9.7
LPPL	54	660	8.2
Total all companies [b]	922	18,521	5.0

Notes: a. Pamol Nigeria includes Cameroons until 1960; thereafter I have
amalgamated the figures for both companies.

b. These totals include other smaller companies not listed separately here.

did not include any large booms or slumps in commodity prices. On
this evidence it should be possible to answer with some confidence
two basic questions about plantations as a form of overseas investment by a multinational company: first, did they, on average, give a
better than 10 per cent return; second, was there any correlation
between the size of the plantation, the type of crop, etc. and its
profitability?

Comparison makes it clear that Pamol (Malaya) was the most
profitable, though the profits varied widely. The poor performance
in 1957/8 was due to the emergency and terrorism, while the disappointing results of 1962–4 were a reflection both of the increased
capital invested in extensions before the new trees came into bearing
and also the prolonged strike of 1964; but the 1965 results confirmed
that this was an excellent investment. Some indication of why
Malaya did best can be deduced from the comparative data in
Table 9.4(c), though these figures are for 1959 only, and the ratios
shown here between total oil production and the area of plantations
cannot be used for a comparison between Malaya and the Congo
because a considerable part of the Congo's oil came from fruit not
grown on the plantations but bought from Africans in the protected
areas. The key to Malaya's superiority lay in its climatic conditions,
and this was reflected in unit costs. Here labour ratios were one of
the critical factors because labour costs were a very large proportion
of total production costs in this labour-intensive industry. In 1959

Table 9.4(c)   Relative Size of Plantations, Labour Force and NSV, 1959

Company	A Acres	B Labour force	C NSV (£'000)	D Trading profit (£'000)	A/B	D/A £	C/A £	D/B £	C/B £
PLC	140,868	41,572	9,622	1,859	3.3	13	68.3	45	231.4
Pamol (Nigeria)	34,160	6,288	1,539	494	5.4	14	45.0	78	244.7
Pamol (Malaya)	10,103	1,030	335	106	9.8	10	33.0	103	325.2
LPP	13,710	1,215	378	88	11.3	6	27.5	72.4	311.1

Notes: a. 1959 was taken as a 'normal' year, when Pamol, Malaya, had nearly reached its full size, when oil prices were relatively high, and before the Congo crisis. It was a 'good year' for all these companies.

b. NSV is taken to include cocoa, rubber and other minority crops.

c. Manpower includes management.

Malaya had the best ratio between labour and NSV with an output of £325 per man. LPPL, which, besides being plagued with a perpetual labour shortage also avoided the cost of cutting fruit from palms, was second with £311; Nigeria and PLC were a rather bad third and fourth. Alternatively, if one takes trading profit before tax in relation to manpower, the primacy of Malaya, with £103 per man, becomes greater, Nigeria takes second place, LPPL third and PLC fourth with a margin of £45 a man.

These contrasts should not be over-stressed, for perhaps the most significant feature of the statistics for 1959 is how relatively close the performance of these widely dispersed and very different enterprises could be; and this in turn demonstrates the wisdom of the policy adopted in the Congo and the Solomons after 1945 of strictly limiting the area under actual cultivation to develop comparatively small palm oil or coconut plantations, using the best available strains of palm and the most scientific methods of cultivation. Had HCB/PLC continued with its original policy of depending on natural palmeries the contrast with other places would have been very striking, for in 1930 total production of palm oil was only 18,000 tons compared with 54,208 tons in 1959. Clearly transformation of HCB into a comparatively intensive plantation enterprise was the condition of its survival once more efficient palm oil plantations were established in South-east Asia; and the continued lag of HCB in the 1950s reflected its continued partial dependence on the collection and purchase of natural fruit.

The first general conclusion must therefore be that at no time after 1920 was it easy to make a profit from the production of tropical commodities such as vegetable oils and that only the efficient producer could compete. The data also suggests that, even when conditions were favourable, as in Malaya, plantation production was neither outstandingly profitable nor secure as a form of investment. By the standards laid down by the Special Committee in 1955 none of these companies succeeded in the next decade: none approached the 15 per cent nett return looked for. Malaya came closest with an average return of 9.7 per cent and LPPL, which had some of its best years in this decade, came next with a surprising average of 8.2 per cent. The two African enterprises in Nigeria and the Congo averaged 5.3 per cent and 4.8 per cent respectively and the eleven-year average of all Unilever plantations was only 5.0 per cent. Other periods would, of course, have provided different results: the average return to capital of all these companies for

1954–60, for example, was 8.4 per cent and, if statistics were available, the profits of the Korean war boom period might have been even higher. But the statistics provide no grounds whatever for believing that plantations were likely over a period of time to provide a return to capital higher than could be obtained in the manufacturing enterprises a company such as Unilever ran throughout the world.

This conclusion is the more significant because plantations appear not to provide security as an alternative to high profits. The evidence surveyed in these chapters makes it clear that commodity production was exceptionally vulnerable to influences beyond commercial control—fluctuations in the commodity market and political events in the host country. Too much has been written about the volatility of the international commodity market as a decisive influence on the life of countries dependent on commodity exports for this factor to need emphasis. The history of LPPL and HCB over half a century demonstrates that the most important factor determining profitability in an 'open' economy (though not where there was state marketing) was the world price of vegetable oils; and, since Unilever's total production of palm oil in 1959 at 69,535 tons was only about 12 per cent of total world exports at 566,000 tons, the concern had no hope of influencing international price levels. To this extent plantations were as much a gamble as dealing in the commodity markets.

From the 1950s, however, politics became an additional and perhaps greater hazard. It has been emphasised in earlier chapters that probably the most important single consequence of decolonisation for a multinational was the disappearance of that political stability which had been the main benefit conferred by colonialism on foreign investors. All foreign investors were vulnerable to the nationalist policies likely to be adopted by successor states, but plantations and other commodity producers more than most other foreign enterprises on three main counts. They were physically very exposed to violence or disorder; they might seem more important to the country's economic and social welfare than, say, a soap factory, because they were large contributors to foreign exchange earnings; and an established plantation might appear easy to run so that the case for continued foreign ownership was weaker than it was for a technically more complex investment such as a copper mine or an electronics factory. Plantations were, therefore, obvious targets for nationalistic policies of public control or expropriation.

The Unilever experience reflects all these dangers. In Malaya Chinese communist terrorists came near to destroying the plantation business in 1957–8 and partly political strikes in 1964 resulted in Pamol (Malaya) making its first loss that year. In the Congo disorder made it impossible for the plantations at various times from 1959 to 1966 to function properly and caused immense damage, while the MARSAVCO factory in Leopoldville did quite well.

In the long run government intervention was the greatest threat to a foreign owned plantation. This might take the form either of state regulation of the market, which determined profitability, or actual take-over. Nigeria provides the best example of the first, since there the selling price of commodities was controlled from 1940 to 1965 and beyond at levels generally well below world prices; and the profitability of Pamol (Nigeria) was determined by what price the colonial and then the regional marketing boards chose to pay. LPPL was tied to the prices paid by the British Ministry of Food until 1957 and was then fortunate that the Protectorate did not establish a marketing board on West African lines. Fears that the Congo might start state marketing after independence proved wrong, but the government did impose a stiff export duty even before 1960 which reduced HCB's profit margins. These were signs of the times. As the 'open' economy of the colonial period disappeared throughout the Third World, so all commodity producers became vulnerable to state regulation of their profit margins in one of these or other ways.

The ultimate hazard was, of course, nationalisation with or without compensation. HCB had always been liable to this because the Convention allowed for compulsory public purchase with compensation for value added by the company. With independence plantations everywhere became dangerously exposed and by the 1960s they had been nationalised in many countries: tea estates in Sri Lanka, all Dutch-owned plantations in Indonesia in 1957, many plantations in India, all foreign plantations in Burma. It was, therefore, not at all surprising that PLZ's plantations in Zaire should have been nationalised in 1975, and far more surprising that the government should have decided to return these in 1977. Almost alone among the new states of Africa and Asia, Malaya chose to maintain the principles of the 'open' economy; and it may be no coincidence that Malaya's share of world trade in her two main commodity exports, palm oil and rubber, should have increased dramatically in the two decades after 1950.

Unilever was, therefore, fortunate that its main new plantations were in Malaysia. But in conclusion it is necessary to consider the wider implications of decolonisation for foreign-owned and run plantations in less developed countries. Two contradictory positions can be adopted. On the one hand the logical extension of what has been said is that plantations belong to an earlier and now defunct phase of world history when only Europeans possessed the technical and financial resources needed to establish and run plantations, together with the facilities for profitable marketing. By the 1970s most LDCs were capable of undertaking production and distribution of commodities on their own account, so that a multinational would be ill-advised to undertake new investment of this kind. The alternative standpoint, which appears to have some support within Unilever itself, is that the technology of plantations production is moving so fast that from the standpoint of a LDC there may be as strong a case for inviting the co-operation of a multinational company in helping to establish and run commodity production (as the Ghana government did in the 1970s) as to build and operate a factory. New oil palm or copra plantations being established in the 1970s are as different from those started in the 1950s as they in their time were from the 'natural palmeries' of HCB in the 1920s and governments now expect local participation in the equity. It therefore remains possible that some LDCs may be persuaded by the dual incentive of increasing the food supply for the home market and providing export commodities to earn foreign exchange that it is worth while to use the resources of a foreign company to establish or expand commodity production. It is, therefore, too soon to conclude that for Unilever the age of plantations is coming to an end.

10

Conclusions

It is easier to ask questions than to answer them; and it is obvious that the evidence in the Unilever records, on which this book has largely been based, does not provide full answers to all aspects of the three main questions posed at the start of Chapter 1: why a capitalist firm should choose to invest in productive enterprises overseas; how its subsidiaries developed and how profitable they proved to their parent; and what effects this investment had on host countries. Still less can evidence concerning a single Anglo-Dutch company which specialised in fats and oils prove anything about the character of other international corporations which did quite different things. It is proposed, nevertheless, to review the evidence briefly in terms of these three questions and then to suggest some tentative conclusions on the general relevance of Unilever's experience overseas to the broader problem of the role of multinationals in less developed countries (LDCs).

Motives for Investment Overseas

The first question turns on the motive for investment in plantations or industrial production overseas. The answers are different and plantations can conveniently be dealt with first because they are a comparatively simple issue.

(a) Plantations

The evidence of Chapters 8 and 9 suggests that at the start William Lever regarded both the production and purchase of commodities broadly in terms of vertical integration. Thinking as a manufacturer, his strategy was defensive; by buying companies that traded in West African vegetable oil and establishing his own coconut and palm oil plantations, he could both assure a supply to his own factories and, by increasing total world production, marginally reduce market prices. As an extension of the same strategy Lever bought a number of ships in and after 1916 which he used on the West African shipping run to break the monopoly previously held by the West African shipping conference dominated by Elder Dempster and Co. [1]

But circumstances alter strategies. As early as 1916–20 Lever's motives for buying ships, taking over the Niger Company and increasing his investment in the Congo plantations were clearly influenced by the prospect of making a profit from dealing in oil as a commodity; and it was at the same time that Anton Jurgens became involved in the commodity trade. [2] Both men, that is, were turning from a defensive strategy of vertical integration to a profit-making policy of horizontal diversification. For both 1920/1 was the moment of truth. The dramatic drop in commodity prices, involving a fall in the Liverpool price of palm oil from £98 a ton in February 1920 to £53 that July and an average of £39 during 1923, made the Niger Company a dangerous liability (because much of the price already agreed was based on its stocks of oil calculated at inflated prices) and made similar nonsense of Jurgens' investment in copra. This marked a turning point. Jurgens stopped operating their oil mills and withdrew from the commodity market. Levers could not get out so easily because their investment in oil production and trade was too large. But the accepted purpose of these activities changed. There was no more talk of the danger of a manufacturing firm being held to ransom by producers, traders or carriers of vegetable oils. Levers, and later Unilever, continued to trade, run plantations and operate ships, but they now did so to make money, if possible; and these enterprises were seen as mere investments of a specialised type, divorced from the rest of the Lever/Unilever business. The West African ships became common carriers, part of the West African shipping conference, and benefited from those very restrictive practices they had been bought to challenge. [3] The Niger Company and Lever's other trading companies, which were amalgamated in 1929 with African and Eastern to form UAC, were no longer thought to have any structural connection with the industrial side of the business; and the plantation companies were judged merely by the financial return they provided. It is true that there were some temporary functional associations: for example, UAC distributed Lever soaps in Nigeria; HCB and SEDEC gave special discounts to SAVCO during the 1930s; and the Australian soap company bought LPPL's copra and provided the plantations with administrative services. Yet these were largely accidental. Unilever did not believe in vertical integration after the early 1920s and all internal transfers were charged on a fixed formula whose aim was to ensure that no part of the business made a profit at the expense of any other part. This was the hallmark of a widely diversified enterprise whose component parts shared only the common purpose of profit maximisation.

It was on this basis that the second generation of plantation ventures was built after 1945. The motive was explicit: to make an above average profit by applying the concern's assets (capital, know-how, etc.) in favourable situations. But to a multinational whose primary function was to manufacture consumer goods from vegetable oils, diversification of this kind had the additional advantage that it provided a small hedge against fluctuations in the commodity market. What Unilever as a manufacturer lost on the swings it might, at least in part, gain on the roundabouts as a commodity producer.

(b) Industry

The grounds on which Levers and Unilever decided to set up overseas manufacturing subsidiaries and the methods they used differed considerably over time and place. Taking the group of eleven companies studied in this book, five distinct motives can be defined, though more than one of these was usually relevant to any one country: to defend an established export market; to increase the profit margins made on exports by taking advantage of relatively cheap factors of production; to penetrate a market not accessible through imports; to create a new market; and to take advantage of attractive conditions created by a host government. None of these should cause surprise for all are found in the standard literature on multinationals. The first is so common that it can be regarded as the norm. Because Lever soaps and, to a lesser extent, margarine, vegetable ghee, etc. made by the Dutch companies, had established export markets in most parts of the world by the first decade of the twentieth century, the home companies stood to lose by almost any change in market conditions overseas. The symptom of danger was the growth in local competition to Lever/Unilever exports; and in most of these countries competition resulted from an increase in effective protection for local producers. Thus the evidence suggests that it was almost a reflex action for an industrial firm with a large international trade to consider local manufacture as a substitute for imports once a host country took decisive steps to protect its domestic producers. Such action was a challenge: tariff walls were built to be jumped over.

The second argument was that it might prove advantageous to use local production factors in order to save costs. By itself the mere fact of a local supply of, say, palm oil was unlikely to constitute a sufficient incentive for investing in a factory because the costs involved (reduction in the use made of existing production facilities in Europe, the high unit cost of overheads in a factory designed to serve a limited market and other diseconomies of scale) would usually offset savings made on the cost of carrying raw materials to Europe and the finished product back to its overseas market. But freight costs in conjunction with even quite moderate import duties might well add up to a cost-benefit analysis that favoured local production and stimulated domestic competition. This combination was particularly evident in Indonesia, Ceylon and Pakistan. Elsewhere local supplies of raw materials often made it possible to achieve other objects—to penetrate existing markets not accessible to imports or to establish new markets. In the Congo there were almost no sales of cheap factory-made soap before the 1920s because freight costs on imported soap eroded potential profits. Local manufacture was therefore seen by William Lever as a means of creating a market for 'filled' soap which could not have been built up by imports. In Nigeria in the same decade and in East Africa after 1944 the market for soap already existed but the availability of cheap 'cottage' soap made from local raw materials made it very difficult for a foreign firm to compete by importing: in each case local manufacture, using as far as possible local raw materials, was the solution. In Turkey Unilever combined three aims: to penetrate a market not accessible to imports (due to import restrictions and very high tariffs); to create a new market for hardened fats; and to take advantage of under-utilised or latent sources of raw materials.

Finally there was the potential attraction of official encouragement by the government of a host country. Strictly speaking, none of the manufacturing enterprises described in this book was the result of an official invitation. Kenya came nearest since the government was a partner with the British-run CDC which actually invited

Unilever to become a half-partner and sole manager of its hardened fats business in Nairobi. In other countries governments never went beyond putting out a welcoming hand, though in a strictly controlled economy such a welcome almost amounted to an invitation. This was what happened in Turkey and Ghana at the start of Unilever's manufacturing activities there; but by the 1960s there were very few LDCs in which Unilever or any other multinational could have invested or expanded its functions without official welcome or at least benediction.

These seem to have been the positive reasons for undertaking productive investment overseas. On the other side the evidence suggests that 'surplus capital' or excess liquidity at home was never a main or sufficient cause. At no point was this ever put forward as an argument for a new investment abroad. It would be more accurate to say that Unilever has almost always had the ability to raise more funds than it actually used, one way or another, but that it judged each investment proposal in terms of its opportunity cost (alternative use of the same resources).

The Character and Profitability of Manufacturing Subsidiaries

The second group of questions relate to the general character of Unilever and its manufacturing subsidiaries, particularly as pin-pointed by the three issues mentioned in chapter one: the growth patterns of subsidiaries, the relationship between them and the centre and their profitability. These will be reviewed briefly in that order.

(a) Growth Patterns

The case studies suggest that there were two distinct patterns of growth by Unilever manufacturing subsidiaries, one characteristic of Europe, North America and the more developed new countries such as Australia, South Africa and New Zealand; the other of LDCs. In the more developed countries, because there was always a local factory-made product by the time Lever Brothers or the Dutch companies came to consider local production, it was never enough to build a single new factory: to achieve a reasonable share of the market one had to buy out the competition, and this was the invariable basis of a successful Unilever business in such countries. This was an expensive process; but if successful it led on to a second 'classical' phase, lasting from about 1914 to the early 1940s, during which Lever/Unilever had market dominance in soap and possibly margarine, which in turn generated relatively high profits. On the other hand this was not a phase in which there was much new investment, diversification or even rationalisation. This was partly due to discouraging economic conditions during part of the 1920s and 1930s, and a contemporary business analyst might well have thought that by the 1930s Unilever companies overseas had lost momentum, becoming stagnant investments. Stagnation ended in the mid-1940s with the major reassessment Unilever then made of its future opportunities at home and overseas and the third, still continuing, phase was one of large investment to expand markets and diversify the product base in all developed countries. Diversification was seen as a way of breaking through limitations imposed by the capacity of markets in which Unilever was already dominant to expand turnover and maximise profits. The means consisted of making in each overseas country to which they were suited any of the new range of products available in Europe or North America: convenience foods, synthetic detergents, animal feeds, chemicals, packaging materials. The initiative for applying these new technologies overseas might come either from headquarters in London or Rotterdam or from the subsidiary whose management could, so to speak, shop around inside the concern's warehouse and select those products it thought best suited to its financial resources and local demand. In assessing such proposals the London management seems to have applied three general tests: portfolio investment was excluded; profit predictions must be realistically optimistic (a nett return of 10 per cent was conventionally looked for, even if it was not always obtained); and new ventures must grow from or be related to Unilever's existing technological base.

The evolutionary pattern of manufacturing subsidiaries in poorer countries in Africa and Asia was significantly different. At the start there was usually no 'modern' factory production of any importance of the products Lever/Unilever proposed to make there. This had two consequences. First, the concern could not save time by buying established local companies and their goodwill: they had, as it were, to start by turning the first sod and laying the foundations of a market. This made early progress slow, but the pay off came later. Precisely because Unilever was the pioneer local modern manufacturer and there was very limited local competition at that quality and price level, the concern could often establish something approaching a monopoly of the market. Provided the experts had got their advance estimates of costs, sales volume and margins right, this might pave the way to satisfactory profits during the second and 'classical' phase. This happened in all the cases studied in this book, though not in some others: Japan in the early twentieth century and Mexico in the 1960s were LDCs which failed to live up to expectations. But these golden ages seldom lasted long and profits in LDCs seem to have been much more volatile than in more developed places. The collapse of the commodity market seriously affected consumer capacity, and therefore Unilever profits, in most parts of Africa and Asia during the 1930s, whereas profit levels in Australia and South Africa remained remarkably stable. Alternatively Unilever's success seemed invariably to stimulate others to follow its example, however undeveloped the host economy might be. In India, for example, vanaspati never recovered that first fine rapture of the mid-1930s because by the next decade total capacity built up by Indians grossly exceeded demand. But the most obvious difference between subsidiaries in more and less developed countries lay in the third phase after about 1945. On the one hand few LDCs offered a market for the typical consumer goods designed for the affluent countries of Europe and North America; on the other hand this third phase coincided with decolonisation in most of the LDCs in which Unilever operated and this in turn commonly led to intensive governmental management of the economy. These governments normally insisted that any new product proposed by a foreign-owned venture should fit into their general economic planning, that it did not duplicate existing products and that it provided backward or forward linkages with the rest of the economy. The combined effect of these two constraints was to narrow down the range of options open to these manufacturing subsidiaries and in some cases to force them, in their attempts to escape from limited markets for established products, to embark on projects that lay on the fringes of Unilever technology or even beyond.

A closely related feature of Unilever manufacturing subsidiaries in LDCs in this third phase was that, because they were distrusted on the grounds that they were alien, the opportunities open to them to grow or diversify were circumscribed. Their survival might be safeguarded on the ground that they had a legal right to exist, that they performed useful functions and that to nationalise them might deter new investment by others; but the host government might nevertheless take the view that an existing foreign enterprise was entitled only to do what it already did or what the authorities wanted it to do. The result might be that the subsidiary survived and made reasonable profits but was so constrained that it lost its vitality and relative importance in the local economy. It is too early to predict the future pattern of a Unilever company which is virtually isolated in a 'managed' economy for long periods; but it is almost certain to differ from that of a subsidiary which has to operate in a state of nature in an 'open' economy and whose survival depends on its being at least as fit as its natural rivals, Colgate–Palmolive and Procter and Gamble.

(b) Central Control and Local Autonomy

The next main question is the relationship between these subsidiaries and their home companies in London and Rotterdam: that is, the balance between central control and local autonomy. It was suggested at the start that in principle a multinational of the type of Unilever, whose subsidiaries mostly manufacture consumer goods for sale in the country in which they are made, is likely to be a federative rather than a unitary enterprise; and the evidence suggests that this was generally so. But the relationship between centre and subsidiary was never constant, and there were evident differences between each of three periods: to 1925; from 1925 to 1945; and from 1945 to 1965.

During the first period the dominant influence in Lever Brothers was, of course, William Lever and his attitude to the autonomy of his associated companies seemed ambivalent. He always maintained that each of them was a separate enterprise, arguing that one major ground for local manufacture was that only local men could properly understand the market. Yet such independence was to some extent legal and illusory. Although Lever called all his subsidiaries 'associated companies', in practice he made a distinction between those which had been founded by him as offshoots of Levers and those which he had bought as established businesses. The first were seen as extensions of Port Sunlight and their managements treated as the employees they were; while companies such as Kitchens were left with much more freedom under their family managements. The future character of Unilever depended to some extent on which model predominated.

This issue was determined during the second, 'classical', period of the older overseas companies. Although this was the main era of rationalisation and concentration within individual countries and the original associated companies almost all lost their identity, the 'national' managements that took over these consolidated enterprises were allowed more autonomy than at any time before or since. Although the routine of making elaborate weekly, monthly and annual estimates and reports continued as Lever had established it, and although the new Overseas Committee developed a system of regular visits, the reports of the visiting executives show that they expected to advise, not dictate. In a sense this was a period of corporate 'salutary neglect' in which the centre put relatively little into established overseas companies and also left them largely to determine their own policies.

By contrast the two decades after 1945 saw a strong latent tension between central control and local autonomy. At a time when the product range was being diversified and the subsidiaries therefore had to rely much more than in the past on the continuous transfer of technology, know-how and capital and when the concept of product 'co-ordination' was gaining force, there was a strong possibility that the balance would tilt the other way. This did not happen. A balance was struck by 1965 which was potentially satisfactory to both central and overseas managements. Provided the subsidiary made a reasonable profit one year with another and could afford to finance its own expansion and diversification over a reasonable period, the local management was allowed a great deal of independence. In cases where the initiative for expansion or diversification came from the periphery rather than the centre, it was up to the chairman of each company to demonstrate to the Overseas and Special Committees that his proposals were viable. This might not be easy and some chairmen might feel that it was as difficult to push a proposal through all the interested departments of Unilever House as it was to clear it through the bureaucracy of their own country. But the impression given both by the records and personal discussion is that the grounds on which projects were assessed were not whether they would provide a large and immediate profit to the centre but whether they were in the long-term interests of the individual company and the host country. This, of course, reflects enlightened self-interest on the part of the London management and was certainly not incompatible with a profit-maximising approach; but it made it possible to allow considerable freedom of initiative to the local management which in turn enabled them to satisfy the host government that they were free to act in accordance with national economic planning.

An impressionistic general view might therefore be that at the end of the period Unilever remained essentially a federation in which the allocation of powers and functions between centre and periphery was flexible and capable of evolution. To project speculatively into the future it seemed likely that as and when both local participation in the equity and indigenous management became predominant, so the relationship between centre and subsidiary would tend to resemble that between an investing company, which also provided a continuing input of technology and know-how, and an independent enterprise in which it held shares. Yet there was a limit to how far this process could go without destroying the special quality of a multinational—its ability to disseminate its capital and skills in return for receiving benefits. A multinational which takes the risk of putting assets into a subsidiary has a claim to management control to match its responsibility. To the possible complaint by a hypothetical indigenous chairman of a thriving subsidiary that his company could do better if it were entirely independent, the centre might legitimately answer that this might well be so in the short term and under fair weather conditions. But in one sense a multinational was a mutual insurance group in which the profits and losses of different parts could balance out and there was a guarantee of product quality, technical progress, etc. No Unilever subsidiary had ever yet gone bankrupt, though several might well have done so in the 1930s if they had been independent. In the last resort a well-run multinational, like any federal organisation, is one in which the centre earns its right to control and tax by the quality of its contribution to the welfare of its subordinate units; and the evidence suggests that the powers retained by Unilever House in the 1960s could be justified on this test.

(c) *Profits*

In the end, of course, a multinational, like any capitalist venture, is in the business for what it can get out of it for its shareholders and from its own standpoint profit is the measure of success. What benefit did Unilever as a European industrial corporation obtain from setting up and running its overseas companies? Advantage, of course, is a matter of relativities and the general question must be broken down into its component parts. First, how did the profits made by all overseas companies compare with profits made by the parent companies in Europe; that is, did the advantage of being a multinational lie in the higher profitability of investments in less developed countries? Second, how does one explain the large variations in the profits made by different concern companies and by particular companies at different times?

It would be impracticable to recapitulate all the evidence provided for each of the thirteen companies studied in this book, particularly that for earlier periods; but for the decade 1956–65 Table 10.1 shows the profitability of all except Lever Brothers (Ghana)—which operated for only two years before 1965—and also includes New Zealand, Argentina and Brazil. Table 10.2 provides a bird's-eye view of the comparative profitability of all Unilever companies in different parts of the world in the same decade. It should be noted that these two tables use different methods of expressing profitability. The figures in Table 10.1 show the economic return to investment, using 'nett profit after statistical tax' as a percentage of 'gross capital employed'; while the data in Table 10.2 is taken from the published accounts, which show aggregated accounting profit as a percentage of the book value of the capital.

Perhaps the most striking feature of all the data on profitability reproduced in this book is how greatly profit levels varied between different companies at particular times and for any one company over a period of time. But for the decade 1956–65 one other feature stands out: on average the profitability of the business in Europe was not only higher than that of any other region but was also less volatile. The ratio between the highest and lowest accounting return to book capital in Europe was 1.5:1, as compared with 1.7:1 for America, 2.5:1 for Africa and 1.6:1 for the rest of the world. In absolute terms Europe provided more than half the total profits in each of these ten years: 50.3 per cent of total capital generated, 58.9 per cent of total sales by value and 61.7 per cent of profits in 1955. In 1965 the proportions were capital 64.7 per cent, sales 64.5 per cent, profits 67.5 per cent. Europe was also the area of largest new investment in these years, the book capital rising by 150 per cent compared with 82 per cent in America, 68 per cent in Africa and 71.9 per cent in the rest of the world. Clearly Europe was the largest generator of profits with the highest return to capital and Unilever became more a European company during this decade.

Yet this must not obscure the great importance of the overseas companies to Unilever as a whole. Statistics for the decade 1955–65, supported by data on profits for the overseas subsidiaries studied in this book, suggests that for this predominantly European enterprise, which did not use foreign subsidiaries to manufacture or assemble

Table 10.1 Post-tax Profitability of 13 Unilever Overseas Manufacturing Subsidiaries, 1956–65, Compared with all Unilever Companies in Europe. Nett Yield after Statistical Tax as a Percentage of Average Gross Capital Employed for Each Year. Losses are Shown in Brackets.

Country	1956	1957	1958	1959	1960	1961	1962	1963	1964	1965	Average
Turkey	19.5	17.3	26.4	19.0	13.5	11.6	14.3	15.2	14.8	9.3	16.09
Australia	6.1	8.9	7.3	8.8	8.3	4.5	8.1	6.6	4.8	4.4	6.78
Ceylon	22.7	13.6	11.3	10.9	11.0	10.6	10.5	9.4	8.2	9.7	11.79
India	7.9	8.3	9.3	13.5	13.2	10.1	9.8	7.2	7.0	6.7	9.30
New Zealand	5.8	5.8	4.8	4.2	9.6	6.1	6.4	6.4	4.9	5.9	5.99
Pakistan	4.3	1.9	1.9	3.9	4.0	3.7	5.1	4.7	4.9	1.7	3.61
South Africa	8.7	8.5	10.2	13.2	16.9	10.2	11.6	10.1	11.5	9.5	11.04
Indonesia	11.5	6.4	4.0	6.7	6.5	9.3	9.5	14.7	6.3	–	7.49
Nigeria: LB(N)	10.4	4.9	0.6	(0.7)	6.2	0.5	2.4	3.2	4.3	10.2	4.20
Congo (MARSAVCO)	(2.4)	(0.8)	1.0	2.0	(0.4)	12.0	22.0	25.0	8.0	9.0	7.54
Kenya (EAI)	10.3	7.3	3.5	11.6	17.3	21.1	25.1	27.5	19.8	20.9	16.40
Argentina	(1.0)	4.5	9.5	2.4	(0.3)	1.5	(10.2)	1.6	7.2	11.7	2.69
Brazil	4.7	(13.4)	(6.3)	(10.8)	3.3	11.1	11.8	17.2	14.5	(3.7)	2.84
All European Companies	11.3	8.2	9.6	10.7	8.2	7.8	8.8	8.9	8.4	8.2	9.0

Notes: a. All calculations are based on local currencies.

b. These figures come from Unilever's 'Statistical Accounts', part of the system of internal management whose purpose is to express financial information in the form that most clearly indicates the economic performance of any part of Unilever and is identical as between any two companies. 'Statistical tax' and 'gross capital employed' are part of this system and are defined in Chapter 2.

c. The 'Average' in the righthand column is the mean of the percentage figures for the ten years. It is not weighted because I have not got the basic data for Europe; but the weighted averages for the overseas companies are not very different.

d. The figures for Indonesia are taken from the data available in London; and for the years 1961–5 they are different from the figures in Table 5.9 which are based on records in Jakarta. The difference probably results from divergent treatment of hyper-inflation; and these 'London results' look unduly satisfactory.

Table 10.2 Unilever Sales, Capital Employed and Profits by Region, 1955–65 (£m)

Total Unilever

	A	B	C		
	Sales	Profit	CE	B/A %	B/C %
1965	1,822	67.8	827	3.7	8.2
1964	1,688	67.3	774	4.0	8.7
1963	1,535	59.9	722	3.9	8.3
1962	1,477	54.3	690	3.7	7.9
1961	1,444	51.7	642	3.6	8.0
1960	1,387	53.2	603*	3.8	8.8
1959	1,329	59.2	571*	4.4	10.4
1958	1,259	47.2	520*	3.7	9.1
1957	1,220	41.0	493*	3.6	8.3
1956	1,182	47.8	465*	4.0	10.3
1955	1,069	42.3	425*	4.0	9.9
Average				3.8	8.9
Standard deviation				0.8	

Europe

	A	B	C		
	Sales	Profit	CE	B/A %	B/C %
1965	1,176	45.8	535	3.9	8.5
1964	1,075	45.2	515	4.2	8.8
1963	959	40.6	472	4.2	8.6
1962	905	39.1	445	4.3	8.8
1961	844	34.9	386	4.1	9.0
1960	800	32.5	359	4.1	9.0
1959	771	38.5	331	5.0	11.6
1958	718	32.6	286	4.5	11.3
1957	708	24.0	260	3.4	9.2
1956	702	30.9	245	4.4	12.6
1955	630	26.1	214	4.1	12.2
Average				4.2	9.9
Standard deviation				1.5	

North and South America

	A	B	C		
	Sales	Profit	CE	B/A %	B/C %
1965	265	10.1	111	3.8	9.1
1964	247	9.6	98	3.9	9.8
1963	237	9.0	94	3.8	9.6

Africa

	A	B	C		
	Sales	Profit	CE	B/A %	B/C %
1965	246	7.3	126	3.0	5.8
1964	238	7.8	109	3.3	7.1
1963	221	5.7	107	2.6	5.3

Year	Sales	Profit	CE	B/A %	B/C %	Sales	Profit	CE	B/A %	B/C %
1962	230	8.0	86	3.5	9.3	235	3.5	116	1.5	3.0
1961	229	7.3	74	3.2	9.9	263	5.0	139	1.9	3.6
1960	211	7.2	70	3.4	10.3	275	8.6	133	3.1	6.5
1959	213	7.1	69	3.3	10.3	252	9.5	131	3.8	7.2
1958	201	5.7	68	2.8	8.4	251	6.1	130	2.4	4.7
1957	184	4.2	63	2.3	6.7	239	9.6	137	4.0	7.0
1956	157	3.7	62	2.4	6.0	234	9.4	125	4.0	7.5
1955	142	4.5	61	3.2	7.4	216	7.6	118	3.5	6.4
Average				3.2	8.8				3.0	5.8
Standard deviation					1.4					1.4

Rest of World

	A	B	C		
Year	Sales	Profit	CE	B/A %	B/C %
1965	135	4.6	55	3.4	8.4
1964	128	4.7	52	3.7	9.0
1963	118	4.6	49	3.9	9.4
1962	107	3.7	43	3.5	8.6
1961	108	4.5	43	4.2	10.5
1960	101	4.9	41	4.8	11.9
1959	93	4.1	40	4.4	10.2
1958	89	2.8	36	3.1	7.8
1957	89	3.2	33	3.6	9.7
1956	89	3.8	33	4.3	11.5
1955	81	4.1	32	5.1	12.8
Average				4.0	9.9
Standard deviation					1.5

*Excluding interests not consolidated of £6m.

Definitions

(a) Sales are to third parties, excluding internal transfers.

(b) Profit is accounting profit after tax but before interest on loans.

(c) Capital Employed in book capital as in published balance sheets and *not* GCE.

(d) Africa includes all operations in that Continent (manufacturing businesses, United Africa operations and plantations interests).

Source: Published Unilever Reports and Accounts.

products for sale in the home markets, direct foreign investment had two major advantages. First, it increased turnover far beyond the limits set by the European market for Unilever's product range, thus providing economies of scale. Second, investment in manufacturing for local markets overseas and in commodity production was an insurance against fluctuations in commercial conditions in Europe or any other region. This dampening effect on fluctuations in overall profit levels is shown by the fact that the standard deviation for Unilever as a whole between 1955 and 1965 was only 0.81 per cent as compared with 1.5 per cent or 1.4 per cent for each individual region. For a company which depended so heavily on commodity prices this was a valuable buffer against the market and was most significant during the first decade after the Second World War. I have been unable to find the relevant figures, but Wilson states that in the years after 1945, when production and profitability were both very low in Europe due to the need to rebuild and reorganise, UAC and the plantations companies, which benefited from the great boom in vegetable oil prices, provided 'between one-third and one-half of Unilever's total turnover'.[4] By 1965 Africa's share was down to 13.5 per cent and America's share had risen from 10.6 per cent to 14.5 per cent. This is not to suggest that these changed proportions necessarily had any permanence: in 1976, for example, after deducting third party shareholding interests, which had by then become significant, Europe provided 60 per cent of total accounting profits, America 13 per cent, Africa 17 per cent and the rest of the world 10 per cent. The point is that to lay off one's bets in the way a multinational of this kind can do is a good insurance against changes in the relative prosperity of different parts of the world and between commodity production and manufacture.

It is more difficult to explain than to demonstrate variations between the profitability of regions and still more difficult between individual companies. In considering this issue one is dealing in two dimensions, place and time. Table 10.1 shows that in the single decade 1956–65 fluctuations in earnings within a single company were likely to be as great as between one enterprise and another. It has also been seen in Chapters 8 and 9 that the profitability of plantations varied very widely; and as these are a totally different and in some respects obverse case to that of the manufacturing companies they can conveniently be dealt with separately and first.

The most striking facts about the profitability of LPPL and HCB, as set out in Tables 8.2(b) and 8.6 for LPPL and 9.2 and 9.3 for HCB, are extreme volatility and low overall yields, particularly down to the mid-1940s. Neither feature is difficult to explain. The profitability of one plantation as compared with another was affected by a wide range of environmental factors, such as soil, climate, labour force and freights, so that some enterprises were likely on average always to be more profitable than others. But the volatility of profits in plantations as a whole was simply a function of the volatility of the vegetable oil market over which Unilever as producer had no control. Plantations were, therefore, necessarily a more speculative investment than a factory. On the other hand the appearance of low profitability in plantations as compared with factories is to some extent misleading. Due to the accident that the two oldest Unilever plantation companies were established before the very long slump in commodity prices that began in 1921 and lasted until the early 1940s, their trading results during the first 30 years look dismal. The figures from 1940 to the later 1950s are very different and suggest that, despite their probably incurable volatility, the profits of well-run plantations might on average be just as high and possibly higher than profits to be got from manufacturing investments.

It is more difficult to generalise about the reasons for varying levels of profitability in Unilever's manufacturing subsidiaries because, whereas the commodity market was common to all producers of vegetable oil (except those who were obliged to sell to some local organisation, such as the West African marketing boards), each overseas manufacturing company was serving a different market and was subject to local influences on its profits. Indeed, if we analyse the main components of production costs and profits, only one element seems to have been sufficiently uniform, and also so small, as to be unimportant: that is, the cost of wages. By sharp contrast with the plantations, the manufacture of most Unilever products was never labour-intensive, though there was scope for adapting the degree of mechanisation in some processes to the level of wages and the efficiency of the local labour force. Thus as between one Unilever factory and another there was a visible hierarchy of technology; and in general the higher local wage rates were in relation to the value of the product, the more sophisticated the equipment was likely to be. But everywhere wages constituted a relatively very small and remarkably consistent proportion of production costs—usually under 5 per cent—which hardly differed between one country and another. Low wage rates therefore neither attracted Unilever nor had any significant impact on comparative profit levels.

Apart from wages almost every other production cost was different as between one country and another and changed over time. The two things most closely examined by Lever/Unilever men when considering whether or not to invest in local production for the first time were the availability and price of raw materials and the size and quality of the local market; and we may safely follow these experts in expecting to find that these were the two most important varying influences on production costs and profit margins. Raw materials were critical because they constituted a very large proportion of total costs: for example, about 60 per cent of the total cost of making and distributing all soaps produced by MARSAVCO in the Congo in 1963, including factory and other fixed expenses, advertising, distribution costs and commissions. The proportion might vary but was always so high that variations were likely to determine profit levels, particularly on low priced products with small profit margins. It is not, therefore, surprising that in every case examined above the decision to build a factory depended on assurance of an ample supply of raw materials—either locally produced or imported—at a price that would enable the factory to compete against imports, taking import duties into account. A modern example was Ghana, which did not then produce enough vegetable oil to supply a large modern factory and where profitable soap manufacture therefore depended on an official assurance that there would be no import duties on imported vegetable oil.

Once local manufacture was started, profits depended mainly on the fluctuating margin between raw material costs and selling prices. Under free market conditions this depended on the world commodity market; and the only case in which a reduction in the price of palm and other vegetable oils did not increase profit margins was in a country such as Nigeria before the 1940s where, because consumer incomes depended so directly on the price received for groundnuts or palm oil, low commodity prices resulted in greatly reduced sales of factory-made soap and so in tight profit margins. But the arrival of the 'managed' economy after 1940 radically altered this equation. In Nigeria raw material prices, both to producers and consumers, were state controlled. Because the price paid to producers was kept artificially low while the price demanded from manufacturers was set at international levels, companies such as WASCO found themselves squeezed between low consumer buying power and high costs. In India Hindustan Lever found itself compelled to use local rather than imported raw materials whose prices were fixed or influenced by official controls. While the price of soap was never controlled, that of vanaspati was at various times, so profit margins were again squeezed. In Indonesia soap prices were controlled during the late 1950s and early 1960s while raw material costs rose with inflation. The result was that the company faced bankruptcy before it was taken over by the trade unions in 1965. Thus, whereas before the Second World War the profits of subsidiaries tended to vary with commodity prices, thereafter their fortunes were more often determined by official policy. In this respect the large foreign firm was worse placed than its small indigenous competitors. Whereas these could often evade official controls the big company, whose activities were too exposed for it to dabble in a black or grey market, could not and found its comparative advantage being eroded.

The other major influence on profit levels was, of course, the character of the local market for which the subsidiary was producing and its position there. Other things being equal, as Unilever men constantly remarked, the most rewarding market was one that could absorb the highest proportion of branded products which sold on consumer preference and could therefore command a premium, as contrasted with one where it was necessary to sell unbranded goods that sold mainly on price. For example, Ceylon, where Sunlight Soap and Lux Toilet Soap formed a large proportion of Lever sales from the start, was predictably more profitable than, say, the Congo, where most sales were originally of unwrapped, almost anonymous, filled bar soaps. Equally important in Unilever eyes was the concern's share of a particular market; and since it is commonly asserted that multinationals make exceptionally high profits precisely because they tend to acquire a monopolistic (or at least dominant) position in the restricted markets of LDCs, the concept demands careful examination. The evidence is ambiguous. Market dominance (50 per cent or more of a market) was certainly a contributory reason why Unilever companies were able to obtain satisfactory profit margins on certain products in certain countries at particular times; conversely a small market share was usually associated with tough competition, high promotional expenditure and low margins. But this does not mean that Unilever (or any other multinational operating under comparable conditions) would normally be able to hold a predominant position even if it once achieved it, nor that predominance alone guaranteed large profits. In fact, success in any product achieved by any of the subsidiaries studied for this book invariably resulted in intensified competition. In an 'open' economy this would probably come from both international and local rivals; in a 'managed' economy typical of a modern LDC it was likely to come at the top of the market from local entrepreneurs or perhaps foreign firms allowed to start production, but at the other end of the market from local 'cottage' producers. In neither case was 'monopoly capital' secure for long, except in those rare occasions when it was government policy to exclude external competition and where at a particular time local competition was ineffective. Of the 13 companies whose results for the decade 1956–65 are summarised in Table 10.1, only three were able to sustain anything approaching a monopoly position for any one product for any length of time. In Turkey this was for margarine and vanaspati, and was due to the government's refusal to allow imports coupled with the inability of the only potential local competitor to solve its technical problems. In South Africa it was for soap and can be attributed to the historic position achieved by William Lever, the limited size of the market, which may have deterred other foreign investors, and the constraints imposed by the government on Indians, 'coloureds' and Africans which made it difficult for these to compete effectively at the lower end of the soap Market. Finally in Kenya the success of EAI can be attributed to the fact that for most of the period covered by this book it was the only modern soap and margarine manufacturer operating within a high tariff and catering to an expanding demand for quality products. By 1965 it had to compete with a local American rival as well as with Indian soap producers and it was unlikely that its dominant position would survive indefinitely.

Dominance was not, therefore, necessarily durable; still less could it guarantee high profits. While in these companies satisfactory profit margins, where they existed, seem normally to have been associated with market leadership, because this made it possible to obtain a premium, the converse was not necessarily true. There were, in fact, many possible reasons why a subsidiary which dominated a local market for one or more products might nevertheless make small profits or even losses. From these studies it is possible to point to three among other possible situations likely to have had this result. First, in an LDC with an 'open' economy (that is, typically under colonial rather than modern conditions), the price of achieving or holding a dominant position against both external and internal competition might be to cut margins to the bone. This happened in Nigeria in the 1930s. In the short term at least these were phyrric victories. Second, in a modern LDC with a 'managed' economy, profit levels are likely to depend far more on governmental policies than on the market: for example, on the prices fixed by the authorities for raw materials and consumer products, on the exchange rates relevant to imported raw materials, on levels of corporate taxation and so on. In fact in all the post-colonial LDCs studied here (though since all were relatively large with comparatively efficient systems of administration they may not be typical of the less developed world as a whole) the main determinant of Unilever's profits was government policy. If Unilever or any other foreign company had a monopoly or near monopoly, and was allowed to make large profits, this was almost certainly by grace and favour of the government. Finally, in a more developed country with a relatively 'open' economy, a Unilever company was most likely to achieve and hold a predominant position in those products which it made there in its early days, after it had bought out the main local firms and before foreign competition became strong. For example, Unilever Australia still retained its near monopoly of laundry soaps in the 1960s. But over time this lost its significance as the profile of the detergents market changed; and it is significant that in no country studied here which had an 'open' economy was Unilever able to achieve as overwhelming a position in any product that became important there for the first time after 1945. This in turn suggests that 'monopoly' may be a transient accident of history rather than an invariable facet of international capitalism.

All this points to a more general and important conclusion as to why a multinational company may appear to make large profits by overseas investment, though, as has been seen, on average those of Unilever Overseas were not as high as those of metropolitan Unilever. Like similar firms, Unilever's basic asset was its ability to spot and make the most effective use of any favourable conjunction of factors wherever this was observed in the non-communist world. In the first place it could be selective and eclectic, whereas competitors in most host countries were tied to their own market. Then, having decided to take the plunge, Unilever had the advantage over those individuals or local companies with whom it was likely to compete that it already possessed all the instruments for immediate production—capital and credit, specialised equipment, technical experience, etc.—and could apply these in the right proportions to the new enterprise. Most important of all, the multinational could put in a team of men trained in the same business who had the full support of the home companies. This is what made Unilever more efficient than its local competitors, whether private or public, for the effect of a team, even of second-class men, is much greater than that of a few outstanding specialists who have an inadequate supporting staff. Thus, providing the multinational has made a reasonably correct estimate of all relevant aspects of the situation, its subsidiary should be able to do exceptionally well so long as the initial assumptions hold good. But because profitability is always contingent on a combination of factors, change in any one of these is likely to affect the whole operation; and the case studies in this book demonstrate how quickly and totally situations and profit levels may change.

We can now sum up the benefits Unilever received from owning and running overseas manufacturing companies and plantations. Although the concern remained primarily a European business, it was valuable for it to be able to expand its turnover beyond the limits it could hope to achieve in Europe, within a given range of products, by making the same things overseas because dividends received from overseas companies to some extent represented an additional profit on the firm's stock of products and know-how and made a contribution to the overheads of the metropolitan business. An ancillary advantage of global distribution of productive capital was that it provided an insurance against fluctuations in the economic health of Europe; and the multiplicity of subsidiaries provided a further cover against loss or destruction of any one of them. Or, to put it another way, in the modern world direct overseas investment performed much the same functions as exports had done during the era of an 'open' international economy before 1914: it provided economies of scale and ensured full use of comparative advantage. This, not above-average profits on capital invested overseas, was the reward a multinational looked for when investing in local production overseas for local consumption; and this is precisely what Unilever received during the seventy years covered by this book.

Unilever and the Host Countries

It remains to examine the other side of the picture—the significance of these Unilever companies for the countries in which they were guests. For an historian who lacks skill in econometrics it is impossible to answer many of the questions an economist might pose. But to ensure that important questions are asked and dealt with methodically it is proposed to review the evidence on these Unilever companies in the light of the main questions examined by Grant L. Reuber in his book, *Private Foreign Investment in Development*, and summarised in Chapter 1 above. Reuber used aggregate data drawn from a very large number of European and American multinationals to answer his questions and it will therefore be possible to consider how closely Unilever's experience conforms to that of its many contemporaries.

The starting point of Reuber's analysis is the proposition that, in terms of games theory, the relationship between a multinational and a less developed host country is not necessarily 'a zero sum game' in which a gain to the investor automatically represents a loss to the host country. 'Although losses may sometimes occur, the process depends upon a return to both parties equal to or in excess of their opportunity costs.' This is, both parties may receive a higher return than either could have obtained if they had invested the same resources in the next-best alternative: for a multinational, investment at home or in some other country, for the host, using the same resources (cost of providing the infrastructure, and possibly capital invested by the government as partner) in some other way.[5] To Reuber, as to most ideologically non-dogmatic economists, each direct foreign investment in each LDC poses the same open question: is there a favourable balance left in the account after deducting from the direct benefits a host country may derive from foreign direct investment whatever advantages it might have received if it had spent the same real domestic resources in some other way? If the balance is positive, the foreign investment was a nett advantage to the LDC; if not, not.

This is the approach that will be adopted here. But it must be pointed out that in a sense this very approach begs the question it purports to ask. To many economists and others, for the most part Marxists, who believe that capitalism is exploitative under all possible conditions, such an open-ended approach is meaningless; and without examining the many arguments put forward to demonstrate this, it is necessary briefly to indicate why they take this view and why it would therefore be pointless to attempt to demonstrate to any committed Marxist that Unilever or any other multinational provided, or might conceivably provide, any nett benefit for a less developed host country.

The basic common denominator of all Marxist criticism of direct investment in LDCs is that, while all capitalism exploits, direct foreign investment exploits absolutely. That is, whereas some at least of the profits made by capitalists within their own countries goes back into circulation and may even benefit the proletariat by increasing demand and therefore employment, the profits made by a multinational are certain sooner or later (sooner if transferred as dividends, royalties, etc., later if ploughed back to increase the capital value of the business to be sent overseas. From the 1940s Marxist writers such as Paul Sweezy, and later Baran and Myrdal and many others, have argued that what they call 'under-development' in Africa, Asia and Latin America was caused by foreign capital.[6] In the first phase local industry was destroyed by an imposed 'open door' to foreign industrial imports and under colonialism agriculture was compelled to produce commodities needed by foreign industry at prices kept artificially low by monopolistic foreign trading companies. In the next stage foreign capital moved in to exploit local resources more intensively by investing in the production of commodities and manufactured goods for export or local consumption. Such investment 'locks' the host country into its state of 'under-development' in two main ways. First, because foreign capital sooner or later exports the 'actual profit' of production, the 'dependent' society is denied the capital accumulation it needs for investment in industrialisation. Second, because foreign capital makes allies of the local élite—proto-capitalists, politicians, army officers and even the better paid workers in foreign enterprises—the host society is led by 'compradors' who put the interests of their foreign allies before that of the country. As a result political decolonisation in the two decades after 1945 made little difference: the successor governments of most LDCs continued to run these countries in the interests of foreign capital, that is as satellites of the international capitalist economy. Such a system condemns the LDCs to perpetual poverty. The only escape is by complete renunciation of capitalism at home and with it direct foreign investment, the destruction of the existing élites and the establishment of socialism in alliance with socialist states overseas.

This is not the place to assess the utility of such arguments. But in the interest of clear thinking it is important to pinpoint the two points on which Marxists are most likely to reject the general argument of this book.

The first has already been indicated. Marxists as a whole believe that in a capitalist system the distribution of rewards is indeed a zero sum game in which all the profits go to the owner of the capital.[7] It follows that any benefits apparently derived by a LDC from the local operations of Unilever would be specious. The second is that much weight has been placed in this book, as in many studies of multinationals, on the role of the host government. The general thrust of most of this evidence is that decolonisation made a fundamental difference to the relationship between foreign capital and the host society because after independence the host government for the first time had the power, if it chose to use it, to regulate the activities of a foreign enterprise in any way it chose; and that in this new relationship even a very large company such as Unilever was weak by comparison with the government of even a small country, provided its function was to manufacture for the local market. This line of argument is excluded in advance by the tenets of contemporary under-development theory. If all governments of capitalist countries, however under-developed, are by definition an expression of the local class structure and if they necessarily perceive their own interests, as an élite, to lie in collaboration with foreign investors, it follows that, as protectors of the interests of their own countries, they are wolves masquerading as watch-dogs. To argue, therefore, that, in doing what a host government wants or permits it to do, a subsidiary can have a good conscience about its relations with the host society is meaningless and all the evidence in this book about Unilever's increasing anxiety to be 'a good citizen' of each country in which it operated is irrelevant. For these and other reasons most of what follows is meaningful only within the context of a non-Marxist critique of the role of multinationals in an LDC that assumes that there is at least a theoretical possibility that a host country may stand to gain from direct foreign investment if this is properly handled by both sides.

Most elements in Reuber's system of cost-benefit analysis are substantive and measurable. But before considering these in turn we must take note of one important factor which evades quantification: the psychological effects of having an alien body operating within one's own country. This is not a new phenomenon, nor one restricted to LDCs. But this sense of 'invasion', as Reuber calls it, may be heightened in Africa, Asia and Latin America by three aspects of the foreign presence which would not necessarily be as important in Europe, North America or Australasia. First, the expatriate staff of a multinational is normally American or European, and their appearance and way of life are in many ways conspicuously alien in most LDCs, whereas they would be camouflaged in most parts of the developed world. Second, white-skinned foreigners holding positions of command in ex-colonial countries are too reminiscent of colonial conditions or may be seen as Trojan horses about to open the gates to foreign political inter-ference. Finally, the system of multinationals appears one-sided. In the more developed world, it can be argued, foreign subsidiaries owned by other industrialised countries are of mutual benefit on the general principle of comparative advantage. But few new states in the ex-colonial world own subsidiaries or extensive capital assets in more developed countries; and to those that do not the fact that foreigners own mines, plantations, factories and other productive assets in their own countries may seem to reflect a hierarchy between more and less developed states. Whatever the actual economic consequences may be, such countries are likely to regard elimination of this unequal 'dependence' on the owners of these productive enterprises as a necessary first step towards the realisation of full equality as sovereign states.

Seen in this way assessment of whether or not a multinational is or is not a good thing from the standpoint of a LDC is likely to start with the premise that all forms of external dependence are to be regretted but that for a poor country some sacrifice of national pride and short-term freedom of action may be necessary and justified, provided the trade-off is satisfactory. In examining the significance of a Unilever manufacturing subsidiary in an LDC we have, therefore, to think at two levels. In strictly economic terms the nett benefit received by the host society equals the increase in nett output of that country that is due entirely to the presence of Unilever, minus profits transferred overseas. But in practice few people (and very few studies of multinationals) insulate economic from other factors in this way; and much of the debate over the impact of these companies on LDCs turns rather on 'externalities', that is, the side effects of foreign direct investment. This necessarily complicates and clouds the issue because many externalities are not susceptible to precise measurement; but it would be unrealistic to ignore the fact that, because of the emotional factors involved, actions by Unilever which succeeded in offsetting the feeling that it was an invader (such as selling part of the equity or replacing expatriate by indigenous managers) might weigh more heavily with its hosts than its efficient use of local resources; and for that reason considerable emphasis will be laid in this analysis on strictly non-economic aspects of Unilever's relations with its host societies.

With so many diverse factors involved, the arithmetic of cost-benefit analysis is necessarily complicated and it will clarify the argument to start by eliminating several of those 'cost' items often imputed to multinationals which Reuber lists in his book [8] but which are clearly not relevant in this case. For example, there is no evidence that Unilever ever stifled an existing export market or, conversely, that they promoted export of their own products to the detriment of a host country. On the political side Unilever subsidiaries appear never to have been involved in non-commercial activities, played politics or attempted to bring with them the laws of their home country. With these potential sins out of the way we can turn to the main profit and loss account, following Reuber in discussing first the two basic issues of 'finance' and 'production and trade', then examining important factors which can be described as 'externalities' or side effects to see how Unilever's record in these fields affects the balance of advantage between host country and multinational.

The first, most important but also most complicated issue relates to the total financial consequences for a host country of entertaining a Unilever subsidiary. The basic question is whether the host country receives a 'reasonable' reward (i.e. at least as good as it could have obtained by using the same resources in some other way) for what it contributes to the productive activities of a foreign enterprise: that is, labour, the cost of the infrastructure, foreign exchange required for repatriating profits, etc. and the social cost of providing protection for that local industry. Potential additional costs to be borne in mind include inflated prices charged in the host country for raw materials or intermediates imported by the multinational. On the credit side of the balance the potential benefits consist of the additional income received by the government (in taxes), by labour (in higher than average wages) and by local capitalists (through opportunities to participate in the equity). Other possible benefits often mentioned in this context (though they are less easy to quantify) are the contributions a foreign firm may make to the balance of payments through import-saving or exporting and by capital imports. Reuber's evidence suggests that, in so far as these items can be measured (and in practice many of them can not), the host countries included in his survey probably benefited from the presence of foreign companies;[9] and the evidence on the Unilever companies studied in this book is broadly in line with his findings. As has been said earlier, Unilever never indulged in artificial internal transfer pricing, so the main emphasis must be on the financial issues; but it will be convenient to get the question of capital imports out of the way first.

In the past much emphasis was placed by development economists and, from a different standpoint, by left-wing critics of imperialism, on the economic importance of foreign capital imported to LDCs. The first group tended to see this as providing the essential resources which would enable the developing country to 'take off' into sustained growth, while the second held that capital exports reflected a 'surplus' of wealth accumulated by European and American capitalists which had to be placed overseas in order to maintain the return to capital in the developed countries. But it is now common ground that multinationals which intend to undertake local production for local consumption are not, and never have been, a major source of new capital in developing countries: this must come mainly from government borrowing and portfolio investment. The reason is obvious: the main asset of a multinational is not its capital but its technology and know-how. A firm such as Lever Brothers expanded in its early years by borrowing or selling shares: at no point did it ever hold a large stock of liquid funds, nor was it ever connected with an investment bank. Thus when the concern decided that it was desirable to set up a local factory overseas—possibly to defend an export market or to expand total sales by creating a new market—its aim was to produce and sell, not to invest. Often the first stage of local production involved investment of large amounts in fixed assets and working capital: even so, Lever/Unilever's preference was to provide these funds in the form of loans from London, which in turn represented the liquidity of the concern as a whole, and were expected to be repaid out of profits as soon as possible. Alternatively, part of the initial capital might be borrowed from local banks or other institutions and repaid as a first charge on profits. For the same reasons Unilever expected that a subsidiary, once established, would finance most of its expansion from local profits. Until 1930 the almost universal convertibility of world currencies meant that there was no inconvenience in putting British or Dutch funds into overseas companies, because loans and investments could always be repaid in the currency of one's choice. But after 1939, and still more when the one-time colonies broke their connections with the currencies of their previous imperial powers and established non-convertible and often highly unstable local currencies, this became a major problem: investment from Europe might never be allowed out again. Thus after about 1945 currency problems provided an additional reason why Unilever preferred to raise development capital locally, repaying it in the same currency in which it had been borrowed.

Reuber's evidence suggests that this was a very common practice after the Second World War and much has been made of it by hostile critics of multinationals. Because they place such great weight on both the economic importance of foreign capital and also on balance of payment problems in LDCs, they tend to argue that a developing country obtains little benefit from a foreign business which makes a restricted contribution to the host country's foreign exchange by capital import and that it is positively harmed if it allows profits, etc. made on locally raised capital to be exported as dividends, royalties and so on. Reuber rightly dismisses this type of argument on the ground that it is conceptually confused.[10] Difficulties only arise as a result of the endemic balance of payments problems faced by most LDCs, and these are properly dealt with by different measures. Yet the important fact remains: the amount of capital injected by Unilever in the form either of capital goods or cash into its overseas companies was, in almost all cases studied here, too small to have much economic impact. It was not the volume of foreign capital it brought in but the way a small input was made to work and grow that might be of value; and the fact that growth was usually financed autonomously did not in any way offset the fact that growth was the product of concern activity.

Thus the financial benefit to these host countries lay primarily in the taxes they could and did impose on the profits made by the combination of foreign and local capital and Unilever skills. Reuber's data shows that in 1966 the total income of the majority-owned foreign affiliates of USA manufacturing companies in all LDCs was divided as set out in Table 10.3.[11] Unilever accounting methods make it impossible to use precisely the same terms, but taking Hindustan Lever as the largest Unilever overseas subsidiary other than that in the USA, and using the figures for 1965, we get the allocation of income shown in Table 10.4.

The figures in Table 10.4 relate to one year's results for a single Unilever subsidiary in a country with very high taxes on corporate profits; and the proportions are different from the average for all

Table 10.3   Allocation of income of U.S. manufacturing affiliates in LDCs,

	Per cent
Goods and services	57.1
Wages and salaries	16.2
Depreciation and depletion	3.6
Foreign income tax	4.6
Other taxes	2.9
Other costs	6.1
Nett income	7.7

Source: Reuber, op cit., p.169. Table 5.7

these American subsidiaries in many countries. But the significant facts are that in India, as in Reuber's aggregate, the greater proportion of the trading profit went to the host government and that in India total taxes, including the distribution tax on dividends, amounted to much more than the total sum transferred overseas. Thus almost all the income of the Indian business was spent within India, as payments for goods, services and wages (the amount potentially transferred on account of expatriate salaries was so small as not to be worth including), as taxes and dividends due to local shareholders, or as reinvested profits put to capital account.

To check whether India in this year was a special case, Table 10.5 sets out the allocation of pre-tax trading profit for six of the other manufacturing companies in LDCs which are included in this study, taking 1963 at random to avoid duplicating 1965. Nothing is

Table 10.4   Allocation of income by Hindustan Lever, 1965 ('000 rupees)

Object	Amount	Per cent
Total income	685,801	100
Nett sales value	678,156	98.88
Production and distribution costs	642,184	93.6
Profit before tax	35,972	5.24
Taxation	26,106	3.8
Nett profit	17,400	2.5
Dividend	12,259	1.8
Unilever share of dividend gross	10,743	1.5
nett	8,657	1.3
Transferred	8,057	1.2
Division of pre-tax trading profit:		
Taxes		60.0
Company		40.0

Table 10.5 Allocation of Pre-tax Trading Profit of Six Unilever Manufacturing Companies, 1963

Country	A Trading profit before tax £'000	%	B Taxes payable £'000	%	C Nett accounting profit £'000	%	D Dividends declared gross £'000	%	E Concern dividend declared gross £'000	%	F Concern dividend declared nett £'000	%	G Interest £'000	%	H Dividends £'000	%	I Fees and Royalties £'000	%	J Total remitted during following year £'000	%
Ceylon/Sri Lanka	601.2	100	364.8	60.7	211.5	35.2	195.5	32.5	195.5	32.5	118.6	19.7	—		84.4	14.0	13.9	2.3	98.3	16.3
Congo/Zaire (MARSAVCO)	305.3	100	38.0	12.4	88.6	29.0	—		—		—		—		—		—		—	
Kenya (EAI)	491.0	100	181.0	36.8	296.0	60.3	500.0	101.8	273.0	55.6	273.0	55.6	—		107.0	21.8	39.0	7.9	146.0	29.7
Nigeria	131.0	100	—		60.0	45.8	—		—		—		57.0	43.5	—		23.0	17.5	80.0	61.1
Pakistan	338.0	100	171.0	50.6	146.2	43.2	145.5	43.0	106.6	31.5	95.9	28.4	—		95.9	28.4	51.3	15.2	147.2	43.5
Turkey (Unilever–Is)	981.8	100	345.5	35.2	699.3	71.2	317.5	32.3	253.9	25.9	253.9	25.9	—		253.9	25.9	—		253.9	25.9
TOTAL	2,848.3	100	1,100.3		1,501.6		1,158.5		829.0		741.4		57.0		541.2		127.2		725.4	
Average	474.7	100	183.4	38.6	250.2	52.7	193.1	40.7	138.2	29.1	123.6	26.0	57.0	12.0	90.2	19.0	21.7	3.7	120.9	25.5

Notes: a. Dividends declared may include profits carried over from the previous year.

b. Dividends for 1963 would normally be transferred the following year. Column H therefore shows dividends, etc. transferred in 1964.

c. In addition to service fees, royalties and interest due, some other deductions or additions are made from or to the pre-tax trading profit before calculation of tax. These have not been shown here.

d. The difference between the gross and nett dividends in columns E and F is that in Pakistan (as in India) there was a distribution tax on dividends.

e. The average is for these six companies only.

f. Local currencies have been converted into sterling at the exchange rate used in Unilever's accounts for 1963.

conclusive; but it seems clear that at least in that year the greater part of the profit resulting from Unilever's industrial activities in these LDCs remained in the countries in which it was made. Only in EAI did the nett dividend exceed the amount paid in taxation. This was because the 1963 dividend included profits carried over; and even there the total amount transferred in respect of 1963 was less than the amount paid in taxes. Governments took the largest share of the trading profit—38.6 per cent on average, plus distribution taxes. Of the post-tax profit, 22.8 per cent was retained in the local business and 21.9 per cent went to non-Unilever shareholders. Only 25.5 per cent of the trading profit before tax was transferred as dividends and fees, etc. Although public revenues did not represent a nett gain, since the host society presumably incurred various costs in entertaining Unilever, it seems difficult to deny that these countries did receive a positive gain from their contribution to enterprises which might not have existed at all, or might not have made comparable profits, had they not been set up and run by Unilever or some other comparably efficient foreign enterprise.

It remains to consider under this first head the strain imposed by even these modest transfers on these countries' balance of payments. In Reuber's view this should not be regarded as a major problem.[12] If monetary and related policies in the host countries are rational, the real income effect of transfer should be small; it is only because of the rigidities of various kinds in LDCs that the transfer of dividends, etc. may have a significant adverse effect on the economy. Furthermore the effect of transfers on a country's balance of payments cannot be discussed in isolation: it has to be considered in the context of all other relevant aspects of a multinational's activities, including import-saving and exports. But two general comments can be made on the evidence provided by these twelve countries. First, Unilever never indulged in speculative transfers of funds which might have had effects on a country's balance of payments. It never contemplated that capital assets built up overseas should be sold and the proceeds repatriated; nor did Unilever ever sell a business outright in order to transfer the capital. Even when, as in India after 1956, part of the equity was sold on government insistence, only that part of the proceeds that represented undistributed profits, less tax, was transferred—necessarily, because if these funds had remained in the business it would have been impossible to reduce Unilever's share in the equity. On subsequent occasions money raised in India by selling shares was used to expand the business and the problem of relative shares was solved by simultaneously increasing the total equity.

The second point turns on the extent to which, within the narrow context of the balance of payments account, a multinational can offset the cost of transfers by its exports and contribution to import substitution. Export earnings are substantive but calculations of import saving are necessarily to some extent hypothetical. The following calculation relating to India in the 1960s and early 1970s probably come as close to a realistic estimate as can be provided. First, for the five years 1968–72 Hindustan Lever's total export earnings at Rs. 222,100,000 exceeded total nett dividend remittances at Rs. 62,200,000 by Rs. 159,900,000. Second, during the period 1962–71 the total 'inflow' hypothetically generated by seven of the British subsidiaries in India (including Hindustan Lever), resulting from actual exports and estimates of import substitution made possible by the research and development work undertaken by these firms, has been calculated at Rs. 1,068,500,000, as contrasted with a total outflow (dividends, royalties, fees, etc.) of Rs. 572,600,000. Exports alone at Rs. 628,300,000 exceeded all transfers. India is not necessarily typical; but at least in principle a multinational should in this way be able to neutralise the adverse effects of the transfer of its profits on the host country's balance of payments.

Reuber's second general test of the impact of a multinational on the economy of a host country concerns its effects on production, trade, employment and productivity: that is, the real income effects of foreign direct capital investment. First, how far were these subsidiaries integrated into the host economy, taking account of the market for their products, the sources of their raw materials, the extent to which they used indigenous management and labour and their systems of distribution? On all these counts the companies studied in this book were intensively integrated. Since all manufactured mainly for local consumption, their products were geared to what the local consumer wanted and could afford: hence the wide variations in brands and types of product in different countries. It could, of course, be objected that quality branded soaps and hardened vegetable fats were luxuries 'unsuitable' for a developing country; but it is also arguably arrogant to suggest that citizens of such countries should not be allowed to buy consumer goods of relatively high quality irrespective of who made them. Exports, by contrast, were always a secondary consideration for these subsidiaries. Before decolonisation lack of interest in the export possibilities of soap, etc., made by these subsidiaries was due mainly to the fact that economies of scale and other factors enabled the concern to produce and export goods more cheaply in Europe than anywhere else. That was still true in the 1970s; and by then new obstacles to exports from LDCs had arisen as some new states adopted fiscal and other measures which tended to raise domestic prices above international levels and as other states adopted quota systems to exclude imports. Unilever subsidiaries therefore placed emphasis on exports only where there were strong local reasons for doing so. Normally this consisted of governmental stimuli to export at a commercial loss in return for credits entitling a firm to import raw materials and intermediates or differential exchange rates to compensate for overvalued local currencies. The success achieved by a company such as Hindustan Lever in increasing its exports in no way affects the fact that its basic concern was with the Indian domestic market with which it was completely integrated.

The question of imported inputs raises different questions. Like all industrial enterprises Unilever preferred to buy in the cheapest market and in the era of 'open' economies before the Second World War these subsidiaries bought freely at home and abroad. In practice this often meant local purchase since the availability of vegetable oil at competitive prices has been seen to be one main ground for starting local production. But many Unilever products require more than one raw material; and in this earlier period Unilever companies felt no hesitation in buying specialised things such as vegetable and essential oils, perfumes, rosin and packaging materials overseas. Indeed, to do otherwise would be commercial suicide if their competitors were free to buy more cheaply elsewhere. The turning point came with shortages caused by the Second World War when most companies had to make do with whatever they could find locally; and thereafter governments of the new states commonly insisted on the use of local products, irrespective of whether they were the best and cheapest for the job. By the mid-1960s 'making-do' had become the rule; and with it for the first time came the incentive to stimulate production of what these subsidiaries needed within the host economy. This could be done by adjusting production techniques so as to make standard products with local substitutes for standard raw materials, and then co-operating with the host government to ensure an adequate supply. Alternatively the company might use its research and development facilities to discover new methods of producing the things it needed from hitherto under-utilised local sources of supply. This might be expensive but it was likely, as in India, to result in valuable backward linkages into the agricultural base of the economy.

It was, however, more difficult, given the fact that most Unilever products were consumer goods which left the factory in their final form, to develop many forward linkages into the local industrial economy except in so far as Unilever needed packaging materials. Hence the most important forward linkage was provided by Unilever's systems of distribution, though these varied widely in different countries and over time. In comparatively developed countries such as Australia local Lever/Unilever subsidiaries could from the start rely on established indigenous wholesalers and retailers of a European type and needed only to develop a sales force to stimulate demand. But in all LDCs Unilever faced an identical problem in different degrees. Initially there was no national market, few if any wholesalers capable of taking the financial and administrative responsibility of buying factory products in bulk and distributing them, and few retailers who could or would hold adequate stocks in good condition. Such problems were not solved easily or quickly. It has been seen that in most countries of this type Lever/Unilever began by using established European importing agents who handled a very wide range of goods from any source and had no interest in pushing Unilever lines or providing adequate distribution facilities. Progress was commonly made in three stages. The first was to establish a network of local depots which would hold stocks and bring the concern into direct contact with local distributors, though this might still involve reliance on the importing agents as intermediaries because they knew the country and had the essential commercial contacts. The second and often simultaneous step was to create a local sales force to promote concern products and to supervise distribution. The third stage was the critical and economically most constructive one, when Unilever broke free from the traditional agents of the colonial period, building up a network of indigenous wholesalers and retailers who would order direct from the local factory and take delivery from the nearest depot; and this involved great effort and costs. In most places it was necessary for the subsidiary to select local men, commonly small middlemen, to train them in modern accounting practice and the use of banking facilities, often to provide them with substantial initial credit. By the mid-1960s this process was well advanced in all the countries included in this book and in some it had reached the stage at which retailers also had been trained and launched. India, where this evolution had gone the furthest, best demonstrates the benefits of the scheme to the host country. Hindustan Lever was the first enterprise in the subcontinent to create a single comprehensive national marketing system and this provided a model which many other public and private enterprises copied. Both India and Pakistan were covered by a network of wholesalers and retailers who depended heavily on concern products and qualified to distribute or sell these by their efficiency and credit. So complete was the mutual trust that wholesalers conventionally deposited a book of signed blank cheques with the local Unilever depot whose staff filled in and cashed each cheque as they fulfilled an order. In countries whose industries were commonly handicapped by defective systems of distribution the stimulus of such a model of national distribution was a considerable economic asset.

The second test of a multinational's economic impact relates to employment effects. Reuber notes that, judging by the numbers directly employed, most subsidiaries had very little significance: they were mostly capital-intensive and usually formed a small part of the economy as a whole. This is certainly true of Unilever's overseas manufacturing activities. The plantation companies were proportionately quite large employers of labour and HCB had some 40,000 workers in the early 1960s. But the factories were not: even Hindustan Lever, the largest overseas subsidiary outside the USA, employed only about 8,000 in the early 1970s. Far more important than numbers was the value of the training these subsidiaries could and did offer to local people. This took two forms: the creation of a modern industrial labour force and the training of staff. In African countries, where the very concept of factory work was novel and alien, Africans had to be trained from scratch and converted from an initially migrant and transitory to an experienced and stabilised work force; and the ablest of them had to be chosen and given further training as foremen and potential managers. Equally important was the training of senior managers and technical staff. Reuber found that in 1966 American expatriates represented only 0.6 per cent of the total payroll of US affiliates overseas. They constituted the same proportion of all managers, 1.7 per cent of technical and professional staff and 0.6 per cent of other salaried staff.[13] Comparable figures for Hindustan Lever show that by 1972 there were eight expatriates in the company—0.1 per cent of the pay roll and 1.9 per cent of the total number of managers. Two of these were on the board, the other six in various technical positions. In the Turkish company, Unilever-Is, there was only one foreigner, the chairman, in 1967; and most other subsidiaries had a comparably small proportion of expatriates. This degree of localisation was, as has been seen, only achieved over a considerable period of time; but once the principle of maximum localisation had been adopted in the early 1950s it moved very rapidly. From the start Unilever took full responsibility for training, both at home and overseas. It preferred university educated men as management trainees but took what it could get and converted those who had the necessary qualities into highly efficient businessmen or technicians. Such men had a high scarcity value and there was a considerable flow from concern companies into other public and private appointments. It is significant that in India, better endowed than any other developing country with administrative and technical skills, the first two indigenous chairmen of Hindustan Lever should have been appointed to be chairmen of major governmental enterprises and that the government relied heavily on the company to provide experts to serve on a variety of public commissions, committees, etc. This suggests that in any developing country a multinational with high technical and administrative standards can contribute more to economic development by setting standards and training staff in the skills of an industrial society than by the mere employment of numbers.

Reuber's third test of the economic impact of multinationals is their productivity—whether they made better use of inputs than other (and normally indigenous) consumers of the same real resources might have done. His general conclusion is that, while subsidiaries manufacturing primarily for the local market are in general more efficient than local competitors, they are also significantly less efficient than manufacturers of the same products in their home countries or than they could be if the environment of the LDC was more conducive to efficiency. It is, as he points out, more difficult to prove or measure these differences. Statistics for private industry in developing countries are even more suspect than for developed countries and in any case accounting conventions differ so widely that margins become meaningless. It seems reasonably certain, however, that Unilever subsidiaries normally made significantly higher profits than competing locally-owned companies in all the LDCs in which they operated; but also that, even where overseas profit levels were higher than those made by Unilever in Europe and other developed countries, concern subsidiaries in

LDCs were usually not as efficient, in terms of costs at world prices, as the home companies. There were various potential causes for this relative inefficiency: diseconomies of scale caused by restricted markets: the relatively high cost of locally-produced inputs and the high cost of doing business in countries where much time and effort had to be spent in dealing with governmental regulations. Perhaps the most dangerous long-term threat to efficiency lay in nationalist economic policies that did not permit an efficient company (local or foreign-owned) to exploit its comparative advantage to the full. Such policies were to be found in almost all the countries studied in this book: in Australia and South Africa they limited production of margarine, in Turkey of soap. But the clearest evidence of the outcome can be seen in India, where the system of licensing productive capacity and allocating imports had the object of diffusing ownership and dispersing industry throughout the country. Unable freely to expand its basic soap and vanaspati production as market leader in both fields, Hindustan Lever felt it necessary to expand by diversifying into products less well suited to Indian needs and of which it was probably a less efficient producer. Taken further over longer periods of time such policies might well dissipate much of the benefit a LDC stood to gain from the relative efficiency of a foreign subsidiary.

This completes Reuber's check-list of the ways in which a multinational might have a direct economic impact on a less developed country, but there remain a number of possible externalities (potentially beneficial side effects or qualifying aspects) of this direct foreign investment to examine. The first, the transfer of technology, has already been considered under the heading of integration; and the conclusion must be that on the whole the technologies transferred by Unilever seem to have been reasonably well-suited to these less developed host countries. Unilever seldom attempted to import sophisticated equipment or methods where simpler techniques would serve; nor did the concern make products for which there was no established demand and then artificially create a demand by intensive promotion. When it developed a 'new' market this was usually for an improved version of something already in common use, such as soap, or for a substitute costing less than the normal product, such as margarine in place of butter. It has been seen that in the decades after about 1944 Unilever was anxious to probe foreign markets for industrial opportunities and an accelerating stream of experts went out from London and Rotterdam to investigate the possibility of introducing products pioneered in Europe or

America; yet the great majority of their reports recommended that no action be taken because these markets were not suited to the more advanced products developed for other environments. In the end, therefore, most Unilever overseas companies still depended, as they had always done, on soap and edible fats. This may suggest that by the standards of some other industries, such as electronics and chemicals, Unilever was not a company that marched in the vanguard of product innovation, however proficient it might be in its own field of oils and fats. This, paradoxically, may have made it better suited to the needs of developing countries which needed to wash and eat but could get by without colour television or atomic power stations.

A second test of the suitability of Unilever subsidiaries is how ready they were to co-operate with government policies in host countries. It is commonly asserted, especially by proponents of under-development theories, that multinationals use their bargaining power to distort local economic policies, breaking the laws and exploiting administrative loopholes in official plans and regulations. The evidence suggests that such accusations are largely irrelevant to these Unilever subsidiaries. While local managements naturally took full advantage of legal opportunities and might press their case on ministers and officials as hard as possible, they clearly accepted that their best long-term interests lay in co-operation rather than evasion and obstruction. Indeed the evidence is fully consistent with Reuber's general conclusion that foreign firms were less likely than indigenous firms to break laws. Because they were foreign, exposure was more dangerous to their prospects. Because they were public and locally-registered companies, with professional rather than family managements, their accounts were likely to be more accurate and they would not attempt illegally to evade taxation. Because they were commonly market leaders it was impossible for them to ignore official price controls: indeed it has been suggested that one reason why the Indonesian government between 1950 and 1965 was well disposed to Unilever, despite its being an Anglo-Dutch enterprise, was that, if Lever soap sold at or below the official maximum price, local producers could not sell above that price. Thus we are again faced with the fundamental fact about Unilever's role in these countries: because it was manufacturing for the local market it was heavily dependent on the goodwill of the host government and society. However much it might dislike aspects of official policy, in the end it had either to submit or withdraw.

The final question turns on foreign ownership of the equity of a subsidiary. It is a common assumption that it is to the economic advantage of a host country if a large proportion of the shares in a locally registered subsidiary of a foreign company—the larger the better—is held by the government or citizens of the host country. This is assumed to produce two good effects: first, it should force the company to follow policies consistent with the national interest; second, it should reduce the adverse effect of the transfer of dividends on the balance of payments. The evidence of these Unilever companies tends, however, to support Reuber's argument that these benefits are largely spurious. Take first the matter of control. It happens that in none of these companies was Unilever's share of the equity less than 51 per cent by 1965, though in some it was less than half by 1977; and by then UAC Ltd also was a minority partner in a number of West African enterprises. There is, therefore, no evidence in this book to show what effect majority local ownership might have on the policy of a Unilever subsidiary; but even so one might have expected that a substantial minority local shareholder, such as the Wazir Ali family in Pakistan, the Ghana government, the CDC and the Kenyan government or the Is-Bank, would have had some marked influence on the policy of the Unilever subsidiaries with which they were connected. Nowhere was this the case. All these local partners accepted that Unilever was more expert in its own field than they could be and none seems to have felt that the policies it adopted were inconsistent with the interests of themselves or the host society. Thus the only two material consequences of dilution of Unilever's equity were, first, that their partners could not or would not always find the necessary additional capital to finance expansion, which made it difficult to maintain the existing balance of share-holding; second, that these partners tended, naturally enough, to expect a reasonable proportion of the profits to be distributed as dividends instead of all being ploughed back into the business or used to pay off loans. This question of dividends was, in fact, a major reason why Unilever generally disliked sharing the equity of a subsidiary. The whole European business had been built up by abstinence and there was a danger that vital growth would be throttled if all profits had to be distributed. In addition there was the technical problem that Unilever found it difficult to employ the proceeds of selling shares satisfactorily because, as payment was in local and commonly unconvertible currencies, the money could not be used for importing capital equipment for further expansion.

Ultimately, of course, Unilever disliked selling shares because it meant sharing control; and like all experts they distrusted the intervention of shareholders who were less competent to take decisions than they were. But there were also strong economic arguments against local ownership of the equity from the standpoint of the host developing country. True, 100 per cent local ownership would mean no transfer of dividends; but what then would be the reward for the foreign company's efforts, assuming that it was still wanted to run the business it had founded? If, say, Unilever agreed still to manage the enterprise it would have to be paid for its skills and technology, as well as for its brands, over and above the salaries of the overseas staff working for the company, possibly by charging service fees, royalties etc.; and it seems at least probable that such payments would cost the host country more on current account than the previous transfers of dividends, etc. But the foreign exchange cost of paying for services in fees, etc. would be the least important defect of such an arrangement from the standpoint of the host country. A company can increase its turnover (NSV) at the expense of its profit margins. If the management has a vested interest in doing this, because its fees and royalties depend on how much it sells, it has no incentive to maximise profits by being efficient; and since the main argument for having the subsidiary of a multinational company in a LDC is its comparative efficiency, this strategy appears to be counter-productive. The conclusion must be that any LDC which wants foreign enterprise does better by allowing it to operate under a sufficient degree of foreign ownership and at foreign risk to ensure that the company has an in-built incentive to be efficient. Local control can then be imposed in many ways—by taxation, regulation of transfers, licensing of imports, restriction on prices and so on.

It is, of course, unnecessary for a host country to ask a multinational to continue to run a company it has founded once the equity has been nationalised: the host country can then simply dispense with alien services altogether. This brings the argument back to fundamentals and to a final conclusion on the value of private foreign direct investment: what would the host country gain or lose if the multinational was totally excluded? Let us, therefore, consider what might happen if any one Unilever manufacturing enterprise was totally nationalised and the concern took no further part in running it. Two of the companies studied in this book, those in Indonesia and Zaire, were in fact nationalised or taken out of the concern's control during the period studied. But in neither case was the period of public ownership sufficiently long to form the basis of a pragmatic verdict; and there is insufficient evidence on what happened to the two concern soap companies in Burma and Egypt which were taken over earlier and were never returned. It is, therefore, better to deal with the problem in theoretical terms, taking India as the subject of a counter-factual proposition.

Two contrasting scenarios are possible. In the first Unilever sells the balance of the equity in Hindustan Lever to Indian citizens and ends all contact with the continuing company. In the other Hindustan Lever ceases to exist and its assets are taken over either by existing Indian companies making the same things, such as Tatas, or by new entrants to the soap and edible fats business. The second of these is more useful for the present purpose because it sharpens the issue. Under total local ownership an otherwise unaltered Hindustan Lever might continue for an indefinite time to operate as effectively as it had done in the past; and what we really want to do is to measure the difference between a company operating along Unilever lines and one which does not. Let us, therefore, consider the position in India if all that was left of Hindustan Lever was its fixed assets, now owned and operated, possibly in different places, by men with no Unilever know-how or experience.

The first and most important conclusion is that there would be no dramatic consequences whatever. Other privately- or publicly-owned firms would, presumably, be allocated Hindustan Lever's production quotas for soap and vanaspati and they or others would quickly take over its share of the market and import licences for these and for goods which were not subject to official control of productive capacity. Quite soon it might seem extraordinary that India should ever have been prepared to tolerate the presence of a foreign concern which, in the terms used above, constituted an invasion of the nation's privacy. The political left would, presumably, rejoice that India no longer paid a 'tribute' to Unilever, that one link with 'imperialism' had been broken and that a major ally of local capitalism had been destroyed. On the right of the political spectrum Indian businessmen might be glad to see a dangerous competitor removed and nationalists would claim a victory for national sovereignty. Consumers would transfer their brand loyalties to other products and wholesalers and retailers would follow their customers. Within a remarkably short time the waters would close, obliterating the effects of the three-quarters of a century during which Lever/Unilever had sold and made consumer products in India.

This might imply that, because India scarcely noticed its absence, the role of Unilever in this or any other LDC had never been of any significance. Yet the evidence and arguments of this book, supporting the general thrust of many other studies covering a far wider spectrum of foreign direct investments overseas, suggest that such a conclusion is false on two counts, the first historical, the second contemporary. Historically it is misleading to suggest that multi-nationals have never performed a dynamic role, even if at some later stage some appear to become comparatively quiescent. In every LDC included in this book Lever/Unilever pioneered the local manufacture of its basic products by factory methods, on a large scale and to standards of quality new to these societies. In some places these subsidiaries effectively created a new market and consolidated it by building for the first time an all-embracing national system of distribution through indigenous middlemen and retailers. In the process the concern trained a corpus of indigenous managers, technicians, industrial workers and traders whose value in a developing economy was disproportionate to their numbers. It is, of course, arguable that the same benefits could have been obtained in different ways by a non-capitalist society; but, as things actually were, under the conditions of these countries at the time, this was what actually happened; and it is difficult to see what other mechanism could have achieved comparable results at comparable cost.

For many other LDCs whose industrial development began later these pioneering functions are still being performed by Unilever and other similar multinationals. But for India and several other countries included in this book that first phase lies in the past. We must, therefore, consider the second question: once a particular multinational has carried out its original task and has become stabilised as part of the host economy, what useful function does it still perform that can be thought to justify continued acceptance of an alien or partly alien presence in a sovereign nation? It can, of course, be argued that innovation never ends: that a multinational will always generate new technology beyond the resources of smaller local enterprises, so that it is pointless to talk of 'old' capital now performing no dynamic function. There is truth in this argument but it can be countered by saying that a LDC can buy all the new technology it wants or needs without allowing a foreign business to exploit each new invention locally; and it is therefore proposed to limit discussion to the mere existence of a manufacturing subsidiary, irrespective of its value as a conduit for new technology or capital. What benefits may a LDC receive in return for tolerating this foreign presence, assuming it to do no more than it does already?

Such a question turns on relativities and margins rather than absolutes; but all profit is marginal and even small margins are worth having. There are many specific marginal advantages an LDC might obtain by allowing a foreign subsidiary to operate in its territory, and several of them have been mentioned in this chapter. But in the last resort the main value of any multinational must lie in its marginal efficiency. It is not more efficient merely because it is large but because it specialises in a particular range of products and has chosen to operate in many countries in order that it can continue to specialise beyond the capacity of its home country to consume all its potential products. Its stock in trade is quality control; and if its subsidiaries thrive in a number of countries, on equal terms with local firms and without cheating (that is, without exploiting opportunities for evading taxes through transfer pricing, or evading import and price controls, etc.), its success must be due to the greater efficiency of its processes and the higher quality of its products. Every Unilever subsidiary studied in this book was in most respects (though not at all times in the past) at least as efficient as any local competitor and the quality of its products was at least as good as that of anything comparable on the market. From the standpoint of a host country this efficiency and quality were advantageous in two respects. First, they ensured the most productive use of real resources. Second, as perhaps the most important of all externalities, they provided competition to keep other local producers efficient. In a free trade world both objects could have been achieved without entertaining foreign subsidiaries in one's own country because imports would have done the job. But in the modern world of partially 'closed' and 'managed' economies, where every country, more as well as less developed, runs the risk of becoming a stagnant backwater, the presence of a comparatively dynamic foreign enterprise may be the cheapest and most effective form of insurance against insulated domestic indolence.

Decolonisation and the Multinational

There remains one general historical issue, the significance of colonialism and decolonisation for a multinational company in the less developed world. This was raised at the start and will be revisited here by way of a coda. The critical question is whether colonialism and its eventual abolition made any substantial difference to foreign direct investment in a LDC. This is an old question and there have been fashions in how it is answered. The current fashion, particularly, though not exclusively, on the political left, is to say that decolonisation made very little difference. Empire had been a tool of monopoly capitalism; but when empire was wound up international capital adjusted its methods and continued to dominate less developed countries through a complex of devices conventionally summed up as 'neo-colonialism'. Without pursuing the implications of this argument let us briefly review the evidence on how Unilever was affected by colonialism and by the end of formal empire.

The central fact is that for a multinational company such as Unilever, whose main object overseas was to manufacture consumer goods for the local market, it mattered much less whether a particular territory happened to be a colony or a sovereign state than what type of economic system it possessed. The main virtue of colonialism was that it normally provided an 'open' economy which closely resembled the economic environment found in Europe, North America, Australasia and South Africa before the Second World War. Colonial governments, though never democratic and seldom representative, were stable and predictable. They were not subject to political coups; they did not act arbitrarily, at least in their dealings with Europeans; they were virtually incorruptible; their currencies were freely convertible into international currencies; they did not threaten compulsory nationalisation nor control imports, exports, prices or profits; and in the last resort there was an appeal to the imperial power against the actions of its subordinates. Such governments did not necessarily or even usually do what a multinational asked: there are a number of examples in this book of colonial officials refusing to do what Unilever proposed, and British colonial administrators, who seldom came from commercial or industrial backgrounds, commonly distrusted business and particularly 'big business'. But at least you knew where you were, just as you did in Australia or South Africa or the USA. You could plan your operations in a particular colony on the assumption that conditions there would not be changed suddenly and that you would be left to get on with your own business.

These were some of the obvious benefits of colonialism; but the 'open' economy of a colonial society also had its limitations when considered from the standpoint of investment in local manufacture. The British, Dutch and Belgian colonial governments believed in free trade until the 1930s. Even the French, who did not, imposed an open door for products of the metropolis; and since protection against overseas competition was clearly the most important single stimulus for investment by Unilever and other similar firms in local production for the local market, colonial rule was likely to prove a deterrent to direct investment. It is very significant that the moment at which Unilever decided to establish large-scale local manufacture in India, Ceylon and Indonesia was the moment when these dependencies were for the first time permitted to act as quasi-sovereign states in establishing a protective tariff against imports from their metropolitan countries and when local competition was beginning to become significant. Conversely, as has been pointed out above, the absence of protection coupled with revenue duties on imported raw materials, which was characteristic of a number of British colonies, was a major deterrent to local investment. The fact that Levers set up soap manufacture in Nigeria and the Belgian Congo in the 1920s, while both had low import duties, does not invalidate this generalisation, for in both places local manufacture was designed to benefit from locally available raw materials and to make only those types of cheap soap which were in the greatest demand in West Africa but on which there was too small a profit margin to stimulate large imports from Europe.

Thus the significance of colonialism for Unilever was two-fold. On the one hand the 'open' economy deterred direct investment except where conditions approximated to those found in independent states; on the other, once conditions were right for local manufacture, it provided a very satisfactory milieu. Decolonisation involved a reversal of these positions. Independent governments, particularly in Black Africa, were seldom stable or democratic and were not always prepared to maintain a conventional rule of law. Foreign companies became generally suspect on nationalist grounds, even where it was thought expedient to tolerate them. Either from preference or because of the exigencies of an adverse balance of payments, all the new states adopted strictly 'managed' economic systems and most announced socialist objectives. In every country studied in this book one practical consequence of the adoption of such broad economic and social objectives was a system of bureaucratic controls which at their best introduced delay and uncertainty

into all commercial activities and at their worst put a private enterprise at the mercy of civil servants and politicians. Other normal
consequences were compulsory sale of part of the equity of subsidiaries, localisation of the senior management, relatively very high
corporate taxation, control over repatriation of profits and the
ultimate threat of nationalisation. None of these were things a
foreign business welcomed in any country and in sum they significantly reduced the attractiveness of many LDCs to Unilever.

But this is only one side of the coin. There were many features of
a 'managed' economy that were attractive to direct foreign investment: high protective tariffs, import controls, tax holidays, state
grants or loans, and expanding markets. Governments of the new
states might dislike dependence on foreign capital and publicly
denounce 'international monopoly capitalism'; but most recognised
their need for it and offered suitable conditions. The result is a
paradox evident throughout this book. Decolonisation meant the
end of security for foreign firms in colonial territories, but it also
meant a widening of opportunities for direct investment. Investment
in production for local consumption in an independent LDC,
whether or not it had recently been a European possession, might
result in very high profits or substantial losses, in expansion or
confiscation. In any case decolonisation and the simultaneous
adoption by virtually all less developed countries during the 1960s
of 'managed' economies clearly constituted the most important
watershed in the history of Unilever overseas. The fundamental fact
was that the sovereign state was prepared to exercise its sovereignty.
This was true of virtually all countries, but it was most obvious in
those which were less developed because this was virtually their only
weapon against international capital. For Unilever the results,
reflected for the decade 1956–65 in Table 10.1, were clearly very
mixed. But these are short-run indications of the consequences of
operating in 'managed' economies. The underlying reality was that
by the 1960s the profitability of any particular Unilever subsidiary
in a less developed country was likely to be determined less by its
efficiency or by the market than by government policy and the way
this was implemented by the bureaucracy: there is no other possible
explanation of the vast contrasts between the fortunes of Unilever
subsidiaries which were in most cases making the same range of
goods from similar materials with the same system of management.
By the date at which this book ends, in 1965, while it was already
clear that the end of formal empire was likely to stimulate rather

than curtail the activities of Unilever overseas, it was also evident
that direct investment in most LDCs must be treated as risk capital.
This for Unilever was the crux of the international revolution
labelled decolonisation.

Notes

CHAPTER 1 Introduction

1. Among the general books I found most useful were the following: M. Kidron, *Foreign Investments in India* (London, 1965); D. Lal, *Appraising Foreign Investment in Developing Countries* (London, 1975); I. Little, T. Scitovsky and M. Scott, *Industry and Trade in Some Developing Countries* (London, 1970); Grant L. Reuber, *Private Foreign Investment in Development* (Oxford, 1973); M. Wilkins, *The Emergence of Multinational Enterprise: American Business Abroad from the Colonial Era to 1914* (Cambridge, Mass., 1970).

2. Reuber, in *Private Foreign Investment*, uses three main categories of foreign direct investment: 'export-oriented', 'market-development' and 'government-initiated' I have broken these down because Unilever was both 'export-' and 'market-development' oriented in respect of its plantations and manufacturing subsidiaries.

3. R. Hilferding, *Finanzkapital* (1910) in *Marx-Studien*, vol. III (Vienna, 1923); V. I. Lenin, *Imperialism, the Highest Stage of Capitalism* (1916) (Moscow Foreign Languages Publishing House, 1947)

4. M. Wilkins, *The Emergence of Multinational Enterprise*, Table V.2, p. 110, shows that there was no US manufacturing investment in Central America in 1914, only seven enterprises in South America, none in Africa and ten in Asia.

CHAPTER 2 Metropolitan Unilever: the Central Organisation

1. Andrew Knox, *Coming Clean* (London, 1976). When a point in the text refers both to Lever Brothers before 1929 and Unilever thereafter 'Lever/Unilever' will be used.

2. William Hulme Lever, Viscount Leverhulme, *Viscount Leverhulme* (London, 1927).

3. The following account is based on the Leverhulme Papers and early minutes of the PTC and PC, Wilson, *The History of Unilever* (2 vols., London, 1954), vol. I, Leverhulme, *Viscount Leverhulme* and Knox, *Coming Clean*.

4. Wilson, *History*, vol. I, appendix 3.

5. Leverhulme, *Viscount Leverhulme*, p. 81.

6. See below, Chapter 3.

7. Wilson, *History*, vol. I, pp. 243 f.

8. Knox, *Coming Clean*, p. 114.
9. Wilson, *History*, vol. II, pp. 301 f.
10. Ibid., pp. 293–7, 336–7, 345–9.
11. Ibid., pp. 385–7.
12. Wilson, *Unilever 1945–1965* (London, 1968), Figure 12, p. 153.
13. Knox, *Coming Clean*, p. 31.
14. Wilson, *Unilever*, p. 31.
15. Ibid., Figures 1, 2 and 3, pp. 34–6.
16. Ibid., p. 41.
17. Knox, *Coming Clean*, pp. 134–42.
18. Ibid., p. 132.
19. Ibid., p. 208.
20. Ibid., p. 30.
21. Ibid., p. 151.

CHAPTER 3   Unilever in Australia and South Africa

1. Wilson, *History*, vol. I, p. 93.
2. Ibid., p. 103, and also in many letters in the Leverhulme Papers.
3. Wilson, *History*, vol. I, p. 198.
4. Modern accounting practice would express the value of fixed assets as a proportion of their replacement value (as is done for Australia in Table 3.4 and for South Africa in Table 3.12), and this would of course reduce profits expressed as a percentage of the capital employed.

CHAPTER 4   Unilever in India and Pakistan

1. Levers acquired a 50 per cent interest in Crosfields and Gossages, who were under the control of Brunner Mond, in 1917. The ordinary capital of both companies was bought by Levers in 1919 for £4 million. See Wilson, *History*, vol. I, p. 246.
2. Andrew Knox describes the system more fully in *Coming Clean*, p. 22.
3. The table from which these figures and also Table 4.1 are drawn is in the Unilever Archives and is headed 'Total and Gossage Shipments from United Kingdom of Household and Fancy Soap'. It is not clear whether 'total' is for all Lever companies or for all UK exports. The former seems possible since these totals are lower than those given in the *Statistical Abstract for the United Kingdom*. But since export statistics for Levers and Crosfields have not survived for the period before 1922 this cannot be proved and it has been assumed merely that Lever exports after 1913 followed the same trend as 'total' UK exports to these markets.
4. The company appears to have taken its name from a still older and very small soap factory at Meerut which was apparently closed down in 1919.
5. There is no mention of Marples' visit in the minutes of the Policy Council and no other evidence of why he was sent.
6. Wilson, *History*, vol. I, ch. 18.
7. Many details of the story cannot be reconstructed because relevant parts of the Leverhulme correspondence, the main source for policy-making in Lever Brothers before 1925, cannot now be traced.
8. A. C. Knight was a senior executive of Lever Brothers.
9. A tentative decision may have been taken earlier. In a report dated 1 March 1923 Hirst commented that 'it has been decided that a factory will not be erected for some years . . .'. But a marginal comment was 'not correct'. Probably the matter was still in the balance throughout the later months of 1923.

10. Knox gives a fuller account of developments in India between 1924 and 1933, in which he was closely involved, in *Coming Clean*, ch. 5.

11. More precisely, the 1931 tariff imposed specific duties of Rs. 4/0/– and Rs. 6/8/– per cwt on plain and 'other' bars of household and laundry soap; 25 per cent *ad valorem* on 'empire' toilet soap (35 per cent on foreign soap); and 20 per cent on 'empire' toilet preparations (30 per cent on foreign goods). From 1934 the *ad valorem* duties were consolidated at 25 per cent while the specific duties remained unchanged.

12. After 1947 the relatively high price of Indian vegetable oils, protected against world market influences by import restrictions, constituted an almost insuperable obstacle to the profitable export of Indian made soap. HL exported refined groundnut oil in the 1960s at a heavy loss to earn import licences for essential raw materials and intermediates, but this was not a strictly commercial operation.

13. See A. K. Bagchi, *Private Investment in India 1900–39* (Cambridge, 1972) for a good account of the growth of the sugar industry.

14. M. Kidron, *Foreign Investments in India* (London, 1965), p. 178.

15. J. N. Bhagwati and P. Desai, *India: Planning for Industrialization* (OECD, Paris: London, 1970), p. 262.

16. *Annual Review of Oil Seeds, Oils, Oilcake and Other Commodities.* (Frank Fehr & Co. Ltd, London, 1947–65.)

17. In November 1960 the Special Committee was hoping to obtain permission to expand soap production above the existing 78,000 tons in exchange for a large investment in a cotton-seed oil extraction plant which would not be commercially profitable but would have promoted the government's policy of developing indigenous raw material supplies. Eventually the project fell through.

18. See Kidron, *Foreign Investments*, ch. 1 & 2.

19. The Pakistan planning system is described in S. R. Lewis, *Pakistan Industrialization and Trade Policies* (OECD, Paris: London, 1970) and in G. F. Papanek, *Pakistan's Development, Social Goals and Private Incentives* (Cambridge, Mass., 1967).

CHAPTER 5   Unilever in Indonesia and Ceylon (Sri Lanka)

1. J. N. Bhagwati, *The Economics of Underdeveloped Countries* (London, 1966), pp. 10–11.

2. See Wilson, *History*, vol. I, chapter 11.

3. Wilson, *History*, vol. II, chapter 10.

4. The following paragraphs are based mainly on the following secondary accounts: B. Dahm, *History of Indonesia in the Twentieth Century* (London, 1971); B. Grant, *Indonesia* (Melbourne, 1964); J. D. Legge, *Sukarno* (London, 1972); G. McT. Kahin, *Nationalism and Revolution in Indonesia* (Ithica, 1962); L H Palmier, *Indonesia and the Dutch* (London, 1962).

5. B. Glassburner (ed), *The Economy of Indonesia* (Ithica and London, 1971), pp. 364–7.

6. R. A. Freeman, *Socialism and Private Enterprise in Equatorial Asia: The Case of Malaysia and Indonesia* (Stanford, 1968), pp. 86–7.

7. Ibid, p. 93.

8. Glassburner, *Economy of Indonesia*, p. 194.

9. Ibid., p. 368.

10. See Legge, *Sukarno*, pp. 349–57 for an analysis of Sukarno's concept of the 'Continuing Revolution'.

11. See W. M. Corden and J. A. C. Mackie, 'The Development of the Indonesian Exchange Rate System', *Malayan Economic Review*, vii, no. 1 (1962), pp. 37–60 for the best account of the very complicated measures adopted by various governments between 1950 and 1961.

12. Glassburner, *Economy of Indonesia*, p. 373.

13. Ibid., p. 11.

14. The following account is based mainly on interviews with Indonesian and expatriate management who were directly involved in the crisis of 1964–5.

15. The material on the Ceylon economy is taken mainly from the following: International Bank for Reconstruction and Development (IBRD), *The Economic Development of Ceylon* (Baltimore 1953); H.M. Oliver Jr, *Economic Opinion and Policy in Ceylon* (Durham, N. C., 1957); H. N. S. Karunatilake, *Economic Development in Ceylon* (New York, 1971).

16. IBRD, *Economic Development of Ceylon*, p. 137.

17. Bhagwati, *Economics of Underdeveloped Countries*, p. 11.

18. IBRD, *Economic Development of Ceylon*, p. 9.

CHAPTER 6 . . . . Unilever in Black Africa

1. Wilson, *History of Unilever*, vol. 1; Sir F. Pedler, *The Lion and the Unicorn* (London, 1974).

2. See in particular P. T. Bauer, *West African Trade* (Cambridge, 1954); P. N. Davies, *The Trade Makers* (London, 1973); W. K. Hancock, *Survey of British Commonwealth Affairs, 1918–39*, vol. II, parts 1 and 2 (London, 1942); A. G. Hopkins, *An Economic History of West Africa* (London, 1973); M. Perham (ed), *Mining, Commerce and Finance in Nigeria* (London, 1948).

3. For an account of these see Bauer, *West African Trade*; G. K. Helleiner, *Peasant Agriculture, Government and Economic Growth in Nigeria*. (Homeword, Ill., 1966.)

4. Peter Kilby, 'Manufacturing in Colonial Africa', in Peter Duignan and L. H. Gann (eds), *Colonialism in Africa*, vol. IV, *The Economics of Colonialism* (Cambridge, 1975), p. 490.

5. J. P. Peemans, 'Capital Accumulation in the Congo', in Duignan & Gann, Ibid., p. 204.

6. Ibid., pp. 194–5.

7. G. Vandewalle, *De Conjoncturele evolutie in Kongo en Ruanda-Urundi van 1920 tot 1939 en van 1949 tot 1958* (Antwerp, 1966), p. 142.

8. *African Research Bulletin*, 2947c.

9. *History of East Africa*, vol. II (Oxford, 1965), p. 472 and vol III (Oxford, 1976), pp. 235–41.

10. For the activities of CDC in East Africa and elsewhere, see Sir W. Rendell, *The History of the Commonwealth Development Corporation* (London, 1976).

11. In 1953 the Kenyan Government transferred its interest to its wholly owned Industrial Management Corporation (IMC) which was from 1975 called the Industrial Development Corporation (IDC) and later still the Industrial and Commercial Development Corporation.

12 See, for example, S. Langdon, 'Multinational Corporations, Taste Transfer and Underdevelopment: a Case Study from Kenya', *Review of African Political Economy*, no. 2 (1975) pp. 12–35 for a clear statement of this argument.

13. A detailed analysis of labour as an element in production costs in this and other industries in Kenya has been made by R. Reichelt in P. Zajadacz (ed.), *Studies in Production and Trade in East Africa* (Munich, 1970), pp. 123f.

14. Government Printing Department, Accra, 1953.

CHAPTER 7   Unilever in Turkey

1. The main secondary sources to which reference was made in writing this chapter were: Z. Y. Hershlag, *Turkey, the Challenge of Growth* (London, 1968);

C. H. Dodd, *Politics and Government in Turkey* (Manchester, 1969); B. Lewis, *The Emergence of Modern Turkey* (Oxford, 1961); G. L. Lewis, *Turkey* (London, 1955); *Facts on Turkey* (New York, 1948); Lord Kinross, *Ataturk: the Rebirth of a Nation* (London, 1964).
2. Unilever later invited Vehbi Koc to participate with the Is-Bank in their edible fats project. He refused on the ground that he did not believe there was a market for margarine but later said that he deeply regretted his refusal.

CHAPTER 8   Lever's Pacific Plantations Ltd

1. Leverhulme, *Viscount Leverhulme*, p. 154.
2. Hopkins, *An Economic History of West Africa*, pp. 32–3.
3. Wilson, *History*, vol. II, appendices 8 and 9.
4. D. Scarr, *Fragments of Empire* (Canberra, 1967), p. 264.
5. Ibid., p. 272.
6. Wilson, *History*, vol. I, p. 162.
7. Scarr, *Fragments*, p. 266.
8. Ibid., pp. 268–9.
9. Ibid., pp. 294–6.
10. H. Tinker, *A New System of Slavery* (London, 1974).
11. Leverhulme, *Viscount Leverhulme*, p. 158.

CHAPTER 9   Huileries du Congo Belge

1. Among secondary sources on the Congo the following were particularly useful: Roger Anstey, *King Leopold's Legacy: the Congo under Belgian Rule 1908–1960* (London, 1966); Fernand Bézy, *Problèmes structurels de l'économie congolais* (Louvain, 1957); Catherine Coquery-Vidtovitch and Samir Amin. *Histoire économique du Congo, 1880–1968: Du Congo français a l'union douanière et économique de l'Afrique centrale* (Paris, 1969); Hopkins, *An Economic History of West Africa;* Georges Hostelet, *L'oeuvre civilisatrice de la Belgique au Congo de 1885 à 1945*, vol. I, *L'oeuvre économique et sociale* (Brussels, 1954); Jean L. Lacroix, *Industrialisation au Congo: la transformation des structures économiques* (Paris, 1966); Pierre Joye and Rosine Lewin, *Les trusts au Congo* (Brussels, 1961); Jean-Philippe Peemans, 'Capital Accumulation in the Congo under Colonialism: the Role of the State', in Peter Duignan and Lewis H. Gann (eds), *Colonialism in Africa 1870–1960*, vol IV, pp. 165–212; Jean Stengers, 'The Congo Free State before 1914', ibid., vol. I (Cambridge, 1969), pp. 261–92; Stengers *Combien le Congo a-t-il coûté à la Belgique?* (Brussels, 1957); Vandewalle, *De conjoncturele evolutie in Kongo en Ruanda-Urundi van 1920 tot 1939 en van 1949 tot 1958.*
2. Wilson, *Unilever*, vol. I, pp. 167–8.
3. 'Mr. Edkins' Notes on the History of HCB', typescript in Unilever House, n.d.
4. Lord Frederick Lugard, *The Dual Mandate in British Tropical Africa*, 3rd ed. (London, 1926).
5. Leverhulme, *Viscount Leverhulme*, pp. 165–6.
6. 'Edkins' Notes', pp. 14–16, 30.
7. This account is summarised from Sikitele Gize, 'Les Racines de la rivalité Pende de 1931', *Etudes d'Histoire africaine*, vol. V (1973) pp. 99–153
8. Peemans, 'Capital Accumulation', pp. 202–10.

CHAPTER 10 . . . . Conclusions

1. See Wilson, *History*, vol. I, pp. 237–40 and Davies, *The Trade Makers*, ch. 7 and 8.
2. Wilson, *History*, vol. II, ch. 10.
3. Davies, *Trade Makers*, p. 331 and Wilson, *Unilever 1945–1965*, p. 221.
4. Wilson, *Unilever*, p. 214.
5. Reuber, *Private Foreign Investment in Development*, p. 22.
6. Paul M. Sweezy, *The Theory of Capitalist Development* (New York, 1942); Paul Baran, *The Political Economy of Growth* (New York, 1957); Gunnar Myrdal, *Economic Theory and Under-developed Regions* (London, 1957).
7. There is an interesting parallel here between modern Marxists and eighteenth-century mercantilists. Both believed that transactions between two countries were part of a zero sum game. This belief survived the assaults of the classical economists, re-emerged in later nineteenth-century protectionist theory and from there became incorporated in modern dependency theory.
8. Reuber, *Private Foreign Investment*, pp. 20–21.
9. Ibid., pp. 141–167.
10. Ibid., pp. 213–5.
11. Ibid., p. 149, Table 5.7.
12. Ibid., pp. 30–40.
13. Ibid., p. 169, Table 5.17.

Index

A and B Oil Industries, Karachi 248,
253, 259
a façon manufacturing arrangement
1, 102, 205, 218, 260, 276, 440
accounting systems 22, 57-62, 234,
352, 583, 591
Accra Chemical Works 409f., 413
administration, central 24-63, *see
also* autonomy, local; control,
central; Committees; Groups
advantage, comparative 314, 573,
576, 580, 592
advertising 63, 73, 118, 120-1, 127,
137, 144f., 219, 262, 267, 281,
377, 404, 428, 431, 444f.
Africa, Black 133f., 143, 339-418,
see also individual countries
African and Eastern Trade Corporation 61, 557
Agreements, Tripartite 517-21, 523,
526-9, 533-7
Ali, Group 246-53, 594; Amjad 246,
249
Alliance Bank of Simla 154, 158
amblypelta cocophaga 467, 473,
476f.
America, Latin 8, 19, 42, 232; North
10ff., 18ff., 31, 77, 135, 137,
217, 270ff., 321, 560f., 599
animal feeds 13, 73, 115, 124, 127,
131-2, 135, 152, 205, 221-2,
227, 229, 258-9, 271, 370, 561
Argentina 18, 146, 268, 340, 566
Arundel, J.T. 452-9
'associated companies' 30f., 34f., 44,
48, 55, 65, 109f., 112, 159, 563
Associated Enterprises Pty Ltd
(AEP) 70, 73, 76
Australia 19, 102, 104, 109, 114f.,
117, 119ff., 137, 153, 232, 243f.,
273, 450, 470f., 474, 560, 589,
592, 599; Lever/Unilever in
64-96, 143-7, and competition 26,
31, 67ff., 81, 87f., 91-3, 104,
107, 121, and distribution 65,
589, and diversification 74ff.,
79-93, and management, localisa-

tion of 93f., and manufacturing,
local 31, 64-7, 91, 102, 173, 243,
and market dominance 81, 107,
575, and ownership. local
participation in 94-6, and profitability 71ff., 82-6, 143-7
autonomy, local 14-16, 19, 21, 25,
30, 34, 43ff., 48, 61, 65f., 70,
110, 163, 168, 345, 450, 563-5,
see also control, central

Bahawalpur 245-6, 249-51; Agency
Ltd 250
Baker, G. and A. Ltd of Turkey
419f.
balance of payments 96, 239-40,
284, 286, 335, 367, 433-4, 439,
583, 586-7, 594
Barnish, C.W. 42, 137, 167, 181
Barraclough, G.W.E. 80, 92
Batchelor Peas Ltd 77, 91
Belgium 31, 62, 496-503, 505, 512,
516, 522, 526-8, 533ff., 541,
see also Congo, Belgian
Bhagwati, J.N. 188, 190
Bibbys 348-9, 351, 354ff., 361, 369,
377, 409
Birds Eye Foods Limited 77f., 88ff.,
129f.
Black, C.F. 62, 539, 544
Bonham-Carter, A.D. 330, 333
Borsumy 266, 276
Boulton Brothers/Boulton Group
153-9, 162f., 249
brand-names 35, 65f., 75ff., 89,
91f., 104, 166, 209, 211, 216,
219; -products 1, 12, 46, 60, 63,
67, 107, 175, 220, 280, 573, 587
Brazil 18, 146, 566
British Ceylon Corporation 323,
324
British Oil and Cake Mills (BOCM)
131, 258
Brock, G.M. 259, 261
Brunner Mond 170, 343
Burford, W.H. and Co. 67, 69f., 73f.,
79, 91f., 94, 121

609